I0343121

State, Society and Islam in the Western Regions of the Sahara

State, Society and Islam in the Western Regions of the Sahara

Regional Interactions and Social Change

Edited by
Francisco Freire

I.B.TAURIS
LONDON • NEW YORK • OXFORD • NEW DELHI • SYDNEY

I.B. TAURIS
Bloomsbury Publishing Plc
50 Bedford Square, London, WC1B 3DP, UK
1385 Broadway, New York, NY 10018, USA
29 Earlsfort Terrace, Dublin 2, Ireland

BLOOMSBURY, I.B. TAURIS and the I.B. Tauris logo are
trademarks of Bloomsbury Publishing Plc

First published in Great Britain 2022
This paperback edition published 2024

Copyright © Francisco Freire and contributors, 2022

Francisco Freire and contributors have asserted their right under the
Copyright, Designs and Patents Act, 1988, to be identified as Editors of this work.

For legal purposes the Acknowledgements on p. xvii constitute
an extension of this copyright page.

Series design by Adriana Brioso
Cover image © Bruno Borges

This work is published open access subject to a Creative Commons Attribution Non-Commercial No Derivatives 3.0 licence (CC BY-NC-ND 3.0, https://creativecommons.org/licenses/by-nc-nd/3.0/). You may re-use, distribute, and reproduce this work in any medium for non-commercial purposes, provided you give attribution to the copyright holder and the publisher and provide a link to the Creative Commons licence.

All rights reserved. No part of this publication may be reproduced or transmitted in any form or by any means, electronic or mechanical, including photocopying, recording, or any information storage or retrieval system, without prior permission in writing from the publishers.

Bloomsbury Publishing Plc does not have any control over, or responsibility for, any third-party websites referred to or in this book. All internet addresses given in this book were correct at the time of going to press. The author and publisher regret any inconvenience caused if addresses have changed or sites have ceased to exist, but can accept no responsibility for any such changes.

A catalogue record for this book is available from the British Library.

A catalog record for this book is available from the Library of Congress.

ISBN: HB: 978-0-7556-4347-9
PB: 978-0-7556-4348-6
ePDF: 978-0-7556-4351-6
eBook: 978-0-7556-4350-9

Typeset by Integra Software Services Pvt. Ltd.

To find out more about our authors and books visit www.bloomsbury.com
and sign up for our newsletters.

This edited volume is part of a project that has received funding from the European Research Council (ERC) under the European Union's Horizon 2020 research and innovation programme (Grant Agreement No. 716467); https://capsahara-cria.fcsh.unl.pt.

Contents

List of Illustrations ix
List of Contributors xi
Preface *Benjamin F. Soares* xiv
Note on Transliteration and Orthography xvi
Acknowledgements xvii

Introduction: Shifting sands: State, society and Islam in the western regions of the Sahara *Francisco Freire* 1

Part 1 State

1 A land of opportunities: Political morphologies at the northwestern Saharan frontier (1934–1960) *Alberto López Bargados* 17
2 A historical perspective on legal practices in Sahrawi society (1958–2019) *Enrique Bengochea Tirado* 43
3 Magnitudes of Sahrawi nomadism throughout colonialism and refugeehood *Juan Carlos Gimeno Martín and Julien Lafontaine Carboni* 69
4 The flexible use of democracy in an Islamic Republic: The case of the Mauritanian President Abdel Aziz (2009–2019) *Elemine Ould Mohamed Baba Moustapha* 87

Part 2 Society

5 Artisanal gold mining in Mauritania *Moustapha Taleb Heidi* 107
6 Unsettling gender and feminism: Views from Mauritania *Maria Cardeira da Silva* 143
7 Funeral orations, the web and politics: The online making of national heroes in Mauritania and the Western Sahara in poems and songs *Sébastien Boulay and Mohamed Ould Ahmed Meidah* 167
8 Haratin activism in post-slavery Mauritania: Abolition, emancipation and the politics of identity *David Malluche* 195

Part 3 Islam

9 On the (body of the) subject in the Sahara: Muḥummadhun Fāl b. Muttālī's *Fatḥ al-ḥaqq* (nineteenth century) *Abdel Wedoud Ould Cheikh* 231

10 The past and present of the *ghuẓfiyya* Sufi order from the western regions of the Sahara *Yahya Ould al-Bara* 261

11 Islamic traditional schooling in a globalized context: A case study from the *maḥẓara* of Teysir (southwestern Mauritania) *Mariem Baba Ahmed and Zahra Horma* 289

12 Islam, blasphemy and realpolitik in Mauritania: The Mkhaitir affair *Francisco Freire* 311

Postscript: Reflections on research ethics in complex contexts: Navigating politics, pragmatics and positionality *Leonardo Villalón and Irina Branco da Silva* 331

Index 346

Illustrations

Figures

1.1	Undated Spanish colonial map of the Ifni territory (c. 1935). © Ministerio de Cultura y Deporte	20
3.1	Panorama of Mahbes in 1974, https://www.lamilienelsahara.net/	72
3.2	Camp where the proclamation of the RASD took place in February 1976. © Archives of the Ministry of Information of the RASD	77
3.3	Diagram of the organization of the camp of Ouenet Bellagra (Dajla since 1978), Source: Julien Lafontaine Carboni	82
5.1	Mining pits in northwestern Mauritania	114
5.2	Miners at work at the Sakina site, 2016 (© Moctar Ould El-Hacen)	115
5.3	Mining trenches at the Container 1 site, near the Tasiast gold mine (© Capsahara, Moustapha Taleb Heidi)	116
5.4	Living conditions available for artisanal gold miners in the Inchiri region (© Capsahara/Moustapha Taleb Heidi)	118
5.5	Processing facilities in Chami (© Capsahara/Moustapha Taleb Heidi)	119
5.6	Gold treatment facilities in Chami (© Capsahara/Moustapha Taleb Heidi)	124
11.1	Teysir's mosque, March 2021 (© Zahra Horma)	303
11.2	Students' housing in Teysir, March 2021 (© Zahra Horma)	306

Maps

0.1	North West Africa	3
3.1	The motions through the Hamada of Tinduf until 1991. Some camps were ephemeral, others were transitioning camps for the population, notably Grarrat Lentilaga. Designed after discussions had in the refugee camps in February/March 2020. © Julien Lafontaine Carboni	73
5.1	Main gold mining locations in Mauritania (2021)	109
5.2	Gold mining locations in northwestern Mauritania	110

Tables

5.1	Field research data	109
A5.1	Sociodemographic data of the sample	131
A5.2	Distribution of miners by occupation	132
A5.3	Previous occupations of artisanal miners	133
A5.4	Source of information about mining	133
A5.5	Satisfaction with mining experience by occupation	134
A5.6	Challenges faced by miners	134

Contributors

Alberto López Bargados (University of Barcelona – GRECS) is Professor of Social Anthropology at the University of Barcelona (UB) and a member of the Grup de Recerca sobre Exclusió i Control Socials (GRECS). He has published on topics such as Saharan 'tribal' systems and their adaptations through colonial processes, as well as Islamic practices in the contexts of diaspora. Between 2017 and 2021 he was a senior scientific consultant to the ERC-funded project Capsahara (Grant Agreement No. 716467) hosted by CRIA – NOVA FCSH in Lisbon, Portugal.

Enrique Bengochea Tirado (CRIA – NOVA FCSH), historian, is currently a post-doctoral researcher in the María Zambrano programme at the University of Valencia. He has published on the Spanish colony of the Sahara and legal pluralism in Islam among the Saharawi from the late colonial to the contemporary period. From 2017 to 2021 he was a post-doctoral researcher at the ERC-funded project Capsahara (Grant Agreement No. 716467) hosted by CRIA – NOVA FCSH in Lisbon, Portugal.

Juan Carlos Gimeno Martín (Universidad Autónoma de Madrid) is Professor of Social Anthropology at the Universidad Autónoma de Madrid. With his fieldwork spanning Spain, Mexico, Guatemala, Nicaragua, Cuba and Western Sahara, he has published work on public-oriented anthropology, public policy, human rights, postcolonial studies and the decolonial epistemological approach. Between 2017 and 2021 he was a senior scientific consultant to the ERC-funded project Capsahara (Grant Agreement No. 716467) hosted by CRIA – NOVA FCSH in Lisbon, Portugal.

Julien Lafontaine Carboni (ALICE laboratory, Swiss Federal Institute of Technology of Lausanne) is an architect and PhD candidate at the ALICE laboratory, Swiss Federal Institute of Technology of Lausanne, Faculty of Natural, Architectural and Built Environment, Institute of Architecture. He has published work in several architecture, philosophy and anthropological journals such as *Architecture and Culture* and *Tabula Rasa*.

Elemine Ould Mohamed Baba Moustapha (University of Nouakchott) is Professor of History and Sociolinguistics at the University of Nouakchott, Mauritania (PhD University of Provence (Aix-Marseille I). An expert in Almoravid history, his more recent focus has explored the political and social transformations of Mauritania from the colonial to the contemporary period. Between 2017 and 2021, he was a senior scientific consultant to the ERC-funded project Capsahara (Grant Agreement No. 716467) hosted by CRIA – NOVA FCSH in Lisbon, Portugal.

Moustapha Taleb Heidi (CRIA – NOVA FCSH, Post-Doctoral Researcher at Capsahara) is a sociologist and a researcher at the Centre d'Etudes et de Recherches sur l'Ouest Saharien (CEROS) at the University of Nouakchott, Mauritania. From 2019 to 2021 he was a post-doctoral researcher at the ERC-funded project Capsahara (Grant Agreement No. 716467) hosted by CRIA – NOVA FCSH in Lisbon, Portugal. He carried out extensive research on international development and cooperation and has served as an expert and consultant for various international organizations. His publications feature social and cultural dynamics of the urban development in the Saharan contexts, legal aspects of the land tenure and traditional artisanal activities on the Mauritanian territory.

Maria Cardeira da Silva (NOVA FCSH – CRIA) is Professor of Anthropology at the Universidade Nova de Lisboa and a researcher at the Centro de Investigação em Antropologia (CRIA). She has published on anthropology of tourism and heritage, as well as gender and human rights in Islamic contexts. Between 2017 and 2020 she acted as senior scientific consultant to the ERC-funded project Capsahara (Grant Agreement No. 716467) hosted by CRIA – NOVA FCSH in Lisbon, Portugal.

Sébastien Boulay (Faculté des sciences humaines et sociales de la Sorbonne, Université de Paris) is an anthropologist, Assistant Professor at the Paris Cité University and research fellow at the UMR 196 CEPED (Population & Development Center). He has been conducting fieldwork since 1999 in Mauritania and since 2011 in the Western Sahara. His current research is focused on the role of artistic productions (especially satirical and humorous) and new media in the political struggles taking place in the western regions of the Sahara. Between 2017 and 2021, he was a senior scientific consultant to the ERC-funded project Capsahara (Grant Agreement No. 716467) hosted by CRIA – NOVA FCSH in Lisbon, Portugal.

Mohamed Ould Ahmed Meidah is a Mauritanian poet, writer and researcher with interest in the topics of culture and heritage. He has served as the Director-General of Arts and Culture of Mauritania and has authored several works on cultural issues.

David Malluche (CRIA – NOVA FCSH, Doctoral Researcher at Capsahara) is Assistant Professor at the department of Islamic Studies and Junior Fellow at BIGSAS, University of Bayreuth. From November 2019 to October 2020 he held a CRIA scholarship as a PhD candidate researcher in the ERC-funded project Capsahara (Grant Agreement No. 716467) in Lisbon, Portugal. His research interests focus on the social and cultural history and contemporary politics of the western regions of the Sahara and the Sahel. His PhD project deals with social and political activism and identity (trans-)formation processes associated with the Ḥarāṭīn population of the Islamic Republic of Mauritania.

Abdel Wedoud Ould Cheikh (Professor Emeritus at the University of Lorraine, France) is a social anthropologist and author of a vast corpus of work on Mauritanian

Moorish society. He acted as senior scientific adviser to the ERC-funded project Capsahara (Grant Agreement No. 716467) hosted by CRIA – NOVA FCSH in Lisbon, Portugal.

Yahya Ould al-Bara (University of Nouakchott) is Professor of Anthropology and linguistics at the University of Nouakchott, Mauritania. His extensively work is associated with the corpus of Islamic scholarly production in the western Saharan region. Between 2017 and 2021, he was a senior scientific consultant to the ERC-funded project Capsahara (Grant Agreement N°716467) hosted by CRIA – NOVA FCSH in Lisbon, Portugal.

Mariem Baba Ahmed (CRIA – NOVA FCSH, Post-Doctoral Researcher at Capsahara) is currently the Director of Scientific Research and Innovation at the Ministry of Higher Education, Scientific Research, Information and Communication Technologies in Mauritania. Having received her PhD in Cultural Anthropology from the University of Lorraine, France in 2015, she has conducted extensive research in Mauritania, and has taught at the University of Nouakchott. Between 2017 and 2019 she was a graduate researcher in the ERC-funded project Capsahara (Grant Agreement No. 716467) hosted by CRIA – NOVA FCSH in Lisbon, Portugal.

Zahra Horma (CRIA – NOVA FCSH, Junior Researcher at Capsahara) is a visual anthropologist. Between 2020 and 2021 she was an early career researcher in the ERC-funded project Capsahara (Grant Agreement No. 716467) hosted by CRIA – NOVA FCSH in Lisbon, Portugal, collaborating with Mariem Baba Ahmed on topics of religious education and transmission of knowledge in contemporary Mauritania.

Francisco Freire (NOVA FCSH – CRIA) is Assistant Professor of anthropology at NOVA FCSH, Portugal, and a researcher at the Centro em Rede de Investigação em Antropologia (CRIA). He was the Principal Investigator of the ERC-funded project Capsahara (Grant Agreement No. 716467) hosted by CRIA – NOVA FCSH in Lisbon. His research focuses on processes of identity reconfiguration among Hassaniyya-speaking populations of the western regions of the Sahara.

Preface

State, Society and Islam in the Western Regions of the Sahara is a very important and timely collection of essays. Although in recent years there has been considerable interest in the Sahara and particularly the conflict in the Western Sahara, the western regions of the Sahara discussed in this volume have not received sufficient attention from scholars and policy makers. Indeed, the object of study in this volume is the vast region stretching from the Atlantic through present-day Morocco, the Western Sahara, Algeria, Mauritania and beyond. This is a region where speakers of Hassaniyya or *klām al-Bīḍān*, a heterogeneous group of people, are numerous, sometimes constitute the majority and whose complex and sometimes fraught history living within and between different political formations – precolonial, colonial and postcolonial – is still not well understood. In contrast to the substantial literature in French about this region, there are surprisingly few, if any, books in English with such a broad geographic scope. However, this edited volume's importance is certainly not limited only to its enormous empirical value for anglophone audiences. Indeed, one of this volume's most important contributions is its focus on the interplay between sociopolitical and religious traditions and political action across space and time through a series of detailed case studies from this vast region. It is a highly interdisciplinary volume with contributors working between the social sciences, including anthropology, geography and political science, and the humanities, including history, Islamic studies and literary analysis. Drawing on various methods from the humanities and social sciences field research, including ethnography, interviews, archival research, textual analysis and/or surveys, we learn here about an array of interconnected topics that illustrate the interplay of sociopolitical and religious traditions in various settings in Algeria, Mauritania, Morocco and Western Sahara. The topics include the implications of French and Spanish colonial rule and postcolonial dispensations for settlement and displacement, how nomads have become more stationary in the Western Sahara, transregional mobility in the case of the recent explosion of artisanal gold mining in northern Mauritania with its many dangers and risks, the complex legal pluralism people in the region experience, as well as populist authoritarianism and a new genre of online elegies for recently deceased political leaders. In addition, we also learn about contemporary forms of activism by the *ḥarāṭīn*, former slaves and/or descendants of slaves in Mauritania, various kinds of feminists in the region, as well as that of historically marginal social groups such as blacksmiths, many of whom have struggled against their subordination, as, for example, in the recent case of 'blasphemy' in Mauritania considered here. The volume is rounded out with a series of chapters about Islam from the exploration of 'the figure of a transregional and transhistorical generic subject' outlined in a nineteenth-century text of a prominent Muslim scholar produced in the region to a careful reconstruction of the history of Mauritania's homegrown but under-studied Sufi order, the *Ghuzfiyya*, and a consideration of Mauritania's distinctive advanced Islamic educational institution, the *mahadra*, seen in a global context.

The volume comes out of a multi-year European Research Council-funded project, Capsahara, about the western regions of the Sahara. This project and this subsequent publication brought together a stellar team of senior and junior scholars from Europe, Mauritania and North America whose work on the project's unified research agenda is clearly reflected in the volume's excellent essays, which complement each other. When taken together, this set of clearly written and accessible essays points to the broader usefulness of this research for comparative reflection about inherited and shifting sociopolitical and religious traditions among other groups in various postcolonial settings elsewhere in Africa, the Middle East and beyond. The research and its output in this volume should serve as a model for regionally focused collaborative research that is so productive, empirically rich and analytically insightful. In fact, it points to the need for other such regionally focused studies which an individual researcher would be unable to undertake and successfully complete. The volume's editor and contributors should be commended for disseminating their excellent research about the Sahara in such a timely fashion. This book deserves to be widely read and debated and stands to inform discussions among scholars, policy makers and broader publics about the Sahara today.

Benjamin F. Soares
(University of Florida)

Note on Transliteration and Orthography

The transliteration of Arabic follows Brill's *Encyclopedia of Islam*, 3rd edition (EI3). The additional phonemes (v) and (g) and the vowel (e) from the Hassaniyya Arabic widely spoken throughout the western Saharan region are also used. Such transliteration of Hassaniyya pronunciation of certain terms has led some authors, for example, to use *maḥẓara* instead of *maḥḍara* and *Bīẓān* instead of the *Bīḍān*.

Arabic words that are now in the English-language lexicon follow the orthography of the *Oxford English Dictionary* (e.g. fatwa, jihad, wadi, shaykh, sabkha, Sufi, Maliki, etc.).

Acknowledgements

The editor is grateful to Hugo Maia for his invaluable help with Arabic transliterations and to Sergiu Pavlocev for the elaboration of the maps used in this volume.

Introduction

Shifting sands: State, society and Islam in the western regions of the Sahara

Francisco Freire
NOVA FCSH, Lisbon, Portugal

Assāvi is a term in Hassaniyya (Ar. *Ḥasāniyya*) – the colloquial Arabic widely spoken throughout the entire western Saharan region, overwhelmingly dominant in Mauritania and the Western Sahara and with speakers also found in Morocco, Algeria, Senegal, Mali and Niger – for a type of light breeze that often sweeps through the western regions of the Sahara, carrying miniscule grains of sand and momentarily blurring one's vision. Although its effects are temporary, it can result in the adoption of a distorted, hazy interpretation of one's immediate surroundings. The contributors to this volume each had to contend with somewhat similar conditions in their attempts to portray and analyse the complexity of the Hassaniyya-speaking groups dispersed throughout this region.[1] While the question of how to interpret this context and convey it to broader publics is a challenge in and of itself, this volume confronts this complexity head-on, tackling the multifaceted character of these populations, the interconnected social landscapes they inhabit and their distinctive albeit shifting socio-cultural characteristics.

The populations of the western regions of the Sahara have undergone significant changes over the past fifty years or so, moving away from a centuries-old history of nomadic pastoralism towards an ontological redefinition of their identity as dwellers of urban spaces.[2] This crucial development is related to yet another revolutionary transformation: the emergence and consolidation of the nation-state as a formal structure for political action. These two major shifts largely overlap chronologically, and both must be taken into consideration when discussing and analysing the region.

In exploring the issues associated with these significant changes, two key concepts have served as guiding threads for the case studies explored in this collection: *society* and *Islam*. In carefully reconsidering these, the contributors to this volume move away from conventional understandings of the region's sociopolitical spheres as based largely on kinship relations and patrilineal genealogical projects, directing our attention to politically significant binding relationships based on proximity, patronage and other affinities and bringing to light new cooperative loyalties and allegiances. The inclusion of more 'informal' bonds has made it possible to highlight the presence of seldom acknowledged protagonists and innovative social constructs in the research (Bonnefoy and Catuse 2013; Dupret et al. 2013; Herrera and Bayat 2010). This has in turn given voice to groups that have often been overlooked in the literature due to their presumed 'irrationality' and pervasive attachment to 'tribal' formations – communities that are currently the subject of negotiation and exchange among (but also under) various state authorities that govern the broader western Saharan region. Using mainly an anthropological lens, this volume aims to reassess questions that are usually only asked in the context of 'traditional' forms of belonging, although they are clearly relevant to the transformations in the region as a result of greater cosmopolitanism and increased access to information (see, for example, Baba Ahmed and Horma's chapter on Islamic schooling in southern Mauritania; Malluche's chapter on Ḥarāṭīn identity and political activism; and Boulay's study of online poetic-political expressions). In short, the chapters that follow provide empirically rich studies of the western Saharan region and analyses that take the current social, cultural and political vocabularies of different segments of Hassaniyya-speaking populations in their complexity and in the context of greater regional integration into consideration.

The missing ethnonym

It is generally understood that the Hassaniyya-speaking groups who inhabit the western regions of the Sahara – geographically bound (but not limited) by the Senegal River to the south and the Guelmim (Morocco) region to the north, extending eastward into southern Algeria, parts of northern Mali and even Niger – share three clearly identifiable markers: the Hassaniyya language, the vital presence of Islam and Islamic-based traditions and the pervasive effects of a *qabīla*-centred social structure.[3] These groups are composed of *bīḍān* communities (etymologically a plural of 'white' and the name attributed to those of 'noble'/'free' status) and various groups of tributary status, the majority of which are *ḥarāṭīn* populations, of slave descent.[4] The diversity of these groups is often obscured through processes of genealogical normalization that associate them with an Arab ancestry (arguably evidenced by the official name given to the Sahrawi *Arab* Democratic Republic). This pervasive yet malleable model – which has already been extensively explored by colonial and postcolonial scholars such as Paul Marty (1919), Julio Caro Baroja (1955), Charles C. Stewart (1973), Abdel Wedoud Ould Cheikh (1985), Harry T. Norris (1986), Sophie Caratini (1989), Pierre Bonte (1990), Alberto López Bargados (2003) and Ghislaine Lydon (2009) – should be treated with caution both when tracing the history of the region and in contemporary debates (Ould Cheikh 2017: 71).[5]

The imposition of ethnic categories is a practice that is common to various colonial contexts, and the western Saharan region stands as a particularly good example of this. The term 'Moor' (Fr. *maure*), for example, has frequently been used to describe these populations as a whole,[6] despite the fact that no all-encompassing ethnonym of

Map 0.1 North West Africa.

this sort is to be found in Hassaniyya. A racializing exonym that emerged in a context of intense competition between Spain, France and Morocco, the term played a key role in colonial efforts to manipulate and control Saharan groups (dating back to the early 1900s).[7] Despite its troubled history, however, this term has been given new life in these ever-shifting contexts and has been re-appropriated and put to different uses. In its more recent re-formulation the term Moorish, apparently separated from a Saharan origin, has, for example, started to be used by Moroccan far-right nationalists (Moreno-Almeida 2021; see also Barreñada 2017).

Efforts to 'domesticate' and re-appropriate ethnic categories – often used to identify taxable subjects governed by colonial administrations based either in St Louis du Senegal or in Sidi Ifni in Morocco – have likewise given new meaning to old formulas, putting them to use in the construction of new social realities.[8] In acknowledgement of its role in these identity-building projects, some of the contributors to this volume (notably the Francophone authors: Ould Cheikh, Baba Ahmed and Boulay) have consciously incorporated the term 'Moor' as a descriptive category. Without in any way seeking to conceal its fraught past, we have chosen to respect the authors' choices and to incorporate the term as one way of referring to the Hassaniyya-speaking populations of the western regions of the Sahara.

With the above in mind, one might ask whether this volume is in fact centred on a 'fictitious identity' (Taine-Cheikh 1997: 86), given the lack of an all-encompassing ethnonym to describe this social universe – a universe that, when it has engaged in self-classification, has always been composite in form, assuming heterogeneity rather than uniformity. For this reason, we use 'Hassaniyya-speaking populations' to refer to the groups and communities of this region, a heuristically richer category for analysing the development of different forms of identity, political allegiance and expressions of religiosity among a population estimated at more than 3 million people.

Will the proliferation of new identities in this context lead to further social fragmentation? Such fragmentation may already be underway, in an area where one finds an Islamic Republic (Mauritania), a monarchy (Morocco) and the non-self-governing territory of the Western Sahara (the UN's official designation for this territory, which is also known as the Saharawi Arab Democratic Republic, the (Moroccan) Southern Provinces, and, perhaps most accurately, a 'hybrid parastate'; Fernández-Molina and Ojeda-García 2020).

The rapid formation and consolidation of a Sahrawi identity constitutes one of the better-known developments in the Hassaniyya socio-cultural milieu.[9] Sahrawi political claims are fundamentally associated with the borders of the former Spanish colony of the Western Sahara. As we know, however, the largely nomadic groups currently affiliated with a Sahrawi identity have always been connected to much broader regional transit routes across southern Morocco, Mali, Algeria and present-day Mauritania. The contributors to this volume offer an innovative perspective on the Sahrawi (both as a tentative national project and as a distinct social identity) that stands in contrast to narratives in which they emerged practically *ex nihilo* in a context of anti-colonial resistance. In this context, López Bargados's chapter in this volume offers a significant contribution to the debate about the intricacies of the western Saharan region's northwestern frontiers. With that said, Spain's colonial efforts in the Sahara – in obvious parallel with those of France further south – did play an essential role in the formation of the Sahrawi identity as it now stands. A long history of nomadic interchanges and Hilali genealogical claims (a well-known motif in the self-description of many Saharan communities, based on a connection with the first Arab groups reaching North Africa and the western Saharan confines) has, somewhat ironically, found political expression in the appropriation of a territory marked by Spanish colonial experimentation dating from the early twentieth century (for an overview of this debate, see Campos-Serrano and Rodríguez-Esteban 2017: 53–6).

The perpetual question concerning statehood and an immemorial allegiance to 'tribal' structures – another recurring theme in this volume – was provocatively posed by Pierre Bonte. His use of the expression 'Sahrawi tribe' (Bonte 2017: 235) implicitly associated the national project of the Sahrawi with the regional *qabīla*-oriented social model, drawing a subtle parallel between them and their Hassaniyya-speaking neighbours to the south and thus undermining (or at least bringing into question) their claim to stand apart as 'modern revolutionaries'. The use of this expression also conflicts with the claim, put forward by the Polisario leadership, that the Sahrawi have been 'liberated' from the bonds of tribal affiliation through a 'coordinated unmaking of tribes' (Wilson 2016: 60), and thus consolidating an eminently egalitarian social project. Making things even more complicated, however, Bonte's 'Sahrawi tribe' would now seem to be adhering to the fundamentally paradoxical concept of a 'tribal state'. My use of the term 'paradoxical' is not aligned with the narratives that nurtured long debates in the 1970s, pointing towards the dissipation (and eventual disappearance) of tribal political structures when in contact with the state. It is particularly associated with the provocative argument recently developed by James C. Scott (2017: 235) in which he asserts that tribal formations may have been 'in the first instance, an administrative fiction of the state; tribes begin where states end'.

While critics might assume that Bonte, like many scholars working in the region before (and after) him, merely fell prey to the common 'compulsive use' of the 'tribal' lexicon (Ould Ahmed Salem 1999: 132), his choice of words can also be illuminating. The state structures (in exile, in this case) that have been implemented in the last four decades by the nationalist Sahrawi movement have now begun to reposition themselves (in a process that can be traced back to the 1990s) as the heirs of centuries of nomadism and Hassaniyya cultural traditions (in which Islam has now also been integrated; see in particular the chapter by Bengochea Tirado in this volume; see also Isidoros 2015; Wilson 2017). The acknowledgement of what might easily be identified as a 'tribal heritage' – both as part of the Sahrawi identity and as a critical element of their understanding of nationhood – could thus have strategic importance.

The implementation of state (and 'parastate') structures has thus played a pivotal role in transformations that have affected the entire western Saharan region.[10] Through a contemporary lens, this volume seeks to highlight how these are currently understood and experienced by those who inhabit the area.

Colonialism, before and after

The period from the late nineteenth century to the early twentieth century proved decisive for the entire western Saharan region. French colonial efforts intensified in this crucial period, putting into action a so-called *Plan de Pacification* developed by one of their most eminent and experienced colonial administrators, Xavier Coppolani, who was subsequently assassinated in Tijikja, in present-day Mauritania, in 1905 (see Désiré-Vuillemin 1955). Significant military operations were conducted prior to *pacification*, which was arduously accomplished in 1912 (see Marty 1915), when the French took control of the Adrar region of present-day Mauritania, thus forming a geographic delimitation that, almost half a century later, would become the Islamic Republic of Mauritania (see Bonte 2017: 151–62; for a broader overview of French policies in West Africa, see Harrison 1988). To the north, Shaykh Maʾ al-ʿAynayn, founder of the city of Smara in 1899, opted to oppose French expansion, thus diverging from the path chosen by his older brother Saʿd Būh, south of the Senegal River, and by Shaykh Sīdiyyā in southwestern Mauritania, both of whom expressed their opposition to an anti-French jihad (see Norris 1972: 160–217; Robinson 2001: 178–93), involving Morocco and Spain in a dispute that by then had engulfed the entire northwestern Sahara (Abitbol 1986).

Although significant social constructs and effects associated with the colonial period are identified and discussed in the chapters that follow, it is important to underscore the ongoing importance of the region's precolonial past in the present. Indeed, some seemingly newly created patterns can be traced to the region's past, which has authoritatively re-emerged in a postcolonial assertion of locality. In Tindouf, for example, the Polisario leadership is now engaged in the promotion of 'nomadic culture' as emblematic of the Sahrawi (see the chapter by Gimeno and Carboni). This should not be taken as a sign of the impending resurgence of camel herding or a return to the nomadic tent as a preferable habitat for the Sahrawi; rather, it highlights the importance the Polisario Front ascribes to re-engaging with precolonial elements in the contemporary definition of statehood. Drawing on extensive fieldwork in Tindouf, Bengochea Tirado's chapter signals the importance of legal pluralism in Sahrawi legal practices. The explicit assimilation of Islamic scholarship in present-day judicial litigation is another clear example of a postcolonial re-appropriation of a social identity.

Such processes cannot be understood as simple amalgams of inherited norms, as 'development in reverse', or as a return to an 'original locality' as a reaction to colonialism (Mudimbe 1994: xiv; see also Bonte 2017: 260). Emerging within a particularly challenging research location (see Villalón and Branco da Silva's Postscript to this volume), such developments reaffirm the adherence of the populations of the western Saharan regions to social mechanisms not originally created by the pressures of colonialism nor through the implementation of nation-states. While clearly associated with the region's past, both colonial and precolonial, these changes are currently being re-implemented from a different set of sociopolitical motives.

To say this is not to deny the impact of the various 'civilizing missions' – understood here as the largely racist policies implemented in this region by French and Spanish colonialism aimed at 'educating' and 'civilizing' (Muslim) groups considered to be inadequately prepared for 'modern' life – that have made their presence felt in the region. The effects of colonization are particularly noticeable in the definition of new political frontiers and the positioning of the nation-state as a privileged model for political action and indeed 'domination' (Mamdani 2020: 330; for a similar argument extended to the central regions of the Sahara, see Georg Klute 1996: 61). These changes made the reinvention of key political arenas possible at the local, regional and international level – arenas that presently encompass the totality of the Hassaniyya-speaking populations of the region, whether they constitute a minority (as in Mali, Niger, Algeria and Morocco) or a majority (in the case of the Islamic Republic of Mauritania and the Western Sahara).[11] It is worth noting that the Treaty of Kayes (February 1963), which established a land swap between Mauritania and Mali, constitutes the only official rectification of colonially inherited geopolitical borders in the region. As we know, the borders of the former Spanish colony of the Western Sahara remain contested, and a swift resolution seems unlikely, at least for the near future (despite the USA's, Israel's, different Gulf states' and more recently Spain's endorsement of the Moroccan pro-autonomy position).

There are thus great risks associated with viewing this context through a linear lens, which, like the *assāvi* wind, may give rise to blurred perceptions that do not align with a much more complex reality. With this in mind, the volume's contributors explore more extensive forms of interplay between pre-modern sociopolitical traditions and contemporary religious expressions, political movements and activism, allowing for the evidence of a multifaceted social history to emerge from the empirical materials the authors use. While confirming the sociological embeddedness of the western Saharan region's sociopolitical culture, this volume seeks to transcend the constraints of colonial academic expertise (and policy), and question the hierarchical structures that have been identified (and denounced) in postcolonial and post-orientalist analyses.

Finding paths on rugged terrain

The volume's focus on anthropology notwithstanding, various methods were adopted for each of the settings analysed. In order to offset the incongruences that inevitably affect multi-sited research, the authors have combined approaches from anthropology, history, geography and political science. Field research was carried out according to anthropological methodological premises, often resulting in descriptive narratives that allowed for an in-depth exploration of the trajectories of the chosen interlocutors. The choice of interlocutors and methodologies brought to the fore the elusive theoretical frontier between 'critical ethnography' (Foley and Valenzuela 2005) and more positivist stances. This triangulation of methods and approaches to field research was a particularly challenging task in the disputed social and political contexts covered in this volume. Indeed, the clash between emic and etic perspectives goes to the very roots of social philosophy as a method and a discipline, to the fundamental differences between constructivist, interpretivist, collaborative and positivist ideas of science. Although 'battling positivism' was not an explicit aim of this project, it cannot be forgotten that the anthropologist is not only a (participant) observer but also a producer of social facts, contributing, sometimes imperceptibly, to changing the actual fabric of the relationships in which he or she is involved (Freire 2017: 150).

A now well-established academic tradition defines the Sahara mainly as a socio-cultural crossroads (Lydon 2009), and this volume confirms the multifaceted social history of the Hassaniyya-speaking peoples and the ubiquitous permeability of their geographic spectrum (on the indefinite social boundaries in/of the western Saharan region, see also Hall 2011; Simenel 2010). This inescapable porosity gives rise to the continual creation of new social, cultural and political coalitions (Mann 2015; Marfaing and Wippel 2004; Scheele 2012), often resulting in the addition of the prefix 'trans-' to the word 'Sahara'. The use of this term has been discussed by McDougall and Scheele (2012), who stress that this focus has yielded a description of the Sahara as a 'crossing': a transnational crossroads of goods and Islamic knowledge (Austen 2010; Ross 2011; see also Taleb Heidi's chapter in this volume). In a conscious departure from this way of thinking about the region, this volume postulates that a much more intimate understanding of the area's multiple social formations and cultural spheres is critical. As such, this collection approaches the western region of the Sahara as much more than a space between two shores, treating its connectivity as an eminently dynamic social, sociopolitical and historical space of its own. Beyond a simple comparative approach, the analyses offered here explicitly attempt to engage with the plural dialogues established between the different political imaginations being pursued across the region.

Another central element of the analysis of the western regions of the Sahara – in stark contrast to what we find further south (Soares 2014) – is of course the ubiquity of Islam. In this context, this volume explores the points of intersection between Islam, including Islamic reformist projects, and the social and political structures conventionally employed to understand the region (see, e.g. Ould al-Bara's and Ould Cheikh's chapters in this volume).

Although Islam has always been a networked civilization – thus 'the nation-state is not necessarily the principal frame of reference within which Islamic intellectual traditions evolve' (Seesemann 2021: 533) – the local character that Islamic belonging has progressively acquired has implications that potentially challenge this pervasive idea (Bayat 2012). The chapters in this volume postulate that the diversity of Islamic understandings observed in the western regions of the Sahara largely transcend the prevailing scripturalist focus of some previous studies. They testify to an explicit adaptation of religiously based discourses that take into account and encompass most aspects of contemporary life (Osella and Soares 2020), likely closer to Soares's suggested reading of Islam in Mali as 'a discursive tradition at the intersection of the local, the supralocal, and the translocal' (2000: 283). These readings now fully incorporate the voices of students (see the chapter by Baba Ahmed and Horma), descendants of hereditary social categories such as blacksmiths (see the chapter by Freire), and other 'uncertified' actors lacking conventional Islamic authority who have questioned the long-established predominant voices in Islamic matters, notably associated with the *zwāya*/'religious' status groups (see the chapters by Cardeira da Silva and Malluche; see also Esseissah 2016, 2021; Frede 2020). One wonders whether we are now witnessing a shift away from viewing Islamic practices in the region through an esoteric episteme (in which they are associated with hierarchy, 'race', and notably a 'Sufi preference' [Amselle 2017; see also Brenner 2000]), toward a perspective that instead focuses on broader social spheres and more 'rational' elements which, for example, emphasize its egalitarian, 'mundane' (Haenni 2005) and presumably democratic aspects.

This volume combines analyses of 'official' and 'public' manifestations of religion with other informal religious practices, often associated with what is called 'lived Islam'. Although this volume engages with the normative social framework that has spread throughout the western Saharan landscape (associated with Islamic-based traditions and the pervasive effects of a *qabīla*-centred social organization), it presents both individual and collective aspirations, as well as the different types of relations that have been established within the 'traditional' model. Complementing and contextualizing the studies drawing on contemporary anthropological field research, the chapter by Ould Cheikh provides not only a significant analysis of a nineteenth-century Saharan textual source, but it serves to highlight the extent and centrality of the tradition of

Islamic scholarship in this region. It thus makes a substantial contribution to our understanding of the importance of scholarly works in Arabic as central elements in the definition of Hassaniyya-speaking social and cultural spheres.

Finally, anchored in a significant range of ethnographic case studies that are deeply rooted in social reality and a comparative methodology, this volume seeks to understand how political expression evolves and is articulated through cultural idioms. Although centred on a relatively remote region, the case studies in this volume and the volume as a whole clearly have important comparative implications that easily connect with the broader Saharan-Sahelian spheres, allowing the articulation of significant dialogues with overarching issues such as state formation, Islamic traditions or the redefinition of perennial social structures. Indeed, the cases explored in the following chapters together offer a new reading of the social experiences that currently define the western regions of the Sahara.

Notes

1 For various reasons – notably related to formal procedures associated with the funding of the underlying project of which this volume is a part and security concerns – it was not possible to cover the entire geographical extent of the Hassaniyya *aire d'influence* (which could have included other notable contributions from Morocco, Algeria and Mali). This collection nevertheless constitutes a significant corpus of scholarship on an important and central part of the region. Following discussions regarding the supervision of the project and academic independence, Moroccan authors and academic institutions in Morocco were unfortunately unable to participate in the research that provided the material for this volume.

2 My use of the expression 'ontology' stresses the significance of these transformations to the self-identification of these populations, at a time when the 'long struggle of competitive cooperation between sedentary societies and their nomadic neighbors' (Curtin 2002: 16) is being questioned.

3 Hassaniyya speakers constitute a clear majority in the central parts of this area (the particular focus of this volume) but are the minority in other locations. In Morocco, where Hassaniyya is spoken by less than 1 per cent of the population (Goeury 2019), the 'Hassani' language is now mentioned in the amended Moroccan Constitution of 2011 (Article 5), in addition to the two official languages of the kingdom, Arabic and Amazigh.

4 If identity is to be considered mainly as an intersubjective phenomenon, formed in opposition to competing social projects and 'progressive differentiation' (Bateson 1935: 181), the term *bīḍān* should be understood in contrast to *kwār*, designating black populations that form the majority to the south. The chronological limitations associated with the use of this terminology can be radically extended if we consider its evident relation with the – much older – expression Bilād al-Sūdān, used by different Arab authors (Levtzion 2001). Despite this, the formal enunciation of such a geography should not lead to caricature-like representations that limit the scope of much more complex and interchangeable social dimensions often observed in the extended western Saharan regions.

5 This social structure, which can be traced with some certainty to the late seventeenth century, was consolidated after the war of Sharbubba (1644–1674, in Leriche and Hamidoun 1948: 525; see also Marty 1919: 60 and Ould Cheikh 2017: 121–37). The first European sources about this region – notably the often forgotten pioneering account by Gomes Eanes de Zurara (written c. 1453–1460) – described the existence of stratified social groups that are reminiscent of the structures that are presently characteristic of Hassaniyya-speaking groups (Horta and Freire 2013: 40–5; see also Freire 2011).

6 Neither the Portuguese word *mouro* nor the Spanish *moro* are directly associated with the Sahara; both can be used generally to describe any Muslim community from northwest Africa to the Philippines.

7 A use to which the term 'Sahrawi' was also put some decades later (in the early 1960s; it was still absent from Caro Baroja's 1955 *Estudios Saharianos*). On the colonial 'invention' of tribal spheres and the ethnic fetishization of African populations, see Amselle and M'Bokolo (1999: 42) and Hall (2011: 113, 174).

8 Hassaniyya speakers in southern Morocco, for example, are unfamiliar with the expression *bīḍān* and use the term *ʿarab* to identify themselves (Taine-Cheikh 1997: 96).

9 The process described in David Malluche's chapter on the Haratin populations of Mauritania in this volume resonates with this description and provides important points of comparison.

10 The questions raised in the conceptualization of the western Sahara as a distinct region parallel many of the theoretical issues faced by scholars of the neighbouring – and indeed partially overlapping – Sahel region (see Villalón 2021).

11 On colonial interactions and the development of new political engagements structured around parties, resistance movements and national liberation platforms, see also Cooper (2005: 232).

References

Abitbol, M. (1986), 'Jihād et nécessité: le Maroc et la conquête française du Soudan Occidental et de la Mauritanie', *Studia Islamica*, 63: 159–77.

Amselle, J.-L. (2017), *Islams africains: la préférence soufie*. Lormont: Le Bord de l'Eau.

Amselle, J.-L. and E. M'Bokolo, eds (1999 [1985]), *Au coer de l'ethnie: ethnies, tribalisme et état en Afrique*. Paris: La Découverte.

Austen, Ralph A. (2010), *Trans-Saharan Africa in World History*. New York, NY: Oxford University Press.

Barreñada, I. (2017), 'Western Saharan and Southern Moroccan Saharawis: National Identity and Mobilization', in R. Ojeda-García, I. Fernández-Molina and V. Veguilla (eds), *Global, Regional and Local Dimensions of Western Sahara's Protracted Decolonization*, 277–93. New York, NY: Palgrave Macmillan.

Bateson, G. (1935), 'Culture Contact and Schismogenesis', *Man*, 35: 178–83.

Bayat, A. (2012), 'Politics in the City-Inside-Out', *City & Society*, 24 (2): 110–28.

Bonnefoy, L. and M. Catuse, eds (2013), *Jeunesses arabes. Du Maroc au Yémen: loisirs, cultures et politiques*. Paris: La Découverte.

Bonte, P. (1984), 'L'émirat de l'Adrar après la conquête coloniale et la dissidence de l'émir Sidi Ahmed (1909–1932)', *Journal des Africanistes*, 54 (2): 5–30.

Bonte, P. (1990), 'L'"ordre" de la tradition. Evolution des hiérarchies statutaires dans la société maure contemporaine', *Revue du Monde Musulman et de la Méditerranée*, 54: 118–29.
Bonte, P. (2017), *Identités et changement socioculturel dans l'ouest Saharien (Sahara Occidental, Mauritanie, Maroc)*. Paris: Karthala.
Brenner, L. (2000), *Controlling Knowledge: Religion, Power, and Schooling in a West African Muslim Society*. London: Hurst.
Campos-Serrano, A. and J.-A. Rodríguez-Esteban (2017), 'Imagined Territories and Histories in Conflict during the Struggles for Western Sahara (1956–1976)', *Journal of Historical Geography*, 55: 44–59.
Caratini, S. (1989), *Les Rgaibāt (1610–1934): Des chameliers à la conquête d'un territoire*. Paris: L'Harmattan.
Caro Baroja, J. (2008 [1955]). *Estudios Saharianos*. Madrid: Calamar.
Cooper, F. (2005), *Colonialism in Question: Theory, Knowledge, History*. Berkeley and Los Angeles, CA: University of California Press.
Curtin, P. D. (2002 [1984]), *Cross Cultural Trade in World History*. Cambridge and New York, NY: Cambridge University Press.
Désiré-Vuillemin, G. (1955), 'Coppolani en Mauritanie', *Revue d'histoire des colonies*, 42 (148–149): 291–342.
Dupret, B., T. Pierret, P. G. Pinto and K. Spellman-Poots, eds (2013), *Ethnographies of Islam: Ritual Performances and Everyday Practices*. Edinburgh: Edinburgh University Press.
Esseissah, K. (2016), '"Paradise is Under the Feet of your Master": The Construction of the Religious Basis of Racial Slavery in the Mauritanian Arab-Berber Community', *Journal of Black Studies*, 47 (1): 3–23.
Esseissah, K. (2021), 'Enslaved Muslim Sufi Saints in the Nineteenth-Century Sahara: The Life of Bilal Ould Mahmoud', *The Journal of African History*, 1–16. doi:10.1017/S0021853721000529.
Fernández-Molina, I. and R. Ojeda-García (2020), 'Western Sahara as a hybrid of a parastate and a state-in-exile: (Extra)Territoriality and the small print of sovereignty in a context of frozen conflict', *Nationalities Papers*, 48 (1): 83–99.
Foley, D. and A. Valenzuela (2005), 'Critical Ethnography: The Politics of Collaboration', in N. K. Denzin and Y. S. Lincoln (eds), *Handbook of Qualitative Research*, 217–34. Thousand Oaks, CA: Sage.
Frede, B. (2020), 'Female Muslim Scholars in Africa', in F. Ngom, M. H. Kurf and T. Falola (eds), *The Palgrave Handbook of Islam in Africa*, 221–32. Cham: Palgrave.
Freire, F. (2011), 'The "Narziguas," Forgotten Protagonists of Saharan History', *Islamic Africa*, 2 (1): 35–65.
Freire, F. (2017), 'The Hemeila Riddle: Genealogical Reconfigurations of Pre-colonial Encounters in Southwestern Mauritania', *History and Anthropology*, 28 (2): 149–65.
Frowd, P. M. (2014), 'The Field of Border Control in Mauritania', *Security Dialogue*, 45 (3): 226–41.
Haenni, P. (2005), *L'Islam de marché: L'autre révolution conservatrice*. Paris: Seuil.
Goeury, D. (2019), 'Y a-t-il un "vote hassani"?', *Tafra*, 18 March.
Hall, B. S. (2011), *A History of Race in Muslim West Africa (1600–1960)*. Cambridge: Cambridge University Press.
Harrison, C. (1988), *France and Islam in West Africa, 1860–1960*. Cambridge: Cambridge University Press.
Hernando de Larramendi, M. (2019), 'Doomed Regionalism in a Redrawn Maghreb? The Changing Shape of the Rivalry between Algeria and Morocco in the post-2011 Era', *The Journal of North African Studies*, 24 (3): 506–31.

Herrera, L. and A. Bayat (2010), *Being Young and Muslim: New Cultural Politics in the Global South and North*. New York, NY: Oxford University Press.
Horta, J. da S. and F. Freire (2013), 'Os Primeiros Contactos Luso-Saarianos: Narrativas Quatrocentistas e Tradições Orais biDan (Mauritânia)', in M. Cardeira da Silva, ed., *As Lições de Jill Dias: Antropologia, História, África e Academia*, 37–53. Lisbon: Etnográfica Press.
Isidoros, K. (2015), 'The Silencing of Unifying Tribes: The Colonial Construction of Tribe and its "extraordinary leap" to Nascent Nation-State Formation in Western Sahara', *Journal of the Anthropological Society of Oxford*, 7 (2): 168–90.
Klute, G. (1996), 'The Coming State. Reactions of Nomadic groups in the Western Sudan to the Expansion of the Colonial Powers', *Nomadic Peoples*, 38: 49–71.
Leriche, A. and M. Ould Hamidoun (1948), 'Notes sur le Trârza: Essai de géographie historique', *Bulletin de l'IFAN*, 10: 461–538.
Levtzion, N. (2001), 'The Almoravids in the Sahara and Bilād al-Sūdān: A Study in Arab Historiography', *Jerusalem Studies in Arabic and Islam*, 25: 133–52.
López Bargados, A. (2003), *Arenas Coloniales: Los Awlād Dalīm Ante la Colonización Franco-Española del Sáhara*. Barcelona: Bellaterra.
Lydon, G. (2009), *On Trans-Saharan Trails: Islamic Law, Trade Networks, and Cross-Cultural Exchange in Nineteenth-Century Western Africa*. Cambridge: Cambridge University Press.
Lydon, G. (2015), 'Saharan Oceans and Bridges, Barriers and Divides in Africa's Historiographical Landscape', *The Journal of African History*, 56: 3–22.
Mamdani, M. (2020), *Neither Settler nor Native: The Making and Unmaking of Permanent Minorities*. Cambridge, MA: The Belknap Press of Harvard University Press.
Mann, G. (2015), *From Empires to NGOs in the West African Sahel: The Road to Nongovernmentality*. New York, NY: Cambridge University Press.
Marfaing, L. and S. Wippel, eds (2004), *Les Relations Transsahariennes à l'Époque Contemporaine: Un espace en constante mutation*. Paris: Karthala.
Marty, P. (1915), *Les Tribus de la Haute Mauritanie*. Paris: Éditions Ernest Leroux.
Marty, P. (1919), *L'Émirat des Trarzas*. Paris: Éditions Ernest Leroux.
Moreno-Almeida, C. (2021), 'The Revival of the Moorish Empire and the Moroccan Far Right', *Jadaliyya*, April 13. (https://www.jadaliyya.com/Details/42600).
Mudimbe, V. Y. (1994). *The Idea of Africa*. Oxford: James Currey.
Norris, H. T. (1972), *Saharan Myth and Saga*. Oxford: Clarendon Press.
Norris, H. T. (1986), *The Arab Conquest of the Western Sahara: Studies of the Historical Events, Religious Beliefs and Social Customs Which Made the Remotest Sahara a part of the Arab World*. Harlow: Longman; Beirut: Librarie du Liban.
Osella, F. and B. F. Soares (2020), 'Religiosity and its Others: Lived Islam in West Africa and South India', *Social Anthropology*, 28: 466–81.
Ould Ahmed Salem, Z. (1999), 'Une "illusion bien fondée": la centralité de la mobilisation tribale dans l'action politique en Mauritanie', *L'Ouest Saharien*, 2: 127–56.
Ould Ahmed Salem, Z. (2005), '"Mauritania: A Saharan Frontier-State', *The Journal of North African Studies*, 10 (3–4): 491–506.
Ould Ahmed Salem, Z. (2007), 'Islam in Mauritania between Political Expansion and Globalization: Elites, Institutions, Knowledge, and Networks', in B. F. Soares and R. Otayek (eds), *Islam and Muslim Politics in Africa*, 27–46. New York, NY: Palgrave.
Ould Cheikh, A. W. (1985), 'Nomadisme, Islam et Pouvoir Politique dans la Société Maure Précolonial (XIe-XIXe siècle)', PhD thesis in Sociology, Paris, Université V.
Ould Cheikh, A. W. (2017), *La société maure: éléments d'anthropologie historique*. Rabat: Centre d'Études Sahariennes.

Ould Mohamed Baba, E. and F. Freire (2020), 'Looters vs. Traitors: The *Muqawama* ("Resistance") Narrative, and its Detractors, in Contemporary Mauritania', *African Studies Review*, 63 (2): 258–80.

Robinson, D. (2001), *Paths of Accommodation: Muslim Societies and French Colonial Authorities in Senegal and Mauritania, 1880–1920*. Athens, OH: Ohio University Press.

Ross, E. (2011), 'A Historical Geography of the Trans-Saharan Trade', in G. Krätli and G. Lydon (eds), *The Trans-Saharan Book Trade: Manuscript Culture, Arabic Literacy, and Intellectual History in Muslim Africa*, 1–34. Leiden and Boston, MA: Brill.

Scheele, J. (2012), *Smugglers and Saints of the Sahara: Regional Connectivity in the Twentieth Century*. New York, NY: Cambridge University Press.

Seesemann, R. (2021), 'Islamic Intellectual Traditions in the Sahel', in L. A. Villalón, ed., *The Oxford Handbook of the African Sahel*, 533–49. Oxford: Oxford University Press.

Scott, J. C. (2017), *Against the Grain: A Deep History of the Earliest States*. New Haven, CT: Yale University Press.

Simenel, R. (2010), *L'origine est aux frontières: Les Aït Ba'amran, un exil en terre d'arganiers (sud Maroc)*. Paris: CNRS.

Soares, B. F. (2000), 'Notes on the Anthropological Study of Islam and Muslim Societies in Africa', *Culture and Religion*, 1 (2): 277–85.

Soares, B. F. (2014), 'The Historiography of Islam in West Africa: An Anthropologist's View', *The Journal of African History*, 55 (1): 27–36.

Stewart, C. C. (1973), *Islam and Social Order in Mauritania: A Case Study from the Nineteenth Century*. Oxford: Clarendon Press.

Taine-Cheikh, C. (1997), 'Les hassanophones du Maroc entre affirmation de soi et auto-reniement', *Peuples méditerranéens*, 79: 85–102.

Taine-Cheikh, C. (2007), 'Ḥassāniyya Arabic', in M. Eid, A. Elgibali, K. Versteegh, M. Woidich and A. Zaborski (eds), *Encyclopedia of Arabic Language and Linguistics*, vol. 2, 240–50. Leiden: Brill.

Villalón, L. A. (2020), 'The Politics of Democratization and State Building in the Sahel', in L. A. Villalón and R. Idrissa (eds), *Democratic Struggle, Institutional Reform, and State Resilience in the African Sahel*, 1–26. Lanham, MD: Lexington Books.

Villalón, L. A. (2021), 'Framing the Sahel: Spaces, Challenges, Encounters', in L. A. Villalón, ed., *The Oxford Handbook of the African Sahel*, 1–11. Oxford: Oxford University Press.

Wilson, A. (2016), *Sovereignty in Exile: A Saharan Liberation Movement Governs*. Philadelphia, PA: University of Pennsylvania Press.

Wilson, A. (2017), 'Ambivalences of Mobility: Rival State Authorities and Mobile Strategies in a Saharan Conflict', *American Ethnologist*, 44 (1): 1–14.

Part One

State

1

A land of opportunities: Political morphologies at the northwestern Saharan frontier (1934–1960)

Alberto López Bargados
GRECS, University of Barcelona

An area of impossible demarcation?

As pointed out by Mary-Louise Pratt (2010), frontiers are 'contact zones', open interstitial spaces often governed by uncertainty. In this chapter, I would like to address a specific frontier – one that lies at the heart of the history of the western Saharan region, the geopolitical limits (*borders*) of which were imposed by two European colonial[1] powers, France and Spain, to mark their respective zones of sovereignty. The territory that stretches from the foothills of the Anti-Atlas mountain range (geographically represented by the Wad Nun) to the basin of the Saguia al-Hamra is a swath of land slightly longer than 300 km from south to north that has served for centuries as a bridge between the Hassaniyya-speaking world (predominantly composed of pastoralists) and Amazigh-speaking groups (mostly sedentary) from southern Morocco.

Drawing inspiration from Igor Kopytoff's (1987) seminal work on African precolonial borders, which portrayed them as favourable to ethnogenesis, I aim to analyse the extent to which the frontier status of this territory throughout history was the key determinant of the emergence of novel political ideologies – ideologies that in turn foreshadowed the appearance of novel collective identities. My analysis traces the recent history of the region, starting in 1934 – the moment of consolidation of the European imperial project in this territory – and ending in the late 1950s with the inception of identity-making processes that would later become decisive to understanding the status quo of this space. This chronology is admittedly unusual compared to other studies on the region; nevertheless, in this chapter I intend to demonstrate the importance of this under-studied period.

Based on a wide range of mostly unpublished documents from Spanish and French colonial archives, I wish to highlight that frontiers are not only areas of resistance to

I am grateful for the help that Prof. Freire and the entire Capshara team provided in preparing this chapter. I would also like to thank Prof. Francesco Correale for providing access to documents at the Centre des Archives Diplomatiques de Nantes (CADN).

the repressive and regulatory actions that states seek to enforce but also stages for creativity and cradles of alternative forms of organization (Das and Poole 2004: 19). Retracing the processes that facilitated these creative endeavours in the immense administrative colonial documentation is not an easy task. Therefore, the principle that should guide our research is that of contrasting the perspectives adopted by the competing powers on this frontier and of grasping (as far as possible) the information, largely marginal and implicit, that the colonial archives offer on the peoples of this area – traces (Ginzburg 2003) that help us to illuminate, however precariously and provisionally, the point of view of the subaltern groups who are the subject of this extensive body of documentation.

As is often the case in frontier areas, the territory under analysis is undefined – one among many as-yet unnamed spaces to which we can allude only indirectly, by means of complicated periphrasis. Geographically, this area constitutes an 'entryway' to the Sahara, where pastoral nomadism has been established as the dominant way of life (Montagne 1930). In addition to marking the traditional boundaries of the area, the Wad Nun to the north and the Saguia al-Hamra to the south have strategic significance, allowing for seasonal crop cultivation. In rainy years, the Saguia al-Hamra used to be considered the 'Sahara's granary', and the Wad Nun basin was subject to intense agricultural exploitation.

The region, with the town of Guelmim as its main historical juncture, has been a crossroads for centuries. Due to its strategic position, throughout the nineteenth century the Ahl Bayrūk trade house established a prosperous commercial network across the Sahara which, in practice, allowed them to make their own pacts and treaties with competing colonial powers of the region – at times in coordination with the *makhzan*, at times enjoying a remarkable autonomy. It is no coincidence that the Ahl Bayrūk belonged to a confederation of lineages and tribes that perfectly embody the hybrid character of the groups inhabiting the region: the Tikna, a political assemblage composed of kinship groups of different origins, whose *frontiersmen* status has more recently been the subject of an interesting debate on the presumed singularity of their identity (Lydon 2009; McDougall 2012).[2] In the precolonial period, this frontier status was due in part to the fact that the area was a space of exchange among those from adjacent cultural areas, given its strategic position in the area of influence of the Moroccan sultanate and Saharan social and political formations, in particular the emirates of central and southern Mauritania (see Ould Hamidoun 1952). But the area's status as a frontier is also due in part to the fact that regional powers lacked the capacity to impose strict control over the territory and its populations, exercising only marginal influence. The interest shown by various Moroccan dynasties in exercising some degree of control over trans-Saharan trade is indisputable, and the long list of cities founded by one or another sultan at the northern ends of the caravan routes is unambiguous evidence of this (Oudada 2012: 216). The Moroccan *makhzan*, for example, exercised symbolic forms of domination, grounded in the religious legitimacy conferred upon the sultan by his status as *amīr al-mu'minīn* (Commander of the Faithful). Yet this authority was not strong enough to guarantee the levying of taxes, and therefore the more assertive sultans, or those whose governments were more consolidated, periodically resorted to the *ḥarka* – a military campaign that was part punitive expedition, part festive parade – in order to 'tame' the border villages which, after years or decades of relative freedom from the *makhzan*'s control, were becoming practically autonomous (Geertz 1994: 159–66; Hammoudi 1999). The Saharan emirates, for their part – in particular the Adrar emirate, closest to the southern limits of the Saguia al-Hamra border region – established aid and protection pacts, ensuring the movement of caravans and occasionally conducting depredatory raids on those living immediately to the north. Nevertheless, they lacked the will and the means to impose effective control over the territories north of the Zemmur region, or the sabkha of Ijil. For their part, the French authorities were equally unsuccessful in imposing control once the Adrar emirate was well integrated within the colony of Mauritania and the colonial border with the Spanish Sahara protected dissident groups who had crossed it.[3]

Indeed, the bonds of obedience that tied these frontier populations to neighbouring political forces were both weak and largely nominal, which raised hopes among the European powers that the ungoverned territories could be claimed and thus exploited. The territory was thus also, on that logic, a frontier for European ambitions, initially commercial in nature (e.g. Donald MacKenzie in Tarfaya; see also Ben-Srhir 2012) and then imperial. It was also a cultural frontier, where colonial powers imposed various administrative boundaries: in the Ifni enclave in 1934, segregating it from the French protectorate over Morocco; in the Wad Draa in 1912, to indicate the beginning of the southern zone of the Spanish protectorate over Morocco; and finally, after the treaties of 1904 and 1912, along parallel 27°40′ north – the boundary separating the Spanish colony of the Sahara and the Moroccan protectorate (López Bargados 2003). Against the will of the local populations, external imperial powers imposed three colonial borders on the territory.

Hybrid morphologies on the northern frontier of the Sahara

Some time ago, Kopytoff (1987, 1999) described the precolonial frontiers of sub-Saharan Africa as open laboratories for ethnogenesis, as 'internal frontiers' to which diverse groups expelled from neighbouring communities would flow (due to economic conflict, politics of membership and allegiance, religious schisms, etc.). Once there, sheltered in relative freedom in a vast habitat not subject to political control, they gave rise to new social and political morphologies. Kopytoff suggested that these frontiers were destined for structural innovation and, at the same time, for cultural continuity, given that the groups that gathered in these autonomous zones brought with them a 'political culture' that was largely shared and that would crystalize into tribes, ethnicities, identities or states (1999: 34). This typology contrasted with Kopytoff's *tidal* frontiers characteristic of imperialism, in which the expansionist power perceives the frontier as an entryway to a 'no man's land', a *terra nullius* that can be conquered in phases depending on the mobilization of forces at any given time (39).

Over the centuries, the regions between Wad Nun and Saguia al-Hamra have indeed taken on the distinct characteristics described by Kopytoff. On the one hand, it was a space that was propitious to the emergence of hybrid forms, hosting large

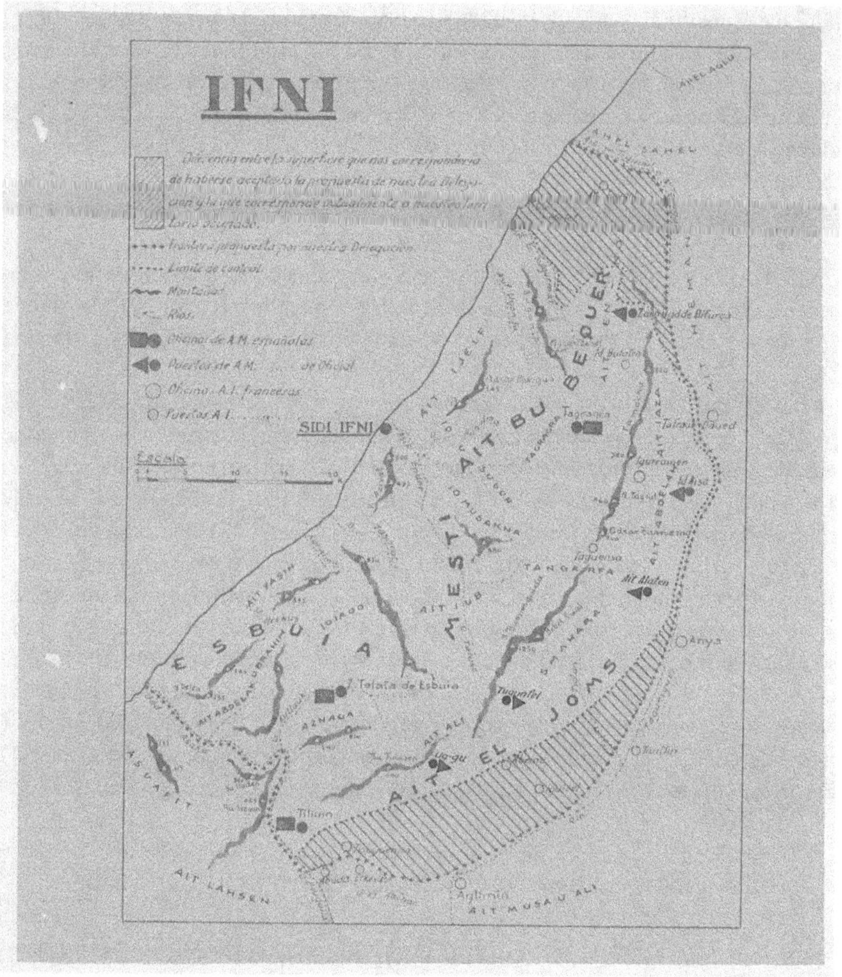

Figure 1.1 Undated Spanish colonial map of the Ifni territory (c. 1935). © Ministerio de Cultura y Deporte. Archivo General de la Administración (Alcalá de Henares, Spain), Fondo Gobierno General del África Occidental Española, IDD (15)023.000, caja S-0065.

aggregations of people with heterogeneous lineages, such as the Tikna, the Rgaybāt and the Āyt Bāʿamrān – a genuine tribal collage composed of rogue lineages who had ended up in an exile of sorts. The '*mestizo*' condition of the frontier was also revealed by the utilization of genealogies borrowed from hegemonic models in Morocco, such as the adoption of *shurfā* genealogies by the Rgaybāt confederation, but also by other frontier groups such as the Awlād Bū al-Sibāʿ; these references were combined, not without distortions, with the classic Saharan hierarchical order, based on the well-known distinction between the *ḥassān* and the *zwāya*, between 'warrior' and 'religious' status clans.

It may be worth paying greater attention to the particular morphology adopted by these frontier groups. The Tikna confederation is the main emergent structural element of the frontier – a heterogeneous agglomeration of clans dating back to at least the sixteenth century. The shared identity of these clans appears to be based more on neighbourly relations and proximity than on filial ties. Over the centuries, these neighbourly relations gave rise to a series of territorial alliances articulated through the distinctive southern Moroccan system of 'dual factions'[4] known as the *liff*.[5] Vincent Montéil (1948a: 10–13), an expert on the region who conducted a well-informed survey in the 1940s, distinguished three forms of affiliation within this confederation: the 'pure' Tikna, with genealogical structures that were homologous to the rest of the Bīḍān clans; the Tikna 'by name'; and the 'factual' Tikna – groups that integrated themselves into the confederation without necessarily extinguishing the memories of their distinct origin. Recently, Ghislaine Lydon (2009: 172–3) has presented a well-documented work on the commercial transnational network operated by the Ahl Bayrūk (Āyt Mūsā ū ʿalī) from Guelmim, which reached its peak in the nineteenth century, emerging as a principal economic and political agent in the frontier (at least until the *ḥarka* of the Mūlay Ḥasan I entered Guelmim in 1886 to limit the autonomy of the trading house). In Lydon's view, these developments underscore the impossibility of integrating the Tikna into the conventional Saharan hierarchical framework. For his part, Mustapha Naïmi (2004: 240), who has studied the Tikna confederation and the complex border dynamics from which they emerged in the most depth, likewise acknowledges that within the confederation, many groups retain the memory of their diverse origins. This is done in a way that does not jeopardize the stability of the confederation, which was forged through political alliances incarnated in the *liff system*, the western 'half' being Āyt Jmal and the eastern half Āyt Billa (according to Hart [1970: 97], these 'halves' could be of quite unequal size).

The Rgaybāt confederacy constitutes yet another group that emerged from this indeterminate frontier. Originating in the seventeenth century around the figure of Sīdī Aḥmad al-Rgaybī and his descendants, they grew significantly during the eighteenth and nineteenth centuries though an alliance policy that allowed for the affiliation of various lineages external to the *nasab* of the founding eponym, through an expansion strategy that contradicted, at least rhetorically, the principles of segmentary filiation followed by Saharan *qabāʾil* (Caratini 1989a, 1989b). On the other hand, the Rgaybāt's claim to be the genealogical descendants of *shurfā*, a genealogical resource frequently used further to the north, was rejected by the majority of the *qabāʾil* Bīḍān, who interpreted it as an attempt to acquire the social capital associated with having *ḥassān* and *zwāya* status (Caratini 1989b: 173).

The emergence of the Āyt Bāʿamrān in the vicinity of the Hassaniyya-speaking area of the Wad Nun can be interpreted as another manifestation of the particular conditions prevailing in that region. The Āyt Bāʿamrān formed an assemblage of mostly sedentary, agriculturalist berberophone lineages living in the foothills of the Anti-Atlas mountain range, just north of Wad Nun/Assaka.

Nevertheless, one of the Āyt Bāʿamrān fractions, the Ṣbūyā, who were predominantly nomadic, moving along the coastal strip between the Wad Assaka and the Wad Draa, used Hassaniyya as a *lingua franca*. Vincent Montéil, who published a small monograph on this confederation in 1948 (1948b: 29; see also Hart 1973: 62), signalled that the specificity of the Ṣbūyā originated in their proximity to the Tikna, and in particular to the Āyt Laḥsan, with whom they interacted in the basin of the Assaka River and in the plains near Taliouine. However, the most detailed information on this area comes from a recent and evocative monograph by Romain Simenel (2010) on the Āyt Bāʿamrān. Because of the ontological and almost immutable status given to the layout of the frontiers between the different societies of southern Morocco, the itineraries of the journeys of various saint(ly) figures have left a footprint on the territories that constitute the tribal space. Simenel describes the Āyt Bāʿamrān as a confederation of allogenic groups stemming from outside the area, making it a true 'place of exile' in which membership is ascribed based on territoriality rather than kinship relations, its non-autochthonous inhabitants lacking common genealogical references (Simenel 2010: 45–51).

These social formations do not necessarily constitute an exclusive frontier model, nor do they make it more of a *sui generis* cultural area. It is likely that the genealogical reconstructions created for the purposes of sanctioning political treaties and strategic matrimonial alliances were present on both sides of the region and that the peoples of the Sahara and the southern regions of Morocco demonstrated some degree of heterogeneity in their internal structure, comparable to the morphologies verified at the frontier. Nevertheless, it would seem that the frontier, with the margin of freedom and uncertainty it provided, enabled the acceleration of specific trends, the intensification of social logics and the establishment of processes of configuration that would have faced greater obstacles under different conditions, where centralization was more of a factor. Sheltered by the expansionary opportunities offered by the frontier, large confederations were able to flourish, while in other territories they inevitably clashed with pre-existing institutions.

A frontier *potlatch*[6]

The frontier was also a land of promise for a number of different entrepreneurs, with some building thriving commercial enterprises in this interstitial space. In this regard, we might highlight the commercial role of the Guelmim-based Ahl Bayrūk, the trading house of Iligh in Tazerwalt (Pascon 1984), and the Casa del Mar, established by MacKenzie in Tarfaya. Of course, the frontier's status as an open field with overlapping zones of influence also gave rise to opportunities for non-commercial pursuits, as demonstrated in particular by the history of Shaykh Māʾ al-ʿaynayn, the founder of the city of Smara, which played a significant (and often contradictory) role in European imperial ambitions in the region. It is no coincidence that the Saguia al-Hamra was for centuries considered fertile ground for sainthood (Bonte 1994, 2013; De la Chapelle 1930; Dermenghem 1954).

Finally, under the yoke of colonialism, the frontier was also a privileged place for ambitious militaries that were eager to add new conquests to the imperial projects they served. Even if the European powers tried to impose their own conceptions of the border upon the Saharan confines, it is important to underscore that any control they managed to establish was bound to be temporary, with lack of security remaining the norm in the management of the Saharan territories. By 1934, the French authorities were under the illusion that they had definitively 'pacified' the frontier, after their advancing troops had defeated the last pockets of resistance in the Anti-Atlas. The Spanish, by contrast, did not even begin to deal with the hinterland of the territory under their jurisdiction until after the Civil War, when the first nomadic units controlling the border were finally established (López Bargados 2003: 549–54). Nevertheless, the border never stopped being a refuge to the exiled and to rebels from both sides. The inherent antagonism between the competing metropolitan powers provoked intense competition for control over neighbouring populations, and neither of the two administrations passed up the opportunity to offer protection to the enemies of the other side.[7] One of the more explicit examples of this frontier *potlatch* was the reception of the nationalist and anti-colonial Moroccan militants in the Spanish enclave of Ifni[8] and the free passage granted by the Spanish authorities to Moroccan Liberation Army (MLA)[9] *ḥarka*s in 1956 and 1957, which facilitated their infiltration into the region of Tarfaya and the north of the Spanish Sahara, their declared objective being to attack the neighbouring French colony of Mauritania.[10] Engrossed in the strategy unfolding at the frontier, anything seemed to be worth securing a short-term advantage. As expected, once the French administration ceased its functions following Moroccan independence in 1956, and especially after the French left Mauritania in 1960, the politics of harassment that had become the norm in frontier management continued, although with one important alteration: instead of the French administration, the competitor was now the Moroccan administration.

The agonistic exchanges between the competing powers who had established the frontiers in the area between Wad Nun and Saguia al-Hamra accelerated the dynamics of mobility that characterized the region. At least theoretically, the colonial powers' aim was to impose their own laws, to segregate the spheres of influence, to allocate towns and, finally, to put an end to the instability and flux of the frontier. What actually played out was completely different, however. The imperial layout created problems for nomadic groups by closing off their traditional pathways and by turning them into a state matter. This resulted in the emergence of incipient mobility between the territories, leading to the diffusion of capital and ideologies through new and unanticipated routes of communication. In addition, it prompted the emergence of a new generation of agents, typical *frontiersmen*, whose experience allowed for the conception of innovative political projects that ultimately led to the formation of new identities in the region.

Frontier incongruities: The case of Ifni

There are few places that provide a better demonstration of the tendencies promoted by imperial gambles than the Ifni enclave, especially its southern parts. Spain, in fact, was always aware of the difficulties inherent in the border layout of Ifni. From the onset of the occupation in 1934, colonel Capaz demanded that the authorities in Madrid sign a treaty with Paris to bring the entire Tikna confederation under the Spanish flag. Capaz and other Spanish officials based in Ifni viewed this 90-km-long swath of borderland – which was under French sovereignty and situated between the estuaries of the Assaka River and the Wad Draa, which was in turn the northern border of the Spanish protectorate over Morocco – as a source of potential problems and requested that Spain annex the corridor.[11] Capaz's likely objective was to attenuate the clash of productive systems in the region, which had traditionally been divided between the Ṣbūyā, a Hassaniyya-speaking group integrated in the Āyt Bāʿamrān confederation who practised sedentary agriculture, and Tikna transhumant groups such as the Yaggūt, which included the Assaka region in their nomadic circuits. As for the Āyt Laḥsan, whose traditional nomadic circuits almost fully coincided with the area between the Wad Draa and the Wad Assaka, they possessed numerous plots of land and settlements in the Taliouine plains, beginning in the territory where the Spanish had established their stronghold.[12] Despite efforts to ensure that the different lineages in the region were segregated in such a way that none would have a dual French/Spanish affiliation, the Āyt Laḥsan were particularly problematic, since many of them had been enrolled in the Spanish army before the official occupation of Taliouine (23 April 1934) and the distribution of the groups between the Spanish and the French, at which point the rest of the Tikna confederation were attributed to the latter.[13] In general terms, as occurred on many other colonial frontiers, treaties regarding the locations of borders established by competing colonial powers were primarily intended to clarify jurisdiction over the populations, as opposed to aligning with abstract considerations of sovereignty or the geographic features of the region. This is largely because the colonial powers sought to avoid being inundated with complaints regarding inaccessible property on both sides of the border (Nugent and Asiwaju 1998).

The tribal charts were inadequate given the conflicts over land tenure and exploitation, livestock and grazing territories, and all this was complicated by the influence of marriage strategies that constantly rearranged alliances and disrupted the coherence that the administrations hoped to achieve with their models. In the case of the Taliouine plains, this resulted in lengthy disputes over the ownership of crop fields and adjacent areas that, in the Spanish territories, had been inherited by the members of Āyt Laḥsan. On the French side, many others were disputed by the Ṣbūyā.[14] The southern border of the Ifni enclave was a permanent source of trouble for the colonial authorities throughout the period of occupation. The rebellion of 1947 is a perfect example of this. After the celebrated speech given by the Sultan Sīdī Muḥammad b. Yūsuf in Tangier on 10 April of that year, in which he seemed to align the palace with the nationalist theses embodied by the *Istiqlāl* party (Zade 2006: 52), the shaykhs of the Āyt Bāʿamrān proclaimed their allegiance to the Moroccan dynasty (to the surprise of the Spanish authorities). In the following weeks, the name of the sultan was invoked in sermons in the mosques, and letters from the palace were read in public recalling that the Spanish colonies of Ifni and the Spanish Sahara, 'from Cape Juby to Lagouira', were part of the sharifian Empire.[15] Not surprisingly, pressure from Spain to grant the population of Ifni a legal status that would cool the growing nationalist fervour intensified. Thus, while France viewed the population of its area of influence – and of the adjoining Spanish area – as 'protégés', and therefore as subjects of the sultan, Spain tried to impose Spanish nationality on the area's inhabitants, as opposed to establishing it as a protectorate. This assimilation strategy, which many

Ifnians still refer to as a shameless attempt to Christianize them,[16] not only caused deep unrest among the Ifni elites but also provoked much more mundane conflicts. From 1945, numerous Ṣbūyā workers, theoretically Spanish subjects, moved to the plains of Taliouine and to the surroundings of Guelmim in order to grow barley and corn. As the weeks passed, some two hundred Ṣbūyā families – a quarter of the *qabīla* – decided to settle permanently in the French zone.[17] This laid bare key complications and unintended consequences of the ambitious legal decisions made by the colonial powers, since from Spain's perspective the Ṣbūyā residents of the French territories had not lost their status as Spanish subjects, while the French considered them Moroccan citizens under a different administration.

The discomfort of the Ṣbūyā shaykhs vis-à-vis the Spanish authorities grew in the following months, to the extent that when Sultan Muḥammad V took over the nationalist project in a famous speech delivered in Tangiers, not only the Ṣbūyā but also the rest of the shaykhs of the Āyt Bāʿamrān decided that the time had come for the Spanish administration to cease its assimilation attempts – which, according to French sources, involved the conscription of tribal leaders into the Spanish army, forcing them to wear military uniforms[18] – and to acknowledge their condition as Moroccan subjects. The outcome was fierce repression, unleashed in August 1947, which resulted in the exiling of many of the Āyt Bāʿamrān to Guelmim,[19] the deportation to Villa Cisneros of *Amghar* Sa'id (a Bāʿamrānī authority who was highly recognized by the Spanish and who supported them in the occupation of 1934), and the exodus to the French zone of large segments of the Ṣbūyā, who were fed up with the humiliation to which they had been subjected by the 'Falangist tormenters', as published on 7 September 1947, in a cartoon in *Espoir* (a publication by the Moroccan Communist Party).[20] The southern boundary of the Ifni colony was once again fertile ground for the mobilization of various competing political actors when Moroccan independence was on the horizon and *Istiqlāl* propaganda began to gain a large number of supporters in the region. One of the first acts of violence attributed by the Spanish authorities to Moroccan nationalists took place in the Sidi Innu mosque, a small Spanish outpost located on the northern bank of the Wad Assaka (on the border with the French zone), close to Warga Tassai, where various Ṣbūyā families held crop fields and small properties. On 2 January 1956, a group of some fifty people (or over one hundred, if those gathered on the other side of the river, in the French zone, are to be included) took over a village mosque, raised the sharifian flag and claimed it in the name of the sultan and the *Istiqlāl*. Since they refused to yield, the head of the outpost requested reinforcements, and later that day, with the help of a captain with two platoons who arrived from Tlata Sbouya, the mosque was recaptured. Three Ṣbūyā were killed in the exchange, and a significant number of them crossed the river into the French zone.[21] In fact, the Moroccan nationalist campaign had begun as early as mid-November 1955, upon the announcement of the reinstatement of Sultan Muḥammad V to the throne following his exile in Madagascar. A legal document (*causa general*) written by the Spanish authorities after these events gives an idea of the scale of the rebellious attitudes germinating in Ifni: A delegation of Sidi Ifni traders approached the Spanish authorities to organize a celebration to honour the sultan. This request was denied, leading to a wave of detentions throughout the enclave followed by deportations to Villa Cisneros.

The determination of the nationalist forces was not stamped out by these setbacks, and in late December a sabotage campaign began, involving the detonation of small explosive devices in the households of those considered to be Spanish collaborators.[22]

The colonial administration had no illusions about the loyalty of the population of Ifni, however. Evidence of this mistrust dates back to the beginning of 1956, when Spanish officials proceeded to disarm indigenous units that had been integrated into the special units created by the army, the *Grupo de Tiradores* (Group of tirailleurs), in Ifni. Although the initiative ultimately failed, the colonial authorities of Sidi Ifni also considered ghettoizing the entire autochthonous population in a single neighbourhood.[23] Throughout the enclave, *Istiqlāl* offices tried to supplant the Spanish administration, subjecting it to continuous acts of sabotage, while the merchants joined the patriotic effort by shutting down their shops, following the instructions of the Moroccan nationalist party. Tensions continued during the spring and summer of 1957, until finally, in November of that year, all-out conflict broke out: in a joint operation, MLA forces attacked Sidi Ifni and different outposts within the enclave, starting the so-called 'Ifni-Sahara War'.

The outcome of this war is well known: the shrinking of the area controlled by Spain to a small defensive perimeter around Sidi Ifni and a precarious status quo that would persist until the definitive retrocession in 1969. What is not so well known is the general dissatisfaction that quickly spread to the Āyt Bāʿamrān zones that had been liberated from the Spanish colonial administration as a consequence of the abuses committed by the MLA. Spanish documents highlight these abuses, since growing disillusion among the Ifni populations fuelled Spanish hopes of regaining control over the territories of the enclave. The French documents highlight the growing anger of the Āyt Bāʿamrān in the face of the despotism of certain *qāʾid*s associated with the MLA, who authorized the confiscation of crops and cattle, as well as violence toward those who had enthusiastically joined the national project.

The construction of roads was another source of anger among the Ṣbūyā, who refused to send family members to perform unpaid labour, which often resulted in abuse.[24] The bureau of the *Istiqlāl* in Tlata Sbouya that was responsible for hiring workers had serious difficulties recruiting a stable workforce given protests by the local population in 1959 and 1960, and even though the Spanish administrative sources were not generally sociologically inclined, they alluded to the significant presence of the Tikna, and especially of the Āyt Laḥsan and Āyt Ūsā, among the ranks of the MLA in Ṣbūyā, Mesti and Amlu villages, until recently part of the Spanish enclave of Ifni.[25] It is extremely difficult to provide plausible estimates regarding the mobility of these populations with regard to the evolution of the colonial frontiers in this area. In case of Sidi Ifni, the conversion of the city into the capital of Spanish West Africa after 1946 resulted in the displacement and concentration of colonial officials, although this mainly affected expatriate personnel of Spanish origin, with the populations from adjacent regions being affected to a lesser extent. On the other hand, the military stronghold – a bastion assumed by the Ifni enclave from the very beginning – had a direct influence on the mobility of the colonial troops, especially starting in 1934, during the Second Republic, with the creation of the Ifni Tirailleurs Battalion (Batallón de Tiradores de Ifni). The *tabores* (companies) of this light infantry unit, joining the insurrectionists, distinguished themselves in numerous battles in the peninsula and in other colonies, such as Spanish Guinea. Of the approximately nine thousand soldiers, 20 per cent were from the Spanish Sahara (Tejero Molina 2013: 434). The formation of the *tabores* therefore involved the presence of some 1,800 Hassaniyya-speaking soldiers, concentrated, for recruitment and training purposes, in Sidi Ifni, a place to which at least some of them would later return to continue their military service once the civil war was over. Given that military personnel constituted a clear majority of the population in the Spanish colony, the presence of these soldiers (and in some cases, of their families) must have had a significant effect on the city. The census mechanisms established by the Spanish colonial administration were usually of poor quality, and thus it is difficult to assess the effects of this mobility in later decades, since the 1957–1958 war restricted the territory under its authority to Sidi Ifni. In this sense, in the municipal census of Sidi Ifni of 1965, and specifically its rectification in 1967, when the retrocession to Morocco was already on the horizon, only the origin of the populations was recorded (according to their provenance), indicating 88 people of Saharan origin, which amounts to about 1.5 per cent of an overall population of 5,608 'natives'. When assessing this seemingly small number, one must consider that among those of 'Moroccan' origin (some 2,126 people, i.e. almost 38 per cent of the total 'native' population), in all likelihood a significant percentage would have come from the bordering provinces of Tarfaya and Guelmim and would therefore have been Hassaniyya-speaking Tikna.[26] Even if we only have indirect information about this, it seems likely that the co-existence, in such close proximity, of two zones of Spanish influence favoured the mobility and circulation of a population that otherwise would not have been as mobile. It should be mentioned that, starting in 1933, the supplying of the Spanish outposts in Ifni and the Sahara was mainly carried out by a commercial company (the 'Kubbāaniyya') managed by a well-known merchant from Sidi Ifni, ʿAlī Būʿayda, and his associates (Āyt Laḥsan, Awlād Bū al-Sibāʿ and a Bāʿamrānī merchant), who owned a fleet of trucks that operated across the Sahara (Naïmi 2013: 162, 268). The fact that a Laḥsanī like Būʿayda was able to assume control of this operation from Sidi Ifni and that from there he also supplied, from 1956, the MLA units that progressively infiltrated the Spanish territory allows us to speak of a certain naturalization of cross-border relations and flows. Simenel's work on the Āyt Bāʿamrān recounts the intensity of the relations with the 'southern provinces' (2010: 33), with the author opting to use the official Moroccan designation for the territories located south of the Wad Nun.

The rise and fall of the MLA in the Sahara

To the south of the Wad Draa, in the southern part of the Spanish protectorate in Morocco and the Spanish Sahara, Pan-Arabist and anti-colonial proclamations also increased significantly from November 1955, following the reinstatement of Muḥammad V to the Moroccan throne. The *Istiqlāl* managed to transmit their slogans of liberation from European domination through the commercial networks that permeated the French and Spanish colonies by mobilizing the language of jihad that, at least since the emergence of the Saadian dynasty in the sixteenth century, had organized the various forms of resistance to foreign occupation throughout the region. This strategy tapped into local collective memory, since both the political initiatives led by Shaykh Māʾ al-ʿAynayn and his son Aḥmad al-Hayba at the beginning of the twentieth century and the more recent initiatives led by Shaykh Muḥammad al-Māmūn wuld Muḥammad Fāḍil wuld Aʿbaydī in the 1930s had also used this terminology (Caro Baroja 1991: 281–6; López Bargados 2003: 519–26). Through an active policy of co-opting Bīḍān notables at meetings in Guelmim, Akka, and even Rabat, and thanks to new means of dissemination (such as portable radios), many of the tribal allegiances on the northern fringes of the *Trāb al-Bīḍān* shifted towards the *makhzan*, although after a short time support both for the *Istiqlāl* and for the MLA began to crack. In any case, the first occasion on which the Spanish administration perceived that the anti-colonial movement in its territories had taken the figure of the sultan as a reference was, as mentioned above, the celebration of the reinstatement of Muḥammad V to the throne following his exile in Madagascar (November 1955) and, immediately afterwards, the announcement by the Spanish administration of new taxes on rural property. It is at this point that Khaṭrī wuld Saʿīd wuld al-Jumānī (also spelled Jatri uld Said Yumani in Spanish) rose to prominence.

Naïmi (2013: 165–67, 191–2) describes the great responsibility taken on by Khaṭrī wuld Saʿīd wuld al-Jumānī in 1951, when, following the passing of his father, he assumed the leadership of the Būyhāt fraction of the Rgaybāt, as well as his allegiance to the sultan and the principles of the anti-colonial movement (at least since 1953). The clearer picture of him that can be drawn from information from the Spanish and French archives is much more gloomy, revealing a cunning and conspiratorial character with purely circumstantial loyalties who collected funds to finance an anti-French sabotage in Morocco just as readily as he had declared himself a sincere supporter of the Spanish government and surrendered to the French in Bir Moghrein (December 1957; see Naïmi 2013: 358). Doubts about the genuineness of his commitment to the sultan to the side, it is reasonable to picture his leadership in the context of a conflict-ridden frontier as a continuous exercise in tacticism, a survival strategy deployed among powers far beyond his sphere of influence, in which ideological considerations were sometimes made to bow down to *realpolitik*. Like so many other shaykhs, Khaṭrī sought only to consolidate his leadership so that local forms of political organization could survive the double challenge posed by accelerated colonial activity and the nationalist steamroller of the *Istiqlāl* and the Moroccan commanders of the MLA.

In any case, the Spanish administrators seemingly agreed with Naïmi's assessment: campaigning against paying taxes was a personal initiative of the Būyhāt leader. The sources in the colonial administration referred to a '*yamaa*' (Ar. *jamāʿa*) of the Legwāsim section of the Rgaybāt confederation (in which the Būyhāt fraction was integrated) that took place in late 1955 in Smara, where Khaṭrī wuld Saʿīd had urged the shaykhs to stop paying taxes since, in the absence of a document from the Spanish authorities confirming their status as subjects of the Moroccan sultan (which the Spanish administration refused to issue), paying taxes made them Spanish subjects.[27] It also follows that the rest of the *qabāʾil* of the regions progressively joined the boycott orchestrated by these Rgaybāt leaders.[28]

The effects of the general uprising organized south of Wad Draa are part of the official story of that war: the infiltration of the MLA into the territories under Spanish rule, the participation of large segments of the local populations in the anti-colonial agitation and finally, a joint French–Spanish military operation, Teide-Écouvillon, which took place in February 1958, aimed at recovering a status quo that seemed to have been irretrievably lost.

If the military operation was a success for the colonial powers in strategic terms, its political consequences were tinged with ambivalence. Spain ceded the southern part of the protectorate (the province of Tarfaya, located between Wad Draa and parallel 27°40′) to Morocco, and the colonial regime became more deeply embedded in the Sahara and what was left of Ifni through its provincialization (Correale and López Bargados 2017). Despite the military defeat of the MLA and the mandatory withdrawal of its *ḥarka*s to the north of parallel 27°40′, the nationalist agitation lasted for months, until, at the end of 1958, a trend toward change was perceived to the south of the Wad Draa.

Several instances occurring over a short period illustrate a growing disaffection, on the part of the populations of the Tarfaya province and the frontier regions in general, with the authority of the Moroccan cadres of the MLA since its integration within an independent Morocco. This is evident in the Spanish documentation, although it is likely that it had been developing over some time.

A turning point was the capture, in early December 1958, of the Tantan arsenal and radio station by an Izargiyyīn contingent under the command of Muḥammad al-Kharr, backed by a Rgaybāt *ḥarka*. This was undertaken in order to fight against the reaction of the *qāʾid* Ṣāliḥ al-Jazāʾirī, who intended to re-establish the authority of the MLA. Tired of the abuses committed by their Moroccan peers, presumably with the tacit permission of the officers, these MLA rebel units, formed by frontier tribesmen, reportedly revolted against their own commanders, seizing weapons and effectively taking control of the town and then cutting off ground communications with Guelmim for several months. Colonial sources differ on the reasons for this move, but they generally mention 'the lack of religiosity' shown by the Moroccan cadres of the MLA – a vague allusion to their lack of respect for local traditions, their continuous requests for cattle and, specifically, the rape of an undetermined number of 'young single women' by Moroccan MLA soldiers.[29]

For his part, Naïmi alludes to other circumstances that led to the progressive disagreements between a large segment of the frontier shaykhs and the Moroccan command of the MLA. He clearly distinguishes the objectives pursued by the Bīḍān tribes, mobilized under the principle of jihad, from those of the leaders of the MLA and the *Istiqlāl*, who he describes as being disrespectful of tribal equilibria and increasingly out of touch with the needs and desires of their Saharan troops. First, Naïmi (2013: 306) notes the inability of Bīḍān notables to rise through the ranks of the MLA and their practical exclusion from strategic decision-making. Second (2013: 333–4), he alludes to the MLA leadership's intention to seize Wad Nun lands, placing them under the jurisdiction of the *makhzan*. Naïmi (2013: 332) also mentions the use of torture and imprisonment to punish 'traitors' (*khawana*) – methods that were completely outside the scope of the Saharan customary code (*ʿurf*). In any case, in the Spanish documentary sources – undoubtedly an interested party in the whole affair – the actions carried out by the MLA in Tarfaya between 1958 and 1959 began to look like the conquest of an occupying army. Having retreated to the Spanish zone (south of parallel 27°40′) to avoid reprisals from the FAR and the MLA commanders, this new avatar of the liberation army (composed only of Bīḍān, whom one Spanish observer presciently described as the 'Saharan liberation army')[30] immediately called for the resignation of the new governor of the province of Tarfaya (appointed by Morocco), the above mentioned ʿAlī Būʿayda – a central figure in the promotion of Moroccan nationalist ideology in the region. Whether because Būʿayda wanted to open fire against the rebel groups who had undermined his authority, or because he had tolerated the abuses committed by the MLA against the nomadic groups of the region, or finally, because the nomadic warriors in rebellion despised this merchant *laḥsanī* made governor, who had mediated in favour of his own lineage and the Āyt Ūsā in the long dispute between them and the Rgaybāt,[31] the situation had gotten out of hand. Within a few short months, Būʿayda was replaced.[32]

Contingent alliances on a beleaguered frontier

It is evident that this shift in the order of alliances between the frontiersmen and the neighbouring powers could not have occurred without the gradual rapprochement with the Spanish administration of Bīḍān groups who had joined the MLA cause, at least in its early stages. All Spanish colonial sources identify this insurgent contingent, formed by the Rgaybāt and the Izargiyyīn. This uprising also counted on the tacit support of the Spanish and French authorities, who were eager to control the MLA units scattered across the region and to limit Morocco's expansionist ambitions across their respective colonies. French sources trace this new coordinated policy in support of Rgaybāt particularism to December 1958, as aiming to 'almost completely disengage the Rgaybāt from the southern Moroccan markets',[33] thus 'effectively protecting Western Sahara against Morocco's expansionist moves'.[34]

This was, once again, muddy terrain, in which different forces and interests converged and in which the significance of established alliances changed rapidly. As always, the main characteristic of the groups established on the frontier was their capacity to survive in a scenario where they were the weakest link and where, once again, external pressures forced them to align themselves with either one or another side of the administrative boundary. At the beginning of 1960, a discussion about whether the still active *ḥarka*s of the MLA should be integrated into the Royal Armed Forces (FAR) was raging; despite its accumulated discredit due to erratic policies marked by abuses, the MLA had not lost its capacity to co-opt the Ifni population.[35] This was perhaps because coordination between the *Istiqlāl*, the FAR and the MLA units was not as exemplary as might be expected. There were continuous announcements of the imminent disbandment of the MLA in the French and Spanish colonial documentation of the time, which a certain number of guerrillas responded to by refusing its disbandment and taking refuge in the rugged terrain of Ifni, acting for a time with complete autonomy from the orders coming from Rabat. These 'activists' (as they were referred to in French sources), acting on their own, exercised almost total control over the former Spanish enclave and engaged in the forced enlistment of Bāʿamrānīs in a policy that, in the words of one French colonial administrator, '... was looking more and more like an endless fight against *Istiqlāl*'.[36] Given the shifting fields of forces on the frontier at the time, diverging ideas easily turned into dissent.

At first glance, this may suggest that the initiative now belonged to the colonial powers, favouring the creation of a 'Rgaybāt state' of sorts, a buffer that would cut off Moroccan ambitions across the frontier and the rest of Bīḍān country. But this amounted to only one part of the story. From the summer of 1960, Morocco redoubled its efforts to co-opt the Saharan tribes who had found refuge and support in the Spanish and French zones, mainly the Rgaybāt, by distributing food and clothing to the groups who were leaving the Spanish zone because of the drought. In February 1961, in Tantan, Moroccan authorities staged a public redistribution ceremony that must have had a strong impact on the frontier groups;[37] in the following months, the French and Spanish observed with concern that their Rgaybāt troops were beginning to desert to the FAR in Tarfaya.[38] The Spanish authorities intended to retain the loyalty of the Rgaybāt and to prevent this slow drain into the area under Moroccan control by extending their already generous aid programme.

In fact, the famous 'sugar pylon policy'[39] applied by the Spanish colonial administration reached its culmination after the end of the 1957–1958 war. Francesco Correale (2019) has recently stated the importance of the *Plan de Ayudas Sociales* (Social Assistance Plan) deployed by the Spanish government after the war: a 'cyclopean economic intervention' (234) accompanied by a compensation programme for damages suffered during the wartime bombardments in which virtually all damages were eligible for reparations. This money, which was distributed among the dense web of tribal fraction leaders that the colonial administration had contributed to consolidating – if not to creating *ex novo* – caused, in Correale's words, 'the creation of a clientelist network and the setting up of a mechanism for surveillance, control and identification of populations ...' (246). This loyalty-buying strategy – with which the Spanish had been familiar since the early days of their presence in the Sahara – was in any case imitated by all of the actors who were intervening at the frontier at the time, each ready to mobilize its own economic and symbolic resources to ensure the extension of its sphere of influence. It is not surprising that one of the first objectives pursued some years later by the incipient Sahrawi independence movement was to end the clientelist policy of control and tutelage that often resulted in shifting loyalties at the price of limiting political autonomy (Barona 2004: 171; Diego Aguirre 1988: 576).

This widespread policy, used in so many other imperial contexts, may indeed have become a psychopathological symptom of sorts – inherent, as Georges Balandier (1951: 9–10) puts it, in any 'colonial situation'. In contexts marked by competition between imperial powers, however, where the frontier represents both a space of uncertainty and opportunities and a limit, these policies were exacerbated to the point of becoming constitutive of imperial action itself. Elsewhere (López Bargados 2003), I describe the extent to which the 'policies of attraction' deployed by France and Spain on a colonial frontier in the western part of the Sahara – the border separating the southern Spanish colony of the Sahara and French Mauritania – led to unusual fractional activity within the groups living on the frontier that nevertheless structured imperial action from start to finish. Perhaps the peculiarities of the space extending from Wad Nun to the Saguia al-Hamra caused an acceleration of these typical frontier processes, as an ideal terrain on which new political projects might grow, among the remnants of the interventions of previous actors.

In the Moroccan case, the incursions at the frontier at that time were directly related to the presence of Ḥurma Wuld Bābānā in the region of Tarfaya, at least since January 1961.[40] Bābānā, an exile of Mauritanian origin who had the support of the sultan (having participated in the creation of the Mouvement Populaire), took on the task of creating the Front de Libération du Sahara et de la Mauritanie (FLSM), to replace the (almost) extinct MLA, recruiting members of factions who had shifted their allegiances to one or the other side of the border in recent months, depending both on their own pastoral interests and on the amount of aid received. The FLSM, which became well known after the attack of 11 March 1961, against eleven oil prospectors with the Italian company AGIP (Naïmi 2013: 254), represented a new avatar of the MLA, at least in terms of the forces it was able to mobilize on the northern frontier of the *Trāb al-Bīḍān*. In June 1961, the French authorities noted with concern that for the first time in a long while the Rgaybāt enrolled in the units created in Tindouf to counter the Moroccan threat were beginning to desert and were heading for Tarfaya.[41]

Once again, and as had occurred on the occasion of the formation of the MLA (of the south) in 1956, the play of interests presiding over Moroccan activities on the frontier clearly exceeded their limits, in line with the nationalist project pursued by the *Istiqlāl*, that is, the idea of a Greater Morocco extending from Tangiers to the Senegal River, under the shadow of the complex personality of Ḥurma Wuld Bābānā and the political programme of the Nahḍa, which broadly supported Moroccan ambitions across the Saharan region. The short-lived FLSM project kept Morocco's claims over the newly independent French colony of Mauritania alive. With the rise of its new avatars and manifestations, it cast a shadow over the border in the years to follow, a spectral threat that would periodically set off alarms at the French and Spanish intelligence services. In February 1963, in a new and dizzying turnaround of the alliances forged at the border, already-independent Algeria's refusal to cede the sovereignty of Tindouf to Morocco, which a few months later would lead to the so-called 'Sand War' (Torres García 2012), brought some segments of the Rgaybāt population closer to the side of the Moroccan government. Thus, the Spanish authorities feared that if the Rgaybāt joined the troops commanded by Ḥurma Wuld Bābānā in Tantan, they would be used to harass the Spanish detachments on the other side of the border.[42] In the summer of 1964, the Spanish administration in Sidi Ifni reported on the transfer and preparation of a Nahḍa army of five thousand men, ready to attack Mauritania from its bases in Tantan.[43]

The demise of a social order

The consequences of the accumulated pressure on the frontier followed soon after. That which ultimately had the most relevant effects was perhaps the breakdown of the tribal alliances that had been firmly established until then. The pacts that had historically united the Rgaybāt confederation with the Tikna were particularly significantly affected. The Spanish and French colonial documentation highlights, with evident surprise, that the relations between the Āyt Ūsā (Tikna) and the Rgaybāt became strained once the latter began to abandon the *ḥarka*s of the MLA en masse to join, among others, the revolt of Tantan and to integrate themselves into the French and Spanish border surveillance units. The open disagreements between the Rgaybāt and the Moroccan leaders of the MLA had already become well known with the surrender of Khaṭrī wuld Saʿīd wuld al-Jumānī and other shaykhs to the French in December 1957. The Āyt Ūsā, on the other hand, remained faithful to the jihadi project and to their membership in the MLA (and, starting in 1960, in the FAR) for some time.[44] Most likely because of this, throughout 1959 several conflicts broke out between the two tribes – disputes that were echoed by the two European administrations. A French document dated 23 July of that year, for example, indicated that the Seventh *Muqāṭaʿa* of the MLA, formed by Āyt Ūsā, had attacked a Rgaybāt camp in the vicinity of Saal,[45] while another note, this time dated 4 November, described a confrontation between the *ḥarka* of Āyt Ūsā, consisting of about two hundred men and led by Ayda wuld al-Tamek, and the Rgaybāt 'enfeoffed' to France or Spain.[46] On the Spanish side, a note from the end of 1959 reported on a request made by the shaykhs of Āyt Ūsā to the French authorities in Tindouf '… to mediate with their protégés, the Rgaybāt, so that the prisoners and cattle retained by the latter as a result of the violent incidents between the two tribes would be returned …'[47] Taking the initiative, the Āyt Ūsā, by then also beginning to abandon the MLA ranks, received logistical support from the FAR for self-defence purposes, since in the following months (January 1960) they continued to suffer from the exactions of the Rgaybāt *ḥarka*s.[48] It should not be assumed, however, that the intense fractional activity that affected the frontier in that period straightforwardly reproduced divisions between lineages, like a mosaic in which each piece has its place. In effect, tensions also ran through the interior of the confederations – tribes and their fractions – due to the individual personalities of each shaykh and the short- and medium-term objectives of each group. Naïmi repeatedly points out the close links between some Rgaybāt fractions and the Āyt Ūsā; Rgaybāt women often married Āyt Ūsā men, and in exchange the latter were in practice integrated into the Rgaybāt *nasab*, alliances that guaranteed mutual access to the regions of Wad Nun, Wad Draa and Saguia al-Hamra (Naïmi 2013: 377). The only thing that jeopardized these alliances, sustained for generations, was the intense pressure exerted by France, Spain and Morocco on the area in question. The Spanish administration in particular had exerted great influence on the coastal groups, namely the *liff* of Āyt Jmal of the Tikna (Izargiyyīn and Āyt Laḥsan) and the Rgaybāt from Sahel or the west, while the eastern sections of Rgaybāt (Legwāsim) had maintained greater loyalty to their pacts with the eastern Tikna (Āyt Ūsā and Azwafīt), thanks, among other things, to the common objective of liberating Tindouf from the French. In any case, tensions between old allies increased in the following years, which shows that some fractures were proving difficult to mend. Thus, at the beginning of March 1964, there were new and harsh confrontations between members of the Rgaybāt and the Āyt Ūsā (with the former capturing a significant number of camels from the latter).[49]

Given increasing confrontations between the rivalling powers for control over the territory, diplomatic efforts at the international level to win allies and increasing sums of money to secure loyalty, it was almost impossible for the delicately balanced social order on the frontier to emerge unscathed. Internal group solidarities imploded, unable to withstand the contradictory pressures to which they were subject. The shaykhs' efforts to maintain their prerogatives and authority clashed with the growing polarization of their own subjects, who frequently occupied a position on the other side of the border, thus giving rise to contradictory alliances. Above all, increased military endowments and new border control technologies rendered the borders increasingly impermeable, making crossings more difficult and, given the punishments imposed on the rebellious groups, condemning them to remain on one side of the border for fear of reprisal. This was the case for many Rgaybāt families and lineages who were condemned for their participation in the *ḥarka*s of the MLA and who had to find refuge in the nearby cities of Wad Nun and the province of Tarfaya, such as Guelmim or Tantan, but also in the north of Mauritania, where they settled, waiting for new political developments.

What is certain is that these changes were taking place as an inevitable effect of the transformations occurring on the frontier. In spite of the dispersion and fragmentation caused by the political and military actions of the rival powers, an awareness of tribal autonomy increased during this period. This was apparently the case with the Rgaybāt, who experienced a demographic expansion thanks to their lax policy of including new members through marriage alliances and whose aversion to the repressive policies exercised by the MLA on the border was early and notorious.[50] These initiatives did not come out of nowhere. On the one hand, they were the result of the negative balance that the frontier groups had to strike in the face of the authoritarian and opaque management exercised by the Moroccan commanders of the MLA, who were not very sensitive to tribal dynamics and even less willing to adapt their action plans to a context they did not know (and likely partly despised). On the other hand, they emerged from the artificial and self-interested policies that the European powers of the area had imposed on a living and complex reality. Perhaps the first signs that a new (and in a certain way unexpected) political project was taking shape on the frontier can be found in the great *jamāʿa* organized by the *makhzan* in Bujchaibiyya, starting on 4 March 1959.

Finally, let us recall that the Tarfaya region was still in turmoil since, months prior, the Izargiyyīn and Rgaybāt (Awlād Mūsā, al-Swāʿid and Būyhāt) had taken control of Tantan, cutting off the land communications and raiding the military objectives of both the MLA and the FAR. In order to defuse an acrimonious situation in which tensions were increasing by the minute, the Moroccan government decided to organize a comprehensive meeting in Bujchaibiyya, a few dozen kilometres south of Tantan, the aim of which was to promote a change of leadership in the MLA and thus to appease the groups at the frontier. The assembly, which reached its high point with the return of Crown Prince Mūlay Ḥasan (future Ḥasan II) on 12 March, tried to convene mainly Rgaybāt and Izargiyyīn groups who were hostile to the MLA and to convince them to join the new Committee for the Liberation of the Sahara. Its success was limited, however, as many of the principal shaykhs who had been active in the rebellion were absent, along with those who were considered allies of the Spanish and the French. Apart from the removal of ʿAlī Būʿayda as governor of the province of Tarfaya and the configuration of the committee's internal structure, it is interesting to note the information obtained by the French intelligence services when, in the presence of the prince, they discussed (albeit vaguely) questions of sovereignty:

> The Prince evoked the history of the great Moroccan dynasties ... whose hegemony extended to Black Africa. The present Reguibats [Rgaybāt] declared loyalty to Muḥammad V and the Alaouite throne (...) However, when the Moroccans spoke of 'indiman' (linkage), they evoked an integration which would turn the Saharan territories into Moroccan provinces; whereas, when the term was pronounced by the Reguibats (and more secretly by the Mauritanians), it evoked a sort of federal link which would leave them the ownership of their nomadic areas (soil and subsoil ...) and their administrative autonomy.[51]

Of course, this information was biased, and it may be a classic case of confounding reality with wishful thinking, to which colonial documentation tends to fall prey. But it is important not to dismiss these assessments, however misplaced they may seem. The most conspicuous of the Rgaybāt leaders present at the assembly, Laḥbīb wuld al-Ballāl, requested a royal pardon for the remaining shaykhs of the confederation (including Khaṭrī wuld Saʿīd wuld al-Jumānī).[52] The mechanisms of agnatic solidarity were still in place, and the ostentatious snubs of the future Ḥasan II (e.g. suddenly leaving the assembly to go to Tantan; calling the representatives of the present sixty-eight tribes 'Rgaybāt') showed signs of a distant and impervious authority, the 'distance of the prince from the tribal milieu' (Naïmi 2013: 369).

Throughout the 1960s, the rains continued to dictate the movements of the Rgaybāt camps (to the extent that the border allowed), together with the payments made by various administrations, competition among which was masterfully exploited by the nomads (skilled, in the words of James C. Scott (2004), in the management of hidden discourses and the art of resistance that characterized the dominated). Yet under these conditions it was difficult not to be tempted by the contrasting promises of the various actors intervening on the frontier. The French had become convinced that the independent spirit and autonomist ambitions of the Rgaybāt had brought about a general rejection of Morocco's expansionist aspirations and that their goal was '... to defend the country against Moroccan interference ...'.[53] On the other hand, doubts about Mauritania's capacity to manage its own territory without the help of the former colonial power, as well as the long history of conflicts between the frontier tribes and those of the Mauritanian Adrar, made the Rgaybāt suspicious of a possible annexation by their southern neighbours. As for the Spanish administration, it had managed to co-opt a large part of the Rgaybāt through the developmental promises of the Franco regime and an accelerated process of sedentarization that was taking place in cities such as El Aaiún and Smara. In exchange for their support for the *pax colonial*, Spain guaranteed the Rgaybāt an artificial bubble of investment and progress. On the other hand, the imminent independence of Algeria was also viewed with distrust by the

Rgaybāt Legwāsim, which is precisely why they approached the Moroccan government, which, in the opinion of French observers stationed at the border, promised to respect the future independence of a *trāb al-Rgaybāt* in order to guarantee its neutrality in the event of an intervention by Moroccan irregular forces in Mauritania.[54]

Thus, in the early 1960s, the strategies employed by the various powers at the frontier converged in such a way as to flame the desire for sovereignty that some Rgaybāt shaykhs may have harboured (Naïmi 2013: 357–8). The documentation produced by the Circle of Atar refers to a report by Lieutenant-Colonel Esquillat, in which it is made clear that the idea of a Rgaybāt state actually arose from an initiative by Moroccan MLA commanders themselves following the defeat of the Teide-Écouvillon operation, which crystallized for the first time at a *jamāʿa* organized in Aïn ben Tili on 11 May 1959. At this stage, it is almost impossible to assess the relevance of this assembly and whether it really served as a founding moment in Rgaybāt – and, by extension, Sahrawi – independence. Putting to the side the irony of the possibility that the Rgaybāt sovereigntist path may have emanated from a suggestion made by retreating Moroccan fighters, and whether or not the Aïn ben Tili *jamāʿa* constituted a turning point, the truth is that the ground had been laid for such developments.

Conclusion

It was to be in Tantan, in the southern part of the protectorate that Spain had pushed back to Morocco in 1958, where the penultimate act of the frontier's story was staged. As the 1960s progressed, the events followed a logic that was guided by regional and increasingly international codes. In 1962, Spain formed the 'Yemaa' (from the Arabic, *jamāʿa*), an embryonic form of self-governance in which the mechanisms of representation made the tribal fraction a form of electoral constituency (Mundy 2005: 5); in 1963, the territory sent its first three *procuradores* (Deputies) to the *Cortes Generales* (General Courts, Parliament) in Madrid (García 2002: 95). In the meantime, France had left the forefront of the regional scene after the independence of Algeria and Mauritania, and Morocco was preparing to sustain its bid for the territory through various political and diplomatic initiatives, not without contradictions. In 1965, the UN issued its first resolution regarding the colony, 'summoning Spain to speed up its exit from the territory' (García 2002: 96). The droughts that mercilessly hit the territory between 1968 and 1973 proved decisive for the sedentarization of its inhabitants, and the 1974 census showed that nomadic life was by then in clear decline, as it was only practised by 16 per cent of the total population (Diego Aguirre 1988: 572). This process must also be considered within the context of the public investment programme undertaken by Spain in the territory during the last years of its administration. According to the World Bank, the income of the Spanish Sahara in 1974 was one of the highest in Africa: $2,550 per capita (García 2002: 86).

This 'Saharan El Dorado' (Andreu 2013) contrasted with the distress that reigned outside the borders of the Spanish colony, in Mauritania and particularly in southern Morocco, where numerous Bīḍān families, coming from the Spanish zone, had sought refuge after the 1957–1958 war, thus overlapping with the rest of the Bīḍān population living between Wad Nun and parallel 27°40′ prior to war. As al-Bashīr wuld Muṣṭafā al-Sayyīd once explained to Alejandro García (2002: 91), the 'losers of that prosperity' living in exile in Tantan were *outsiders*, keenly aware of the homes that they and their parents had abandoned. García himself (2002: 111–2) offers a picture of what a border town like Tantan might have been like in those days:

> Tantan was the ideal place to recruit a core of young people willing to do anything. Almost half of its population were Sahrawi refugees who had fled from the Écouvillon operation, old nationalist mujahideen of the Liberation Army. Their children had been educated on the legends of war; they were inflammable material (…) Although the majority of its people were Sahrawi and in its streets dominated the darrah (Ar. *drāʿa*), the turban and the melfa (Ar. *melḥafa*), the administration and power were managed by people from the north, civil servants, teachers, police officers (…) Not everyone in Tantan were refugees; thousands of Sahrawis settled here for decades, had gardens and were farmers. In spite of their cultural uniqueness, over time they had become Moroccan people; some were soldiers in the FAR, others were policemen, official drivers or truck drivers. The first Sahrawis graduated from the high schools and several dozen entered universities.

Some of these young students, who pursued higher education, played an important role in the later – tragic – history of this frontier. Practically all of them were part of the Rgaybāt confederation, such as Baṣīrī (born in Tantan in 1942), al-Wālī wuld Muṣṭafā al-Sayyīd (whose father was a member of the MLA), and the group of young people who played a decisive part in the Zouérat Congress of 29 April 1973, which led to the formation of the Polisario Front (Bárbulo 2002: 105). In an unexpected plot twist, the frontier was once again presented as an ideal context for the crystallization of new political projects forged from the remnants of the immediate past.

Sources

AGA	Archivo General de la Administración. Alcalá de Henares, Madrid
AGMA	Archivo General Militar de Ávila.
CADN	Centre des Archives Diplomatiques de Nantes
SHD	Service Historique de la Défense. Château de Vincennes, Paris

Notes

1 'Colonial' is an imprecise term. *Stricto sensu*, when referring to European political initiatives in the western Saharan region, following Said (1994: 9), I consider them an expression of 'imperialism', understood as 'the practice, the theory, and the attitudes of a dominating metropolitan center ruling a distant territory', reserving the term 'colonialism' specifically for the 'implanting of settlements on distant territory'. Therefore, colonial practices are not limited to imperial actions deployed by Western

European states, and it is possible to view as 'colonial' any settlement of a metropolitan population in a distinct, but not necessarily remote, territory (as was the case with the occupation and colonization of the Western Sahara by Morocco, starting in 1976).

2 In particular, the debate raised the question of whether the border status of the Tikna allowed them to be integrated into an eventual common Saharan identity or whether it reduced them to being 'outsiders' within the Saharan space.

3 This is the most studied episode of resistance to colonial activity in the region's history. For a broad perspective on the interactions between the groups living in the Adrar and their northern neighbours prior to and during colonization, see Bonte (2008).

4 Hart (1970) explains this system in detail. For the purposes of this chapter, it is important to note that only neighbouring clans could form this type of alliance (Hart 1970: 96).

5 Hart (1996: 194) signals the orthography *liff* (plural *lfuf*, for 'faction, coalition, league'), a term that is usually spelled '*leff*' in French.

6 A ceremony celebrated by the Indigenous peoples of the Pacific Northwest (widely practised up to the height of colonial interventions in the late nineteenth century) in which valuable items are given away or destroyed. Studied extensively by Franz Boas, the potlatch was viewed by Marcel Mauss as a paradigmatic example of what he called 'agonistic exchange', in which the goods introduced into the relationship were expected to increase with each new intervention by the actors involved (Mauss 1979: 155–263).

7 Paul Marty (1915: 26), a shrewd French colonial administrator, had already detected this agonistic distribution of lineages and tribes on the border between the Spanish Sahara and Mauritania at the beginning of colonial activities.

8 A note dated 27 January 1956 states that the number of political refugees in Ifni amounted to 123 people, with a significant number (66 people) being sent to Villa Cisneros to be deported (AGA, S296).

9 In Spanish, *Ejército de Liberacíon Marroquí* (ELM).

10 An information note from Sidi Ifni, dated 16 March 1957, stated that the first parties of the MLA had penetrated the perimeter of Spanish Sahara in October 1956 (AGA, S161).

11 *Situación política de la zona de Ifni en relación con sus límites*, Sidi Ifni, 6/1/1935 (AGA, S65).

12 In Taliouine, according to the documentation collected by the French in 1945, eleven houses belonged to the Āyt Bū Meggūt, an Āyt Laḥsan lineage. See *Bulletin special de renseignements*, Guelmim, 9/6/1945 (SHD, 3H, 2210).

13 *Carta del capitán De Oro al capitán Maldonado*, Sidi Ifni, 6/5/1934 (AGA, S92).

14 *Bulletin special de renseignements*, Guelmim, 9/6/ 1945 (SHD, 3H, 2210)

15 *Affaire des Sbouyas, 1945–1955* (SHD, 3H, 2210).

16 The accusations of attempted 'Christianization' trace back to 1942, when Spain wanted to introduce personal ID cards, as stated in a letter sent by El Hajj Abdelkrim ben El Hassan – a significant actor in IFNI – to the Spanish authorities in Sidi Ifni on 22 August 1949 (AGA, S296).

17 *Affaire des Sbouyas, 1945–1955* (SHD, 3H, 2210).

18 *Affaire des Sbouyas, 1945–1955* (SHD, 3H, 2210).

19 Among them the *qāʾid* Aḥmad of the Ṣbūyā, considered by the Spanish to be the instigator of this 'seditious movement' (*Nota informativa*, Sidi Ifni, 3/1/1956; AGA, S160).

20 SHD, 3H, 2210. *La Falange Española* (the Spanish Falange) was a fascist party founded by Jose Antonio Primo de Rivera in 1933. After joining the Franco-led military uprising, it played a crucial role in the Spanish Civil War (1936–1939).

21 *Nota informativa*, Sidi Ifni, 3/1/1956 (AGA, S160).

22 *Causa general de los incidentes ocurridos en el A.O.E. con motivo de la restitución del sultán de Marruecos, Mohammed V*, without date (AGA, S160).

23 As indicated in a six-page undated draft, s.d. (AGMA, box 32725, folder 1).

24 *Nota informativa sobre la situación política en Ifni y Marruecos*, Sidi Ifni, 29/3/1959 (AGA, S25).

25 *Nota de información interior sobre la situación política en el territorio de Ifni*, Sidi Ifni, 2 April 1960 (AGA, S25).

26 AGA, S95.

27 *Informe sobre reunión efectuada en Semara de chiujs y cabezas de familia más importantes de la yemaa de Reguibat El Guasem, para el pago de impuesto de rústica*, El Aaiún, 3/12/1955 (AGA, S160).

28 The *Causa general* indicates the *qabā'il* and the lineages that refused to be taxed: the Rgaybāt, the ʿarūsiyyīn, the Āyt Laḥsan, the Yaggūt, the Ahl Shaykh Māʾ al-ʿaynayn and the Awlad Tīdrārīn (AGA, S160).

29 *Nota informativa sobre la situación política en Marruecos*, Sidi Ifni, 4 March 1959 (AGA; S25). Sources indicate from twenty to over a hundred.

30 *Nota de información interior sobre la situación política en Marruecos*, Sidi Ifni, 13/2/1959 (AGA, S25).

31 *Nota de información interior sobre la situación política en Marruecos*, Sidi Ifni, 5/12/1959 (AGA, S25).

32 *Nota de información interior sobre la situación política en Marruecos*, Sidi Ifni, 20/7/1959 (AGA, S25).

33 *Mise en oeuvre d'une politique commune à l'égard des tribus R'guibat*, Paris, 10/12/1958 (SHD, 6Q, 28)

34 *Politique à l'égard des R'guibat*, Paris, 4 May 1959 (SHD, 6Q, 28).

35 *Nota de información interior sobre la situación política*, Sidi Ifni, 9/3/1960 (AGA, S25).

36 *L'ALM su Sud et la situation à Ifni*, 22/2/1960 (SHD, 9Q5, 77).

37 Note of 18 March 1961, from the French Embassy in Rabat to the Ministry of Foreign Affairs (SHD, 9Q5, 71).

38 Note dating 6 June 1961, from the French embassy in Rabat to the Ministry of Foreign Affairs (SHD, 9Q5, 71).

39 In reference to the strategy of co-opting shaykhs and eminent tribal figures through the offering of gifts and negligible salaries which, in the context of the Spanish colonization of the Sahara, dates back to Governor Francisco Bens (1903–1925).

40 Note of 18 March 1961, from the French Embassy in Rabat to the Ministry of Foreign Affairs (SHD, 9Q5, 71). On the other hand, the Foreign Information Note on Political Situation, Sidi Ifni, 21 February 1961 (AGA, S25), states that Ḥurma wuld Bābānā arrived in Tantan, along with other political personalities linked to the *makhzan*, on 13 February of that year.

41 Telegram sent by Roger Seydoux from the French Embassy in Rabat to the Ministry of Foreign Affairs, 12 June 1961 (SHD, 9Q5, 71).

42 *Nota de información sobre situación política*, Sidi Ifni, 19 February 1963 (AGA, S25).

43 *Nota de información exterior sobre la situación política en Marruecos*, Sidi Ifni, 30 June 1964 (AGA, S25).

44 Telegram from R. Seydoux, from the French Embassy in Rabat to the Ministry of Foreign Affairs, 19 January 1960 (SHD, 9Q5, 71).
45 *Les R'guibat et l'A.L.M.*, 23/7/1959 (SHD, 9Q5, 77).
46 *Situation de l'A.L.M. du sud*, 4/11/1959 (SHD, 9Q5, 77).
47 *Nota sobre la situación política en Marruecos*, Sidi Ifni, 5/12/1959 (AGA, S25)
48 *Nota de información interior sobre la situación política*, Sidi Ifni, 16/1/1960 (AGA, S25).
49 *Nota de información interior*, Sidi Ifni, 12/3/1964 (AGA, S25).
50 According to the 1974 Spanish census (the only rigorous statistical source produced by the Spanish administration during the colonial period), the Rgaybāt constituted practically half of the territory's population, 49.5 per cent of the total. See Gobierno General del Sáhara (1975).
51 *La conjuration de Bou Khchibia*, 17/3/1959 (CADN, c.113, subdossier 1, file 6).
52 *Situation en régions sahariennes*, 17/4/1959 (CADN, c.113, subdossier 1, file 6).
53 *Synthèse de renseignements Regueibat*, Fort Trinquet, 1 to 25 August 1961 (CADN, c.113, subdossier 3).
54 *Synthèse mensuelle de renseignements*, Fort Trinquet, January 1961 (CADN, c.113, subdossier 3).

References

Andreu, B. (2013), 'La busqueda del Dorado en el Sahara. Intereses, colonizacion y proceso migratorio de los canarios en la ultima colonia espanola durante el franquismo'. PhD Thesis, Universidad de Las Palmas de Gran Canaria.

Balandier, G. (1951), 'La situation coloniale: approche théorique', *Cahiers Internationaux de Sociologie*, 11: 44–79.

Bárbulo, T. (2002), *La historia prohibida del Sáhara Español*. Barcelona: Destino.

Barona, C. (2004), *Los Hijos de la Nube*. San Lorenzo del Escorial: Langre.

Ben-Srhir, K. (2012), *British Documents Respecting the Establishment of the North-West African Company by Donald MacKenzie in Tarfaya, 1878–1895*. Rabat: Bouregreg.

Bonte, P. (1994), 'Figures historiques de sainteté dans la société maure', *Annuaire de l'Afrique du Nord* XXXIII: 283–91.

Bonte, P. (2008), *L'Émirat de l'Adrar Mauritanien: Harîm, Compétition et Protection dans une Société Tribale Saharienne*. Paris: Karthala.

Bonte, P. (2013), *La Saqiya al-Hamra: Berceau de la Culture Ouest-Saharienne*. Casablanca: EDDIF.

Caratini, S. (1989a), *Les Rgaybat*, vol. 1. Paris: L'Harmattan.

Caratini, S. (1989b), *Les Rgaybat*, vol. 2. Paris: L'Harmattan.

Caro Baroja, J. (1991 [1955]), *Estudios saharianos*. Madrid: Júcar.

Correale, F. (2019), 'Enmascarar el colonialismo: las "ayudas sociales" en la provincia española del Sáhara entre 1898 y 1975', in M. E, Rios, G. Maire, P. Alvarez, I. Cabana and M. Galvez, eds, *Nuevos Diálogos: Asia y África desde la Mirada Latinoamericana*, 232–54. Mexico: Colégio de México.

Correale, F. and A. López Bargados (2017), 'Rashōmon au Sahara Occidental. Perspectives, contradictions et défis dans l'interprétation du conflit de 1956–1958', in S. Boulay and F. Freire (eds), *Culture et Politique dans l'Ouest Saharien*, 211–42. Igé: L'Étrave.

Das, V. and Poole, D. (2004): 'State and its Margins: Comparative Ethnographies', en V. Das and D. Poole (eds), *Anthropology in the Margins of the State*, 3–33. Oxford: Oxford University Press.

De La Chapelle, F. (1930), 'Esquisse d'une histoire du Sahara Occidental', *Hespéris*, 11: 35–95.

Dermenghem, E. (1954), *Le Culte des Saints dans l'Islam Maghrébin*. Paris: Gallimard.

Diego Aguirre, J. R. (1988), *Historia del Sáhara Español*. Madrid: Kaydeda.

García, A. (2002), *Historias del Sáhara. El mejor y el peor de los mundos posibles*. Madrid: La Catarata.

Geertz, C. (1994), *Conocimiento local*. Barcelona: Paidós.

Ginzburg, C. (2003), *Tentativas*. Michoacán: Universidad Michoaca de San Nicolás de Hidalgo.

Gobierno General del Sáhara (1975), *Censo de población*. Aaiún: Gráficas Saharianas.

Hammoudi, A. (1999), 'The Reinvention of Dar al-Mulk: The Moroccan Political System and its Legitimation', in R. Bourqia and S. Gilson Miller (eds), *In the Shadow of the Sultan: Culture, Power, and Politics in Morocco*, 129–75. Cambridge, MA: Harvard University Press.

Hart, D. M. (1970), 'Conflicting Models of a Berber Tribal Structure in the Moroccan Rif: The Segmentary and Alliance System of the Aith Varyaghar', *Revue de l'Occident musulman et de la Méditerranée*, 7: 93–9.

Hart, D. M. (1973), 'The Ait Ba 'Amran of Ifni: An Ethnographic Survey', *Revue de l'Occident Musulman et de la Méditerranée*, 15 (1): 61–74.

Hart, D. M. (1996), 'Berber Tribal Alliance Networks in pre-Colonial North Africa: The Algerian Saff, the Moroccan Liff and the Chessboard Model of Robert Montagne', *The Journal of North African Studies*, 1 (2): 192–205.

Kopytoff, I. (1987), *The African Frontier: The Reproduction of Traditional African Societies*. Bloomington, IN: Indiana University Press.

Kopytoff, I. (1999), 'The Internal African Frontier: Cultural Conservatism and Ethnic Innovation', in M. Rössler and T. Wendl (eds), *Frontiers and Borderlands: Anthropological Perspectives*, 31–43. Frankfurt: Peter Lang.

López Bargados, A. (2003), *Arenas coloniales. Los Awlad Dalīm ante la colonización franco-española del Sáhara*. Barcelona: Bellaterra.

Lydon G. (2009), *On trans-Saharan trails: Islamic Law, Trade Networks, and Cross-Cultural Exchange in Nineteenth Century Western Africa*. Cambridge: Cambridge University Press.

Marty, P. (1915), 'Les tribus de la haute Mauritanie', *Renseignements Coloniaux*, 5, 6–7, 8: 73–82; 118–26; 136–45.

Mauss, M. (1979), *Sociología y antropología*. Madrid: Tecnos.

McDougall, E. A. (2012), 'On Being Saharan', in J. McDougall and J. Scheele (eds), *Saharan Frontiers: Space and Mobility in Northwest Africa*, 39–57. Bloomington, IN: Indiana University Press.

Montagne, R. (1930), 'La limite du Maroc et du Sahara atlantique', *Études, notes et documents sur le Sahara Occidental, VIIème congrès de l'Institut des Hautes-Études Marocaines*, 111–8. Rabat: Institut des Hautes-Études Marocaines.

Montéil, V. (1948a), *Notes sur les Tekna*. Paris: Larose.

Montéil, V. (1948b), *Notes sur Ifni et les Aït Ba-ᶜAmran*. Paris: Larose.

Mundy, J. (2005), 'The Colonial Formation of Western Sahara National Identity', Paper presented at the international conference *The Berbers and Other Minorities in North Africa: A Cultural Reappraisal*. Portland: 1–33.

Naïmi, M. (2001), 'Saillances et négotiation de l'identité au Sahara', VV. AA., *Pratiques et strategies identitaires au Sahara*, 191–221. Rabat: Institut des Études Africanes.

Naïmi, M. (2004), *La dynamique des alliances ouest-sahariennes*. Paris: Maison des Sciences de l'Homme.

Naïmi, M. (2013), *L'Ouest Saharien. La perception de l'espace dans la pensée politique tribale*. Paris: Karthala.

Nugent, P. and A. I. Asiwaju (1998), 'La paradoja de las fronteras africanas', in P. Nugent and A. I. Asiwaju (eds), *Fronteras Africanas. Barreras, Canales y Oportunidades*, 31–51. Barcelona: Bellaterra.

Oudada, M. (2012), 'Notes on Informal Economy in Southern Morocco', in J. McDougall and J. Scheele (eds), *Saharan Frontiers: Space and Mobility in Northwest Africa*, 215–21. Bloomington, IN: Indiana University Press.

Ould Hamidoun, M. (1952), *Précis sur la Mauritanie*. Saint Louis, Senegal: Centre IFAN.

Pascon, P. (1984), *La maison d'Iligh et l'histoire sociale du Tazerwalt*. Rabat: SMER.

Pratt, M. L. (2010), *Ojos imperiales. Literatura de viajes y transculturación*. México: FCE.

Said, E. (1994), *Culture and Imperialism*. New York, NY: Vintage Books

Scott, J. C. (2004), *Los dominados y el arte de la resistencia*. México: Era.

Simenel, R. (2010), *L'origine est aux frontières. Les Aït Ba'amran, un exil en terre d'arganiers*. Paris: MSH.

Tejero Molina, J. (2013), *El Sáhara Español, de la 'A' a la 'Z'*, vol. 1. Madrid: Torres de Papel.

Torres García, A. (2012), *La guerra de las arenas. Conflicto entre Marruecos y Argelia durante la Guerra Fría*. Barcelona: Bellaterra.

Zade, M. (2006), *Résistance et Armée de Libération au Maroc (1947–1956)*. Rabat: Kawtar.

2

A historical perspective on legal practices in Sahrawi society (1958–2019)

Enrique Bengochea Tirado
CRIA – NOVA FCSH

This chapter traces legal institutions in Sahrawi society from the mid-1950s to the present, showing how a multiplicity of practices are intertwined in a shared 'legal culture' (Lydon 2009: 276–8). It is organized chronologically into three periods: 1) late Spanish colonialism (1958–1975); 2) the first revolutionary period and the founding, by the Popular Front for the Liberation of Saguia el-Hamra and Rio de Oro (the Polisario Front), of the Sahrawi Arab Democratic Republic (SADR)[1] (1975–1991); and 3) current efforts to institutionally develop the Sahrawi state in exile in a context of diplomatic conflict (1991–present). My research mainly focuses on different legal institutions, the practices they have brought about, and the discourses they have helped to form. Since this study aims to situate the legal phenomenon broadly, including the mechanisms of informal conflict resolution, I provide a diachronic analysis of a geographically fluid area, which will allow me to establish the contexts of and connections between different legal practices.

Franco-Spanish colonization resulted in the political fragmentation of the cultural unit of the hassanophone space, or *trāb al-bīḍān*,[2] which lies between the Draa and the Senegal Rivers, entering inland to the Azawad region of northern Mali. The hassanophone social landscape is historically grounded in a nomadic way of life,[3] the linguistic prevalence of the *Ḥassāniyya* dialect of Arabic, a *qabāʾil*-centred (sing. *qabīla*) form of social organization,[4] and Islam (predominantly influenced by Mālikī legal reasoning, Ashʿarī theology and Sufism (Ould al-Bara 2014; Warscheid 2017). Until the 1960s, the word '*sahrawi*' was a purely geographical term, linked to the Spanish administration of a colony that later became a province.[5] The social transformations of the 1950s, however, prompted a growing number of inhabitants of cities such as El Aaiún and Villa Cisneros (present-day Dakhla) to identify with the geographic location in which they lived (San Martín 2010). At the end of the 1960s, that identification was drawn on by the liberation movements in the territory (e.g. *Ḥarakat al-Taḥrīr*, also known as OALS, the Advanced Organization for the Liberation of the Sahara). The Polisario Front, referring to the two regions of the Spanish colony (Saguia al-Hamra and Rio de Oro), used the term as a synonym for the Sahara (Baddou

2008). This anti-colonial identity was further developed and deepened in the refugee camps managed by the Polisario Front near Tindouf. Since 1976, when used to refer to a community, the term 'sahrawi' has been strongly linked to the community of people who have resolute aspirations for the sovereignty of this former Spanish colony (Anderson 1983).

Imperial fragmentation gave way to a reality in which nation-states were confronted with sovereignty issues across these territories, especially in the northwest, where the SADR struggled to establish the sovereignty of the territory of the Western Sahara, over two-thirds of which is still occupied by Morocco (Fernández-Molina and Ojeda-García 2020) and the remaining one-third of which, controlled by the Sahrawi army, is a scarcely inhabited but hyper-connected area (Drury 2019).

Consequently, most of the institutions of the Sahrawi state are located in several refugee camps around the Algerian city of Tindouf. This is the settlement of one of the oldest refugee populations in the world (since the end of 1975), displaced mainly from the territories previously colonized by Spain. By tracing the sinuous flow of history in this region, this chapter examines the legal practices formed during the period of late colonialism in the Spanish Sahara colony, followed by those that can be observed in the Sahrawi refugee camps around Tindouf since 1975. These practices, closely linked to the exercise of power and the delimitation of sovereignty, shed light on the process of defining the Sahrawi people.

The main material for this research comes from a set of forty-five interviews conducted in the Sahrawi refugee camps, which represent over five months of fieldwork divided into three visits between 2017 and 2019 within the scope of the Capsahara research project. These interviews were conducted jointly with the Sahrawi sociologist Mohammed Ali Laman of the Sahrawi Oral Memory Collection Department of the Ministry of Culture of the SADR and the researcher Lahsen Selki Sidi Buna, who helped me with translation and who hosted me during my visits.[6] We interviewed people who had extensive experience in legal practice and conflict resolution from the late Spanish colonial period to the present. The average age of the interviewees was 71, and 76 per cent of them were men. They came from all refugee camps and from a wide variety of families.[7] Most, both men and women, had memorized the Qur'ān at some point in their lives. We tried to include the greatest possible cross-section when selecting our interviewees, including *quḍāt* (sing. *qāḍī*, judges), lawyers, politicians and women of the popular committees. The interviews had a biographical structure and sought to identify moments in which they or their ancestors had participated in legal processes. I also worked with archived documents related to the colonial period, such as the collection on Quranic justice in the General Archive of the Administration, in Alcalá de Henares (AGA), Spain, as well as the archive of the Ministry of Information of the SADR in Rabouni, the administrative centre of the Sahrawi refugee camps.

In terms of historical perspective, some works trace the legal practices of certain *qabā'il* in the region (Caratini 1989; Caro Baroja 2008; Stewart 2006) or include a description of the legal structure of the colony (Barona 2004; Mercer 1976). Nonetheless, the literature on the legal systems in the Western Sahara has always been more focused on international law and on the conflict in which the very existence of the refugee camps is framed.[8] With that said, it is worth noting anthropologist Alice

Wilson's recent efforts to insert legal logics into her analysis of sovereignty practices in the camps. Wilson points out that the Polisario Front's revolutionary programme tried to implement revolutionary practices in its early years, a process that was reflected in the economy, political participation and legal practices (Wilson 2016). Over time, however, the practices that were intended to be overwritten 're-emerged' and, as in a palimpsest, could be detected in the background, pointing to an important tension within such concepts as 'tradition' (Wilson 2015, 2018b). There is a problem with the present 're-emergence' of social practices linked to the *qabāʾil* universe, since these were practices that the revolutionary project of the Polisario Front was meant to eliminate. In this sense, anthropologist Konstantina Isidoros's reading of the revolution in the refugee camps as a phenomenon that can be understood through the nomadic categories of the Sahrawi people seems especially pertinent (Isidoros 2015, 2018; Lafontaine and Gimeno 2021). Whereas Wilson focuses on revolutionary overwriting, Isidoros points out how the background survives, finding in the coalescent practices of the *qabāʾil* the possibility of the emergence of a nation. The Polisario Front's ability to combine revolutionary elements linked to modernity and traditional elements rooted in the ways of life of the Sahrawi people should not be underestimated (Allan 2010; San Martín 2010; Solana 2019).

Another element of the following analysis is an understanding of the legal phenomenon through the prism of pluralism (Scheele 2008). Hassanophone populations have historically relied on a wide range of institutions and conflict resolution practices that can be understood in terms of what has been called the 'Islamic legal triangle' (Benda-Beckmann and Von Benda-Beckmann 2006). Here, however, I aim to consider these practices in a way that moves beyond essentialism and recognizes the importance of the religious dimension, offering an analysis that is more akin to an anthropology of law in an Islamic context than an anthropology of Islamic law (Dupret and Ben Hounet 2015). As far as 'traditional' legal practices in the hassanophone context are concerned, several overlapping logics can be observed: *fiqh* (Islamic jurisprudence), *ʿurf* (customary norms of the most influential *qabāʾil*) and *ṣulḥ* (Islamic amicable settlement) (Charre 1966). Each of these logics involves the mobilization of different authorities, although in many cases they overlap. The process of colonization and the subsequent development of the modern state resulted in greater institutional variety and the inclusion of positive law, defined by its relation to the state.

On the one hand, there is clear evidence of the appeal to *sharīʿa* through *fiqh*, applied by the *quḍāt* (judges) or *fuqahāʾ* (*fiqh* specialists) (Hall and Stewart 2010). These figures were traditionally associated with a *shurfā* lineage (descendants of the prophet) and/or belonging to *qabāʾil* who were regarded as bearers of a *zwāya* status (religious specialists). Their popularity varied among different individuals and families, however, as did their influence and status. The importance of these individuals depended on their charismatic ability to attract followers and earn their recognition in conflict resolution. Because of their charisma, these figures could become mediators in conflicts between different *qabāʾil* (Hernández Moreno 1988: 156). The legal solutions offered in this way were based on Mālikī interpretations of *sharīʿa* (one of the interpretative schools of Islamic jurisprudence), although these individuals were often influenced by different schools throughout their training, depending on their life experience (Ould al-Bara 2009; Vikør 2005).

These individuals could also impart trustworthiness to judgements made by *jamāʿāt* (plural of *jamāʿa*, tribal assemblies) (Ould al-Bara 2001) formed by *shuyūkh* (plural of *shaykh*, tribal chiefs). Powerful *qabāʾil* issued their judgements in accordance with their own *ʿurf* and *ʿudūt* (customs). The *jamāʿāt* were held at different levels, although they were normally convened at the level of the nomadization unit, the *frīg* (nomad camp). They also gathered when, for different reasons, various factions met in one place: Sophie Caratini refers to the *Āyt Arbaʿīn* (Council of Forty) of the Rgaybāt (Caratini 1989), one of the major *qabāʾil* confederations in the territory. These meetings also served as assemblies between *qabāʾil* and could coordinate several of them against common enemies. The decisions arrived at in these meetings were unquestionable; the neutrality of their members and their capacity to act lent authority to their resolutions. The protected *qabāʾil* and those of dependent status inside the *qabīla* (*mʿallemīn, ḥarāṭīn, ʿabīd*)[9] were placed under the *ʿurf* of those with power. Within the fluctuations of the status of different *qabāʾil*, it was possible for the *ʿurf* of a *qabīla* that had at one time been dominant to become dependent and thus considered internal (Caro Baroja 2008: 137). Although their justification depended on the participation of *quḍāt* and religious discourse, this form of justice seemed to be more effective than the previous one since it was more easily enforceable.

The form of justice practised at these gatherings sought to restore the damage done by the guilty party via payment of compensation such as *diya* (in the case of murder or physical injury) or *targhība* (a gift given as compensation in certain cases) (al-Dāf 2015: 154–5). In such solutions, the responsibility was shared by all of the individual's family members, making the *qabāʾil* a network that ensured legal responsibility. Thus, if an individual was sentenced to ostracism, he or she was deprived not only of a subsistence network but also of the legal protection provided by his or her extended family. In her analysis of the *diya* among the Mauritanian hassanophone populations, anthropologist Marta Alonso Cabré points out that this practice is not a mere payment of a 'blood price', since it also includes elements of cohesion. She describes it as involving two elements: reconciliation between the parties and the transfer of goods to the victim or their representatives as compensation for homicide or physical harm (Alonso Cabré 2016: 114). Although Islamic jurisprudence establishes fixed amounts of compensation depending on the severity of the offence, the amount paid in practice is negotiated collectively between the *qabāʾil* and the factions involved in the conflict. This process avoids mediation by a political authority (Ben Hounet 2010) while creating cohesion between the affected parties (Wilson 2018a).

Finally, there is the practice of *ṣulḥ*, which is endorsed by *sharīʿa* and was often the preferred solution.[10] In this practice, authority figures, the shaykhs of the involved *qabāʾil* or a *qāḍī*, mediate between the parties. The conflict is resolved when the parties agree on a *diya* or *targhība*, depending on the case. This allowed for the modulation of elements prescribed by *sharīʿa* or *ʿurf* and for the adaptation of payments to the opposing parties' means. This fluidity between different juridical logics was especially evident in the resolution process, as conflicts were for the most part resolved by mobilizing the least amount of resources possible. As the institutional enforcement capacities of hassanophone society were very limited, consensus between parties was imperative to the practical application of the verdicts. The decisions made by individuals could involve the entire *qabā'il*, and thus unresolved lengthy conflicts could potentially escalate to violence via razzias.

This pluralist legal system began to be intertwined with positive law issued by the state during European colonization. From the 1930s onward, state institutions began to emerge and compete as French and Spanish armies gained control over inland areas. In the context of Spanish colonization, this became evident from the 1950s, although the fragmentation of the territory and the destruction of customary ways of living had already begun prior to this.

1958–1975: Late Spanish colonialism

In his *Kitāb al-bādiya*,[11] Muḥammad al-Māmī b. al-Bukhārī al-Bārakī (d. 1282/1865) (Ould Cheikh 2016; Warscheid 2018) defined the hassanophone space as a *bilād al-sība* ('anarchic' country) since it was an area with neither *sikka* (currency) nor *ṣulṭān* (central political power) (Ould Cheikh 2011). As the anthropologist Yahya Ould al-Bara points out, the term *sība* was used over the centuries by *fuqahā'* across this territory to define the reality in which they lived. This term seemed to fall into disuse in the Mauritanian context from the early twentieth century, coinciding with French colonial penetration (Ould al-Bara 2001: 269). Under French military pressure, due to the lack of centralized political control, the region that was nominally under Spanish sovereignty became a de facto autonomous redoubt until the 1950s (Correale 2018).

Incrementally, colonialism contributed to the decline of the status dynamics of hassanophone society. Several interviewees indicated the perception that Spanish colonial powers gradually broke the initial pact, which had been based on respect for property and had thus precluded the expropriation of cattle in the form of tribute. Another initial condition was the permission to possess weapons – which was of great symbolic importance, especially for warrior status groups – and freedom of religion, including the application of *sharī'a* in the framework of the exercise of justice.[12] Over time, the colonizing powers went against these covenants by gradually increasing their control over weapons and requisitioning livestock.[13] In 1954, the Spanish anthropologist Julio Caro Baroja documented the words of a member of a prestigious *qabīla* who was lamenting the new situation of colonial control and taxation: 'Now we all are *znāga* ["tributaries"] . . . Now we all have to adjust to laws which are not ours . . . The only "people of the gun" are the government soldiers' (Caro Baroja 2008: 33).

The circumstances in the territory changed qualitatively after the Ifni-Sahara War (1957–8) and its subsequent transformation into a Spanish province (Correale 2019). Several dynamics, including its attempt to control its African colonies in an increasingly adverse international context, led Spain to declare the Sahara as a metropolitan territory in 1958.[14] This decision was taken after a war in which the Spanish army, helped by the French, tried to control an anti-colonial uprising in Spanish North African colonies led by the Liberation Army – a liberation movement supported by the Kingdom of Morocco (Correale and López Bargados 2017; see also the chapter by López Bargados in this volume). From this date, Spain began to establish a dual political system in the province, in which the institutions of *cabildo* and the municipalities under the governance of the Franco dictatorship coexisted with institutions such as the *Yemaa* – a consultative parliament which took the name of the tribal *jamā ʿāt*.

In this context, Spanish colonizing powers proposed a plural legal system that can be characterized as 'weak legal pluralism' (Griffiths 1986: 8). It was a dual system with metropolitan institutions on the one hand and Quranic and customary courts on the other, similar to the French colonial institutions in southern Algeria. In 1961, the laws imported from the Spanish protectorate in northern Morocco were reorganized, designating four legal areas: civil, labour, military and Sahrawi legislation.[15] The first three corresponded to those of the Franco regime in the metropolis, while the latter involved two types of courts: Quranic and customary. These courts were formed by the Sahrawi and were responsible for crimes not involving bloodshed or metropolitan Spaniards (Mercer 1976: 201). The different courts were governed according to different logics: *fiqh* was used mainly in relation to personal, family and inheritance matters, and customary law was applied to criminal matters. The colonial government tried to control legal practices by including these institutions in a legal hierarchy, however, ultimately making them subsidiaries of metropolitan positive law (Barona 2004: 112). The application of this legislation required the participation of various figures, including *cadis* (individuals renowned for their knowledge of religion and conflict resolution) and *chiuj* (authorities linked to the tribes).

The terms 'cadi', 'chiuj' and 'tribu' in this context refer to figures created by colonial legislation, while *qāḍī*, *shuyūkh* and *qabīla* designate figures and practices of Sahrawi society. The former found obvious inspiration in the latter, but they were inscribed in different institutional logics. Spanish colonization tried to co-opt certain elites by institutionalizing authority figures of Sahrawi society. Thus, the *chiuj* (Spanish for the Arabic noun *shuyūkh*), for example, were ultimately defined by the colonial 'law' (*ordenanza*) of 30 April 1973 titled 'New structuring of the *Chiuj* and *Yemaas* and their rules' (*Nueva estructuración de chiuj y Yemaas y sus reglamentos*), which made them intermediaries between those they represented and the colonial administration (Lázaro Miguel 1974: 638), an appointment that was revocable by the General Government of the province. These individuals participated in other institutions, such as town halls, the *cabildo* and the *Yemaa*, erected as a provincial assembly within the framework of the 'organic democracy' that marked Franco's regime. On the other hand, *cadis* were assigned by the tribal *chiuj* in coordination with the Spanish administration. These courts where then composed of a *cadi*, an *ʿadl* (a figure similar to a notary) and a *kātib* (secretary). They had the ability to issue fines up to five thousand pesetas (Spanish currency) and sentences of up to one month in prison, but all of their sentences could be revoked by the courts, led by metropolitan judges.

The authority of the main *cadis* of the colonial period is still recognized in Sahrawi institutions. Many of these *cadis* took part in the creation the of the refugee camps' first legal system, and their names are still remembered.[16] The background training of the interviewees who held the position of *cadi*, *ʿadl* or *kātib* in the colony varied greatly. Some received traditional training in Mālikī jurisprudence in *maḥẓaras* in 'the North', especially in Tantan, Fez and Meknes and other learning centres in the Spanish protectorate, and later in the Kingdom of Morocco. Others were trained in '*Shinqīṭ*', used in this context as an umbrella term for training centres located in the north of present-day Mauritania/*Bilād Shinqīṭ*. Some were trained by live-in paid *ṭulba* ('teachers'), who accompanied nomadic families. According to the data available in Spanish censuses (Gobierno General del Sahara 1974), *South shurfā*, the *qabāʾil* dedicated to religious education, had a strong presence in the territory of contemporary Mauritania. In this light, some of the *cadis* belonging to learned families received their training directly from their relatives in the south. No matter what form religious education took, the core curriculum remained largely the same (Hall and Stewart 2010). It started with training in reading and writing using a *lawḥ* (a wooden slate), partial or full memorization of the Qurʿān, and the study of the major texts of the Mālikī tradition. Lifelong learning was not uncommon, and individuals tended to draw from various sources in their religious education. This type of religious education also taught about the main *fuqahāʾ* of the time, notably the Mauritanian *faqīh* Bouddah Ould Bousseyri, who was often cited. In all cases, students remained highly mobile throughout their training, often disregarding the constraints of the colonial frontiers.

To boost their control, the colonial powers used a discourse linking colonial authority to the 'traditional' practices of the Sahrawi population (Lawrance et al. 2006). In this framework, certain sectors of the colonized population engaged with the colonial powers on their own terms, which had a profound impact on social practices. With that said, we should be wary of a double temptation when attempting to grasp the inner workings of the legal system put in place in the (Spanish) province of Sahara. On the one hand, we should not fall prey to the mirage of absolute colonial control over life in the colony. On the other hand, the force of the dynamics of social change put into play through colonization must not be ignored. The extent of the changes brought about by European colonization is difficult to estimate, but, as the historian Sean Hanretta masterfully puts it (referring to the case of French colonization of the Senegal River valley), '[t]he density of social change may have increased with European conquest, but the density of evidence of change certainly did' (Hanretta 2009: 45).

The courts and other institutions associated with colonial control were located in the cities and urban centres. We must also take into account the context of geopolitical and economic changes resulting from the fragmentation of the territory and the series of droughts that hit the area in the 1960s and 1970s, which led to significant migration to urban centres such as El Aaiún and Villa Cisneros (Bengochea Tirado and Correale 2020). Despite a relative increase in the sedentary way of life, reflected in the censuses of the time (Gobierno General del Sahara 1967, 1974; Molina Campuzano 1954), the population effectively maintained a strategic relationship with urban settlements (Isidoros 2015). The population of the Western Sahara viewed the *bādiyya* as a space in which to negotiate the scope of Spanish imperial and postcolonial national state agencies, once it was located away from Spanish control (Boulay 2014). Coexisting with this system and subverting the narrative of total imperial control, the Sahrawi people's legal practices overlapped with those of European institutions in an attempt to use the latter to their benefit.

Regarding French colonial penetration, Yahya Ould al-Bara (1997) identifies different attitudes – of resistance (either violent or 'silent'), cohabitation and collaboration – by

Mauritanian theologians. A first reading of the interviews shows parallel attitudes among legal authorities in the Western Sahara. Despite the decline of armed resistance in the aftermath of the Ifni-Sahara War, at least until the founding of the Polisario Front in 1973, such resistance had not completely vanished (Martín and Picón 2015). In addition, attitudes linked to 'silent resistance' are confirmed throughout this period. They are characterized by an aversion to the colonial state, with different *bādiyya*-based authorities providing legal solutions that were unfamiliar to the colonial institutions. Cohabitation involves toleration of the colonial state without participation in it. In this context, the grey area in relation to *sharīʿa* and the appeal to Islam emerged. The imperial administration built its discourse on the colonial 'Other' around the essential distinction between a Spanish Christian nation and a Muslim Sahrawi population.[17] In this regard, it should be borne in mind that *sharīʿa* is not a legal code but a framework for diverse political and legal practices. As one interviewee stated: 'We are a peaceful people. We have never invaded anyone; we were only colonially administered by Spain, but we also know that we must respect and comply with our *sharīʿa*, which is our law for how to deal with each other or with anyone.'[18] Thus, whereas for Spain references to Islam served to justify an expectation of respect for differences between the colonizers and the colonized (and ultimately for the continuity of colonization), strategically, for the Sahrawi people, it served as a starting point for building autonomous spaces beyond the reach of colonial institutions.

Moving from this grey area to collaboration, a whole series of agents involved in the exercise of justice were employed by Spain. These included justice-related paid professionals, notably the abovementioned *cadis* and a number of teachers, *ʿudūl* (sing. *ʿadl*) and *kātibs*. In this sense, it is worth noting the connection between the educational and the legal professions in terms of the importance they attributed to *fiqh*. The *quḍāt* involved in the Spanish administration were relatively few and were loosely controlled. The shaykhs found themselves in a similar situation, participating in customary justice. Because of their political role as intermediaries acting on behalf of colonial institutions, however, they were heavily criticized by anti-colonial movements such as *Ḥarakat al-Taḥrīr* (1969–1970) and, later, by the Polisario Front (San Martín 2010).

Colonial institutions established a rigid hierarchy among the different instances of justice by dividing the cases between different courts. This logic was opposed to the fluidity that had existed in the Sahrawi legal context, where there was competition between different authorities. In addition, there were different logics for providing solutions to conflicts, with the *quḍāt* applying *fiqh*, the *jamāʿāt* applying *ʿurf* and peaceful settlements applying *ṣulḥ*. Participation in colonial justice was strategic in its approach, however. Throughout the interviews, *ṣulḥ*-based conflict resolution was referred to as the preferred type. It involved a creative process in which the authority that mediated the agreement could be required to contribute resources. This kind of solution was reached not only through the legal institutions established by the metropolis (the Quranic or customary courts) but also through people not related to the colonial administration.

An example of this horizontal logic is found in the following excerpt from one of the interviews. The interviewee, currently hired as a *ʿadl* in Hagunia, talked about a case presented to the *cadi* with whom he worked. This case had previously been given to several *quḍāt* but has yet to be resolved. The interviewee relates how the *cadi* proposed a solution in the form of *ṣulḥ*, to which both parties agreed. The key point of the solution was not legal enforcement but the ability to mobilize resources (in this case, buying bags of wheat). Upon providing a solution, this individual gained a good reputation and joined the network of individuals renowned for conflict resolution:

> There was a problem, I remember, among members of the same family. This family went on to live in Hagunia. There was a man who owed twelve bags of wheat to another man, and they had gone through many judges to solve this conflict. There was a great conflict; it was no longer a conflict between individuals, but between two families (…) So what was the problem? Those who sold it [the wheat] lived in the city of Hagunia, while those who bought it lived in the city of El Aaiún. Those who had purchased it were arguing that this wheat had to be moved to El Aaiún, and those who had sold it said 'no,' so they had to go there with bags. And they went to look for me. And when I saw them I said '*Oh!*' Luckily we have gathered both sides of the conflict, which has been brought before so many judges.' There was one among them named Hamoudi Abdala, who said, 'I swear, the solution this man tells us is the one that will be carried out.' Sidi Mohammed said: 'What has the other one done?' Then he started to recite the whole problem because he was aware of it. [Sidi Mohammed said] 'I think that this is the moment to find a solution to this easy problem. May God bless those who give.' The problem was that the wheat was not in sacks but in wells. So Sidi Mohammed said: 'Look, I'm going to buy you eighty bags, and those eighty bags will remain here in Hagunia, so you should carry them to El Aaiún.' We killed a camel and ate it, and we were all there. We went to his tribe with them. The tribe said it was fine, that is, they should pay no more, no less, and that's it; the problem was over.[19]

Navigating between different legal logics did not exclusively occur at the level of the *quḍāt* and *shuyūkh*; different segments of the population employed plural legal practices, switching between appeals to colonial law and local traditional law. Joanna Allan analyses the use of these practices by Sahrawi women at the intersection of anti-colonial struggles and female empowerment, in cases where they have appealed to colonial institutions to influence trials (Allan 2019: 40). The Spanish archives contain documentation of several cases situated at the intersection between different legal and institutional logics (Bengochea Tirado 2019: 111). As the following fragment of a report shows, the services of social workers were sometimes used strategically to influence Quranic trials:

> The other case we had was in the month of March. The Chief Captain of the Local Office of this city [El Aaiún] sent us a one-week-old girl who had been abandoned by her mother and whose father, who was very old, could not take care of her. For five days, she was in the *Escuela Hogar de Patronato* [a Spanish boarding school], until the mother came to pick her up because she had already reached an agreement with her husband before the Quranic judge; the ex-husband had to give

> her 1,500 pesetas monthly to raise the girl on milk replacement formula, since the mother had no milk. Once this problem was solved, she told us she had decided to leave her daughter because she thought it was the only way to have this money assigned.[20]

This institutional map was altered after the Green March, in which Morocco sent civilians and military personnel into the Western Sahara. On 14 November 1975, the Tripartite Agreement was signed in Madrid, and the sovereignty of the territory was transferred from Spain to Morocco and Mauritania starting in February 1976. The Polisario Front opposed this decision, arguing for the decolonization process. By the end of 1975, the entire territory had turned into a battlefield. In short, Morocco eventually implemented its own legal system in almost the entire territory (Pazzanita and Hodges 1994: 241),[21] especially after Mauritania's withdrawal from the war in 1979, abdicating, at the same time, its position in acquiescence to the Polisario Front's demands.

In the meantime, a significant part of the population of the Western Sahara (up to 45 per cent of the total population of the colony) fled to the *bādiyya*. After a difficult journey throughout the territory, those who did not settle in the Mauritanian- or Moroccan-controlled cities ended up in refugee camps in Algeria run by the Polisario Front. After Mauritania's withdrawal, the population increased significantly in the camps, where a new legal system was born – one rooted in hassanophone logics combined with the practices of the liberation movements of the 1970s.

1975–1991: The revolutionary period

From October 1975, small refugee camps began to form throughout the territory of the Western Sahara. The violence of Moroccan and Mauritanian armies forced them to move, until they settled near the city of Tindouf, Algeria, where the Polisario Front had a military base. Thanks to Algerian support for the Polisario's claims, the refugee camps had autonomy. At that time, the camps were intended as an interim solution, initially experiencing a severe shortage of means and humanitarian aid (San Martín 2010: 113). The Polisario Front, which just a few months earlier had used these positions to carry out attacks on Spanish outposts, suddenly faced a full-fledged war across the Western Sahara territory.

The organization employed rhetoric drawing from the language of other third-world liberation movements, such as the Palestinian PFLP (Allan 2010), coupled with practices of cohesion inherited from the historical anti-colonial struggle in the hassanophone space (Solana 2019: 365). The origins of the founding members of the Polisario Front were very diverse, spanning the entire region. They came from different geographical and ideological backgrounds and included young people from the Moroccan Marxist-Leninist left (such as the founder of the Polisario Front, Uali Mustafa Sayed), exiled activists from the *Ḥarakat al-Taḥrīr* established in Mauritania (Diego Aguirre 1988) and former combatants of the Liberation Army of 1958, who had been residents of Tarfaya.

Historical events developed rather quickly. In November 1975, most of the shaykhs who were participants of the Spanish *Yemaa* signed the declaration of Guelta, recognizing the authority of the Polisario Front in a 'National Unity Pact'. It was a powerful action, revolutionary in itself, and it affirmed the need to eliminate social divisions and inequalities originating in differences at the level of inherited status, gender and age. At the time, the Polisario Front had assumed not only the anti-colonial struggle and management of the still-forming camps but also the leadership of Sahrawi society (Caratini 2007). By 1976, the nomadic movements of the population had completely come to an end, and the society was divided between the refugee camps and militarized cities (Simenel 2017: 83–4). On 27 February 1976, the Sahrawi Arab Democratic Republic was proclaimed. It claimed the entire territory of the Western Sahara Spanish colony (although to this day it controls only part of it), and the majority of the population under its administration was placed in the refugee camps near Tindouf, Algeria. There, the revolutionary moment brought to life by the young leaders of the Polisario Front met the encampment practices of the nomadic population (Isidoros 2018). Thus, although the organization of the refugee camps was a matter of extensive political improvisation, it did not take place in a discursive vacuum.

In this sense, the imagined legal practices of an idealized past were not at odds with the revolutionary possibilities of the future postcolonial state. Some of the Polisario's publications described these ideal legal practices. An article in the *20 de Mayo* magazine from May 1975 ('De las costumbres' 1975) described the precolonial society as having been organized around a tribal assembly, the *Āyt Arbaʿīn*, representing all of the *qabāʾil* in the territory. According to this article, assembly gatherings became progressively rare throughout the nineteenth century, with each tribal *jamāʿāt* remaining part of the whole that represented the (Sahrawi) people. The article presents the *Āyt Arbaʿīn* as a source of law above the level of the *quḍāt* and as carrying out bureaucratic functions (Healy 2011).

The Polisario Front was called upon to rebuild the unity that the *Āyt Arbaʿīn* had once represented and that colonization had broken, corrupting some shaykhs in the process (Awad 2017). This first discourse distinguished those shaykhs who had been corrupted by colonial powers from those who supported the anti-colonial cause (San Martín 2010). In addition, it presented a Jacobin political programme that allowed the *qabāʾil* to gather around the people/nation narrative. Here, the Polisario Front, as the heir of the *Āyt Arbaʿīn*, was to restore the unity of the people and expel the evils of colonization. As far as justice was concerned, this political programme would involve recognizing the primacy of Polisario political power over the authority of the *quḍāt* in legal matters. The Polisario would thus assume the authority of the *jamāʿāt*, leaving space for the *quḍāt* when it came to resolving conflicts.

Upon the creation of the refugee camps, this discourse was immediately put into practice. In Rabouni, the administrative centre of the camps, a team with the main *quḍāt* was organized, many of whom actively collaborated with the colonial system.[22] This team had been operating prior to the establishment of the SADR. The assembly was placed under the authority of the Polisario Front (Bengochea Tirado 2020), and in November 1976 its members were appointed to the *Superior Council of Justice*.[23]

The Council worked as an appeals tribunal while local structures were built in *dawāʾir* by assigning a *qāḍī* to each of the camps.[24] Popular committees were established to organize the day-to-day activities in the camps by late 1977,[25] an idea borrowed from Gaddafi's Libya (Wilson 2016: 97). There were five such committees – governing education, health, justice, food supplies and crafts. Along with the cells, they were part of the organizational structure of the camps.[26] The committees were formed mainly by women and the elderly, since adult men were at the battlefront, and were organized by the Polisario military structure (Pazzanita and Hodges 1994: 89). The *quḍāt* of each *dāʾira*[27] were integrated into these justice committees as advisers (*mukhtaṣṣ*). The functions of these committees included registering marriages and divorces (Firebrace and Harding 1987: 15–16), responding to certain religious questions (related, for example, to burial procedures), producing goods for celebrations and serving as courts in conflict resolution and mediation. In this sense, the committee dealt with some matters that had traditionally been dealt with by the *quḍāt* and the *qabāʾil*. With regard to their legal work, an informant described her work during the years in which she belonged to the popular justice committee as follows:

> As a committee, what we did was find out about the problem; we found out what the problem was when there was a problem between two people in an argument or whatever. We wrote down what there was and followed the steps to arrange the meeting with the *qāḍī* so that he could decide on anything at the level of the *wilāya* or at the level of the *dāʾira*. But really, as a committee, what we did was to investigate what the problem was and intermediate to solve it, which would be *ṣulḥ*, and if it could not be solved through advice or *ṣulḥ* it was sent to the *qāḍī* in order to solve it through *sharīʿa* or some other means.[28]

Some of the collected testimonies refer to the practices carried out by the women of the popular committees as *ṣulḥ*. In this sense, women were carrying out a practice that had previously been carried out within the *qabāʾil*. The official participation of women in *ṣulḥ* processes allowed for the continuation of certain traditional social practices while shifting the locus of the authority of the *qabāʾil* to the movement. As the anthropologist Alice Wilson points out, the predominant role of women in friendly settlement processes at the time resulted in a deep popularization of justice (2016: 90–115), parallel to what had occurred in other revolutionary contexts, such as Cuba.

According to the anthropologist Konstantina Isidoros, the role of women in promoting alliances in Sahrawi refugee camps should not be overlooked (Isidoros 2017). These camps, understood as war *firgān* (sing. *frīg*), were matrifocal organizations in which feminine lines of solidarity served to create alliances. The formalization of extensive associations through the cohabitation of matrifocal nuclei was not entirely a novelty in Sahrawi society. Just as women's mobility had served the formation of such alliances in hassanophone society (Caratini 2000), in the refugee camps women helped to organize the great alliance that would become the Sahrawi nation. Understanding the liberation movement and the state as a *khayma kbīra* (Solana 2019) – the successor of *Āyt Arbaʿīn* – sheds light on women's participation in legal practices.

These legal practices were constrained by the material context of refugeehood. The forced migration to the camps resulted in the decapitalization of a large part of society, which was deprived, among other belongings, of much of their cattle. The cattle were crucial not only to the survival of the people but also as part of the material composition of the *diya*. Because of the circumstances, the requested retribution payments were only partial, with the rest treated as debt or forgiven,[29] reinforcing the symbolic component of reconciliation. Conflict resolution agreements did not involve significant material exchange but greatly reinforced the symbolic unity taking shape in the camps.

Women on these committees received religious training from the *qāḍī* in order to facilitate the argumentation of their decisions. The *quḍāt* were treated as experts in Islamic jurisprudence, while the popular committees served as representatives of the popular organization. The *quḍāt* exercised justice within the institutions of the movement, recognizing their authority. At the same time, women, who held the authority of the movement in the justice committees, were ultimately subject to the decisions of the *qāḍī*. Nevertheless, many interviewees pointed out the importance of reaching agreement through *ṣulḥ* in order to prevent the conflict's going to the *qāḍī*. In practice, this meant that much of the weight of conflict resolution fell on the shoulders of women, despite the authority of the *qāḍī*.[30] The participation of women in the legal field played a central role in facilitating the resolution of conflicts such as *nujush*[31] and *ʿalaqa*.[32] From that time, changes to the settlement pattern of the new families began to take shape, leading to a form of matrilocality that continues to this day.

Another task carried out by the committee was the preparation of clothing for those who were about to marry. In this sense, the committee directly carried out the task, which had previously been taken care of by the family of the contracting parties. The committee also enrolled in the social control and birth increase policy advocated by the Polisario Front, keeping a registry of unmarried women to assist in marriages. This activity was combined with a shift from materially significant to largely symbolic dowries, which was meant to facilitate marriage and to prevent social inequality (Caratini 2007). The justice committee was engaged in a number of practices related to social celebrations, such as preparing bodies for burial. Traditionally, someone would have been hired to do this, but the coalescence of different *qabāʾil* and social equality led to a shortage of people who had chosen this function as a means of securing their livelihood. As early as 1976, there were documented complaints regarding the difficulty of finding personnel to handle burials. Eventually, the state stepped in through the justice committees, responding to a need that arose in the aftermath of the revolution.

In this sense, life in the refugee camps, as spaces of identification within the nation, was governed by a series of practices that were part of a broader egalitarian programme. Gradually, various scattered camps were rearranged to form three large camps, organized in *wilayāt* and named after main urban centres of the Western Sahara: Smara, El Aaiún and Dakhla. In turn, these were organized into *dawāʾir* in which people of different tribal and statutory origins lived together in rows of equal *khaymāt*. Strategies for unifying the community included participation in the frequent festivities and anniversaries linked to the war, the dual system of administrative and party structure membership (popular committees and cells), the emergence of public services as a concrete manifestation of the state, prohibition of the use of genealogies and the names of tribes, and cooking the same food in each administrative unit (Caratini 2003). These revolutionary practices resulted in the deepening of an anti-tribal discourse in an attempt to erase tribal idioms from society.

Constant mobilization during the war effort gave rise to a liminal context that supported these social transformations (Wilson and McConnell 2015). This process produced tensions, however, since these social changes occurred in a context where there was little democratic control over institutions. 1976 saw the creation of the Council for the Command of the Revolution, which functioned as the 'supreme executive power of the SADR' and tended to rule by decree (Pazzanita and Hodges 1994: 87). This can be seen as a form of detribalization (Wilson 2016: 101) that in practice eliminated the different *ʿurf* and the inequality between the *qabāʾil*. In turn, since all of the inhabitants of the refugee camps were militants of the Polisario Front, this institution had the power to try them in the State Security Court.[33]

This institution's monopoly on decision-making generated tension, however, which came to a head in 1988. In that year, a series of mobilizations in the refugee camps calling for greater democratic participation in decision-making and counterweights within the power system took place. These mobilizations, which continued throughout the years, occurred in a context in which the Polisario Front was negotiating a ceasefire with Morocco. At a time when political tensions could disrupt the national cause, the figure of the *shuyūkh* became the key to maintaining social cohesion through reconciliation (García 2001: 229–93). These were years of profound change to Sahrawi mobilization, and when the ceasefire was signed with Morocco in 1991, it started a new phase in the struggle, marked by diplomatic negotiation.

In 1991, the Executive Committee and the Political Bureau of the Polisario Front were abolished (Pazzanita and Hodges 1994: 87). This process of change, which the Sahrawi historian Mohamed-Fadel Ould al-Sweyih calls the Sahrawi *perestroika* (Ould Es-Sweyih 1998), involved the institutional re-formulation of the Sahrawi state to give it a statelier image. This occurred in the context of abrupt changes to the framework of world politics following the fall of the Berlin Wall and the end of the bipolar world of the Cold War. Meanwhile, Sahrawi society had to process the return of almost half of its population to civilian life, with the gradual demobilization of men and the return to the refugee camps of the first generations of young students from abroad.

1991–today: Institutionalization

From the early 1990s onward, this context changed, marked by hope for a quick resolution of the conflict. Following the recognition of the SADR by Mauritania in 1979, the peace talks with Morocco seemed to indicate the beginning of the end of the years-long conflict. However, the failure of the United Nations framework agreement plans in the early 2000s deepened the social and institutional changes that began to occur in that period. An institutional building process that sought to implement more counterweights and to improve the representativeness of the state was initiated, and this alleviated the tension caused by the political demands of 1988 to some extent. This period was marked by the institutionalization of the state and the introduction of a market economy, which consequentially increased inequality (Mundy 2007).

This process of institution-building was accompanied by extensive legislative activity in the constitutional sphere. From 1991 to the present, more than half a dozen constitutions have been written, delineating the organization of the future Sahrawi state.[34] In the Constitution of 1991, the State Security Court was removed. From 1999 onward, the legal system was organized in courts of first instance, courts of appeal and the Supreme Court, which also created settlement courts as sections of the first instance courts and military courts. In compliance with the 2011 Constitution, and highlighting the role of the state in the application of justice, the reconciliation courts ceased to be part of the courts of first instance. Although this process was initially linked to the construction of the state following independence (Ould Es-Sweyih 1998: 84), the frustration of hopes for a rapid end to the conflict caused the institutions in the camps to gradually become more like the ideal described by the constitutions. This institutionalization process also led to the recognition of certain institutions that had been obscured by the revolutionary process. As of the Constitution of 2005, for example, a Consultative Council represents the different *qabāʾil* of the refugee camps through their shaykhs.[35]

In early 1992, a commission formed by judges, politicians and law students began to work on a report on the reforms to the legal system. The problems they faced concerned how to implement checks and balances, dismantle the old political system and incorporate generations of young people trained abroad. The document was presented to the popular committees and subsequently debated in the different *wilāyāt* before its official presentation to the ninth congress of the Polisario Front (19–22 August 1995). Although broad sectors of the Polisario Front argued that the peace plan had been a failure, calling for a return to armed struggle, it was decided that the peace talks would continue regardless. This resulted in the gradual demobilization and consequent inclusion of battlefield returnees in the management of the camps. Around the same time, a training programme for judges took place, eventually becoming part of the judicial framework. Simultaneously, to support the emerging judicial system, institutions such as the *gendarmerie* and the judiciary police, which replaced the militia, were created.[36] Rather than emerging in the national territory following a referendum, a state that sought to be seen as viable in the eyes of the international community began to take shape in the camps.

With regard to the justice system, these years were marked by professionalization. Since the late 1980s, individuals trained in law in countries such as Libya, Cuba and Algeria had been returning to the refugee camps and had become part of a new judicial system that replaced the popular committees. Despite their different backgrounds, these individuals received training in the RASD's own legislation upon their return to the camps, forming a new judicial system that sought the broader implementation of positive law. A legal system with courts of first instance and courts of appeal eventually replaced popular justice committees in 2007. The first instance courts are present in each of the *wilāyāt*, formed by judges trained in the *fiqh* and judges trained in positive justice. There is currently a criminal court in Boujdour that oversees criminal matters in compliance with the penal code. This tribunal, composed exclusively of judges trained in positive law, also serves as the appeal court (Embārik 2015).

The development of positive justice involves the incorporation into the legal system of those who have studied law at universities abroad. The co-existence of legal personnel trained in traditional forms of *fiqh* and those trained in positive justice at foreign law schools is established through practice. In this regard, one of the interviewees commented on how the young people studying law receive training in *fiqh* and in the practical resolution of conflicts:

> When you are studying in the schools of positive law you receive the basic information of the *sharī ʿa* in order to know how to proceed with the solution of a case in a trial, and it will be your experience in the field of practice with what you have at the level of *wilāyāt*. People trained in positive law have both as they have also been taught the Quranic law throughout their academic training, while the *qāḍī*, which comes from *sharī ʿa*, does not have knowledge of positive law. That is why it is envisaged that the appeals court will be chaired by a person who is academically trained in positive law but must also have knowledge of the Quranic laws … [W]e issue laws according to what we need and based on what we have. Then, through *sharī ʿa*, we have been able to move forward in the resolution of conflicts and to maintain the unity of the people by solving problems through the *ṣulḥ*, and for this reason the Sahrawi state still maintains the applicability of the Quranic laws and *sharī ʿa*.[37]

The diversity of the judges' backgrounds is reflected in the composition of the Supreme Council of Justice, the institution responsible for monitoring and protecting judicial practice. It is an important organ in the organization of the Sahrawi Republic as it watches over the legal branch. As set out in the Constitution, this institution has seven members, the eighth being the president of the Republic. Of these seven, two are elected by the president, two by the National Council and three by the institution of justice. The idea behind this is to ensure that all three branches of government (executive, legislative and judicial) are represented in this institution. As noted in the interviews, however, it also aims to balance the representatives of the *quḍāt* and those of positive justice, in an attempt to reach consensus among both kinds of judges.[38]

Several interviewees expressed the view that legal developments have progressed slowly.[39] This lack of concern for the full development of the legal system has been possible insofar as there are other means of solving disputes in this context. The traditional practices linked to *fiqh* and the practice of *ṣulḥ* coexist with the penal code. Various interviewees reflected that this practice is preferred to the involvement of the state in legal conflicts. In many cases, complaints are withdrawn when the involved parties and their families reach agreements through *ṣulḥ*. These agreements involve judicial figures such as judges or *ʿudūl*, *shuyūkh* from the advisory council and renowned individuals.

With the development of the penal code, certain criminal cases (such as those dealing with theft or murder) do not allow for the withdrawal of sanctions upon agreement, even if the *ṣulḥ* complements the sanction applied by the state.[40] Nevertheless, given the international demand for the standardization of the Sahrawi legal system, these practices can be a source of judicial uncertainty. In addition, although these practices are applied to the daily lives of the population in the camps, political dissent is handled by the military courts. This has raised concerns about the keeping of political prisoners (Human Rights Watch et al. 2008).

The importance of *ṣulḥ* also reveals the limitations of the state when it comes to dealing with certain types of conflict. On the one hand, there are problems that the Sahrawi state is ill equipped to address directly. One example is drug trafficking, which is common in hyper-connected spaces such as the Algerian southwest region. These activities can mobilize resources that exceed the capacity of the Sahrawi state and its ability to apply *ṣulḥ* due to economic inequalities. Beyond cultural analysis, there are also geostrategic difficulties with establishing the rule of law. The insecurity resulting from dependence on foreign aid and the attraction of humanitarian aid continues to weaken the Sahrawi legal system.[41]

Conclusion

This chapter has traced the development of legal practices in the Western Sahara for over half a century. During this period, various configurations mainly associated with four logics can be found: *fiqh*, *ʿurf*, *ṣulḥ* and positive law. With regard to the colonial period, I have described how Spanish colonization tried to adapt these logics and to include them in a plural – albeit hierarchical – system, which allowed local legal practices to survive beyond colonial control. The administration of justice during the colonial period was thus situated in a context of relative autonomy. These grey areas left by colonization – notably associated with Islamic legal traditions – demonstrate that although '*law may be essential to sovereignty ... the reversal is not necessarily true*' (Wilson 2016: 115).

The autonomy of legal practices became a challenge for state-building, however. In this sense, the Polisario Front always had to negotiate with the logic of legal practice, giving it proper space but ensuring the primacy of the political. Settlement in the refugee camps led to the implementation of a wide range of legal logics inherited from the precolonial period, into which the Polisario Front began to be drawn as a central element of authority. This was especially true after the establishment of the popular committees. Following the ceasefire and subsequent international rebalancing, the Polisario Front needed to highlight the structure of the state in the face of the movement, giving greater exposure to positive law. The construction of the state in more contemporary instances involved continued negotiation with the authorities, although the permanence of the Sahrawi people in the camps has also led to these authorities' being increasingly co-opted by the Polisario Front.

Participation in a common process of war and state-building, as a liminal life experience, has contributed to the transformation of social practices. Alice Wilson notes how the state movement[42] managed its relation to the social relations of the *qabā'il*, indicating their potential compatibility in carrying out the project of sovereignty (2016: 89). Despite the state's efforts to control these practices, they seem to disappear and re-emerge over time, changing in each incarnation.

The Polisario Front's ability to hegemonize legal authority is evident, although this has occurred in a 'legal culture' that has traditionally distrusted state authority. In this changing institutional panorama, it has been possible to re-signify this plural set of legal practices. The practice of *ṣulḥ*, the relevance of which in legal systems in Islamic contexts should not be neglected (Othman 2007), plays a prominent role in this process. It has served to minimize conflicts and to maintain balance between heterogeneous actors. The popularization of this practice has influenced the reconciliation element of the *diya*. In turn, these practices continue to escape the logic of positive law, which is nonetheless gaining in populatity among the younger members of the refugee camps.

Notes

1 Initially organized as an anti-colonial front against Spanish colonialism in the Spanish Sahara colony in 1973. Its efforts led to the declaration of the RASD in 1976, following Spain's withdrawal of its former colony (which was left to Morocco and Mauritania) through the 'tripartite agreements' (14 November 1975).

2 The expression *trāb al-bīḍān* translates as 'land of the whites'. The term *bīḍān* refers to a particular strata of the Hassaniyya-speaking populations of the western Saharan region, namely those of 'free'/'noble' status. Following discussion with the editor of this volume, I have decided to use the expression 'hassanophone space', in order to surpass eminently racial and hereditary status markers (Freire 2014).

3 Here, the evocation of a 'nomadic way of life' should be understood from a cultural perspective in a sense that is similar to the Khaldunian notion of *'umrān badawī* (nomadic civilization), as opposed to *'umrān ḥaḍarī* (sedentary civilization). Although the term 'Bedouin' has similar roots, I would like to avoid its possible negative connotations, in particular its relation to the French *bedouin*. I would also like to add a nuance to its direct application to Arab lineages by pointing out the cultural intermixing of Amazigh, African and Arab populations in the Western Sahara. I would like to thank Professor Abdel Wedoud Ould Cheikh for his insights on this subject.

4 This can (problematically) be translated as 'tribe' (Stewart 2006: 239).

5 The term '*saharaui*' was used jointly with '*sahariano*' as a demonym for the people who inhabited the colony of the Spanish Sahara.

6 I would like to thank Juan Carlos Gimeno for introducing us. His many years working in the refugee camps allowed for the creation of this research team, which follows a collaborative methodology (Rappaport 2008).

7 I have not included information on the *qabā'il* of the interviewees insofar as this was often not explicitly communicated to me and because in certain cases interviewees requested that I maintain discretion in this regard.

8 I should highlight the efforts made by CESO, the Center for Studies on Western Sahara of the University of Santiago de Compostela, https://www.usc.gal/es/institutos/ceso/.

9 For a reflection on the meaning of the word *ḥarāṭīn*, see, for example, McDougall (2020) and the chapter by David Malluche in this volume.

10 Throughout the interviews, this practice is referred to as 'primary', to be carried out in order to 'avoid' appealing to justice.

11 Recently published by the Centre des Etudes Sahariennes (al-Māmī 2014).

12 Interview in the refugee camp of Dakha, 29 November 2017.

13 Interview in the refugee camp of Bujdur, 3 April 2018.

14 Among the motivations for carrying out this movement was pressure from the United Nations to bring the non-autonomous territories under Spanish control. The Spanish response, which was to make these colonies 'provinces', initially mirrored that of the Salazarist regime of Portugal in the same situation (1951), although it should not be forgotten that the incorporation of colonial territories into the metropolis was a strategy used by other empires at the time, such as France.

15 This kind of justice was already articulated in the *Decreto de 23 de enero de 1953, orgánico de la administración de justicia del Africa Occidental Española*, which indicated two types of justice, 'Muslim law in the Quranic Courts and consuetudinary law in the Consuetudinary Courts' (Yanguas Miravete 1960: 208).

16 '*waraqa ḥawla wizārat al-ʿadl wa-l-shuʾūn al-dīniyya muʿadda bi munāsabat al-dhikra al-khāmisa wa-l-thalāthūn li-iʿlān al-jumhūriyya al-ʿarabiyya al-ṣaḥrāwiyya al-dīmuqrāṭiyya*', RASD Information Ministry Archives, Rabouni.

17 The role reserved for Islamic legal practices under Spanish colonization seems to have been more important than that given to them under French colonization, where the Quranic courts had the least power and the least funding (Feria 2002: 33–4). In this sense, the relationship between the practice of Islam and Spanish colonization in the Sahara should be highlighted. An essential part of Spanish colonial discourse declared respect for the Islamic religion. The discourse of racial and cultural continuity on both sides of the Mediterranean, typical of Spanish imperialism, was used as an argument for the supposed appropriateness of the Spanish state's colonization of this region. Nonetheless, this also put the colonial relationship in danger (Martin-Márquez 2008), making it difficult to differentiate between metropolitan and colonial subjects. Only the Catholic core of the Spanish nation differentiated it from colonized subjects, who were essentially Muslim. Respect for the Islamic faith thus produced a continuous slippage that made these colonized subjects 'almost the same, but not quite' (Bhabha 1984: 127).

18 Interviews in Smara refugee camp, 12 and 17 April 2018.

19 Interview in Aousserd refugee camp, 26 November 2017, translated from Ḥassāniyya to Spanish by Lahsen Selki Sidi Buna.

20 'Informe 1er semestre de 1974' (El Aaiún, 7 August 1974), AGA, Cultura, 237.

21 Although most of the Moroccan legal system formally rested with the local Pasha (governor) and the judges, there was broad judicial discretion. Concerning the numbers of Sahrawi people killed or disappeared under the Moroccan regime, 'in percentage terms with respect to the whole of the population, they are close to those of the war in El Salvador or to countries that have suffered genocide such as Guatemala or East Timor' (Martín Beristain and González Hidalgo 2012: 49).

22 Interview in El Aaiún refugee camp camp, 21 April 2018.

23 *'waraqa ḥawla wizārat al- 'adl wa-l-shu'ūn al-dīniyya mu'adda bi munāsabat al-dhikra al-khāmisa wa-l-thalāthūn li-i'lān al-jumhūriyya al- 'arabiyya al-ṣaḥrāwiyya al-dīmuqrāṭiyya'*, RASD Information Ministry Archives, Rabouni.

24 According to an IFHR report from 1979, in October 1976 there were twenty-two camps around Tindouf, the largest of which had 7,800 inhabitants in 660 tents. Of these inhabitants, 80 per cent were women and children; only 10 per cent of the tents were made according to the traditional nomadic Sahrawi practices (Mercer 1979: 18).

25 Interview in Smara refugee camp, 20 October 2018.

26 The organization of the refugee camps took place on two levels. The popular committees organized the production and day-to-day matters in the camps on behalf of the state. On the other hand, the cells organized political activity in the camps within the structure of the Polisario Front, to which all its inhabitants belonged.

27 The *dā'ira* was the basis of the organization of the refugee camps until the formation of the *wilāyāt.*

28 Interview in Aousserd refugee camp, 19 March 2018, translated from Hassaniyya by Lahsen Selki Ssdi Buna.

29 Interview in Aousserd refugee camp, 27 November 2017.

30 In this regard, a *qāḍī* complained that the elimination of the justice popular committees meant an increase in the work to be done by the *quḍāt* since, from that moment on, they had to take care of not only justice through *fiqh* but also the *ṣulḥ*, which had previously been carried out by the committees. Interview in El Aaiún refugee camp, 21 April 2018.

31 This practice, which has been described to me as 'women's anger', is a way in which wives can claim a *targhībah* from their husbands when they have a grievance against them, for example if the husband takes on a second wife against the wishes of the first.

32 These are cases in which a husband does not wish to recognize a divorce. In such cases, women remain in a compromised situation since they are not officially divorced.

33 *'waraqa ḥawla wizārat al- 'adl wa-l-shu'ūn al-dīniyya mu'adda bi munāsabat al-dhikra al-khāmisa wa-l-thalāthūn li-i'lān al-jumhūriyya al- 'arabiyya al-ṣaḥrāwiyya al-dīmuqrāṭiyya'*, RASD Information Ministry Archives, Rabouni.

34 The constitutions can be found at Universidade de Santiago de Compostela, Constituciones de la Rasd, https://www.usc.gal/es/institutos/ceso/RASD-Constituciones.html.

35 These gained new importance as a consequence of the voting censuses for the self-determination referendum (which would have been carried out had the peace plan proposed by the United Nations been successful).

36 Interview in Boujdour refugee camp, 28 April 2018.

37 Interview in Rabouni refugee camp, 17 October 2018.

38 Interview in Rabouni refugee camp, 17 October 2018, and interviews in Smara refugee camp, 12 and 17 April 2018.

39 Interview in Rabouni refugee camp, 17 October 2018.

40 Alice Wilson also notes that some parts of the penal code redirect to the *'urf* (2016: 108).

41 Interview in El Aaiún refugee camp, 21 April 2018.

42 Alice Wilson refers to the pair composed of the Polisario Front and the SADR as a 'state movement'.

References

Al-dāf, Ḥamdī ʿAllāl (2015), *Aḍwāʾ ʿalā al-sāqiya al-ḥamrāʾ wa wādī al-dhahab lahjatan wa taqālīda: munjid al-lahja al-ḥassāniyya wa baʿḍ al-ṭuqūs wa-l-taqālīd al-muntashira ladā sukkān al-ṣaḥrāʾ al-gharbiyya*. Régaïa: ENAG.

Al-māmī, Muḥammad b. al-Bukhārī al-Bārakī (2014), *Kitāb al-bādiya wa nuṣūṣ ukhrā*. Rabat: Centre des Études Sahariennes.

Allan, J. (2010), 'Imagining Saharawi women: The question of gender in POLISARIO discourse', *The Journal of North African Studies*, 15 (2): 189–202.

Allan, J. (2019), *Silenced Resistance: Women, Dictatorships, and Genderwashing in Western Sahara and Equatorial Guinea*. Madison, WI: University of Wisconsin Press.

Alonso Cabré, M. (2016), 'Responsalidad compartida: El rol de la composicion de la diya en la resolucion juridica de los accidentes de circulacion en la Mauritania contemporanea', PhD thesis, Universitat de Barcelona. http://www.tdx.cat/handle/10803/399649.

Anderson, B. (1983), *Imagined Communities: Reflections on the Origin and Spread of Nationalism*. London: Verso.

AwaH., B. M. (2017), *La entidad política precolonial saharaui en el ideario de la República Saharaui*. Madrid: Bubok.

Baddou, R. (2008), 'Nueva Palestina en tierra del Sahara', *Revista de Estudios Internacionales Mediterráneos*, 4. https://revistas.uam.es/index.php/reim/article/view/768.

Barona, C. (2004), *Los hijos de la nube: Estructura y vicisitudes del Sahara Español desde 1958 hasta la debacle*. El Escorial: Langre.

Ben Hounet, Y. (2010), 'La tribu comme champ social semi-autonome', *L'Homme*, 194: 57–74.

Benda-Beckmann, F. and K. Von Benda-Beckmann (2006), 'Changing One is Changing All: Dynamics in the Adat-Islam-State Triangle', *The Journal of Legal Pluralism and Unofficial Law*, 38 (53–54): 239–70.

Bengochea Tirado, E. (2019), *La Sección Femenina en la provincia de Sahara: Entrega, hogar, imperio*. Barcelona: Bellaterra.

Bengochea Tirado, E. (2020), 'Debating Theology and the Performance of Nationhood: The Case of *taqsīr al-ṣalāh* (the shortening of prayer) among the Sahrawi', *History and Anthropology*, 31 (5): 545–62.

Bengochea Tirado, E. and F. Correale (2020), 'Modernising Violence and Social Change in the Spanish Sahara (1957–1975)', *Itinerario*, 44 (1): 33–54.

Bhabha, H. (1984), 'Of Mimicry and Man: The Ambivalence of Colonial Discourse', *October*, 28: 125–33.

Boulay, S. (2014). 'Poétique et politique de la migration au Sahara occidental. Les 'a'idın: Repentants, migrants ouralliés?', in C. Canut and C. Mazauric (eds), *La migration prise aux mots: Mise en récits et en images des migrations transafricaines*, 91–109. Paris: Le Cavalier Bleu.

Caratini, S. (1989), *Les Rgaybāt: 1610–1934*, vol. 2 Paris: L'Harmattan.

Caratini, S. (2000), 'Système de parenté sahraoui', *L'Homme*, 154–155: 431–56.

Caratini, S. (2003), *La république des sables: Anthropologie d'une révolution*. Paris: L'Harmattan.

Caratini, S. (2007), 'La prison du temps. Les mutations sociales à l'œuvre dans les camps de réfugiés sahraouis. Première partie: La voie de la révolution', *Afrique Contemporaine*, 221 (1): 153–72.

Caro Baroja, J. (2008 [1955]), *Estudios saharianos*. Madrid: Calamar.
Charre, J.-P. (1966), 'Les Reguibat L'Gouacem. Système juridique et social', *Revue de Géographie Alpine*, 54 (2): 343–50.
Correale, F. (2018), 'Reconfigurations politico-territoriales de l'Ouest saharien dans la longe durée', in F. Correale and S. Boulay (eds), *Sahara occidental: Conflit oublié, population en movement*, 35–62. Tours: Presses Universitaires François Rabelais.
Correale, F. (2019), 'Enmascarar el colonialismo: las "ayudas sociales" en la provincia española del Sáhara entre 1898 y 1975', in M. E. Rios, G. Maire, P. Alvarez, I. Cabana and M. Galvez (eds), *Nuevos Diálogos: Asia y África desde la Mirada Latinoamericana*, 232–54. Mexico: Colégio de México.
Correale, F., and A. López Bargados (2017), 'Rashōmon au Sahara Occidental. Perspectives, contradictions et défis dans l'interpretation du conflit de 1956-1958', in S. Boulay and F. Freire (eds), *Culture et politique dans l'Ouest saharien: Arts, activisme et État dans un espace de conflits: (Algérie, Mali, Maroc, Mauritanie, Sahara occidental)*, 211–42. Igé: L'Étrave.
'De las costumbres de la sociedad precolonial de Saguia el Hamra y Rio de Oro' (1975), *20 de Mayo*, 19, May.
Diego Aguirre, J. R. (1988), 'La lucha del frente polisario: 1973–75', *Historia*, 16 (151): 12–22.
Drury, M. (2019), 'On the Border in Northern Mauritania', *L'Année du Maghreb*, 21: 325–40.
Dupret, B. and Y. Ben Hounet (2015), 'Pratique du droit et propriétés au Maghreb', *L'Année du Maghreb*, 13: 9–15.
Embārik, I. M. (2015), *Tajribat al-qaḍā ʾ fī al-Ṣaḥrā ʾ al-Gharbiyya. Al-maḥākim al-jazā ʾiyya wa ijrā ʾāt al-taqāḍī namūdhajan*. Régaïa: ENAG.
Feria, M. (2002), 'Conflictos de legitimidad jurídica en Marruecos: el impacto del protectorado', in F. R. Mediano, F. Rodriguez Mediano and E. de J. de Felipe Rodríguez, *El protectorado español en Marruecos: gestíon colonial e identidades*, 37–62. Madrid: CSIC.
Fernández-Molina, I. and R. Ojeda-García (2020), 'Western Sahara as a Hybrid of a Parastate and a State-in-Exile: (Extra)territoriality and the Small Print of Sovereignty in a Context of Frozen Conflict', *Nationalities Papers*, 48 (1): 83–99.
Firebrace, J. and J. Harding (1987), *Exiles of the Sahara: The Sahrawi Refugees Shape their Future*. London: War on Want.
Freire, F. (2014), 'Saharan Migrant Camel Herders: Znāga Social Status and the Global Age', *The Journal of Modern African Studies*, 52 (3): 425–46.
García, A. (2001), *Historias del Sahara: El mejor y el peor de los mundos*. Madrid: Catarata.
Gobierno General Del Sahara (1967), *Censo de la población, año 1967*. Gráficas Saharianas SA.
Gobierno General Del Sahara (1974), *Censo 1974*. Servicio de Registro de Población, censo y estadística.
Griffiths, J. (1986), 'What is Legal Pluralism?', *The Journal of Legal Pluralism and Unofficial Law*, 18(24): 1–55.
Hall, B. S. and Stewart, C. C. (2010), 'The Historic "Core Curriculum" and the Book Market in Islamic West Africa', in G. Krätli and G. Lydon (eds), *The Trans-Saharan Book Trade: Manuscript Culture, Arabic Literacy, and Intellectual History in Muslim Africa*, 109–74. Leiden and Boston, MA: Brill.

Hanretta, S. (2009), *Islam and Social Change in French West Africa: History of an Emancipatory Community*. Cambridge: Cambridge University Press.
Healy, P. O. (2011), 'Making history in the Sahara: Historiography in the nationalist discourse of the Polisario Front, 1973–1976', Master's thesis, Beirut, American University of Beirut.
Hernández Moreno, A. (1988), *Economía y sociedad del Sáhara occidental en el siglo XIX*. Murcia: Universidad de Murcia.
Human Rights Watch (Organization), Eric Goldstein, and Bill Van Esveld, eds. 2008. *Human Rights in Western Sahara and in the Tindouf Refugee Camps: Morocco/Western Sahara/Algeria*. New York, NY: Human Rights Watch.
Isidoros, K. (2015), 'The Silencing of Unifying Tribes: The Colonial Construction of Tribe and its "extraordinary leap" to Nascent Nation-State Formation in Western Sahara', *Journal of the Anthropological Society of Oxford*, 7 (2): 168–90.
Isidoros, K. (2017), 'Unveiling the Colonial Gaze: Sahrāwī Women in Nascent Nation-state Formation in the Western Sahara', *Interventions*, 19 (4): 487–506.
Isidoros, K. (2018), *Nomads and Nation-Building in the Western Sahara: Gender, Politics and the Sahrawi*. London: I.B. Tauris.
'La religión por los suelos' (1976), *La opinión de las masas*, 6, 19 April.
Lafontaine, J. and J. C. Gimeno (2021), 'Inmóviles, pero no quietos. La sedentarización de los saharauis como estrategia de adaptación y respuesta a la supervivencia. Sobre la posibilidad de un nomadismo inmóvil', *Tabula Rasa*, 37: 17–48.
Lawrance, B. N., E. L. Osborn and R. L. Roberts (2006), *Intermediaries, Interpreters, and Clerks: African Employees in the Making of Colonial Africa*. Madison, WI: University of Wisconsin Press.
Lázaro Miguel, H. (1974), *Legislación de Sahara, años 1965 a 1973*. Madrid: Dirección General de Promoción de Sahara y Instituto de Estudios Africanos (CSIC).
Lydon, G. (2009), *On Trans-Saharan Trails. Islamic Law, Trade Networks, and Cross-Cultural Exchange in Nineteenth-Century Western Africa*. Cambridge: Cambridge University Press.
McDougall, E. A., ed. (2020), 'Devenir visibles dans le sillage de l'esclavage. La question harātin en Mauritanie et au Maroc', *L'Ouest Saharien*, 10–11. Paris: Khartala.
Martin-Márquez, S. (2008), *Disorientations: Spanish Colonialism in Africa and the Performance of Identity*. Yale: Yale University Press.
Martín Beristain, C. and E. González Hidalgo (2012), *El Oasis de la Memoria: Memoria Histórica y Violaciones de Derechos Humanos en el Sáhara Occidental*, vol. 1. Bilbao: Hegoa.
Martín, J. C. G. and J. I. R. Picón (2015), 'Hacia una contrahistoria del Sahara Occidental', *Les Cahiers d'EMAM. Études sur le Monde Arabe et la Méditerranée*, 24–25. https://doi.org/10.4000/emam.872.
Mercer, J. (1976), *Spanish Sahara*. London: Allen & Unwin.
Mercer, J. (1979), *The Sahrawis of Western Sahara*. London: Minority Rights Group Report.
Molina Campuzano, M. (1954), *Contribución al Estudio del Censo de Población del Sahara Español*. Madrid: CSIC.
Mundy, J. A. (2007), 'Performing the Nation, pre-Figuring the State: The Western Saharan Refugees, Thirty Years later', *The Journal of Modern African Studies*, 45 (2): 275–97.
Othman, A. (2007), 'And Amicable Settlement is Best:' Sulh and Dispute Resolution in Islamic Law', *Arab Law Quarterly*, 21 (1): 64–90.

Ould al-Bara, Y. (1997). 'Les théologiens mauritaniens face au colonialisme français: Étude de fatwa-s de jurisprudence musulmane'. In David Robinson (ed.), *Le temps des marabouts: Itinéraires et stratégies islamiques en Afrique occidentale française* v. 1880–1960, 83–117. Paris: Karthala.

Ould al-Bara, Y. (2001), *Fiqh, société et pouvoir: Étude des soucis et préoccupations socio-politiques des théologiens-légistes maures (fuqahā) à partir de leurs consultations juridiques (fatāwā) du XVIIème au XXème siècle*, thesis, Paris, EHESS. http://www.theses.fr/2001EHES0205.

Ould al-Bara, Y. (2009), *Al-majmū'a al-kubrā: al-shāmila li-fatāwā wa nawāzil wa aḥkām ahl gharb wa janūb gharb al-Ṣaḥrā'*. 12 vols. Nouakchott: al-Sharīf Mawlay al-Ḥasan b. al-Mukhtār b. al-Ḥasan.

Ould al-Bara, Y. (2014), 'Le milieu culturel et social des *fuqahâ* maures', in P. Bonte and H. Claudot-Hawad (eds), *Élites du Monde Nomade Touareg et Maure*, 151–66. Paris: Institut de recherches et d'études sur les mondes arabes et musulmans.

Ould Cheikh, A. W. (2011), 'Théologie du désordre. Islam, ordre et désordre au Sahara', *L'Année du Maghreb*, VII: 61–77.

Ould Cheikh, A. W. (2016), 'De quoi le Sahara est-il le nom? Images du Sahara et des Sahariens dans Kitâb al-bâdiyya d'al-Shaykh Muḥamd al-Mâmi', in R. Boubrik (ed.), *Le Sahara, Lieux d'Histoire et Espaces d'Échange*, 51–70. Rabat: Centre des Études Sahariennes.

Ould Es-Sweyih, M.-F. O. I. (1998), *Les Sahraouis*. Paris: Harmattan.

Pazzanita, A. G. and T. Hodges (1994), *Historical Dictionary of Western Sahara*. Metuchen: Scarecrow Press.

Rappaport, J. (2008), 'Beyond Participant Observation: Collaborative Ethnography as Theoretical Innovation', *Collaborative Anthropologies*, 1: 1–31.

San Martín, P. (2010), *Western Sahara: The Refugee Nation*. Cardiff: University of Wales Press.

Scheele, J. (2008), 'A Taste for Law: Rule-Making in Kabylia (Algeria)', *Comparative Studies in Society and History*, 50 (4): 895–919.

Simenel, R. (2017), 'Bojador/Boujdour, 1975–1977: Les tribus sahariennes face au conflit', in F. Correale and S. Boulay (eds), *Sahara occidental: Conflit oublié, population en movement*, 81–92. Tours: Presses Universitaires François Rabelais.

Solana, V. (2019), 'Hospitality's Prowess: Performing Sahrāwī Sovereignty in Refugee Camps', *PoLAR: Political and Legal Anthropology Review*, 42 (2): 362–79.

Spear, T. (2003), 'Neo-Traditionalism and the Limits of Invention in British Colonial Africa', *The Journal of African History*, 44 (1): 3–27.

Stewart, F. H. (2006), 'Customary Law among the Bedouin of the Middle East and North Africa', in D. Chatty (ed.), *Nomadic Societies in the Middle East and North Africa*, 239–79. Leiden: Brill.

Vikør, K. S. (2005), *Between God and the Sultan: A History of Islamic Law*. Oxford: Oxford University Press.

Warscheid, I. (2017), *Droit musulman et société au Sahara prémoderne: La justice islamique dans les oasis du grand Touat (Algérie) aux XVIIe-XIXe Siècles*. Leiden: Brill.

Warscheid, I. (2018), 'Le Livre du désert: La vision du monde d'un lettré musulman de l'Ouest saharien au xixe siècle', *Annales. Histoire, Sciences Sociales*, 73 (2): 359–84.

Wilson, A. (2015), 'Refracting Custom in Western Sahara's Quest for Statehood', *PoLAR: Political and Legal Anthropology Review*, 38 (1): 72–90.

Wilson, A. (2016), *Sovereignty in Exile: A Saharan Liberation Movement Governs*. Philadelphia, PA: University of Pennsylvania Press.

Wilson, A. (2018a), 'To Compensate or Not to Compensate? Law, Property and Sahrawi Refugees in Algeria', in Y. Ben Hounet and B. Dupret (eds), *Law and Property in Algeria: Anthropological Perspectives*, 142–63. Leiden: Brill.

Wilson, A. (2018b), 'Gifts that Recalibrate Relationships: Marriage Prestations in an Arab Liberation Movement', *Ethnos*, 83 (2): 296–315.

Wilson, A. and F. McConnell (2015), 'Constructing Legitimacy without Legality in Long Term Exile: Comparing Western Sahara and Tibet', *Geoforum*, 66: 203–14.

Yanguas Miravete, J. (1960), *Antecedentes históricos, organización politico-administrativa y legislación de las provincias de Ifni y Sahara*. Sidi Ifni: Imprenta de Sidi Ifni.

3

Magnitudes of Sahrawi nomadism throughout colonialism and refugeehood

Juan Carlos Gimeno Martín
Professor of Social Anthropology at the Universidad Aut.noma de Madrid
and Julien Lafontaine Carboni
Architect and PhD candidate at the ALICE laboratory, Swiss Federal Institute of Technology of Lausanne

Introduction

The nomadic/sedentary binary, which opposes the desert, the mobile and the primitive to the civilized, the urban and the state, has come under question as a cultural construction that the West has imposed on the rest of the world (Isidoros 2018; Wilson 2014). The deconstruction of this binary is all the more necessary in contexts where nomadic populations have become refugees for climatic, political and/or economic reasons, twentieth-century examples of which include Somali refugees in Kenya, Malian Tuaregs in Mauritania and Sahrawis in refugee camps in Algeria. Nomadism is associated with constant movements, independent domestic productions, and thus a highly specialized way of life and array of knowledge. Nevertheless, in some instances, the magnitude of the distances covered by nomadic populations is less significant than the Western gaze tends to imagine, and temporary sedentarization has been proven to be an adaptation strategy (Salzman 1980).

On several occasions, the camps near Tindouf have been compared to the nomadic forms of pastoral life that existed prior to the conflict with Morocco (Caratini 2003; Wilson 2014). Within this context, we would like to consider the variety of the movements and the different magnitudes of Sahrawi nomadism. The Sahrawi's forced

Universidad Autónoma de Madrid, Departamento de Antropología Social y Pensamiento Filosófico Español. A previous version of this text was published (in Spanish) in 2021 in the journal *Tabula Rasa* with the title 'Inmóviles, pero no quietos. La sedentarización de los saharauis como estrategia de adaptación y respuesta a la supervivencia. Sobre la posibilidad de un nomadismo inmóvil'. [Juan Carlos Gimeno Martín]

ALICE, Swiss Federal Institute of Technology of Lausanne, Faculty of Natural, Architectural and Built Environment, Institute of Architecture. Research for this chapter has been funded by the Swiss National Fund (SNF) as a PhD Mobility Fellowship. [Julien Lafontaine Carboni]

loss of mobility due to protracted conflicts and their subsequent refugee status have given rise to a temporary resistance and survival strategy involving the unification of the *qabāʾil* (former political units based on lineage) in a 'coalescence' of sorts (Isidoros 2018). As we will argue, in order to understand nomadism in this context, it is necessary to approach the phenomenon from various temporal and geographic scales or perspectives, from the movements of the individual body, its gestures, to the distance of the movements of the populations. This widening of perspective is necessary if we are to avoid imposing Western scales of analysis, thus reproducing epistemic violence toward Sahrawi society (Spivak 1988).

We will first discuss the significant elements of the *firgān* (sing. *frīg*), the traditional Sahrawi encampments, across various scales of time and motion and in the context of French and Spanish colonization, revealing temporary 'sedentarization' as an adaptive strategy stemming from traditional Sahrawi nomadic practices. We will then introduce elements that allow us to draw an analogy between the refugee camps and Sahrawi *firgān*. Next, in light of accounts gathered by different twentieth-century anthropologists, we will present, given the various regimes and temporalities of motion within Sahrawi pastoral nomadism prior to the conflict, the history of the Sahrawi refugee camps from 1975 to 1991, unveiling its temporal and spatial complexity. As a means of conclusion, based on the various debates that have shaken Sahrawi society since the 1990s and in relation to the non-linear histories of the camps, we will outline the apparently paradoxical immobilization of a specific part of the Sahrawi population as a form of nomadic movement, the apparent immobility of which derives from reliance on a particular (and ultimately limiting) temporal and geographic scale. This narrative is accompanied by numerous visual documents from the archives of the Sahrawi Ministry of Information, the work of anthropologists (in particular Caratini 1989a, 1989b; Caro Baroja 1955), and our own documents.

Sahrawi spatio-temporal organization in the twentieth century: Movements and gestures

The territories inhabited by the populations that composed the Sahrawi nation at the time of the revolution and the creation of the SADR extends from the Senegal River to southern Morocco and from southern Algeria to the north, from the Atlantic Ocean in the west to Mali, and through present-day Mauritania. The population was composed of several *qabāʾil* (sing. *qabīla*), imprecisely translated as 'tribes' in most Western scholarship (see Caratini 2003; Isidoros 2018; Wilson 2014). Until the Spanish invasion of the Western Sahara and the French colonization of Mauritania, Algeria and Morocco, the *qabāʾil* shared this territory more or less peacefully (even if conflicts over the control of pasturelands were frequent), coordinated until the sixteenth century by a pan-tribal political organization called the Āyt Arbaʿīn, with a defined border (Awah 2017), which disappeared under colonialism.

These different *qabāʾil* possessed cultural habits on which present Sahrawi identity and nationhood projects are grounded. The spatial and temporal organization of the *qabāʾil* and their smaller familial units all followed regular patterns that favoured nomadic practices in the Saharan desert's harsh conditions. To understand the spatialities associated with the Sahrawi territory and the habits of its populations, including under diverse colonial regimes, we must closely analyse the movements of the populations at each time scale. In Sahrawi nomadic practices, the territory is constantly re-enacted through motions and gestures that are deeply anchored and entrenched in the culture as survival techniques; each situation, location and season is associated with different forms of encampment and daily territorial organizations. By following the evolution of these motions and gestures, we can better understand how both colonialism and the protracted refugeehood of the Sahrawi have affected their nomadic mode of life.

Motions of tents and people

Daily motions

Under the colonial regimes and in precolonial times, the camps were usually organized into *firgān* camps hosting people with familial ties, with slaves and sometimes with blacksmiths. The spatial boundaries of the *frīg* were a half-day's walk, which means that one could visit another tent and be back by sunset for the evening prayer (Caratini 1989a: 122–31). The tents were more or less aligned, depending on the distance between each tent, to respect the privacy of each household; the *khayma* (pl. *khiyām*), the traditional wool tent, was open to the north and to the south, with the east and west sides touching the ground. The familial ties established a genealogical hierarchy between the different members, and thus with regard to the tents' positions, the elderly living at the centre of the encampment.

This model was the most common kind of encampment when the population was pasturing their livestock. Its low density allowed the entire *qabīla* to spread and take advantage of the pastureland. The *firgān* moved several times during the year in search of water and food for their herds, from October to May/June (according to the evolving conditions and resources).

In her anthropological research with the Rgaybāt (demographically the largest *qabīla* of the region), Caratini described the spatialities in which each individual moved around the *frīg*. These motions are highly gendered and depend on age. Women stayed close to the tent (a maximum of 10 km away) to accomplish the domestic tasks and to care for the young, watching over the family's goods and transforming raw products into food and crafts. They were also in charge of smaller livestock (mainly goats), with the help of the children.

From 10 to 50 km away from the tent, at the limits of the *frīg*, men (including free young men and young slaves) conducted their own activities. Here, their tasks were mainly related to caring for female camels in nearby pastures and bringing them back each night. The dawn and sunset prayer determined the time of departure and return.

Then, from 50 to 100 km away from the tent, male slaves, hired shepherds and free young men took care of the male camels in the peripheral pastureland. Given their distance from the encampment, they didn't return to the tent every night, and sometimes only occasionally (less than once a month).

Finally, the space beyond 100 km from the tent was a masculine space dedicated to economic trade and political decisions. This was both a highly 'domestic' space

Figure 3.1 Panorama of Mahbes in 1974. Photograph taken by a Spanish military during his service in the Western Sahara. We can see an encampment at the left of the photo, near the military installations. Source: *La Mili en el Sahara* (https://www.lamilienelsahara.net/).

(involving the use of tents) and a de-centred political space (involving significant movements through the territory). This set of motions, organized around the *frīg*, took place during rainy and temperate times of the year, when gathering around wells was not necessary (Figure 3.1).

Seasonal motions

In response to political, climatic, economic and safety reasons, the encampment took on new forms. However, these more significant tent groupings (between 50 and 150, according to Caratini) disappeared at the beginning of the twentieth century, undoubtedly because of the dissolution of the Āyt Arbaʿīn, a war council and its fragmentation when it made contact with the colonial authorities, which fostered the dissension between the *qabāʾil* and the shaykhs (Bárbulo 2002).

During the summer (when the population usually gathered around wells) or when the Āyt Arbaʿīn was summoned, the tents were arranged in the form of a *maḥṣar* (pl. *mḥaṣir*). This consisted of several *firgān*, with the tent of the shaykh, the most influent elder, at the centre of the encampment. The parallel perspective permitted a clear view, which allowed the population to spot potential enemies from far. In the summer, encampments could host four *mḥaṣir* – situated at the northeast end of the area, the other at the northwest corner, etc. – each orientated toward the pastureland. Thus, the motions of the members of a family were quite similar, transforming the circles into quadrants.

When family members approached cities or unsecured land for economic reasons, or when the density of the population was higher, the Sahrawis arranged the tents in a circular form (*anawāl*). This allowed them to protect the herd from thieves at night. The circle was closed with a simple barrier after all the goats and camels had returned. A guard ensured that the tents and animals were safe. Caratini also argues that the *anawāl* may correspond to a time of higher equality between the households (economically and politically) – a period where there were no dependent families – as the circle eliminates the spatial hierarchies characteristic of the *frīg* and the *maḥṣar*. As recounted by Rabiia Eslaiman Ijiar, an influential women living in the Dakhla refugee camp, the circle as a spatial and formal way to create equality between the members of a community is central to Sahrawi culture. It is used as a symbol in jewellery and other art forms and to create equality between guests and hosts in the quotidian ritual of tea-making. The first 'protocols' (administrative buildings) that women built in the refugee camps in the 1980s took this design, evoking the equality of all in the SADR. In the *anawāl*, the everyday spatialities of motion were much denser than in other forms of encampment, as the risks were greater.

Life motions

Over the years, the Sahrawi populations moved across a vast territory. Both 'wedding-scapes' (Solana Moreno 2017) and economic conditions influenced these motions, the magnitudes of which were highly affected by the colonial border defined at the Berlin Conference. While the extent of the men's movements was broader due to the types of tasks they were assigned, the women were far from sedentary. No patterns can be extracted from the work of Caro Baroja or from our discussions with the elderly in the Sahrawi refugee camps. Nevertheless, despite its refugee status, the Sahrawi population remains extremely mobile (with notable transits towards Mauritania and

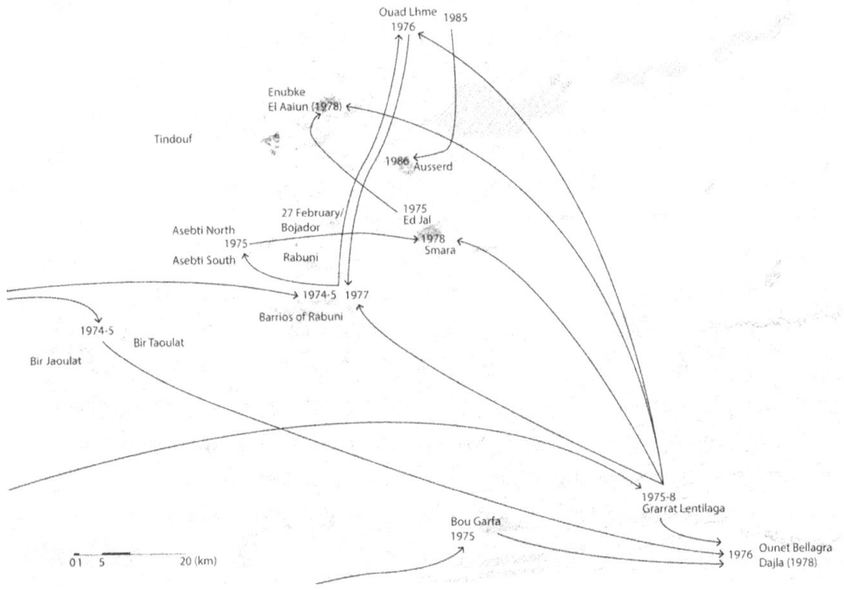

Map 3.1 The motions through the Hamada of Tinduf until 1991. Some camps were ephemeral, others were transitioning camps for the population, notably Grarrat Lentilaga. Designed after discussions had in the refugee camps in February/March 2020. © Julien Lafontaine Carboni.

northern Algeria), and this mobility grew with increased access to countries such as Spain, Syria and Cuba.

Exceptional motions

War and times of conflict

During periods of war or territorial conflicts between *qabāʾil*, the members of a *qabīla* would reunite in several *maḥṣar* called a *ḥalla* – the camp of the emir/shaykh, the space of political decision-making. These spatialities allowed the Āyt Arbaʿīn to meet and organize the defence of the camps and herds. In an Āyt Arbaʿīn, all of the factions of the *qabāʾil* were represented. A *muqaddam* was elected to 'preside' over the assembly and took honorific responsibility for deciding cases of internal disagreement. Beyond the merely defensive role of the council, the Āyt Arbaʿīn also organized the use of wells and pastureland and the spatial arrangement of each encampment. This setting was beneficial as it permitted a common response to an immediate threat without the need for centralized and permanent power. While the Āyt Arbaʿīn is the name for the council that summons different *qabāʾil*, the same system existed on a smaller scale when a coordinated response was needed in a regular *maḥṣar*.

The Āyt Arbaʿīn ('Council of Forty') also produced a series of 'laws' standardizing the sentences for each crime. In an interview in May 2016, the poet Mohamed Lamin[1] gave us a copy of a manuscript written by his grandfather, Mulay Brahim Ben Omar, a judge and scribe for the 'Council of Forty'. In his book, Mohamed Ali Laman translates the text as follows:[2]

> The laws and measures that were adopted by the Council of Forty were mandatory for the organization of the social life of the population. They took the form of defined requirements, among which we can cite the following:
>
> 1. Whoever helps or takes sides, even with his father or brother, or any other person, must provide dinner and lunch to each of the members of the Council of Forty separately.
> 2. Whoever threatens another with a sword shall be punished by having to pay five *mathāqil* (*pesos*).
> 3. Whoever threatens another with a gun will be sanctioned with a five-*pesos* fine. If he harms another, he will have to surrender a two-year-old camel, and if he causes death, he will have to pay monetary compensation.
> 4. Whoever unjustly seizes the fortune of his neighbor will be sanctioned, and those who are accomplices will have to surrender a two-year-old camel and return everything that was stolen.
> 5. Whoever denies justice to one who asks for it must pay ten *pesos*.
> 6. Whoever enters another's *khayma* with the intent to corrupt, as the corrupt do to women, must surrender a pregnant camel; those who are found to have committed infidelity with a foreigner must pay five *pesos* each, as long as they were not found in the same bed, in which case each must provide a pregnant camel and will receive one hundred lashes, in addition to the punishments provided for in the law.

7. Anyone who breaks an agreement with a Muslim, whoever he may be, or who has broken the rules of the Qur'ān, as well as those who helped him to do so, must hand over ten pregnant camels and return to the victim his belongings or whatever was taken from him.
8. Whoever strikes his neighbor must hand over a two-year-old camel, and if he leaves a black eye he must hand over another two-year-old camel and must provide dinner to the Council of Forty. Any clan that helps another clan to break the law shall be punished by having to surrender ten pregnant camels.
9. Any person who plunders his neighbor's belongings, whether found elsewhere or at his place of dwelling, must pay one hundred silver *pesos* and must return what he has consumed or plundered to its owner.
10. Any person who, in self-defense, causes the death of a member of a tribe shall not assume any penalty if the victim is proven to be guilty of assault, and the tribe shall be responsible for compensation.

(Laman 2022)[3]

Spanish colonialism

The borders established between the Spanish- and the French-dominated area limited nomadic practices, particularly in periods of drought. In these times, the peripheral pastureland was essential to free grazing and to providing enough resources for the herds and the people. Insofar as they prohibited the movements of the Sahrawis, the borders intensified the consequences of drought. Beyond this, the borders gained a strategic and political significance for the Sahrawis when they fought against the French Army, which had invaded the Sahara from the Mauritanian side (Eastern Border).[4] They could withdraw across the Spanish border, where they were protected by the Spanish metropolitan decision to prohibit the persecution of Sahrawi dissidents in the Spanish Sahara (Martínez Milán 2003). The fighting ended in 1934, the year called 'Melgā Laḥkāma' (literally, a meeting of governments) by the Sahrawi.

After the conflict between the French and the Spanish armies ceased, the *anawāl* and the *maḥṣar* completely disappeared from everyday encampment models. The *frīg* developed markedly insofar as the direct threats to tents and herds had disappeared, as the Spanish enacted institutions to create a dialogue between the *qabā'il* from the Western Sahara and to find consensus through centralization (which they would later use to provoke dissent. Without the need to protect themselves from robbery or attack, the familial units navigated more freely across the land, rendering the *maḥṣar* and the *anawāl* obsolete and leading to the emergence of trans-*qabā'il firgān*.

At this time, the colonial cities in Spanish Sahara were small. Until 1934, the Spanish army couldn't reach Smara; only border checkpoints and the homes of the 'indigenous soldiers' existed. These positions were abandoned by the Spanish authorities during the war in 1957–1958 (see the chapter by López Bargados in this volume) so that Spain could concentrate its forces in the cities. As a consequence of the terrible droughts at the end of 1950 and the beginning of 1960, in addition to Spain's contribution to sedentarization, the immobilization of the Sahrawi and their settlement around colonial cities developed rapidly. Through a process that can hardly be called 'sedentarization', the families maintained urban-rural lifestyles, living for part of the year in the *bādiyya* (pastureland/'countryside') and investing in farming resources.

Nevertheless, another type of camp emerged, prompted by Spanish policies (Bengochea Tirado 2019). Their location was imposed, and thus the camps were not organized as *maḥṣar* (around the presence of an elder). During colonization, Spain aimed to sedentarize the Sahrawi population so as to 'educate' them and better control them (Portillo 2019). As such, they used a Sahrawi workforce to build roads and extract resources (such as phosphates from the mines of Bucraa). In this photographic series, we see the parallel development of colonial cities/military installations and the growth of Sahrawi encampments on their margins (Hodges 1983: 130–2).

In the 1960s, on the site of the first encampment, the Spanish government installed housing programmes, hoping to fully sedentarize the population (Rodriguez and Barrado Timón 2015), accompanied by different institutions aiming to 'civilize' the population based on the Spanish model (Bengochea Tirado 2019). The cities of the Western Sahara grew significantly, and a large segment of the Sahrawi population moved to find work and food due to severe droughts coupled with the spreading of a disease that killed entire herds of camels. Nevertheless, the Sahrawis commonly said that men were living in the cities to work but that the women and the extended family remained in the pasturelands. The Spanish census of 1974, used by MINURSO as a basis for the preparation of a list of voters for the promised independence referendum, is still debated, particularly with regard to the percentage of 'sedentarized' Sahrawis it reports, even if it is generally accepted that the majority of them were still labelled as nomadic.

The Oum Dreyga encampments

From 1970, a large part of the Sahrawi population who lived near the colonial cities left for Oum Dreyga, a riverbed in the centre of the colony of the Western Sahara. Following repression by the Spanish army against civil movements and strikes for independence, which began in El Aaiún from 14 to 20 June 1970, the population was worried about a possible invasion of Mauritania from the south and of Morocco from the north, as both claimed sovereignty over the territory. Thus, from 1970 to 1975, until the phosphate bombing of the civil population by the Moroccan army, whole families began to install themselves in this region, where wells had been dug. According to Rabiia Eslaiman Ijiar and Gurba Mohamed Lehbib, two elderly women with whom we spoke in the refugee camps and who lived in the camps of Oum Dreyga, the families settled quite freely along the riverbed, in the form of *firgān*. As most had left some of their goods behind, the tents were largely made of light white cotton structures customarily used for newlyweds. Their construction was faster and easier, and as most of the herds had died out by then, women didn't have enough camel hair to manufacture the traditional *khayma*.

Prior to this, Oum Dreyga had been largely uninhabited, as the available water was too deep underground and mostly inaccessible through the techniques available to the Sahrawi. Thanks to Spanish pumps and tools, they could dig new wells and survive in the area for several years. When the Spanish army left without warning, Mauritania and Morocco invaded the Western Sahara, and thousands of people from all cities joined the camp. According to our information, these camps were highly dense and lasted until the Polisario Front left for the region of Tindouf. Oum Dreyga, like Tifariti and other Sahrawi encampments, was bombed with napalm and white phosphates by the Moroccan air force in February 1976 (Martín Beristain 2015: 17–28).

Throughout the first three-quarters of the twentieth century, the forms of encampment and movement of the Sahrawi nomadic population evolved significantly due to climatic conditions on the one hand and as a consequence of Spanish and French colonialism on the other. As such, the motions and gestures implied in Sahrawi nomadism were multiple and heterogeneous. The Sahrawis currently living in the refugee camps are claiming their right to nomadism (as well as their right to call themselves nomads), even though they have been physically immobilized for over forty years. In the face of international observers' 'fascination' with the refugee camps, which have become increasingly subject to the Western gaze, we must further consider the possibility of 'immobile nomadism', which would seem to characterize the current mode of life of Sahrawi refugees.

Figure 3.2 According to different interlocutors this photography represents the camp where the proclamation of the RASD took place in February 1976. © Archives of the Ministry of Information of the RASD.

An immobile nomadism?

Is the settling of the Sahrawi in the refugee camps an evolution of their form of nomadism? Does nomadism cease to exist in contexts of immobilization? The SADR, like the Sahrawi refugees, claims a right to call its people nomads, despite their protracted refugeehood. Along these lines, some scholars have argued that the refugee camps were built on the model of the nomadic encampment, and thus that this forced 'sedentarization' is a temporary adaptive strategy (Marx 1980) to deal with the present situation (see in particular Isidoros 2018). We wish to contribute to this debate by first dismantling the assumption that the refugee camps have a linear history of development, unveiling the multiplicity of motions across the hamada of Tindouf and between the camps, and then by introducing insights from internal debates within Sahrawi society on the politics of the camps' materialities.

The analogy between the refugee camps and the *frīg*: Realities and limits

The relationship between nomadism and sedentarization had been shown to be more complex than it first appears. There is no progress from nomadism to sedentarism, from mobility to settlement, as the use of the pejorative term 'tribe' associated with nomadism implies. An extensive literature has attempted to deconstruct this opposition (see, among others, Humphrey and Sneath 1999; focusing more closely on the Mauritanian and Sahrawi contexts, see Bonte 2007; López Bargados 2003; Mundy 2007; Villasante-de Beauvais 1998). Sedentary and nomadic communities are interdependent, the one developing on the margins of the other. The transition from a nomadic way of life to a sedentarized one involves a broader type of socio-cultural change than mere immobilization (Salzman 1980), is reversible, and contains ambiguities (Marx 1980).

The Sahrawis have been involved in this dynamic throughout their history, from movements of significant magnitude to partial immobility, the sedentarization process being emphasized by the politics of Spanish colonialism. Long engaged in trans-Saharan trade routes and the development of several *qṣūr* (economic centres on the routes), in parallel with the *qabāʾil* from Mauritania, the Sahrawi population has historically settled several times as a tactical strategy for survival, as in Oum Dreyga.

One particularity of the new Sahrawi state is that the structure created to govern the camps is not unfamiliar to the system of the Āyt Arbaʿīn (Mahmud Awah 2017) and that the election of the national parliament or council of elders suggests that 'the visual image is different, but the idea remains the same' (Isidoros 2018: 233). Thus, the adoption of a Western nation-state model is mainly tied to an imported vocabulary, as the Sahrawi state model is grounded in an image of a detribalized nomadic ideal.

Alice Wilson has emphasized the ambiguity of the Sahrawi encampments, which lie somewhere between being refugee camps and being nomadic encampments (2014). While several of their features suggest their standing as 'traditional' refugee camps – such as the constraint of movement due to conflict (an extension of the restrictions posed by colonial borders), political control over the populations and the disappearance of the domestic mode of production characteristic of Sahrawi nomadic pastoralism – Wilson notes, following Caratini, that the layout of the camps can be interpreted as *firgān* situated between the square forms of a *maḥṣar* (in response to the war situation) and the circular shape of the *anawāl* (signaling radical equality between members). This fusion of the two forms resulted in the grid-like layout of each *dā ʾira*, while organizing them in a circle around the administrative buildings. This is despite the fact that the refugee camps are not called *firgān* in the Sahrawi lexicon, but rather the eminently Arabic word *al-mukhayyam* (Wilson 2014: 15–16), which means 'the tented place'. Nor can they be considered sedentary spaces, as they remain, despite the protracted conflict, spaces and states of exception that also constitute a fundamental right of refugees from which exception is constantly re-enacted as a political means of struggle (Lafontaine Carboni and Gimeno Martin 2020).

Isidoros also insists on a further persistent dimension of nomadic encampment in the refugee camps: the capacity of the tents to coalesce, a capacity of fusion and fission among a group of individuals, enacting a moving political constellation and forming a 'tented-state' (Isidoros 2018: 235). Arguing on this dimension, she insists that the 'public space' of the camp was created for the international humanitarian programme that 'echoes emptily' (Isidoros 2018: 214) when it leaves in the summer. This constellation is based on the fact that in the nomadic culture of the Sahrawis, one tent always moves toward another, and this motion is at the basis of the emergent quality of their political power. Furthermore, this nation-building as tent-dwellers began prior to the exodus to the region of Tindouf (and thus prior to the construction of the 'public infrastructure'), when the Sahrawis began to claim their right to independence in the 1960s. As Isidoros argues, this moving political space – a space provided by women's tents and hospitality, blurring the traditional opposition between states and different *qabā ʾil*, nomadism and sedentarism, citizens and refugees – characterizes the persistent presence of nomadism in the changing culture of the Sahrawi, suggesting an analogy between the refugee camps and the nomadic encampments.

Motions and spatial histories of the refugee camp (1975–1991)

Looking closely at the motions of the Sahrawi in the refugee camps, there are myriad surviving forms of the pastoral way of life. A further scale that we can also acknowledge is the non-linearity of the spatial histories and motions of the refugee camps as a whole in the first two decades of the camps' existence. Building on the little information we have on this period, international observers have tended to describe this history in terms of a linear development. Nevertheless, the camps did move several times through the hamada of Tindouf to search for safety and resources (water and firewood). Thus, in the following we offer insights into these motions based on a series of discussions held with elderly women in February/March 2020 in the refugee camps of Smara and Dakhla.

Territorial motions

There is now an extensive body of literature on the political and armed struggles of the Sahrawi against Moroccan occupation from a political science perspective (Mundy 2007) and from a counter-historical perspective (see, among others, Gimeno Martín and Robles Picón 2015). Some anthropologists have intensely studied the identity and cultural transformation of Sahrawi society through exile and revolution (among others, see Caratini 2003; Gimeno Martín 2007; Isidoros 2018). The camps have even been analysed from an urbanistic perspective (Herz 2013). Nevertheless, the memories and histories of the refugee camps in themselves have not been addressed. From the hamada of Tindouf, the Sahrawis, the great majority of which (around 90 per cent) are women, have outlined and performed the camps and the nation-state that is to govern it.

Thus, the history of the refugee camps encompasses much more than the settling of the population in a single place and the steady growth of infrastructure. Almost all of these eminently nomadic camps and their spatialities have disappeared; the harshness of the climate coupled with the flimsiness of the installations mean that barely any traces have been left behind. In addition, none of the motions, gestures and spatialities enacted by women have been archived or recorded (Lafontaine Carboni 2021).

After the Spanish left without warning on 30 October 1975, Mauritania and Morocco's armies simultaneously invaded the Western Sahara. Thousands of Sahrawis, both in cities and in pastureland, suddenly had to leave the territory, as they did not want to live under another colonial regime. We don't know precisely how many people arrived in the precarious refugee camps installed in the region of Tindouf from 1975 to 1976; the number is thought to be around sixty thousand. At first, there were no tents to protect the families from the heat during the day and from the cold at night. Despite help from Algerian authorities, the population was lacking almost all necessities. As most of the men were at war in the disputed territories, women began to organize political cells and committees to improve living conditions with the Polisario. As water and firewood were lacking, and as remaining in the open air was unsafe (the Moroccan army could attack using planes), they decided to spread throughout the hamada of Tindouf. At this point, the population was already partly spread out but disorganized; some of them first settled in the camps of Bir Taoulat and Bir Jaoulat (on the Algerian border), which existed until the beginning of 1974. Others had already lived for years in Ouenet Bellagra – which would later become Dakhla, a well-known site for nomads as water there is less than one metre underground – because they felt insecure in the territory of the Western Sahara. Others settled in Bou Garfa, south of Rabouni, where a relative abundance of water permitted them to begin agricultural experimentations.

Thus, following the founding of the SADR, the population was dispersed throughout the hamada, in places where firewood and water could be found and in the riverbeds, to reduce their visibility from afar. In order to do so, they developed a scalable system of *barrios*, *dawāʾir* (sing. *daʾira*) and *wilāyāt* (sing. *wilāya*) to organize the camp's food supplies, distribution and autonomous administration without the help of external or foreign institutions and NGOs. The result was the establishment of the camps of Asebti North and Asebti South (which would later change location and join to become

Smara), with two *dawāʾir* each, the camp of Ed Jal (at the north of Smara, which would later be relocated to El Aaiún), also with two *dawāʾir*, the camp of Enubke (renamed El Aaiún), with four *dawāʾir*, the camp of Ouad Lhme, with three *dawāʾir*, and the camp of Ouenet Bellagra.[5] They also created the camp of Grarrat Lentilaga, literally the camp 'for the immigrants', for newcomers who would then be assigned a tent in another camp. Each *daʾira* and *barrio* was relocated with the aim of finding resources and safety. In 1978, they were renamed to organize the return to the Western Sahara, each *wilāya* now bears the name of an administrative region of the Western Sahara, and each *daʾira* bears the name of a smaller administrative unit around a city. Further infrastructure was later built, such as the women's school and the national hospital.

For over a decade, the Sahrawi population in exile moved through the hamada to improve their living conditions. None of these movements ever stopped entirely; for example, one of Dakhla's *dawāʾir* was relocated to the *wilāya* of Smara in 2012 due to desert encroachment.

Spatialities of the camps: Analogies to former encampment models

As Caratini and Wilson have underscored, the Sahrawi refugee camps were built on the basis of a productive ambiguity between the political ideals of the newborn SADR and nomadic pastoralist values. While the administrative model was inspired by the Algerian system of governance and enacts a return to the occupied territories, aligning it with national ambitions (in terms of education, health, social services, police, etc.), the spatiality and arrangement of the tents was defined and inspired by the *maḥṣar* and *anawāl* models. In 1976, with the foundation of the SADR, a series of laws were enacted on the spatial layout with a view to 'detribalizing' society and promoting radical equality among the Sahrawis.

These regulations were precise and lasted until 1991, the year of the ceasefire with Morocco, when a general relaxation occurred. In this model, the reference to the *anawāl* is only metaphoric; by promoting the 'detribalization' of society, the SADR and the popular congress prohibited grouping tents according to *qabīla* membership. No hierarchies existed between the tents, and as such the equality enacted by the circular form was re-enacted in another spatial setting. Along these lines, familial groupings were also largely prohibited until the mid-1980s, after the strikes in Dakhla.

On the contrary, we can hypothesize that the spatialities of the camp were borrowed from the *maḥṣar* encampment structure. The tents had to be aligned on the north/south and west/east axes. This alignment permitted fluid mobility throughout the camps and an unobstructed view of the desert (and thus of any oncoming enemy attacks). In addition, the proximity between the tents (around 4 metres), as in the *maḥṣar*, fostered solidarity between the households thanks to the circulation of goods, information and help. One of the significant shifts between the spatialities of the *maḥṣar* and the refugee camps is that, due to the protracted armed conflict and the absence of men, who were occupied on the battlefront, the camps and the family were up to that point matrilocal; husbands would move into the tents of their wives, who traditionally lived in close proximity to their mothers' *khiyām*. The absence of men profoundly changed the gendered division of labour during the wartime effort, as the women had to manage the *wilāyāt* and *barrios* in their husbands' absence. These new dynamics between the tents and politics in the encampments were characterized by what Konstantina Isidoros called a 'political economy of affection' (Isidoros 2018: 76). The grid-like organization of the camp did not seem to follow common international models for refugee camp construction, instead resembling the traditional *maḥṣar*, an exceptional form of encampment enacted in times of war, danger or for the temporary unification of the *qabīla*. Prior to the development of public infrastructure, which was secondary, this model further entrenched their status as ideal refugees (Fiddian-Qasmiyeh 2014).

While it would be inaccurate to say that the refugee camps, the *al-mukhayyam*, are nomadic encampments, we can nevertheless underscore the 'genetic dynamism' associated both with the *maḥṣar* encampments and with the *firgān* throughout the twentieth century and the encampments of the hamada of Tindouf. The camps can be interpreted as exceptional spatialities enacted to unify the *qabā'il*, derived from nomadic *qabā'il*-centred traditions and built upon the ideal of radical egalitarianism

Figure 3.3 Diagram of the organization of the camp of Ouenet Bellagra (Dajla since 1978). All the daïras were outlined by rows of stones from which we can find traces at some places. Source: Julien Lafontaine Carboni.

as a temporary (and essentially reversible) strategy for survival and adaptation. In this sense, through the lens of the long history of Sahrawi culture, this relative immobilization does not lie in tension with nomadic culture and its perpetuation over generations. On the contrary, the maintenance of affective and material dimensions of nomadism, despite the lower mobility of the Sahrawi population – whose movements have been reduced only in terms of magnitude – outlines the existence of new forms of Sahrawi nomadism in exile. These magnitudes of nomadism are deeply inscribed in the history of the twentieth century, a period in which the pastoralist population reinvented forms of nomadism and economic/ecological modes of life as a strategic adaptation for survival. Moreover, this portrays a strategy for reclaiming and resisting attempts to undermine their status as refugees, a necessary political subjectivity used to legitimate and pursue their struggle for self-determination.

Conclusion: The short-circuiting of knowledge circulation

Beyond the spatial analogy and the inscription of the refugee camps in a broader spatial history of Sahrawi culture, Sahrawi nomadism is an entire socio-cultural set of gestures and motions, from tea-making to the ways in which the tents have been positioned in relation to each other. The material culture of the Sahrawi evolved in exodus, shaped by the economic and material reality; among other factors, the absence of herds of camels and goats rendered the maintenance of the traditional *khayma* impossible. As such, with a view to sustaining their nomadic culture, numerous Sahrawis refused, for a time, to improve their quality of life as refugees; as they argued, replacing the lightness of the *firgān* with individual blocks built of sand bricks – for kitchens, bathrooms, and 'living rooms' – jeopardized their right to claim to belong to a nomadic culture. For the same reason that the Sahrawi have refused (and continue to refuse) to call the refugee camps 'cities', they have resisted building infrastructure and undertaking material improvements to their households. Just as their status as refugees and the acknowledgement of the camps as refugee camps is a right, the nomadic continuation of their culture is also a right, despite their protracted refugeehood and immobilization. This persistence reflects their unyielding will for self-determination as a people and sends a message to those who are working to improve the situation.

This perseverance is part of a political project that articulates modernity and nomadism. The Sahrawi project promoted by the Polisario Front and by the institutions of the SADR has sought to break with institutions of the past that are typical of Bedouin societies, where the segmentation of the social structure was accompanied by a classificatory system in which artisans and slaves occupied an inferior position. This entailed the rejection of their tribal condition and of slavery, which were abolished with the aim of building a society in which all people are equal. The struggle for the self-determination of the Sahrawi people has been accompanied by their will to mould themselves into a modern society. However, the nomadic condition of Sahrawi society, which we have highlighted here as its central cultural feature, has in a sense redeemed the term 'Bedouin'. Its positive significance, associated with freedom of movement, denotes a radical freedom of thought (within the framework of a nomadic and Muslim culture). In this way, the term 'Bedouin' has been reclaimed in ways that resist the tendency toward 'abjection' that is often at play when it is situated within the global hierarchy of values of the contemporary world (Peutz 2011).

Although we can argue that the spatialities of the refugee camps are inscribed in nomadic culture as an exceptional constellation of tents, we must nevertheless emphasize that nomadic culture isn't based solely on the presence of physical movements. In this contribution, we have not emphasized the movements of individual Sahrawis since their exodus, despite their significant mobility – notably to Mauritania and the occupied territories, to liberated territories, to European countries and allied countries such as Cuba (through Algeria) and even inside the camps themselves for work or weddings. Beyond these movements, we argue that, in addition to the spatial analogy between the refugee camps and the nomadic encampments, the coalescence of the tents (Isidoros 2018) and the unification of the *qabā ʾil* as an adaptive strategy for survival and independence is now the main argument for the existence of new forms of Sahrawi nomadism.

The biggest threat to Sahrawi nomadic culture isn't immobilization but the short-circuiting of the dissemination of pastoralist knowledge, which lies at the heart of their culture. Sahrawi nomadism is at base a set of motions: cultural and ecological practices that ground a collective capacity to survive, exist and freely develop in the harsh conditions of the Western Sahara. To the extent that they become dependent on the international neoliberal economic system, however, these networks, based on oral and embodied knowledge circulation, risk losing their strength and resiliency. The very motions that constitute their knowledge, spatialities and practices can be sustained despite their immobilization. Nevertheless, they would seem to be further endangered by the increasing imposition of a neoliberal economy on the refugee camps, justified on the grounds of improving living conditions and thus using the same mechanisms on which colonial Spain relied to acquire a cheap workforce.

Acknowledgements

We are grateful to Mohamed Ali Laman, responsible for the Oral Memory preservation programme at the Ministry of Culture of the SADR, and Lahsen Selki Sidi Buna, an excellent translator and investigator.

Notes

1 Mohamed Lamin Mehdi Mulay Zein participated in the attack on Nouakchott, a legendary assault in the struggle for Sahrawi independence in which Luali Mustapha Sayed was wounded and imprisoned in Mauritania, where he eventually died in June 1976.

2 The forthcoming book *Sáhara Occidental. Sociedad y Cultura* (2022) is now being translated to Spanish by Mohamed Abdelfatah.

3 Translation into English by the authors.

4 Since the Berlin Conference in 1885, the French Army stopped its operations at the Rio de Oro, which marked the border between the Spanish Sahara and French West Africa. In 1932, after the French Army was attacked by the Saharan resistance in Oum Tounsi (80 km north of Nouakchott), the French prepared a plan to more consistently conquer parts of northwestern Sahara. In the following years French colonial efforts produced cartographic descriptions of northern Mauritania and southern Western Sahara, starting to more actively control this territory (see Caratini 2003).

5 This information results from a series of interviews and discussions led by Lahsen Selki Sidi Buna and Julien Lafontaine Carboni in the refugee camps in February/May 2020 on the history of the refugee camps between 1975 and 1991. The results of this research will be presented in the forthcoming PhD thesis of Julien Lafontaine Carboni.

References

Awah, B. M. (2017), *La Entidad Política Precolonial Saharaui en el Ideario de la República Saharaui*. Madrid: Bubok.

Bárbulo, T. (2002), *La Historia Prohibida del Sáhara Español: Las Claves del Conflicto que Condiciona las Relaciones entre España y el Magreb*, Spanish edn. Madrid: Destino.

Bárbulo, T. (2017), *La Historia Prohibida del Sáhara Español: Las Claves del Conflicto que Condiciona las Relaciones entre España y el Magreb*. Madrid: Destino.

Baroja, J. C. (1955), *Estudios saharianos*. Madrid: Consejo Superior de Investigaciones Científicas/Instituto de Estudios Africanos.

Bengochea Tirado, E. (2019), *La sección femenina en la provincia de sahara: entrega, hogar e imperio*. Barcelona: Edicions Bellaterra.

Bonte, P. (2007), *Essai sur les formations tribales du Sahara occidental : Approches comparatives anthropologiques et historiques*. Waterloo: Luc Pire.

Campuzano, M. M. (1954), *Contribución al estudio del censo de población del Sahara Español*. Madrid: Consejo Superior de Investigaciones Científicas/Instituto de Estudios Africanos.

Caratini, S.(1989a), *Les Rgaybāt (1610–1934)*, vol. 1: Des Chameliers à la conquête d'un territoire, Paris: L'Harmattan.

Caratini, S. (1989b), *Les Rgaybāt (1610–1934)*, vol. 2: Territoire et société. Paris: L'Harmattan.

Caratini, S. (2003), *La république des sables: anthropologie d'une révolution*. Paris: L'Harmattan.

El Hasnaui Ahmed, Z. (2017), *El Silencio de las Nubes*. Sevilla: Arma Poética.

Fiddian-Qasmiyeh, E. (2014), *The Ideal Refugees: Gender, Islam, and the Sahrawi Politics of Survival*. Syracuse: Syracuse University Press.

García, A. (2010), *La Historia del Sáhara y su Conflicto*. Madrid: Catarata.

Gimeno Martín, J. C. (2007), *Transformaciones socioculturales de un proyecto revolucionario: la lucha del pueblo Saharaui por la liberación*. Programa Cultura, Comunicación y Transformaciones Sociales. Caracas. Universidad Central de Venezuela.

Gimeno Martín, J. C. and J. I. Robles Picón (2015), 'Vers une contre-histoire du Sahara occidental', *Les Cahiers d'EMAM*, 24–25. https://journals.openedition.org/emam/866.

Herz, M., ed. (2013), *From Camp to City: Refugee Camps of the Western Sahara*. Zurich: Lars Müller.
Hodges, T. (1983), *Sahara Occidental: Origines et Enjeux d'une Guerre du désert*. Paris: L'Harmattan.
Humphrey, C. and D. A. Sneath (1999), *The End of Nomadism? Society, State, and the Environment in Inner Asia*. Durham, NC: Duke University Press.
Isidoros, K. (2018), *Nomads and Nation-Building in the Western Sahara: Gender, Politics and the Sahrawi*. London: I.B. Tauris.
Lafontaine Carboni, J. (2021), 'Undrawn Spatialities. The Architectural Archives in the Light of the History of the Sahrawi Refugee Camps', *Architecture and Culture*, 9 (3): 505–22.
Lafontaine Carboni, J. and J. C. Gimeno (2020), 'Reinvindicar un derecho al Campamento', *Boletín de la Sociedad Geográfica Española*, 66: 94–105.
Laman, M. A. (2022), *Sáhara Occidental. Sociedad y cultura*. Málaga: Última Línea.
López Bargados, A. (2003), *Arenas Coloniales: Los Awlād Dalīm ante la Colonización Franco-Española del Sáhara*. Barcelona: Edicions Bellaterra.
Martín Beristain, C., ed. (2016), *Los Otros Vuelos de la Muerte: Bombardeos de Población civil en el Sáhara Occidental*. Bilbao: Universidad del País Vasco/Sevilla: Asociación de Amistad con el Pueblo Saharaui de Sevilla.
Martínez Milán, J. M. (2003), *España en el Sáhara Occidental y en la Zona Sur del Protectorado en Marruecos, 1885–1945*. Madrid: UNED.
Marx, E. (1980), 'Wage Labor and Tribal Economy of the Bedouin in South Sinai', in P. C. Salzman (ed.), *When Nomads Settle: Processes of Sedentarization as Adaptation and* Response, 111–23. Santa Barbara CA: Praeger.
Mundy, J. A. (2007), 'Performing the Nation, Pre-Figuring the State: The Western Saharan Refugees, Thirty Years Later', *The Journal of Modern African Studies*, 45(2): 275–97.
Peutz, N. (2011), 'Bedouin "Abjection": World Heritage, Worldliness, and Worthiness at the Margins of Arabia', *American Ethnologist*, 38(2): 338–60.
Portillo Pasqual Del Riquelme, J. (2019), *Los Saharauis y el Sáhara Occidental*. Madrid: Editorial Círculo Rojo.
Rodríguez-Esteban, J. A. and D. A. Barrado Timón (2015), 'Le processus d'urbanisation dans le Sahara espagnol (1884–1975). Une composante essentielle du projet colonial', *Les Cahiers d'EMAM*, 24–25. https://doi.org/10.4000/emam.743.
Salzman, P. C. and E. Sadala, eds (1980), *When Nomads Settle : Processes of Sedentarization as Adaptation and Response*. New York, NY: Praeger.
Solana Moreno, V. (2017), 'Regenerating Revolution: Gender and Generation in the Sahrawi Struggle for Decolonization,' PhD thesis University of Toronto.
Spivak, G. C., N. Cary and G. Lawrence (1988), 'Can the Subaltern Speak?', in C. Nelson and L. Grossberg (eds), *Marxism and the Interpretation of Culture*, 271–313. Champaign: University of Illinois Press.
Villasante-de Beauvais, M. (1998), *Parenté et politique en Mauritanie: Essai d'antropologie historique*. Paris: L'Harmattan.
Wilson, A. (2014), 'Ambiguities of Space and Control: When Refugee Camp and Nomadic Encampment Meet', *Nomadic Peoples*, 18 (1): 38–60.

4

The flexible use of democracy in an Islamic Republic: The case of the Mauritanian President Abdel Aziz (2009–2019)

Elemine Ould Mohamed Baba Moustapha
University of Nouakchott

The protesters associated with the social movement that some call 'the second Arab Spring' (Ayoob 2019) gathered around the slogan 'All, meaning all!' (*Kullkun ya'nī kullkun*), calling for the removal of all politicians, without exception, from governing positions. This chapter investigates whether the contempt for political elites felt by large segments of various populations scattered throughout the southern Mediterranean served as an inspiration for Mauritanian President Mohamed Ould Abdel Aziz (hereafter Aziz), who, after coming to power in 2007 (officially elected in 2009), decided to launch a direct attack on the country's former ruling class.

Aziz's answer to prominent Mauritanian politician Ould Khatri – a political leader from the eastern regions of the country who promptly offered his services in the aftermath of Aziz's coup d'état – may be revealing in this respect: 'I do not need you [i.e. authority figures and politicians] to run the country anymore.' This statement put an end to the Mauritanian 'tradition' of governance by an unchanging political elite with a grip on the reins of power, in some cases since the country's independence in 1960. This radical attitude, hardly expected of a putschist seeking support,[1] may in truth have been a Machiavellian exploitation of the unpopularity of politicians, who were often seen as opportunistic and willing to acquiesce to any ruling power in order to maintain the privileges provided by this patronage system. Aziz surfed the populist wave that allowed him to dominate the political scene by virtually eliminating a de facto unpopular ruling class while assuming what can only be described, as we will see, as authoritarian rule over Mauritania 'dressed up' as a democracy.

What explains the ascension to power of this ex-general, who has marked Mauritania's political landscape for the past fifteen years?[2] Can it be associated with 'strongman' forms of neopatrimonialism (see Bratton and Van de Walle 1994: 474–5, who classify Mauritania as a 'military oligarchy') or with the hybridization of power, as defined by Dufy and Thiriot (2013; see also Driscoll 2020)? Perhaps it is comparable to the pretorianism described by Abdel Wedoud Ould Cheikh and the so-called 'Sultanian' form of governance, supposedly explained by the notion that Mauritanians are intrinsically predisposed to 'despotic rulers' (Ould Cheikh 2003, 2006)? Far from this line of questioning, most of the authors who have addressed the Mauritanian context in recent years have focused on the political reality and on statements evoking economic and diplomatic questions on both a local and a global scale – recurrent coups, institutional crises, the populist nature of President Aziz's campaign, the destabilization of the region and its consequences for militant activities and drug trafficking. The dynamics of political promotion and social mobility were noted more than twenty years ago by Zekeria Ould Ahmed Salem (1998), who referred in particular to the 'ascension routes' of the *ḥarāṭīn* elite.[3] Antil and Lesourd (2014) have provided an account of the different facets of Aziz's policies[4] and his form of government, emphasizing, in an article with the telling title 'I must control everything', the 'highly centralized and vertical character of his governance' (2014: 275).[5] Despite their familiarity with the subject, however, these authors mainly stress the continuity of his methods of exercising power (through the manipulation of ethnic identities, regional interests and tribal allegiances), which, according to them, were not so different from those used by his predecessors. In this chapter, I will offer arguments to the contrary by analysing President Aziz's will to remove an entire political class from power, thus characterizing his reign as a rupture with Mauritania's postcolonial political traditions. This action proved decisive to Aziz's legitimation, but the processes he engaged with require further exploration, beyond describing Aziz's actions as an attempt to create a new ruling class – or indeed, in Aziz's own words, 'a new Mauritania' – via 'tacit lustration'. In this vein, it seems relevant to reconsider his centralizing tendencies and the autocratic inflections that marked his presidency.

This study draws on empirical data, including Aziz's speeches, the administrative and legal acts of his government, and further analysis of his actions, notably towards the local political elite. The political class is here defined as 'actors who hold positions of power or political resources (ministerial posts or elected offices) and who are likely, in a Weberian sense, to earn their living off them' (Genieys 2006: 133). The chapter begins with an overview of the categories and typologies of transitional power in general, proceeding to the presentation and analysis of the Mauritanian context under President Aziz.

Intermediate political categories

The governance exercised by President Aziz between 2009 and 2019 can be seen as a particular use of the democratic system, quite different in practice from that which he claimed to promote. Behind formally democratic structures we can easily observe autocratic practices that make it appropriate to characterize this regime as an intermediate or hybrid one, falling somewhere between the democratic and the autocratic.

Such regimes are studied by the emerging discipline of transitology, which, as the name suggests, is dedicated to examining forms of political power that are no longer dictatorships but not yet democracies – many of which first arose in the shift away from totalitarianism in Eastern Europe (Saxonberg and Linde 2003), Latin America (Brinks et al. 2014) and Africa from the beginning of the 1990s (for the West African Sahel, see Villalón 2010). Transitology presupposes in principle that the regimes in question are evolving towards democratization. This has often been far from the case, however, with significant setbacks leading to a return to totalitarian rule, in some cases even leading to civil war (Dufy and Thiriot 2013; Levitsky and Way 2002).

To designate the regimes of this grey zone, 'for which the qualification of a totalitarian regime did not apply in all rigor', some authors have introduced the concept of authoritarianism (Droz-Vincent 2004: 946). To further emphasize the hybrid nature of these powers, researchers have specifically evoked the concept of neo-patrimonialism, which combines traditional heritage with modern state institutions while manifesting a tendency to conflate the public and the private sphere (Brossier 2019). This category of governance, previously applied mainly to sub-Saharan African countries, has gradually expanded to embrace most mixed-regime countries outside the West.

One of the most extreme expressions of neopatrimonialism is dictatorship in which a single individual governs the entire state apparatus, gradually reducing the power held by institutions and other elements of the political system. Their monopoly on power and the elimination of opponents generally allows such leaders to declare themselves president for life (Bratton and Van de Walle 1994). This weakening of democracy directly undermines the usual path established by transitology (one *towards* democracy) and may signal a need for the new category of 'post-transition', in which formal compliance with the standard criteria of democratic life is accompanied by a substantive movement beyond forms and labels (Dufy and Thiriot 2013). This formal respect for democratic rules runs parallel to totalitarian acts.

Although elections in such states are regularly held and generally free of widespread fraud, incumbents routinely abuse state resources, deny the opposition adequate media coverage, harass opposition candidates and their supporters, and in some cases manipulate electoral results. Journalists, opposition politicians and other government critics may be spied on, threatened, harassed or arrested. Members of the opposition may be jailed, exiled or – less frequently – even assaulted or murdered. Regimes characterized by such abuses cannot be called democratic. Rather than openly violating democratic rules (for example by banning or repressing the opposition and the media), incumbents are more likely to use bribery, co-optation and more subtle forms of persecution (through tax authorities, compliant judiciaries and other state agencies) to 'legally' harass, persecute and extort cooperative behaviour from critics (Levitsky and Way 2002: 53).

This type of competitive authoritarianism falls under a category that combines 'free elections with the authoritarian use of power', the cornerstone of which 'is the unequal access of parties to financial, media and legal resources[,] inequality that largely undermines the opportunities available to the opposition to contest by the ballot the domination of the ruling elites' (Dufy and Thiriot 2013: 24). Yet another political category, that of 'defective democracy', is also relevant in this regard. In this context, we may be witnessing a gradual shift from the 'democratic transitions' model to other types of power structures, which further undermines the notion that the regimes studied by transitology are moving toward the implementation of democratic institutions (Droz-Vincent 2004; Levitsky and Way 2002).

In this critique of transitology, the fundamental question regarding adherence to democratic norms is complicated by the extent to which the regimes in question, supposedly moving towards democratization, continue to demonstrate a decidedly authoritarian inflection. This tension is in part explained by the longevity of these regimes and their apparent 'stability' (Droz-Vincent 2004: 963).

It is important to emphasize that the inefficiency of the opposition also plays a key role in the 'normalized' political and institutional landscape that is undermined by autocrats. It is no longer the opposition that threatens the longevity of authoritarian powers but their inability to secure a monopoly on the distribution of material resources and the manipulation of the levers of legitimacy. In order to grasp the reasons for the resilience of authoritarianism, various mechanisms must be described and analysed. Given that democracy in its ideal form cannot be described as standard practice in most countries – which are usually more concerned with security than with fully realizing democratic norms – it is necessary to look at how these systems function and their strategies for intervening in different segments of society and the economy. It is equally important to question the dynamics of these political regimes since, as Genieyes (2006: 139) confirms, 'the transformation of the social structure of the elite, as an adaptation to changes in society, has always been regarded as a reliable indicator of regime change'.

In the remainder of this chapter, these approaches will be applied comparatively to the Mauritian case, with the aim of better understanding how President Aziz exploited a well-known set of processes to secure legitimacy and ensure a quasi-monopoly on authority while keeping up democratic appearances – a form of window dressing that was crucial to his relationship with Western partners.

The (populist) fight against mismanagement

Aziz's inauguration was marked by a series of populist measures, including the allocation of plots of land, a reduction of the price of essential goods, major road works and bringing water and electricity to the poorest districts of Nouakchott (El Haycen 2016: 22). He gave himself the moniker 'president of the poor' (*ra'īs al-fuqarā'*), indicating his primary commitment to the more disadvantaged among the population (Makhmutova 2020: 610; Villasante Cervello 2013: 17). His announcements and promises were usually made in the presence of large crowds and took place while visiting hospitals, construction sites and at political meetings while touring the country.

Independence Day celebrations presented another special opportunity for Aziz to announce his agenda.[6] His speeches centred on several key issues, some of which borrowed heavily from positions previously taken by the opposition, such as the topic of diplomatic relations with Israel, his 'anti-system' stance and his focus on social inequities (against the backdrop of the 'president of the poor' narrative). Other common themes of his public addresses included the fight against mismanagement and the valorization of anti-colonial resistance – promises that were portrayed as part of a fearless crusade against the political elite who had preceded him and who, in his opinion, were responsible for the population's current penury. The fight against the mismanagement of public funds was often a major focus of his allocutions. Aziz, self-acknowledged as the embodiment of economic righteousness,[7] repeatedly stated that the eradication of all forms of financial misdealing was his government's main objective:

> We are pleased with the positive results achieved since 6 August 2008, particularly in the fight against mismanagement and harmful practices that have marked our society in recent decades (...) The government continues to fight the moral crisis the eradication of which is a prerequisite for any development policy and the success of any serious enterprise (...) I take this opportunity to once again urge the corrupt and all those who capitalize on trading in influence, lies and hypocrisy, to repent and to renew our Islamic values and virtues.[8]

For President Aziz, mismanagement of public resources was a social scourge that had run rampant in the country for too long; fortunately, he claimed, with the events of 6 August (the day of his coup), this situation was finally about to change. He insisted that combatting this 'moral crisis' was the condition *sine qua non* for the effectiveness of his policy in this area. He called for the repentance of those involved in these nefarious practices and directly addressed the 'lost souls' (*al-ḍāllīn*) involved. Calling for a renewal of Islamic values and virtues, he equated the fight against corruption with a sacred struggle to end the deleterious atmosphere that had pervaded in Mauritania before his coup.

Aziz was by then also engaged in a merciless fight against the political actors of the previous regime, referring to them as 'symbols of mismanagement' (*rumūz al-fasād*). Demonizing his enemies, Aziz launched a witch hunt against the entire political class – a purge that was baptized by the official press as *Muḥārabat al-fasād wa-l-mufsidīn* ('the fight against mismanagement and the corrupt'). As a result, former Prime Minister Yahya Ould Mohamed al-Waqf was incarcerated following an obscure accusation known locally as the 'spoiled rice' affair (*mārū al-khāmir*).[9]

At the same time, the authorities were imprisoning businessmen from the inner circle of ousted President Ould Taya, namely Mohamed Ould Noueigedh, Chérif Ould Abdellahi and Abdou Maham. According to Lesourd and Antil (2014: 368–9), these powerful men had been 'vassalized' by Ould Taya and 'given disproportionate access to State resources'. It should be noted that those, now convicted of illicit enrichment, had supported Ahmed Ould Daddah, Aziz's main political opponent in the July 2009 presidential election. It is therefore possible that underneath Aziz's campaign for ethical governance was an underlying desire to settle the score with his political opponents. It also seems relevant that the dropping of the lawsuit against Ould Waghef coincided with the withdrawal of his party, the ADIL, from the coordination of the democratic opposition after it opted to ally itself with the presidential majority in support of Aziz.

The sympathy expressed by opposition leaders towards the detained businessmen offered Aziz further justification for denouncing his political opponents.[10] He claimed that any parties that defended mismanagement, protected those who had defrauded the country or organized rallies for such purposes should not be called an opposition.

To consolidate his popularity, he began to portray himself as a 'proper gentleman' (*rājil naẓīf*), in stark contrast to his political opponents, who were defined as 'corrupt politicians' or, at best, their auxiliaries and accomplices.

Aziz alternated diatribes addressed to his opponents with reports of his campaign against the mismanagement of public funds, frequently returning to this strategy to assert his perseverance in this struggle and to highlight its achievements. It should be remembered that tools such as the General State Inspectorate and the Audit Office were by then conspicuously used for this purpose (El Haycen 2016: 188). Aziz assessed the results of the anti-mismanagement campaign in a speech delivered on 13 March 2010:

> With regard to the fight against mismanagement and misappropriation of public funds, it is important to point out that 5,650,000,000 ouguiya [equivalent to over 15 million euros], squandered by certain people, has been recovered by the public treasury. We have recovered 600 million ouguiya from managers this year, and we will continue with these efforts. These measures will be improved, and this is a message to the civil servants. To them we say that henceforth, and within the framework of the 2009 and 2010 budget, any diversion will be treated with rigor, and the perpetrators will be required to refund the embezzled funds, sanctioned and brought to justice.
>
> (Extract from a speech delivered during a meeting in Nouakchott's southern suburb of Arafat on 13 March 2010; see Agence Mauritanienne d'Information 2010a)

This speech exhibits one of Aziz's more characteristic rhetorical devices – his use of numbers. He often resorted to the manipulation of these 'objective' parameters, leading some in Nouakchott to call him *al-muḥaṣṣil* ('the tax collector'). The abundant use of numbers in his speeches lent credibility to his assertions, not to mention that it obviously helped to impress his predominantly low-income audience, for whom even a few thousand ouguiyas represented an impressive amount. With that said, this period saw the retrocession of several billion ouguiyas to the state coffers (El Haycen 2016: 198).

Aziz enjoyed presenting himself as the protector and curator of the public treasury, overseeing it closely and keeping its records. The second part of the above excerpt shows that the president was not content to target only the top members of the administration, politicians and businessmen but was also focused on 'managers' – accountants, treasurers and financial officials. At this point in the campaign against mismanagement, he was on a treasure hunt for 600 million ouguiya. He warned that more effective measures would be taken and that enforcement actions would be strengthened, explaining that any case of misappropriation of public funds would lead to the exposure of the perpetrators and to a reimbursement of the funds without immunity from prosecution and criminal penalties. As he stated in yet another public address:

> We have rigorously built momentum to ensure the sound and transparent management of public resources and state assets. In this sense, we have given firm instructions that the perpetrators of the crimes of misappropriation of public

> funds, corruption, embezzlement and marginal practices, which are foreign to the traditions of our Muslim society, should be punished.
>
> (Speech delivered by Aziz on the occasion of the fiftieth anniversary of independence on 27 November 2010; see Agence Mauritanienne d'Information 2010b)

Public Treasury officials were eventually condemned and imprisoned after the dismantlement of a large network engaged in the misappropriation of public funds in 2014.[11] This action gave some credit to Aziz's anti-corruption campaign, but most of the economic scandals made public during his presidency carried a strong political flavour. The judicial chronicles of Aziz's reign were in fact filled with financial scandals and the imprisonment of managers of some of the country's leading institutions, including Mauritanian Airlines, the board of directors of the savings bank CAPEC and the National Society of Import and Export (SONIMEX) (see Agence Mauritanienne d'Information 2008; Nouakchott Info 2011; Tawary 2016). These scandals were the subject of much gossip in the country and put president Aziz's anti-corruption initiatives in something of a good light. The end result of these initiatives was not impressive, however, as none of these scandals ultimately went to trial.

In addition to their significant media impact, these cases can also be understood as a coercive political strategy aimed at pushing opponents towards the presidential majority. As for those who were already members of his majority, this procedure forced them to openly state their loyalty and to assume an overtly militant posture. The wrongdoers were often obliged to repay the sums but, paradoxically, tended to be reinstated in their positions thereafter, as occurred with the Director of the ENS (École Normale Supérieur), for example. The same technique was replicated in the area of fiscal policy with more impressive political results, for instance with the chairman of the Mauritanian Leasing Company.

This process amounted to the clear instrumentalization of the judiciary system and other state institutions, with the particular aim of controlling or eliminating Aziz's political opponents. Aziz seemed determined to demonize an entire political class who, in his eyes, were responsible for all of Mauritania's problems. This campaign, while seriously handicapping the opposition, made Aziz appear as the chosen saviour of the country and the protector of the poor against 'a corrupt political class of exploiters'.

A crusade against the political class

During a meeting in the populous Nouakchott suburb of Arafat, President Aziz continued his litany, affirming that the use of public funds for personal enrichment was a characteristic of previous political actors in Mauritania:

> I thank you for your patience during the last thirty years, in which you lived in these conditions. I apologize to you on behalf of the previous regimes that have left you like this. They are the ones who are responsible for this situation.
>
> (Agence Mauritanienne d'Information 2010a)

Aziz accused the entire political class who had preceded him of being responsible for the precarious conditions in working-class neighbourhoods and the hazardous areas established on illegally occupied land, which lacked water, electricity and sanitation. Aziz pushed this point by insisting that he was obliged to apologize on behalf of the previous governments who had kept the population in misery, thus underlining his solidarity with those who were suffering. Covering the last forty years, Aziz blamed government officials from the Ould Haidallah period (1979–1984) and those who worked with Ould Taya (1984–2005). He was particularly harsh on Ould Taya and his administration, from which many of the voices opposing Aziz stemmed. At the same time, he hit two birds with one stone by denouncing his political opponents and soliciting support from the population that had suffered as a result of the policies of previous governments, thus gaining popularity and legitimacy to the direct detriment of his political rivals. Reiterating his decisive action against previous governments, he said:

> You will not be forced from the places you have lived for thirty years so that others can be assigned to them, and we will not abandon you (…) We will proceed with the opening of roads, the distribution of plots of land, the guaranteeing of safety …
> (Agence Mauritanienne d'Information 2010a)

He thus specifies the lines of action that will remediate the injustices caused by past governments. Unlike what happened with previous governments, Aziz promised that populations would not be displaced from the occupied lands where they lived; more than that, land rights would finally be granted to them. The allocation of land rights was another of his promises and arguably the most popular measure of his presidency.[12]

Since the 1980s, thousands of precarious and illegal settlements, known locally as *gazra*, had been established on the flanks of the capital, representing one of the manifestations of the accelerated and anarchic urbanization that had been fuelled by a rural exodus and land speculation in the country (McDougall 2015). One can only imagine the high hopes raised among the inhabitants of these neighbourhoods upon hearing of the possibility of being granted a new plot of land or the immanent legalization of those they already occupied. Aziz's speech in fact provoked a new exodus that mobilized a considerable part of the population from the countryside, causing serious problems for public services as a result of a dramatic increase in the number of beneficiaries now settled in Nouakchott. One of the president's first speeches was delivered in the al-Hay Assakin neighbourhood, one of the capital's oldest *gazra*, solidifying this promise into yet another pillar of Aziz's rule that differentiated him from his predecessors, who had been unable to solve the problem:

> If we compare this situation with what has prevailed in the past, we will find that billions of external funds have been misplaced in recent decades for the settlement of the *gazra* without any significant achievement. You also know that during the last eight years of this operation, all that was achieved was the displacement of poor people, leaving their dwellings open to the benefit of influential people who were close to the previous regimes.
> (Agence Mauritanienne d'Information 2010a)

Here, Aziz argued that housing policies had not succeeded because of the misappropriation and poor governance that prevailed, despite the considerable financial resources available to his predecessors. Moreover, what had been achieved was only made possible in the context of patronage and favouritism. Aziz emphasized his role as 'protector' of the poor and champion of social justice – a commitment that he openly declared on various occasions: 'I tell you today that this situation is gone forever, and priority will be given to the poor' (Agence Mauritanienne d'Information 2010a).

In order to emphasize his role as the protector of the poor, he – a military man – spoke with disdain of the country's political class. He devoted an important part of his Arafat speech to criticizing senior officials of previous governments, blaming them for the dismal state of Mauritania, its social and political crises and the serious dysfunctions of the state. For him, all of Mauritania's ills originated in the actions of the previous powers, who had accumulated failures and bottlenecks.

It should be remembered that Mauritania experienced a major upheaval following the fall of Ould Taya in 2005, with the subsequent reorganization of political parties following a massive 'transhumance' to opposition parties. The plotters of the 2005 coup initially tried to 'deconstruct' the state party (PRDR) that had dominated the country during the Ould Taya era, which was emptied through the creation of so-called 'independent' parties (El Haycen 2016: 55). The PNDD-Adil was torn apart, and the elites of the Republican Democratic and Social Party (PRDS)/Republican Party for Democracy and Renewal (PRDR), 'the backpacks of the presidential parties', joined Aziz. The parliamentary battalion widened, and the 'slingers' were joined by former Ould Taya supporters such as Louleïd Ould Weddad and Kaba Ould Eleywa. The Hatem, Temam and Al Vadhila parties showed support for the new power. The Rally of Democratic Forces (RFD), led by Ahmed Ould Daddah – which many Europeans and even Mauritanians viewed as 'the eternal opponent', the 'best candidate for a truly democratic presidency' – made a pact with Aziz and joined the pro-putschist movement (Antil 2009: 371).

The 2008 elections saw the ascension to power of former Ould Taya ministers and a large group of businessmen who had been in the opposition (El Haycen 2016: 155). By then, Aziz found himself confronting both the opposition parties (RFD, UFP, APP) and former members of the ADIL state party. This is possibly why Aziz decided to fight against the entire Mauritanian political class, assigning it responsibility for all of the country's tribulations and associating it with the classic opposition parties in order to reinforce his line of defence and his populist agenda. He highlighted the privileges enjoyed by this class, which were revoked in a restructuring of state spending through the adoption of new legislation.[13] This new law implied, among other things, the end of government subsidies for officials (meaning free utilities, including water, electricity, telephone and housing) and of governmental cars, which from then on would only be consigned to ministers: 'With regard to water and electricity [subsidized for government officials], this was terminated and is no longer the privilege of a minority' (Agence Mauritanienne d'Information 2010a). Moreover, the operating budgets of the state administration were drastically reduced. These measures, which clearly affected the governing officials' lifestyle, were presented by Aziz as a collective punishment imposed on a corrupt political class. The removal of their privileges, often accompanied by public exposure, undoubtedly aimed to achieve more than the mere optimization of public spending.

With these actions, Aziz intended to persuade the population that the only difference between them and the class of privileged officials consisted in this series of advantages, which they enjoyed and which he abolished. Even more explicitly, Aziz claimed that whereas his predecessors had marginalized the population, his administration would be closer to the people. Here, Aziz would seem to have been tacitly exploiting the situation by, on the one hand, claiming to solve economic problems and, on the other, shifting the burden of responsibility onto his predecessors while playing them against the population. For the ordinary citizen, these populist measures – punishment inflicted on the upper-level administration, who were responsible for the dire condition of the popular classes – represented an achievement in themselves, and they were most likely the card that Aziz's populist instinct told him to play.

Aziz's denunciation of the political class led, in his own words, to a generalized opposition to his policies as he was allegedly trying to end mismanagement and to launch a reform of public institutions that would benefit the overall population, not only the political elite:

> This may not be good for some who have benefited for decades from the wealth of the country and have made a profession of mismanagement to the detriment of the 3 million Mauritanians. It is this minority who today cries and who says that the country is collapsing.
>
> To them we say: You must be reasonable! If you have devastated the country for forty years, it is up to you now to beg forgiveness from the Mauritanian people, including those whom death might surprise while on this erroneous path.
>
> (Agence Mauritanienne d'Information 2010a)

Such appeals can be interpreted as an incitement to rebellion against a political class who, according to Aziz, had squandered the country's wealth and were now lamenting the loss of their privileges. They are presented as perpetrators of crimes of which only 'the people' can absolve them.

Here, he again introduces the religious dimension, already perceptible in his mention of their need to repent. Aziz also decided to sermonize those 'whom death might surprise on their evil path'. He thus associates the officials who served under the old regimes with 'misguided souls' (*al-ḍāllīn*), a concept with a very strong resonance with disbelief among Muslims. His recourse to the religious dimension in reflects the mental universe of Mauritanians and reveals a high level of opportunism on his part. Do we not say that 'words stop when they reach Allah' (*leklām yūgaf ilā al-ḥagg mūlāna*)?

In Mauritania, the best way to win any debate or controversy is to resort to religious arguments. One's opponent is thereby obliged to appeal to religious grounds, at the risk of being accused of apostasy. The most effective way to promote an opinion is to find a religious motive for it. In a deeply Islamized society, the mere mention of Islam alleviates all suspicion and attracts immediate support. In all mobilization campaigns, it is always the religious argument that represents the last resort and the most effective weapon in guaranteeing the support of the population. Because of this, religious arguments were decisive in shifting public opinion on female genital mutilation. Similarly, very recently, the speech of the ulemas referring to the plague epidemics during the time of the prophet Muḥammad, played a large part in raising awareness about the spread of Covid-19.

By appealing to the religious dimension, Aziz therefore sought to strike a chord in the Mauritanian 'subconscious'. This Manichean understanding of reality distinguishes between those who follow the path of the good (*al-rāshidūn*) and the lost (*al-ḍāllīn*), who follow no path and necessarily choose evil. The association of corrupt politicians (and by extension the old regime) with the 'damned' and with disbelievers is certainly the best way to articulate their downfall. Globally, the invocation of the religious dimension and its concepts allows Aziz to also appear as a champion of Islam.

A call to young people

The struggle against the 'old' political class led Aziz to claim the creation of a 'new' political class, calling for young people to get involved in political life. In most of his speeches, he repeatedly stressed the slogan 'rejuvenate the political class' in order to ensure the succession of a 'deliquescent' political class that had constantly shown its shortcomings and failures.[14] Following online consultations involving thousands of young people in March 2013 (on media uses in Africa, see, for example, Hackett and Soares 2015), a large event was organized under the patronage of Aziz, who occasionally entered into direct dialogue with youth representatives. At the end of this process in 2015, a High Council of Youth (HCY; HCJ abbreviation in French) was created. This structure was placed under the direct control of the Presidency of the Republic, and its president was raised to the rank of minister, with all its advantages, while the thirteen members of the HCY executive office were made deputies in the prime minister's office.

Despite its incorporation into the ranks of the state apparatus, the HCY had no impact on the actions of the government, and no executive tasks were ever assigned to it. Although some observers, like Ould Sneib (Mohamed Sneiba 2013) viewed this approach as an attempt to take the youth out of the streets (during a period that coincided with the civil unrest associated with the so-called Arab Spring; for other interpretations of Aziz's attempts to nullify the influence of the Arab Spring in Mauritania, see Makhmutova 2020: 608), it seems to be in line with Aziz's strategy of 'cutting the grass under the feet' of the old ruling class in order to neutralize it while dismantling the opposition by poaching some of its more prominent leaders. As a result of this continued undermining, the opposition failed to run a single candidate in the presidential election of June 2019 (Sahara Media 2019), and several of its top leaders rallied with the presidential majority, while others supported a former Ould Taya prime minister for president.

To complete his battle against the political class, President Aziz worked hard to rid the administration of the old guard and their allies. Through the demonization of the former leaders of the country, Aziz associated all of his political opponents with administrations formed by 'incompetent old men' (al-Akhbar 2012). In their place, he often installed young people who lacked previous experience in the public sector. The opposition continuously denounced this scuttling of the administration (Antil 2019: 280).

In full accordance with the slogan 'rejuvenate the political class', young ministers such as Amal Mint Maouloud and Ould Abdel Fettah (born in 1983 and 1977, respectively) were appointed to the government. In the eyes of the president, the recruitment of inexperienced staff had the advantage of making them particularly malleable and well suited to his authoritarian paternalism. Such actions made Aziz's government the most stable ever known in the country, and the longevity of the ministers was exceptional, as they represented, one might argue, 'smokescreens' for Aziz's own exercise of power.

Alan Antil has stressed the heightened levels of control exercised by Aziz, the consolidation of his inner circle, and especially 'the low turnover of ministers and their low decisional weight'. Antil also highlights one of the characteristics of Aziz's appointment techniques, which distinguishes him from his predecessors:

> The opportunistic loyalty of men no longer operates by offering them carte blanche to public funds, but rather by maintaining pressure on their necessary probity. In case of "error"—real or fake—they are immediately put to the media and legal guillotine.
>
> (Antil 2014: 278)

Unlike Ould Taya, who offered his ministers and administrators the opportunity to embezzle public funds with impunity, Aziz used coercion, and his collaborators could only claim the crumbs he portioned to them. Far from scrutinizing this attitude from the perspective of moral integrity, Aziz's opponents justified this through his particular relationship with money and his propensity for personal enrichment. Another of Aziz's well-known traits was his public scrutiny of his ministers through the active exposure of the slightest of slip-ups, which forced them to choose inaction out of fear of making missteps.

Because of this, the ministers only had symbolic power, while the administration, stripped of its financial means and its more efficient human resources, sunk into paralysis, thus opening the way to the only available recourse: President Aziz himself was to take on the tasks of the most modest officials in the administrative hierarchy. Those with any sort of grievance would then have to turn to the sole 'manager' of the country. Whether the problem was in downtown Nouakchott or in the most remote corner of Mauritania, it could only be resolved by taking direct recourse to the president. Aziz's visits to the countryside provided another opportunity for citizens to talk to him directly about their problems during private hearings or to hand him their complaints when he appeared at public gatherings. This approach to power, as we know, can easily be manipulated by actors with privileged access to the administration, thus favouring corruption.

Zekeria Ould Ahmed Salem (1999) has emphasized the exaggerated personification of state power in Mauritania and the fact that 'the different regimes are systematically identified in collective memory as "the epoch of so and so"' – this even more so for Aziz: Whereas his predecessors had sometimes strengthened the administration, or at least allowed their collaborators room for manoeuvre, Aziz combined the executive and the administrative function of government in a single person, thus becoming the state itself. From the ordinary citizen's point of view, only President Aziz was likely to find a solution to their problems. He thus wanted to take the place of the entire state apparatus, to intervene in all levels of the administration, and to disavow it. This *l'état c'est moi* approach was also evident in his personal overseeing of all aspects of the public budget (Antil and Lesourd 2014: 277–8).

These actions made President Aziz the sole 'master' of the country, with a neutralized political opposition and young and inexperienced collaborators who would never aspire to overshadow him. It is therefore legitimate to ask whether the ultimate goal of his presidency – facilitated by his efforts to demonize the old political class and to surround himself with neophyte government officials – was not simply to secure a monopoly on power while obtaining total control over the country's resources.

Conclusion

Aziz's strategy therefore consisted first of demonizing the old elites by accusing them of corruption and positioning them as the cause of Mauritania's problems. At the same time, his speeches continually included a call for the political engagement of the youth to give some semblance of coherence to his propaganda calling for the need to replace the old elite. This call was merely a tactic to co-opt inexperienced but dedicated staff, which suited Aziz's unquenchable thirst for material gain. This was a component of the populist character of Aziz's policies, which had been revealed during his first term in office. Nonetheless, Aziz was quick to change his approach by returning, paradoxically, to a better disposition towards the old political elite.

Indeed, after a short period of political turbulence, he rapidly secured the legitimation of his positions. Aziz started by making concessions to the political class that had preceded him in office, especially towards some of its more notable actors, who had proved quite useful during the electoral period. He also put his fight against misappropriation on hold by keeping in office figures known to have diverted public funds. At the same time, he vigorously pursued the dismantling of the opposition parties, notably by offering future promotions and government posts to defectors. Finally, Aziz balanced his fight against the old political elites with their partial rehabilitation, which came with political dividends. These two apparently irreconcilable processes can hardly be acknowledged as signs of democratization. One might even argue the opposite: that they helped the executive – mostly represented by the figure of Aziz – to steadily strengthen its grip on power.

President Aziz sought a third term in office and gradually implemented the necessary political and legal tools to achieve this outcome. He continued to take advantage of the options available to him in order to obtain a third presidential mandate, despite the fact that the Constitution forbade it. He vehemently questioned this constitutional clause and encouraged his ministers and collaborators to openly state that the president deserved a third term in office and that the articles of the Constitution were insignificant details that could easily be curbed. It was only after a dramatic reversal – announced in a presidential statement read on state television, in the absence of the president (who was visiting the United Arab Emirates) – that those campaigning for a third term were formally ordered to suspend their actions, paving the way for elections that included a (reluctant) candidate who was part of Aziz's establishment.

In general terms, the political practices of President Aziz were largely marked by his authoritarianism and by Machiavellian political tactics that often ran contrary to the spirit of democracy. Rather than leading Mauritania towards democracy, the political regime under Aziz had an authoritarian character that makes it appropriate to describe it as either a 'deficient democracy' or a form of 'competitive authoritarianism'.

Nevertheless, Aziz's Mauritania remains an interesting case study that can be drawn on by different fields (particularly political studies), as evidenced by Ould Cheikh's research on the 'mirror of the Sultan' (2019), Ould Ahmed Salem's work on new conceptions and perceptions (1998, 1999, 2020), Villasante's studies on the involvement of tribal identities (2013), Lesourd and Antil's research on Aziz's mode of governance (2009, 2014), and Pettigrew and Evrard's (2019) work on the Mauritanian political system.

Notes

1 Immediately following his takeover and the overthrowing of Sidi Mohamed Ould Cheikh Abdellahi, Aziz found himself ostracized by the international community, and an internal front was set up for the first time to thwart military action.

2 As a colonel, in 2005 Aziz took part in a coup that overthrew President Ould Taya, becoming one of the strongmen of the transitional 'Military Committee for Justice and Democracy'. He later became the chief of staff of the elected President Ould Abdallahi. Ould Abdallahi promoted Aziz to General but in 2008 dismissed him due to his alleged involvement in a parliamentary vote of no confidence against Ould Abdallahi. Supported by the military and the parliament, Aziz would go on to overthrow President Ould Abdallahi and was thus instrumental in the restoration of national unity (which he had previously disrupted). He ran for presidential office and won the election in 2009. He stepped down from the role of president in 2019 after two terms (see N'Diaye 2009).

3 The *ḥarāṭīn* (a significant segment of the Hassaniyya-speaking populations of Mauritania) are historically associated with a dependent/servile status. Their current mobilization has challenged the country's political equilibrium. See the chapter by David Malluche in this volume for a more in-depth analysis.

4 El Haycen's book *Mohamed Ould Abdel Aziz: Construire la Mauritanie Autrement* is dedicated, in the author's own words, to the 'simplified reconstitution of the political events that Mauritania had known from 2008, the date that marks the beginning of the political rise of President Mohamed Ould Abdel Aziz', but its panegyric character makes it useful only for illustrating factual aspects.

5 My translation from the French. All translations are my own.

6 Antil (2019) has emphasized Aziz's 'ability to sell himself as a good communicator'. He is probably the most public Mauritanian President, organizing frequent meetings with the press which he called 'the meeting with the people' (*Liqā ʾ al-sha ʿb*), a sort of press conference where he engages in disjointed conversation with a panel of journalists on various issues, replicating a model that is well known, for example, in parts of South America.
7 Ironically, in 2020 it was Aziz's turn to be investigated for 'suspected embezzlement' (https://www.france24.com/en/africa/20210311-mauritanian-ex-president-mohamed-ould-abdel-aziz-charged-with-corruption).
8 See the AMI website, https://fr.ami.mr/Depeche-9292.html.
9 Yahya Ould Ahmed Waghef, Ould Cheikh Abdellahi's prime minister, was arrested during the coup of 6 August 2008. He was accused of selling a stock of spoiled rice to traders during his time as the head of the Food Aid Commission (CSA). He was freed a few months later (Tawary 2016).
10 Leaders of the opposition (RFD/Rassemblement des Forces Démocratiques and UFP/Union des Forces Progressistes) organized support rallies for the detainees and publicly expressed their support for the detained businessmen, denouncing an action which could have serious economic repercussions.
11 See for example the journal *Points Chauds* at: https://pointschauds.info/fr/arrestation-a-nouadhibou-de-cinq-comptables-de-la-tresorerie-regionale-suite-a-la-disparition-dune-importante-somme/.
12 Land speculation is among the more profitable enrichment schemes in Nouakchott. Land sales have transformed the lives of many of the capital's inhabitants, turning what were once very poor families into wealthy communities overnight. This explains the enormous hope and high expectations that followed President Aziz's promise.
13 'Decree No. 2010-033 of 9 February 2010 on housing allowance, transport and water and electricity and amending certain provisions of Decree No. 2006-003 / PM amending the value of the index point, flat rate increase to benefit of categories C and D abrogation and modification of certain provisions of the Decree No. 99-01 of 11 January 1999 and its modifying texts' (*Journal Officiel de la République Islamique de Mauritanie* (2010): 506).
14 Ibid.

References

Agence Mauritanienne d'Information (2008), 'Mauritanie: Arrestation de l'homme d'affaires Abdallahi Ould Moctar et de Mohamed Ould Vilaly', 15 November. https://fr.allafrica.com/stories/200811160035.html.

Agence Mauritanienne d'Information (2010a), 'Le Président de la République rassure les populations de Arafat que la priorité sera donnée dans l'attribution des terrains au citoyen dans le besoin', 13 March. https://fr.ami.mr/Depeche-9292.html.

Agence Mauritanienne d'Information (2010b), 'Le président de la république adresse un discours à la nation à l'occasion du cinquantenaire de l'indépendance nationale', 27 November. https://fr.ami.mr/Depeche-11455.html.

al-Akhbar (2012), 'Aziz à Nouadhibou: La diatribe a noyé le discours programmé', 15 March. www.fr.alakhbar.info/3078-0-Aziz-a-Nouadhibou-La-diatribe-a-noye-le-discours-programme.html.

Antil, A. (2019), 'Mohamed Ould Abdel Aziz l'alchimiste', *L'Année du Maghreb*, VI: 357–72.

Ayoob, M. (2019), 'Will the Second Arab Spring Go the Way of the First?', *The National Interest online*, 20 April. https://nationalinterest.org/feature/will-second-arab-spring-go-way-first-53357?page=0%2C1.

Bates, R. H. (2010), 'Democracy in Africa: A Very Short History', *Social Research*, 77 (4): 1133–48.

Bekoe, D. A. (2012), *Mauritania: On the Road to Democracy or Just More Violence?* Alexandria: Institute for Defense Analyses.

Boserup, R. A. and L. Martinez (2018), *Europe and the Sahel-Maghreb Crisis*. Copenhagen: Danish Institute for International Studies.

Bratton, M. and N. Van de Walle (1994), 'Neopatrimonial Transitions in Africa', *World Politics*, 46 (4): 453–89.

Brinks, D., M. Leiras and S. Mainwaring, eds (2014), *Reflections on Uneven Democracies*. Baltimore, MD: The Johns Hopkins University Press.

Brossier, M. (2019), 'Imaginaires et pratiques de la famille et du politique en Afrique: sortir du tout néopatrimonial par un dialogue "indiscipliné"', *Cahiers d'Études Africaines*, 234 (2): 323–57.

Driscoll, B. (2020), 'Big Man or Boogey Man? The Concept of Big Man in Political Science', *The Journal of Modern African Studies*, 58 (4): 521–50.

Droz-Vincent, P. (2004), 'Quel avenir pour l'autoritarisme dans le monde arabe?', *Revue française de science politique*, 54 (6): 945–79.

Dufy, C. and C. Thiriot (2013), 'Les apories de la transitologie: quelques pistes de recherche à la lumière d'exemples africains et post-soviétiques', *Revue Internationale de Politique Comparée*, 20 (3): 19–40.

El Haycen, M. L. (2016), *Mohamed Abdel Aziz, Construire la Mauritanie Autrement*. Saint-Estève: Les Presses Littéraires.

Evrard, C. and E. Pettigrew (2019), 'Du baptême du nouvel aéroport de Nouakchott à la réforme constitutionnelle (fin 2015–2018): Politiques de l'histoire en Mauritanie', *L'année du Maghreb*, 21 : 295–319.

Fatton, R. (1990), 'Liberal Democracy in Africa', *Political Science Quarterly*, 105 (3): 455–73.

Genieys, W. (2006), 'Nouveaux regards sur les élites du politique', *Revue Française de Science Politique*, 56 (1): 121–47.

Hackett, R. I. J. and B. F. Soares, eds (2015), *New Media and Religious Transformations in Africa*. Bloomington, IN: Indiana University Press.

Journal Officiel de la République Islamique de Mauritanie (2010), year 52, 1214, 30 April.

Lesourd, C. and A. Antil (2009), 'Non, mon Président! Oui, mon général! Retour sur l'expérience et la chute du président Sidi Ould Cheikh Abdallahi', *L'année Politique*, V: 365–83.

Lesourd, C. and A. Antil (2014), 'Je dois tout contrôler moi-même. Changement d'un mode de gouverner', *L'Année du Maghreb*, 11: 275–97.

Levitsky, S. and L. A. Way (2002), 'The Rise of Competitive Authoritarianism', *Journal of Democracy*, 13 (2): 51–66.

Makhmutova, M. M. (2020), 'The Features of the Domestic Political Development of Mauritania during the Reign of Mohammed Ould Abdel Aziz (2009–2019)', *Vestnik of the Saint-Petersburg University. Asian and African Studies*, 12 (4): 607–21.

McDougall, E. A. (2015), 'Hidden in Plain Sight: "Haratine" in Nouakchott's Niche-Settlements', *The International Journal of African Historical Studies*, 48 (2): 251–79.

Morelle, M. and S. Planel (2018), 'Appréhender des "situations autoritaires." Lectures croisées à partir du Cameroun et de l'Éthiopie', *L'Espace Politique*, 35 (2). http://journals.openedition.org/espacepolitique/4902.

Nalepa, M. and E. J. Powell (2016), 'The Role of Domestic Opposition and International Justice Regimes in Peaceful Transitions of Power', *The Journal of Conflict Resolution*, 60 (7): 1191–218.
N'Diaye, B. (2009), 'To "midwife" – and Abort – a Democracy: Mauritania's Transition from Military Rule, 2005–2008', *The Journal of Modern African Studies*, 47: 129–52.
Ninsin, K. A. (2006), 'Introduction: The Contradictions and Ironies of Elections in Africa', *Africa Development*, 31 (3): 1–10.
Nouakchott Info (2011), 'Entretien Exclusif avec Ahmed Ould Khatri: Ancien Directeur National de Procapec', 26 April. https://cridem.org/C_Info.php?article=55002.
Ould Ahmed Salem, Z. (1998), 'Sur la formation des élites politiques et la mobilité sociale en Mauritanie', *Nomadic Peoples*, 2 (1–2): 253–76.
Ould Ahmed Salem, Z. (1999), 'Une "illusion bien fondée": la centralité de la mobilisation tribale dans l'action politique en Mauritanie', *L'Ouest Saharien*, 2: 127–56.
Ould Cheikh, A. W. (2003), 'La science au(x) miroir(s) du prince. Savoir(s) et pouvoir(s) dans l'espace arabo-musulman d'hier et d'aujourd'hui', *Revue du Monde Musulman et de la Méditerranée*, 101–102: 155.
Ould Cheikh, A. W. (2006), 'Les habits neufs du sultan. Sur le pouvoir et ses (res)sources en Mauritanie', *Revue Maghreb-Machrek*, 189: 29–52.
Ould Cheikh, A. W. (2019), 'Autoritarisme compétitif, diversité ethnique et démocratie'. https://www.academia.edu/6157344/Autoritarisme_comp%C3%A9titif_diversit%C3%A9_ethnique_et_d%C3%A9mocratie.
Ould Cheikh, A. W. (n.d.), *Prétorianisme et Autoritarisme Compétitif: Les Militaires et le Pouvoir en Mauritanie*, ACADEMIA https://www.academia.edu/6157263/Pr%C3%A9torianisme_et_autoritarisme_comp%C3%A9titif.
Owusu, M. (1997), 'Domesticating Democracy: Culture, Civil Society, and Constitutionalism in Africa', *Comparative Studies in Society and History*, 39 (1): 120–52.
Sahara Media (2019), 'Mauritanie: échec de l'opposition dans le choix d'un candidat unique pour les présidentielles', 12 March, online issue. https://fr.saharamedias.net/mauritanie-echec-de-lopposition-dans-le-choix-dun-candidat-unique-pour-les-presidentielles/.
Saxonberg, S. and J. Linde (2003), 'Beyond the Transitology–Area Studies Debate', *Problems of Post-Communism*, 50 (3): 3–16.
Schmitter, P. C. (2014), 'Reflections on "Transitology": Before and After', in D. Brinks, M. Leiras and S. Mainwaring (eds), *Reflections on Uneven Democracies*, 71–86. Baltimore, MD: Johns Hopkins University Press.
Sneiba, Mohamed (2013), https://medseib.mondoblog.org/2013/02/19/facebook-la-revolution-des-jeunes-un-appoint-a-lopposition/.
Tawary (2016), 'Découverte de Documents Relatifs au Scandale de la Sonimex de Rosso dans un Magasin', 21 August. http://tawary.com/fr/index.php?option=com_content&view=article&id=4257.
Thurston, A. (2012), 'Mauritania's Islamists', *Carnegie Endowment for International Peace*, 1 March. https://carnegieendowment.org/2012/03/01/mauritania-s-islamists-pub-47312.
Villalón, L. A. (2010), 'From Argument to Negotiation: Constructing Democracy in African Muslim Contexts', *Comparative Politics*, 42(4): 375–93.
Villasante Cervello, M. (2013), 'De la chute du régime de Ould Sid'Ahmed Taya au désordre politique actuel sur fond de guerre au Mali (janvier-juin 2013)', in M. Villasante Cervello (ed.), *Chronique politique de la Mauritanie*, 11: 9–39.

Part Two

Society

5

Artisanal gold mining in Mauritania

Moustapha Taleb Heidi
CRIA – NOVA FCSH, Post-Doctoral Researcher at Capsahara

Introduction

In August 2020, a 50-gram fragment from the lunar meteorite NWA 12691, polished into a moon-like sphere just 3 cm in diameter, was sold at a Christie's auction in London for $17,500 (Hyslop 2020). The meteorite itself, reportedly the largest of its kind ever found (104 kg) (Gattacceca et al. 2020: 1147), was discovered a few years prior, somewhere between southwestern Algeria and northern Mauritania.[1] How, exactly, it found its way from a desert in Africa to London is unclear,[2] signalling the geographic porosity of this remote corner of the Sahara, which is swirling with (often clandestine) flows of people and goods (Ould Ahmed Salem 2005; Scheele 2012). Rare space rocks are not the only gifts of the desert, however; its depths contain valuable minerals and precious metals, among them gold, which attracts bounty hunters from far and wide. This issue is widespread in Africa, the Sahara and the Sahel regions, with certain locations being affected earlier and then contributing to the spread of know-how elsewhere (Chevrillon-Guibert and Magrin 2018: 237, 277). This chapter aims to shed light on the inception of the full-fledged gold rush in Mauritania that, since 2016, has displaced thousands of artisanal miners and those providing logistical support to the northern and northwestern regions of the country.[3] This chapter elaborates on the profound economic, social and political changes triggered by this movement, questioning both its local and global reach and its sustainability.

A Saharan meteorite's finding its way to a high-end London auction house bears witness to the extent of the involvement of global actors in this remote location and makes clear that the processes analysed in this chapter should not be categorized as merely internal, regional or even continental, but should instead be seen as part of a globally integrated reading of the Saharan region.[4] Here, as in other African locations, precious metals extracted by artisanal miners often change hands without much official oversight because of a lack of regulation and insufficient enforcement of what rules there are, as authorities struggle to control the informal entrepreneurial efforts of the impoverished population – a reality that has been well documented by various international organizations and individual researchers (Bazillier and Girard 2019;

Gagnol, Magrin and Chevrillon-Guibert 2019; Hunter 2020; Maconachie and Hilson 2011; Spiegel 2015).

Although mention of a London auction brings to mind images of wealth and success, we should not ignore other stories of this facet of African globalization that are significantly less glamorous, and even tragic – for example a court decision in Tindouf, a town in the southwest of Algeria that has hosted Saharawi refugee camps for over forty years. On 20 June 2017, twenty nine Mauritanian and five Sudanese artisanal miners were released from jail following several months of detention. They had been arrested by Algerian authorities for border trespassing and illegal extraction activities carried out on Algerian soil.[5] Their release was the result of Mauritanian diplomatic efforts, strongly incentivized by popular pressure[6] by Mauritanians who were sympathetic to these unfortunate men, whom they viewed as having braved the unknown, renewing a widely shared hope for a better life. A second, much more sombre, example comes from an artisanal mining camp in Mauritania, not far from the Tasiast gold mine, a Canadian-owned industrial open-pit mine. On 4 December 2017, seven miners lost their lives following the collapse of a mining well. Accidents of this sort put into perspective the hardships faced by the actors involved in artisanal gold mining in Africa and the risks inherent to this activity (for other examples from around Africa, see Bolay 2014; Jønsson and Fold 2011; Mégret 2008; Werthmann 2017).

In light of the above, the aims of this chapter are twofold: it seeks to analyse the emerging artisanal mining trade from the point of view of the agents – who hope to make a fortune in the Sahara – while also revealing the inherent structural adversities they face. The subject of the study presented in this chapter, even if articulated in connection to its global dimensions, is the artisanal gold mining phenomenon in Mauritania, and particularly its relation to the country's political and socioeconomic environment. The following argues that the development of artisanal mining activities may entail significant changes to the country's socioeconomic and political spheres, the impact of which the following attempts to anticipate. In this context, it seems important to draw attention to the resurgence of abolitionist activism in Mauritania's public debate (see Malluche in this volume), and indeed, actors and activists from this movement were observed and interviewed in the mining camps under study. Their presence and political work in these locations parallels a broader, emerging national debate involving voices that are rarely publicly heard in the country (a fact that is largely associated with the region's hierarchical social stratification).[7]

From an analytic perspective, a close reading of the firsthand experiences of both artisanal miners and those from other professional groups suggests that these seemingly heterogeneous groups of miners form a 'community' (Douglass 1998). By questioning these processes of 'community formation', this chapter seeks to establish their potential impact on the structure of Mauritanian society as a whole. In particular, it seeks to understand and explain how this recent Saharan mining venture, while related to a larger phenomenon covering territories from Sudan in East Africa to West African countries such as Mali and Burkina Faso (Bazillier and Girard 2019; Chevrillon-Guibert and Magrin 2018; Hunter 2020; Maconachie and Hilson 2011), permeates current social and political realities in contemporary Mauritania (Table 5.1).

Table 5.1 Field research data

Regions (*wilāyas*)	Community	Population	Mining site	Date of establishment	Estimated number of miners
Dakhlet Nouadhibou Inchiri	Chami Benichab	4,500	Sakina	2016	3,000
			Container 1	2018	2,500
			Container 2	2019	1,000
Tiris Zemmour	Bir Moghrein	1,599	Gleib N'Dour	2019	10,000
			Chegatt	2018	2,500
			M'kelbouha	2019	3,000
			Tenawmer	2019	2,000

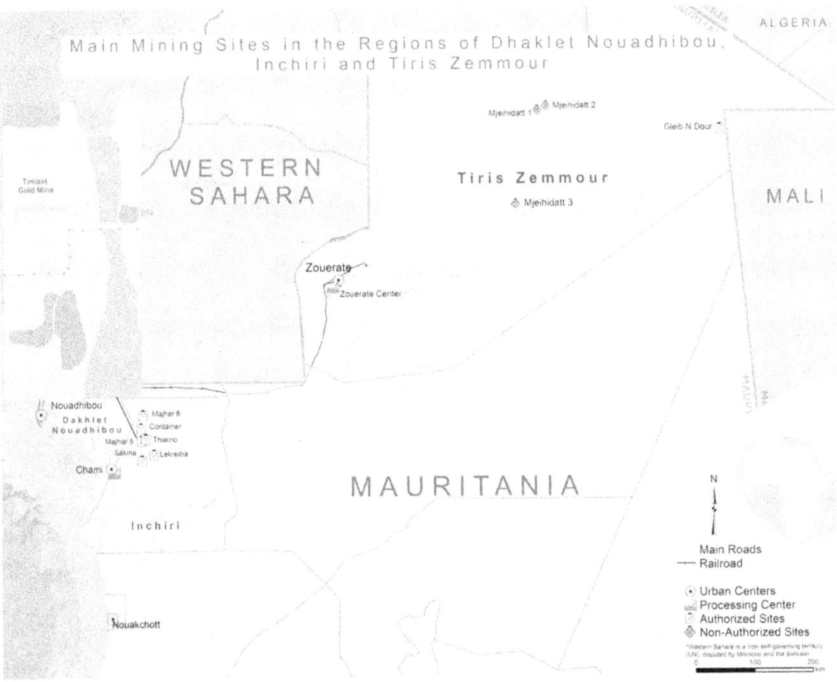

Map 5.1 Main gold mining locations in Mauritania (2021). Source: Capsahara, November, 2020.

The artisanal mining sector (AMS) in Mauritania and in Africa more broadly

Over the past twenty years, the AMS in Africa has experienced significant growth (Banchirigah 2006; Maconachie and Hilson 2011: 293; Østensen and Stridsman 2017: 33, 37). In 2019, an estimated 10 million people were engaged (with or without

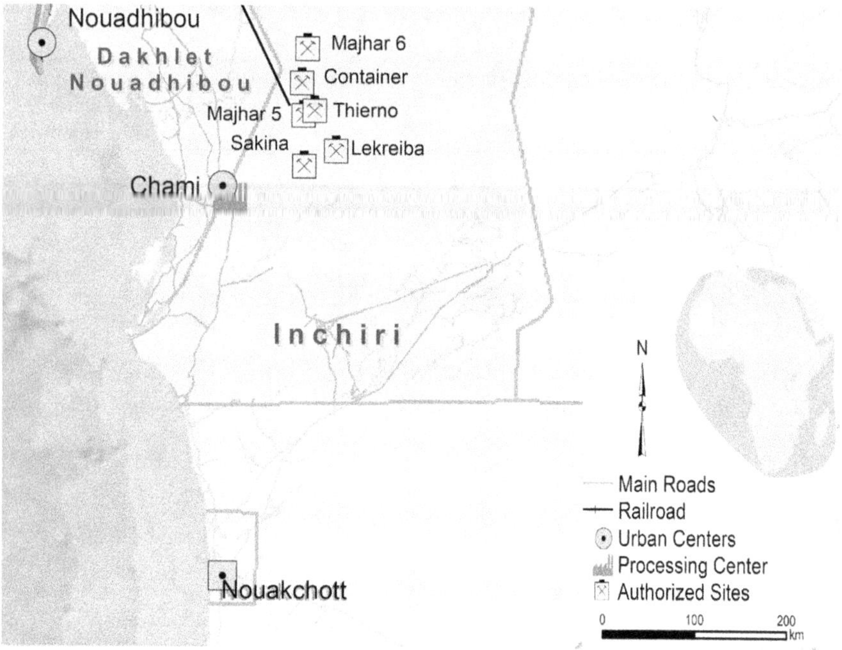

Map 5.2 Gold mining locations in northwestern Mauritania. Source: Capsahara, November, 2020.

official authorization) in artisanal and small-scale mining activities, covering gold, diamonds and coltan (tantalite) deposits (World Bank 2019: 13). This sector represents an important source of income in a context still largely marked by poverty and political instability. It is also a source of concern, particularly regarding health and environmental issues (Huggins, Buss and Rutherford 2016; Persaud et al. 2017: 4) and, in the case of Mauritania, regarding security issues associated with the infiltration of insurgent groups in these new mining sites (situated in remote areas of the country).

A commonly used definition of the AMS signals three main characteristics: its low levels of technology, the intensive labour it involves, and its minimal financial resources (D'Avignon 2018: 180; Persaud et al. 2017: 4). The rich and diverse body of knowledge on the AMS mainly considers the socioeconomic dynamics of this activity and its increasing contributions to the development of low-income countries, with a particular focus on Africa (e.g. Banchirigah and Hilson 2009). Another significant focus of this literature has to do with the use of chemicals, and mercury in particular, and their adverse effects on human health and the environment (Bose-O'Reilly et al. 2010; Dooyema et al. 2012; Hilson and Garforth 2012; Hunter 2020).

The available literature offers various explanations for why certain communities lean towards the AMS despite its challenges (high operational costs, uncertain results) and risks. In countries such as Tanzania and Zimbabwe, AMS activities are considered a complementary source of income (Kitua 2006). In other cases, e.g. Ghana (Hilson and Potter 2003), the AMS presents itself as the only option available to those affected by critical events such as droughts. In some cases, the AMS option is an indirect result of the implementation, in low-income countries, of structural adjustment mechanisms required by international institutions (such as the World Bank and the International Monetary Fund). The implementation of these measures often includes significant cuts to the available workforce, thus increasing unemployment rates, which then push more people towards the AMS (Hilson and Potter 2005).

Legal questions also have important weight in the literature on the AMS. Regulatory mechanisms and authorizations (including individual licences by operators) and processes related to the delineation of areas reserved for this activity have also been widely explored (D'Avignon 2018: 180; Hunter 2020; ILO 1999; Jønsson and Fold 2011). The umbilical links between the AMS and the official industrial mining sector are also commonly acknowledged in the above literature (for an interesting account of the potential co-existence of the two elsewhere see, for example, Holley et al. 2020), a factor that takes centre stage in examinations of the AMS in Mauritania in particular.

In the last twenty years, the mining sector in Africa has shown tendencies toward liberalization in an attempt to attract potential foreign investment. According to some actors, this situation favours the institutionalization of asymmetric power relations that could lead to an unsatisfactory balance between local interests and actors with primarily global agendas (Campbell 2010; Persaud et al. 2017). Bonnie Campbell traces the origins of African mining legislation, established under pressure from the Word Bank, to the logic of 'free mining'. This strategy, which was adopted for some time in North America (especially in Canada, a mining country par excellence), assumes a right of free access to publicly own mineral deposits, the right to take possession of them through staking a claim, and the right to exploit the discovered resources (Baron 1993, cited in Campbell 2010: 198). It could be argued that the free mining regime contributes to an unequal distribution of power between various actors, as it can enable mining companies, who benefit from close relationships with the country's authorities, to impose extracting activities on communities in these territories, regardless of their own development model preferences. Although various developing countries have put forward specific AMS legal regimes (Giraldo and Muñoz 2012), state bureaucracy, associated with the illiteracy of many of the miners and inefficient capacity-building programmes, has too often dragged the AMS into a grey zone of illegality (Fisher 2008; Hunter 2020; Østensen and Stridsman 2017).

The artisanal processing of minerals relies heavily on products known for their toxicity; this constitutes another grave concern associated with the AMS. Mercury (and cyanide), used frequently in Mauritania, was even the subject of an international convention (in 2013) aimed at reducing its 'informal' use (Bell et al. 2014: 8). In practice, gold miners use mercury on a large scale in gold separation processes (Chevrillon-Guibert and Magrin 2018: 286), which is potentially responsible for several public health problems.[8] Its widespread use is explained in part by its affordable price and a lack of awareness of its dangers (Heemskerk 2005; Veiga et al. 2020).

A final element of particular significance in the Sahelo-Saharan context has to do with security issues, following the proliferation of armed groups defying public authority and sowing terror in some of these remote regions.[9] The crossover between these armed groups and gold mining (as a source of funding and recruitment) is no longer a grim possibility but in some cases a reality, as pointed out by the International Crisis Group (2019) in Mali, Burkina Faso and Niger.

The Mauritanian mining context

The exploitation of mineral resources is enshrined in the contemporary history of Mauritania. During the colonial period, this aspect constituted a main focus of economic policy, expressed particularly through the foundation of MIFERMA (Mines de Fer de Mauritanie) and MICUMA (Mines de Cuivre de Mauritanie). The geological studies that led to industrial mining in Mauritania were carried out before the Second World War, but the first geological survey was only finalized in 1946, revealing the existence of significant deposits of iron ore in the French colony (Gallet 2008). This discovery drew interest from different international mining companies (notably from North America). MIFERMA was finally created in 1951, with the direct involvement of the Canadian group Frobisher Limited.[10] The company was responsible for the geological studies and industrial development of the particularly rich F'derick deposits, in the Tiris Zemmour region of northern Mauritania. The lack of infrastructure and the geographical remoteness of the extraction sites constituted a real challenge for the project, which only came to fruition in 1963 – the date of the arrival of the first cargo train to Port Etienne/Nouadhibou. Since then, mining has helped to promote significant transformations in Mauritania, including the creation of the town of Zouérat in the upstream part of the mineral industry supply chain (De Dominicis 2017). However, the development of the vast territories to the north (Tiris Zemmour, where industrial mining was located) and northwest (Dakhlet Nouadhibou, the Atlantic port from which iron ore was exported) has above all highlighted the slow pace of effective economic development in these regions.

In its aftermath, the mining activities initiated by MIFERMA led to a strong shift toward sedentarization around the new mining centres of Fort Goureau (present-day Zouérat) and Port Etienne (present-day Nouadhibou). The change to the status of the Mauritanian territory, with its shift to independence in 1960, did not fundamentally alter the fact that a largely nomadic population continued to suffer from a lack of modern infrastructures that might have otherwise facilitated a general transition to sedentary forms of living. In fact, it was the onset of a new cycle of drought in the late 1960s, and not the implementation of public policies, that led to profound social transformations. At that point, a desperate population in search of economic opportunities took refuge in these new urban/mining centres, creating slums and what has been described as de facto 'poverty belts' around Zouérat and Nouadhibou (Bonte 2001: 80–2).

In this particularly complex environment – bringing together nomadic populations and large-scale industrial projects – Mauritania's mineral resources became the state's most important source of financing and remains a topic of intense debate in domestic politics (Bonte 2001: 368). President Mokhtar Ould Daddah (1960–1978) received significant pressure from opposition leaders, who were demanding changes to the prevailing economic order inherited from colonial days and the urgent nationalization of MIFERMA (Audibert 1991). This process was in fact accomplished in 1974, giving rise to a new entity called the Société Nationale Industrielle et Minière (SNIM), which continues to explore the iron ore deposits of northern Mauritania.

After decades of governmental investments in the SNIM, the Mauritanian state decided to open its mining industry to foreign capital. The SNIM's capital was partially shared with rich Arab countries (such as Iraq and Kuwait), and, more recently, new mining concessions were granted to private investors for the exploration of copper, iron, gold, phosphate and quartz. The Mining Code, enacted in 1999 (and amended in 2008, 2012 and 2014), stipulates that all mining activities are subject to the acquisition of a mining permit delivered by the authority in charge of the sector (Art. 8). The overall strategy provides attractive conditions for investors (Mining Code 2012),[11] and in 2016 mining permits were distributed among 105 private operators (Moore Stephens LLP 2018: 25). This policy reaffirmed the importance of mineral resources for the Mauritanian economy. In 2012, for example, the mining sector contributed 29.4 per cent of the GDP (Moore Stephens 2014: 10), more than doubling from 2006 (IMF 2013: 14), and the production of the SNIM – the second largest producer of iron ore in Africa[12] – amounted to 11.17 million tons (Moore Stephens 2014:11). The total GDP of iron ore in 2018 climbed to $5.2 billion (World Bank 2019), equivalent to $1,160 per capita,[13] and production is expected to grow fivefold from 2013 levels by 2025 (International Monetary Fund 2015: 6).

Sixty years after the dawn of the mining industry in Mauritania, the country's natural resources are still fuelling economic hopes. This time, however, the actors involved are not only passionate explorers, geologists and international bankers seeking the support of a central administration (whether colonial or national)[14] but ordinary Mauritanians, closely followed by Malian and Sudanese migrants (with both countries having solid experience in the domain of artisanal gold mining).

Gold panning and artisanal mining started to boom in Mauritania in 2016 following rumours of the discovery of 2 kg of gold in Tijirit (in the Inchiri region of Mauritania), 160 km northwest of Nouakchott (see Figure 5.1). Thousands of people crossed the desert in hopes of making a fortune. At the same time, the government grew understandably concerned about the security risks involved in this 'occupation' of remote parts of the Mauritanian hinterland (Interview with the head of the mining office in Zouérat, 22 December 2019). In 2020, the most recent study estimated number of artisanal miners approaching twenty-nine thousand people (Diagana 2020: 5).

At the regulatory level, the Ministry of Mining and the Ministry of Finance swiftly issued two decrees in 2016 and 2018. The first (now revoked) defined the geographical limits of the mining zones (N356 of 22 April 2016), and the second set out the conditions that had to be met for permits to be granted (N002 of 2 January 2018). According to these regulations – with the exception of waste processing – artisanal mining was reserved for Mauritanian nationals. The cost of a permit depended on the category of the mining activity: i) workforce; ii) geophysical equipment of detection; iii) wells; iv) physical processing units (crushing, grinding); v) chemical processing units (amalgamation); or vi) waste management. The permits issued to these different types of operators had a duration of one year, with the possibility of renewal.

Figure 5.1 Mining pits in northwestern Mauritania (© Capsahara/Moustapha Taleb Heidi).

Field study

The data presented in this chapter results from a corpus of thirty-four in-depth interviews with artisanal miners and a questionnaire answered by 296 participants working in mining areas around Chami, Benichab and Bir Moghrein. The results provide a rough profile of the mining actors involved in this economic activity in 2020.

After more than sixty years, the extracting industry's impact on Mauritania's economy has been slow to develop. The country has not experienced the economic boost expected from the profits of industrial mining, with poverty remaining a major issue that affects more than 30 per cent of the country's population (ONS 2020: 50; World Bank 2017a; World Bank 2019[15]). The enthusiasm accompanying the development of industrial mining activities in Mauritania was ultimately short lived. It did not serve as an impetus either for establishing sustainable values and developmental ethics of prosperity or for propelling the state into a take-off economic transition in the Rostowian sense (Rostow 1971 [1960], 1978). The industrial development model remained unchanged.[16] Despite numerous investments and successive reforms, the mining resources did not meet these high expectations. Frustration with the lagging prosperity from mining only increased with the discovery of new reserves that were now being exploited, such as the Inchiri copper and gold deposits (see Figures 5.2 and 5.3).

Figure 5.2 Miners at work at the Sakina site, 2016 (© Moctar Ould El-Hacen).

In light of this observation, the current gold rush can be understood as a popular movement that directly questioned Mauritania's moribund economic situation via the direct appropriation of natural resources by populations that had been condemned by the country's endemic crises. The distributary function of artisanal and small-scale mining has already been examined in the academic literature.[17] In this sense, this movement may also represent a significant social transformation in the guise of an economic venture. The impressive scale of this venture may even suggest another complementary reading of the restructuring of the country's social landscape, marked for centuries by territorial and political disputes. Hence, artisanal mining may one day reconfigure the hereditary social stratification acknowledged among Mauritania's Hassaniyya-speaking populations (Bonte 2001, 2008; Norris 1986; Stewart 1973). Currently, competition for power (and social prestige) is not exclusive to those groups that traditionally hold the reins of political and religious authority (the 'warriors'/*ḥassān* and the 'religious'/*zwāya*). Indeed, what the following portrays is a much more heterogeneous situation that includes new dominant actors (from new political spheres and from a growing autonomous merchant class) and those stemming from clearly disadvantaged social milieus, notably the *ḥarāṭīn* population (of slave descent). By taking risks in this new economic arena, these groups seem to be beginning to blur traditional status positions through the acquisition of significant financial means and/or prestige and through their conquest of the – often deemed indomitable – Saharan confines.

The occupation of remote corners of Mauritania and the demographic scale of this still largely unregulated mining venture is a growing concern for public authorities,

Figure 5.3 Mining trenches at the Container 1 site, near the Tasiast gold mine (© Capsahara, Moustapha Taleb Heidi).

who are aware of the possibility of losing control over a significant flux of people and financial resources scattered across 'under-governed' territories. The volatility of these areas is easily confirmed when we incorporate in a single location a disfranchised group of people in search of wealth, international mining interests, migrant populations, Islamic militant groups and state interests from countries such as Mali, Algeria, Morocco, Mauritania and the neighbouring Saharawi refugee population. Despite the spontaneous nature of these mining expeditions and their extensive geographic breadth, the Mauritanian state is trying to assert its sovereignty over (and supervision of) the sector (see the official newspaper *Horizons* 24 June 2016; *Horizons* 3 September 2019). However, as mentioned above, the state does not seem to be considering or directly addressing the – mainly economic – reasons behind the popularity of artisanal mining activities, and its engagement often translates to the development of specific regulations and the (tentative) implementation of measures that reflect an interest in the security of international borders. Nonetheless, the situation is far from being under strict state control, and the relations between miners and state representatives (including those in charge of security) are often tense.[18]

Results

In 2016, different groups of artisanal miners seeking gold deposits seized areas in Tijirit (in the Inchiri region), in the vicinity of the Tasiast industrial gold mining concession managed by the Canadian company Kinross.[19]Consequently, artisanal mining activity – to the surprise of many of these actors – began to be labelled 'illegal'. The possibility of some sort of regulation of the desert was difficult to understand, running against the 'informal' character (identified by the Hassaniyya moniker *Tsheb-Tshib*; see Ahmed Ould Salem 2001) of most economic activities in Mauritania. At this early stage, mining activities required only the use of simple metal detectors.[20] The technology associated with digging wells and following gold 'veins' was then unknown to most of those who left in search of gold. This knowledge emerged in a process of discovery through hands-on, day-to-day experience passed down by the Malians and especially the Sudanese AMS pioneers, who for various reasons embarked on this journey in search of the precious metal and whose sociopolitical history in the historical and cultural area of present-day Mauritania (see the medieval empires of Ghana and Mali) is marked by mystery, violence and even rumours of curses (Farias 1974).[21]

Reasons for joining the AMS and the constraint of 'illegality'

The profiles of the artisanal miners reflect a multitude of trajectories and motivations. For the pioneer groups engaged in this activity, however, the idea of venturing into the desert in search of gold is often perceived as a last resort in a desperate attempt to curb an endemic cycle of poverty:

> [W]e saw that state companies closed their doors, there was no more recruitment, no jobs, tourism was "closed" because of security problems, smuggling was no longer possible because of border controls, we really had no choice.
>
> (Interview with a miner from the first wave of 2016, Nouakchott, 12 December 2019)

Extreme economic conditions were therefore the main motivation for most of our interviewees, who reported engaging in an activity they knew practically nothing about and did not plan to make a permanent activity.

Figure 5.4 Living conditions available for artisanal gold miners in the Inchiri region (© Capsahara/Moustapha Taleb Heidi).

Was artisanal mining becoming a new form of 'squatting', a phenomenon that had swept through Nouakchott in the late twentieth century with the occupation of public land (Choplin 2016; McDougall 2015)? To classify it as usurpation, we would have to juxtapose this practice with its legal character, which until that point was non-existent insofar as artisanal mining was not regulated by law in Mauritania. Nonetheless, the state reacted swiftly in intervening in this phenomenon, and a legislative corpus was rapidly produced. Since most of the mining activities were carried out without licensing and the findings were not officially declared, the miners were invited to custom clear the materials and to obtain individual authorizations. This policy resulted in an immediate shift among miners towards 'collectivism'. Even though the activity began as an individual endeavour, the state's legislative intervention constituted a turning point that forced artisanal miners to regroup and organize more complex operations. The leader of a group would usually acquire the permit, declaring his 'associates' as 'fellow travellers'. This 'arrangement' may explain why, in August 2016, the number of authorizations issued by the Ministry of Mines amounted to five hundred permits, while the effective number of miners working in these camps was at least ten times this figure. Y. A., a gold prospector based in Chami, recalls this shift in the position of the state, while explaining the overall excitement concerning the search for gold (see Figure 5.4):

> Popular mobilisation around gold was such that the state had to intervene to bring some order to the situation. They introduced authorizations for the use of the

equipment. Illegal prospectors were manhandled by law enforcement agents and their expensive equipment was often confiscated. From then on our operations became really serious: we had to unwrap the turban (on checkpoints), stating who we were and that we wanted to become gold prospectors (*munaqqib*).

(Interview with Y. A., a first-wave miner, Chami, 20 January 2020)

News of the gold mining possibilities in Mauritania spread rapidly through the media, social networks and the Mauritanian diaspora. Most importantly, they also resulted in the prompt arrival of hundreds of Sudanese and Malian migrants specialized in this field (similarly to what happened in other locations; see Chevrillon-Guibert and Magrin 2018). The know-how passed on by these migrants has since marked artisanal mining activity in Mauritania, in particular regarding the implementation of new mineral extraction techniques (see Figure 5.5), contractual arrangements between partners, more efficient technological choices and, crucially, organizing the distribution of benefits among the different groups of workers involved in these operations.

The 'luck' economy

Thousands of people engaged in the AMS faced numerous physical and material challenges in order to settle in the desert. The cost of the trip and the expense of

Figure 5.5 Processing facilities in Chami (© Capsahara/Moustapha Taleb Heidi).

staying on the sites are high; as noted above, however, this study showed variations in the individual budgets allocated to this activity. In many cases, after having exhausted their savings, miners would offer their services as paid workers to more affluent actors who could afford to employ them for digging operations or to scout for new drilling locations.

Among those considered in this survey, the findings vary from a few grams of gold ('hardly enough to cover expenses'), to more significant gains (between $1,143 and $1,428). In fact, much depended on finding a significant vein. There are anecdotal accounts of a miner who tried to sell 6 kg of the precious metal (Interview with a miner in Sakina, 12 January 2020), but these are rare events, against the much more common trend of total failure. Despite this, and in contrast with other types of activity (such as agriculture), the artisanal mining gamble continues to enjoy a good reputation, and those seeking their fortune can usually find private funding in their chain of commercial relations (workforce, logistics, equipment owners, etc.).

The 'invasion' of the vast Tijirit region by miners – Tasiast is a well-known natural corridor carved by a large wadi (dry riverbed) – has been translated by some interlocutors through an idiom that they directly identify with nomadic culture. Venturing into the Saharan hinterland in the search for hidden riches can in fact be easily associated with the traditional camel herding trails with which many of these miners were acquainted. This was summed up by one of the miners, acknowledging the resemblance of gold mining to his former pastoralist activity:

> And indeed, like grazing camels moving through the Saharan expanse, large groups of gold hunters began to arrive in the remote Zouérat region (800 kilometers to the northeast of Tijirit) towards the end of 2016.
>
> (CRIDEM, November 2016)

In Zouérat, the cradle of the Mauritanian mining industry, the emergence of gold panning meant good news. Mining is by now a pervasive mark of the region, more than sixty years after the opening of the MIFERMA/SNIM industrial iron ore extraction operations.

Scattered throughout the working-class districts of Zouérat, the artisanal gold miners began working at different locations on the outskirts of Zouérat and F'Derick. These operations expanded to the north, to M'Jeihidatt and Tenoumer (400 km and 200 km north of Zouérat, respectively). Unlike in the first phase of the Tijirit explorations, the gold miners who reached the Tiris Zemmour region quickly moved from surface exploration to the subsoil. For logistical reasons, the rock-crushing phase took place in the town of Zouérat. Massive rock piles became an element of the town's landscape, as did the sound of the processing machines. The situation soon became unbearable for the town dwellers, who organized protests that led to the relocation of the activity 20 km west of the city's urban perimeter. The extraction sites gradually moved even further north, towards the Algerian border (800 km to the north of Zouérat), replicating the trans-border artisanal gold mining phenomenon that had already permeated the eastern region bordering Algeria and Mali.[22]

An actor directly associated with these transits told us about the relentless efforts made in the search of gold, international borders notwithstanding:

> We sometimes went beyond the Mauritanian borders, looking for new places not yet explored. Once, with my group of workers, I clandestinely crossed the Algerian border around Ain Bintili. It was during the night, and this was, of course, dangerous. We could even hear the voices of the border guards, but we were very hopeful and took all the precautions. We entered some 30 km into Algerian territory, but it was only for surface exploration. It's the adventure that took us this far.
>
> (Interview with M. S. B., investor, Zouérat, 23 December 2019)

From nomadism to sedentarization

By late 2017 to early 2018, artisanal gold mining in Mauritania entered a new era, with the widespread use of mercury in the treatment of extracted materials. Given the large numbers of new arrivals, the spreading of artisanal mining activities to larger areas and the use of chemical extraction techniques, mastered by the more experienced Sudanese and Malian artisanal miners, seemed inevitable. Previously 'nomadic' short-term practices slowly began to consolidate on the ground, becoming long-term operations.

In the sites of Sakina, Container 1 and Container 2, miners have dug hundreds of wells, with depths between 20 and 40 metres (see Figure 5.5). In Gleib N'Dour, in the Tiris region, the depth of the wells can reach over 60 metres. Some of these wells are lined up to form a trench approximately 150 metres long (Figure 5.6), following a vein of quartz, which can indicate the presence of gold. Given the scale of these operations, miners have begun to remain at the sites for longer periods of time. A more complex system has thus been necessary, with various service providers starting to follow the miners in a mutually beneficial arrangement (a similar multi-tier organization has been reported in other artisanal mining geographies; see for example Huggins et al. 2016: 144; Persaud et al. 2017: 4). Among these service providers are highlight drillers, well diggers, merchants (funding drilling operations or buying gold nuggets) and processed rock collectors (*qawlāba*). The latter subgroup, lacking sufficient funds to organize their own mining expedition, recover certain minerals from the abandoned rock piles. Their presence reflects a spirit of solidarity that is common among miners of all profiles. In this constellation, the *qawlāba* are considered the most dispossessed of all mining agents, even though destitution is a ubiquitous quality shared among the whole mining population. L. B. provides us with a first person account of the hardships associated with this activity:

> I move from one site to another collecting abandoned rocks. A *qawlāb* has no means to own detection equipment or a mining pit. Some of us are also limited by poor health and cannot work in the wells ... Yes, we depend on the solidarity of others in order to survive, sometimes truck drivers help us out and give us a ride for free. However, after spending time here, we start feeling that we belong in this

> activity and that we may be also useful to others. The circulation of information concerning the pits is made by us. The 'generosity,' kindness (*karam*), and charitable works (*shi zayn*) are done by us. We are a 'contact point' both for the people on the field as well as for those in the treatment centres. It is true – there are people who despise the *qawlāba*, accusing us of all the sins, not letting us even touch the rock piles. Fortunately, those are only a minority.
>
> (Interview with L. B., Container 1, 8 January 2020)

Among service providers, one could single out drivers of tank trucks delivering water and fuel and transporting mineral loads to the processing centres (which can be quite far from the extraction sites). In Zouérat, for example, the closest extraction site is 220 km away from the processing plant; in the Inchiri, the most distant extraction site is 200 km away from the Chami treatment plant. In fact, the distance between extraction sites and processing plants constitutes a critical element in the value chain of mining operations, one that can easily jeopardize the profitability of the activity as a whole. The remoteness of the mining sites has also led to the establishment of an array of services that directly depend on these operations, from groceries stores and water shops to gasoline vendors and traditional bread-baking ovens (similar dynamics are seen in other AMS regions; see, for example, Jønsson and Fold 2011: 480). As far as the extraction sites are concerned, the miners use pick hammers and power generators in their work. This also bears witness to the intensity of the extraction operations and the tendency towards the 'sedentarization' of these mining activities, leading to important changes in the overall socioeconomic environment.

The opening of a centre for mining services in the town of Chami symbolizes the consolidation and official recognition of the AMS as a significant activity. This centre, inaugurated by the Ministry of Mining in 2017, is open day and night, receiving the bagged loads of rock from extraction sites for different types of treatment, including chemical processing. The available equipment includes machinery for breaking, grinding and washing 'raw' rock materials (see Figure 5.3). Apart from the government-imposed prohibition on processing gold at the extraction sites, the elevated costs of water and energy strongly contribute to the impossibility of in situ processing.

Organization of work

The organization of work in the AMS is rather convoluted and involves complex relations between various actors (it may appear 'chaotic' to the outsider, but this would be an inaccurate assessment; see Huggins, Buss and Rutherford 2016: 144). Certain relational practices have become more standardized among miners, but written contracts are virtually non-existent. As a general rule, the investors offer the drillers 30 per cent of the profits and cover their expenses on the ground. Independent workers can expect to be offered 50 per cent of the profits. Each mining pit employs three to four workers directly.

In some processing centres, operators control the extraction sites and the equipment, offering remuneration to the miners based on a share of the production. Others may have preferential agreements with miners to buy their product or 'sub-contracting' mineral processing services. These schemes equally apply to transportation – some are forming partnerships, while others are paid for their services (Focus group with miners, Chami, 9 January 2020).

The workforce present in the mining locations under study comprises a mix of Mauritanian and other African nationalities, with a preponderance of Sudanese and Malian migrants (see Annex, Table A5.1). Officially, foreigners are excluded from these sites; in reality, however, the control measures ensured by the Mauritanian authorities (*Gendarmerie*) are not strict in this regard, and foreign workers, who have a positive professional reputation, make up a significant part of this social landscape. Sudanese migrants are prevalent in the gold filtering stage, competing only with Mauritanian *m῾allemīn* – 'smiths' (see the chapter by Francisco Freire in this volume) – who have also started to invest in this sector.

Each mining spot usually has semi-industrial units of processing equipment, often belonging to Sudanese investors. Another notable presence consists of Mauritanians who have recently returned from other African countries, such as Angola and Guinea Bissau. They also tend to own their own processing equipment and sometimes offer other services such as vending, transport and the provision of fuel supplies.

Living conditions

Judging by the visited sites, within a 200 km radius around Chami, the conditions in which the miners live their daily lives are deplorable (similar observations have been made in numerous other reports; see, for example, Maconachie and Hilson 2011: 295, 301). In addition to the extreme thermal amplitudes of the naturally harsh desert environment, the miners must live in crowded conditions, in small tents (see Figure 5.6). The inflated water and food prices condemn workers to a frugal existence. A lack of sanitary services is yet another serious problem, especially for miners who are unaccustomed to desert life and for those with health issues. In Chami, the desert town with the most industrial processing plants for the treatment of gold, most people live in barracks or small rooms near processing units, where toxic products are used in abundance. In addition to the extreme climate conditions, workers are exposed to mercury, as they often work without protective equipment (see Figures 5.7 and 5.8).

Politics and society in the artisanal mining sector

Public authorities in Mauritania welcome artisanal mining as a contribution to the battle against poverty, since it offers self-employment opportunities to many Mauritanians. Nonetheless, the government has yet to address an extensive array of risks associated with this activity. During our fieldwork, all of our interlocutors indicated dissatisfaction with the limited level of public intervention in the sector. The state has not enforced any regulatory measures regarding employment, workers' safety

Figure 5.6 Gold treatment facilities in Chami (© Capsahara/Moustapha Taleb Heidi).

or child labour (a phenomenon that is easily verified in the field and that has been reported by other sources, e.g. Maconachie and Hilson 2011: 301, and, in the Malian case, Østensen and Stridsman 2017: 30, 38, 40). The miners do not report any visits by public officials and often complain about salaries and the complete absence of health and safety measures. Isolation is yet another problem often reported by the mining population.

A further facet of this activity has to do with the emergence of political leadership figures among the miners. Some of the more prominent political actors in this sector are part of Biram Dah Abeid's abolitionist movement, IRA-Mauritania. One of these activists gave a clear account of what, in his opinion, was happening in the artisanal mining sector (comparing it to a pervasive phenomenon common to various economic activities in Mauritania):

> In the beginning, gold mining was a free and noble activity, but it was later overtaken by feudal lords who brought with them their games of corruption.
>
> (Interview with a miner/activist, Chami, 22 January 2020)

A visit by Biram Dah Abeid (a local politician and vociferous advocate for the abolitionist cause) to Chami during his 2019 presidential campaign provided significant support for this sentiment. This political event was largely thought to confirm that the 'feudal-like' conditions still prominent in many Mauritanian social and economic spheres were also a feature of the artisanal mining sites. The emancipatory narrative provided by Biram's movement has often been heard in the different mining locations visited during this survey. Whereas in the 1960s and early 1970s the disputes between the Mauritanian government and the workers of the mining industry (MIFERMA/SNIM) had the 'communists' (of different tendencies) as their main political interlocutors, a quite different political landscape is now associated with the AMS.

The management of this sector presents a serious challenge due to mass migration to mining sites by an impoverished population. Today, artisanal gold mining is a popular choice among the unemployed who have been left behind by the government in the cities and among young people who have grown increasingly disillusioned with the failure of governmental programmes aimed at integrating them into the job market. This view was also conveyed by participants, confirming that for them, joining AMS was a last resort:

> We came here for a different experience. We were in the fishing business, but it failed because of the competition of the industrial fleets … I also worked in the real estate sector, but the taxes were unbearable. Finally, the insertion program in which I enrolled only brought me despair. That's why I came here where at least you can earn your living freely.
>
> (Interview with a miner, Container 1, 25 January 2020)

Economic instability has forced a low-income population (which often represents a significant part of the total population, as we see in Mauritania) to seek alternative sources of income, with increasing numbers turning to AMS for its low-level technology and low entry barriers (see Østensen and Stridsman 2017: 30; Spiegel 2015). Described as a 'do-or-die' enterprise (Stoop and Verpoorten 2020: 1203), this labour-intensive activity may be the only way for local populations to sustain themselves and their families during intermittent droughts (Banchirigah and Hilson 2009: 161). This is not a recent trend or in any way particular to Mauritania. Robyn d'Avignon (2018: 195) reports that the populations in neighbouring Senegal and Mali have also resorted to artisanal mining as a survival strategy since as early as the 1980s, bartering gold for grain. The AMS also serves as a source of additional income for seasonal workers, such as those employed in agriculture (Persaud et al. 2017: 9) and serves as an incentive for the repopulation of rural areas (Persaud et al. 2017: 9). Paradoxically, however, AMS may also contribute to the degradation of agricultural lands (Hilson and Garforth 2012: 440).

A recent World Bank report (International Development Association 2018) acknowledges that the abundance of mineral resources in Mauritania has the potential to create a strong base for alleviating inequalities and reducing poverty, instead of one-off benefits to rural agricultural sector, given that the extractive industry, and in particular 'mineral and petroleum exports[,] together represent approximately 25 per cent of Government revenues' (International Development Association 2018: 22). The plans to optimize the use of mineral resources rely on the significant involvement of private sector, including in the artisanal mining sector (22). It remains to be seen how the government and international organizations will manage to harness the potential of small-scale mining due to the informal nature of this activity, often dispersed in remote corners of the country. Efforts to formalize artisanal and small-scale artisanal mining in other West African countries have had mixed results and remain a 'considerable challenge' (Maconachie and Hilson 2011: 293; Persaud et al. 2017). The need for 'context-sensitive formalization' (Jønsson and Fold 2011: 479, 489–90) is as strong in Mauritania as it is in other African countries with growing AMSs, since the root cause of the continuous spread of this high-risk, high-potential-gain informal entrepreneurship is a complex socioeconomic and political issue that requires careful examination and strategic planning. The World Bank's Country Partnership Framework for 2018 to 2023 states the need for direct investment, strengthening public–private partnerships, and policy development. Efforts to improve the state's ability to tax mining operations would have much better results, however, if they were to focus on large-scale, foreign-owned mining facilities, as can be seen by the more than doubled value of the royalties paid to Mauritania by the Canadian-owned Tasiast Kinross mining operations in 2020, in comparison with 2019.[23] Taxing small-scale and artisanal mining operations can have a completely different effect on the economy, and it would not be the first time that the formalization of the AMS resulted in significant drops in official exports and the rise of illicit flows of minerals, serving as an incentive for smugglers (Hunter 2020: 22).

As suggested by some of the interviewees, the sense of freedom inherent in the practice of gold mining is a clear motivation. In other words, the miners are choosing a new economic activity where they can negotiate their contribution and remuneration outside the mores of the established traditional sectors. However, they also mention their fear of reproducing the unfavourable social relationships that exist elsewhere in Mauritanian society. As mentioned above, artisanal mining has the potential to reshape relations between the labour force and capital owners, since the choices made by both are limited by factors such as geographic distance, limited supply and the high cost of the means of survival (water and food). Chami has recently seen a series of riots as a reaction (ultimately unwarranted, since it was based on a misunderstanding) to the taxation imposed by the government on gold mining in its attempt to regulate the AMS. These scenes of violence, which are rare in Mauritania, reflect the deep malaise felt by certain sectors of the population. When we take into account the demographic structure of the country, the connection between artisanal gold mining and the IRA abolitionist movement becomes clearer.

Contrary to the situation in other West African countries (for a detailed overview of the cases of Mali, Ghana and Sierra Leone, see Maconachie and Hilson 2011), where artisanal mining constitutes a transient activity that is often combined with other professional activities such as agriculture (for a clear example from Guinea, see Bolay 2014; for a case study of how re-agrarization was used to fight the growth of the artisanal mining sector in Ghana, see Banchirigah and Hilson 2009), in Mauritania mining seems to be the main professional activity of those involved in it and an effective source of financing for other activities of lesser significance, such as agriculture. For each miner involved in the AMS, there is an estimated average of six people who depend 'on the sector for their livelihoods',[24] a number that puts the significant contribution of the AMS to the overall economic landscape of Mauritania into perspective.

Conclusion: A new 'desert' is born in a changing socio-geography

Compared to other African locations, artisanal gold mining is a very recent activity in Mauritania. Given its potential economic impact and the strong mobilization it has attracted (from a population the majority of which continues to live in poverty), the Mauritanian government has attempted to regulate this activity. Despite significant legislative interventions, however, the AMS remains a largely informal activity, due to public institutions' lack of experience in the management of such activities and because of the remoteness of the actual mining sites, some of which are located beyond the effective reach of the Mauritanian state. Many of the mining sites have thus been established in sparsely populated desert areas, causing logistical difficulties unknown to neighbouring countries such as Mali (since their artisanal mining activities generally occur in the proximity of urban areas). Artisanal mining, particularly in Africa, is thus intimately connected with the surrounding environmental (Teschner 2014). The significant problems associated with this recent practice in Mauritania are undoubtedly linked to this reality, making it more difficult for the state to impose law and order in the mining sites and for complementary activities to adhere to this hazardous venture.

The territories in which this activity is carried out in Mauritania may first appear – especially in the eyes of the miners – as a 'no man's land', an area without an autochthone population that could claim rights or authority over it. This impression is rooted in the low population density of the local communities of the north of Mauritania.[25] As noted above, in the 1950s, mining operations intensified in northern Mauritania, leading to the industrial exploration of iron ore in Idjil, in the Tiris Zemmour region. There are indications that this sabkha was the only mining activity ever known to the groups living in these regions – according to Kunta families referenced by one of the first directors of MIFERMA in 1955, Jean Audibert (on the initial implementation of the MIFERMA iron ore industrial compound in Zuerate, see Audibert 1991).

In a famous poem describing his native Inchiri and the nomadic areas frequented by his Ahl Bārikallāh kin, the scholar and poet al-Shaykh Muḥammad al-Māmī (1785–1861) prophesied what might occur following the discovery of iron ore, gold, and copper deposits in northern Mauritania:

الأرض من المعادن حطره
لو كانت رات إدوارن
نتف زغبته ما تبره
من طول اجرب فيه حارن

The land is full of mines
If only there were explorers!
Their work would never end
Their tasks, like picking dead skin from a plague-ridden body

These verses state that the apparent barrenness of the Sahara can be misleading, since it is full of underground mineral riches that, if exploited, could change the lives of the local communities for the better. It can also be interpreted as a formal invitation to explore mineral resources. Coming from a prominent religious figure, the poem can almost be interpreted as a *fatwā*, and in fact it has been used by some actors in the mining sector to legitimize their activities. This element touches on the intricate social design of the Hassaniyya-speaking populations of the region and their pervasive commitment to a structure that reveres the opinions of esteemed Islamic scholars.

Five years into artisanal gold mining in Mauritania, a certain amount of friction is already being felt between the largely nomadic populations who traditionally inhabit these regions and the workers (who have come from different parts of the country and from abroad) who have settled around the mining sites. This relation may lead to open hostilities and resistance to the mining venture as a whole, should the corridors of communication between these two camps continue to be neglected. The matter is even more pressing since there are plans to establish a significant industrial mining infrastructure in Chami (a cyanide treatment centre) (Sidya 2020).

Most of the mining agents mentioned above have some level of education, and 10 per cent have a secondary school or even university education. This may facilitate the implementation of the regulations in the sector while mitigating health and environmental risks. This educational advantage is in stark contrast to the situation in countries such as Burkina Faso, where illiteracy levels among artisanal miners are rampant (Ouedraogo and Mundler 2019). This element may also bring into question the possible negative impact of mining on the agricultural and farming sectors, and potentially on school dropout levels – consequences that have been observed in the other countries in the subregion, including Mali and Burkina Faso (World Bank 2017b).

In his pivotal work on MIFERMA and SNIM, Pierre Bonte (2001) examines the social reconfigurations prompted by this enterprise from the beginning of its existence in 1974. The central element to which he draws attention is the impact, particularly in Zouérat, of the implementation of a complex industrial operation in the middle of the desert, as well as the emergence of a capitalist mode of production (associated with profound technical challenges) in a nomadic social environment. This triggered the emergence, for the first time in Mauritania's history, of a politically active (and now unionized) 'civil society' that is not solely constrained by traditional social norms. Bonte (2001) has enquired into the enormous challenges that Mauritanian and French group faced in their efforts to transfer the European industrial model to the Sahara. Showing the depth of the relevant dissimilarities, ranging from political systems to cultural traits, he speaks of a 'cultural crisis' (Bonte 2001: 189).

Almost fifty years after his initial observations on the implementation of an industrial hub in northern Mauritania, one wonders what Pierre Bonte's reaction to the current mining frenzy in the region would be, with convoys of off-road trucks now hurrying towards Gleib N'Dour, 800 km away from Zouérat. Indeed, the consequences of these developments can be expected to be at least equally significant. The *aire d'influence* of the current artisanal mining experiments cover a much more extensive area and involve many more actors. There is no central administration regulating mining practices or salaries. Not only do these workers risk putting into question local communities of scattered nomadic populations, but they are raising awareness at the international level, as these operations currently occur between international borders.

Territorial encroachment onto official mining areas is a widespread phenomenon. Even though it may be a coincidence, sparked by the artisanal miners' desire to get closer to certain, established gold deposits, this also reflects the spontaneous and even anarchic nature of the movement. The emergence of a new economic sector linked to artisanal exploration of gold deposits in Mauritania has given rise to a social structure that has the characteristics of yet another 'internal frontier' (Kopytoff 1987; see also Chapter 1 by López Bargados, drawing on Kopytoff's proposition in the definition of the northern frontiers of the western Saharan region) in comparison to traditional economic sectors such as commerce and agriculture. The restructuring and consolidation of this initially entry-level activity – as it matures and develops both internally (labour division and structure) and externally (regulation), creating more obstacles and 'frontiers' for newcomers – will determine its level of dependence on various others sectors. Contrary to other West African locations, where gold mining is considered a transitory situation (since workers are less dependent on it, maintaining links to agricultural production; see Bolay 2014), the data obtained in this survey suggests that mining is considered a principal source of income in Mauritania, used to finance agricultural and cattle farming activities. With that said, the significant financial pull of the mining sector has exacerbated the challenges faced by the agriculture and animal husbandry sectors, which have seen a significant drop in their available workforce.

Artisanal mining in Mauritania is becoming an enduring marker of the region and an important – albeit non-quantifiable – source of income for a large number of Mauritanians and immigrants. The remoteness of the areas in which these activities are conducted makes it difficult, if not impossible, for the government to effectively supervise it. In addition, this activity represents the illusion of a fast and easy fortune that can lead to unpayable debts and the moral and physical collapse of many hopes and dreams. Located in the remote desert regions of Mauritania, workers are exposed to daily challenges to their health and well-being; in the absence of a law-enforcing public authority, the risk of human rights violations is ubiquitous (see a detailed account on human rights risks of artisanal mining in Mauritania country study by Carlowitz and Danz 2018). Although mining in Mauritania is a recent development, it has already proved to be an activity that involves the entire population, shedding light on structural problems that require immediate attention.

Annex

Qualitative results

Sociodemographic indicators of miners

Table A5.1 presents a profile of the miners in three mining sites (Sakina, Container 1 and Container 2) located on the border of the Inchiri and the Dakhlet Nouadhibou regions, as well as a profile of workers settled at the Chami processing centre (80 km away).

Age distribution

Those aged 19 to 35 constitute the largest tranche (62.5 per cent), while around one-third of miners are 36 to 50 years old. It should be borne in mind that this is a labour-intensive activity that requires significant physical strength. The average age of the interviewees was 33, with the oldest being 65 years old and the youngest 15. The presence of minors, even in the sampling for this study, is strong evidence for the precarious working conditions and the use of child labour.[26]

Place of origin

Mauritanian nationals constitute 75 per cent of the sample, with the remaining 25 per cent being divided by migrant African communities (from Sudan, Mali and Senegal). Mauritanian nationals from five eastern and central regions (both Hodh's, l'Assaba, Brakna and Tagant) make up the bulk of the sample (52.3 per cent of the entire sample, regardless of professional category). Bearing in mind that a very small percentage of the population identifies with the capital Nouakchott as their place of origin, the northern regions of the country (Dakhlet Nouadhibou, Adrar, Inchiri and Tiris Zemmour, which include the mining areas) come last, with only 8.7 per cent. This apparently paradoxical situation can be related to a combination of two factors: 1) the very low demography of the northern regions of Mauritania; and 2) the other economic opportunities available to these populations, notably in the official mining sector, fishing and tourism.

Foreigners working in the sector mostly hail from Sudan and Mali (each around 12 per cent). Their presence in the sector has been strong from the beginning (2016) given the extensive and comprehensive gold production know-how to be found in these countries, which distinguishes them from Senegalese migrants, which amount to only 0.4 per cent. This finding is corroborated by other researchers, who have pointed out that the Sudanese miners' gold deposit detection skills are especially valued in low-tech and information-poor artisanal mining conditions (e.g. Chevrillon-Guibert and Magrin 2018: 278, 284).

Table A5.1 Sociodemographic data of the sample

Variable	Criteria	Result
Age (in %)	< 18	1.0
	19–35	62.5
	36–50	29.2
	51 and >	7.3
Education (in %)	Absent	5
	Primary	24
	Secondary	24
	Secondary school diploma	3
	University diploma	6
	Quranic school	38
Origin (in %)	East	37.4
	Centre	14.9
	North	8.7
	Senegal River basin	12.2
	Nouakchott	1.4
	Sudan	12.2
	Mali	12.8
	Senegal	0.4
Ethnic group	Moor (hassanophone including some Ḥarāṭīn)	65.1
	Ḥarāṭīn (exclusively)	25.8
	Other	9.1

Source: Fieldwork, 2019–2020.

Level of education

The vast majority of miners (95 per cent) reported some level of instruction (which is higher than usual in the AMS; see Obiri et al. 2016: 11): 57 per cent pursued studies at regular schools, and 38 per cent at Quranic (religious) schools. Among those attending regular schools, an equal percentage (24 per cent) had a primary education and continued on to the secondary level without concluding it. Only 3 per cent of the sample had attained a secondary education, and 6 per cent had a university education. This last group was mostly present in the processing centres as owners or managers of sites to which the raw minerals were brought from the extraction sites.

Ethnicity

Despite the country's multi-ethnic landscape, according to the obtained data, artisanal gold mining in Mauritania is an activity that predominantly involves the Hassaniyya-speaking population (90.9 per cent). Table A5.2 distinguishes between *Bīḍān* and *Ḥarāṭīn* °ethnicities', even if this point can be contested, covering a culturally unified population (see David Malluche's chapter in this volume, which discusses the emergence of a distinct *Ḥarāṭīn* ethnic identity). It was nevertheless useful for this research to attempt this separation when it comes to the economic actors involved in this activity and the overall social dynamics of Mauritania. Our questionnaires showed that 65 per cent of participants reported their ethnic identification as 'Moor' (which could be *Bīḍān* or *Ḥarāṭīn*). In any case, it was observed that the *Ḥarāṭīn* undoubtedly have a strong presence among artisanal miners in Mauritania, whether they are included under the category of 'Moor' or claim their own identity.

Professional distribution

Table A5.2 distributes participants by type of activity. The variance among the occupations is high. The table does not address the importance of each occupation and only provides an idea of the existing profiles: drillers, artisans, investors, merchants, gold filterers, waste processors, etc. Artisanal mining is an activity that involves the

Table A5.2 Distribution of miners by occupation

Occupation	**% of sample**
Accountant	0.4
Artisan	1.5
Atelier supervisor	7.3
Collector of mineral waste	2.9
Driller	17.9
Equipment mechanics	2.2
Equipment owner/ renter	4.0
Gold Filterer	10.6
Investor	6.9
Maintenance	28.5
Merchant	3.6
Metal detector worker	0.4
Qawlāb (collector of rock waste)	3.3
Subcontractor	0.4
Transporter	2.9
Welder	0.7
Well operator	6.2
Other	0.4
Total	**100.0**

Source: Fieldwork, 2019–2020.

participation of various other actors, thus opening up the scope of this operation to different professional profiles.

Table A5.3 shows that the majority of those involved in artisanal mining have had a previous occupation. More than half of the participants were involved in an informal economy before venturing into the AMS (c. 55 per cent). The business sector also provides a significant part of the actors involved in this activity (31 per cent), with those with salaried jobs amounting to only 8 per cent. Only 3 per cent of the sample had been working in the agricultural sector.

Table A5.3 Previous occupations of artisanal miners

Previous occupation	% of sample
Agriculture	4.9
Commerce	31.1
Informal employment	44.8
Salaried job (guard, clerk)	8.4
Unemployed	10.8
Total	**100.0**

Source: Fieldwork, 2019–2020.

Table A5.4 shows that more than half of the sample (55.4 per cent) became aware of this working opportunity through word of mouth, about a third through social networks, with media being the least effective source of information. Participants reported that their decision to venture into the AMS was based on general information received through word of mouth and from inner circles characterized by higher level of trust (families, friends, etc.).

Table A5.4 Source of information about mining

Source of information	% of sample
Contacted by an acquaintance	33.1
Press/media	4.6
Word of mouth	54.4
Other	7.8
Total	**100.0**

Source: Fieldwork, 2019–2020.

Table A5.5 presents the impact that mining activity has had on the quality of life of those involved. It reflects responses to the open question: Did mining change your life? The answers obtained are varied. Overall, those who reported positive changes equal those who stated the contrary – 50 per cent in each case. However, further analysis by occupation shows that the general workforce and the drillers share this overall 50/50 split, while service providers present much more positive answers, with 79.3 per cent of the sample having experienced positive results from their engagement with mining.

Table A5.5 Satisfaction with mining experience by occupation

		5. Did your quality of life change after your involvement in artisanal mining?	
		Yes %	No %
Occupation	Driller	48.8	51.2
	General workforce	50.0	50.0
	Service provider	79.3	20.7
	Other	41.7	58.3
Total %		**50.0**	**50.0**

Source: Fieldwork, 2019–2020.

Main challenges

Table A5.6 presents the main problems encountered by the different actors involved in artisanal mining activities. The data indicates a variety of challenges ranging from poor living conditions at the extraction sites and mining centres (food, accommodation, medical care) to work conditions (payment, working hours), along with transversal considerations such as violence and isolation, for example.

Table A5.6 Challenges faced by miners

Challenged with . . .	**% of sample**
Discrimination	9.2
Distance from accommodation	1.5
Food	15.1
Insufficient quality of communication/ GSM service	14.4
Medical care	24.8
Payment	5.7
Solitude	14.4
Violence	2.2
Working hours	12.7
Total	**100.0**

Source: Fieldwork, 2019–2020.

Notes

1 Hence the 'NWA' part of its identifier, which stands for 'North West Africa'.
2 In Nouakchott, Mauritania, for example, a network of antique dealers buys these kinds of findings from artisanal miners and then sells them to clients ranging from European businesspeople to archaeologists, philanthropists and regular tourists. This type of sale is not regulated.
3 This type of exchange also takes place in Western Sahara. However, a lack of reliable information on this topic (which is managed very discretely by the Polisario administration) makes it impossible to present concrete data.
4 Similar examples have been reported in the African context, revealing the economic connection between the African hinterland and the largest international markets (e.g. the famous case of the 'Togolese gold' imported by Switzerland and traced back to a Burkina Faso artisanal origin (Guéniat and White 2015).
5 *Al-Salām* 21 June 2017, quoted by djazairess.com.
6 The Mauritanian press echoed the government's position on the subject, reporting an accidental case of border trespassing that was attributed the character of the Saharan geography, where borders are not clearly demarcated.
7 Another aspect, only briefly mentioned in this article (but one that deserves further consideration in a future publication), has to do with its contextualization in the country's Islamic traditions. This involves a series of practices concerning praying and social behaviour in mining sites and other less visible aspects associated with Maliki jurisprudence (prominent in Mauritania and in the entire North African region) in relation to the gold trade and its (il)licit character.
8 Upon short-term exposure, mercury vapour directly affects the respiratory tract, with symptoms including chest pain, dyspnoea, coughing, haemoptysis, impaired lung function and pneumonia (Justice et al. 2019; Levin and Polos 1988).
9 Mauritania serves as the headquarters of the 'G5 Group' (*Force Conjointe du G5 Sahel* or FC-G5S), which comprises five countries of the region (Mali, Burkina Faso, Niger, Mauritania and Chad) that cooperate on security issues (for more information, see Cooke, Toucas and Heger 2017).
10 With mostly French shareholders and some Canadian, British, German and Italian interests (Gallet 2008).
11 Loi no. 2008-011 du 27 avril 2008 portant Code minier (2008), *Journal Officiel de La République Islamique de Mauritanie, smhpm.mr/fr2/Loi_2008-011_portant_Code_Minier.pdf.*
12 SNIM, https://snim.com/e/index.php/produits/markets.html.
13 The socioeconomic benefits of artisanal gold mining amounted to 9.8 billion MRU per year, 51 per cent coming from Chami and 49 per cent from Zouérat. The activity has created 6.6 billion MRU of value added, 51 per cent in Zouérat, and 49 per cent in Chami. These numbers, not yet assumed in the national GDP, represent 73 per cent of the added value of the gold mining activity carried out by the two foreign companies operating in the sector (Tasiast and MCM), and it almost parallels the total added value created by iron ore exploration (6.5 billion MRU in 2018). The contribution from artisanal gold mining to the national GDP is thus 3.5 per cent, equal to other important sectors such as fishing. AMS contributes 30 per cent to the added value obtained from all the mining activities developed in Mauritania, and 12 per cent of the added value accorded to secondary sector activities. In terms

of revenue, the activity generates approximately 4 billion MRU per year, which is distributed through eleven regions of the country (Alassane 2020: 9, citing a GTZ [German Technical Cooperation] report from 2018; author's translation from French).

14 BUMIFOM (currently BRGM, French), FINSIDER (Italy) and the Rothschild bank are MIFERMA/SNIM's historical partners (United States. Congress. Senate. Committee on Interior and Insular Affairs 1959: 96), and the current stakeholders include Kuwait Investment Authority (with a 7.7 per cent stake) and the Arab Mining Company (Jordan, with a 5.6 per cent stake), as well as companies from Iraq and Morocco with smaller stakes (see the official SNIM page at https://www.snim.com/e/index.php/societe/shareholders.html).

15 Capitalist industrialization was carried out through MIFERMA – a colonial enterprise, the nationalization of which (in 1974) was strongly supported by socialist Algeria. Immediately following its nationalization, it employed a large workforce trained in communist countries such as the USSR and Iraq.

16 See, for example, Bazillier and Girard (2019) for a quasi-experiment in Burkina Faso that supports the claim that artisanal mining, not industrial mining, correlates to an increase in household spending in the adjacent areas.

17 When rumours spread of the potential abundance of gold in different parts of the country in November 2016, the political landscape of Mauritania immediately experienced significant tensions. They were apparently taken as a lifeline of sorts by President Abdel Aziz, whose political legitimacy was being questioned by the country's senate (for more on this topic, see Ould Mohamed Baba's chapter in this volume).

18 The Tasiast gold mine, which opened in 2007, produces between 6,000 and 7,000 tons of gold annually (Sims 2019).

19 Because of the growing demand for these devices, their price in Nouakchott rose from approximately 500,000 to over 1,500,000 MRU.

20 It should be noted that in some tribes of northern Mauritania, such as the Awlād Dalīm, gold was considered a source of bad luck and was not used in social life, including as jewellery.

21 From a legal perspective, most of these mining sites have not been officially authorized. Until 2020, the only location recognized by the Mauritanian authorities was Gleib N'Dour, on the Algeria–Mali border (more than 870 km northeast of Zouérat). The survey presented in this chapter does not incorporate data from these locations that could not be obtained due to bureaucratic constraints, security issues and logistical complications.

22 As confirmed, for example, by CRIDEM in a publication from the 16 July 2021 entitled *La Mauritanie augmente de 3% à 6,5% les redevances de l'exploitation de l'or* (citing the Chinese Xinhua agency as a source of information). https://cridem.org/C_Info.php?article=747149

23 A calculation based on Persaud et al. (2017: 2) (citing Jønsson and Fold 2011).

24 Known as the *qabā ʾil al-sāḥil* ('northern tribes'), or 'the tribes of Mauritania's highlands', in the early twentieth-century colonial parlance. Paul Marty (1915) emphasized that the Tiris Zemmour region was occupied by groups such as the Awlād Dalīm (renowned camel herders who have more recently migrated towards the Inchiri region, the second mining site treated in this chapter), the Rgaybāt and the Tikna (the first preponderant in the Dakhlet Nouadhibou region of northwestern Mauritania, and the latter especially significant in the Wādī al-Dhahab/Rio de Oro).

25 For research ethics reasons, minors were excluded from questionnaires and interviews.

26 The Adrar region is Mauritania's tourist hub, with charter flights from the capital, Atar, connecting to various European cities, notably in France.

References

Alassane, A. (2020), 'Un arrêté conjoint pour réglementer l'orpaillage', *Horizons* (3): 7–9.

Artignan, D., G. Maurin, A. O. Bellal, A. Dieye and A. O. Taleb (2000), 'Discovery of a New Auriferous Province in the Tasiast and Tijirit Archean (Mauritania)', *Chronique de la recherche minière*, 538: 3–16.

Audibert, J. (1991), *MIFERMA: Une Aventure Humaine et Industrielle en Mauritanie*. Paris: L'Harmattan.

Azarya, V. (1998), 'Reordering State-Society Relations: Incorporation and Disengagement', in D. Rothschild and N. Chazan (eds), *The Precarious Balance: State and Society in Africa*, 3–21. Boulder, CO and London: Westview Press.

Banchirigah, S. M. (2006), 'How Have Reforms Fuelled the Expansion of Artisanal Mining? Evidence from sub-Saharan Africa', *Resources Policy*, 31 (3): 165–71.

Banchirigah, S. M. and G. Hilson (2009), 'De-Agrarianization, Re-agrarianization and Local Economic Development: Re-orientating Livelihoods in African Artisanal Mining Communities', *Policy Sciences*, 43 (2): 157–80.

Bazillier, R. and V. Girard (2019), 'The Gold Digger and the Machine: Evidence on the Distributive Effect of the Artisanal and Industrial Gold Rushes in Burkina Faso', *LEO Working Papers* 2545. Orleans: Laboratoire d'Economie d'Orleans.

Bell, L., J. DiGangi and J. Weinberg (2014), *An NGO Introduction to Mercury Pollution and the Minamata Convention*, IPEN.

Berramdane, A. (1992), *Le Sahara occidental: enjeu maghrébin*. Paris: Karthala.

Bolay, M. (2014), 'When Miners Become "Foreigners": Competing Categorizations within Gold Mining Spaces in Guinea', *Resources Policy*, 40 (1): 117–27.

Bomsel, O. (1989), 'Competitiveness and Prospects for the African Mining Industry: A Case Study of the Guelbs Complex in Mauritania', *Natural Resources Forum*, 13 (4): 285–93.

Bonte, P. (2001), *La Montagne de Fer. La SNIM (Mauritanie), une Entreprise Minière Saharienne à l'Heure de la Mondialisation*. Paris, Karthala.

Bonte, P. (2008), 'L'Émirat de l'Adrar Mauritanien'. *Harîm, Compétition et Protection dans une Société Tribale Saharienne*. Paris: Karthala.

Bose-O'Reilly, S., K. M. McCarty, N. Steckling and B. Lettmeier (2010), 'Mercury Exposure and Children's Health', *Current Problems in Pediatric and Adolescent Health Care*, 40 (8): 186–215.

Campbell, B. (2010), 'Revisiting the Reform Process of African Mining Regimes', *Canadian Journal of Development Studies*, 30 (1/2): 197–217.

Carlowitz, L. and J. Danz (2018), *Human Rights Risks in Mining BGR/GIZ Country Study Mauritania*. Hannover: Deutsche Gesellschaft für Internationale Zusammenarbeit (GIZ).

Centre Mauritanien d'Analyse des Politiques (CMAP). Ministère des Affaires Economiques et du Développement (2014), Étude sur les filières attachées aux industries minières. http://cmap.mr/Etudes%202013/Rapport_Mines_version_%20definitive_290614.pdf.

Cheikh Sidya (2020), 'Mauritanie: des manifestants s'opposent à l'implantation d'une usine de traitement de l'or à Chami', Kassataya online. https://kassataya.com/2020/02/07/mauritanie-des-manifestants-sopposent-a-limplantation-dune-usine-de-traitement-de-lor-a-chami/.

Chevrillon-Guibert, R. and G. Magrin (2018), 'Ruées vers l'or au Soudan, au Tchad et au Sahel: logiques étatiques, mobilités et contrôle territorial', *Bulletin de l'association de géographes français*, 95 (2): 272–89.

Chevrillon-Guibert, R., L. Gagnol and G. Magrin (2019), 'Les ruées vers l'or au Sahara et au nord du Sahel. Ferment de crise ou stabilisateur?', *Hérodote*, 1 (1): 193–215.

Choplin, A. (2016), 'Post-Politics and Subaltern (de)Mobilization in an African City: Nouakchott (Mauritania)', *Journal of Asian and African Studies*, 51 (4): 398–415.

Cooke, J. G., B. Toucas and K. Heger (2017), 'Understanding the G5 Sahel Joint Force: Fighting Terror, Building Regional Security?'. Washington DC: Center for Strategic and International Studies. https://www.csis.org/analysis/understanding-g5-sahel-joint-force-fighting-terror-building-regional-security.

CRIDEM (2017), 'Décès de 7 prospecteurs de l'or, à la suite de l'effondrement d'un puits près de l'usine aurifère de Tasiast', 5 December. https://www.cridem.org/C_Info.php?article=705367.

CRIDEM (2020), 'Des orpailleurs refusent l'installation de concasseurs près de Bir Moghrein', *CRIDEM*, 16 September. https://cridem.org/imprimable.php?article=740428.

CRIDEM (2021), 'La Mauritanie augmente de 3% à 6,5% les redevances de l'exploitation de l'or', *CRIDEM*, 16 July. https://cridem.org/C_Info.php?article=747149.

D'Avignon, R. (2018), 'Primitive Techniques: From "Customary" to "Artisanal" Mining in French West Africa', *The Journal of African History*, 59 (2): 179–97.

De Dominicis, F. (2017), 'Reports from Sahara. Transitions and Contradictions in Afro-European Modernities: The Case of Cansado-Zouérat, Mauritania', *Clara*, 4 (1): 127–46.

De Waele, B., A. Aitken, M. Van Mourik, K. O. L. Laab, M. E. O. M. Yeslem and T. Mohamedou (2019), 'From a Mining Mindset to Regional Discovery: A Case Study for Hematite Iron Ore Exploration in Mauritania', *ASEG Extended Abstracts*, 1: 1–3.

Diagana, B. (2020), 'L'activité artisanale de production de l'or : La Mauritanie recèle d'importantes potentialités', *Horizons*, 3: 5–6. https://filefr.ami.mr/pdf/maghorizons003.pdf.

Dooyema, C. A., A. Neri, Y. C. Lo, J. Durant, P. I. Dargan, T. Swarthout et al. (2012), 'Outbreak of Fatal Childhood Lead Poisoning Related to Artisanal Gold Mining in Northwestern Nigeria, 2010'. *Environmental Health Perspectives*, 120: 4. doi: 10.1289/ehp.1103965.

Douglass, W. (1998), 'The Mining Camp as Community', in A. Bernard Knapp, C. Vincent, E. W. Herbert, A. B. Knapp and V. C. Pigott (eds), *Social Approaches to an Industrial Past: The Archaeology and Anthropology of Mining*, 1st edn., 97–108. London and New York, NY: Routledge. https://doi.org/10.4324/9780203068922.

Farias, P. F. d. M. (1974), 'Silent Trade: Myth and Historical Evidence', *History in Africa*, 1: 9–24. doi: 10.2307/3171758.

Fisher, E. (2008), 'Artisanal Gold Mining at the Margins of Mineral Resource Governance, a Case from Tanzania', *Development Southern Africa*, 25 (2): 199–213.

Gagnol, L., G. Magrin and R. Chevrillon-Guibert (2019), 'Chami, ville nouvelle et ville de l'or. Une trajectoire urbaine insolite en Mauritanie', *L'Espace Politique* [online], 38, 2019-2. http://journals.openedition.org/espacepolitique/6562.

Gallet, M. (2008), 'La société des mines de fer de Mauritanie (MIFERMA)', in P.-H. Bourrelier, and J. Lespine (eds), *Les opérations minières outre-mer. Le BRGM, acteur*

central de la politique publique. Annales des Mines: Réalités industrielles, 8: 12–14. http://www.annales.org/ri/2008/ri-aout-2008/Bourrelier-annexe1.pdf.
Gattacceca, J., F. M. McCubbin, A. Bouvier and J. N. Grossman (2020), 'The Meteoritical Bulletin no. 108', *Meteoritics and Planetary Science*, 55: 1146–50.
Gerson, J. R., C. T. Driscoll, H. Hsu-Kim and E. S. Bernhardt (2018), 'Senegalese Artisanal Gold Mining Leads to Elevated Total Mercury and Methylmercury Concentrations in Soils, Sediments, and Rivers', *Elementa: Science of the Anthropocene*, 1: 6–11.
Giraldo, J. and J. C. Muñoz (2012), *Informalidad e ilegalidad en la explotación del oro y la madera en Antioquia*. Medellín, Colombia: EAFIT-Proantioquia.
Guéniat, M. and N. White (2015), 'Golden Racket: The True Source of Switzerland's "Togolese" Gold. A Berne Declaration Investigation'. Lausanne an Zurich: Berne Declaration.
Heemskerk, M. (2005), 'Collecting Data in Artisanal and Small-Scale Mining Communities: Measuring Progress towards More Sustainable Livelihoods', *Natural Resources Forum*, 29 (1): 82–7.
Heron, K., M. Jessell, K. Benn, E. Harris and Q. G. Crowley (2016), 'The Tasiast Deposit, Mauritania', *Ore Geology Reviews*, 78: 564–72.
Hilson, G., and C. Garforth (2012), '"Agricultural Poverty" and the Expansion of Artisanal Mining in Sub-Saharan Africa: Experiences from Southwest Mali and southeast Ghana', *Population Research and Policy Review*, 31 (3): 435–64.
Hilson, G. and C. Potter (2003), 'Why is Illegal Gold Mining Activity so Ubiquitous in Rural Ghana?', *African Development Review*, 15: 237–70.
Hilson, G. and C. Potter (2005), 'Structural Adjustment and Subsistence Industry, Artisanal Gold Mining in Ghana', *Development and Change*, 36: 103–31.
Hilson, G., A. Hilson and R. Maconachie (2018), 'Opportunity or Necessity? Conceptualizing Entrepreneurship at African Small-Scale Mines', *Technological Forecasting and Social Change*, 131: 286–302.
Hoffman, D. (2019), 'Yellow Woman: Suspicion and Cooperation on Liberia's Gold Mines', *American Anthropologist*, 121 (1): 138–48
Holley, E. A., N. M. Smith, J. A. Delgado Jimenez, I. C. Cabezas and O. J. Restrepo-Baena (2020), 'Socio-Technical Context of the Interactions between Large-Scale and Small-Scale Mining in Marmato, Colombia', *Resources Policy*, 67: 101696. https://doi.org/10.1016/j.resourpol.2020.101696.
Huggins, C., D. Buss and B. Rutherford (2016), 'A "Cartography of Concern": Place-Making Practices and Gender in the Artisanal Mining Sector in Africa', *Geoforum*, 83: 142–52.
Hunter, M. (2020), 'Illicit Financial Flows: Artisanal and Small-Scale Gold Mining in Ghana and Liberia', *OECD Development Co-operation Working Papers*, 72, Paris: OECD Publishing. https://doi.org/10.1787/5f2e9dd9-en.
Hyslop, J. (2020), 'NWA 12691 — Rare Lunar Sphere, *Online Auction 18513 Deep Impact: Lunar and Rare Meteorites*. New York, NY: Christie's. https://onlineonly.christies.com/s/deep-impact-lunar-rare-meteorites/nwa-12691-rare-lunar-sphere–12/82795.
ICG (2019), 'Reprendre en main la ruée vers l'or au Sahel central'. *Report Nº 282 / Africa*, Dakar, Brussels: International Crisis Group (ICG). www.crisisgroup.org/fr/africa/sahel/burkina-faso/282-reprendre-en-main-la-ruee-vers-lor-au-sahel-central.
International Development Association, International Finance Corporation and Multilateral Investment Guarantee Agency (2018), Report No. 125012-MR, *Country Partnership Framework For The Islamic Republic Of Mauritania For The Period FY18–FY23*. http://documents1.worldbank.org/curated/en/288231531625439579/pdf/MAURITANIA-CPF-NEW-06192018.pdf.

International Labor Organization (ILO) (1999), *Social and Labor Issues in Small-Scale Mines. Report for Discussion at the Tripartite Meeting on Social and Labor Issues in Small-Scale Mines*. Geneva: International Labor Organization, Sectoral Activities Program, International Labor Office.

International Monetary Fund (IMF) (2013), IMF Country Report No. 13/188 Islamic Republic of Mauritania. https://www.imf.org/external/pubs/ft/scr/2013/cr13188.pdf.

International Monetary Fund (IMF) (2015), *Islamic Republic of Mauritania*. IMF Country Report, 15: 36. https://www.imf.org/external/pubs/ft/scr/2015/cr1536.pdf.

Jønsson, J. B. and N. Fold (2011), 'Mining "From Below": Taking Africa's Artisanal Miners Seriously', *Geography Compass*, 5 (7): 479–93.

Justice, A., O. Y. Kwaku, G. E. Ofori, A. George and R. D. Sorkpor (2019), 'The Clinical Importance of the Mercury Problem in Artisanal Small-Scale Gold Mining', *Frontiers in Public Health*, 7: 131.

Kitula, A. G. N. (2006), 'The Environmental and Socio-economic Impacts of Mining on Local Livelihoods in Tanzania: A Case Study of Geita District', *Journal of Cleaner Production*, 14: 405–14.

Kopytoff, I., ed. (1987), *The African Frontier: The Reproduction of Traditional African Societies*. Bloomington, IN: Indiana University Press.

Levin, M., J. Jacobs and P. G. Polos (1988), 'Acute Mercury Poisoning and Mercurial Pneumonitis from Gold Ore Purification', *Chest*, 94 (3): 554–6.

Maconachie, R. and G. Hilson (2011), 'Safeguarding Livelihoods or Exacerbating Poverty? Artisanal Mining and Formalization in West Africa', *Natural Resources Forum*, 35 (4): 293–303. doi: 10.1111/j.1477-8947.2011.01407.x.

Marty, P. (1915), *Les Tribus de la Haute Mauritanie*. Paris: Comité de l'Afrique Française.

Marutami, M., M. Higashihara, Y. Watanabe, H. Murakami, G. Kojima and B. Dioumassi (2005), 'Metallic Ore Deposits in the Islamic Republic of Mauritania', *Shigen-Chishitsu*, 55(1): 59–70. https://www.jstage.jst.go.jp/article/shigenchishitsu1992/55/1/55_1_59/_article.

McDougall, E. A. (2015), 'Hidden in Plain Sight: "Haratine" in Nouakchott's "Niche-Settlements"', *The International Journal of African Historical Studies*, 48 (2): 251–79.

Mégret, Q. (2008), 'L'or "mort ou vif." L'orpaillage en pays lobi burkinabé', in M. Cros and J. Bonhomme (eds), *Déjouer la mort en Afrique. Or, orphelins, fantômes, trophées et fétiches*, 15–41. Paris: L'Harmattan.

Moore S. (2014), 'Rapport de l'Administrateur Independant de l'ITIE pour les Revenus de l'Année 2012'. http://www.cnitie.gov.mr/index.php/fr/publications/rapports-itie/67-rapport-de-l-administrateur-independant-de-l-itie-sur-les-revenus-de-l-annee–2012.

Moore Stephens LLP. (2018), Rapport ITIE - Mauritanie exercice 2016. http://www.cnitie.gov.mr/index.php/fr/publications/rapports-itie/45-rapport-itie–2016.

Norris, H. T. (1986), *The Arab Conquest of Western Sahara: Studies of the Historical Events, Religious Beliefs and Social Customs Which Made the Remotest Sahara a Part of the Arab world*. Harlow: Longman; Beirut: Librarie du Liban.

Obiri, S., P. A. Mattah, M. M. Armah, F. A. Osae, S. Adu-kumi and P. Yeboah (2016), 'Assessing the Environmental and Socio-Economic Impacts of Artisanal Gold Mining on the Livelihoods of Communities in the Tarkwa Nsuaem Municipality in Ghana', *International Journal of Environmental Research and Public Health*, 13 (2): 160. doi: 10.3390/ijerph13020160.

Ouedraogo LS, Mundler P. (2019), 'Local Governance and Labor Organizations on Artisanal Gold Mining Sites in Burkina Faso', *Sustainability*, 11(3):616. https://doi.org/10.3390/su11030616

ONS. Office National de la Statistique. Département des Statistiques Economiques et de la Conjoncture (DEEC) Service des Statistiques Générales et Environnementales (2020), Annuaire Statistique 2019. https://ansade.mr/fr/publications/?row=RGPH.

Ould Ahmed Salem, Z. (2001), "*Tcheb-tchib*'et compagnie: Lexique de la survie et figures de la réussite en Mauritanie', *Politique Africaine*, 2 (2): 78–100.

Ould Ahmed Salem, Z. (2005), 'Mauritania: A Saharan Frontier-State', *The Journal of North African Studies*, 10 (3–4): 491–506.

Østensen, Å and Stridsman, M. (2017), 'Shadow Value Chains: Tracing the link between Corruption, Illicit Activity and Lootable Natural Resources from West Africa', *U4*, 7. Bergen: Chr. Michelson Institute.

Penfield, A. (2019), 'The Wild Inside Out: Fluid Infrastructure in an Amazonian Mining Region', *Social Anthropology*, 27 (2): 221–35.

Persaud, A. W., K. H. Telmer, M. Costa and M.-L. Moore (2017), 'Artisanal and Small-Scale Gold Mining in Senegal: Livelihoods, Customary Authority, and Formalization', *Society & Natural Resources*, 30 (8): 980–93.

Rostow, W. W. (1971 [1960]), *The Stages of Economic Growth: A Non-Communist Growth*. Cambridge: Cambridge University Press.

Rostow, W. W. (1978), *The World Economy: History and Prospect*. Austin, TX: University of Texas Press.

Schapendonk, J., M. Bolay and J. Dahinden (2020), 'The Conceptual Limits of the "Migration Journey". De-exceptionalising Mobility in the Context of West African Trajectories', *Journal of Ethnic and Migration Studies*, 47 (14): 3243–59.

Scheele, J. (2012), *Smugglers and Saints of the Sahara: Regional Connectivity in the Twentieth Century*. Cambridge: Cambridge University Press.

Sidya, C. (2020), 'Mauritanie: des manifestants s'opposent à l'implantation d'une usine de traitement de l'or à Chami'. Kassataya, Nouakchott. https://kassataya.com/2020/02/07/mauritanie-des-manifestants-sopposent-a-limplantation-dune-usine-de-traitement-de-lor-a-chami/.

Sims, J. (2019), 'Kinross Gold Corporation, Tasiast Project, Mauritania, NI 43–101 Technical Report'. (https://s2.q4cdn.com/496390694/files/doc_downloads/technical_reports/2019/Kinross-Tasiast-NI-43-101-Technical-Report-Oct-2019-FINAL.pdf.

Spiegel, S. J. (2015), 'Shifting Formalization Policies and Recentralizing Power: The Case of Zimbabwe's Artisanal Gold Mining Sector', *Society & Natural Resources*, 28 (5): 543–58.

Stewart, C. C. (1973), *Islam and Social Order in Mauritania: A Case Study from the Nineteenth Century*. Oxford: Clarendon Press.

Stoop, N. and M. Verpoorten (2020), 'Risk, Envy and Magic in the Artisanal Mining Sector of South Kivu, Democratic Republic of Congo', *Development and Change*, 51: 1199–24.

Taleb, M. (2015), 'Chami, nouvelle ville du désert: quels nouveaux apports à l'urbanisation en Mauritanie?', *Les mutations de la ville saharienne. Approches croisées sur le changement social et les pratiques urbaines*, Faculté des Sciences Sociales et Humaines-Université Kasdi Merbah, Ouargla, Algérie, 13. https://halshs.archives-ouvertes.fr/halshs-01235703/document.

Teschner, B. A. (2014), '"*Orpaillage* pays for everything": How artisanal mining supported rural institutions following Mali's coup d'état', *Futures*, 62: 140–50.

United States. Congress. Senate. Committee on Interior and Insular Affairs (1959), *Mineral Resources of and Background Information on the Eastern Hemisphere including the Soviet Union and Satellite Countries*. Washington: U.S. Govt. https://babel.hathitrust.org/cgi/pt?id=uiug.30112069633649&view=1up&seq=3.

Veiga, M. M. and O. Fadina (2020), 'A Review of the Failed Attempts to Curb Mercury Use at Artisanal Gold Mines and a Proposed Solution', *The Extractive Industries and Society*, 7 (3): 1135–46.
Verbrugge, B. and S. Geenen (2019), 'The Gold Commodity Frontier: A Fresh Perspective on Change and Diversity in the Global Gold Mining Economy', *The Extractive Industries and Society*, 6 (2): 413–23.
Werthmann, K. (2017), 'The Drawbacks of Privatization: Artisanal Gold Mining in Burkina Faso 1986–2016', *Resources Policy*, 52: 418–26.
World Bank (2009), 'Mining Together: Large-Scale Mining Meets Artisanal Mining—A Guide for Action', Technical Report; Washington, DC: World Bank Group.
World Bank (2017a), 'Islamic Republic of Mauritania: Turning Challenges into Opportunities for Ending Poverty and Promoting Shared Prosperity'. Washington, DC: World Bank Group, 7. https://openknowledge.worldbank.org/bitstream/handle/10986/27997/MAU-SCD-06292017.pdf?sequence=1.
World Bank (2017b), 'Mauritania. Transforming the Jobs Trajectory for Vulnerable Youth'. Washington, DC: World Bank Group.
World Bank (2019), 'State of the Artisanal and Small-Scale Mining Sector'. Washington, DC: World Bank Group.

6

Unsettling gender and feminism: Views from Mauritania

Maria Cardeira da Silva

NOVA FCSH – CRIA, Lisbon, Portugal

Introduction

In a very eloquent and elegant text, E. Ann McDougall (1998) tell us the story of the slave Fatma Barka, who was born somewhere in Mali between 1900 and 1910 and died in 1995 in Guelmim, Morocco. As McDougall puts it, when Fatma told her story, she did not formulate it in terms of enslavement and freedom. Her narrative does not begin linearly with her enslavement or end with her 'liberation'. Rather, it started with a desert crossing in the caravan of Mohamed Barka, Fatma's master at the time, for whom she would become a concubine. Her life was encoded in that particular story. Presenting Fatma Barka's narrative, MacDougall intends to allow historians access to her experiences expressed in their own terms, and Fatma's access to history (McDougall 1998: 287).

At the time when feminist oral history on slavery was already making efforts to liberate itself from liberal ideals, feminist debate around Islam remained encapsulated in a redemptionist concept of liberty. The discussion between leftist (secularists) and Islamic feminism that occurrted in the very same decade as MacDougall wrote her paper was still pretty much impassioned by that conception (see, among many others, Moghadam 2002). Leftists feminists criticized, for instance, Iranian Islamic feminists for the fact that, while working *from inside*, they were not fighting the (Islamic) system which was the source of their oppression. Islamic feminists aptly replied that secular feminists were not, either, fighting against their oppressive system (capitalism) but the women's oppression by itself (McDougall 1998). In both cases liberty was, after all, illusory. The real difference between these two 'feminisms' is that the secular/liberal idea of emancipation is closely attached to that of liberal freedom, while other desired paths of empowerment or cultivation of selves within Islam – as Mahmood (2005) came to affirm – may not be so.

Sabah Mahmood opened the floor to a post-structural and post-secular feminism with her ethnography on the women's piety movement in the mosques of Cairo, but her exclusive focus on *self* and Islam may have contributed, even if inadvertently, to the exacerbation of the polarization of feminist debate within Muslim contexts (or even more broadly, regarding Muslim women in general), keeping it focused on the secular/religious pair; or, in other words, it may have fostered the Islamization of the feminist discussion (not to mention the feminization of Islam debate in general) until today. This paradoxical resilience of a certain kind of orientalism – or 'sexularism' (Scott 2012) – in the feminist forum may partly explain why Arab feminisms themselves discarded until late – or were left out of – the confederation and association spirit of other subaltern feminists ('third word feminisms', 'black feminisms', etc.): it was difficult for them to get rid of the secular/religion debate.

If, as we know, 'woman' is a debatable category (Butler 1990), 'Muslim woman' is all the more contentious. There is no single cause for women's subordination and no single approach towards dealing with it. This Islamization of feminist debate in certain areas of the globe has obscured the different configurations, constraints and aspirations of feminine *selves* behind which, according to a secular view, religion is inscribed. If we go further, one could even ask if this did not contribute to the diffusion of a current liberal categorization of Muslims: the one that separates 'good Muslims' – either men or women, the secular ones, those that adapt their views and actions, for instance, to the liberal regime of women rights – from 'bad Muslims' (Mamdani 2002) – those that follow other non-conformist paths.

The intersectional approach (Crenshaw 1989) came to describe how race, class, gender and other individual characteristics intersect and overlap with one another, and how the experience of this imbrication is more than the sum of its parts. Intersectionalism tries to illuminate the connections between all struggles for rights and empowerment. But this view was scarcely used in majority Muslim contexts, being mostly applied in secular and often Islamophobic ones (especially in the contexts of immigration), and it was often combined with decolonial proposals (Salem 2014; Tariq and Syed 2018). In the light of this theoretical (and political) contamination, Islam became, in some trends and specially in diasporic contexts, racialized: not only because on some occasions race and religion (in this case Islam) overlap in the discrimination processes but also because religion became synonymous with race in the sense that both can be – and historically were – instrumentalized categories of biopolitics, of social engineering and domination. Nevertheless, once again, these approaches were hijacked by a, somehow, religion-centric approach even when they intended to dismantle the secularist lens. Once more, this prevented a crystalline observation at the level of micro-cultural, social and political settings for *selves* and self-ideas configurations and aspirations illuminated by class, status and ethnic components.

Since Clifford Geertz's *Islam Observed* (1968), there has been a call, in anthropology, for a 'local Islam' approach (even though Geertz's work keeps a certain essentialization, since he speaks of a 'Moroccan' and an 'Indonesian Islam') and later, reacting to the centrality of Islam in the discipline forum of Muslim societies, another call to the production of ethnographies on 'every-day Islam'. Women were especially affected by this ethnographic turn. The focus on women and private life induced a certain 'privatization' of Islam, in a secular fashion, while it 'liberated' women from both oppressive 'orthodox Islam' and orientalist-colonial essentializations. It could also be inferred from the universe now unveiled by these ethnographies that Islam, after all, was not so irreconcilable with secularization since it could be *interpreted*, performed and experienced as a private matter.

These attempts to counter orientalist approaches and desencapsulate Islam have, in fact, contradicted the lack of Muslim women's agency reflected in previous studies. But they were not cautious enough to prevent the side-effects of its new incidence in everyday practices (Fadil and Fernando 2015; Hirschkind 2014): disregarding Islam relevance as a discursive tradition (Asad 1986) they end up neutralizing its political force as micro power – important for the constitution of *selves* – and macro power – important for the constitution of political communities and projects.

Islam (singular, and with a capital 'I', as a discursive tradition) must, of course, be considered in all spheres where it is pervasive; moreover in places where religion by itself is called into play as a social marker and capital, as it happens in Mauritania.[1] Nevertheless, feminist discussion must not allow religion's centripetal force to overshadow the debate before finding its place in women's own speeches.

As ethnographies precluded grand narratives in favour of historical and cultural particularities, anthropology moved progressively from the anthropology of women to the anthropology of gender and then to feminist anthropology. This move challenged a range of assumptions – starting with the universal category of woman and, even before that, with the very idea of person (Strathern 1987) – and thus to intercede against unreflexive impositions onto other cultures and to monitor the categories of social scientific research itself. Difference and specificity (Kingfisher 2016: 256) have garnered the field and anthropologist's activism is currently mainly engaged on cross-cultural feminisms. Rather than favour the particular over the universal *or* vice versa, we should focus on the details of how the conversations between the two play out and draw attention to the importance of transnational feminisms through the analysis of the travel of neoliberal policies of welfare state restructuring, and welfare reforms targeting women (Deeb 2009). I would add to this that we should also pay attention to the travel of other non-liberal transnational movements. These assumptions pave the way for new approaches that the historical, and until recently persistent, opposition between universalism and difference did not allow.

Even if we agree with Kingfisher and Deeb, we must remember that global policies can only affect individuals through the mediation of gender policies at the level of states and nations. Focusing on national and state narratives and policies concerning and affecting women (directly and collaterally) is an important part of the analysis of women's movements and actions. Moreover, in states – like Mauritania – that politically mobilize the gender issue, the woman category overshadows an enormous social and ethnic diversity. Nevertheless, and taking in consideration the geographic outlines and ethnic diversity of Mauritania – finding itself, due to historical and political reasons, between the north and the so-called sub-Saharan Africa – we still cannot ignore the narratives and political trajectory of transnational African and Muslim feminisms.

In this article I will try to show how the complexity and entanglement of Mauritanian political, religious, ethnic and racialized structures by themselves – along with its territorial, religious and political emplacement in a world of nations – force us to delve deep into the previous conundrum of feminism debates, and how they can inspire epistemological and methodological challenges to future ethnographies of gender and feminism in general, and in Mauritania in particular.

Although acknowledging the importance of transnational feminist analysis in the ethnographic approaches on women's rights and action in Muslim contexts, I will attempt here to underline the need to go ethnographically deeper and theoretically further, using Mauritania's geographic and politic borders as heuristic boundaries for research,[2] carefully avoiding, nonetheless, to take nationality as a *frozen metonymy* (Appadurai 1988) or as a marker of difference by itself.[3] Lastly, I hope to highlight the significance of private and intimate spaces – where women also assert their status, formulate positions, exchange perspectives and feel themselves empowered – away from the formal political or deliberative arenas of feminist action, which are usually excluded from the global project of liberal genderification of democracy (Cornwall and Goetz 2005).

Women, academy and nation-building

Like most African countries, Mauritania is a recent and multi-ethnic nation whose borders ignore previous ethnic settings and mobilities. During the French colonization its territory was included in the *Afrique-Occidentale Française* (AOF, between 1895 and 1958) under a general government that grouped together within a single federation eight French colonies in West Africa.[4] This French political design pushed Mauritanian territory to 'black Africa' during its mandate. The capital of the AOF was established in Saint Louis and this separated Arab and Berber dwellers[5] from other co-ethnic groups of the Western Sahara and Maghreb. It has also, somehow, disenfranchised Mauritania from both of the academically established cultural (and racialized) areas – the Arab Studies and/or the African Studies, both treating Mauritania as a peripheral country and research field. Most of the research on colonial and postcolonial Mauritania was francophone, usually included into, and influenced by, the orientalist studies of Algeria and Morocco, and, later, into the academic lineage founded by Pierre Bonte. Its liminality notwithstanding, it can be said that until very recently the academic production on Mauritania was simultaneously Arabist and Arabizing. This has to do with a colonial engineering mirrored in academic competencies both at ethnological and linguistic level. But this project of 'Arabization' is further complicated by the fact that if colonial French policy gave cultural prevalence to Arabs (and Berbers), creating the *Moorish* category, it relied on the 'black African' functionaries of the Senegal valley to support the administration, submitting them to an assimilationist project through francophone education, and supporting them during the transition process to independence. Beyond the Moorish (*bīḍān*)/black African binary tension, French policies strongly explored the frictions between *bīḍān* warrior tribes – the *ḥassān*, which they considered 'Arab' – and the religious ones – *zwāya*, also designated as *maraboutiques*, and ethnicized as *berbers*, perceived as more embedded in previous local and ethnic environment and taken as the privileged *bīḍān* interlocutors of the French to seize control over the transition towards independence (Ould Mohamed Baba and Freire 2020).[6]

At the independence, in 1960, Mauritania became a pluri-ethnic state which gathered Arabs – generally assumed as the emic category of *bīḍān* – Halpulaaren, Soninké, Wolof and Bambara (gathered under the generic term *kwār*, meaning 'black'), all contained in the same territory. This diversity is complexified by the imbricated social stratification of the *bīḍān* tribes – literally meaning 'the whites' and including the 'noble' status groups of the *zwāya* and the *ḥassān*, their tributary groups – the *znāga* or *lahme*, the *ʿabīd* and *harāṭīn* (slaves and descendants of manumitted slaves), some of them considering themselves *bīḍān* and attached to their master's tribes.[7]

This complex and stratified model of the Mauritanian society stemming from the colonial and nation-building processes has rarely been analysed as a whole in a cross-ethnic, linguistic, gendered and racialized manner. We can say that, until the twentieth century, most of the prominent references and studies (particularly those focused on women) either by ancient Arab sources (Ibn Khaldun 1982; Ibn Battuta 1887), colonial French and other orientalist accounts (Park 1815; Caillié 1830; Hamet 1911; Du Puigaudeau 1937, 1992), and even some postcolonial approaches focused on the *bīḍān*, neglecting or obscuring 'their' *ḥarāṭīn* and subaltern members, as 'their' other racialized and gendered groups. And even those focusing on *bīḍān* free/noble women, often neglected relevant distinctions between *zwāya* and *ḥassān* women.

This convergence of academic and hegemonic local views that prevailed until today had to do, in part, with the focus on two academic tropes of the Arab world conditioned by political interests: the tribe and Islam (Abu-Lughod 1989). Women were long absent from these masculinized tropes and were only brought in through the voices of their fellow women European researchers. Nevertheless, these often reproduced the male-oriented map of academy and research on North Africa and Middle East, focusing on a private and feminine 'world' disconnected from the political and public sphere of action.

Mauritanian history, as well as part of its anthropology, was framed under a *bīḍān* essentialized and masculine tent. Later, even the tentative attempts by male researchers to 'rescue' Mauritanian women from their silence were often voiced from the point of view of a men's political interest, taking place in masculinized settings, using male interlocutors, where women's voices were barely heard. While emphasizing the exceptional role that some women played in the genealogical architecture of tribes (Bonte 1987; Freire 2013, 2017), they end up maintaining them under the gatekeeping concept (Appadurai 1988) of the cultural areas where they *should* be academically placed: that of the tribe.

Although there is a solid and diversified French research specifically focused on women in Mauritania between the 1980s and the first decade of this century (Tauzin 1984b, 2001, 2007a, 2007b; Caratini 1996; Simard 1996; Fortier 2000, 2003, 2010, 2011; Lesourd 2007a, 2007b, 2008, 2010), it often finds itself under the influence of the theoretical circle of francophonie and – occasionally male-oriented – Arab studies, even when it aims to challenge its paradigms. In other works, even in those works written by female researchers, Mauritanian women are often presented as objects of desire and infatuation, but still deprived of – or with limited – agency, under a masculinized explanatory rationale where they stand little chance of being taken as actors by themselves. That might be the case, for instance, of Fortier's otherwise brilliant and revealing work on love and poetry (2003, updated in 2021), tempered by Tauzin's work on the feminine poetry (1989)[8] and the '*ruse des femmes*' across Mauritanian tales (1984b).

Nevertheless, female researchers were, in fact, able to overcome gender dichotomies more successfully than men, covering in their research topics as diverse as 'tribal' world of the *bīḍān*, the *Rgaybat* (Caratini 1989) and trans-Saharan trails and caravan economy (Lydon 2008, 2009) and the *ḥarāṭīn* universe (Ann McDougall 1988, 1998), while some male researchers that ventured into the feminine realm addressed more tangential – although important – issues, like Sébastien Boulay (2003) who while researching the topic of the *khayma* in broader terms also analysed the social hierarchization of the chores carried out by women as a function of the tribal structuration, and Ruf (1999) exploring, in innovative ways, gender hierarchy, dependency and gender, and paving the way for intersectionalist approaches like that of Ann Wiley in Kankossa (2014, 2018). The work of the latter authors, along with the pioneering work of Ann McDougall progressively open the field to closer approaches on *ḥarāṭīn* women and come to invest in the entangled way slavery and gender interweave and configure each other. This will be especially evinced in Ann McDougall work (2014).[9]

However, without the academic participation of Mauritanian women actively voicing their diverse views and claims – including those of non-Hassaniyya-speaking women – it is difficult to get free of a restrictive view which frames women's agency as something subversive, exclusively moved by the resistance against a male and 'Arab' order, and a *bīḍān*-centred academy. Unfortunately, and despite a remarkable presence in activist and NGOs *fora*, Mauritanian women were rarely engaged in gender and feminist global debates within the MENA arena academia.

Academic interests and policies and its focus on *bīḍān* have also contributed to a colonial and now self-proclaimed idea of 'Mauritanian exceptionality of women status', which ignored self and gender mutual and interconnected configuration within and between the different groups. This does not mean, of course, that there are not some particularisms in Mauritania – precisely among *bīḍān* women – that may indicate a more 'favourable' situation for women (according to feminist liberal criteria) than in some other neighbouring, and especially Arab, countries. Maybe, as we shall see, these 'good' particularisms are underlined by national rhetoric's, overshadowing some other less 'favourable' cultural practices which are not so common in Arab neighbour countries like genital cuts[10] (Tauzin 1988), early marriage[11] and forced-feeding (Tauzin 2001). The established idea of a nationwide 'special status' of women was an important ingredient of asserting ethnic specificity and *bīḍān* leadership in the country, and an important and pervasive instrument for Mauritanian biopolitics. This, in fact, transcends gender and reproductive administration to become a relevant tool for ethnic management: one that contributes for the *bīḍānization* of the nation.

These exercises of imagination evince two points in need of critic analyses: the first one concerns the acritical use of the designation of 'Mauritanian woman status'; and the second – the unguarded essentialization and reification of the 'Arab' and 'Muslim' paradigm of women discrimination (even if that is the price to pay to assert Mauritania's exceptionality against the very same orientalist frames which produced this essentialization).[12] One can speak here of a double orientalization: an internal one, and an external and colonial-induced one.

In fact, my preliminary interviews, and most anthropological scholarship, does not show such an exceptionality (which, in any case and as we've seen, is built against an imagined and essentialized Islamic or Arab rule): rather they talk about different cultural and social configurations of gender that, nevertheless, point to female segregation and lack of political participation, like in most Arab and non-Arab, Muslim and non-Muslim countries and contexts. And several international recent reports and academic works (Evrard and Pettigrew 2020) refer to the growth of violence against women, and the low literacy levels and poverty especially affecting rural women, among other situations in need of clear amelioration (UNDP 2020), namely women's access to rights and political participation (Lesourd 2007a).

Moreover, while not neglecting the extraordinary life of certain women, like last century's transnational traders (Caratini 2011; Lesourd 2007a; Lydon 2009; Simard 1996) and nowadays businesswomen/*batrônat*, this scholarship presents them as some sort of exceptional heroines (Lesourd 2014: 280). One could think that maybe Mauritania's exceptionality is thus built upon exceptions and regret the fact that only women – more often *bīḍān* – with great willpower and strength manage to achieve a certain 'status'.

The configuration of social and ethnic categories – which, in fact, and according to a substantial historiography, we can never take as stabilized under colonial and independentist regimes – and its later disruption according to different economic and political crises under the influence of both global Islam and liberal human rights regime, opens the field for unremitting gender reconfigurations, constraints, challenges but also opportunities and ways of *self* and gender empowerment that challenge previous orders and hierarchies and claim renewed approaches.

A pseudo-confessional state, a pseudo-feminist nation?

The first Mauritanian Constitution (1961), with unmistakable French influence, states that 'The Islamic Republic of Mauritania is a republican, indivisible, democratic and social state'. But its second article goes on to state that 'The religion of the Mauritanian people is the Muslim religion'. Mauritania thus created the second Islamic Republic in the Islamic world (after Pakistan) and the only one in Africa. While assuming its dedication to liberal democratic principles and inalienable human rights as expressed in the Universal Declaration of Human Rights – granting, in the second article the freedom of worship and conscience to the citizen – the text underscored the state's determined quest for independence and unity by proclaiming Islam as the official religion. This has been seen by some as a semantic dissonance.[13]

In the 1980s, while maintaining the pre-existing (colonial) French model, Mauritania introduced *sharīʿa*-inspired laws in civil and penal codes (in regards to heresy, apostasy, atheism, refusal to pray, adultery and alcoholism, as well as punishments such as lapidation, amputation and flagellation), which persisted later in the 2001 Personal Status Code, the 11th article of which states that when there are difficulties of interpretation, reference should be made to *sharīʿa* (Serge 2009). Even if in the 2001 Code we can find some improvement regarding women rights (according to international law), such as the requirement of a woman's consent before marriage, the fact that the (male) tutor can marry off a woman under eighteen if *he* determines it is in her interest, allows for the perpetuation of forced marriages. And whilst Mauritania is a signatory of the Convention on the Elimination of All Forms of Discrimination against Women (since 2001), it has also stated that its ratification is only 'valid in the parts which are not contrary to Islamic Sharia and are in accordance with our [its] Constitution'.[14]

Even if these alleged dissonances did not go unnoticed, there is another one that has been neglected and deserves our attention. In article 1 of the country's first Constitution (1961), it is also declared that the Republic ensures 'all its citizens equality before the law, without distinction as race, religion, or social condition'. No mention is made to 'sex (or gender) distinction'. This only came to be included in the revised Constitution text of 1991, where it is stated that it is ensured 'all its citizens equality before the law, without distinction as to origin, race, sex or social condition' (while religion distinction was omitted in this article).

In spite of no constitutional acknowledgement at the time of independence, women were, in addition to religion, an important cultural ingredient to cement the nation: as we have seen before, the 'exceptionality' and power of Mauritanian woman – inherited from an allegedly previous (Berber?) matriarchal system – was used in nation-building, exported as a trademark rhetoric and embodied henceforth as an identity and national symbol. This exceptionality was expressed in different manners stretching and displaying women's inscription and importance in genealogies, underlying monogamic practice and the refusal of polygamy,[15] women's public circulation, the political and economic leadership of some women in history among other things that distinguished them from other Arab and/or Muslim women[16] and through a sort of colonial inspired 'state feminism'.

After independence, in 1961, and under the leadership of the French wife of the first president – Marie-Thérèse Daddah – a movement to establish childcare, better nutrition and civic education of illiterate women was promoted, and this will become the MNF (National Women's Movement) in 1966. Other women, opposing the regime which they considered to be under French tutelage, resorted to the local forms of oral feminine expression using the lyrics of their lullabies (*t'mari*) to convey political messages and information.[17] In the second phase of contestation, between 1972 and 1974, some women aligned with the *kādiḥīn* movement[18] came to use these same lullabies songs to incite the men to the fight – something that Ould Ahmed Salem (1997) described as 'rhymed guerrilla' – engaging in covert actions that lead some of them to prison. Several of these lullabies specifically denounced the governmental politics of 'feminine emancipation', while others, markedly feminist ones (Ould Ahmed Salem 1997: 785–6), clearly called for liberty and gender equality in a democratic framework, urging women to go work and study, in a pronounced rebuttal of 'patriarchy'.[19] If those early movements, and especially the political enunciation through the poetic practice of *t'mari*, did not result in large contributions to a new gender economy, they still allowed women to enter the camp of political mobilization in a way that still occurs, as epitomized, for instance, by the popular international singer, songwriter and politician, Malouma Mint el-Meidah.[20]

In addition to ignoring the constitutional rights of women from the dawn of the statehood, the governmental structures curtailed the momentum that women assembled during its foundation. Even though the circles close to President Ould Daddah included quite a few active women, the need to leverage the support from traditional and conservative religious powers, as well as that of the reformist movement *Nahḍa* (tuned with the Moroccan *Istiqlāl* movement), might be one of the reasons why they were soon contained. As in many other countries (Traboulsi 2003), women's rights were the first concessions the Arab regimes made under the pressure of conservative or Islamist voices, and this seems to still be the case in Mauritania. But the fact is that this movement did not echo outside the capital, as it did not reach the Halpulaaren and Soninké groups, since they did not agree with the polygamy ban, one of the movement's main demands (Lesourd 2016).

After the military coup of 1978, successive governments did not include women, until 1986, when President Mouaouiya Ould Taya resumed a 'feminist' rhetoric for the state. Women in positions of power or holding more significant political posts re-appeared, becoming more numerous, but they were assigned to the areas of health, social affairs or education, and always with a significant predominance of *bīḍāniat* (Lesourd 2010). The official representation of women would only become recognized under the transitional government of Mohammed Vall with the advent of gender quotas and representation law in 2006.[21] This law reserved a minimum of 20 per cent of municipal council seats for women and in 2012 was reformed to add fifty-one new seats to the National Assembly, of which twenty are solely reserved for women. The instauration and subsequent (several) enlarging attempts of this law introduced a vivid – and polarized – debate regarding women in 'the public sphere'. Yet, if it is important to emphasize the significant evolution of women's 'para-political' action taking place behind the scenes of formal domain and their eventual 'official' entrance at the level of municipal circles (Lesourd 2007a, 2010), the truth is that they are underrepresented in public service, especially in the ministerial, judiciary and foreign service:[22] 'all in all, the presence of women in the Mauritanian state apparatus and official organs of power has remained merely symbolic despite 20 years of a pro-women discourse. While women engaged in politics, politics did not engage with women' (Lesourd 2016: 85).

Excluded from the governmental political sphere, many politically active women at the dawn of statehood channelled their activism through the 'public sphere' enacted by the global NGO-ization.[23] Following the BTI Country Report of 2020,[24] many Mauritanian NGOs are empty shells or schemes to siphon off state authority or solicit international aid. Among them, only a few play a significant role in addressing social problems, notably those dedicated to the interests of ethnic, racial and gender groups, such as IRA (Initiative de Résurgence Abolitionniste en Mauritanie), SOS-esclaves, Touche pas à ma nationalité and the Association of Female Household Chiefs (Association des Femmes Chefs de Famille).

But in the meantime, Mauritania suffered different political conflicts and social and economic setbacks caused by drought, desertification and the resulting acceleration of urban consolidation (some call it Nouakchottization). These turbulent dynamics and consequent social demands can partially explain why among this blossoming of

NGOs, so few were focused specifically on women's rights, something that would make them more likely to secure financing from the dedicated structural funds that fostered support for women. But there might be other reasons for it. Capitalist liberalization and its globalization was not the only thing to affect the Mauritania state. From the end of the 1980s, like in many other Muslim countries, we will assist to what some call a 'gulfization' process. This process of urban re-Islamization tends to replace 'local rural Islam' (Ould Cheikh 2018: 2–3) and that is something that would really deserve a deeper assessment,[25] especially in what concerns its collateral effects in terms of Islamic ONG-ization, its narratives and practices.[26]

As in many regional Islamic countries the euphoria of the Arab Spring has ultimately given way to some backlash against women's rights. Elections brought to power politicized Islamist movements that rose from the atmosphere of dictatorship, economic crises, unemployment, inequalities and corruption, expanding its charitable activity, noticeable among the urban poor since the early 1980s. If the ideologies of these movements often undermined women's 'human rights and gender equality' one must also stress the role of some of the women also stress the key role of some women in opposing extremism (UNDP 2016). Maybe it was within that complexified framework that the usual tag of 'Human Rights Association' – the label other countries give to most of the NGOs' secularist fighting for civil and minorities rights – were not authorized or obliged to change their name to another less vindictive and more charitable, therefore in unequivocal compliance with Islamic ethics and commitment.[27]

A clearer display of feminist transversal activism occurred recently, when women from different organizations (secularist and Islamicists) strongly engaged in their fight together against gender violence. This culminated in April 2020 with a public demonstration close to National Assembly halls by fifty female NGOs pleading for the ratification of the law punishing rape and all the aggression against women.[28] This was a draft bill which had its first sketch during Mohamed Ould 'Abdel Aziz's mandate and which never achieved unanimous approval by the National Assembly until today.[29] The public debate around women and violence was further inflated by the intervention of Saadani Mint Khaïtoure, a *Tawāṣul* partisan, who supported claims for the law approval while inviting her party to do the same and refuse male pre-eminence and obscurantism. Several voices intervened, from different religious, social and ethnic fields, including the *Initiative de Résurgence Abolitionniste en Mauritanie* (Ira-M) and Mahfoudh Ould Waled (alias Abu Hafs, Bin Laden's former *muftī*).[30] In November 2021, on the day of the International Day for elimination of violence against women and girls, the law had not yet been approved.[31]

In his chapter in this volume, Freire contests the idea proposed by Zekeria Ould Ahmed Salem of Mauritania as a 'pseudo-confessional' state (Ould Ahmed Salem 2013). In his reasoning he takes special consideration of President Abel Aziz's funding of a state-sponsored version of Islam through a Fatwā Office, the opening of Radio Qur'ān, the Mahadra TV channel, and the announced construction of the country's largest mosque in Nouakchott. But women's rights policies in Mauritania – swinging between inflated feminist rhetoric and governmental demission regarding pivotal matters – makes us wonder if we may not be facing a 'pseudo-feminist state': one based on the ambiguities of a dual legal system and *sharīʿa*-inspired laws in civil and penal codes which finds reason enough to delay or block its own alleged feminism, thereby reinforcing its confessional dimension.

Power, Islam and feminism on women's own terms

In my earlier discussion, and especially when it comes to the involvement of the state, I refer to feminist concerns in a liberal and UN-esque sense of the term. As emphasized by Frede and Hill (2014) in relation to en-gendering Islamic authority in West Africa, many approaches on Muslim women operate within the Habermasian notion of the 'public sphere', which assumes that power and influence are exercised in public and formal spaces. By only taking seriously formal and public forms of power frequently dominated by men, and depicting women as subjects of men's agency and not as agents in their own right (Frede and Hill 2014: 141), such a stance ends up perpetuating an androcentric bias. This concern is barely new and only adds to the issues described at the beginning of this chapter, and tallies with the views abundantly expressed by Sabah Mahmood. We should also, without a doubt, highlight the importance of intimate spaces where the power of differently situated women is experienced and negotiated, if we want to counteract the uncritical exaggerations of numerous works that assign to women 'peripheral', 'marginal' and 'oppressed' positions. This extension of the notion of empowerment, on the other hand, should not end up mirroring the error of discarding women's struggles for participation in official political life, just reinforcing the contested idea that 'men are to women as the public is to the private' (Frede and Hill 2014: 131), hence ultimately reifying the private vs public dichotomy presiding over the challenged idea of the 'public sphere'.[32]

Furthermore, this could also lead to the exclusion of the voices of women that believe that their true empowerment can solely be conquered in the framework of democratic representation and those, even more numerous, but also more silenced, that develop their tactics of empowerment while navigating undifferentiated spheres of political action. To articulate these two points of view – one more centred on publicly acknowledged political action and another, partly constructed to contradict the first one, on intimate spheres of feminine power – seems to me a fundamental objective to achieve a comprehensive perception of women's positions in Islamic contexts and surpass the limitations of the categories established by secularism and the liberalism. Attaining this objective would imply a strenuous ethnographic work both extensive and intensive that would follow numerous diffused and pervasive paths of empowerment, some of which were until recently largely ignored.

My first visit to Mauritania took place in 2002. The Paris-Dakar rally was still crossing the territory at that point and, among other things, brought more tourists to oases such as Ouadane (in the Adrar region of northern Mauritania). This is where I met Zaida, a young black woman, divorced and mother of two, the owner of a successful and very popular hostel. The way other residents looked upon her with respect and admiration intrigued me. My previous extensive fieldwork in a Moroccan urban setting (Cardeira da Silva 1998, 1999a, 2003) had colonized much of my academic imagination and, despite all the training and critical thinking against any generalization or essentialization of Muslim women (Cardeira da Silva 1999b), I was still captivated by the fact that Zaida did not fit into any of the 'logical' categories I was carrying from my previous experience. The fact of 'being' young, woman and black (more likely slave-descendant), divorced, a single householder, in an eminently 'Moorish' environment, would readily set her up for misery, social immobility and disadvantage. And yet, here she was, fully engaged and most respected. In hindsight, I understand now that my surprise regarding Zaida reflected my astonishment of her success interpreted through the lens of my previous and misplaced ethnographic experiences, but also biased by a certain naturalization of women's and other minorities disempowerment instilled by the Charter of Human Rights.

At that time it was still very visible – through the modest development of tourism that brought more life to some of the Adrar's oases – the growing presence of paradoxes arising from the expansion of liberal economic models and humanist ideas, as well as the ways in which various local agents actively reacted to them, managing to adapt or not, as they always have done, after all, facing numerous changes in their own worlds (Cardeira da Silva 2006, 2010, 2016). The traumatic droughts of the 1960s and 1970s were still fresh in memories, once they led to forced sedentarization depriving the oases of many of its inhabitants (who were now slowly starting to come back). There were also memories of political and military convulsions (a chain of successive transitional governments and especially the violent conflict across the Senegalese border and the killing and expulsion of black, non-Arabophone populations from Mauritania in 1989 and 1990) and the disruptive social changes that peaked (however, not ended) with the prohibition of slavery (see Malluche in this volume). The use and appropriation of religion had somehow been democratized by the expansion of educational opportunities, the diffusion of new media and technologies, and most of all, mobile phones. All of the above led to a liberalization of religious legitimization and, consequently, to increasing possibilities of empowerment through it. In order to understand Zaida's case, I had to start paying attention, among other things, to the specificities of gender, hierarchization, racialization, status and age and their mutual configurations in Mauritania. But Zaida showed me how, to a certain extent, Islam also played an important role in her success story and in her struggle for empowerment.[33] She frequently sought the counsel, in person or by mobile phone, of a shaykh who advised her on the Islamic conformity of many of her social and economic actions, which could be a delicate issue, taking in consideration her tourist business and direct contact with non-Muslims (generally labelled by the term *naṣrānī*). For example were the profits from her business eligible for *zakāt*? Could she use it for the *Hajj*? Was it acceptable to shake hands with her foreign guests, since they would stay in 'her home'? After these consultations, she widely and strategically publicized its results, and often repeated them when she sensed the need to protect herself from potential defamation.

While Fortier (2001, 2011), Tauzin (1984b, 2001, 2007a), and infinitely more modestly, myself, opened the field to explore how Mauritanian women make use of Malikite Islam as a form of subversion or resistance and an authoritative resource for specific tactics of empowerment (for instance regarding marriage, divorce and public performance or, in Zaida's case, building a reputation and status), the work of Frede

(2014) and Frede and Hill (2014) started unveiling the significant participation of women and their central roles in the early spiritual education of children's, as well as in the *maḥāẓir* – either by founding their own schools or by composing texts for a broader public, potentially including *ḥarāṭīn* women. The groundbreaking work of Britta Frede (2014) paved the way for a broader analysis of women's place in various Islamic spheres in Mauritania. Her work is furthermore important, not only because it fills up and corrects important ethnographic and historical gaps, but mainly because it places women into an eminently public dimension of Islam thus restoring their power and religious legitimacy.

When I returned to Mauritania in 2019, I carefully restrained myself from introducing the words Feminism and Islam in my interviews. However, since we were discussing women and power, many of the interlocutors felt compelled to state their own understanding of what feminism was, and none of them has referred to Islam as a source of women's oppression and restriction of their empowerment.

Overall, based on the conversations that we had, the mobilization of Islam as a source of empowerment for women can be heuristically summed up in at least five distinct, sometimes overlapping, ways.

The first one, that we can call 'transnational Islam',[34] (often taken by the secularists as the *evil twin* of the transnational liberal feminism) is fashioned by a globalized Islam, and not very different from that of other 'sisters' in Muslim countries: this came up in the speeches and performances of the partisan women of *Tawāṣul* party, but it was also be performed by others, as an allegedly apolitical 'gulfism' (Ould Cheikh 2018; Ould Mohamed Baba Moustapha 2014). This approach to Islam emphasizes the pre-existence of women's rights, allegedly enshrined only by the Charter of Human Rights, already in the Qu'ran and in Islamic doctrine. In the words of one of the female leaders of the *Tawāṣul* party that I interviewed, Islamic and liberal values do not necessarily conflict.[35] A high-ranking member of the *Tawāṣul* party saw no contradiction between Islam and the Charter of Human Rights, as she defended equity (a more '*sharīʿa*-friendly' concept) as synonymous with equality (a secular requisite for 'women's rights'), transferring gender problems in Mauritania – which significance she acknowledged – to ethnic and cultural illiteracy and lack of education.[36] To that woman, it is precisely that primacy of *sharīʿa* and the universality of Islam in Mauritania that makes it possible to speak of *a* Mauritanian woman and sustain a national emancipatory project that overcomes ethnic and cultural diversity by means of education.[37]

The second stance, a conservative one, appeals to traditional education and the direct knowledge of Islam as anchored in society, and to the historic monopoly on religious knowledge and power maintained by the *zwāya*.[38] This may be called 'culturalized Islam' and it is a hallmark of Mauritanian national identity together with its alleged 'women's exceptionality' – although both are related, the former is much broader than the latter. 'We are powerful princesses in our houses and that is where power is! And this is because our mothers educated us so well in what regards our rights according to Islam', said an old *zwāya* woman, while her granddaughter, nodding her head in agreement, told us why, against her first decision, she decided to wear the *ḥijāb* (curiously not the *milḥafa*) during travel to the USA for a medical appointment, because of her strong sense of cultural displacement and discomfort.

The third manifestation can be called 'status Islam'. As in most Islamic majority countries, the development and growth of non-religious education allowed, as we have already noted, for a knowledge democratization and autonomy that liberated most of the marginalized groups and women from the dependency on religious elites. This process led to the enlargement and multiplication of religious knowledge and interpretations: in some cases, this took the form of individuation, self-attribution of authority and empowerment; in other cases, religious authority was transferred to newly created circles of proselytism. The individual choice and engagement in these modern paths depend, among other things, on the social value that followers of those processes ascribe to these new forms of predicament and its performers. On the other hand, this 'status Islam' may, on some occasions, take a neo-traditionalist tone, mobilizing ethnic closeness with notables *bīḍān*, and thus capitalizing the *zwāya* religious 'status', pointing towards an ethnic self-definition or redefinition of social mobility. For example, when I've asked one of my interlocutors – a woman that 'acted', and was socially perceived, as a *bīḍān*', but which genealogy and ethnic requirements (as fluid as they go) she did not fulfil – what is it that leads a person to be considered *bīḍān* and if one could 'become *bīḍān*', she answered me with a whimper saying that it would be difficult to nail down, but not impossible. It could be done based on the embodiment of some intricate daily routines, performances and details, such as discreet and elegant preparation of the house for the prayers, especially those at the end of the day, when *ṣalāt al-maghrib* is approaching. The details of those performances can be learned 'naturally', she emphasized, as a result of a prolonged and immersive co-existence. This type of discourse can be also found among some *ḥarāṭīn* women that consider themselves *bīḍān* by status.

The fourth approach or dimension (once again not exclusive of the others and often overlapping with the first that we called, heuristically, 'transnational Islam') is what we could name as a 'virtuous Islam' – one that demands some ethnographic delving. This is the path of a more individual or individualistic quest for *self*-cultivation through Islamic knowledge and embodiment. Even if this individual quest may keep women who engage in it apart from the collective arena of women rights, one should not discard it. It should be taken, instead, as a way of empowerment on their own terms, as part of the reconfigurations of the idea of person and the womanhood. This approach to Islam can also be mobilized for statutory goals. Some of the women in the process of cultivating the Islamic knowledge and their inner self develop coaching skills and predicate the ethos of this 'modern Islam' from house to house, organizing elegant gatherings and feminine *soirées*. 'Modern Islam' can thus serve, alternatively, for social upgrading.[39]

Finally, the fifth expression of Islam voiced by my interlocutors corresponds to a secularly framed narrative where Islam emerges in a fragmented manner, as a tactical defence of some rights and liberties, casuistically – and sometimes paradoxically – combined with other liberal arguments: let's call it 'tactical Islam'.[40] When I questioned one of the most controversial and provocative media figures of the self-proclaimed Mauritanian feminists about the liberating potential of 'secret marriage' (*as-sirriyya*),[41] she did not hesitate to voice her support to this religiously sanctioned practice, despite the secularly radical positions she often defends in public which may have been one of the reasons for her imprisonment in 2020.

In parallel to these dimensions and attitudes that mobilize Islam in a more or less coherent way, presenting it as compatible with women's rights, we witnessed some more secularizing attitudes. One of those is often voiced by women directly involved in the combatant times of the *kādiḥīn* and who are now leaders of the most important NGOs that assume a feminist stance without questioning it, taking the global regime of human rights as an horizon and a goal of their struggles, assuming, often uncritically, a more UN esque formula consistent with liberalism and, accordingly, accepting the necessity to consider Islam in the struggle for women's rights, even if 'merely' in its 'cultural' dimension. Another, voiced by younger women but, in fact, more in line with the old views of the *kādiḥīn*, radically refutes Islamic interference in any area of political and private life, as they refuse any other identity and gender policy that might go against universal and egalitarian rights. In the words of one of these politicized female students, women's problems were said to be a 'strict matter of citizenship, freedom of choice and rights: thus, no Islamic text should be called to regulate it; and because it is a matter of citizenship above all, women struggles should be diluted in broader ones through a general opposition to "the system"'. For this reason, she protests against the quota system: 'take the example of that woman – elected to the parliament by the quota system – who recently argued against the law of gender-based violence using Quranic arguments. Is she talking as a woman, or just voicing the party (the *Tawāṣul*) and their men?'. Here she resonates with Lesourd (2016), when referring to the clientelist ambiance of the political system and how it prevents women in positions of power to embrace broader causes, including the very cause of women, because the female element is not reduced to the single argument of gender: 'women belong to a family, embody a tribe, reflect a region. The quotas, in the end, reinforce this clientelist trend' (Lesourd 2016: 92).[42]

Even if some older women commented that I would never find a 'feminist' in Mauritania that would speak out against Islam, and taking in consideration that the word 'Islam' never spontaneously dominated the discussions I had with these women, the secularism/Islam divide (and not Islam per se), appears to be, at least on some level, a major obstacle for a common project of empowerment.

Conclusion

If Islam never came up in my conversations as the source of women's oppression, the state and the tribes were often mentioned by both younger and older women, which frequently merge them in their speeches, denouncing its political promiscuity and corruption, projecting on them an assembled idea of male interests and patriarchy.

In February 2020, fourteen Human Rights activists were arrested without formal condemnation. Among them were two of the country's most well-known feminists: Mekfula Mint Brahim (awarded with the French-German Prize for Human Rights in 2018) and Aminetu Mint El Moktar (leader of the NGO, The Association of Women Heads of Households). Until then, female activists and gender topics were relatively spared by the state persecutions against Human Rights defenders or alleged offenders against *sharīʿa*. This can be explained by four facts: 1) the fact that there is a general assumption that women don't have an effective political power, so they won't constitute a dangerous opposition; 2) the fact that there is social reluctance towards violence against women; 3) the fact that, actually, the state delegates women's issues to feminine NGOs (treating them as 'technical problems' instead of 'political problems' (Fisher 1997) and raises international funds through them; and 4) the fact that the state complacency toward female activism is used to 'pink wash' human rights policy (or lack of it) in Mauritania, making it seem more acceptable to liberal standards.

The growing violence against women in the last five years led to demonstrations for the approval of the Law Against Gender Violence gathered women (and some men) from different cultural, ethnic and political congregations. This seems to suggest a turning point for both female collective mobilization and state attitudes regarding women's political demands. The 'gender topic' can no longer be dismissed or treated as a merely 'cultural problem' as it encompass society as a whole. This public and collective mobilization cannot be understood, on the other hand, if we only focus on the state and the NGOs sector, ignoring the daily battles of women striving for their rights on their own terms, in less formal and more private arenas. Neither can we ignore the internet 'sphere' and the vibrant virtual 'feminist' engagement voiced by women rights 'influencers' or online associations. This is only attainable through thick, but extensive ethnographic and collaborative work.

Notes

1 The same way as Christianity or other religions should be, perhaps, more evidenced in other contexts when it comes to feminist claims. Secularist projects naturalized the idea that religion explains 'other's' behaviours, not 'ours'.

2 To put it clearly, and at the risk of this being interpreted as a positivist and authoritative stance, I will take the Mauritanian state as a privileged laboratory to put gender and feminist anthropology to the test, although acknowledging the risk of the arbitrariness of this exercise. I will do that based on documentary and bibliographic research, and on three short field trips to Nouakchott, Ouadane, Chinguetti and Teysir, carried out within the scope of the Capsahara project (ERC-2016-StG-716467), and in a previous individual fieldwork in Ouadane (under the Castles Abroad Projects I and II, funded by the Portuguese Public Agency for Science, Technology and Innovation between 2003 and 2011; see Cardeira da Silva 2013). The Capsahara project's main objective is to analyse how political expression is articulated through different cultural idioms, and thus, of course, the political expression of half the population could not be ignored or silenced. Mariem Baba Ahmed, Elemine Moustapha, Abdel Wedoud Ould Cheikh and Isabel Fiadeiro inspired my thoughts in very fruitful and different ways, not to mention, of course, the women that I've interviewed with the crucial help of Elemine and Mariem who allowed me to quickly expand and diversify the sample (which never aimed to be representative) and translate those conducted in Hassaniyya. Some other interviews – especially those with non-Hassaniyya-speaking women – were conducted in French or English but they did not fully reach the number necessary to fulfil one of the major requirements of my argument in this text: the need to diversify women's voices and their cultural, statutory and linguistic identities. Elemine provided me with

important surveys that complemented my views. Long and friendly conversations with Mariem generously allowed me to expand and go freer and deeper in more complex and subtle topics.

3 This does not mean that I will not consider the state and nation as gender markers and sources of oppression as well.

4 Along with current Senegal, French Sudan (present-day Mali), Guinea, Ivory Coast, Niger, Upper Volta (now Burkina Faso), Togo and Dahomey (now Benin).

5 The term for Berber, now in residual use in Mauritania, also designates the disadvantageous tributary category (*znāga*, from *Sanhāja*). For colonial and national historic reasons that have been touched upon (for more detailed accounts, see Ould Mohamed Baba 2002; Freire 2014), the 'Berber identity' claim was never fully voiced, being agglutinated in the process of Arabization. This can explain the indifference to the term 'Berber' (from Greek 'barbarian' – 'that who speaks a different language' or 'uncivilized') in contrast to what happened in Morocco, for example, when this term was replaced by the emic term *Amazigh*. Apart from the tensions stemming from the colonial exploitation of interethnic divisions between Arabs and, allegedly, Berbers, endemic to what Ould Mohamed Baba calls 'bicephalous aristocracy' (1984), this latent duality also finds its reflection in the 'feminine issue'. For a general overview of the Arab/Berber colonial divide and gender, see Claudot-Hawad (2006); for a broader discussion on the ideological 'invention' of 'berbers', see Rouighi (2019).

6 Inverting the power relations to their advantage and supporting their project of 'pacification' against the resistance of some northern *ḥassān qabīla*s.

7 On Mauritania's statuary hierarchies associated with different ethnic and racialized groups, racialism and statistics, see Malluche's chapter in this volume.

8 *Tebra*; see note 19.

9 Where she argues that in twentieth-century Mauritania, the fertility of slave women enabled and, indeed, underpinned, the diminished fertility of 'fattened' free wives.

10 The law punishes any act or attempt to damage a girl's sexual organs, but it is seldom applied. According to a UNICEF study in 2015, 67 per cent of women aged 15 to 49 have undergone this practice, much more prevalent in the southeastern part of the country where the prevalence was higher than 90 per cent (UNICEF Data Warehouse, https://data.unicef.org/resources/data_explorer/unicef_f/?ag=UNICEF&df=GLOBAL_DATAFLOW&ver=1.0&dq=MRT.PT_F_20-24_MRD_U18.&startPeriod=1970&endPeriod=2022).

11 According to the same UNICEF report, 37 per cent of girls were married before the age of 18, and 18 per cent were married before the age of 15.

12 For something similar regarding 'Sahrawi Women' in Algerian-based refugee camps, see Fiddian-Qasmiyeh (2010).

13 Notwithstanding that, as Freire points out in this volume, some distinguished Islamic scholars recognized evidence of freedom of religion.

14 See United Nations Human Rights, 'Ratification of 18 International Human Rights Treaties', https://indicators.ohchr.org/ and UN Women, http://www.un.org/womenwatch/daw/cedaw/reservations-country.htm.

15 Monogamy is, in fact, a *bīḍān* prerogative and motif of religious discordance with other ethnic groups, namely the Halpulaaren, the Soninké and the Wolof.

16 It is important to note again that this 'exceptionality' was never built against other close cultural complexes, where an alleged 'feminine liberty' and even 'matriarchy' was explored by colonial authors, like the Touareg (see Keenan 2003; McDougall 2014).

17 In Mauritania, lullabies were written to celebrate the end of a woman's forty-day seclusion after giving birth (Wiley 2020). While not always demonstrating an activist dimension, the political axis of lullabies has been signalled throughout the world. See, for example, Kurd and Armenian cases in Amy de La Bretèque and Bilal (2013).

18 Fem. sing *kādiḥa*. Clandestine Maoist protest movement, drawing inspiration in May 1968 and driven by students, intellectuals and trade unions, triggered by the repression of a strike in the mining town of Zouérat. This was an important movement fighting for civil and social rights and the root of PKM (the Party of the Mauritanian *Kādiḥīn*). It was also very important to understand the genealogy of feminist agenda in Mauritania. We can say that the stronger national and international feminist voices belong to this lineage. I've interviewed some of them, from different ethnic groups.

19 In Mauritania there are two types of feminine poetic composition, *t'mari*, without a clear metric and addressed to a child (this is the most common form) and *Tebrā*ʿ, romantic poetry that evokes a loved one. The choice of the first form over the second demonstrates once again, as in many other countries, that the Mauritanian women, even when opposing men, enters the struggle above all in her role of a mother.

20 Malouma became politically active as a member of Ahmed Daddah's RFD opposition party in 1992 and was elected as senator in 2007. She was arrested the following year after a coup d'état. In the 2009 elections she became a senator for the opposition party. In 2014, she left the opposition and joined the ruling party Union for the Republic, on the grounds that she could participate more effectively in building Mauritania by standing behind the policies of the then leader President Aziz. At the time of my fieldwork in 2018 she was under house arrest (where I could visit her) and forbidden to play in public and give concerts because she rejected the referendum which approved the dissolution of the Upper Chamber among other constitutional revisions. Her first song 'Habibi Habeytou' harshly criticized the way in which women were treated by their husbands and her 2014 album *Knou* expresses her views on human rights and women's place in society.

21 See Lesourd (2007a, 2016) for an extensive analysis and update of this process.

22 See International IDEA, Gender Quotas Database, https://www.idea.int/data-tools/data/gender-quotas/country-view/214/35 for current data regarding quotas.

23 Ould Cheikh (2018) mentions the current existence of eight thousand NGOs in Mauritania. Most of them are headed by women. For a deeper analysis of this topic, we should engage here in the general anthropological debate on the uses and abuses of public sphere and NGOs category. But this goes far beyond of both Ould Cheikh's and my scope. For specific aspects of NGO-ization of Arab Women Movements, see Jad (2004).

24 The Bertelsmann Stiftung's Transformation Index (BTI), https://bti-project.org/en/reports/country-dashboard/MRT.

25 See Ould Ahmed Salem (2007) and also Ould Mohamed Baba Moustapha (2014) for the negotiation of Islamic revival and public religiosity in Nouakchott.

26 For a general and comparative view, see Soares and Otayek (2007). Until 9/11, Western observers ignored these organizations since they seemed to contradict conventional ideas about civil society (see p. 12).

27 The historical and current leader of the Association of Women Heads of Households, one of the women whose political career is inscribed into the *kādiḥīn* genealogy, told me how she was forced to change the name originally proposed for her organization – closer to the UN notion of Human Rights – for the one it now carries

in order to be approved by the official entities. However, one may also think that it was her activist career among the *kādiḥīn* and, later, its engagement on the 1980s transversal humanitarian crisis that moulded its participation in a rather more general political frame than an exclusively feminist one.

28 CHEZVLANE, 'Des organisations féminines réclament une loi réprimant les violences à l'égard des femmes', 30 April 2020, https://www.chezvlane.com/Des-organisations-feminines-reclament-une-loi-reprimant-les-violences-a-l-egard-des-femmes_a19233.html. This was concurrent with the #MeToo global movement and similar demonstrations in Morocco, but triggered by the rape and assassination of another victim, Khadijetou Oumar Sow.

29 See Evrard and Pettigrew (2020) for an extensive analysis of this process.

30 CHEZVLANE, 'Mauritanie : de la femme-objet au martyre muet (projet de loi en pdf)', 12 May 2020, https://www.chezvlane.com/Mauritanie-de-la-femme-objet-au-martyre-muet-projet-de-loi-en-pdf_a19432.html; Evrard and Pettigrew (2020: 5).

31 CHEZVLANE, 'Journée Internationale pour l'élimination de la violence faite aux femmes et aux filles', 25 November 2021, https://www.chezvlane.com/Journee-Internationale-pour-l-elimination-de-la-violence-faite-aux-femmes-et-aux-filles_a25316.html.

32 The spread of new media technology came to complexify this private/public sphere and brings new challenges for anthropology, expanding the boundaries of relevant 'fieldwork'. This is a very important arena for 'feminist activity' (in a broader sense) in Mauritania which unfortunately I did not have the opportunity to explore virtually. Nevertheless, some of my interlocutors mentioned their engagement in feminine causes acting either as 'influencers' on women rights, or through the participation in online sites like that of *EtKelmi* (Speak!), an associative platform denouncing women's rights violations. Exploring this universe is most urgent as it can also unveil ethnic – Halpulaaren, Soninké, Wolof – Associations for women's rights much less visible in the immediate public sphere, and underexplored in academic production.

33 In addition, Zaida also used, however discretely, the fact of being related (through milk kinship) with the *commune*'s president. It was, actually, more him than her who felt the need to justify this kinship and the closeness of their mutual treatment (Cardeira da Silva 2006). See Fortier (2001) for more on milk kinship.

34 Generally coinciding with the meaning given by Olivier Roy (2004) but updating the term to transnational to emphasize the transit of not only ideas and things but also of people.

35 Other women inside the Tawāṣul party support this: see J. Spiegel, 'Droits des femmes en Mauritanie: Saadani Mint Khaytour fait face à son propre camp', jeuneafrique, 28 September 2020, https://www.jeuneafrique.com/mag/1049052/societe/droits-des-femmes-en-mauritanie-saadani-mint-khaytour-fait-face-a-son-propre-camp/.

36 Thereby resonating a very ONUsian slogan.

37 Not specifying if she means Islamic or secularized education. On the prospects of women's expectations regarding Islamic education, and hybrid knowledge conceptions, see Frede (2021).

38 I am not including here the more traditionalist, although radical, voices, such as that of the Teysir women I met when accompanying Mariem Baba Ahmed to their *maḥẓara*. Their zeal for Maliki tradition prevented me, because I am not Muslim, from sharing the plate they ate from.

39 We can include here the case of the so-called 'Dedew mosque' mentioned in this volume by Mariem Baba Ahmed.

40 In this designation, we can find a symmetry with the 'tactical secularism' of some religious feminists, not only the Islamic ones (cf. Engelke 2009).

41 Secret marriage is not legally recognized in the Mauritanian Personal Status Code, but it was socially accepted (more than polygamy) as a common practice. According to Fortier (2011: 221) it was declining some ten years ago because of sedentarization. Nevertheless, she also states – and several girls confirmed it during my conversations – that it is nowadays used by young people as a means of legalizing premarital sexual relations. More than the juridical problems it causes, some of my interlocutors' complaints about the way *as-sirriyya* is nowadays used against them as a veiled, but sanctioned invitation for sexual favours.

References

Abu-Lughod, L. (1989), 'Zones of Theory in the Anthropology of the Arab World', *Annual Review of Anthropology*, 18: 267–306.

Amy de La Bretèque, E. and M. Bilal (2013), 'The Oror and the Lorî: Armenian and Kurdish Lullabies in Present-Day Istanbul', in C. Allison and P. G. Kreyenbroek (eds), *Remembering the Past in Iranian Societies*, 125–40. Chicago, IL: Chicago University Press.

Appadurai, A. (1988), 'Putting Hierarchy in its Place', *Cultural Anthropology*, 3(1): 36–49.

Asad, T. (1986), *The Idea of an Anthropology of Islam*. Washington, DC: Center for Contemporary Arab Studies, Georgetown University.

Bonte, P. (1987), 'Donneurs de femmes ou preneurs d'hommes?: Les Awlād Qaylān, tribu de l'Adrar mauritanie', *L'Homme*, 27 (102): 54–79.

Bonte, P. (1990), 'Les risques de l'alliance. Solidarités masculines et valeurs féminines dans la société maure', in F. Héritier and E. Copet-Rougier (eds), *Les complexités de l'alliance, IV*, 107–49. Paris: Archives contemporaines.

Boulay, S. (2003), 'Organisation des opérations techniques féminines de fabrication de la tente dans la société maure (Mauritanie)', *Journal des Africanistes*, 73(2): 107–20.

Butler, J. (1990), *Gender Trouble Feminism and the Subversion of Identity*. New York, NY: Routledge.

Caillié, R. (1830), *Travels through Central Africa to Timbuctoo; and across the Great Desert, to Morocco, performed in the years 1824–1828*, 2 vols. London: Colburn & Bentley.

Caratini, S. (1989), *Les Rgaybat (1610–1934)*, 2 vols. Paris: L'Harmattan.

Caratini, S. (1996), 'Le rôle de la femme au Sahara occidental', *La Pensée*, 308: 115–24.

Caratini, S. (2011), *La fille du chasseur*. Vincennes: Éditions Thierry Marchaisse.

Cardeira da Silva, M. (1997), *O Islão Plástico. Transformações da Intimidade em Contexto Popular Marroquino Etnográfica*, I (1): 57–72.

Cardeira da Silva, M. (1999a), *Um Islão Prático. O quotidiano feminino em meio urbano popular marroquino*. Oeiras: Celta.

Cardeira da Silva, M. (1999b), 'Etnografias de Alfândega: Exercícios simples com vista à desterritorialização do trabalho de campo', *Ethnologia*, 6–8: 147–62.

Cardeira da Silva, M. (2003), 'O *hammam*, alguns anos depois: revisitação etnográfica de um contexto marroquino', *Etnográfica*, 7 (1): 187–205.

Cardeira da Silva, M. (2006), 'Hospedaria Vasque. Cultura, raça, género e expediente num oásis da Mauritânia', *Etnográfica*, X (2): 355–81.
Cardeira da Silva, M. (2010), 'Mauritanian Guestbook: Shaping Culture while Displaying It', in C. Palmer, J.-A. Lester and P. Burns (eds), *Tourism and Visual Culture, Theories and Concepts*, 181–91. Wallingford: CAB International.
Cardeira da Silva, M. (2013), *Castelos a Bombordo: Etnografias de Patrimónios Africanos e Memórias Portuguesas*. Lisbon: CRIA.
Cardeira da Silva, M. (2016), 'Old Maps, New Traffics: Political Itineraries around Scattered Heritage of Portuguese Origin', in L. Bourdeau, M. Gravari-Barbas and M. Robinson (eds), *World Heritage, Tourism, and Identity. Inscription and Co-production*, 227–36. London: Routledge.
Claudot-Hawad, H., ed. (2006), *Berbères ou Arabes ? Le tango des spécialistes*. Paris: Non Lieu/Aix-en-Provence, Iremam.
Cornwall, A. and A. M. Goetz (2005), 'Democratizing Democracy: Feminist Perspectives', *Democratization*, 12(5): 783–800.
Crenshaw, K. (1989), 'Demarginalizing the Intersection of Race and Sex: A Black Feminist Critique of Antidiscrimination Doctrine, Feminist Theory and Antiracist Politics', University of Chicago Legal Forum: vol. 1989, Article 8.
Deeb, L. (2009), 'Piety Politics and the Role of a Transnational Feminist Analysis', *The Journal of the Royal Anthropological Institute* (Special Issue: Islam, politics, anthropology), 15(1): S112–S126.
Du Puigaudeau, O. (1937), *La grande foire des dattes: Adrar Mauritanien*. Paris: Plon.
Du Puigaudeau, O. (1992), *Pieds nus à travers la Mauritanie. 1933–34*. Paris: Phébus.
Engelke, M. (2009), 'Strategic Secularism: Bible Advocacy in England', *Social Analysis*, 53 (1): 39–54.
Evrard, C. and E. Pettigrew (2020), 'Encore une nouvelle victime ... Le long chemin d'une législation à l'égard des femmes en Mauritanie', *L'Année du Maghreb*, 23: 271–302.
Fadil, N. and M. Fernando (2015), 'Rediscovering the "everyday" Muslim: Notes on an Anthropological Divide', *Hau: Journal of Ethnographic Theory*, 5(2): 59–88.
Fiddian-Qasmiyeh, E. (2010), '"Ideal" Refugee Women and Gender Equality Mainstreaming in the Sahrawi Refugee Camps: "Good Practice" for whom?', *Refugee Survey Quarterly*, 29 (2): 64–84.
Fisher, W. F. (1997), 'Doing Good? The Politics and Antipolitics of NGO Practices', *Annual Review of Anthropology*, 26: 439–64.
Fortier, C. (2000), 'Corps, différences des sexes et infortune. Transmission de l'identité et des savoirs en Islam Malékite et dans la société maure de Mauritanie'. Paris, EHESS, thèse de doctorat en anthropologie.
Fortier, C. (2001), 'Le lait, le sperme, le dos. Et le sang?: Représentations physiologiques de la filiation et de la parenté de lait en Islam malékite et dans la société maure de Mauritanie', *Cahiers d'études africaines*, 41 (161): 97–138.
Fortier, C. (2003), 'Épreuves d'amour en Mauritanie', *L'Autre. Cliniques, cultures et sociétés*, 4(2): 239–52.
Fortier, C. (2010), 'Le droit au divorce des femmes (khul ') en Islam: Pratiques différentielles en Mauritanie et en Égypte', *Droit et cultures: Revue internationale interdisciplinaire*, 59: 59–83.
Fortier, C. (2011), 'Women and Men Put Islamic Law to Their Own Use: Monogamy versus Secret Marriage in Mauritania', in M. Badran (ed), *Gender and Islam in Africa: Rights, Sexuality, and Law*, 213–32. Washington: Woodrow Wilson Center Press with Stanford University Press.

Fortier, C. (2021), 'Passion Love, Masculine Rivalry and Arabic Poetry in Mauritania', in C.-H. Mayer and E. Vanderheiden (eds), *International Handbook of Love: Transcultural and Transdisciplinary Perspectives*, 769–88. New York, NY: Springer International.

Frede, B. (2014), 'Following in the Steps of 'Aisha: Hassaniyya Speaking Tijānī Women as Spiritual Guides (*muqaddamāt*) and Teaching Islamic Scholars (*limrābuṭāt*) in Mauritania', *Islamic Africa*, 5 (2): 225–73.

Frede, B. (2021), 'What Does Traditional Islamic Education Mean? Examples from Nouakchott's Contemporary Female Learning Circles', in O. Kane (ed.), *Islamic Scholarship in Africa: New Directions and Global Contexts*, 300–20. New York, NY: Boydell & Brewer.

Frede, B. and J. Hill (2014), 'Introduction: En-Gendering Islamic Authority in West Africa', *Islamic Africa*, 5 (2): 131–65.

Freire, F. (2013), *Tribos, Princesas e Demónios: Etnografias do Encontro Pré-colonial no Sudoeste do Saara*. Lisbon: Colibri.

Freire, F. (2014), 'Saharan Migrant Camel Herders: Znāga Social Status and the Global Age', *The Journal of Modern African Studies*, 52 (3): 425–46.

Freire, F. (2017), 'The Hemeila Riddle: Genealogical Reconfigurations of pre-Colonial Encounters in Southwestern Mauritania', *History and Anthropology*, 28 (2): 149–65.

Geertz, C. (1968), *Islam Observed: Religious Development in Morocco and Indonesia*. New Haven, CT: Yale University Press.

Hamet, I. (1911), *Chroniques de la Mauritanie Sénégalaise*. Paris: Ernest Leroux.

Hirschkind, C. (2014), 'Everyday Islam', Cultural Anthropology. https://journal.culanth.org/index.php/ca/everyday-islam-charles-hirschkind.

Ibn Batoutah (1877), *Voyages d'Ibn Batoutah*, IV, trans. Defremy and Sanguinetti. Paris: Imprimerie Nationale.

Ibn Khaldun (1982), *Histoire des berbères et des dynasties musulmanes de l'Afrique Septentrionale*, trans. M. le Baron De Slane. Alger: Imprimerie du Gouverneur.

Jad, I. (2004), 'The NGO-isation of Arab Women's Movements'. *IDS Bulletin*, 35 (4): 34–42.

Keenan, J. (2003), 'The end of the Matriline? The changing roles of women and descent amongst the Algerian Tuareg', *The Journal of North African Studies*, 8 (3–4): 121–62.

Kingfisher, C. (2016), 'Studying Gender and Neoliberalism Transnationally: Implications for Theory and Action'. In E. Lewin and L. M. Silverstei (eds), *Mapping Feminist Anthropology in the Twenty-First Century*. New Brunswick, NJ: Rutgers University.

Lesourd, C. (2007a), 'Femmes mauritaniennes et politique. De la tente vers le puits ?', *L'Année du Maghreb*, 3: 333–48.

Lesourd, C. (2007b), '"Capital beauté". De quelques riches femmes maures', *Politique Africaine*, 107 (3): 62–80.

Lesourd, C. (2008), 'Le *mesrah*. Regard sur la "culture matérielle du succès" à Nouakchott', *L'Année du Maghreb*, IV: 325–38.

Lesourd C. (2010), *Mille et un litres de thé: Enquête auprès des businesswomen de Mauritanie*. Paris: Ginkgo.

Lesourd, C. (2014), *Femmes d'affaires de Mauritanie*. Paris: Karthala.

Lesourd, C. (2016), 'The Lipstick on the Edge of the Well: Mauritanian Women and Political Power (1960–2014)', in F. Sadiqi (ed.), *Women's Rights in the Aftermath of the Arab Spring*, 77–93. Cham: Palgrave Macmillan.

Lydon, G. (2008), 'Contracting Caravans: Partnership and Profit in Nineteenth and Early twentieth-Century trans-Saharan Trade', *Journal of Global History*, 3 (1): 89–113.

Lydon, G. (2009), *On Trans-Saharan Trails: Islamic Law, Trade Networks, and Cross-Cultural Exchange in Western Africa*. New York, NY: Cambridge University Press.

Mahmood, S. (2005), *Politics of Piety: The Islamic Revival and the Feminist Subject*. Princeton, NJ: Princeton University Press.
Mamdani, M. (2002), 'Good Muslim, Bad Muslim: A Political Perspective on Culture and Terrorism', *American Anthropologist*, 104(3): 766–75.
McDougall, E. A. (1988), 'A Topsy-Turvy World: Slaves and Freed slaves in the Mauritanian Adrar, 1910–1950', in S. Miers and R. L. Roberts (eds), *The End of Slavery in Africa*, 362–88, Madison, WI: University of Wisconsin Press.
McDougall, E. A. (1998), 'A Sense of Self: The Life of Fatma Barka', *Canadian Journal of African Studies [Revue Canadienne des Études Africaines]*, 32(2): 285–315.
McDougall, E. A. (2014), '"To Marry One's Slave Is as Easy as Eating a Meal": The Dynamics of Carnal Relations within Saharan Slavery', in G. Campbell and E. Elbourne (eds), *Sex, Power, and Slavery*, 40–66. Athens, OH: Ohio University Press.
Moghadam, V. M. (2002), 'Islamic Feminism and Its Discontents: Toward a Resolution of the Debate', *Signs*, 27 (4): 1135–71.
Ould Ahmed Salem, Z. (1997), 'Le prétexte de la berceuse: femmes, poésie populaire et subversion politique en Mauritanie', Annuaire de l'Afrique du Nord 1995, 771–89. Paris: CNRS Éditions.
Ould Ahmed Salem, Z. (2013), *Prêcher dans le Désert: Islam Politique et Changement Social en Mauritanie*. Paris: Karthala.
Ould Cheikh, A. W. (2018), 'Mai 68 et les Kadihin', La Nuit des Idées Nouakchott, Institut Français Mauritanie.
Ould Mohamed Baba Moustapha, E. (2014), 'Negotiating Islamic Revival: Public Religiosity in Nouakchott City', *Islamic Africa*, 5 (1): 45–82.
Ould Mohamed Baba, E. (1984), *La société beidhane face à la colonisation française*. Mémoire, ENS., 12–13.
Ould Mohamed Baba, E. (2002), 'La discrimination Arabes/Berbères aurait-elle partiellement inspiré la politique coloniale en Mauritanie?', *MASADIR: Cahiers des Sources de l'Histoire de la Mauritanie*, 3: 101–07.
Ould Mohamed Baba, E. and F. Freire (2020), 'Looters vs. Traitors: The Muqawama ("Resistance") Narrative, and its Detractors, in Contemporary Mauritania', *African Studies Review*, 63(2): 258–80.
Park, M. (1815), *The Journal of a Mission to the Interior of Africa: in Year 1805*. London: John Murray.
Pettigrew, E. (2019), 'The History of Islam in Mauritania', History and Arab Crossroads Studies, New York University, Abu Dhabi. https://doi.org/10.1093/acrefore/9780190277734.013.628.
Rouighi, R. (2019), *Inventing the Berbers: History and Ideology in the Maghreb*. Princeton, NJ: Princeton University Press.
Roy, O. (2004), *Globalized Islam: The Search for a New Ummah*. New York, NY: Columbia University Press.
Ruf, U. P. (1999), *Ending Slavery: Hierarchy, Dependency and Gender*. New Brunswick, NJ: Transaction Publishers.
Salem, S. (2014), 'Islamic Feminism, Intersectionality and Decoloniality'. *Tabula Rasa* [online], n. 21: 186–93.
Scott, J. W. (2012), *The Fantasy of Feminist History*. Durham, NC: Duke University Press.
Serge, Z. N. (2009), *Researching the Legal System and Laws of the Islamic Republic of Mauritania*. https://www.nyulawglobal.org/globalex/Mauritania.html#_edn22.
Simard, G. (1996), *Petites commerçantes de Mauritanie: Voiles, perles et henné*. Paris: Karthala.

Soares, B. F. and R. Otayek (2007), *Islam and Muslim Politics in Africa*. New York, NY: Palgrave Macmillan.

Strathern, M. (1987), 'An Awkward Relationship: The Case of Feminism and Anthropology', *Signs: Journal of Women in Culture and Society*, 12(2): 276–92.

Tariq, M. and J. Syed (2018), 'An Intersectional Perspective on Muslim Women's Issues and Experiences in Employment', *Gender, Work & Organization*, 25(5): 495–513.

Tauzin, A. (1981), *Sexualité, mariage et stratification sociale dans le Hodh mauritanien*. Thèse de 3e cycle.

Tauzin, A. (1984b), 'La ruse des femmes. Présentation d'un corpus de contes mauritaniens'. Paris, Littérature orale arabo-berbère, (15): 89–118.

Tauzin, A. (1988), 'Excision et identité féminine. L'exemple mauritanien', *Anthropologie et Sociétés*, 12(1): 29–37. https://doi.org/10.7202/015003ar.

Tauzin, A. (1989), 'A haute voix. Poésie féminine contemporaine en Mauritanie', *Revue du monde musulman et de la Méditerranée*, 54: 178–87.

Tauzin, A. (2001), *Figures du féminin dans la société maure (Mauritanie)*. Paris: Karthala.

Tauzin, A. (2007a), 'Femme, musique et Islam: De l'interdit à la scène', *Clio*, 25: 133–53.

Tauzin, A. (2007b), 'Women of Mauritania: Cathodic Images and Presentation of the Self', *Visual Anthropology*, 20 (1): 3–18.

Traboulsi, F. (2003), 'An Intelligent Man's Guide to Modern Arab Feminism', *Al-Raida*, 20(100): 15–19.

UNDP (2016), *Études des perceptions des facteurs d'insécurité et d'extrémisme violent dans les régions frontalières du Sahel*. UNDP Radicalisation et citoyenneté Ce que disent 800 sahéliens Rapport National Mauritanie.

UNDP (2020), *The Next Frontier: Human Development and the Anthropocene*. Human Development Report 2020. http://hdr.undp.org/sites/default/files/Country-Profiles/MRT.pdf.

Wiley, K. (2014), 'Joking Market Women: Critiquing and Negotiating Gender and Social Hierarchy in Kankossa, Mauritania', *Africa*, 84 (1): 101–18.

Wiley, K. (2018), *Work, Social Status, and Gender in Post-slavery Mauritania*. Bloomington, IN: Indiana University Press.

Wiley, K. (2020), 'Women in Mauritania', in K. Shillington (ed.), *Encyclopedia of African History*. Oxford: Oxford University Press.

7

Funeral orations, the web and politics: The online making of national heroes in Mauritania and the Western Sahara in poems and songs

Sébastien Boulay
Faculté Sociétés & Humanités, Université Paris Cité
and Mohamed Ould Ahmed Meidah
Mauritanian poet, writer and researcher

For some years now, we have been collecting funeral tributes composed by artists from Mauritania and the Western Sahara, paid to influential political figures or to individuals whose deaths have had a significant impact in the broader public sphere. These poems, either spoken or sung in classical Arabic or in the Hassaniyya dialect, are abundant on the web. This study[1] is based on the hypothesis that these performances and their dissemination participate in the making of West Saharan political figures and have something to say about the values of a changing society. We are also interested in these tributes because they represent a large proportion of the poetic and musical material from this area available on the web and because they seem to us to be under-studied by researchers, although they are no less valued by society than love poetry (*ghazal*), the poetry of attachment to place (*nasīb*), secular (*shekr*) or religious praise (*madḥ*), satire (*shemt*) and eulogies (*t'heydīn*), the latter genre being exclusive to griots.[2]

This research is original to the extent that it studies the evolution of these funeral tributes within the framework of a comparative approach and within the context of Mauritania and the Western Sahara, territories in which Moorish or *Bīẓān* communities have had very different political and social destinies since the 1960s. These contextual differences largely explain why the making of national martyrs is currently 'running at full speed' in the Western Sahara – at a time when the founders of the liberation movement, the Polisario Front, have been passing on one after the other – but is still relatively rare in Mauritania, which has focused on the commemoration of figures of anti-colonial resistance.[3] The *Bīẓān* of the Western Sahara and Mauritania share the same language, Hassaniyya, and an attachment to poetic expression and to the music of the griots, with the exception that the Sahrawis do not have griot families, most of whom live in the south of Mauritania. This absence of griot families, keepers of the West Saharan musical and oral tradition,[4] has not prevented the Sahrawis, who have rallied behind the banner of the Polisario Front and who have been living in the refugee camps of Tindouf (southwest Algeria) since the end of 1975, from inventing a form of popular music that has long conveyed the struggle of the Sahrawi people (during the Western Sahara War from 1975 to 1991 in particular) (Ruano Posada 2016).

This research thus consisted of assembling a corpus of poems and songs that were available online and then transcribing and translating them in order to explore their richness and to evaluate the possible renewal of the elegiac genre in the West Saharan oral tradition, as well as the possible transgressive nature of putting these tributes online, given the artistic and religious canons they are meant to respect. As Bornand and Derive observe, the canonicity of a performance can relate as much to the form of the work (its stylistic and rhetorical features) as to its theme or topic, or even its poetic form, these canonical features 'signaling both the identity of the genre and its ideal in the eyes of the audience that expects and enjoys these clichés' (2018: 14). It is also a question of understanding how these exceptional political journeys are narrated, 'the narrative act participating to varying degrees in transforming the protagonists, *post mortem*, into heroines or legendary heroes' (Clerc-Renaud and Leguy 2016: 14). These tributes also make it possible to question the political power of these heroic figures in the context of the mobilizations in Mauritania and the Western Sahara, in divergent political and historical situations. We will therefore attempt to explore the different ways in which these deceased personalities are portrayed in the media and the arts.

How are 'exceptional figures' (Bromberger and Mahieddin 2016) constructed in West Saharan society, depending on the context in which they are found? What do these exceptional figures say about society, its contemporary values, norms, etc.? While these questions have been explored by the social sciences (Centlivres 2001; Centlivres et al. 1998; Schmitt 1983) in the Arab and Muslim world (Mayeur-Jaouen 2002; Mohammad-Arif and Schmitz 2006), the Mande region and West Africa (Diawara 2014), they have not been explored in the region of interest to us, and even less so from the perspective of artistic and mediatic productions.

Drawing on two examples of funeral tributes to two regional political figures of comparable stature – Mahfud Ali Beiba, in the Western Sahara, and Ely Ould Mohamed Vall, in Mauritania – we will attempt to illustrate the richness of this corpus and the questions it raises in the global context of the expression of mourning on digital social networks (Georges 2020: 70). Rather than providing a long series of examples of tributes paid to a wide variety of prestigious people, we have chosen to confine this reflection to two contemporary political figures who have been the subject of different types of tribute. Our approach to these tributes will not be limited to their wording and literary features alone but will encompass both 'the aesthetic use of speech—voice and words' (Dupont 2010: 10) and performative practices, starting from the postulate, from ethnopoetics, that 'it is the delivery that produces meaning, not the wording [...]' (Dupont 2010: 11).

The stereotypical dimension of these eulogies will be evaluated, and the differences between *marāthī* (sg. *marthiyya*) dedicated to martyrs and *marāthī* dedicated to national personalities who were not 'martyred' will be questioned from the point of view of the content or wording of the tribute, its delivery and its dissemination. What do these exemplary lives say about the models and values promoted by society? In what way does the internet offer a new 'place' for commemorating the deceased, and what does it mean for a poet or singer to pay tribute to these political figures, especially when these tributes are meant to circulate on the web? These are the questions we will address in this chapter.

Paying tribute to deceased prestigious figures in Mauritania today

It is logical to begin this reflection by first considering funeral poetry in Mauritania – a country almost devoid[5] of a poetic tradition dedicated to the martyrs of the nation but still considered the home of West Saharan poetry and music – and then moving on to consider a national production geared towards a cult of the martyrs of the nation, organized within the framework of the Sahrawi revolutionary movement. We shall thus begin by shedding light on this genre in West Saharan poetry, composed either in classical Arabic (which designates poetry as *shiʿr*) or in the Hassaniyya dialect (which designates it as *ghne*), before evoking the transformations it has undergone in the two fields of investigation that interest us.

Marthiyya in the West Saharan poetic tradition

Funeral poems, called *marthiyya* (pl. *marāthī*) both in classical Arabic and in Hassaniyya, are part of the genre, well known in Arabic poetry, of *rithā'* (elegy or lament). These funeral elegies, present in funerary rituals since the pre-Islamic period, were historically divided into two parts: a first part in which the poet reflects on the inevitability of death and describes his or her pain, and a second, longer part that emphatically recalls the virtues of the deceased (Toelle and Zakharia 2003: 87). These poetic tributes had a strong social function – strengthening bonds within the group – and women seemed to play a key role in staging the mourning process (Toelle and Zakharia 2003: 88). While they sometimes had the political function of recalling the tragic destiny of a political or religious figure, *marāthī* more often took the form of 'courtly poetry in which professional poets mourn the death of a patron in order to retain his favor, or sing about a deceased patron in the hope of pleasing his heirs, rarely expressing real loyalty to the memory of a deceased benefactor' (Toelle and Zakharia 2003: 89), an analysis that we must bear in mind with regard to West Saharan elegiac performances. While these orations tended to repeat clichés and themes, Pellat notes that this genre has nevertheless allowed many poets to become famous and to express their creativity (1990: 588).

In present-day Mauritania, poetic orations are composed on the occasion of the death of a loved one (whether family or not) and recited during the condolences (*taʿziyya*) immediately following the death.[6] As poetic expression is very popular and lively in this West Saharan society, a deceased person might be the subject of several poems if he or she was a highly esteemed and/or well-known figure. In this (Sunni Malekite) Muslim society, it is thought that the more the deceased is praised, the better he or she will be treated in the beyond. Unlike classical Arabic poetry, the West Saharan *marthiyya* always includes three aspects: a commemoration of the qualities of the deceased, the imploring of divine mercy and the consolation of his or her descendants. In order to reach the audience, the pain must show through in the poet, and the appropriateness of these feelings must be felt in his or her sadness.

Marāthī can theoretically be composed in different poetic metres, although *l-əbtayt* (characterized by eight-foot hemistiches) seems to be the most commonly used metre, one that traditionally expresses nostalgia and sadness and is sung in the musical mode of the same name, along with *l-əbhayr* (characterized by seven-foot hemistiches) recited in the musical mode *lə-byāḍ*, as Taine-Cheikh (1985: 530) observes. It was very rare for a *marthiyya* to be sung, however, as this would have been contrary to the festive and recreational dimension of music in Moorish society. *Marāthī* can be composed in classical Arabic, especially when composed by a man from a prestigious maraboutic family (*zwāya*), in which case it is acceptable for[7] a *qaṣīda* to be long. Such poems are much longer than those composed in Hassaniyya, a language in which funeral tributes, purely oral in nature, are composed in as few words as possible (although this canon is not peculiar to funeral poetry). Poems composed in Hassaniyya have the advantage of being shared more easily and understood by more people, whereas classical Arabic is reserved for a literate elite.

Marāthī are normally dedicated to men, the most visible figures in the political arena; as the history of Arabic poetry has revealed (Pellat 1990: 589), however, we are beginning to see elegies dedicated to women, such as the diva of Moorish music Dimi Mint Abba, whose death in 2011 attracted a plethora of tributes. Men also tend to compose these poems, as is the case with all other poetic genres, with the exception of the *tebra*ʿ, a two-line poem reserved for women. This is changing, and women now sometimes compose *marāthī*, just as they are beginning to compose in other poetic genres normally reserved for men. Moreover, since political roles are still largely entrusted to members of the Moorish aristocracy, it can be assumed that these poetic orations are mainly dedicated to members of these classes, whether they belong to maraboutic or warrior groups, and more rarely to those belonging to other social groups (families of tributaries, blacksmiths, descendants of slaves, griots).

Today, any poet who did not compose *marāthī* would be frowned upon – so much so that there is currently much competition and great pressure to compose tributes to the country's key personalities. According to Abdel Wedoud Ould Cheikh, this trend is coupled with a dialectalization of these tributes that is linked to the context of sedentarization: '[i]n facilitating the gathering around the dead, sedentarization has democratized the mortuary tributes and promoted the passage to Hassaniyya' (quoted in Taine-Cheikh 2018: 163). In the same way, we are beginning to see the staging of these funeral tributes on the web, as in the three examples of tributes to Ely Ould Mohamed Vall presented below. Is this development a response to a demand for the heroization and popularization of great national figures? Does it reflect a shift in values in Mauritanian society and political life? Social networks and modern means of communication such as WhatsApp[8] have played a significant role in the proliferation of funeral tributes on the web. These tools allow poets to be informed of the subject's death immediately and to compose a poem within the timeframe of the funeral, whereas previously news of his or her death often arrived too late.

Three tributes to Ely Ould Mohamed Vall

Ely Ould Mohamed Vall, a soldier long in the shadow of President Maaouya Ould Sid'Ahmed Taya (himself a former soldier) and head of national security for eighteen years (1987–2005), took over as head of the junta that overthrew President Taya in August 2005 with the help of his first cousin, Mohamed Ould Abdel Aziz – then in charge of the BASEP (a battalion assigned to presidential security) – and the army. Presiding over the Military Council for Justice and Democracy, he was head of state and supervised the 'democratic transition' from August 2005 to April 2007, the date of the first free elections in Mauritania, which brought to power Sidi Mohamed Ould Cheikh Abdallahi, who emerged at the time as 'le candidat des militaires'. The latter was soon overthrown by General Mohamed Ould Abdel Aziz in August 2008 in a coup that was legitimized by new elections in 2009. Ely Ould Mohamed Vall ran in the 2009 elections, although he did not do well. He then joined the democratic opposition to the regime of his cousin and former comrade in arms, taking part in anti-regime demonstrations. He was also close to another enemy and cousin of Mohamed Ould Abdel Aziz, the businessman Mohamed Ould Bouamatou, who will be discussed later. He died on 5 May 2017, following a heart attack in the north of the country at his residence, located 100 km from the mining town of Zouérat. A national mourning period of three days was decreed.[9]

At the time of his death, Ely Ould Mohamed Vall was the only person with whom the opposition had managed to reach agreement, still haloed by the end of Taya's long 'reign' and the success of the 'democratic transition' he had overseen. He remained controversial in the minds of many Mauritanians, however, since he had been in charge of the police during the events of 1989 (when many serious abuses were committed against the black populations of the Senegal River valley) and because he seems to have benefited greatly from the misappropriation of public funds, which was common under Taya (and which would continue to be so under the presidency of Mohamed Ould Abdel Aziz).

Among the tributes that have been paid to Ely Ould Mohamed Vall, three have had some success on the web[10] and will be discussed below.

A song by Ely Salem Ould Eleyya

Coming from a prestigious griot family from the Brakna region, and nephew of the famous artist and griot Seymali Ould Hamed Vall, Ely Salem Ould Eleyya was a known critic of the Mohamed Ould Abdel Aziz presidency (2009–2019), to the point of seeking exile in the USA in 2017. His song is composed in the musical mode '*lə-byāḍ*' (white way), a mode dedicated to sentimentalism and nostalgia. The poem that is sung was composed in classical Arabic, in a type of metre called '*rajaz majzū*'' ('contracted'), which has eight feet. The video clip was published on 11 May 2017, on the *bellawarmedia* website.

Credited with more than 148,000 views at the time this chapter was written,[11] the video clip begins with a reading of the poem against a backdrop of images of the deceased when he was head of state. The song itself then begins, accompanied by video footage of the singer and his lute in the recording studio, followed by new images of the deceased, this time in an opposition demonstration alongside Ahmed Ould Daddah, one of his historical leaders. Finally, we see superimposed images of the arrival of the body of the deceased in Nouakchott and the funeral prayer, led by the imam of the Great Mosque of Nouakchott, in the presence of various political figures of all persuasions and President Mohamed Ould Abdel Aziz, dressed in a large boubou (*derrā ʿa*)

REFRAIN (bis)	صَبْرًا بَني وطني جَلَدْ / فَقَدْ مَضَى أمَلُ الْبَلَدْ	Extreme patience, O dear compatriots / The country's hope has faded away
	مَاتَ الشُّجَاعُ اعْلِ الذي / مَا خَانَ يَوْمًا مَا وَعَدْ	The brave Ely who / has never betrayed his principles
1	مَاتَ الزَّعيمُ الْقَائدُ / اعلِ الأَبِيُّ الَماجِدُ	He died the recognized leader / Ely the clean, the glorious
2	أسَدُ الحُرُوبِ الصامِدُ / اعْلِ الطليعَةُ والمَدَدْ	The lion of wars, the enduring / Ely, in the front row and in the back row
3	مَاتَ الرَّئيسُ المُحْتَرَمْ / الشَّهْمُ والطَّوْدُ الأشَمْ	The respected president is dead / The horseman, the high monument
4	مَنْ ذِكْرُهُ بَيْنَ الأمَمْ / فِي كُلِّ نَفْسٍ قَدْ خَلَدْ	His memory among nations / Immortalized himself in all minds
	REFRAIN (bis)	
5	يَا رَبَّنَا رٌحِمَاكَ لهْ / فِي الخُلْدِ وَسِّعْ مُدْخَلَهْ	O God! Grant him Forgiveness / And in the Beyond, give him a welcome worthy of him
6	واغْفِرْ لِمَنْ يَدْعُوكَ لَهْ / ولِوَالِدَيْهِ وَمَنِ وَلَدْ	Spread your forgiveness over all those who pray for him / His parents and children.
	REFRAIN (bis)	

The text follows the canons of the elegiac genre, although it is sung to rather lively, almost joyful music. It underlines the national scope of the character, courage and pugnacity of the deceased and finally implores a divine welcome worthy of the man and forgiveness for his children. In this video clip, the artist is clearly on stage: we see him rehearsing in front of a microphone in the recording studio, which we imagine is in North America, participating in arrangements with the sound engineer.

A poem in classical Arabic by Mohamed Ould Taleb

The author of this second work is considered one of Mauritania's best and most recognized contemporary poets, ever since his participation in the finale of the 2007 'prince of poets' (*amīr al-shuʿarā*') competition, organized in the United Arab Emirates (a programme that was broadcast throughout the Arab world). He belongs to the *qabīla*[12] of the Awlād Bū al-Sibāʿ, the tribe of the deceased and of his cousin, then-President Mohamed Ould Abdel Aziz. He worked at the Ministry of Culture as a chargé de mission and was an adviser to the president in 2017. Mohamed Ould Taleb is therefore an 'official' poet and very close to power: he was (socially) close both to the deceased and to the president of the Republic, who had become adversaries. He composes mainly in classical Arabic, in a language that is nevertheless accessible, thus following the current trend of contemporary Arabic poetry.

The video, which has had more than 43,000 views,[13] was published on 10 May 2017, on the news website *bellawarmedia*.com. It shows the poet in a still frame slowly declaiming his poem in a sorrowful tone, struggling to contain his emotion, with a photograph of the deceased looking up to the sky in the background. The author uses the eleven-foot '*al-khafīf*' metre, a highly musical metre that promotes sentimentalism. In this poem, Mohamed Ould Taleb sends his condolences, first to the Mauritanian president in office and then to the Mauritanian people, in a very solemn tone:

1	غمَرَ الحزنُ ذرْوَةَ العَلْيَاءِ / وبَكى المجدُ فارِسَ الصحْرَاء	Sadness has invaded the summit of values / And glory mourned the rider of the Sahara
2	وَ رَوَتْ عَنْ عَلِيِّها كُلَّ فَضْلٍ / وَ فَخَارٍ وعَزْمَةٍ وإبَاءِ	And brought back from his Ely all virtue / All pride, determination and self-sacrifice
3	عَنْ فَتى ثَابِتِ الجَنَانِ كريمٍ / يتمَشى كَالليثِ في الهَيْجَاءِ	From an accomplished, exemplary, generous man / Who prowls around like a lion in the jungle
4	عَرَفَ العزَّ يافِعًا ونَمَتْهُ / للمَعالي شَهادَةُ الأعْداءِ	He knew happiness at a very young age and was attributed / The greatness of the very confessions of his enemies
5	نَجْلُ فَالٍ مِنْ مخْتدي الشرفِ الفَذِّ / ونسلِ الأرومةِ الشمَّاءِ	Vall's son, of reliable Cherifian stock / Descendant of the purest glory
6	كَانَ كَالسَّيْفِ في الحُروبِ مَضاءً / وضياءً كالبدر في الظلماء	He was like a sharp sword in wars / As bright as the moon on a dark night
7	طَاهِرَ القَلْبِ لا يَبِيتُ بِغِلٍ / ساهرا أو يخوض في شحْنَاء	He fell asleep with a light heart, without hatred / Without getting involved in futile polemics
8	ولئنْ كَانَ المَوْتُ غَيَّبَ وَجْهًا / من جَمَال الأفعال والأصداء	And death took away a figure / Beautiful actions and their echoes
9	فستبكي عليه سمر العوالي / وبنود الكتيبة الحمراء	He will be mourned by what makes values / And by the red units of the regiment
10	وستبكي مواثق العهد عهدا / من شموخ وطيبة ووفاء	Respect for commitments will mourn an era / Of greatness, kindness and fidelity.
11	وستبكي عرى الندى وسأبكي / والقوافي لو كان يجدي بكائي	And will weep the roots of generosity, and I will weep / And the poems (would weep) if my weeping were useful

12	أيها الشهم إن شنقيط ضاقت / بثياب الحداد يوم العزاء	O hero, see Chinguetti who could not bear / The mourning clothes, the day of condolences.
13	ودعت فيك قائدا عربيا / هَاشِمِيَّ الأجداد والآباء	In you she said goodbye to an Arab leader / Hashemite by his grandfathers and fathers
14	ودعت فيك ماجدا ما توانى / عن أداء وخدمة وعطاء	In you she has lost a brave man who never backed down / When it was necessary to serve, act, share
15	إخوة الحرفِ عذرَ شِعري وبَوحي / هكذا فعل الحزن في الأحشاء	O brothers of letters, forgive my poetry and my tears / Tributes to the sadness infiltrating my heart
16	رحل الشهم عن سمانا فقولوا / رحم الله فارس الصحراء	The Righteous One has left our skies … Say / May God grant forgiveness to the horseman of the Sahara

The poem here emphatically depicts a prestigious, exemplary, virtuous man of noble ancestry – a man of principle and commitment, an Arab leader, a celebrated 'horseman of the Sahara'. The religious dimension is limited to a simple plea for divine forgiveness, and the descendants of the deceased are not mentioned.

A poem in Hassaniyya by Mohamed Yahya Ould Lemseydev

Mohamed Yahya Ould Lemseydev is a young poet whose precocious talent has received widespread recognition in Mauritania. He has a large following on social networks and is said to belong to the statutory group of 'blacksmiths' of the Kunta tribe (Tagant), a devalued social category but known for its role in transmitting knowledge (religious, technical, etc.) and its linguistic mastery. Some people say that he 'takes advantage' of his social status, saying things that others would not dare to express publicly. He has thus made a name for himself, notably through his satirical and even defamatory poems addressed to President Mohamed Ould Abdel Aziz. Having become a fierce opponent of the latter's regime, he went into exile in Morocco (Rabat), where he was said to have been financed by a Mauritanian businessman, a bête noire of the ruling power and once its promoter and financial backer, Mohamed Ould Bouamatou (also a very close relative of President Mohamed Ould Abdel Aziz). In fact, when Bouamatou returned to Mauritania in April 2020 (under the presidency of the successor of his cousin, Mohamed Ould Ghazouani), he was ostensibly accompanied on his private jet by the young and talented poet – a development which likely surprised no one.

The following is a poem, this time in Hassaniyya, composed in the '*lə-bteyt ət-tāmm*' metre (with eight feet), in twenty-four verses. The poem is in the form of a long *ṭal'a* with a final *gāv*,[14] marked by a change of rhyme in the last two verses. It features lively, fiery words (characteristic of this poet's works). The poem, which has the 'flaw' (relative to the expectations of a poem in Hassaniyya) of containing a few pleonasms, takes the form of a soundtrack featuring the poet's voice. This is played over a frozen image of the poet, who is dressed in a white *derrāʿa* without ostentatious embroidery and wearing a black turban. Published on 11 May 2017, on the website Tawatur.net and credited with more than 21,000 views, the poem includes the quick diction that is also characteristic of the author.[15]

1	مُوريتَان ازْكِلْ شانْ مَانْ / واطيَبْ واتْفَكْرِيشْ وتـهْدَانْ	Mauritania has lost its glory, its serenity / Its maturity, bravery and tranquility.
2	ذُو لَيَّامْ ازْكِلْ مُوريتان / يَاسِرْ منْ مَعَالِ لُمُورْ	These days Mauritania has lost / Many of its values:
3	إعلِ ولْ اعْلَيَّ سلْطَانْ / مُوريتَانْ الْ مَاهُ مَحْكُورِ	Ely Ould Eleya, Sultan / From Mauritania, the one who never disappointed
4	امْشَ مُودَّعْ للرخمانْ / وامْشَ بَعْدْ افِكْراشْ ابْصور	He is gone, God protect him / He's off to a good start
5	الشجْعَانْ وكِيفْ الشجْعَانْ / ذَات وقوْلْ وفِعْلْ وحُضورْ	A brave man among the brave / Brave in body, brave in spirit.
6	وامْشَ راجلْ مَا كَطْ اليَانْ / ولا كطْ اضعضعْ لَهْلْ الجورْ	There went the man who never bent / Who never wavered before the wickedness of the mighty
7	وامْشَ مَشْكُورْ افْكِلْ ازْمَانْ / وامْشَ حَاكِمْ عَهْدُ مشْكُورْ	He left honoured at all times / Unshakeable in his position
8	حَاكِمْ كَلْبُ مَاهُ عجلانْ / ولاهُ عنْ تِخْمَامُ مَفْدُورْ	Brave and courageous, quiet / And acting according to what his thoughts dictate.
9	يَعْطيهْ الرَّحْمَ والغُفرانْ / ذَأكْ ال كَانْ ابْذَاكْ ادَورْ	May Allah grant him mercy and forgiveness / This is what he aspired to.
10	واحْسَانْ الْ عدلْ منْ لِحْسَانْ / تَلْكَاهْ الْفَرْحَ والسرُورْ	May He welcome him / With joy and happiness
11	والجن قصورْ وجنانْ / والولدَانْ وتلْكاهْ الْحُورْ	In the palaces of Paradise / With young people and women (from Paradise)
12	يالله أعْطِيهْ أعْلَ مَكَان / لَدِيبْ المُهابْ المنْصُور	O God, reserve the best seat for him / To him, the wise, the respected and the kind.
13	وذَاكْ الّ خِلْفُ منْ لَعْيَانْ / فِيهْ اتْبَاركْ ناثِ واذكُورْ	And on those he left behind / Spread your *baraka*, boys and girls
14	لَمِينْ ويُوسفْ يالسبحَانْ / فِيهمْ ديرْ البَرْكَ والنُّورْ	Lamine and Youssef (his children) O my God / Let them be guided and enlightened …
15	والدنيَ لامِتْهَ بُهْتَانْ / حكْ انْ الدنْيَ كذْبْ وزُورْ	Companionship in life is false / Of course, life is a lie and an illusion
16	أمَّ سلْطَانْ اخْدِمْ لَوْطَانْ / واكْطَعْ فاجْرِيمِتْهُمْ لبْحُورْ	But a leader who served his country / And who, in order to serve it, crossed the oceans

17	واخْبَطْ فمَقُونْ ومَيْدَانْ / الحَرْبْ الينْ ادخلْ لِغْرُورْ	And who fought valiantly on the field / of battle and braved all dangers
18	واسْلِمْ مِنْ ذَاكْ وفَازْ وبَانْ / وجَابْ افْقْصُورْ الحكمْ ادْهُور	Then came back safe and sound with a resounding victory / Who spent a long time in the palaces of power
19	والقصور اوخَظْهُمْ فرحَانْ / مَاهُ مَنْشُوعْ ولا مَنْتُورْ	But from the palaces, he emerged with happiness / Neither dislodged nor abused
20	خَاظْ اطْيَبْ وانْصَافْ و عِرْفَانْ / بجْمِيلْ الشَّعْبْ ال مَنْكُورْ	He went away with the blessing and the gratitude / Of the people
21	سلطانْ افْذَ الصور امن الشَّانْ / كَوْنُ بِيهْ انْزَادِتْ لِقْبُورْ	A chief of such great value / When his grave was added to the cemeteries
22	تَوجَعْ غَيرْ ادْلِيل وبُرهانْ / عَنْ مَا خَاللكْ كُونْ المَقْدُورْ	For us, what a pain, but also the proof / That only destiny is the law . . .
23	وال منَّ يَسْمَعْ واشُوفْ / يظْهرْ لُ عَنْ لَيَّام ادُّورْ	And he among us who hears and sees / Will see that the days are not the same
24	وعَنْ لِقْبُورْ أكثَرْ حَظْ اتَوْفْ / اعْيَاتْ اتْعُودْ امنْ الْقْصُورْ	And that the graves are sometimes luckier / Than the palaces.

For the author, the disappearance of Ely Ould Mohamed Vall is a loss for the whole of Mauritania. He insists on the values of courage and quiet strength of character; he implores God to give him a hero's welcome in Paradise and asks Him to extend his *baraka* (blessing) on those he has left behind. He concludes by saying that cemeteries are sometimes luckier places than palaces, a line the thunderous tones of which are underscored by the final *gāv*[16] and which is clearly aimed directly at the incumbent president, the object of all of his fiery compositions.

Here we have three compositions likely to reach a large audience, performed by three fairly famous artists. The song will be easily disseminated because it will be taken up by everyone. The poem in Hassaniyya will also reach a very large audience, and while classical Arabic normally reaches a smaller audience, the fact that Mohamed Ould Taleb's poem was composed and performed by a television star with close ties to power also increases its chances of being heard, including in the wider Arab world. At first glance, these three compositions are very similar in terms of content, and all respect the canons of the genre, although in different ways. They each insist on the unanimously recognized qualities of the deceased – moral qualities that are implicitly sought after in a leader.

But isn't this a form of courtly poetry, in which these highly politically committed poets compete artistically? It is in fact the political position of these three men that gives particular significance to these compositions. Although very close to the president in office, who was a political opponent of the deceased, Mohamed Ould Taleb addresses the president of all Mauritanians, displaying the grief that is expected of him and the funeral tribute of a country that has lost one of its most valiant subjects. Obliged to pay tribute to his president and cousin, he plays the card of national harmony. On the other hand, the voices of the two opposition artists underline the difficult tomorrows, the loss of all hope, the disappearance of the qualities of the president, qualities that are lacking in the incumbent, who has the respect neither of the people nor of other nations. In a society where poets are reluctant to write critical works and thus expose themselves to reprisals, a strong tribute to one person is one of the most common means of criticizing another, as the famous Hassaniyya proverb 'praise of one is criticism of the other' (Taine-Cheikh 2004) reminds us. Filling the silence is the incumbent president, whose personality, diametrically opposed to the deceased, is not mentioned in the poem but is on everyone's mind.

Funeral tributes to Sahrawi personalities

Orations to the martyrs of the nation

Rithā' is a very important type of Sahrawi nationalist poetry and song, largely devoted to the 'martyrs' (*shuhadā'*) of the nation. In the Sahrawi refugee camps of Tindouf, where the exiled government of the SADR (Sahrawi Arab Democratic Republic) is located, anyone who played a role in the defence of the territory, the organization of the state and helping the victims of war becomes a martyr. The status of martyr can therefore be granted to combatants (*muqātilīn*), civil activists (*munāḍilīn*) and activists (*nushaṭā'*). Because the Sahrawi refugees are in exile, anyone who dies in the camps thus becomes *shahīd*. Here we find the different categories of martyrs identified by Hamid Bozarslan (2002) within the Kurdish liberation movement (PKK), including those he calls 'emblematic martyrs':

> a very limited number of figures who occupy the Kurdish symbolic universe and who, beyond commemoration, structure the nationalist syntax through poetry and visual art. They are either leaders of the armed struggle who fell on the battlefield or were assassinated ... or founding martyrs of an organization ... or finally militants or sympathizers who made a singular act of self-sacrifice for the nation.
>
> (2002: 339)

The majority of songs and poems dedicated to the dead are devoted to those considered *rumūz al-waṭan*, 'symbols of the nation' in the Sahrawi political imagination.

The war (1975–1991) resulted in thousands of deaths, both military and civilian: mourning was thus part of daily life for Sahrawi families (and of course for the combatants) for many years. According to Za'īm 'Allāl al-Dāf,[17] a poet-soldier encountered several times in the Tindouf camps, it is therefore normal for poets to compose many *marāthī* because the poet expresses what the people feel: '*al-qaṣīda lisān al-jumhūr*'. He does not choose the circumstances; he composes his poems – or rather, he corrects himself, the poem imposes itself on him, depending on the circumstances. He insists that the *marthiyya* must be sincere (*ṣadīq*) in order to touch its audience; his language is recognizable in its lyricism, for which *lə-bteyt* is the most appropriate metre. The poet does not hesitate to compare the very sensitive and passionate tone of the *marthiyya* to a love poem (*ghazal*). Although it is not customary when it comes to *marāthī*, Za'īm 'Allāl has recently composed several, including one in classical Arabic dedicated to the late President of the SADR Mohamed Abdelaziz (who died in 2016), composed an hour after the announcement of his death, and another in Hassaniyya recited on television on the day of the funeral. He says he is more at ease in Hassaniyya, a language that, according to him, reaches more people than classical Arabic, which is more popular among young Sahrawis who have studied in Arab countries.

All Sahrawi families have had martyrs in their midst, and a special policy has been put in place within the SADR government to facilitate the daily lives of martyrs' family members.[18] Today, an entire generation of fighters and activists is passing on, giving rise to new tributes to national heroes. The Polisario Front invested in its martyr figures very early on: Sidi Brahim Bassiri, the first Sahrawi independence leader, kidnapped by the Spanish colonial authorities during the peaceful demonstrations in Zemla in 1970 and missing ever since; Bachir Lahlaoui (who died on 8 March 1974), the first official martyr of the Polisario Front, celebrated every year in the refugee camps; and above all El-Ouali Moustapha Sayed, the emblematic leader of the movement, who died prematurely but heroically in a military raid on Nouakchott on 9 June 1976. These figures are enthroned in the pantheon of national martyrs, recently joined by SADR President Mohamed Abdelaziz (1976–2016) and by artists like Mariem Hassan (disappeared in 2015), who for many years was the great voice of resistance to Moroccan occupation and of Sahrawi nationalism.

In the Sahrawi revolutionary tradition, unlike the poetic practice of the Moors of Mauritania, no tribute is paid to individuals in their own lifetime (*shekr*), for fear of stirring up competition between groups and undermining national unity; instead, tribute is paid only to deceased personalities.[19] This principle is said to predate the Sahrawi revolution and Spanish colonization and, as Bechir Ould Ely told us, is linked to the political organization of the Ayt Arbaʿīn ('the Forty'), who exercised power collegially. For this poet, 'a people that has not staged a revolution as we have can have no *shuhadāʾ*!'[20] According to him, the *shahīd* is a point of pride for his people and an example of *ʿahd* (commitment) to be followed by the younger generations, to quote the famous song performed by Mariem Hassan, *ʿAlā ʿahd al-shahīd*.[21]

According to Mohamed Ghali, a man of the theatre in the refugee camps and author of a successful one-man show[22] recounting a disillusioned refugee's visit to the grave of a martyr, a zany character who uses self-mockery to denounce the situation of refugees:

> The martyr is the source of legitimacy; he is the reference. For example, for Muslims, the Qurʾān is the source. And in our political cause, the reference is the martyrs, because they have given everything for the national cause. For us we are accountable to God and to the martyrs, so for each Sahrawi, either his father is a martyr, or his brother, or his cousin, or he himself is a future martyr, etc. So we must respect the person who has given everything. Moreover, for us, martyrs are a red line. If you've made a mistake, they say, 'Watch out! It's the martyrs who will hold you to account'.[23]

In terms of its form, the Sahrawi *marthiyya* respects the canons of classical poetry. As Bechir Ould Ely assures us, in Hassaniyya, composed in the *lə-bteyt* metre (hemistiches of six or eight feet), the funeral poem does not have to be long to touch the audience. Its primary objective is *taraḥḥum*, a request for mercy and a homage to the values of the deceased. It rests on the three common pillars of the West Saharan *marthiyya*. On the question of whether setting the *marthiyya* to music is frowned upon by some, Bechir Ould Ely affirms that music can only give importance to the poem, enhancing it and lending it strength and beauty. As in Mauritania, the poems are usually composed in Hassaniyya (the most popular language for poetry), but some are also composed in classical Arabic, given that the Hassaniyya currently spoken by Sahrawis in the refugee camps of Tindouf is heavily mixed with classical Arabic, likely due to the common use of Arabic political vocabulary in daily life and to students' extended visits to other Arabic speaking countries, Algeria in particular.

A national hero becomes a martyr: The example of Mahfud Ali Beiba

Born in 1953 in El Aaiún, then Spanish Sahara, Mahfud Ali Beiba was one of the founders of the Polisario Front. He was chosen to take over the interim leadership of the state and the movement following the death of El-Ouali Moustapha Sayed on 9 June 1976, even if for a very short time (June to August 1976). He subsequently held many high-profile political posts: twice prime minister, minister on several occasions, governor, president of the SADR parliament and member of the National Secretariat, the executive body of the liberation movement. Mahfud Ali Beiba was a much-appreciated personality in the refugee camps and in the network of international solidarity with the Sahrawi people. Now deceased (he died on 2 July 2010), he has been the subject of various tributes that are accessible on the web, of which we will give just a few examples.

The first of these is his official funeral oration. Likely filmed at the time by the newly created SADR TV, this tribute was the subject of a video published on YouTube on 9 August 2010, by Selwan Esmra (a cyber activist from the 'occupied territories', the city of Smara). The video,[24] credited with more than 12,300 views, combines still and moving images of the deceased in public life, on the one hand, with images filmed at his official funeral, on the other. The coffin is wrapped in the SADR flag and is carried by six soldiers before a line of official figures of the regime, including the president of the SADR (who died in 2016), who is in mourning. The video then shows Mahfud Ali Beiba in his role as an official at political conferences and responding to journalists on television, as well as older footage filmed at the beginning of the armed struggle. The speech presents the man as a 'symbol of the Sahrawi nation'. It recalls his human qualities: wisdom, loyalty, dignity, modesty and devotion to the common good. It then recalls the highlights of his public career, including his participation in the first clandestine activities of the organization. The funeral tribute ends with a promise to the deceased to remain 'faithful to his commitment, just as he was faithful to the pact of martyrs', presenting him not only as 'the son of Fala and Hammed but the son of all Sahrawis', for whom divine mercy is implored.

A 'statement of condolences' given by nine prisoners of conscience incarcerated in Tiznit prison, filmed clandestinely with a mobile phone, has also been published on the web. The video,[25] which has had more than six thousand views, begins with a collective recitation of *al-Fātiḥa,* the opening *sūra* of the Qurʾān. The names of the nine prisoners present in the room are then given. This is followed by a collective recitation of the *Sūra* of Dawn (*al-Fajr*). The homage reminds us that the subject of the tribute 'has given himself to the cause of the Sahrawi people'. The condolences are addressed 'to the Saharawi people, the national leaders, the government and his small family', which marks the subject as a personality of national stature. It is above all the living character of the figure of the martyr that is underlined in this video: 'You remain among us, because not all of the martyrs have gone, and they will never be gone, because they are a light on our path. The path of struggle continues until victory is achieved.' The subject is presented as a model, a reference and as an example for future generations to follow, 'a symbol for awaiting the arrival of dawn, the day of liberation and independence'.

More surprising – but also more interesting – is an online tribute featuring a song by the famous Mauritanian artist and griot Maalouma Mint el-Meidah, which accompanies a slideshow[26] of images of the life of the deceased. This video features a famous song that Maalouma had written for her friend, the satirical journalist Habib Ould Mahfoudh, who died in 2001 – a beautiful tribute that highlights the interpretative talent of the artist, expressing the sadness caused by the disappearance of the writer, whose humorous 'Mauritanides' columns were eagerly anticipated by the readers of *Le Calame* each week. In the song, the Sahrawi blogger rhymes the name *Maḥfūdh* with the word 'disappeared', *mafqūd*, associating it with the deceased Sahrawi dignitary. The first image of Mahfud Ali Beiba, whose gaze is fixed on the photographer and who is comfortably seated on a sofa, bears the following words in Arabic: 'The martyr who taught us what it means to die for a cause is Mahfud Ali Beiba.' The slideshow then displays images of Ali Beiba, the national funeral and a wake featuring Sahrawi women from the occupied territories, all wearing black veils and silent, some holding photos of the deceased. This transplantation and remixing of songs and poems – apparently without the original artists' knowledge – is a common practice in the hassanophone space, one that gives free rein to a certain inventiveness. Maalouma is not just any artist, however: highly involved in political life and opposed to military regimes in Mauritania, long boycotted by the regime of Maaouya Ould Sid'Ahmed Taya, whom Habib Ould Mahfoudh never ceased to satirize, she is the daughter of a prestigious family of griots from the Trārza and the most popular singer in Mauritania, alongside Dimi Mint Abba (who died in 2011). On the other hand, she is not known for being sympathetic to the Sahrawi cause, much like Habib Ould Mahfoudh.

1	حبيبنا المفقود / يهدي لنا الورود	Our friend, the departed / He offers us flowers,
2	في عينيه وعود / وأسرار الوجود (حبيبنا المفقود)	In his eyes promises / And the secrets of existence, (choir) Our friend, the disappeared /...
3	مضى فاين هو / كنا هنا نلوم	He's gone, and where is he? / We were here complaining,

4	عن حزننا مسؤول / حديثه يزول (حبيبنا المفقود) (مرتين)	Of our grief, he is the one responsible / His word disappears (choir) ×2
5	في وكره الأخير / أزهار وعبير	In his (last) moving refuge / [one finds] flowers and [their] perfume,
6	أسراب وصفير / تداعب القدير	Clouds [of birds] whistling / Touching the water,
7	للوح ولطير... (حبيبنا المفقود) (مرتين)	Which suddenly appear and then fly away (choir) ×2
8	رحلت كالاحلام (أحقا لم تعد) / هوت بنا الايام (وأين رحلت؟)	You left like [the dreams do] (really you don't come back anymore) / The days let us down (and where did you go?),
9	بل هاجر الحمام / وجفت الاقلام (هُنالك صعد)	Yet the pigeons have gone on migration / And the feathers have stopped writing [for you] (and there he went to heaven)
		Refrain (1–2)

This song reveals the artist's creative freedom and taste for transgression[27] as she departs from the canons of the classic funeral homage to sing of her love for the deceased, lending her performance an intense, passionate tone. The 'hijacking' of the song, originally written in a completely different context, is surprising, however, given the artist's lack of connection to the Sahrawi political movement. The text, originally commemorating a journalist who unceasingly satirized Taya's regime, seems to be out of step with the usual funeral tributes to Sahrawi political figures. Does Maalouma know that her song was used to commemorate another person? We don't know, but the result is quite impressive. The web link may have been removed at the request of the artist or the family of Habib Ould Mahfoudh, or perhaps by the SADR government, which was worried about its diplomatic relations with Mauritania.

An oration in classical Arabic sung by a Mauritanian griot

The online tribute to Mahfud Ali Beiba that has had the greatest impact is a long poem in classical Arabic, sung by a famous Mauritanian griot and accompanying a slide show posted on YouTube on 3 June 2011, almost a year after his death. The slideshow presents still images of the official funeral mixed with images of the deceased throughout his public career. The images are of poor quality (very pixelated). The author of the montage uses the pseudonym 'Sahrawi assarasdtv', which indicates that he is a Sahrawi activist, potentially from the town of Assa in southern Morocco, home to a large hassanophone population. This pseudonym also indicates that the cyber activist is claiming a connection to RASD TV, the official channel of the Sahrawi government founded in 2004 (but active since 2009–2010), and that he is using video clips that were originally broadcast on this channel. All the other documents available on the web under this pseudonym confirm this identity.

The author of the poem is Abbe Sellahi, an official of the SADR government, in charge (in 2017) of twinning and cooperation. Although he is not one of the regime's official poets, Abbe Sellahi is a respected poet in the refugee camps of Tindouf, known for his compositions in classical Arabic. The text of this elegy, in twenty-two verses, is as follows:

أتمسكُ الدمعَ عندما يُبكي الحجرا / أم دمعُ عينكَ جفَ بعدما انهمراَ	How can you contain your tears when even the stones are crying / Or your tears have dried up after seeing them run down in abundance	1
تلومُني كلما عينُ العزَا دمعتْ / ومنكَ دمعُ الأسى ينسابُ مُنحدراَ	You reproach me with every tear of sorrow / And it is because of you that the tears of my pain flow freely	2
وتمنعُ النفسَ أن تشكو السماء قدرا / دع النفوس تشكو لربها القدرا	And you forbid the spirit to complain to heaven about its fate / ah, let the spirits complain to their God about their fate	3
سلِ النجومَ بليلٍ غابَ كوكبُهُ / والأرضَ والبحرَ والأريافَ والحضراَ	Ask the stars on a night without a planet / (whether you are) on land, sea, countryside or city	4
واحبسْ عواطفَ قد أدمنتَها طربًا / واهجرْ نديمكَ والمُدامَ والسَمراَ	And remember the happy feelings/ and leave your companion, habits and night-time pleasures	5
وابكِ الحبيبَ الذي عاهدتَه زمنًا / فما تحايَل في عهدٍ وما مَكراَ	And weep for your erstwhile friend / who never cheated or disappointed you	6
خَلِّ الكرى واعتكفْ ليلًا إلى سحرٍ / عسى الحبيبَ يعودُ طيفُهُ سَحراَ	Abandon sleep and meditate at night until dawn / the friend's spirit, it is likely, will return during the night	7
هو اعلي بيبا الذي أعلامُ سيرتِه / تَهدي الأحبة والرفاق والنظراَ	It is Ali Beiba, and the merits of his life / guide his admirers, companions and peers	8
هو اعلي بيبا الذي ضَمتْ شمائلُه / بعد البصيرةِ والعطاءِ والوقراَ	It is indeed Ali Beiba, whose merits / farsightedness, generosity and respectability are among the most important	9
هو اعلي بيبا الذي عرفته رجلا / عفّت يداه فأعطى كل ما ادخرا	It was Ali Beiba whom I knew as a man / a man of integrity and full of liberalities	10
حياتُه مَعلمٌ لمن أرادَ هُدىً / وموتُهُ عبرةٌ لمن لهُ اعتبراَ	His life is a reference for those who want to find the right way / and his death is a lesson for those who want to understand	11
رحيلُه سفرُ وفي حقائبهِ / يلُمّ من دُررِ الأخلاقِ ما ندراَ	Its departure is a journey and its luggage / contains the rarest of morals	12

جئتك ربي شجيَ القلبِ مبتهلًا / وجئتُ مستسمحاً عنهُ ومُعتذراً	I have come, my God, with a pure heart to implore you / and I have come to ask for your forgiveness and mercy for him	13
بردْ مضاجِعَهُ وسِعْ مداخلَهُ / يسِر عليهِ من الحساب ما عسراً	Make his last refuge pleasant and open your doors wide to him / make it easier for him to ask questions about the Last Judgment	14
يا ربي طَيبْ ضريحاً ضَم أضلُعهُ / واحضر لخير نزيلٍ فيه خيرَ قَرى	O my God purify the tomb that will receive his body / and let this distinguished guest be accompanied by the best of his companions	15
ضم الصمود وضم الصبر في زمن / لا حظ في ظله إلا لمن صبراً	(Among his merits) are resistance, patience at a time / when there was no chance except for those who know how to wait	16
طيّبه للموت واجعل فيه راحته / من بعد ما تعب الترحال والسفراً	Prepare him for death so that he can rest in peace / having worn himself out so much by moving and travelling	17
وارحمه فكرا نقيا ظل متزنا / وفيا في ما خفا منه وما ظهراً	And have mercy on his pure and measured spirit / faithful to himself (inside) and to others (outside)	18
وارحمه قولا كريما طابَ مَنطِقهُ / فلم يُعكر صفاً ولم يَجرح بشراً	And have mercy on his well-considered good word / he has never offended or even hurt anyone	19
لا نقص في فعله جرى اللسان بهِ / ولا عيوبٌ بها حبرُ اليراع جرى	No one has (ever) testified to any shortcomings in his actions / no criticism has been written about him	20
فاخدم ثوابته التي في خدمتها / أفنى الطفولة فالشباب فالعمراً	And serve the principles to whose service / he has dedicated his childhood, youth and (all) his life	21
ثابر على دربه واسدي الوفاء له / فالفجر يشرق طال الليل أم قصراً	Follow his path and be faithful to him / and the dawn will surely come, whether the night is long or short	22

This seems to be a fairly classic poetic oration, in terms of content: the text mixes the expression of the poet's pain (verses 1, 2 and 3) with praise for the many virtues of the martyr (9, 10, 16) and the principles that guided his life (verse 21), his irreproachable conduct (verse 20), principles that should serve the living as a reference and a path to follow (verses 11 and 22), and finally, with an imploration of divine mercy (verses 13, 18 and 19).

The setting of the poem to music and song took place in a second phase, commissioned by Mohamed Salem Ould Meidah, a famous Mauritanian artist, son of

Ahmeddou Ould Meidah and cousin of Maalouma Mint Meidah. In a long prologue, the singer recites the poem and names its author, followed by lively music saturated with synthesizers. The music contrasts with the idea of sadness and sorrow developed in the poem. The homage thus becomes almost festive and colourful. The fact that this poem is sung in a mode (*lə-byāḍ*) that is specific to the expression of feelings and sadness is strongly counterbalanced by the thunderous interpretation of Mohamed Salem Meidah, an artist who is used to singing at a very high register.

The music of the Ahl Meidah (Ar. *Ahl Maydāḥ*) is sophisticated and often praises the Prophet (*madḥ*) in particular. This line of griots also compose songs in classical Arabic, a language that is usually reserved for the literate elite and the maraboutic milieu, to which the singer's father was very close. He himself recently hosted a programme on a Mauritanian television channel on *madḥ* during Ramadan. This family story may explain, at least in part, the artist's skill in setting the eulogy to music. When interviewed in Nouakchott in July 2019, Mohamed Salem Meidah went back over the reasons that led him to agree to perform this poem, as he had no known links to the Polisario Front, to the deceased or to the author of the poem, Abbe Sellahi (whom we were unable to meet in Tindouf in 2017):

> People phoned me and came to see me and told me about the poem. I told them that if the poem was a poem of pure *rithā'*, I wouldn't be against it, I'd agree to do it. But if in the poem there were something against X, I wouldn't take that on! I'd do that for anyone. Even here in Mauritania, if someone brings me a poem where there is something against such and such a family, I won't take it on. But I can praise you all you want, without offending anyone! They brought me the poem. It was an extraordinary poem! … quite simply! A poem about the values of this person who, according to the poem, is extraordinary! The poem touched me greatly! By the way, when I hear myself presenting this poem, I start to feel hoarse, as if I were going to start crying! No, I was really touched by the poem. It's an extraordinary poem! Hats off to Abbe Sellahi, who wrote it!
>
> *Why do you sing it in this joyful way?*
>
> Because *lə-byāḍ* is the best way to do this! It is *lə-byāḍ* that allows the poem to be presented seriously, as it is! And it worked! To each *beyt* [verse], I gave the right value, the right tone, and I weighed the letters properly to give it the flavor of a real *rithā'*!
>
> *Is it common today to put rithā' on the internet?*
>
> Before, it wasn't very appropriate, and I was afraid that parents wouldn't like it. But it's better! There is no better way to preserve and spread these tributes. I even did another one that worked very well too!

Mohamed Salem Meidah has indeed sung another *marthiyya*, this time composed by ʿAllāl al-Dāf, father of Zaʿīm ʿAllāl, and dedicated to Khalil Sidi Mhamed, another

Polisario personality, who died in 2013.[28] According to Zaʿīm ʿAllāl, '[the song] gives value to the poem, and it touches more people'. It is likely that the setting of Abbe Sellahi's poem to music has contributed to its success on the web. In fact, the song was taken up by a Mauritanian blogger (who no doubt has links to the Sahrawis), who presented it against the backdrop of images of heavenly natural landscapes, perhaps referring to images of the luxuriance and abundance of Paradise. In this last montage, there are no images of the deceased or any mention of him in the description of the video; on the other hand, the author of the poem is well cited. The Arabic transcription of the poem is superimposed on the images.[29] Put online on 4 September 2014, the video has had over 1,736,000 views on YouTube.

Performativity and political significance

The political value of these productions is clearly inseparable from their artistic performativity. Indeed, if these poems seem rather constrained, both in their form (metre, rhyme, structure, lexicon) and in the messages they deliver, it seems that their success is measured by the quality of the artist's performance and the way in which the statement is put to images, but also by the identity and notoriety of the artist and the political context in which the poetic orations are composed and disseminated.

The canonicity of these tributes and the renewal of the elegiac genre?

If they are to have a chance of reaching a broad audience and being broadcast on digital social networks, these tributes normally have to respect certain conventions, as we have seen. Usually composed in a specific metre, the poem will first be judged by these poetic canons, but also by the message it delivers about the deceased, his or her exemplary values and the sincerity of the poet in expressing his or her sadness. In addition to these formal literary canons, the accessibility of the language, whether classical Arabic or Hassaniyya, is decisive to the reception of the tribute, given that Hassaniyya poems are meant to be short (a standard which, for example, the young poet Ould Lemseydev does not quite manage to meet). It is possible that his *marthiyya*, in dialect, was influenced by the structure of funeral orations in classical Arabic, such as that composed by Mohamed Ould Taleb.

Once these textual conventions have been evaluated in the tribute, the vocal performance of the poetic text and the creativity of the artist (poet) or artists (poet, singer and blogger) are decisive to its success and reception.[30] These funeral poems are either recited by the author, live or recorded, on a news channel (Mohamed Ould Taleb) or a video-sharing platform – an author whose voice, eloquence and diction can then be clearly recognized – or recited by another person, often an artist/griot who provides an original interpretation of the text, as in Mohamed Salem Meidah's case. Note that the latter, like Ely Salem Ould Eleyya, recites the Arabic poem for the first time in a sort of prologue before singing it, thus emphasizing the textual properties of the utterance. The talent and passion with which these artists perform their tributes gives strength to the poetic text, to the point that the identity of the celebrated hero takes a back seat or is even forgotten. Maalouma's and Mohamed Salem Meidah's passionate interpretations strengthen the lyricism of the text exponentially. The competence and professionalism of these artists are given centre stage.

In addition, the quality of the editing or video plays a significant role in the success of these tributes. In the Sahrawi context, what seems to be occurring is the normalization of photomontages dedicated to martyrs of a certain weight: the recitation of a poem or song spoken or sung over a succession of still images of the deceased, taken in different situations. The slideshows and photomontages that belong to the category of *rithā'* have, in the Sahrawi context, formed a genre of their own with its own canons, the most important of which is having a Mauritanian griot, if possible a famous one, lend his or her voice to the tribute. From the death of Mahfud Ali Beiba to that of Mhamed Khaddad in 2020 – another important personality of the Polisario Front whose death inspired many orations – these montages have followed largely the same conventions, although the quality of the images has improved (no doubt benefiting from increased internet coverage and speed in the region). In some montages, the text is displayed in beautiful calligraphy (a technique used by the blogger who used the song from Mohamed Salem Meidah), highlighting the importance of the written word and the Arabic text in its diffusion.

These photomontages feature highly complimentary images of the deceased, both in private life – in a relaxed, smiling, comfortable armchair, dressed in a traditional blue or white *derrā'a* – and in public life – in 'Western' clothes while carrying out his official duties. In the case of Ely Ould Mohamed Vall, only images of his 'glory years' (following the 2005 coup against Taya) are shown, while his darker years are left out. In the case of Ali Beiba, archive images retrace the stages of his life as a statesman, seeking to show the exemplary nature of his life. Photographs of the man are intermingled with photographs of the state funeral. A Sahrawi blogger even takes the liberty of using (again 'hijacking') a funeral song written for another to commemorate Ali Beiba, a move which is likely to be shocking to Mauritanian audiences who know both Maalouma, the author of the song, and the figure to whom she originally paid such poignant tribute, the journalist Habib Ould Mahfoudh. With this noted, it should be remembered that 'covering' poems and songs is commonplace in the oral tradition and seems to remain fairly widespread on the internet.[31]

The question of temporality is also essential to the renewal of the elegiac genre. We know that these poems are usually composed in the moments or days following the subject's death and on the occasion of funerals. It is on such occasions that tributes are most likely to have an effect on the audience, composed and recited on the spot and in circumstances in which poets can best express the grief that is being experienced collectively. Forms of 'secondary orality' (Ong 1982), mediated by audiovisual technologies but interpreted in the context of death, or 'neo-orality' (Ong 1982), made after the fact and recorded for editing and dissemination on the internet, then take precedence over 'primary orality'.[32] The homage is no longer necessarily performed in a funeral context and gives rise to a more sophisticated creation that will have more of a commemorative dimension. The mediatized and deferred homage and the oralized written word take precedence over the immediacy of a rhyming oration. Even when the tribute is paid in the days following a death and posted on the internet, it loses its ephemeral character, now preserved on the web. Given the political dimension of these tributes, these new temporalities can pose problems for the authors, their relatives, the political movement to which the deceased belonged, etc., in shifting political contexts (in Mauritania in particular).

Do these new ways of paying homage to political figures reconfigure the *rithā*ʾ genre, and do they contribute, as Robin Azevedo proposes, 'to the development of a visual culture of death and the afterlife that energizes ancestral principles of homage to the dead by adapting them to the new dematerialized context of the internet' (2020: 20–1)? The creation of such works, Dauphin-Tinturier and Derive remind us, 'is situated in principle in relation to a certain number of canonical rules, often unspoken but nevertheless perceived, with which the creator plays in a subtle dialectic between respect and transgression' (2005: 11). To address these questions, we must return to the notion of genre, helped by the field of ethnopoetics: '[I]f there are indeed generic constraints at the origin of successful performances … it is difficult, if not impossible, to enunciate a corpus of rules that would objectify this genre. Counter-examples always arise' (Dupont 2010: 14). As Dupont goes on to note, '[t]he borderline cases make it possible to see how the invariants can be varied without transgressing the genre' (15). Initially isolated, these poems – sung and put to images – become models for other artists and bloggers, who eventually compete. This is the conclusion we came to (Boulay 2018a) when examining another sensitive poetic genre, the *shemt*, which is more widely publicized today via social media and the internet, although these types of satirical and defamatory poems, smearing the reputation of the subject and his family and exposing the performer to reprisals, were not intended to be widely shared.

Our 'borderline cases' transgress traditional canons in different ways, whether because they 1) are sung to joyful music; 2) 'pirate' or 'hijack' songs originally dedicated to one deceased person to pay tribute to another who has no connection to the first; 3) appear online, where they are preserved; 4) emphasize the qualities of the deceased such that listeners are likely to view the poem as false and hypocritical; 5) are sung by a woman passionately paying tribute to a man to whom she was not related; or 6) are used (politically) to overshadow an enemy of the deceased (as in Lemseydev's poem). These different types of transgression are each capable of disrupting the canons of the genre.

It is therefore interesting to consider whether this new type of funeral tribute (involving spoken messages, musical performances and photomontages) will generate new canons and whether the contrast between funeral poems and joyful songs will itself become canonical.

Death, memory and politics: The semantic 'hijacking' of the West Saharan rithāʾ

The political force of a funeral tribute primarily comes down to the identity of the artist who performs it, in particular his or her authority in the artistic, public and even political arena. The idea would seem to be that it takes artists of a certain stature, authoritative artists (Bourdieu 2001), to commemorate heroic figures, just as it takes artists of a certain weight to dare to address satirical poems to well-known traitors

(Boulay 2018b). An artist's proximity to power (Mohamed Ould Taleb), relation to the opposition (Lemseydev, Eleyya, Maalouma) or national/international fame (Mohamed Ould Taleb, Maalouma, Mohamed Salem Meidah) all contribute to the poem's meaning and reception. What is decisive is not merely the artist's talent but his or her image and reputation. Moreover, recognition of some of these artists as 'committed' necessarily gives their tributes a special dimension: the tribute to the opposition figure Ely Ould Mohamed Vall portrayed him as having so much national and international significance, for instance, that the poem inevitably served to denigrate those currently in power. Especially in the Mauritanian context, these tributes have become spaces of confrontation and competition, where artists attempt to gain favour or seek recognition from the relatives of the deceased and/or his or her political movement.

On the Sahrawi side, the griot remains a sought-after spokesperson for political messages. Of central importance to the Sahrawis is finding the griot or griotte who will perform the relevant poetic oration in the most beautiful way and who will thus allow it to be disseminated as widely as possible on social media and the internet. Mohamed Salem Meidah is typical in this regard, and other Mauritanian griots regularly agree to sing for pro-Moroccan or pro-Polisario Sahrawi poets. By restricting themselves to singing poems that have been written by others, such singers circumscribe their role as (simple) performers, maintaining their political immunity as griots and thus protecting themselves from reprisals. Because of their social role and statutory position, griots are not considered responsible for the content of the poetic compositions they perform; they are enlisted by others to praise or denigrate different figures, for which they are compensated financially. Whether or not they express civic commitments, griots continue to play a very important role in the political arena and in competition between groups – both on the national scale and on the broader scale of the hassanophone West Saharan area, where their travels receive much publicity – since their ability to amplify the political messages and positions of their sponsors is well known and feared.

These online tributes have become full-fledged modes of political action – of infrapolitics, in the sense discussed by Scott (2019 [1992]) – which, when the public sphere no longer offers people the chance to express themselves, allow people to give free rein to their political positions from the private sphere and under the cover of pseudonyms, protecting them from reprisals from the regime. As in other areas of resistance in the Arab world and elsewhere, Sahrawi bloggers have demonstrated a certain creativity in dramatizing the lives of these martyr figures. The author of the photomontage featuring Maalouma's song inserts a video of Sahrawi women from the occupied territories gathered at one of their homes, wearing black veils as a sign of mourning and brandishing photos of the 'martyr Mahfudh Ali Beiba', an iconic protest grammar that Cécile Boex has described in the context of the war in Syria (2012: 128).

In addition to the type of media used (official, protest, amateur, local/regional/national, etc.), which gives the internet user information on the 'provenance' and political tone of the work, the reception of these tributes depends on the proximity (political, but also social, tribal, geographical, generational, etc.) of the audience to the deceased. Mahfud Ali Beiba enjoys fairly broad popularity in the Sahrawi independence community, and above all, as Eric Butel recalls in relation to the victims of the Iran–Iraq War, '[t]he martyr bears witness to the ontologically just nature of the struggle between true Islam and the forces of evil' (2002: 306). To celebrate the martyrdom of Mahfud Ali Beiba is to say that he belongs to this Sahrawi nation, an 'imagined community' that is struggling to exercise its rights and to recover its land. Yet it is also to mark its difference from a part of the Sahrawi population that subscribes to Moroccan views and disagrees with the nationalist and pro-independence rhetoric of the Polisario Front. The same goes for Ely Ould Mohamed Vall, whose coup against Taya cannot eclipse, in the eyes of many Mauritanians, his many years as the head of the national police under the same leader. Despite his 'less glorious' past, the three tributes aim to make him an undisputed and indisputable national hero, capable of reconciling Mauritanians around a single nation. These commemorative acts are as much a reminder as they are a cover for certain pages of the past (Ricoeur 2000), and these policies of remembrance aim to situate the heroic figures in political contexts and histories in which they did not enjoy widespread approval and even provoked much criticism. As Robin Azevedo reminds us, these memories 'are rarely consensual and remain a constantly disputed field' (2019: 19).

Like satirical poems (*shemt*), which remain rare but in which the poets recall the values to be respected in political life and the red lines not to cross (Boulay 2018b), these tributes are aimed at the descendants of the deceased, and by extension the rest of the community, reminding them of what brings them together: first and foremost a commitment to Islam and its values, but also the qualities of responsibility, wisdom and courage associated with political commitment. In the Sahrawi revolutionary tradition, which bestows the status of martyr on anyone who has played a role, however modest, in resisting the occupation of their land, these prestigious martyrs are above all models of commitment and sacrifice. They represent the way forward for the young, in service of 'the cause'. In Mauritania and the Sahrawi context, the images of flags and uniforms are there to underscore the tension between these individual lives and the collective destiny of the nation. Like the body of the sovereign in Kantorowicz (1989 [1957]), the dead body of the hero, whether a martyr or not, plays a role in constructing the nation (Kastoryano 2020: 177).

Commemorating these national heroes in the most beautiful way possible is a way of dealing with the collective loss of highly esteemed personalities while remobilizing their political entourages, who will now be able to follow their examples and continue the fight in their memory. The online preservation of these hagiographic stories offers the political community of the deceased an opportunity to re-immerse itself in his or her exemplary life. Pierre Centlivres reminds us that '[b]y accepting martyrdom, the *shahīd* testifies doubly; firstly to his attachment and fidelity to Islam, and secondly to the truth and legitimacy of the cause for which he allows himself to die' (2002: 322). This takes on its full meaning in the SADR, where this commemorative tradition has been deeply rooted and organized in national social and political life since the Western Saharan War (1976–1991), which plunged the families in the Tindouf refugee camps into mourning. Any festivity, any political event (the Polisario Congress, for example), no matter how minor, is an occasion to pay tribute to a famous and recent martyr, not to mention the days of homage, such as 9 June, the date of the death of El-Ouali, or 8 March, the anniversary of the death (in 1974) of the first anti-colonial martyr of the Polisario Front, Bachir Lahlaoui (Tabet and Boulay 2020). Civilian victims of Moroccan repression in the occupied territories are also celebrated, as are the disappeared, who are held up as quasi-martyrs. For the Sahrawis, the challenge seems to be to ensure the continuity of the struggle among the new generations, at a time when the first cadres of the Polisario Front are passing on. The different media used to portray these martyrs – poems, songs, portraits and parades on national holidays – structure Sahrawi collective memory, which must reach the greatest number if it is to transform a situation of political fragility into a message of strength and hope for the living.

While each of these tributes has its own 'national' audience, delimited on the Sahrawi side by the lexical field of martyrdom (and therefore of jihad) and by a particular style of photomontage, and while an oration to Mahfud Ali Beiba will essentially affect Sahrawis, in particular those who are militants or who sympathize with the Polisario Front, their reception nonetheless seems capable of going beyond the borders of this 'imagined community' to possibly reach, perhaps with less intensity, a wider hassanophone audience. The Moors of Mauritania, and in particular the Moors of the north of the country (the Ahl al-Sāḥil, who are often related to the Sahrawis), are quite receptive to cultural productions from Western Sahara, whether from the Moroccan channel TV Laayoune, which targets the Sahrawi and, more broadly, Hassanophone public,[33] or from the refugee camps of Tindouf, where Mauritanians appreciate these poets.[34] In the same way, the Sahrawis continue to admire the Mauritanian poets and the griots, keepers of West Saharan music, whom they do not hesitate to solicit to convey their messages. These two national traditions of *rithā'* are therefore not hermetically sealed from each other and reveal numerous bridges – bridges that are strengthened by social media and web platforms for sharing audiovisual material, but also by the physical circulation of artists on a regional scale.

Acknowledgements

This text benefited from valuable feedback and suggestions from Nadia Belalimat, Abdel Wedoud Ould Cheikh, Jean Derive, Mick Gewinner and Catherine Taine-Cheikh, for which we are very grateful.

Notes

1 Work carried out as part of the MINWEB programme (2015–2017, funding Emergence-Ville de Paris), then the Capsahara programme (European Research Council (ERC) under the European Union's Horizon 2020 research and innovation programme, Grant Agreement No. 716467), and presented at the World Congress for Middle-Eastern Studies (WOCMES), Seville, July 2018.

2 On these different poetic genres, see in particular the work of Taine-Cheikh (1985, 1994, 2004 and 2018) and Tauzin (2013). On contemporary poetic practice, see the very fine ethnographic study by Schinz (2009).

3 Figures represented by the two red stripes that frame the new Mauritanian flag. On political issues surrounding the memorializing of anti-colonial resistance in Mauritania, see in particular Mohamed Baba and Freire (2020).
4 On this learned musical tradition, see the reference work by Michel Guignard (2005).
5 These poems date back to the period (spanning the 1910s to the 1930s) of resistance to French colonial occupation and were the subject of a new national interest in the context of the state's desire to rewrite national history, under the presidency of Mohamed Ould Abdel Aziz (2008–2019). On the history of resistance literature in Mauritania, see Boyé (1988).
6 On funeral rituals in Mauritania, see Lagdaf (2017).
7 This is the classic form of the Arabic poem: '[…] the *qaṣīda* (pl. *qaṣā'd*) is a poem of at least seven verses, usually much longer, monorime and plurithematic, built on the same meter' (Toelle and Zakharia 2003: 63).
8 WhatsApp is an instant messaging application for smartphones, where messages (along with images, videos, audio recordings, etc.) are sent and received via the internet.
9 Ely Ould Mohamed Vall, Wikipedia, https://fr.wikipedia.org/wiki/Ely_Ould_Mohamed_Vall.
10 Assuming we can rely on the number of views these productions have had – an indicator that should be taken with caution, since we know that these figures can be artificially inflated.
11 Mohamed Ould Taleb, YouTube, https://www.youtube.com/watch?v=_YvF0pLuJWg.
12 Still widely translated in the anthropological literature as 'tribe', the term designates a group of agnatic filiation whose members claim a common ancestor.
13 Mohamed Yahya Ould Lemseydev, YouTube, https://www.youtube.com/watch?v=q8R0bCKXZsI&t=120s.
14 The *gāv* is the most widespread form of Moorish dialectal poetry, a poem usually consisting of two lines (rarely three), each made up of two hemistiches. The rhymes are crossed: the first hemistich rhymes with the third, the second with the fourth (ab/ab). The *ṭle'* (pl. of *ṭal'a*) are longer poems that usually follow an aa/ab/ab/ab/ structure. A poem can thus have several *ṭle'* with different themes and rhymes, interspersed with the same *gāv*. See Taine-Cheikh (1985) and (2018).
15 https://www.youtube.com/watch?v=tSIwj86nxIk.
16 And it is the hallmark of *the gāv* to be more incisive, to the point of being able to be said alone (personal communication with C. Taine-Cheikh, February 2021).
17 Za'īm 'Allāl al-Dāf is one of the most important contemporary 'national' poets (Gimeno Martín et al. 2020). Interviews conducted in the Tindouf refugee camps in February 2017 and March 2019.
18 On the place of martyrs in the Sahrawi society of the Tindouf camps, see the documentary film we made in the framework of the Capsahara project: Tabet and Boulay (2020).
19 For C. Taine-Cheikh, this attitude may also be related to the fact that there are no griots among the Sahrawis. However, it is the role of griots in Mauritania to praise – a role that is almost forbidden to non-griots because giving praise in dialect puts the one giving praise in a position of social inferiority (personal communication, February 2021).
20 Interview conducted in February/March 2017 in Smara camp. Bechir Ould Ely is one of the best-known 'national' poets in the camps, as well as the long-time host of a radio and TV programme dedicated to poetry and music.
21 An excerpt of the song can be found here: https://www.youtube.com/watch?v=atm1NnVdWDU. Also see Wikipedia, Mariem Hassan (1958– 2015), https://fr.wikipedia.org/wiki/Mariem_Hassan.

22 This work was analysed in Boulay and Dahmi (2020).
23 Interview conducted in Smara camp on 6 March 2015.
24 https://www.youtube.com/watch?v=qIuVOqe-eB0.
25 https://www.youtube.com/watch?v=dgaYnyV6Xk4.
26 https://www.youtube.com/watch?v=hahbWMW5zeA (note: this link is no longer accessible or searchable).
27 See the article that Taine-Cheikh (2013) devoted to this very committed artist.
28 Photomontage posted online on 24 March 2015: https://www.youtube.com/watch?v=87Ap07nFbzM.
29 https://www.youtube.com/watch?v=qd8pFNClvPk.
30 'These canonical norms more or less consciously form a frame of reference, and conformity to or, on the contrary, transgression of these conventional features can be one criterion among others for assessing the degree of creativity at work in a particular interpretation' (Dauphin-Tinturier and Derive: 2005: 10).
31 Personal communication with Mick Gewinner (February 2021).
32 On the relationship between oral and written works in Moorish society, see the concept of 'aurality' in Taine-Cheikh (1998: 175), which emphasizes the importance of hearing in the teaching and transmission of texts that are intended to be 'uttered and heard as well as read' (Cheikh 2020: 328).
33 A channel which had some success in Mauritania when it was launched in the mid-2000s, at a time when the audiovisual sector in Mauritania had not yet opened up to private channels.
34 A large segment of Mauritanian society remains largely sealed off from what is happening in the Western Sahara and from everything that concerns the Sahrawi population, however, as the Western Sahara War, in which Mauritania took part from 1975 to 1979, has left dark traces on the collective imagination, first because of its victims, and second because of its consequences for Mauritanian national political life (the coup against President Ould Daddah and the seizure of power by the military, which still controls the country today).

References

Boex, C. (2012), 'Montrer, dire et lutter par l'image', *Vacarme*, 61: 118–31.

Bornand, S. and J. Derive (2018), 'Introduction', in S. Bornand and J. Derive (eded.), *Les canons du discours et la langue*, 11–23. Paris: Karthala.

Boulay, S. (2018a), 'Une poésie offensive et offensante du Sahara occidental … à l'épreuve des canons', in S. Bornand and J. Derive (eds), *Les canons du discours et la langue. Parler juste*, 169–96. Paris: Karthala.

Boulay, S. (2018b), 'Sismique de la dissidence et diffamation poétique au Sahara Occidental. Quand les artistes sahraouis condamnent ou défendent les puissants', in P. Chaudat and M. Lachheb (eds), *Transgresser au Maghreb. La normalité et ses dépassements*, 147–71. Paris: IRMC-Karthala.

Boulay, S. and M. Dahmi (2020), 'Humor, Mockery and Defamation in Western Sahara: How do Sahrawi Artists use New Media to Perform Political Criticism?', in S. Damir-Geilsdorf and S. Milich (eds), *Creative Resistance: Political Humor in the Arab Uprisings*, 79–101. Bielefeld: Transcript Verlag.

Bourdieu, P. (2001), *Langage et pouvoir symbolique*. Paris: Seuil.

Boyé, M. O. (1988), *Contribution à l'histoire littéraire de la Mauritanie, de la pénétration coloniale à nos jours*, doctoral theis, université de la Sorbonne nouvelle Paris III.

Bozarslan, H. (2002), 'La figure du martyr chez les Kurdes', in C. Mayeur-Jaouen (ed.), *Saints et héros du Moyen-Orient contemporain*, 335–47. Paris: Maisonneuve et Larose.

Bromberger, C. and E. Mahieddin (2016), 'Introduction. Penser l'exception', *Ethnologie française*, XLVI, 3: 389–93.

Butel, E. (2002), 'Martyre et sainteté dans la littérature de guerre Irak-Iran', in C. Mayeur-Jaouen (ed.), *Saints et héros du Moyen-Orient contemporain*, 301–17. Paris: Maisonneuve et Larose.

Centlivres, P. (2001), *Saints, sainteté et martyre. La fabrication de l'exemplarité*. Neuchâtel: Éditions de l'Institut d'ethnologie/Paris: Éditions de la Maison des sciences de l'homme.

Centlivres, P. and M. Centlivres-Demont (2002), 'Les martyrs afghans par le texte et l'image (1978-1992)', in C. Mayeur-Jaouen (ed.), *Saints et héros du Moyen-Orient contemporain*, 319–33. Paris: Maisonneuve et Larose.

Centlivres, P., D. Fabre and F. Zonabend, eds (1998), *La fabrique des héros*. Paris: Éditions de la Maison des sciences de l'homme.

Clerc-Renaud, A. and C. Leguy (2016), 'Editorial', *Des vies extraordinaires: les territoires du récit, Cahiers de la littérature orale*, 79: 13–20.

Dauphin-Tinturier, A.-M. and J. Derive, eds (2005), *Oralité africaine et création*. Paris: Karthala.

Diawara, M. (2014), 'La fabrique des héros en Afrique subsaharienne', *Présence africaine*, 190: 31–60.

Dupont F. (2010), 'Introduction', in C. Calame, F. Dupont F., B. Lortat-Jacob and M. Manca (ed.), *La voix actée. Pour une nouvelle ethnopoétique*, 7–20. Paris: Éditions Kimé.

Georges F. (2020), 'Éternités numériques', in V. Robin Azevedo (ed.), *[Im]matérialités de la mort*, 69–87. Paris: CNRS Éditions, Les essentiels d'Hermès.

Gimeno Martín J. C., M. A. Laman Robles, J. I. Robles Picón, B. M. Awah, M. S. Abdelfatah and V. Solana Moreno (2020), *Poetas y poesía del Sahara Occidental. Antología de la poesía nacional saharaui*. Málaga: Última Línea.

Guignard, M. (2005), *Musique, Honneur Et Plaisir Au Sahara*, French edn. Paris: Librairie Orientaliste Paul Geuthner.

Kantorowicz, E. (1989 [1957]), *Les deux corps du roi*. Paris: Gallimard.

Kastoryano, R. (2020), 'La mort et le djihadiste. Redéfinir le territoire dans la globalisation', in V. Robin Azevedo (ed.), *[Im]matérialités de la mort*, 171–85. Paris: CNRS Éditions, Les essentiels d'Hermès.

Lagdaf, S. (2017), 'The cult of the dead in Mauritania: between traditions and religious commandments", *The Journal of North African Studies*, 22 (2): 283–300.

Mayeur-Jaouen, C., ed. (2002), *Saints et héros du Moyen-Orient contemporain*. Paris: Maisonneuve et Larose.

Mohammad-Arif, A. and J. Schmitz, eds (2006), *Figures d'Islam après le 11 septembre. Disciples et martyrs, réfugiés et migrants*. Paris: Karthala.

Mohamed Baba, E. O. and F. Freire (2020), 'Looters vs. Traitors: The Muqawama ("Resistance") Narrative, and its Detractors, in Contemporary Mauritania', *African Studies Review*, 63 (2): 258–80.

Ong, W. J. (1982), *Orality and Literacy. The Technologizing of the World*, London and New York, NY: Methuen.

Ould Cheikh, A. W. (2020), 'Anthropologie et/ou histoire entre oralité et écriture', in Y. Ben Hounet, A.-M. Brisebarre, B. Casciarri and A. W. Ould Cheikh (eds), *L'anthropologie en partage. Autour de l'œuvre de Pierre Bonte*, 327–47. Paris: Karthala.

Pellat, C. (1990), 'Marthiya', in *Encyclopédie de l'Islam*, 587–92. Leiden, Brill, Paris: Maisonneuve & Larose.

Ricoeur, P. (2000), *La Mémoire, l'histoire et l'oubli*. Paris: Seuil.

Robin Azevedo, V. (2019), *Sur les sentiers de la violence. Politiques de la mémoire et conflit armé au Pérou*. IHEAL Editions.

Robin Azevedo, V. (2020), 'Communiquer (avec) la mort hier et aujourd'hui. Gestion, présence et circulation des défunts', in V. Robin Azevedo (ed.), *[Im]matérialités de la mort*, 9–31. Paris: CNRS Éditions, Les essentiels d'Hermès.

Ruano Posada, V. (2016), '"Sahara Ma Timbah" "The Sahara Is Not For Sale"): Music, Resistance, and Exile in Saharawi Culture', PhD thesis, School of Oriental and African Studies (SOAS), University of London.

Schmitt. J.-C., ed. (1983), *Les Saints et les Stars. Le texte hagiographique dans la culture populaire*. Paris: Beauchesne.

Schinz, O. (2009), *Dans le feu de la parole. Jouer avec les mots en Mauritanie*, doctoral thesis de la Faculté des lettres et des sciences humaines, Université de Neuchâtel, Neuchâtel.

Tabet, M. and S. Boulay (2020), *SAHARA – Les voix des martyrs* [film] Paris, prod. Capsahara and CEPED.

Taine-Cheikh, C. (1985), 'Le pilier et la corde: recherches sur la poésie maure', *Bulletin of SOAS*, XLVIII/3: 516–35.

Taine-Cheikh, C. (1994), 'Pouvoir de la poésie et poésie du pouvoir. Le cas de la société maure', *Matériaux arabes et sudarabiques*, 6: 281–310.

Taine-Cheikh, C. (1998), 'Langues, savoirs et pouvoirs en milieu maure', in P. Bonte and H. Claudot-Hawad (eds), *Savoirs et pouvoirs au Sahara, Nomadic Peoples*, 2 (1–2): 215–34.

Taine-Cheikh, C. (2004), 'De l'injure en pays maure ou 'qui ne loue pas critique', in E. Larguèche (ed.), *L'injure, la société, l'islam. Une anthropologie de l'injure, Revue des mondes musulmans et de la Méditerranée*, 103–4: 103–26.

Taine-Cheikh, C. (2013), 'Les chansons de Malouma, entre tradition, world music et engagement politique', in L. Bettini and P. La Spisa (eds), *Au-delà de l'arabe standard. Moyen arabe et arabe mixte dans les sources médiévales, modernes et contemporaines*, 337–62. Dipartimento di Linguistica, Università di Firenze (coll. Quaderni di Semistica no. 28).

Taine-Cheikh, C. (2018), 'Canons poétiques et poésies canoniques dans la culture maure', in S. Bornand and J. Derive (eds), *Les canons du discours et la langue. Parler juste*, 141–68. Paris: Karthala.

Tauzin, A. (2013), *Littérature orale de Mauritanie. De la fable au rap*. Paris: Karthala.

Toelle, H. and K. Zakharia (2003), *A la découverte de la littérature arabe du VIe siècle à nos jours*. Paris: Flammarion.

8

Haratin activism in post-slavery Mauritania: Abolition, emancipation and the politics of identity

David Malluche

CRIA – NOVA FCSH, Doctoral Researcher at Capsahara

Introduction: Post-slavery and citizenship struggles in West Africa

The history and legacies of African slavery and contemporary social and political mobilizations have received increased scholarly attention in recent years.[1] These studies are often situated in the context of 'post-slavery', a conceptual approach comparable to that of postcolonialism in that it equally stresses the resilience and legacies of ideologies, mentalities and social hierarchies of slaveholder societies in a chronological 'after', despite the legal abolition and official 'end' of slavery. Benedetta Rossi (2015: 304) has criticized this field of scholarship for its linear historical view when considering the transition from slavery to emancipation and the tendency to define the moral illegitimacy of slavery (and other extreme forms of dependency) as a universal norm – a normative stance not reflecting the reality of many post-slavery societies, notably in Africa. In certain contexts, legal and normative pluralism account both for the partial perpetuation and reactivation of master–slave relations despite abolitionist legislation and for conflicting understandings and discourses of emancipation.

This conceptualization of post-slavery conforms with the situation that can be observed in the Islamic Republic of Mauritania, where slavery and hierarchical distinctions among descent-based status groups seem particularly unaffected by colonial rule and abolitionist policies. Whereas 'traditional' forms of slavery have gradually receded due to extensive ecological, economic and social transformations, descent-based status hierarchies largely persist in the country. The same holds true for many other states in the extended region. Eric Hahonou and Lotte Pelckmans (2011) take a comparative perspective on West African anti-slavery movements and interpret them as 'citizenship struggles' of slaves and slave descendants in the context of the conflicting political ideologies of democracy and aristocracy, which can be mutually contextualized within such plural legal landscapes. They therefore propose a social movement theory perspective – an approach that has been developed and used mainly in the context of Western societies, although it has been increasingly (and fruitfully) applied in African contexts in recent years (Ellis and van Kessel 2009) – applied to abolitionist and emancipatory struggles. Based on this comparative perspective, they argue 'that social movements such as anti-slavery struggles concerning identity are not replacing struggles over material issues, as observed by social movement theorists in European contexts, but are closely interlinked', as 'in West African contexts of political and institutional reform implementation, demands for recognition of new identities are a way of accessing resources' (Eric Hahonou and Lotte Pelckmans 2011: 141). The anti-slavery movements they analyse emerged in francophone West Africa in the late 1970s, but they have grown in scale since the 1990s, thanks in part to the democratization and decentralization policies that have been increasingly advanced since that period.[2] These political processes have created new possibilities of participation and organization for formerly marginalized status groups in the region and had an impact on local notions of social identity, resulting in renegotiations of traditional hierarchies, religious normativity and the (attempted) creation of new ethnicities (Pelckmans and Hardung 2015: 19).

The renegotiation of identity and status among the various groups of slave descendants in West Africa thus exhibits certain parallels with what has come to be known as 'identity politics' in the context of multicultural Western democracies, as they often strive to transform the stigmatized social identity that has historically been ascribed to them by the dominant strata of their respective societies into a source of positive group identification and collective mobilization.[3] In this sense, they use the affirmation of difference and pursue strategies associated with the 'politics of recognition' (Taylor 1994) as a means of emancipation and of claiming collective rights as citizens. However, the explicit claim to be recognized as a distinct 'ethnic group' seems to be a peculiar feature of some of these West African anti-slavery movements, which might well be related to the special nexus of ethnicity and citizenship created through colonial rule in Africa (see Keller 2014; Mamdani 1996).

This chapter focuses on the development of an abolitionist and emancipatory social movement among the Mauritanian Ḥarāṭīn, from its emergence in the late 1970s to the present. In particular, it examines the ways in which the members of this socio-ethnic group, usually defined as hassanophone[4] slave descendants of Black African origin in the Mauritanian context,[5] have challenged the hierarchical social model that is largely acknowledged in the region, attempting to remove the stigma still attached to their (supposed) slave ancestry and formulating demands for civil rights, political inclusion and positive discrimination on the grounds of their specific socio-ethnic identity. In this context, I argue that the question of 'ethnogenesis' in relation to the profound socioeconomic transformations experienced by the extended hassanophone society and political activism among the Mauritanian Ḥarāṭīn since the 1970s constitutes a gap in the scholarship devoted to the region. Furthermore, the observation of distinctive identity politics in relation to the Mauritanian and other West African anti-slavery movements may also be linked to debates on culturally defined (ethnic) minorities and collective rights in international human rights law (Thompson 1997) and to a global shift in the articulation of social movements and political demands from class issues to cultural identities (Hechter 2004), a process that is rarely discussed in non-Western contexts. As globalization has now reached even the remotest corners of the Sahara (Choplin 2009; Hill 2012; Scheele 2012), these developments also deserve to be considered in such supposedly 'peripheral' African contexts as the Mauritanian one. In order to fully grasp this phenomenon, we must pay attention to larger political conflicts related to identity issues, which have been engendered by colonial and postcolonial state-building and nationalist ideologies.

Constructivist anthropological perspectives on ethnicity help to shed light on the current renegotiation of traditional social designs and identities in the Islamic Republic of Mauritania.[6] Whereas the primordialist conception of ethnicity has largely been abandoned due to its analytical flaws (primordial notions of ethnicity cannot serve as an explanation, but rather require explanation themselves), purely instrumental accounts of ethnic phenomena as resulting from the strategic mobilization of certain identities for contemporary political or economic purposes have often tended to neglect history and 'culture' as deeper sources of group dynamics in the *longue durée*. Although ethnic identities are continually re-elaborated in response to changing circumstances, they cannot be 'invented' arbitrarily in short periods of time for purely instrumental reasons and without the necessary 'historical material' to work with. In the context of African politics, primordialist and instrumentalist approaches to ethnicity alike have tended to focus on ethnic phenomena related to the notion of 'political tribalism', as an obstacle to modern statehood, inclusive citizenship and a driver of 'ethnic conflict' (see, for example, Alumona and Azom 2018). More nuanced constructivist approaches to ethnicity and nationalism that have been developed since the 1980s can help us to make sense of Mauritania's postcolonial history and the claims voiced by Ḥarāṭīn activists.[7] Based on his research on ethnic politics in Africa, Lonsdale (1994) argues that the language of ethnicity came to serve as a vehicle for disputes within groups regarding the normative basis of political community, a development that he describes as 'moral ethnicity'. In this sense, he argues, contemporary African ethnicity should not be directly equated with 'political tribalism' and should instead be understood 'as *a form of nationalism*, an intellectually imaginative political project of liberation that makes modern claims on behalf of civil rights, directly comparable with European nationalisms, if also sharing their Janus-faced potential for exclusive, jealous evil'. He urges us to think of ethnic nationalism in Africa 'as, in large part, a moral struggle with all the complexities of social change that our previous analyses had barely begun to understand' (Lonsdale 1994: 136). This notion of 'moral ethnicity' resonates with what Hahonou and Pelckmans describe as 'citizenship struggles' of slave descendants in francophone West Africa. Post-slavery societies in Africa are strongly characterized by such moral struggles, as different ideologies concerning the normative basis of community and political authority coexist and wage a 'war of position'.

Slavery, race and social order in precolonial Bīḍān society

Like many other West African and Saharan populations, the Bīḍān have historically adhered to a hierarchical model in which genealogical bonds and institutionalized relations of patronage and dependency served to legitimize and stabilize social stratification, including slavery.[8] Bīḍān culture and society developed after Arab 'tribes'[9] migrated from North Africa towards the western fringes of the Sahara from the fourteenth to the seventeenth centuries, successively subjecting the local population of Amazighs and Black Africans to a tributary position and eventually Arabizing the region following their victory over a Amazigh coalition in the religiously inspired rebellion of *Shurbubba* (c. 1644–1674; see Norris 1986).[10] The formally acknowledged social order of the larger hassanophone sphere distinguishes the 'noble'/'free' status groups of the 'warriors' (*ḥassān*) and 'marabouts' (*zwāya*) from their tributaries and dependents: tributary herders of Amazigh origin (*znāga*); 'blacksmiths' (*m'allemīn*) specialized in craftsmanship; 'griots' (*iggāwen*); the descendants of manumitted slaves (*ḥarāṭīn*); and slaves (*'abīd*). These kinship and status groups were integrated into a 'segmentary' system of dynamic alliances based on the principle of patronage and protection in return for submission and tributes, which gave rise to the four precolonial Moorish emirates of Trarza, Brakna, Adrar and Tagant in the eighteenth and nineteenth centuries (Bonte 2008; Ould Cheikh 2017). The historical existence of slavery among the Bīḍān, as in most parts of Muslim Africa, was regulated by local traditions of Maliki Islamic jurisprudence (Oßwald 2016, 2017). It has been argued that local *zwāyā* scholars strove to sacralize the institution of slavery and the larger social order of descent-based status groups as a God-given natural order by instrumentalizing their proficiency in Islamic knowledge and excluding those of slave descent from religious education (Esseissah 2016). They undoubtedly asserted a cultural hegemony that continues to reverberate in contemporary society.

The Bīḍān share an ethno-linguistic identity vis-à-vis neighbouring Sub-saharan African populations (Halpulaaren, Soninké, Wolof and Bambara, collectively referred to as *kwār* in Hassaniyya Arabic) that is based on their nomadic cultural heritage (whereas the Black African communities were largely sedentary agriculturalists)[11] and the Hassaniyya dialect of Arabic (also referred to as *klām al-bīḍān*, 'language the Bīḍān', which additionally differentiates them from neighbouring populations like the Tuareg and North African Arabs). One might therefore argue that Bīḍān identity has no racial connotations, as in its broader ethno-linguistic sense it includes hassanophone black slaves and Ḥarāṭīn and because, after centuries of intermarriage and blending between the various ethnic groups of the region,[12] skin colour does not necessarily correlate with alleged genealogical origins. However, historians Bruce Hall (2011) and Chouki El Hamel (2013) have convincingly argued that indiginous concepts of race developed in the West African Sahel well before the arrival of the European colonizers and formed an integral part of the way in which precolonial social identities and hierarchies that legitimized the large-scale enslavement of Black Africans were constructed, as 'blackness' became deeply associated with non-Muslim/pagan origins and therefore with a generalized eligibility for slavery.

The Arabic ethnonym *bīḍān* literally translates as 'the whites'. In the context of the Sahara, this colour terminology refers to Arab-Muslim origins. When applied internally to Bīḍān society, the term *bīḍān* has a statutory meaning and refers exclusively to the free/noble (*ḥurr*) status groups of the *ḥassān* and the *zwāya*, whereas slaves and Ḥarāṭīn are subsumed under the label *sūdān* ('the blacks') (Brhane 1997, 2000).[13] Although skin colour alone is not a definitive marker of social status and alleged patrilineal descent, there is undoubtedly a strong overlap between 'blackness' and inferior social rank in Arab-Muslim social and cultural history (see also Lewis 1992). Race must therefore also be considered an important element of social identification and stratification in the Sahara, although individuals and groups were historically considered 'white' or 'black' because of their (alleged) genealogical origins and associated status categories, not because of their skin colour or other phenotypical features. Only with the advent of French colonial rule were earlier indigenous conceptions of social identity supplanted by the modern 'scientific' European concept of race (Villasante-de Beauvais 2007b), which exerted an important influence on their subsequent transformations. Based on European conceptions of racial difference, the French categorized the hassanophone population into 'black Moors' (slaves and Ḥarāṭīn) and 'white Moors' (Bīḍān) based on skin colour.

The etymological origin of the term *ḥarāṭīn* (sing. *ḥarṭānī*) is disputed. A popular version claims that it derives from the Arabic words *ḥurr* ('free') and *ṯānī* ('second') and conveys the meaning 'freemen of second degree'. Others trace it to the Arabic verbal root *ḥ-r-th*, which means 'to cultivate', and translate *ḥarāṭīn* as 'cultivators'. Linguist Catherine Taine-Cheikh (1989) in turn refutes the thesis of an Arabic etymology and argues that it most likely derives from the Berber lexeme *āḥarḍān*, which denotes a mixture of races (of animals or humans) and colours, especially in the sense of 'becoming darker/black'. Corinne Fortier (2020) recently argued that in Hassaniyya the term *ḥarr* can also carry the meaning of 'pure' and that *ḥarṭānī* translates as 'unpure' in opposition to it. Ḥarāṭīn populations can be found throughout the entire western Saharan region and the Sahel, in a region that includes (apart from Mauritania) southern Morocco, northern Mali and southwestern Algeria (the precolonial *Trāb al-Bīḍān*, 'land of the whites'). The Islamic Republic of Mauritania, however, is the only contemporary state with a Hassaniyya-speaking majority population, in which the Ḥarāṭīn form the largest demographic group (approx. 40 per cent), ahead of the Bīḍān (approx. 30 per cent) and the Halpulaaren, Soninké and Wolof (together approx. 30 per cent).[14]

As membership in a *qabīla* in the Arab-Muslim world is generally expressed symbolically in terms of genealogy (*naṣab*) and kinship (Bonte et al. 1991), the case of the Ḥarāṭīn is a curious one: they are considered part of their respective Bīḍān *qabīla*, but only as subordinate clients who are excluded from genealogical affiliation with the constitutive kinship groups.[15] Their attachment to the *qabīla* is generally based on the Islamic legal concept of *walāʾ* – which designates a contractual clientelist relation of mutual solidarity with their former masters into which former slaves automatically enter following their formal manumission – and not on reciprocal kinship, as men of slave origin generally were (and to a large extent still are) forbidden to marry women from the higher social strata.[16] According to the locally acknowledged conception of social status, which is based on supposedly inherent moral qualities grounded in genealogical credentials (Klein 2005), and, in the case of *zwāya* lineages with divine blessing (*baraka*), those of slave origin, although nominally free Muslims, remain inferior to those of freeborn status.[17] This stigma can attach to them indefinitely, even if their ancestors were manumitted generations ago, as long as the collective memory of their slave origin is kept alive. Furthermore, contrary to more common interpretations of this institution, certain Bīḍān scholars have argued that the concept of *walāʾ* justifies legal discrimination against the subordinate *mawālī* (Ould Cheikh 2020: 119–21). Most Ḥarāṭīn were obliged to pay tribute (in the form of shares of their annual harvest or occasional unremunerated labour) to their respective Bīḍān patrons and in this sense continued to suffer from economic exploitation despite their liberation from slavery.[10]

Revolutionary times: Historicizing the emergence of Ḥarāṭīn activism in Mauritania

When the French began to establish colonial rule in the western regions of the Sahara at the turn of the twentieth century, slavery was soon formally abolished, as it had been in the rest of French West Africa.[19] Razzias and the slave trade were banned; as the French colonial administration had limited resources to control the vast desert territory and depended on the support of the Bīḍān nobility for their project of 'pacification', however, they opted to accommodate them by preserving their local sovereignty and autonomy, including their control over the 'servile population', as slaves and slave descendants were now called in official reports, largely untouched (Klein 1998; Robinson 2000). Hereditary slavery was tolerated because it was considered an essential pillar of the local social fabric that could not simply be abolished 'from above' without causing the collapse of traditional authority and jeopardizing the strategy of indirect rule. Therefore, it was still widespread when Mauritania became independent in 1960,[20] although French colonial policies during the first half of the twentieth century also gave way to important changes in the statuary mobility of slaves and Ḥarāṭīn (McDougall 2007). It was only after the devastating droughts of the late 1960s and 1970s had severely undermined the traditional pastoralist economy that a genuine abolitionist movement emerged in Mauritania. Slaves and Ḥarāṭīn left their masters and patrons in large numbers and settled in segregated agricultural hamlets (*adwābe*, sg. *adabay*) or on the outskirts of the developing cities. Ould Cheikh (2020) argues that the spatial separation between former slaves and masters during this period played a key role in the re-formulation and re-creation of Ḥarāṭīn identity out of this new experience of a certain amount of autonomy.

In addition to this process of sedentarization and urbanization, the war in the Western Sahara that broke out after the chaotic decolonization of the Spanish colony in 1976 also had an impact on the situation of the Ḥarāṭīn in Mauritania (and likely those in the Western Sahara), as enrolment and service in the Mauritanian army provided men of slave origin with another opportunity for individual emancipation and the cutting of ties with their former masters (Ould Ahmed Salem 2009: 160). Perhaps more importantly, the emergence of the 'Frente Polisario' independence movement in the colony of the Spanish Western Sahara was itself related to the proliferation of revolutionary socialist ideologies in the region, which radically questioned the traditional model of society based on hierarchical principles.[21] The ideology of socialist Pan-Arabism that emanated from the Middle East (notably

Egypt, Syria and Iraq) also took roots in the Islamic Republic of Mauritania in the 1960s. Nasserist and Baathist political currents among the Bīḍān opposed President Ould Daddah's unitary party government due to its initial proximity to France and the idea of a multicultural Mauritanian nation that would function as a 'bridge' between the Arab world and sub-Saharan Africa, opting instead for ideological commitment to the superiority of Arab-Islamic civilization and Arabization policies.[22] Given the socialist orientation of those Pan-Arab ideologies, Baathists criticized statuary and racial discrimination against the Ḥarāṭīn and invited them to join their ranks and thus affirm their identity as 'black Arabs' (Freire and Taleb Heidi forthcoming). In addition to socialist Pan-Arabism, a local movement of communist-Maoist inspiration called 'Kādīḥīn' attracted many followers among Mauritania's nascent urban 'working class' and 'progressive' intellectual circles between the late 1960s and early 1970s. Simultaneously, with neighbouring Senegal's President Léopold Senghor embracing and prominently representing the Pan-Africanist 'Négritude' movement (Villasante 2007b), anti-colonial revolutionary ideologies also poured into Black African political milieus in the Senegal valley. In reaction to the establishment of a new territorial and political border by the French, the Black African communities living on the northern bank of the Senegal River strove to retain their local autonomy and started to organize on a regional and ethnic basis, as they had suddenly become 'national minorities' (Abdoul 2004).[23]

Against the background of these revolutionary times, a small elite of Ḥarāṭīn educated in French colonial schools founded the clandestine movement El-Hor (Ar. *al-Ḥurr*, 'the Freeman', short for 'Organisation pour la libération et l'émancipation des Haratines') in 1978. The Ḥarāṭīn intellectuals behind El-Hor felt that the problem of slavery had not yet been adequately addressed by the Baathists and the Kādīḥīn, as these movements were framed in more 'global' terms that tended to neglect locally specific mechanisms of domination and oppression. In their founding charter, they stated their motivation as follows:

> Fondamentalement inspirés par la religion, aggravés par une interprétation abusive de cette même religion par les couches sociales privilégiées, entretenues par l'ambiguïté, voire le silence quasi complet de la législation du pays, les inégalités dont souffrent les Haratines sont non seulement d'ordre économique, social, politique et religieux, mais elles sont aussi, et surtout, inhérentes à une mentalité puissamment ancrée par des siècles de conditionnement psychologique. Lutter contre tout ceci constitue la raison d'être de El-Hor.
>
> (El-Hor 2004)

The critique of anchoring slavery in local Islamic traditions and the goal of reforming respective mentalities and juridical-religious norms in Bīḍān society were thus at the core of this abolitionist movement. In this reformist vein, El-Hor called for the removal of 'all the contradictions that exist between Muslim and modern law, in particular those having to do with the slave status, namely: the problems related to the incapacitation of slaves (property rights, testimony, inheritance) and to matrimony (marriage, concubinage)' (El-Hor, cited in Ould Ahmed Salem 2009: 162).

The second essential aspect of El-Hor's emancipative project concerns the need for the development of a collective consciousness among hassanophone slaves and Ḥarāṭīn in order to enable collective action and to effectively push for such a social revolution. Until El-Hor's attempt to shift its meaning, the term *ḥarāṭīn* (sg. m. *ḥarṭānī*, f. *ḥarṭāniyya*) generally applied to legally manumitted former slaves and their descendants – those nominally free but dependent clients (*mawālī*) who were distinguished from other such groups within extended hassanophone society by their association with a slave background and Black African origin. By contrast, the *ʿabīd* formed another category of people who were seen as the mere 'property' of their masters, frequently compared to livestock in the local legal literature.[24] El-Hor wanted to erase these distinctions and unite all 'black Moors' under the Ḥarāṭīn label. This was no easy task; at the time, the attachment of the Ḥarāṭīn to the *qabīla*-centred social and political structures of the Bīḍān was not yet contested, apart from those few civil servants with a 'modern' French education who initiated the movement. In general, the territorially dispersed Ḥarāṭīn communities depended on their affiliation with local Bīḍān lineages for protection in case of conflict and for land use rights and therefore primarily identified with their respective *qabīla*, not with other 'black' hassanophones. In addition, many 'established' Ḥarāṭīn (those who managed to distance themselves from their slave past or completely denied that their ancestors had ever been enslaved) most likely opposed being lumped together with slaves in a single category, as this would have diminished their actual social status.[25] The founding members of El-Hor therefore stated the 'necessity of raising their collective awareness and of their unified struggle' and strove for the 'radical elimination of particularisms among the social class of the Ḥarāṭīn'. Independent of their current social status and tribal affiliations, they aimed to integrate all hassanophone slaves and Ḥarāṭīn within a supratribal 'imagined community' capable of organized, collective action. The Ḥarāṭīn, the El-Hor charter claims, are a 'people' characterized by a distinct hybrid culture, which is the result of their forced assimilation into Bīḍān society through the historical experience of slavery:

> La double appartenance des Haratines au monde négro-africain dont ils sont originaires d'une part et au monde arabo-berbère qui constitue leur milieu « d'adoption » détermine leur spécificité culturelle qui apparaît à travers divers aspects de leur vie … « El-Hor » s'engage également à *reconstituer l'histoire authentique des Haratines* afin de fournir aux générations futures la somme des souffrances que *leur peuple* a endurées durant les siècles. Par ailleurs, *la revalorisation de la culture des Haratines implique nécessairement qu'elle soit considérée sur le même pied d'égalité que les autres cultures nationales et bénéficie comme elles des mêmes préoccupations de l'Etat.*
>
> (El-Hor 2004, emphasis added)

This clearly shows that El-Hor's agenda also had an ethnopolitical aspect; official (state) recognition of the Ḥarāṭīn as a distinct 'national community' on equal footing with the Bīḍān, the Haalpulaaren, the Soninké and the Wolof was a stated goal. The cultural elements that Ḥarāṭīn activists draw on to substantiate these claims are certain musical genres, notably *medḥ* (religious music in praise of the Prophet Muhammad) and *benj* (popular music performed by Ḥarāṭīn women on the occasion of weddings and other profane festivities), musical instruments (the *nayffāra* flute, among others), or the *la ʿb al-dabbūs* (a ritual stick fight performed by Ḥarāṭīn men). These traditions were created by slaves and Ḥarāṭīn within the distinct social spaces they inhabited and historically served to express a moral subjectivity that subtly or overtly contested their representation in the dominant Bīḍān culture (Baba Ahmed 2017; N'gaïde 2008). In the context of the Ḥarāṭīn movement's political project, however, these traditions were now put to a different and distinctively 'modern' use, meaning that they can be understood as 'invented traditions' in Hobsbawm and Ranger's sense (Leservoisier 2004). Given the diverse historical and cultural background of slavery among Black African ethnic groups, El-Hor did not aspire to include all Mauritanian slave descendants in their abolitionist movement and instead focused exclusively on hassanophone spheres. In this context, they defined the new Ḥarāṭīn community they were striving to bring to life in a double contrast with the other 'Black African' ethnic groups and the 'white' Bīḍān.

Emerging as an underground movement, they spread their message and attracted followers in the rural *adwābe* and in the rapidly growing suburban slums (Ould Ahmed Salem 2009: 163). When Moktar Ould Daddah's unitary party regime was overthrown by the military in 1978, El-Hor's leaders seized the opportunity to present the movement on the national political stage, publicly declaring their support for the junta. Although state authorities continued to repress El-Hor's anti-slavery mobilization, the new military rulers realized the necessity of responding to the public outcry against slavery voiced by the movement.[26] On 5 July 1980, president Ould Haidallah announced the abolition of slavery in a national radio broadcast (Ruf 2000: 243). This declaration was followed by a formal decree the following year. Despite the ambiguities involved in the government's political reaction,[27] this was a big success for El-Hor, as the legitimacy of the Ḥarāṭīn's emancipatory aspirations was officially acknowledged. The abolition decree was followed by an important land reform in 1983, which abrogated traditional land tenure systems based on collective ownership of locally established kinship groups and supplanted it with new regulations inspired by Islamic law that enabled individual ownership (Ould Cheikh and Ould al-Barra 1996). This was meant to assist the Ḥarāṭīn in acquiring the land they had cultivated for generations without holding any property rights, thereby creating material conditions under which emancipation and economic development could proceed.[28]

Despite these concessions, the Ḥarāṭīn activists of El-Hor were not incorporated into the political system until president Ould Haidallah was overthrown in another coup d'état in 1984, which brought long-time authoritarian ruler Colonel Maaouya Ould Taya to power. The following year, he appointed Messaoud Ould Boulkheir (one of El-Hor's most prominent leaders) as Minister of Rural Development. This strategy of appeasement led to a decline in El-Hor's mobilization efforts at the grassroots level in the following years. The expansion of Ḥarāṭīn activists' involvement in official politics would only gain way when Ould Taya announced, under increasing internal and external political pressure, the democratic opening and decentralization of the political system at the beginning of the 1990s. Before that, however, Mauritania went through the darkest chapter of its recent history, when the salience, politicization and racialization of the country's multi-ethnic make-up reached a tragic peak. This chapter would have a profound and lasting impact on intergroup relations and the hardening of communitarian boundaries.

Rising ethno-racial tensions: FLAM and African counter-nationalism

While El-Hor denounced the persistence of slavery and statuary discrimination, another conflict developed between Black African ethnic minorities and the Bīḍān dominated regime. In the late colonial period, the sedentary Black African communities of the Senegal River valley had formed political alliances on an ethnic basis and rallied around demands for local autonomy, as they feared being marginalized in a nation-state with a hassanophone majority, in which political and military power was in the hands of the Bīḍān (Abdoul 2004; Ba 1998). Paradoxically, whereas the Bīḍān were recognized as the culturally and politically dominant majority population by the French, the indigenous colonial administration was largely made up of Black Africans who profited from their enrollment in French schools, whereas the Bīḍān remained mostly committed to a nomadic lifestyle and traditional Islamic education (Ciavolella 2014: 336).[29] This contradictory state of affairs, resulting from French colonial policy, prevailed when the country became independent under Ould Daddah and his 'Parti du People Mauritanien' (PPM), which managed to integrate various political factions under the umbrella of his nation-building project. Ould Daddah initially stressed the country's role as a 'bridge' between the Black African and the Arab world in his nationalist rhetoric, while retaining close ties with France. Lacking administrative structures in the interior and a feasible alternative, his government initially adopted the French school system and continued to rely on the francophone functionaries from the Senegal valley. As the anti-colonial Pan-Arabist ideologies of Baathism and Nasserism began to take root among the political elite, however, Ould Daddah's regime was put under pressure to cut its ties with the colonizer. Arab nationalism and the anti-colonial sentiments it fostered were soon translated into concrete policies.[30]

Conflict emerged when Ould Daddah's government reformed the colonial education system and the state's language policies. This involved the introduction of Arabic as a compulsory subject in secondary education (in 1966) and its elevation to an official langue alongside French (in 1968). Although this may seem justified in a country with an arabophone majority population, Black African civil servants and intellectuals perceived this as cultural repression and a first step towards an imposed Arabization, with the ultimate aim of displacing them from the state administration and marginalizing them culturally, politically and economically. In response to the 1966 decree, Black African pupils from the college in Rosso went on strike, and a group of Black African functionaries published a document entitled 'Manifeste des 19', in which they expressed their fears and demanded a federalist reform of the nation-state order. The signatories of the 'Manifeste' were subsequently arrested. After this incident, the conflict around language and education policy and the distribution of power and state revenues between Black African communities and the Bīḍān continued to deteriorate, especially after Ould Daddah was deposed and the military came to power in 1978. Eventually, Black African intellectuals and functionaries hostile towards their subordinate inclusion in an Arab nation-state formed a clandestine organization – mainly made up of Haalpulaaren, the largest Black African minority in Mauritania – called the 'Forces de Libération Africaines en Mauritanie' (FLAM) in 1983. In 1986, they published the 'Manifeste du Négro mauritanien opprimé', in which they rearticulated and intensified the discourse of the collective cultural, political and economic marginalization of Black Africans in a nation-state dominated by a 'white' Arab-Berber elite, and called for an armed uprising against Ould Taya's authoritarian regime.[31] FLAM's discourse framed oppression and inequality (including slavery) exclusively in racial terms and questioned the basic legitimacy of the nation-state in its present form:

> On se demande comment on peut donc parler d'Unité Nationale en Mauritanie, alors que les principes directeurs de l'Etat Unitaire sont bafoués par un Système (le système beydane) qui s'est toujours préoccupé de défendre les intérêts d'une *nationalité racio-culturelle (arabo-berbère) au détriment des autres (…)* Le refus de résoudre correctement les problèmes de la coexistence politique et économique des deux communautés raciales, sous le prétexte de préserver une "Mauritanie Unitaire" engendre petit à petit dans la conscience des Négro-mauritaniens un doute sur le principe même de l'Etat Unitaire.
>
> (FLAM 1986, emphasis added)

The publication of this manifesto was followed by strong repression. When a group of Black African army officers affiliated with FLAM mounted a failed coup d'état in 1987, resulting in the execution of three of them, tensions were at a maximum. The regime used this move as a reason to further purge the administration and the armed forces of Black Africans deemed disloyal, replacing them with hassanophones.

As FLAM's Manifesto states, Black African nationalists considered the Ḥarāṭīn to be part of a 'Afro-Mauritanian' (Fr. *Négro-Mauritanien*) community, which they defined in racial terms as opposed to the 'Arab-Berber' Bīḍān. In this sense, they also embarked on a project to unite wider parts of the Mauritanian population politically while creating a new 'imagined community' explicitly based on race, under the label and narrative of the 'oppressed Black Mauritanian'. With the Baathists already appealing to them to join the 'Arab' camp, FLAM directly addressed the Ḥarāṭīn in their underground newsletter and demanded their political cooperation by appealing to 'racial solidarity':

> La lutte que je mène est celle de *la communauté négro-mauritanienne à laquelle tu appartiens*. Je lutte contre le racisme d'État mauritanien, je lutte contre l'esclavage, je lutte pour la libération de notre pays …
>
> (quoted in Ould Saleck 2000: 259, emphasis added)

In the light of these developments, Ḥarāṭīn activists found themselves between two competing nationalist camps. In this period of intense political tensions, the El-Hor movement split into two opposed tendencies (Ould Ahmed Salem 2009, 2018a). Some of their members took up positions within Ould Taya's administration and joined the Arab nationalist camp, now arguing for the closure of the debate around slavery and stressing the historical and cultural bonds between the Ḥarāṭīn and the Bīḍān.[32] The adherents of the other tendency, associated with Messaoud Ould Boulkheir and Boubacar Ould Messaoud, kept their distance from the regime and refused ideological alignment with either side. While criticizing the government for its racist policies, they also rejected the appropriation and instrumentalization of the abolitionist cause by FLAM activists (see Ould Ahmed Salem 2018a: 138).

Ḥarāṭīn activists accused the Black African intelligentsia of silencing and denying the problem of slavery in their own ranks and misrepresenting the abolitionist cause of the Ḥarāṭīn. FLAM's framing of slavery in Mauritania as a purportedly purely racial problem restricted to the 'white'/'Arab-Berber' community was clearly refuted as a misleading political manoeuvre by El-Hor:

> *Slavery is not a racial problem.* There are in Mauritania black-skinned slave-owning feudal potentates, just as there are white ones. Likewise, there are democrats and opponents of slavery both among the white Moors and among the Poulars, Wolofs and Soninkes … The conservative elements among the Poulaars, Wolofs and Soninkes are trying to sidetrack it [the emancipation movement] in order to use it in their struggles against the Arab-Berbers for the sharing of power.
>
> (quoted in McDougall 2005: 967, emphasis added)[33]

These statements from El-Hor's leaders exemplify the complex interconnections between the issues of slavery, race and ethnicity/nationality within postcolonial Mauritania and the Ḥarāṭīn activists' dissatisfaction with the Black African nationalists' attempt to interfere with their emancipatory project by associating the problem of slavery with the marginalization of the Black African ethnic minorities and framing both in terms of race.

The ethnic tensions that had built up in the Senegal valley finally escalated following an incident in the Mauritanian-Senegalese borderland in 1989, resulting in pogroms on both sides of the border and the subsequent expulsion of around eighty thousand Black Africans from the southern regions of Mauritania to Senegal and Mali.[34] These pogroms were to a large extent supported by local Ḥarāṭīn, instigated by security forces and local officials. Members of the military carried out extrajudicial executions of several hundred Black African officers and soldiers accused of having ties to FLAM.[35] The conflict eventually calmed down in 1991, not least due to the increasing international isolation of Ould Taya's regime, but also because he had achieved his goal of expelling FLAM's leadership from the Senegal valley. Although most of these refugees have now returned to Mauritania, either on their own or in the framework of a UNHCR resettlement programme between 2008 and 2012, the underlying conflicts around arable land and national belonging remain unresolved (Fresia 2009). The crimes committed by members of the armed forces during this period at the orders of military leaders and President Ould Taya have not been punished or dealt with and were instead covered up by an amnesty law in 1993.[36]

Entering institutional politics and advocacy

Because of its dependency on foreign financial aid and the isolation of its main ally, Iraq, in the wake of the Gulf War (1991), Mauritania's government came under increasing pressure to address criticism from the international community concerning its suppression of oppositional political voices and its ethnic cleansing policies towards Black African communities in the Senegal valley in the early 1990s. Once the threat of FLAM had been neutralized, Ould Taya therefore announced the political liberalization of the country towards a pluralist democracy in 1991 and initiated constitutional reform. The Ḥarāṭīn activists of El-Hor now saw a chance to advance their cause through active participation in the electoral process.

In preparation for the first pluralist presidential elections, scheduled for 1992, the various political opponents of Ould Taya's regime united as the 'Union des Forces Démocratiques' (UFD). Although the results were highly contested, the incumbent Ould Taya managed to claim victory and remained in place. The El-Hor faction associated with Ould Boulkheir eventually left the UFD and finally created the 'Action pour le Changement' (AC) party in 1995. The AC was legalized by the state authorities, forming the first Ḥarāṭīn-controlled political party.[37] Even though the party clearly wanted to represent the Ḥarāṭīn population and the political goals of El-Hor (which included ending racial discrimination and the repression of Black African communities), it did not explicitly refer to identity, as this was criminalized by the new Constitution of 1991. The first article stated: 'Toute propagande particulariste de caractère racial ou ethnique est punie par la loi.' The decree regulating political parties stated: '[A]ucun parti ou groupement politique ne peut s'identifier à une race, à une ethnie, à une région, à une tribu, à un sexe ou une confrérie.' In practice, these regulations were applied quite selectively and mainly served to discredit the political opposition among the Ḥarāṭīn and the Black Africans as racist, segregationist and particularistic, where most other parties were controlled exclusively by Bīḍān (and often had a regional or tribal base), and (Pan-)Arabism had been adopted as the official state ideology. The AC also supported the creation of the union 'Confédération libre des travailleurs de Mauritanie' (CLTM), under the presidency of El-Hor member Samory Ould Beye, in order to back the political organization of the urban working class, largely constituted by Ḥarāṭīn (Ould Ahmed Salem 2018a: 128).[38] Whereas the Ḥarāṭīn activists associated with Ould Boulkheir chose to engage in party politics (as the circumstances of relative democratic liberalization allowed for this), Boubacar Ould Messaoud opted instead to anchor the fight against slavery and discrimination in a developing 'civil society' and an international human rights framework by creating the NGO 'SOS-Esclaves'. Although his organization was denied legal recognition by the government, Ould Messaoud and his fellow activists managed to reach out to human rights organizations like Amnesty International and quickly became the principal interlocutor for Western governments on the issue of slavery. SOS-Esclaves essentially aimed to provide victims of slavery with the support and protection the government had failed to supply, despite its official commitment to fighting against the 'vestiges' of slavery. For this purpose, they set up a network of activists throughout the country who approached victims when they discovered cases of slavery and spread awareness about the illegality of such practices in order to facilitate self-emancipation on a broader scale.[39]

In the wake of this ambiguous process of partial democratization during the 1990s, slavery came to be debated more publicly. Despite lacking authorization SOS-Esclaves published annual reports on slavery and discriminatory practices against slave descendants in cooperation with their international partners. Whereas the activists affiliated with Ould Boulkheir and Ould Messaoud insisted on the recognition of slavery as a contemporary reality that must be tackled by the judicial system and specific programmes targeting the Ḥarāṭīn population, the government maintained that slavery had been abolished and now needed to be addressed only in terms of its economic and social 'aftermath'. Abolitionist activists were accused of instrumentalizing an outlawed 'historical' practice for political purposes and threatening the fragile 'national unity'. To support this official narrative, Ould Taya's regime set up the 'Comité national pour l'éradication des séquelles de l'esclavage en Mauritanie' (CNESEM) in 1997 and staffed it with former El-Hor members who had joined Ould Taya's 'Parti Républicain Démocratique et Social' (PRDS).[40] After the opposition boycotted the 1997 presidential elections and Ould Taya was re-elected for another six-year term, he began to severely cut back on democratic liberties and finally banned the AC in 2002. The dissolved party's leadership and members then eventually joined the small Arab nationalist party 'Alliance populaire progressiste' (APP), which led to an unlikely coalition of Arab and Black African nationalists under the leadership of Ḥarāṭīn activists, held together under the umbrella of a socialist political agenda.

At this stage, the Ḥarāṭīn movement had made its way into both organized party politics (both in the government camp and in the opposition) and into a nascent 'civil society' that developed in the cities.[41] Although the 'abolition decree' and the land reform of the early 1980s and the political liberalization of the 1990s had not brought forth the collective empowerment of the Ḥarāṭīn as full-fledged citizens, their demographic weight now made them a central bargaining chip in the electoral process. Sedentarization, urbanization and democratization had allowed the Ḥarāṭīn to renegotiate their position vis-à-vis their tribal patrons and towards the state.[42]

Political change and the revitalization of the Ḥarāṭīn movement after 2005

Ould Taya was re-elected for a third term in 2003, but the legitimacy of his dictatorial regime had already been seriously damaged. After two attempted coups, he was eventually ousted by the military in 2005. The junta pledged to lead the country back to a democratic path and announced free presidential elections for 2007. Ould Boulkheir, who stood as a candidate but placed far behind with only 9.79 per cent of the vote, decided to support the independent candidate Sidi Ould Cheikh Abdallahi in the second round, who was eventually victorious. In exchange for his support, he negotiated four ministerial posts for the APP and the presidency of the National Assembly for himself. What is more, he insisted that the new parliament immediately pass a law criminalizing slavery so that the abolition decree of 1981 could finally be enforced in practice.[43]

Despite general satisfaction with the democratic character of the transition, the newly formed government of Cheikh Abdallahi did not remain in power for long. He was deposed by another coup under the leadership of General Ould Abdel Aziz in 2008, which led the country into a deep political crisis. Together with other political parties who remained loyal to Cheikh Abdallahi, Ould Boulkheir vigorously opposed the coup and assumed the leadership of the coalition 'Front National pour la Défense de la Démocratie' (FNDD). After an agreement was reached under international mediation, new elections were held in 2009, and Ould Boulkheir stood as the joint candidate of the FNDD coalition. He was clearly defeated by Abdel Aziz, placing second with 16 per cent of the votes. Despite the political turmoil, Ould Boulkheir remained president of the National Assembly until the 2013 parliamentary elections, which the APP and other oppositional parties had decided to boycott. As a result, the APP lost its grip on the political institutions. Although he remains a respected political father figure and a symbol of the fight against slavery, Ould Boulkheir and the rest of the El-Hor generation lost their appeal among many Ḥarāṭīn, especially its disaffected youth. As El-Hor increasingly lost its coherence as a movement and split into various political factions,[44] and as the marginalization of the Ḥarāṭīn continued under the new regime of Abdel Aziz, a new generation of militants stood up to revive the Ḥarāṭīn cause.

In the wake of the renewed commitment to democratization following Ould Taya's ouster, younger Ḥarāṭīn activists again began to organize and mobilize at the grassroots level. An example of this is the 'Front uni pour l'action des Haratines' (FUAH), a group that published a document entitled '50 ans de marginalisation et d'exclusion systématiques des Haratines' in 2008 (Ould Ahmed Salem 2018a: 132). Like El-Hor's charter, this manifesto insists on the Ḥarāṭīn's distinctive cultural identity and additionally stresses their 'autochthone' history, clearly defining them as an ethnic group alongside the Bīḍān and the other Black African communities:

> Les Haratines sont donc *un peuplement noir descendant des aborigènes, autrement dit, la première population de la sous-région* et que trouvèrent sur place respectivement les berbères et les arabes. Ils se définissent comme *une communauté nègre d'origine et arabo- berbère de langue (Hassania), mais qui n'est, par-dessus tout ni nègre ni Beïdane; car ils ont leur spécificité socioculturelle propre et partant une identité* qui a su résister à toutes les adversités sociales et temporelles: les tentatives de phagocytose, de dissolution et d'aliénation.
>
> (Front uni pour l'action des Haratines 2008, emphasis added)

The organization that would become the spearhead of the revitalization of the Ḥarāṭīn, however, was the 'Initiative pour la résurgence du mouvement abolitionniste' (IRA), founded in 2008 by the former secretary general of SOS-Esclaves, Biram Dah Ould Abeid. Like many younger Ḥarāṭīn militants, he was displeased with the conciliatory and pragmatic stance adopted by many El-Hor leaders and Ḥarāṭīn politicians who had become 'part of the system'. Ould Abeid now argued for the necessity of (re-)radicalizing the Ḥarāṭīn movement. IRA's goals are stated as follows in the movement's charter:

> Le but de l'Initiative pour la Résurgence du Mouvement Abolitionniste en Mauritanie (IRA-Mauritanie) est d'interpeller et de conscientiser les pouvoirs publics et les partenaires sur la situation sociale, économique et politique du pays. Elle devra à terme constituer une plateforme et un forum réel d'expression, de contestation, de dénonciation et de concertation en vue de diagnostiquer les problèmes des citoyens et de proposer des solutions optimales. IRA-Mauritanie s'inscrit dans une dynamique de défense des droits humains, de dénonciation et de lutte contre l'injustice pour la *déconstruction du système de domination érigé en mode de gestion de l'Etat mauritanien.*
>
> (IRA, Statuts et Règlement Intérieur, Arts. 3 and 4, emphasis added)

A decisive strategic novelty that distinguished IRA from its predecessors was the young militant's skilfull and large-scale use of social media. IRA quickly attracted a large number of followers, especially among the youth, and vehemently attacked the government and traditional authorities for their alleged compliance with the persistent practice of hereditary slavery. They helped victims escape from their 'masters', organized sit-ins at police stations to compel the authorities to take action on their complaints and mobilized for public demonstrations that frequently led to clashes with the police. As a consequence of this militant anti-slavery activism, Ould Abeid was discharged from his position as senior adviser to the president of the National Commission for Human Rights in Mauritania in 2010. In early 2011, he was sentenced to a twelve-month jail term for his 'illegal activities' but quickly received a pardon from President Abdel Aziz.

IRA's strategy crucially relies on its relations with Western governments, international NGOs, and UN and EU institutions, from whom the association gathers significant moral and political support. The Black Mauritanian diasporas in the USA and Europe constitute an important pool of activists, underscoring the transnational nature of contemporary social movements, even when they spring from very specific local issues.[45] IRA has skilfully used the Mauritanian state's relations with foreign governments to draw attention to human rights violations and to mobilize international support against internal repression (Freire 2019: 497–501).

Breaking with the earlier stance taken by El-Hor's leaders, who had distanced themselves from FLAM's political discourse during the 1980s, IRA adamantly stressed the racial nature of both slavery in the Bīḍān community and the country's overall power structure. In this spirit, Abeid adopted the African nationalists' narrative of 'racial oppression' and called for an end to 'Bīḍān hegemony' and the collective marginalization of Black Africans in Mauritania, going so far as to compare the situation of the country to the apartheid system. Although IRA did not call for an overthrow of the regime (as FLAM had in its day), instead committing themselves to non-violent means of protest and claiming the status of aa apolitical human rights organization, their discourse represented a declaration of war against the status quo upheld by the political and religious establishment, pairing the fight against slavery with a demand for the rearrangement of ethno-racial power relations in the nation-state.

Notwithstanding the cultural sensitivity of this endeavour, Biram Ould Abeid fiercely challenged the local tradition of Islamic scholarship and the country's established *ʿulamāʾ* (Islamic religious scholars), whom he accused of 'obscurantist' religious teachings that distorted the true essence of Islam. In April 2012, Ould Abeid and other IRA activists publicly burned books on classic Islamic jurisprudence, among them Khalīl ibn Isḥāq's *al-Mukhtaṣar*.[46] IRA activists argued that these classic legal standard compendiums should no longer be used in the country's religious educational institutions because they were outdated and presented slavery as a legitimate institution, comparing them to the 'code noir'. This act of rebellion against traditional religious normativity was a national scandal and prompted the religious establishment, state authorities and members of the public to accuse him of blasphemy, resulting in his temporary imprisonment. The imam of Nouakchott's central mosque delivered a sermon in which he called Abeid and IRA militants 'devils … criminals who will also burn Korans, the *ʿulamāʾ* and the whole country if nothing is done to stop them' (BBC 2012). IRA subsequently issued an apology for this controversial act of protest, and, under national and international pressure to release Abeid, the case was eventually dismissed. This controversy exemplifies the difficulties faced by abolitionist activists in their attempts to shift the boundaries of Islamic normativity without transgressing them.[47]

With the multiplication of religious schools (*maḥāẓir*, sing. *mahẓara*) and the opening of advanced religious education beyond traditional statutory boundaries, the Ḥarāṭīn have striven to gain access to religious knowledge and to demonstrate the immorality of slavery and descent-based discrimination from an Islamic perspective (see the chapter by Baba Ahmed and Horma in this volume). In light of the growing 'democratization' and globalization of Islamic religious education and knowledge, a process that is also connected to the increasing availability and use of new types of media,[48] some Mauritanian scholars have managed to establish themselves as part of a new generation of religious teachers and preachers who are critical of many aspects of local Islamic traditions and are putting forward arguments connected to the internally diversified reformist movement in contemporary Islam (Ould Ahmed Salem 2013).[49] As an overwhelming majority of Mauritanians self-identify as devout and pious Muslims, any strategy that relies on a discourse of emancipation and social change that is overtly critical of locally acknowledged sources of Islamic normativity faces great challenges. It is notable that a growing number of Ḥarāṭīn have attained positions as Imams of small neighbourhood mosques, tackling their community's discrimination from an Islamic religious angle rather than arguing from a human rights perspective, the proponents of which are easily accused by conservative circles of being under the influence of a Western, anti-Muslim ideology. Against this background, Ḥarāṭīn activists are confronted with the task of developing paths and narratives of emancipation that resonate with popular religious and cultural values and achieve what Bruce Hall (2020) calls 'Muslim citizenship'.

On the formal legal level, SOS-Esclaves and other human rights organizations have continued to advocate for changes to the 2007 anti-slavery law, notably to enable third parties to represent victims in court and to introduce higher sentences. The anti-slavery law was eventually tightened according to their demands in 2015, and the government set up three specialized regional courts (in Nouakchott, Nouadhibou and Nema) which were assigned the task of handling slavery-related crimes.[50] A constitutional revision in 2012 additionally raised slavery to the status of a 'crime against humanity'. Notably, there were also signs of growing solidarity and cooperation between the revived Ḥarāṭīn movement and Black Mauritanian activist groups. In 2014, IRA militants and the NGO 'Kawtal' organized a '*caravane contre l'esclavage foncier*' in the Senegal valley.[51] The purpose of this campaign was to denounce the increasing appropriation of arable land by rich Bīḍān businessmen from the northern regions to the detriment of the local Ḥarāṭīn and Black African communities, who actually cultivate the land since generations. In a small village near the border town of Rosso, an area particularly ridden with land conflicts, the police violently stopped the march and arrested Abeid and IRA's then Vice President Brahim Bilal Ramdhane, several other IRA militants and Kawtal's President Djiby Sow. In early 2015, the two IRA leaders and Sow were sentenced to two years in prison for 'non-authorized assembly' and the former two additionally for 'membership in an illegal organization'. Despite the protests of foreign governments and human rights organizations, the sentence was upheld by the court of appeal, and Abeid and Ramdhane had to serve their prison sentences (Sow was released a couple of months later). This was clearly meant to deter the activists, but Abeid's repeated imprisonment had the opposite effect and instead boosted the IRA leader's image as a staunch and courageous human rights militant.

Biram Abeid's reputation as a radical and adamant anti-slavery militant resisting threats and repression eventually propelled him to embark on a political career. As the state authorities did not recognize IRA as an NGO, however, they also refused to accredit Abeid's IRA-affiliated political party 'Parti radical pour une action globale' (RAG). When the opposition, now regrouped as the 'Forum national pour la démocratie et l'unité' (FNDU), largely boycotted the elections, Biram Ould Abeid participated as an independent candidate and gathered 8.7 per cent of the vote, which placed him second after the incumbent Abdel Aziz. In his campaign to the elections, Abeid styled himself primarily as the candidate of all 'oppressed Black Mauritanians' and vowed to end the 'Arab-Berber hegemony' in the country:

> Il faut d'abord rétablir l'équité. Pourquoi sur 35 ministres, il est de coutume d'en placer 30 Arabo-Berbères? Pourquoi les 18 banques du pays appartiennent aux Arabo-Berbères? Pourquoi sur les 13 gouverneurs de région, 12 sont Arabo-Berbères? Pourquoi sur 54 préfets, 52 sont Arabo-Berbères? *Les Harratines et les autres ethnies noires* doivent se réapproprier leur place.
>
> (Abeid in Spiegel 2014, emphasis added)

For Abeid and his fellow IRA activists, there are no 'black Moors'; this was merely an invention of the Bīḍān, he states, supported by French colonial policies to justify their vision of an Arab nation, which the Ḥarāṭīn should refuse to support (Maimone 2018). This argument fuelled allegations of extremism and racism against Abeid, making him very unpopular among the Bīḍān population. But despite Abeid's rapprochement with non-hassanophone Black African activists and the African nationalist camp, IRA activists continue to insist on the recognition of the Ḥarāṭīn as an ethnic group. On the occasion of a hearing session in the European Parliament, the (then) head of the European section of IRA, Abidine Ould Merzough, demanded that the Mauritanian state 'recognize the Haratin's identity, as the majority group, as a separate ethnic group, independent of the Arab-Berbers, with whom they share a language as a legacy of slavery relations' (Diagana et al. 2016).

Despite this insistence on ethnic boundaries, Abeid sharpened his profile as representative of all 'oppressed Black Mauritanians' by strengthening his cooperation and demonstrating solidarity with political parties and civil society associations representing Black African minorities. Most notably, he vigorously denounced the amnesty pertaining to the massacres of Black African soldiers during the years of violent ethnic conflict under Ould Taya's rule and, together with other human rights activists and civil society associations, initiated a commemorative event at Inal.[52] Against this background, the electoral alliance between his unrecognized RAG party and the Baathist 'Sawab' party (whose leaders had expressed worries about the increasing 'negrification' of Mauritania some years ago), forged in the run-up to the municipal, legislative and regional elections of 2018 and the presidential elections of 2019, surprised observers and estranged many Black Africans who sympathized with Abeid.[53] IRA and Sawab presented the alliance as a sign of rapprochement between historically antagonistic political camps and affirmed their commitment to common political goals. This alliance allowed IRA/RAG members to appear on Sawab's electoral list in the upcoming elections, and Abeid himself was elected deputy to the National Assembly from his prison cell, after he had again be arrested on dubious charges of having threatened a journalist. In the presidential elections of 2019, he again placed second, this time with 18.6 per cent of the vote (more than doubling his 2014 results). Abdel Aziz respected the constitutional limit of two mandates, and it was the candidate of his ruling UPR, Mohamed Ould Ghazouani, who came out victorious and took over the presidential office.[54] Since his election to parliament, Abeid has markedly moderated his political discourse and reached out to Ghazouani's new government, who in turn broke with his predecessor's strategy of repression and entered into dialogue with IRA's leader. Although they have yet to be legalized, IRA's and RAG's activities are presently tolerated. Abeid's rapprochement with Ghazouani, however, earned him heavy criticism from the movement's militant base. This change of course led to many defections within IRA's ranks, which left it significantly weakened.

Alongside the militant approach pursued by IRA during the last decade, a coalition of activists formed a joint committee in 2013 and published a document entitled 'Manifesto for the political, economic and social rights of the Haratin within a united Mauritania, egalitarian and reconciled with itself.' The 'Manifeste des Haratines', as this coalition came to be known, subsequently initiated an annual march to be held every 29th April (the date of the documents publication) in Nouakchott that has attracted huge crowds. The document describes the Bīḍān and the Ḥarāṭīn, again, as 'two entities [which are] increasingly different' and holds that the Ḥarāṭīn should be recognized as a 'socio-ethnic category' of its own. In addition to demanding the effective implementation of existing anti-slavery legislation, the manifesto urges the government to resort to 'positive discrimination' in favour of the Ḥarāṭīn in order to help overcome the long-term socioeconomic effects of their historical marginalization. The manifesto claims to represent a new historical stage of the Ḥarāṭīn movement initiated by El-Hor and restates the need for a 'social and political revolution':

> [L]a présente initiative a pour ambition de traduire une nouvelle prise de conscience de la communauté Haratine pour capitaliser les acquis des luttes menées depuis la création *du Mouvement El Hor* en mars 1978, tirer les leçons de ces combats et concevoir un nouveau projet à la fois fédérateur et en rupture franche avec le système des hégémonies particularistes, tribales en particulier, et ce dans le but de servir les intérêts supérieurs de la nation. Le grand mouvement civique que ce Manifeste voudrait susciter et animer, s'inscrirait à contresens de l'ordre ancien, esclavagiste et féodal, pour créer les conditions d'une *révolution sociale et politique* portée par une forte mobilisation citoyenne, pacifique et démocratique, associant toutes les forces, issues de toutes nos communautés nationales et transcendant les appartenances partisanes de culture, d'opinion ou de couleur.
>
> (*Manifeste des Haratines* 2013)[55]

Whereas in the beginning these activists faced difficulties convincing larger segments of society to participate in a march for the rights of the Ḥarāṭīn, they have managed to broaden their mobilization base in recent years. In 2019, members of the ruling UPR party participated for the first time, and in 2020 representatives of the 'Coalition Vivre Ensemble' (CVE), which spans the most important political factions of the Black African opposition (among them former FLAM leaders), also expressed their interest in participating.[56] At the same time, these recent initiatives still suffer from perpetual internal divisions. Dissension in the committee behind the manifesto led to a split in the organizational structure. As a result, as of 2018, two separate meetings and marches now take place simultaneously every year. Despite these constant fissions into conflicting camps and political factions, what seems to have increasingly crystallized with the revival of the Ḥarāṭīn movement by IRA, the manifesto and other small groups and organizations that have multiplied in recent years is a demand for official recognition of the Ḥarāṭīn's specific 'socio-ethnic' identity as a basis for claims to collective rights and positive discrimination, full and equal citizenship, and representation in national politics and institutions.[57] Boubacar Messaoud describes the social change since the early days of El-Hor to the present as follows:

> À l'époque, tu ne pouvais pas dire à un Mauritanien que les *Ḥarāṭīn*, c'est une nationalité … Ça, c'était en 1980. Aujourd'hui, nous sommes en 2018, ce n'est pas la même chose. Il y a des *Ḥarāṭīn* qui disent qu'ils veulent être des *Ḥarāṭīn*, ils sont nombreux. Il y a des *Ḥarāṭīn* qui ne sont même pas instruits, qui ne veulent pas être des Maures, ils sont déjà nombreux. Et c'est pour cela donc, aujourd'hui, c'est ça qui explique l'essence du Manifeste.
>
> (Interview with Boubacar Messaoud, April 2018)

This new attitude is pronounced among the Ḥarāṭīn whom I met and spoke to during my fieldwork in Nouakchott (March–April 2018; October 2021), whether or not they were engaged in militant activist circles. Most of them clearly refused to be included in the Bīḍān category, and the pervasiveness of tribal affiliation is often criticized as a relict of the past impeding the country's development. The growing cultural self-consciousness among the Ḥarāṭīn is a central element of the proliferation of NGOs and activist groups during recent years. An example of this 'cultural turn' in the Ḥarāṭīn movement is the success of the NGO 'Teranim', founded in 2014 by Mohamed Ali Bilal, which promotes *medḥ* and other artistic genres associated exclusively with the Ḥarāṭīn as a hitherto neglected part of the national cultural heritage. In this way, he seeks to contribute to the recognition and valorization of a distinct 'Ḥarāṭīn culture' in the Mauritanian public sphere:

> I pondered how I could add something to the struggle that started in 1970s … The identity problems are [always] there—some Ḥarāṭīn say that we are not like the white Moors, others say no. We all drink tea, we eat couscous, we wear the boubou, we speak Hassaniyya—what is so different? What is it that in fact distinguishes us from others? The white Moors, the Peuls, the Wolofs, the Soninkés—we are all different. We are different through our culture … Therefore, there is a difference, but this difference was always downplayed; it was actually downplayed by ourselves, the Ḥarāṭīn.
>
> We have been working [on the Ḥarāṭīn identity] for 10 years now … so if Ḥarāṭīn public officials, politicians, and human rights activists now want to tackle the question of Ḥarāṭīn cultural identity, there is something tangible they can refer to. If you look on our website, on our YouTube channel, there is something that says—here it is, this is the difference between ourselves and the others! The other thing concerns Ḥarāṭīn artists. Before, if you said that this was Ḥarāṭīn music, people would have felt ashamed. We have done workshops with those artists so that they can say: Hey, this is our song, this is our music, this is our dance! This is your culture, and it is different from the culture of the griots; it is different from the culture of the Moors … You should be proud of your music; you should be proud of your culture!
>
> (Interview with Mohamed Ali Bilal, October 2021)

Another interesting new actor within the Ḥarāṭīn activist scene is the 'Movement of the Supporters of Change' (*ḥarakat anṣār al-taghyīr*), created in 2018 by a group of young militants who had left IRA due to their disagreement with Abeid's leadership. Their discourse equally professes a growing ethno-racial self-consciousness and their goals include the recognition of the Ḥarāṭīn as a separate 'national community' in the Constitution:

> Nous voulons que les Ḥarāṭīn soient reconnus comme communauté séparée dans la constitution Mauritanienne. Ils nous disent encore, vous êtes Maures blancs, nous, nous sommes Maures blancs?! Je ne suis pas Maure blanc, je suis Africain comme tous les Africains. Je suis Ḥarṭānī mauritanien! Il faut alors reconnaitre [les

Ḥarāṭīn] comme communauté nationale. La constitution Mauritanienne reconnait les Bīḍān, les Peuls, les Wolofs, les Soninkés ... pas les Ḥarāṭīn. Ils te disent que tu n'es pas Ḥarṭānī, mais que tu es Bīḍānī ... *[Les* Ḥarāṭīn*] ne sont pas des* Bīḍān. *Nous ne sommes pas des Maures noirs (khaḍar). Nous sommes des nègres Mauritaniens,* nous sommes des Africains comme les Congolais, les Togolais, les Ivoiriens, ou et les Gambiens ...

(Interview with Mohamed Lemine Seck, October 2021, emphasis added)

Conclusion: Remaking Ḥarāṭīn identity in post-slavery Mauritania

The renegotiation of Ḥarāṭīn identity in terms of ethnicity and nationality, and of the region's traditional social model more broadly, is a dynamic and controversial process that deals with innovative forms of sedentarization and urban life, and with the consolidation of the state- and nation-building. Its sensitivity is related not only to the emotional and socioeconomic legacies of slavery but also to the intricate political and identity-based conflicts that resulted from the uneven integration of different ethno-linguistic constituencies in the Mauritanian nation-state, giving rise to the formation of new 'imagined communities' on the basis of ethnic and racial identities. Notions of ethnic or racial differentiation – both indigenous as well as colonially imported – and traditional statuary hierarchies have interfered with postcolonial state- and nation-building in the Islamic Republic of Mauritania and have hardened into ideological cleavages between conflicting nationalist projects. A distinguishing feature of the Mauritanian case, when compared to other anti-slavery movements in West Africa, is its standing as the only nation-state in which slave descendants constitute a demographic majority, thus rendering the process of emancipation all the more potentially threatening for former masters. The development of the Mauritanian Ḥarāṭīn movement confirms Hahonou and Pelckmans' (2011) assessment that the turn towards questions of identity in West African anti-slavery movements didn't replace the struggle against material inequalities but is instead closely related to it. Although the country suffers from generalized poverty, which also affects large swathes of the traditional 'noble' class, the Ḥarāṭīn constitute the bulk of the country's most vulnerable and marginalized population (McDougall 2015) and largely depend on physically demanding and poorly paid labour in the vast sector of the informal urban economy and agriculture, remaining largely excluded from the country's religious, political and economic institutions, which are still dominated by people with Zwāya or Ḥassān descent. For Ḥarāṭīn activists, the goal of more equality in terms of representation within these institutions can only be reached by first recognizing their difference from the rest of society.

The Ḥarāṭīn embody several intersecting identity traits that account for their particularly contested position in Mauritania: although they are 'racially' defined as black, they are linguistically and culturally described as Arab/Bīḍān, and within the traditional *qabīla*-centred model they are collectively ascribed to the inferior social status of slave descendants (*mawālī*). The constant debates around these issues in the context of abolitionist and post-slavery emancipation efforts and postcolonial conflicts regarding national political integration in the last few decades have led to the progressive ethnicization of the Ḥarāṭīn category in Mauritania, independently of the strong internal divisions and divergent opinions concerning their 'Arab' or 'African' identity. Ḥarāṭīn activists consistently argue that such a unifying and class-transcending collective identity is a necessary basis for claims to recognition and joint political action towards effective emancipation from their historical marginalization. The 'ethnic turn' of the Mauritanian Ḥarāṭīn movement was likely fostered by the decisive role that ethnicity played in the colonial administrative order and the subsequent construction of postcolonial state- and nationhood, which effectively took the path of informal power-sharing on an ethnic basis but structurally favoured groups within the extended Bīḍān society who claim a 'white' (that is, Arab) identity. It may also be related to the fact that 'ethnic minorities' occupy a special place in the global human rights discourse, to the effect that they can claim certain 'collective rights' and measure such as 'positive discrimination' on the grounds of their cultural difference from the majority population.

Against this background, it stands to reason that Ḥarāṭīn activists use strategies associated with the concept of identity politics in their attempts to achieve a twofold goal: getting rid of the social stigma associated with slave ancestry by proudly embracing it as part of their identity, on the one hand, and asserting their claim to equal citizenship and political participation by resorting to ethnicity as a historically and structurally favoured path for negotiating national integration and moral subjectivity on the African continent, on the other. To acknowledge the potential influence of such structural and political factors on Ḥarāṭīn ethnogenesis is not to say, however, that Ḥarāṭīn activists and politicians are acting in a purely instrumental, manipulative way in working towards the creation and recognition of a new 'imagined community'. Like all nationalists and 'ethnicists', they are seriously convinced of the historical and sociological accuracy of their claims, and their arguments are no less valid than those put forward by the proponents of the Ḥarāṭīn's 'Arabness', who advocate for their integration within the Bīḍān community. The constuctivist approach to ethnicity I advocated holds that it is exactly this kind of social engagement and political struggle that can lead to changes in ethnic identification.

Today, forty years after the abolition of slavery, relations between the descendants of slaves and their masters have undergone major transformations, but many Ḥarāṭīn – especially in the rural hinterland – remain integrated within the hierarchical socio-cultural framework of the *qabīla* as subordinate clients, at times re-enacting those social bonds with their respective Bīḍān 'patrons' through various forms of symbolic and economic exchange (Brhane 1997; Wiley 2018). Despite the profound socioeconomic and political transformations of the postcolonial period, which have shaken its material basis in the past few decades, the social order of statuary stratification and its religiously imbued ideological framework continue to prove their resiliency and to thwart initiatives for social change. Because of its historical and cultural embeddedness, the notion of hereditary social status and associated moral qualities survived legal abolition and remains an important aspect of social differentiation in the Islamic Republic of Mauritania, defying the concept of equitable citizenship in a state-centred and democratic political order. Nevertheless, the effects of the changes that have swept the socioeconomic and ideological basis of the traditional social order cannot be overlooked, as disadvantaged groups are articulating their claims and fierce social critiques in an increasingly concerted manner, garnering never-before-seen levels of public acknowledgement, both internally and globally. The Ḥarāṭīn's quest for emancipation, recognition and political participation and the reinvention of traditional social and cultural identities in the context of political modernity and globalization remain central issues for Mauritania's future as a nation-state.

Notes

1 For an overview of the field, see Pelckmans and Hardung (2015). Villasante (2000) and Rossi (2009) have edited collective volumes dealing with the evolution of slavery, servility and dependency in the region from a comparative perspective.
2 For the effects of democratization and decentralization policies on the emancipation of slaves and slave descendants in the Sahara and the Sahel during the 1990s, see Botte (1999).
3 For an exploration of various cultural expressions of political resistance and dissidence in the western regions of the Sahara, see Boulay and Freire (2017).
4 Speakers of the Hassaniyya dialect of Arabic.
5 In southern Morocco (and possibly also in southern Algeria), where Haratin populations also live, the situation is different. There, the Ḥarāṭīn are seen not as slave descendants but as indigenous black populations who are distinguished from black communities who are known to have been enslaved by Berber and Arab groups, who are still called 'slaves'/ *'abīd* (McDougall 2020).
6 For a concise recapitulation of different normative approaches within social constructivist theories of ethnicity and their appreciation of ethnic politics in Africa, see Yeros (1999).
7 See notably Benedict Anderson's *Imagined Communities: Reflections on the Origin and Spread of Nationalism* (1983) and Eric Hobsbawm and Terence Ranger's *The Invention of Tradition* (1983).
8 For a historical overview of the development of 'caste systems' in West Africa, see Tamari (1991).
9 The notions of 'tribe' and 'tribalism' have received much well-founded criticism in anthropology. In order to avoid misleading associations in relation to these concepts, I will refer to these units of social and political organization by using the original Arabic term *qabīla*, which generally denotes a kinship group constituted around a patrilineal genealogy connecting its members to a common ancestor (Bonte et al. 1991).
10 This includes not only the supersession of the Amazigh by the Arabic language but also the imposition of an Arabo-centric Islamic historiography that excludes the history of earlier populations indigenous to the Western Sahara (Freire 2011) and supports the superiority of groups who claim genealogical links to the Arabian Peninsula and the early Muslim community.
11 This dual representation of 'white' nomads and 'black' sedentary agriculturalists (with each group settled in its respective 'ecological habitat') that developed with French colonial policies is not fully adequate, however (Ciavolella 2014). The Bīḍān

also relied on oasis agriculture (although they assigned this work exclusively to slaves and Ḥarāṭīn), and some Halpulaaren groups traditionally practised nomadic pastoralism as well.

12 Whereas the widely acknowledged rule of female hypergamy (*kafā ʾa*) prohibits marriage between men of lower status and 'noble' women, *concubinage* and marriage between 'freeborn' men and female slaves (the latter case implying the woman's formal manumission) were common.

13 I will use the term 'Bīḍān' mostly in this statuary sense, referring only to the *ḥassān* and the *zwāya*. The *znāga*, the *m ʿallemīn* and the *iggāwen*, who like the Ḥarāṭīn are relegated to subordinate positions in the traditional social hierarchy and equally lack prestigious genealogical connections, tend to identify themselves as 'Bīḍān' in the cultural sense and are usually also included in this category. Whenever I use the expressions 'extended/larger Bīḍān society', I am referring to the whole/Hassaniyya-speaking population of the western Saharan region, independently of statuary differences.

14 There are no official statistics on ethnic proportions, as the government refuses to collect such data because of its political sensitivity. The given proportions are therefore based on estimates, conservatively extrapolating from the last available census data and group-specific rates of population growth. Many local activists claim that the Ḥarāṭīn account for even more than 50 per cent of the whole population.

15 The incorporation of 'exogenous' elements (who lack genuine genealogical affiliation with the constitutive kinship groups) such as the *znāga* or the Ḥarāṭīn into a *qabīla* is locally conceptualized as *dkhīla*.

16 Many official and symbolic representations nevertheless convey the image of kinship between Bīḍān and Ḥarāṭīn in order to gloss over the statuary barrier and the rule of female hypergamy. Local interlocutors often present the Ḥarāṭīn as 'cousins' of the Bīḍān (see Bonte 1998). Another way of representing kinship bonds and reciprocity despite the boundary of social status is the Islamic tradition of 'milk kinship' (*riḍā ʿa*), which establishes significant bonds between children who were breastfed by the same woman, independently of their respective inherited social status (Fortier 2001; see also Ould Cheikh's chapter in this volume).

17 A model not exclusively targeted at the Ḥarāṭīn but associated with all other dependent status groups within the larger Bīḍān sphere. For the persistence of negative stereotypes and social boundaries concerning the *m ʿallemīn* and the *znāga*, see Villasante-de Bouvais (2004) and Freire (2014), respectively.

18 There were exceptions to the rule, however, with certain Ḥarāṭīn communities associated with ruling *ḥassānī* families enjoying high standing, as Ould Cheikh (2020: 111) shows.

19 France formally abolished slavery in its West African colonies in 1905 but largely abstained from implementing the decree. For abolitionist policies and their effects on slavery in colonial West Africa, see Klein (1998); Klute (1998) and Roberts (1988).

20 When the Islamic Republic of Mauritania became independent in 1960, it implicitly confirmed the abolition of slavery in its Constitution and by subscribing to various international legal norms. Again, this did not have much effect on the local level due to the lack of effective state structures.

21 The Polisario's socialist and nationalist political project, aimed at creating a unified 'Sahrawi' people in the territorial boundaries of the former Spanish colony, starkly objected to the segmentary and statuary divisions traditionally acknowledged among the Bīḍān (Caratini 2003).

22 Some of the Pan-Arab nationalist factions within the Islamic Republic of Mauritania even supported the claims of sovereignty over the whole western Saharan region voiced by Moroccan politicians, notably by the leader of the Istiqlāl-party, Allal al-Fassi.

23 Whereas the *al-Nahḍa al-Waṭaniyya* ('National Renaissance') party, which was based in the northern regions of Mauritania, supported the claims of the Moroccan Istiqlāl party and wished to become part of 'Greater Morocco' in the 1950s, the 'Union Nationale Mauritanien' (UNM), based in the Senegal valley, at the same time campaigned for the attachment of Mauritania's southern region to a union of Senegal and Mali (Du Puigaudeau 1961).

24 There were further differentiations according to slaves' occupations and their relative status. The term *khādim*, for example, designated female domestic slaves. Slaves who had been inherited within a single Bīḍān family for generations were called *nānma*, implying a deeper emotional bond with their masters and likely a higher social status than recently acquired slaves. The term *khaḍara* (pl. of 'greenish/blueish', somewhat avoiding the inferiority in social status associated with 'blackness') was used, especially in the eastern regions of Mauritania, to designate slave descendants who had been manumitted and emancipated over many generations, or communities of hassanophone blacks who claimed that they had never been enslaved. The label *ḥarāṭīn* in turn tended to carry the connotation of recent liberation and emancipation. Though they were obviously still considered inferior to Bīḍān 'nobility' because of their slave origin, *khaḍara* and *ḥarāṭīn* were legally free and sometimes even possessed slaves themselves.

25 As Ann McDougall (1988) has demonstrated, individual Ḥarāṭīn managed to attain high social standing, economic power and political influence during the colonial period and acquired numerous slaves themselves.

26 After El-Hor organized demonstrations against the sale of a slave girl in Atar in early 1980, eighteen of the movement's leaders were put on military trial (known as the 'trial of Rosso'), accused of threatening the security of the state (punishable by death), before being finally acquitted (Messaoud 2000: 296).

27 The text of the decree provided for the compensation of slave owners by the state and thereby implicitly acknowledged the legitimacy of slavery as it was practised in accordance with the local Maliki legal tradition. Although most local Islamic scholars who were consulted for their legal opinion concerning the possibility of abolishing slavery by the government approved of the plans, some also expressed their opposition to this move as they considered the institution of slavery an undisputed provision of Islamic *sharīʿa* (Ould Ahmed Salem 2013: 202–6). Because those slaves who were still in a formal servile relationship with their masters had been proclaimed free by the government without the latter's consent to the manumission, and because the promised 'compensation payments' for expropriated slave owners were never realized, there was mocking talk about 'Haidallah's Ḥarāṭīn'.

28 In reality, those who profited most from this reform were rich Bīḍān businesspeople close to the regime in power, who increasingly appropriated arable land in the southern regions mainly populated by the Black African communities, rather than the Ḥarāṭīn, who were now simply employed as cheap tenants (Ould Cheikh 2004: 295).

29 Until its independence in 1960, Mauritania shared most colonial services with neighbouring Senegal and was administrated from the post of Saint Louis in Senegalese territory. The new capital, Nouakchott, was created from scratch on the eve of decolonization.

30 Notably the nationalization of the MIFERMA (now called SNIM), the French consortium that extracted iron ore from the mines of Zouérat (which accounted for roughly 80 per cent of Mauritania's export trade at the time), and in the introduction of the Ouguiya as a national currency instead of the CFA franc.

31 That these claims of economic and politic marginalization had a solid basis was demonstrated by Phillipe Marchesin (1992) in his study on Mauritania's postcolonial political system.

32 This group prominently includes Sghaîr Ould Mbarek and Mohamed Ould Haimer, who both became influential figures in national politics.

33 On the legacy of slavery and the current situation of slave descendants among Black African ethnic groups, see Leservoisier (2008) (on the Halpulaaren) and N'Diaye (2016) (on the Soninké). Concerning the Wolof, the smallest of Mauritania's minorities, to my knowledge no significant works have yet been written on the contemporary relevance of traditional statuary hierarchies.

34 The expulsions mainly targeted Halpulaaren communities, who constituted the driving force behind FLAM and who the government perceived as the greatest danger to 'national unity' because of their demographic weight in southern Mauritania and because of the 1987 attempted coup, which had apparently been orchestrated by Halpulaaren officers. On the other hand, 160,000 Mauritanian nationals were also expelled from Senegal. See also Fresia (2009) and Ciavolella (2014).

35 An especially heinous event took place on Mauritania's national Independence Day on 29 November 1991, at the prison of Inal, a remote village located in the Dakhlet Nouadhibou region of northwestern Mauritania. In a macabre symbolic act, twenty-eight Black African soldiers who had been arrested in the previous weeks for their alleged ties to FLAM were tortured and hanged by members of the military at the local police station. This event continues to figure prominently in the discourse of Black African activists and politicians.

36 The abrogation of the amnesty law and the criminal investigation into the acts committed by security forces during this period of ethnic cleansing is still a central theme among opposition parties dominated by Black Africans and led by former FLAM members, such as the 'Alliance pour la justice et la démocratie' (AJD) and the 'Forces progressistes pour le changement' (FPC), which united in the 'Coalition vivre ensemble' (CVE) in the run-up to the 2019 presidential elections.

37 Although the AC's base was mainly made up of Ḥarāṭīn, the new party also incorporated some Black African nationalists, which led to accusations of creating a 'Black racial party' (Ould Ahmed Salem 2018a: 128).

38 While the abolitionist movement of the Ḥarāṭīn had to situate its fight in a political context that was increasingly polarized around identity issues, this step can be interpreted as an attempt to recalibrate attention and activism with regard to class inequalities as well.

39 For a firsthand account of the organization's approach, see Messaoud (2000).

40 Among them where Mohamed Salem Ould Merzough (who later became Minister of Hydraulics and Energy), Sid'Ahmed Zahaf, Breika Mbarek and Daha Ould Teiss.

41 This internal diversification may justify speaking of Ḥarāṭīn movements in the plural. With this noted, I will use the term 'Ḥarāṭīn movement' in the sense of a broader 'identitarian' movement aimed at the social and legal recognition of the Ḥarāṭīn as a distinct 'national community', in contrast to other Ḥarāṭīn groups and most Bīḍān, who have instead opted for a strategy of assimilation within the hassanophone majority population.

42 For the evolution of statuary hierarchies and slavery in Bīḍān society in the late twentieth century, see Bonte (1989, 1998, 2002); Botte (1999, 2005); Ould Cheikh (1993); Ruf (1999, 2000); and Villasante (1991).
43 The practical effects of this new anti-slavery law were quite limited, however. On the Mauritanian state's failure to implement its abolitionist legislation, see Ould Ciré (2014). To my knowledge, there have only been four convictions for slavery in the Mauritanian courts thus far. Dozens of cases filed with the police in recent years are pending in the Mauritanian courts, apparently stalled. Reports on slavery and related forms of discrimination and exploitation are regularly published by international NGOs such as Anti-Slavery International, Minority Rights Group and the Society for Threatened Peoples, who cooperate with Mauritanian anti-slavery and Human Rights NGOS (especially SOS-Esclaves and IRA) to obtain data on the phenomenon and to implement projects aimed at its eradication and victim support. For an overview, see for example the joint report by ASI, IRA, MRG, SOS-Esclaves, STP and UNPO (2015). The concrete number of actual 'slaves' is a highly controversial issue, based on estimates that depend on disputed definitions of slavery.
44 A new political split in El-Hor's ranks occurred in 2010, when Samory Ould Beye and Mohamed Bourbos were expelled from the APP for their opposition to Ould Boulkheir's plan to fully integrate the movement into the party. They created their own party, 'al-Mustaqbal' ('The Future'), which remains a small group without real political influence but, unlike the APP, openly speaks in the name of the original El-Hor movement (Ould Ahmed Salem 2018: 132).
45 Kawtal, which has been legally recognized as an NGO since 2010, has defended positions and claims similar to those voiced by TPMN and advocates for the civil rights of Black African Mauritanians, especially the rural, agricultural communities in the Senegal valley, who are facing land expropriation to the benefit of national and international investors.
46 On Maliki jurisprudence and its significance in the western Saharan region, see Ould Bah (1981).
47 Another example of this is the 'Mkhaitir affair' involving a young blogger who was accused of blasphemy; see Freire's chapter in this volume.
48 For an exploration of this development and its manifestations in different African religious contexts, see Hackett and Soares (2015). For a perspective on Muslim societies, see Eickelman and Anderson (1999).
49 The pioneer of this trend is Cheikh Mohamed Ould Sidi Yahya, who was the first Mauritanian preacher (*dā ʿī*) to record and spread his sermons on cassettes in the local Hassaniya dialect rather than classical Arabic, which is not understood by many Mauritanians. He is extremely popular among the Ḥarāṭīn population because of his anti-racist, egalitarian stance.
50 This amendment allows legally recognized NGOs such as SOS-Esclaves to legally represent victims of slavery, who are often deterred and discouraged from pressing formal charges due to social pressure (by state agents, traditional religious authorities and their 'master's' families) and informal offers of compensation (far below the financial compensation prescribed by law) in return for dropping the accusations and settling the case. Penalties were doubled to ten to twenty years' prison.
51 Besides the Mauritanian mother organization, IRA has branches in Senegal, Belgium, France, Italy, Germany, the Netherlands, the USA and Canada.
52 The ceremonial event has taken place two times thus far, in 2011 and 2019. Its coincidence with the national holiday adds to its symbolic weight.

53 After IRA Mauritanie sealed this political alliance, the regional American chapter of IRA, which has many Halpulaaren members who went into exile during the ethnic clashes of the late 1980s, announced a split from the Mauritanian mother organization.

54 On the populist style of 'democracy' implement by President Abdel Aziz during his time in office, see Ould Mohamed Baba's chapter in this volume.

55 The document is available on the homepage of the 'Association des Haratine de Mauritanie en Europe' (AHME): https://haratine.com/Site/?p=6291.

56 Following this announcement, however, the 2020 march had to be cancelled due to the Covid-19 pandemic.

57 These 'Ḥarāṭīn NGOs' include the Fondation Sahel, Elawassir, Flambeau de Liberté, Maison de la Liberté, and the Association Ennour pour l'Éducation et l'Engagement Social. Fondation Sahel and Elawassir were founded by former IRA members who left the organization because they disagreed with its increasing politicization under Abeid's leadership. Flambeau de la Liberté was founded by a cousin of Messaoud Boulkheir, an El-Hor and former SOS-Esclaves member. The latter two organizations are close to the Islamist Tawassoul party. In addition to these established and officially recognized NGOs, there are many other small organizations and informal activist circles, especially among young Ḥarāṭīn with a higher education.

References

Abdoul, M. (2004), 'Démocratisation, ethnicité et tribalisme: jeux identitaires et enjeux politiques en Mauritanie', *L'Ouest Saharien*, 4, 'Regards sur la Mauritanie', 16–76.

Alumona, I. M. and S. N. Azom (2018), 'Politics of Identity and the Crisis of Nation-Building in Africa', in S. O. Oloruntoba and T. Falola (eds), *The Palgrave Handbook of African Politics, Governance and Development*, 291–306. New York, NY: Palgrave.

Anderson, B. (1983), *Imagined Communities: Reflections on the Origin and Spread of Nationalism*. London: Verso.

ASI, IRA, MRG, SOS-Esclaves, STP and UNPO (2015), 'Enforcing Mauritania's Anti-Slavery Legislation: The Continued Failure of the Justice System to Prevent, Protect and Punish'. https://minorityrights.org/wp-content/uploads/2015/10/MRG_Rep_Maur2_Nov15_ENG_2.pdf.

Ba, O. M. (1998), 'The State, Elites and Ethnic Conflict in Mauritania', in O. N. Okwudiba (ed.), *Ethnic Conflicts in Africa*, 235–58. Dakar: CODESRIA.

Baba Ahmed, M. (2017), 'Chants et danses profanes des Ḥrāṭīn de Mauritanie: entre stigmates de la servitude et quête de reconnaissance social et politique', in S. Boulay and F. Freire (eds), *Culture et politique dans l'Ouest saharien: arts, activisme et etat dans un espace de conflits*, 335–60. Igé: Éditions de l'Etrave.

BBC (2012), 'Mauritanian Activist Sparks Religious Storm', 31 May. https://www.bbc.com/news/world-africa-18209011.

Brhane, M. (1997), 'Narratives of the Past, olitics of the resent: Identity, Subordination and the Haratines of Mauritania', PhD thesis, University of Chicago.

Brhane, M. (2000), 'Histoires de Nouakchott: discours des *hrâtîn* sur le pouvoir et l'identité', in M. Villasante (ed.), *Groupes serviles au Sahara. Approche comparative à partir du cas des arabophones du* Mauritanie, 195–234. Paris: CNRS Éditions.

Bonte, P. (1989), 'L'«ordre» de la tradition: évolution des hiérarchies statuaires dans la société maure contemporaine', *Revue de la monde musulman et de la méditerrané*, 54: 118–29.

Bonte, P. (1998), 'Esclaves ou cousins: évolution du statut servile dans la société mauritanienne', in B. Schlemmer (ed.), *Terrains et engagements de Claude Meillassoux*, 157–82. Paris: Khartala.
Bonte, P. (2002), 'L'esclavage: un problème contemporaine?', *L'homme*, 164 (4): 135–44.
Bonte, P. (2008), *L'émirat de l'Adrar mauritanien: Harīm, compétition et protection dans une société tribale saharienne*. Paris: Khartala.
Bonte, P. et al., eds (1991), *Al-Ansâb: La quête des origines*, Paris. Éditions de la Maison des sciences de l'homme.
Botte, R. (1999), 'Riimayɓe, Ḥarāṭīn, Iklan: les damnés de la terre, le développement et la démocratie', in A. Bourgeot (ed.), *Horizons nomades en Afrique sahélienne. Sociétés, développement et démocratie*, 45–78. Paris: Khartala.
Botte, R. (2005), 'Les habits neufs de l'esclavage: Métamorphoses de l'oppression au travail', *Cahiers d'études africaines*, 3–4 (179–180): 651–66.
Bulay, S. and F. Freire, eds (2017), *Culture et politique dans l'Ouest saharien*. Igé: L'Étrave.
Caratini, S. (2003), *La république des sables: anthropologie d'une révolution*. Paris, L'Harmattan.
Choplin, A., ed. (2009), *Nouakchott: Au Carrefour de la Mauritanie et du monde*. Paris: Karthala.
Ciavolella, R. R. (2014), 'Representing the Nation Horizontally and Vertically', *Middle East Law and Governance*, 6: 327–54.
Diagana, A. et al. (2016), 'Marches et grèves. Les tourments d'une gouvernance face aux tensions sociales et politiques (2014–2015)', *L'Année du Maghreb*, 15: 257–77. https://journals.openedition.org/anneemaghreb/2904#bodyftn62.
Du Puigaudeau, O. (1961), 'Mauritanie, république des sables', *Esprit*, 292 (2): 230–48.
Eickelman, D. F. and J. W. Anderson, eds (1999), *New Media and The Muslim World: The Emerging Public Sphere*. Bloomington, IN: Indiana University Press.
El Hamel, C. C. (2013), *Black Morocco: A History of Slavery, Race, and Islam*. Cambridge: Cambridge University Press.
El-Hor, Organisation pour la libération des Haratines (2004 [1978]), 'Charte Constitutive', in *L'Ouest Saharien*, 4, 'Regards sur la Mauritanie', 183–88. Paris: L'Harmattan.
Ellis, S. and I. van Kessel, eds (2009), *Movers and Shakers: Social Movements in Africa*. Leiden: Brill.
Esseissah, K. (2016), '"Paradise Is under the Feet of Your Master": The Construction of the Religious Basis of Racial Slavery in the Mauritanian Arab-Berber Community', *Journal of Black Studies*, 47(1): 3–23.
Fortier, C. (2001), 'Le lait, le sperme, le dos. Et le sang?', *Cahiers d'Études Africaines*, 161: 97–138.
Fortier, C. (2020), 'Genre, statut et ethnicisation des harâtîn de Mauritanie'. In E. A. McDougall (ed.), *L'Ouest saharien*, vol. 10/11, 'Devenir visibles dans le sillage de l'esclavage: la question ḥarāṭīn en Mauritanie et au Maroc', 171–86.
Freire, F. (2011), 'The "Narziguas," Forgotten Protagonists of Saharan History', *Islamic Africa*, 2(1): 35–65.
Freire, F. (2014), 'Saharan migrant camel herders: Znāga social status and the global age', *The Journal of Modern Africa Studies*, 52(3): 425–46.
Freire, F. (2019), 'Weapons of the Weak, and of the Strong: Mauritanian Foreign Policy and the International Dimensions of Social Activism', *The Journal of North African Studies*, 24 (3): 490–505.
Freire, F. and M. Taleb Heidi (forthcoming), 'Nouakchott y Baghdad: Baazismo y movilizaciones sociales en Mauritania', in A. López Bargados and F. Correale (eds), *Movilizaciones colectivas en el Sáhara Atlántico*. Barcelona: Bellaterra.

Fresia, M. (2009), 'Les enjeux politiques et identitaires du retour des réfugiés en Mauritanie: Vers une difficile 'réconciliation nationale'?', *Politique Africaine*, 114 (2): 44–66.

Front uni pour l'action des Haratines (2008), '50 ans de marginalisation et d'exclusion systématiques des Haratines'. http://mauritanie2007.unblog.fr/bilan-50-ans-de-marginalisation-et-dexclusion-systematiques-des-haratines/.

Hackett, R and B. F. Soares, eds (2015), *New Media and Religious Transformations in Africa*. Bloomington, IN: Indiana University Press.

Hahonou, E. and L. Pelckmans (2011), 'West African Antislavery Movements: Citizenship Struggles and the Legacies of Slavery', *Stichproben: Wiener Zeitschrift für kritische Afrikastudien*, 20: 141–62.

Hall, B. S. (2005), 'The Question of "Race" in the Pre-colonial Southern Sahara', *The Journal of North Africa Studies*, 10 (3–4): 339–67.

Hall, B. S. (2011), *A History of Race in Muslim West Africa 1600–1960*. Cambridge: Cambridge University Press.

Hall, B. S. (2020), 'Memory, Slavery and Muslim Citizenship in the Post-Emancipation Circum-Saharan World', in E. A. McDougall (ed.), *L'Ouest Saharien: cahier d'études pluridisciplinaires*, vol. 10–11, 'Devenir visible dans le sillage de l'esclavage: La question Ḥarāṭīn en Mauritanie et en Maroc', 95–108.

Hechter, M. (2004), 'From Class to Culture', *The American Journal of Sociology*, 110(2): 400–45.

Hill, J. (2012), 'The Cosmopolitan Sahara: Building a Global Islamic Village in Mauritania', *City & Society*, 24(1): 62–83.

Hobsbawm, E. J. and T. Ranger, eds (1983), *The Invention of Tradition*. Cambridge: Cambridge University Press.

Kamara, O. (2000), 'Les divisions statutaires des descendants d'esclaves au Fouta Tooro mauritanien', *Journal des Africanistes*, 70: 265–89.

Keller, E. J. (2014), *Identity, Citizenship, and Political Conflict in Africa*. Bloomington, IN: Indiana University Press.

Klein, M. (1998), *Slavery and Colonial rule in French West Africa*. Cambridge: Cambridge University Press.

Klein, M. (2005), 'The Concept of Honour and the Persistence of Servility in the Western Soudan', *Cahiers d'Études Africaines*, 3–4(179): 831–52.

Klute, G. (1998), 'Réflexions sur la politique coloniale de l'esclavage en Afrique Occidentale Française: le cas des Touaregs', *L'Ouest Saharien*, 1: 113–23.

Lecocq, B. and E. Hahonou (2015), 'Introduction: Exploring Post-Slavery in Contemporary Africa', *International Journal of African Historical Studies*, 48(2): 181–92.

Lonsdale, J. (1994), 'Moral Ethnicity and Political Tribalism', in P. Kaarsholm and J. Hultin (eds), *Inventions and Boundaries: Historical and Anthropological Approaches to the Study of Ethnicity and* Nationalism, 131–50. Roskilde: Roskilde University.

Leservoisier, O. (2004), 'Enjeux des traditions inventées chez des groupes d'origines serviles: Les Harâtîn de Mauritanie', in D. Dimitrijevic (ed.), *Fabrication des traditions: Invention de modernité*, 163–74. Paris: Éditions de la Maison des sciences de l'homme.

Leservoisier, O. (2008), 'Les héritages de l'esclavage dans la société haalpulaar de Mauritanie', *Journal des Africanistes*, 78(1–2): 247–67.

Lewis, B. B. (1992 [1990]), *Race and Slavery in the Middle East: An Historical Enquiry*. New York, NY: Oxford University Press.

Maimone, G. (2016), 'The fight against Slavery in Mauritania as a Tool for Socio-political Claims between Military Coups and the Arab Spring Contagion', in L. El Houssi et al. (eds), *North African Societies after the Arab Spring: Between Democracy and Islamic Awakening*, 222–39. Newcastle: Cambridge Scholars.

Maimone, G. (2018), 'Are Haratines Black Moors or just Black?', opendemocracy.net. https://www.opendemocracy.net/beyondslavery/giuseppe-maimone/are-haratines-black-moors-or-just-black.

Maimone, G. (2020), 'IRA Mauritanie: Legacy and Innovation in the Anti-slavery Fight in Mauritania', *Antropologia*, 7(1): 67–92.

Mamdani, M. (1996), *Citizen and Subject: Contemporary Africa and the Legacy of Late Colonialism*. Princeton, NJ: Princeton University Press.

Manifeste des Haratines (2013). https://haratine.com/Site/?p=6291.

Marchesin, P. (1992), *Tribus, ethnies et pouvoir en Mauritanie*. Paris: Karthala.

McDougall, E. A. (1988), 'A Topsy-Turvy World: Slaves and Freed Slaves in the Mauritanian Adrar, 1910–1950', in S. Miers and R. Roberts (eds), *The End of Slavery in Africa*, 362–82. London: University of Wisconsin Press.

McDougall, E. A. (2005), 'Living the Legacy of Slavery: Between Discourse and Reality', *Cahiers d'Études Africaines*, 45(179–180): 957–86.

McDougall, E. A. (2007), '"Si un homme travaille il doit être libre …": Les serviteurs hrâtîn et le discours colonial sur le travail en Mauritanie', in M. Villasante Cervello (ed.), *Colonisations et Héritages Actuels au Sahara et au Sahel: Problèmes Conceptuels, État des Lieux et Nouvelles Perspectives de Recherche (XVIIIe-XXe siècle)*, vol. 2, 229–64. Paris: L'Harmattan.

McDougall, E. A. (2010), 'The Politics of Slavery in Mauritania: Rhetoric, Reality and Democratic Discourse', *The Maghreb Review*, 35(2): 259–86.

McDougall, E. A. (2014), 'Affirming Identity in the Islamic Republic of Mauritania: the "Abolition Crisis" of 1980–1983', *The Maghreb Review*, 39(2): 191–207.

McDougall, E. A. (2015), 'Hidden in Plain Sight: Haratine in Nouakchott's "Niche-Settlements"', *International Journal of African Historical Studies*, 48(2): 251–79.

McDougall, E. A., ed. (2020), *L'Ouest Saharien*, vol. 10-11, 'Devenir visible dans le sillage de l'esclavage: La question ḥarāṭīn en Mauritanie et au Maroc'.

Messaoud, B. (2000), 'L'esclavage en Mauritanie: de l'idéologie du silence à la mise en question', *Journal des Africanistes*, 70 (1–2): 291–337.

N'Diaye, S. (2016), 'Des "restes" résistants en milieu soninké: esclavage, sens de l'honneur et mécanismes d'émancipation', *Critique Internationale*, 72 (3): 113–25.

Ngaïde, A. (2008), 'Musique et danse chez les Haratin de Mauritanie: Conscience identitaire et/ou dissidence culturelle?', *Afrika Zamani*, 15–16: 1–25.

Norris, H. T. (1986), *The Arab conquest of the Western Sahara*. Harlow: Longman.

Oßwald, R. (2016), *Sklavenhandel und Sklavenleben Zwischen Senegal und Atlas*, Mitteilungen zur Sozial- und Kulturgeschichte der islamischen Welt, vol. 39. Würzburg: Ergon.

Oßwald, R. (2017), *Das islamische Sklavenrecht*, Mitteilungen zur Sozial- und Kulturgeschichte der islamischen Welt, vol. 40. Würzburg: Ergon.

Ould Ahmed Salem, Z. (2009), 'Bare-Foot Activists: Transformations in the Haratine Movement in Mauritania', in S. Ellis and I. van Kessel (eds), *Movers and Shakers: Social Movements in Africa*, 156–77. Leiden: Brill.

Ould Ahmed Salem, Z. (2013), *Prêcher dans le désert: Islam politique et changement social en Mauritanie*. Paris: Karthala.

Ould Ahmed Salem, Z. (2018a), 'The Politics of the Haratin Social Movement in Mauritania, 1978-2014', in O. Abi-Mershed (ed.), *Social Currents in North Africa*, 117–42. London: Georgetown University Qatar.

Ould Ahmed Salem, Z. (2018b), '"Touche pas à ma nationalité": enrôlement biométrique et controverses sur l'identification en Mauritanie', *Politique Africaine*, 152(4): 77–99.

Ould Ahmed Salem, Z. and B. Samuel (2011), 'Aux frontières du printemps arabe: crises sociales et contestations populaires en Mauritanie', Centre d'études et de recherches internationales (CERI). https://www.sciencespo.fr/ceri/sites/sciencespo.fr.ceri/files/art_zoas_bs.pdf.

Ould Bah, M. E. M. (1981), *La Littérature Juridique et l'Évolution du Malikisme en Mauritanie*. Tunis: Publications de l'Université de Tunis.

Ould Cheikh, A. W. (1993), 'L'évolution de l'esclavage dans la société maure', in E. Bernus et al. (eds), *Nomades et Commandants: Administration et Sociétés Nomades dans l'Ancienne A.O.F.*, 181–92. Paris: Karthala.

Ould Cheikh, A. W. (2004), 'Mutations de l'espace public et nouvelles formes de citoyenneté: la difficile sortie des débats sur l'esclavage en Mauritanie', in Z. Ould Ahmed Salem (ed.), *Les trajectoires d'un État-frontière: espaces, évolution politique et transformations sociales en Mauritanie*, 281–304. Dakar: CODESRIA.

Ould Cheikh, A. W. (2017), *La Société Maure: Éléments d'Anthropologie Historique*. Rabat: Centre des Études Sahariennes.

Ould Cheikh, A. W. (2020), 'Géographie de la liberté: Emancipation légale, émancipation foncière et appartenance tribale en Mauritanie', in E. A. McDougall (ed.), *L'Ouest Saharien* 10–11, 'Devenir visible dans le sillage de l'esclavage: La question Ḥarāṭīn en Mauritanie et en Maroc', 109–24.

Ould Cheikh, A. W. (n.d.), *Islam et esclavage en Mauritanie*. https://www.academia.edu/6157206/Islam_et_esclavage_en_Mauritanie.

Ould Cheikh, A. W. and Ould Al-Barra, Y. (1996), 'Il faut qu'une terre soit ouverte ou fermée. Du statut des biens fonciers collectifs dans la société maure', *Revue des Mondes Musulmans et de la Méditerranée*, 79–80: 157–80.

Ould Ciré, M. Y. (2014), *L'Abolition de l'esclavage en Mauritanie et les difficultés de son application*. Paris: L'Harmattan.

Ould Saleck, E.-A. (2000), 'Les Haratin comme enjeu pour les partis politiques en Mauritanie', *Journal des Africanistes*, 70(1–2): 255–63.

Ould Saleck, E.-A. (2003), *Les Haratins: Le paysage politique mauritanien*. Paris: L'Harmattan.

Pelckmans, L. and C. Hardung (2015), 'La question de l'esclavage en Afrique: politisation et mobilisations', *Politique Africaine*, 140 (4): 5–22.

Robinson, D. (2000), *Paths of Accommodation: Muslim Societies and French Colonial Authorities in Senegal and Mauritania, 1880–1920*. Oxford: James Currey.

Rossi, B., ed. (2009), *Reconfiguring Slavery: West African Trajectories*. Liverpool: Liverpool University Press.

Rossi, B., ed. (2015), 'African Post-Slavery: A History of the Future', *International Journal of African Historical Studies*, 48(2): 303–24.

Ruf, U. P. (1999), *Ending Slavery: Hierarchy, Dependency, and Gender in Central Mauritania*. Bielefeld: Transcript.

Ruf, U. P. (2000), 'De neuf dans le vieux: la situation des harâtîn et 'abîd en Mauritanie rurale', *Journal des Africanistes*, 70(1–2): 239–54.

Scheele, J. (2012), *Smugglers and Saints of the Sahara: Regional Connectivity in the Twentieth Century*. New York, NY: Cambridge University Press.

Spiegel, J. (2014), 'Biram Dah Abeid: "Ma candidature va totalement transformer la carte politique mauritanienne"', jeuneafrique.com, 17 June. http://www.jeuneafrique.com/52116/politique/biram-dah-abeid-ma-candidature-va-totalement-transformer-la-carte-politique-mauritanienne/.

Stewart, C. C. (1973), *Islam and Social Order in Mauritania: A Case Study from the 19th Century*. Oxford: Clarendon Press.

Taine-Cheikh, C. (1989), 'La Mauritanie en noir et blanc: Petite promenade linguistique en hassâniyya', *Revue des Mondes Musulmans et de la Méditerranée*, 54: 90–105.

Tamari, T. (1991), 'The Development of Caste Systems in West Africa', *The Journal of African History*, 32(2): 221–50.

Taylor, C. (1994), 'The Politics of Recognition', in C. Taylor et al. (eds), *Multiculturalism and the Politics of Recognition*, 25–73. Princeton, NJ: Princeton University Press.

Thompson, R. H. (1997), 'Ethnic Minorities and the Case for Collective Rights', *American Anthropologist*, 99 (4): 786–98.

Villasante, M. (1991), 'Hiérarchies statutaires et conflits fonciers dans l'Assaba contemporain (Mauritanie). Rupture ou continuité?', *Revue du Monde Musulman et de la Méditerranée*, 59–60: 181–210.

Villasante, M. (1999), 'Mauritanie: catégories de classement identitaire et discours politiques dans la société bidân', *Annuaire de l'Afrique du Nord*, 36: 79–100.

Villasante, M., ed. (2000), *Groupes serviles au Sahara: approche comparative à partir du cas des arabophones de Mauritanie*. Paris: CNRS Éditions.

Villasante, M. (2004), 'They Work to Eat and They Eat to Work. *M'allemîn* Craftsmen Classifications and Discourse among the Mauritanian *Bidân* Nobility', in J. C. Berland and A. Rao (eds), *Costumary Strangers: New Perspectives on peripatetic Peoples in the Middle East, Africa and Asia*, 123–54. Westport, CT: Praeger.

Villasante, M. (2007a), 'Négritude, *tribalitude* et nationalisme en Mauritanie: Des héritages coloniaux en matière d'idéologie et de commandement', in M. Villasante (ed.), *Colonisations et héritages actuels au Sahara et au Sahel: Problèmes conceptuels, état des lieux et nouvelles perspectives de recherche (XVIIIe-XXe siècles)*, 2 vols, 445–98. Paris: L'Harmattan.

Villasante, M. (2007b), 'Quelques réflexions sur le devenir des catégories coloniales de classement collectif: races, tribus et ethnies. La question des identités sociales élargies et restreintes', in M. Villasante (ed.), *Colonisations et héritages actuels au Sahara et au Sahel: Problèmes conceptuels, état des lieux et nouvelles perspectives de recherche (XVIIIe–XXe siècles)*, 2 vols, 67–126. Paris: L'Harmattan.

Yeros, P., ed. (1999), *Ethnicity and Nationalism in Africa: Constructivist Reflections and Contemporary Politics*. Houndmills: Macmillan Press.

Wiley, A. K. (2018), *Work, Social Status and Gender in Post-Slavery Mauritania*. Bloomington, IN: University of Indiana Press.

Part Three

Islam

9

On the (body of the) subject in the Sahara: Muḥummadhun Fāl b. Muttālī's *Fatḥ al-ḥaqq* (nineteenth century)

Abdel Wedoud Ould Cheikh
Professor Emeritus at the University of Lorraine, France

In any case, one thing is certain,
and that is that the human body is the principal actor in all utopias.
–Michel Foucault

Introduction

The remarks proposed here are part of an ongoing research project on the presence (or absence) of something along the lines of a *thinking subject* in the scholarly traditions associated with the western Saharan region, namely among the Moorish *zwāya* ('religious') scholars. Their contributions demonstrate an appreciable degree of sophistication, evidenced in the accumulation of sometimes very extensive works in all fields of the Arab-Muslim scholarly corpus, dating back to the sixteenth century: Arabic language sciences (grammar, rhetoric, prosody, lexicography, etc.), religious sciences (Quranic exegesis, *ḥadīth*, theology, jurisprudence, prophetic history) and even secular knowledge such as mathematics, astronomy, logic and medicine.[1]

The question presiding over this research was inspired by anthropological literature that underlined the contrast between *holistic societies* – functioning essentially on a communal basis – and those resulting from the development of capitalism, where the individual has progressively become the centre of the social and political game.[2] The more general side of this undertaking also brought me back to philosophical debates between structuralists, Marxists, psychoanalysts and phenomenologists around *the question of the subject*. I will not enter into these debates here, however. When one undertakes to question the notion of the *thinking subject*[3] in the remote corner of Arab-Muslim culture that is the Moorish world of the western Saharan region, one is confronted with related themes that range from the 'person', to 'consciousness' and 'perception', to 'identity', 'understanding', 'the intellect', 'memory', 'the will', 'freedom' and the like. There is then of course the related theme of *the subject's body*, its singular physical properties and indigenous ways of thinking about the genetic processes that determine its sex, bodily appearance, character, membership in the father's or mother's kinship group, whom it may or may not touch, marry, etc. The subject's body and the way it is (ideally) perceived in *zwāya* culture is the focus of this chapter.[4]

I will start with a brief presentation of the Islamic view of the genesis of the human subject and some of its sociological consequences in the Sahara, particularly with regard to what might be termed the 'external contacts' of the subject.[5] In a second section, I will discuss elements of the Saharo-Islamic discipline of the body, as summarized in the *Fatḥ al-ḥaqq fī ḥuqūq al-khāliq wa-l-khalq*, written by the Moorish scholar Muḥummadhun Fāl b. Muttālī (d. 1287 H/1870 CE). The connection between these two points may not seem obvious, but they both participate – a point I would like to stress – in the idea that the body of the subject is above all a social construction: before (eventually) becoming a thinking subject, the Saharan subject is *a thought subject.*

Saharan Islamic embryology

Maurice Godelier (2007: 115) has suggested that 'nowhere are a man and a woman enough to make a child'.[6] The intervention of agents and powers outside the direct 'operators of reproduction', if we can call them that, is generally acknowledged, even if in modern Euro-American culture and its avatars the focus has progressively been established around the nuclear family, based on the individual,[7] whereas in so-called 'traditional' societies the hold of extended kinship and the spirit world continues to assert itself.

Who are the protagonists involved in the production of a human embryo in the – profoundly Islamized – Moorish society of the Western Sahara? There must be a man and a woman, of course, but the Devil and the Good Lord also bestow benefits and curses on the embryo, starting with the attribution of the vital breath, the soul. Let us consider the respective contributions of men and women in the light of the considerations developed by Françoise Héritier (1994a; where she dealt directly with milk kinship in the Arab-Muslim context) on the three bodily fluids, *blood*, *sperm* and *milk*, which are the essential vectors of the links, real or symbolic, of kinship. What weight do they carry in the genesis of the (Saharan) embryo? What kind of proximity/distance or prohibitions are they vectors of?

I mention Françoise Héritier because most of the questions that revolve around the problem of the genesis of the embryo considered here are closely linked to that of incest, her central theme. We know that for Lévi-Strauss (1949) – a close associate of Héritier – the prohibition of incest was considered universal and was present at the foundation of all human cultures.[8] But whereas for Lévi-Strauss incest is limited to the prohibition of sexual relations with certain classes of consanguineous persons (mother, sister, daughter, etc.) for the purposes of exchanges with third parties, Héritier suggests that, alongside this 'direct incest', we should take into consideration what she calls 'second type incest', associated with the circulation of essential bodily fluids (blood, milk, sperm) and the risks, in her words, of 'short circuits' that this circulation could generate (Héritier 1994a: 11). The matter is not so much a question of identifying a category of individuals who are prohibited from having sexual relations as protection against forms of harmful circulation, particularly the circulation of sperm. Lévi-Strauss interpreted incest as a negative prescription (don't marry your sister) coupled with a positive perspective of exchange (the exchange of the sister for another), whereas Françoise Héritier's 'second type' incest aimed to prevent the bringing together, the putting into contact, of identical 'humors' (see, for example, the Islamic prohibition of a man's marrying two sisters, or a daughter and her mother, etc.).

In the western regions of the Sahara, which have long been Islamized, matrimonial prohibitions are defined by legislation derived from the Qurʾān, in particular verse 23 of surah IV (*al-Nisāʾ*, 'The Women').[9] They are based on degrees of closeness commanded by genealogy: through blood kinship (the ties that are created as a result of marriage; for example the father's wife, the wife's mother, even if the union has not been consummated, the wife's daughter only if the marriage has been consummated …), and through milk kinship.

These details seemed useful for addressing the formation of embryos, the consequences for unborn subjects, and the network of constraints, prohibitions and obligations that are imposed on their future freedom of action and thought. In both the scholarly realm and Moorish popular culture, the reproduction process is involved in a representation of the body that inscribes it in a set of dichotomies, bearing, on the literate side, the mark of Greek medicine (Hippocrates, Aristotle, Galen), distilled through more recent authors from the eastern Mediterranean such as Ibn Sīnā, al-Rāzī, al-Suyūṭī, al-Inṭākī and al-Ṣunbarī. These dichotomies are based on the four elements (water, earth, fire and air), associated with four 'humors' (blood, phlegm, yellow bile and black bile), hot and cold, wet and dry, belly and back, hard and soft, left and right, etc.[10] Awfā b. Abī Bakr al-Idātfaghī (d. 1300 H/1882 CE), the leading authority on traditional medicine in the Moorish Sahara, summarizes the foundations of Saharan physiology in his *al-ʿUmda*, a treatise in 1,219 verses in *rajaz* metre:

The first chapter of the (science of) nature	And what it contains of creative wisdom
Figure in the initial appearance of *heat*,	Which comes from the movement of beings
Then the *cold*, associated with immobility,	Born of the absence of motion in the universe
Dryness comes from the heat of the earth	And *wetness* from a contrary mixture
From the mixture of these four properties	Came the following elements
From the combination of dry and hot	Our Almighty God created *fire*
From the combination of the moist and the hot	Gave birth to the *air*
From the combination of *water* and cold	Comes moisture
The combination of dry and cold	Gave birth to the *earth*
This happened in two rotations of the celestial vault	Operated for the mixture by the Lord Almighty.

(*al-ʿUmda*, manuscript, verses 38–47)

Awfā continues with the table of the humours and their 'locations': yellow bile (*al-ṣafrā ʾ*) comes from fire and is located in the gallbladder. It is subdivided into five varieties associated with five different pathologies. 'Blood is created from air', and its organs are the liver (*al-kabid*) and the heart (*al-qalb*). Phlegm (*al-balgham*), on the other hand, comes from water (*al-mā ʾ*). Its seat is in the kidneys and the lungs (*wa li-l-kilā thumma li-l-riyyat nusib*). Black bile (*al-mirra al-sawdā ʾ*) is related to the earth and has its seat in the spleen (*al-ṭiḥal*) (verses 50–63).[11]

The Sunni conception of the formation of the embryo, associated with these various polarities, gives a role to both the man and the woman (surah XLIX, *al-Ḥujurāt*, verse 13), even if it conceives of the latter above all as a receptacle, a 'ploughing field' (*nisā ʾukum ḥarthun lakum*), as stated in verse 223 of surah II (*al-Baqara*), which her husband may frequent at will (*fa ʾtū ḥarthakum annā shi ʾtum*). But while the female fluid is supposed to contribute to the genesis of the embryo, the sperm, of osseous origin since it emanates from the spinal column (*al-ṣulb*) of the man, is credited with forming the solid frame – the skeleton – of the unborn child. The mother's physiological contribution is limited to the 'soft' parts of the future baby, i.e. the formation of its flesh.

The process of the 'coction' of the embryo takes it, according to the path suggested by verse 5 of surah XXII (*al-Ḥajj*), from the state of a 'drop' (*nuṭfa*), to that of a 'flaccid mass' (*muḍgha*), passing through that of a 'blood clot' (*ʿalaqa*), before it becomes, at the end of six months minus five days, a small living human being (*al-Ḥajj*, XXII, verse 5). In the meantime, an angel will have passed by and breathed a soul into the embryo and assigned a gender, which only God knows before birth, although guesses can be made from certain clues. Boys are presumed to be heavier (thus the belly of the future parturient is 'lower') and are more likely to be located on the right than on the left, the side associated with girls (Fortier 2000: 643). The physiological impact of the father extends far beyond the children's time in the maternal womb, however. Breastfeeding, the main condition for their survival, is far from being independent of the father's powers. Rather than entering into the arcana of milk kinship in the Sahara,[12] I will limit myself to highlighting a few aspects that touch on the future of adult Saharan subjects and the limits and constraints that they face.

The questions related to milk kinship stem from the different degrees of proximity and/or distance associated with breastfeeding. Any woman who breastfeeds a child generates the same network of prohibitions and freedoms (in terms of male/female relations) as that conferred by blood ties. The child becomes her own children's brother, her mother's grandson, her grandchildren's uncle, etc. A *ḥadīth* attributed by al-Bukhārī to ʿĀ ʾisha states that 'the (matrimonial) prohibitions of breastfeeding are the same as those of genealogy' (*yaḥrum min al-riḍā ʿ mā yaḥrum min al-nasab*; al-Bukhārī, *Bāb al-shahāda ʿalā al-ansāb wa al-riḍā ʿ*, number 2645).[13] Breastfeeding must, of course, be carried out by a woman and not by any other mammal (goat, sheep, etc.), and most Sunni legal scholars maintain that this should take place before the age of weaning, set at 2 years (although this agreement has not prevented long debates on the possibility of breastfeeding an adult). Things become more complicated, however, with the intervention of the husband or the father, whatever his legal status. According to Muslim theologians, in fact, the milk of the breastfeeding woman is not so much her own as that of the 'stallion' (*al-faḥl*), according to Bousquet's translation, or of the 'male', as Benkheira prefers to translate it (Benkheira et al. 2012: 208), who is associated with her. Maḥanḍ Bāba Ibn Aʿbayd, a nineteenth-century Moorish commentator of Khalīl's *Mukhtaṣar*, writes that 'milk belongs to the *faḥl* in two ways: either by reason of the fact that his semen (*māʾihi*) is the cause (*sabab*) of the existence of milk (*wujūd al-laban*), such as one who marries a woman who at first lacks milk but then acquires it as a result of her sexual relationship with him (*fatadurru bi-waṭʾihi*), becomes pregnant, gives birth, and thus nurses (*aw taḥmalu fa-talidu fa-turḍiʿu bi dhālika*), or by reason of being the cause of its abundance (*sababan li-kathratihi*), such as one who marries a nursing woman, copulates with her and dispenses his semen to her because his semen increases the milk (*yakthuru bihi al-laban*), of which he thus becomes a part (*fa-shāraka fīhi*)'; Ibn Aʿbayd 2016, vol. II: 649; see also Ibn Isḥāq 1981: 163). In other words, if a woman is lactating, this is because she has copulated with a man, who becomes ipso facto its co-producer. This entails the imposition of the same restrictions and rights on the agnatic kin of the beneficiary of this milk as those that apply to his matrilineal kinship network. Whether based on blood or on milk, kinship engenders both matrimonial prohibitions and permissions in the context of what the *fuqahāʾ* call *maḥramiyya* ('intimacy'),[14] touching or looking, which is otherwise prohibited. The *maḥārim* (the mother and her children, sisters and brothers, uncles/aunts and their nephews/nieces …) are people (both women and men) who may touch and see each other, but among whom marriage is prohibited.

The *fuqahāʾ* discuss the number of feedings or the amount of milk required to establish a legally admissible milk relationship, who can legitimately attest to this relationship, whether 'illegitimate' milk (i.e. the result of an illegitimate sexual relationship) can be used to establish a legitimate milk relationship, the duration of a woman's lactation, and the basis (or lack thereof) of a shared 'ownership' of a woman's milk supply in cases where she has had more than one husband in successive alliances without any interruption of lactation. In the latter case, I cannot resist mentioning the example of a kind of 'UHT (ultra-high transmission) milk', mentioned by Maḥanḍ Bāba in his *Muyassar*:

> Whoever marries a woman who is lactating due to a previous husband and has sexual intercourse with her and then repudiates her, let that woman come to marry a third man, such that her milk supply continues and the period of sexual intercourse with the second husband is prolonged, the (transmitting) power of the latter vanishes and the powers of the first and third remain; for the power of the middle husband was related to increase (*kāna bi-l-takthīr*), and the prolonging of the duration annihilates it. As for the first husband, he is the cause of the existence of the milk, and his power (of transmission) disappears only if the lactation stops.
>
> (Ibn Aʿbayd 2016, vol. II: 650, referring to al-Lakhmī (d. 478 H/1085 CE)

Let us imagine that a man marries a nursing woman who has a previous husband, copulates with her and separates from her after some time. She marries a third husband. The milk relationship between this woman's offspring and the relatives of the second husband, whose only role was to maintain lactation for a certain period of time, will not be taken into account. On the other hand, the network of relatives of the first husband, considered the initial trigger of the woman's lactation, as well as the third husband, associated with the perpetuation of her milk supply, will be fully considered as milk kin.

One might think that this is a simple carry-over from a bygone era now that bottle feeding is steadily replacing breastfeeding. And yet, particularly in the case of Moorish society, where at least 70 per cent of the population remained nomadic until the early 1970s, this would not seem to be the case. If we consider the *fatāwā* collected by Yaḥyā w. al-Barrā' in his voluminous compilation of western Saharan legal responses, for example, it is clear that this topic continues to have importance for contemporary Saharan authors such as Muḥammad ʿĀlī b. ʿAbd al-Wadūd ("ʿAddūd', d. 1401 H/1980 CE), Muḥammad Faḍil Allāh b. Ahl Aydda al-Jakanī (d. 1407 H/1987 CE), Muḥammad Sālim b. al-Mukhtār b. al-Maḥbūbī (d. 1412 H/1992 CE), and b-Bāh w. ʿAbdallāh, who is still alive and even authored the preface to w. al-Barrā''s 2009 *Mawsūʿa*.

Even before birth, and during the early years of life, the future Islamic-Saharan subject is therefore marked by blood, sperm and milk, through a prescribed association with communitary life that is normatively inscribed in his body and which, like a multi-layered palimpsest, will grow with the person, imprinting itself in each part of his body, as witnessed in the work of Muḥummadhun Fāl w. Muttālī.

Images of the body

The *Fatḥ al-ḥaqq* and its author: Muḥummadhun Fāl w. Muttālī

Muḥummadhun Fāl w. Muttālī belongs to the Idägfūdyä 'faction' (*fakhdh*) of the Tandgha *zwāya qabīla* ('tribe'), which is genealogically associated with the Lamtūna, founders of the Almoravid Empire (eleventh–twelfth centuries CE). Within this larger context, the Idägfūdyä stand out through their claim to sharifian ancestry, i.e. as descendants of the Prophet of Islam, via the legendary character of al-Shrīf bu-Bazzūl.[15] This group lives in the Gibla, the southwestern region of present-day Mauritania, an area known for its many literati. The Gibla was the main theatre of a conflict (known as *Shurbubba*) in the 1670s, the main protagonist of which, al-Imām Nāṣir al-Dīn (d. 1674 CE), attempted to establish an Islamic state. Muḥummadhun Fāl's *qabīla*, the Tandgha, vigorously contributed to the mobilization led by Nāṣir al-Dīn, and since then they have played a significant part in the dissemination of scholarly traditions.

Born in 1205 H/1790 CE (according to his nephew and biographer, Ḥaymidda w. Ndyubnān), Muḥummadhun Fāl is said to have been hidden from view for sixty days by his father (*Fatḥ* 16).[16] The latter died when Muḥummadhun Fāl was only 3 years old. According to his biographers, Muḥummadhun Fāl had the power to perform miracles from an early age and had wonderful intellectual abilities, learning everything largely on his own.[17] After establishing himself as a teacher and as a 'leader of souls', he saw an important influx of students and disciples, some of whom would become notable figures in the region's intellectual landscape.[18] In addition to being a recognized scholar in the field of material knowledge (*al-ʿilm al-ẓāhir*), an area in which he authored several works,[19] and an accomplished poet, he was known above all for his therapeutic skills. As was natural at the time and in this particular milieu, his skills combined proven experimental knowledge and the miraculous effects of charisma (considered to have a divine essence). Muḥummadhun Fāl is also credited with significant writings in this field, notably associated with his *Shifā' al-abdān*. He undoubtedly passed on some of this medical knowledge to at least one of his disciples, Awfā, whose *al-'Umda*, the main reference work of traditional Moorish medicine, is mentioned above. Muḥummadhun Fāl was also a prominent figure in the shādhiliyya,[20] considered the Sufi order 'of the scholars', with limited expansion among the 'common people' except for the circumscribed membership of a few small groups among its ghuẓfiyya branch (on this subject, see the chapter by Yahya Ould al-Bara in this volume). As a major regional intellectual figure surrounded by an aura of sanctity, Muḥummadhun Fāl also took part, as a mediator and head of a *zāwiya* Sufi lodge, in events of some importance that shook the region at the time.[21] He died in 1287 H/1870 CE.

Fatḥ al-ḥaqq

An initial word on the title, *Fatḥ al-ḥaqq fī ḥuqūq al-khāliq wa al-khalq*. The term *fatḥ* means 'conquest', 'opening' and also 'inspiration'. *al-Ḥaqq* is one of the multiple Arabic names for God. Etymologically, it can be rendered as 'the true', but also as 'the right'. In this second sense, it has the plural *ḥuqūq* ('the rights'), which appears in the title of Muḥummadhun Fāl's work. This way of qualifying the divine is particularly popular with mystics (*mutaṣawwifūn*), who like to contrast *al-ḥaqīqa* ('the reality'), derived from the same root as *ḥaqq* (*ḥ.q.q*), and *sharī'a* ('the norm of the visible'), thus emphasizing the contrast between the universe to which they alone have access (the true/real/hidden sphere) and the (visible/tangible/everyday) world of the common man. *Khāliq* can be translated as 'creator' and *khalq* – a collective noun – as 'creatures'. This would render the title as a whole (without, of course, the Arabic alliterations, highly prized, as we know, in the 'old-fashioned' titles of the works of Arab-Muslim scholars): *Divine Inspiration in Relation to the Rights of the Creator and His Creation*. While this title emphasizes 'rights' (*ḥuqūq*), an expert on the text asserts that the work was known instead by the abbreviated title *Lā yajūzu* … ('It is not permitted …'), which is in fact the introductory sentence of the work: 'It is not permitted for the responsible adult to undertake any action until he or she is aware of the judgement of Allāh pertaining to it' (*Lā yajūzu li-l-mukallafi an yaqdima 'alā fi'lin min al-af'āl ḥattā ya'lama ḥukma allāhi fī dhālika al-fi'l*). *Lā yajūzu* seems in fact to be closer to the normative and injunctive content of the work than the title suggesting the existence of a right on the part of creation in relation to the Creator. Its general approach tends towards the inscription of each of the created beings' organs in a network of obligations and prohibitions, the ultimate goal of which appears to be the transformation of the entire body into a text of law. And indeed, the expression that recurs like a leitmotif throughout the work is *wa yajibu 'alayh* ('it is obligatory for him …'), its negative counterpart being *lā yajūzu* ('it is not permitted'), as well as the expression stating that a given type of behaviour with regard to such and such an organ is 'prohibited' (*ḥarām*).[22] Where these two specifications do not appear in the book, we find the attenuated forms assigned to them by *fiqh*: *yundab* ('it is recommended to'),[23] and *yukrah* ('it is inadvisable, reprobate to'). These injunctions leave little room for leeway, especially as they are specified for each part of the body, as we shall see, invoked as parts of a subject that can only find unity in the conformity of all of its components to divine law, a law which was already beginning to be imprinted on it at its embryonic stage.

Although I will only be examining a small part of this book in detail, which is some five hundred pages in length, it will be useful to provide a brief overview of its overall content. The book does not appear to follow any rigorous outline. It is a summary of the popular, mystical and normative Islam practised by nineteenth-century Western Saharans, drawing its material and arguments largely from the classics of Muslim jurisprudence and mysticism,[24] in addition to the Qur'ān and the main collections of *ḥadīth*. In a clear Sufi tone, its introductory section emphasizes the system of obligations and prohibitions the observance of which is a prerequisite for the salvation of the soul, here and in the Hereafter. This is followed by details of the obligations and prohibitions applied to each of the main organs of the body. As an extension, there are warnings against killing animals by fire, warnings to be uttered to snakes that have entered one's dwelling before attacking them, and considerations on the care of the body related to circumcision, hair (armpits, beards, moustaches, the tuft of hair under a person's lower lip …), as well as nails, wigs and tattoos. The discussion continues with considerations on magic squares (*al-awfāq*), clothing and eating habits, sleep, the 'legal' way to satisfy one's natural needs (bowel movements and urination), what to say to a person who sneezes, conduct inside the mosque, observations on dreams and their interpretation, the behaviour that should be adopted with relatives (ascendants, descendants, spouses) and elements of sexual morality. The rights of the slave and the legal forms of subjection to this status are also discussed, as is proper conduct towards animals and plants, master–disciple relations, greetings and the legitimate forms of contact they allow, yawning and sneezing, visits to the sick and to the tombs of saints, conduct at meetings and while welcoming visitors, and the like.

The remainder of the book deals with the rules of behaviour that should be adopted towards the deceased and their relatives and associates. It sets out moral considerations on the power of the emirates, on apostasy and what is permitted or forbidden with regard to the prophets, observations relating to medicine, and general remarks on the salvation of the soul and the world of the Hereafter: the prayers that must be performed to access it; how to shorten/soften the final moments of life, providing oneself with a happy end (*khātima*); on coping well with the interrogation of the two angels (Munkar and Nakīr) in the grave; and how to avoid the perils of the Last Gathering (*ahwāl al-ḥashr*). Finally, the author examines the Sunni Ashari view of the Hereafter, or the elements of classical Muslim eschatology: the lifespan of the universe (seven thousand years), the signs of the Hour (*al-sā'a*), the 'Rightly Guided' (*al-mahdī*), the 'Imposter' (*al-dajjāl*), the return of Jesus, 'The Beast' (*al-dābba*), the reversal of the course of the sun, the resurrection and the Last Judgement (*al-ḥashr, al-qiyyāma*), the intercession (*shafā'a*) of the Prophet and how to cross The Bridge (*al-ṣirāṭ*).

These elements, schematically enumerated, are the main subjects that Muḥummadhun Fāl w. Muttālī saw fit to deal with more or less extensively. I will focus in detail only on those that have to do with the legislative dissection of the body of the subject, to which I alluded at the beginning of this chapter. The 'intra-organic interpellation', as it were – i.e. organ by organ, as expressed in this work by the shādhilī master, even if he is far from being the first to do so[25] – participates in the legislative geography of the body associated with the obsessive ritualism of Islam, to which entire library shelves devoted to the major juridical-theological themes (ritual purity, prayer, pilgrimage, fasting, etc.) bear witness. The desire for exhaustiveness in the limb-by-limb control of the Muslim subject's body expounded by Muḥummadhun Fāl finds its cardinal legitimation in verse 56 of *sūrat al-Dhāriyyāt* (LI, 56), which states: *wa mā khalaqtu al-jinna wa al-insa illā li-ya'budūnī* / 'I have created demons and men only that they may worship me' (50) – although, as Muḥummadhun Fāl observes, invoking exegetes such as Ibn 'Abbās, Mujāhid, al-Rāzī, and al-Suyūṭī, this interpretation of the Qur'ān must take into account the possibility of sin, which also enters into God's design and omnipotence. *Fatḥ al-ḥaqq*'s legislative physiology – which indeed contains some redundancy insofar as organs can have various functions and are, in the end, only (partial) vectors of the conduct of the (Muslim) human being in general – therefore operates on organs that are invested with a juridical-theological individuality of their own. At the same time, it carefully considers their interactions with the surrounding universe, establishing the rules of conduct imposed on them by this 'external contact'.

The dismembered body

The dissection that Muḥummadhun Fāl carries out in his book aspires to update normative prescriptions the roots of which he strives to reveal in practices attributed to the Prophet of Islam. The text is not concerned with the physiological specificities that are attributable to these organs outside what justifies their legislative interpellation. There is no concern for the 'self', no 'subjectivation' that could inscribe them in any individual idiosyncrasy. Instead, what he provides is a pure panorama of what each member must or must not do according to *sharī'a*, as perceived by the author.

The heart

It is the heart (*al-qalb*) that is charged first and foremost with conforming to the pious and unique function devolved upon demons and men in the above-quoted verse. 'The heart', writes the author of the *Fatḥ al-ḥaqq*, 'was created (*khuliqa*) and has been tasked with knowledge as well as with all the obligations of which it is the seat' (49), for in Muḥummadhun Fāl's physiology, it is the heart, not the brain, that is the seat of intellection, discernment, memory and will. The first knowledge to be acquired is that of the foundations of faith (*'ilm al-'aqā'id*). Next comes the 'four foundations of Islam' (*qawā'id al-islām al-arba'a*): prayer (*al-ṣalāt*), legal almsgiving (*al-zakāt*), fasting (*al-ṣawm*) and pilgrimage (*al-ḥajj*) (53). These essential foundations laid, Muḥummadhun Fāl explores the difference between 'true' and 'deviant' forms of knowledge, especially those that fall under 'magic' (*al-siḥr*), which are called 'the obscure sciences' (*al-ʿulūm al-ẓulmāniyya*; 60), no doubt aware that there are sometimes tenuous boundaries between beneficial knowledge, which conforms to the Islamic norm, and what he describes as a 'simulacra of knowledge'. 'The knowledge that the heart has been made obliged to acquire', he writes, 'is that which generates light for its holder' (54). Muḥummadhun Fāl also warns against delving into 'philosophical knowledge' (*ʿulūm al-falsafa*) and 'logic' (*al-manṭiq*), as they can generate perplexity that is detrimental to faith (73). Referring to al-Ghazālī's *Iḥyaʾ ʿulūm al-dīn*, he notes that even 'natural philosophy' (*ʿilm al-ṭabīʿiyyat*), despite its kinship with medicine (*al-ṭibb*), is to be avoided (73–74). As for the third component of philosophical knowledge mentioned by al-Ghazālī – namely his considerations relating to the divine (*ʿilm al-ilāhiyyāt*), which deal with the divine essence and attributes of God – it is said to be part of a speculative theology (*ʿilm al-kalām*) which does not belong to the philosophers in its own right, even though some of them have been guilty of 'misusing' the *kalām*, of disbelieving opinions (*kufr*) or blameworthy innovations (*bidʿa*).[26]

Muḥummadhun Fāl continues to explore the duties of the heart by enumerating the faults to be avoided and the virtues to be cultivated, thus making this organ the seat and conveyor of Sufi ethics, as already developed by predecessors such as al-Ghazālī and Ibn ʿAṭāʾ Allāh. The responsible adult (*al-mukallaf*), he says, must 'purify his heart from the evil of jealousy' (*al-ghill*), of deceit and fraud (*al-ghishsh*), resentment (*al-ḥiqd*), envy (*al-ḥasad*), anger (*al-ghaḍab*), pride (*al-kibr*), complacency (*al-ʿujb*), hypocritical conformity (*al-riyyāʾ*), concern for reputation (*al-sumʿa*), greed (*al-bukhl*), fear of poverty (*khawf al-faqr*), 'celebrating the rich because of their wealth' and having 'contempt for the poor because of their poverty' (82–83), as well as any competition for the goods of 'this world' (*al-dunyā*). The heart 'is forbidden to venture into speculations about the divine nature' and must purify itself of scepticism about the divine goodness of Allāh's blessings (86). It must also guard against wishing misfortune upon other believers, cultivating the idea of the 'durability of life', thinking of oneself as 'safe from divine punishment' and 'despairing of Allāh's mercy' (94).[27]

The tongue

Continuing his normative interpellation of the organs of the human body, Muḥummadhun Fāl turns to the tongue. Of all the organs, the tongue has 'the most sway over the subject' (*amlaku shayʾin li-ṣāḥibihi*; 95), for it can both elevate him and lead to his downfall. The other parts of the body beg it, in the name of Allāh, to save them from the perils that it can bring about. The tongue is associated with the heart for its ability to signify the best and the worst in a parable attributed to Luqmān, the Quranic archetype of wisdom as presented by the surah (XXXI) that bears his name. As Muḥummadhun Fāl reports, a king is said to have proclaimed: 'Here is a beast to be slaughtered, and I ask you to present me with the best it offers.' Luqmān brought the heart and the tongue back to the ruler and, in the face of his perplexity, said to him: 'there are none better than these two organs if they follow the path of good, nor worse if they take the path of evil' (95).

The duties of the tongue are associated with a kind of Islamic moral common sense. It must invoke Allāh (*dhikr allāh*), deliver sermons (*al-waʿẓ*), remind the 'misguided' of their duties (*irshād al-ḍāll*), educate the ignorant (*taʿlīm al-jāhil*) and foster concord among Muslims. It must command good and proscribe evil (96). It must speak the truth and pronounce fair judgements (97). It must praise Allāh and pray for the Prophet, and it is forbidden to lie (99), to commit slander (*al-ghība*), to make slanderous denunciations (*al-namīma*), to speak in malice (*al-buhtān*) or to divulge the secrets of others. The tongue must also avoid uttering profanity or reporting what happens in the intimacy of couples and must guard against songs that may encourage fornication and other illicit relations between the sexes (105–106). The tongue should not be complicit in self-celebration (*tazkiyyat al-nafs*), nor should it be used as a tool to celebrate the misfortunes of an enemy or to report for its advantage the blessings bestowed on others. The tongue should not inveigh against the orphan or insult the Muslim. It must not curse (*al-laʿn*) nor seek at any cost to recall the errors of another's words (*al-mirāʾ*). It must avoid controversy (*al-jidāl*) and refrain from mockery or expressing disdain (*al-istihzāʾ*). The tongue should neither lend itself to excessive praise (*al-iṭrāʾ fī al-madḥ*) nor praise iniquitous actions (*al-madḥ bi-l-ẓulm*). Preciousness and 'Gongorism' (*al-tafayhuq*) are forbidden to it. It should tease (*al-mazḥ*) only in moderation and avoid reporting remarkable facts (*maqāmāt*) attributed to great sinners (*al-fussāq*). The tongue is also prohibited from indulging in a personal interpretation (*bi-l-raʾī*) of the Qurʾān and the *ḥadīth* and – which may seem contradictory – from adhering to the apparent meaning (*ẓāhir al-lafẓ*) of ambiguous passages (*mā tashābaha*) in these two major sources of law or resorting to interpretative sources other than those approved by Sunnism (113).

The tongue is also prohibited from assigning 'forbidden names' (*al-asmāʾ al-muḥarrama*) because they are only used for Allāh. It must guard against attributing any evil deed to Allāh or crediting anyone other than Him with eternal power (116). It is forbidden to wish death (*tamannī al-mawt*) on anyone, to speak during the Friday sermon, to accuse a Muslim of disbelief (*takfīr al-muslim*) or to seek divine forgiveness for a non-Muslim (118). The tongue must not use lawful terms to describe unlawful actions, so as to give them an air of legitimacy, such as the imposition of an illegitimate tribute (119). The tongue is also forbidden to exclude a third person from a conversation between two people and should be very careful not to deal with complex legal matters (*al-ughlūṭāt*) reserved for experts. It is forbidden for an interpreter of dreams to attribute a meaning to them that differs from what he thinks he has understood (120), just as it is forbidden for the *qāḍī* (judge) to formulate a judgement on a matter of which he is ignorant. It is also forbidden to seek knowledge 'for the purpose of worldly preeminence' (*ṭalaban li-l-riʾāsa al-dunyawiyya*; 121). Nor should the tongue charge the *dhimmī* more than what he is legally required to pay.[28] Espionage is also forbidden (122), as is giving credence to the divinations of the 'diviner' (*al-kāhin*) and the 'astrologer' (*al-munajjim*), this prohibition also being part, as Muḥummadhun Fāl points out, of the prescriptions that are binding on the heart (*al-maḥārim al-qalbiyya*).

It is forbidden to use the tongue to deny one's relatives through kinship (126), just as it is forbidden to boast of one's genealogy (*iftikhārihi bi-nasabih*) or to attempt to have one's ancestors vilified (127). It is forbidden to intercede on behalf of someone who oversteps any of the 'limits' (*ḥadd*, pl. *ḥudūd*) imposed by Allāh or to lead someone towards a prohibited thing or act. It is also forbidden to work towards a husband's rejection of his wife, or a wife's rejection of her husband. The tongue is also forbidden to promote the rebellion of the slave against his master (130). Muḥummadhun Fāl concludes his record of the obligations and prohibitions of the tongue by mentioning the prohibition against 'seek[ing] material goods' (*su'āl al-māl*) from those who are unwilling to give them gladly. He then moves on to the ear.

The ear

'The ear is required, at the age of adulthood (of the "listener"), to hear what is said and to follow the best of it' (131). Because of this legal assignment and its relation to the responsible status of an adult person, Muḥummadhun Fāl concludes that the ear 'was created for this purpose' (*khuliqat li-ajlihi*). Moreover, 'the prohibitions that are imposed on the ear are exactly the same as those that are addressed to the tongue' (131). This resemblance, however, does not exclude the addition of further restrictions. As the author continues, invoking the opinion of Zarrūq commenting on the *al-Waghlīsiyya*,[29] the ear is forbidden to listen to the music of prohibited instruments, that is, virtually all musical instruments. He lists specific examples: *al-būq* ('the trumpet'), *al-qay'a* (unknown), *al-ṭumbūr* ('the mandolin'), *al-'ūd* ('the lute') and *al-ṭār* ('the tambourine'). He clarifies, however, relying on the opinions of 'Iyyāḍ and al-Zurqānī,[30] that an exception should be made for 'the drum' (*al-duff*) during wedding ceremonies. Citing the chapters on hearing (*kitāb al-samā'*) in al-Ghazālī's major Sunni doxographic encyclopaedia, *Iḥyā' 'ulūm al-dīn* (vol. II: 232–64), Muḥummadhun Fāl notes that the sung recitation of poetry (*al-ḥadā'*) is an old (and therefore 'good') Arab tradition, practised in the time of the Prophet to quicken the march of camels or simply for pleasure (133). Moreover, he emphasizes that our reactions to music (joy, laughter, melancholy, etc.) are not so much an effect of the music itself as of the conjunction between a category of sounds and 'dispositions' of the mind that are somehow 'activated' by this or that type of sound arrangement. These dispositions mean that a crying baby can be soothed by a lullaby and that a camel can forget its painful burden as a result of hearing a rousing chorus. Thus there are positive aspects of music, provided it is used to awaken a disposition that is itself positive, i.e. in accordance with Islamic moral law. In terms of the moral obligations of the ear, it is also specified that it should guard against eavesdropping on neighbours who clearly wish to escape attention. The ear should also refrain from listening to an *ajnabiyya*[31] for the pleasure of hearing her.

The eye

The teleological physiology of the *Fatḥ al-ḥaqq* states that the eye was created in order to 'observe the divine wonders attesting to the oneness of God' (134). It is forbidden to look at any part of the body that should not be seen (grouped under the generic term of *ʿawra*). There is a discussion in this regard, says Muḥummadhun Fāl, about one man's seeing the thighs (*al-fakhdhayn*) of another man. Some believe that they may be 'visible' to 'intimates' (*al-khāṣṣa*) but not to other (male) people. It is forbidden to look with concupiscence on those whom it is ordinarily lawful to look at, whether a 'beardless man', an old man (shaykh), a *maḥrama*[32] woman, a child or a slave. A woman is to treat an ugly slave (*wakhsh*) as she would a brother-in-law (*ka-maḥramihā*) in terms of the licence she has to look at him and be face-to-face (*fī al-khulwa*) with him. On the other hand, a beautiful slave, even if he is castrated (*majbūb*),[33] is an *ajnabī* to her. He is therefore presumed to be a possible sexual partner. These rules regarding a woman's relations with her own male slaves also apply, the author points out, to her husband's slaves.[34]

It is forbidden to touch the face or hands of the *ajnabiyya*. It is forbidden (for the eye) to explore a house in which it has been permitted entry. It is impermissible to look at that which another strives to hide, for whatever reason, from one's gaze, just as it is *ḥarām* to look through books in which a person may have hidden a secret. It is forbidden to look with deference and approval at 'iniquitous despots' (*al-ẓalama al-mutajabbirīn*). It is impermissible to look at or to consult 'that which it is impermissible to write and teach' (*lā yaḥillu al-naẓaru fī-mā lā yaḥillu katbuhu wa taʿlīmuhu*; 138), such as magic spells or poetry that contains forbidden things. It is prohibited to look with wrath (*bi-l-shuzr*) upon anyone other than iniquitous or arrogant people, just as it is impermissible to look with disdain and contempt upon 'the weak among the believers' (*al-ḍuʿafāʾ min al-muʾminīn*; 139).

The belly

'Allāh has placed in the womb many benefits for the organism and for carrying out his requirements' (140). The organism, the author adds, is 'the mount' (*maṭiyya*) of the soul (*al-nafs*, *al-rūḥ*). The latter 'rides' it to realize its most perfect aspirations, but unlike the (contingent) relationship between the mount and its rider, the bonds between the body and the soul are imposed, and their exact nature is unknown. The body can, however, serve the noble purposes of the soul, which should lead it to obey its Creator, to know its unity and to draw closer to it. But the body, and with it the soul, is dependent on the 'productions' of that 'field' (*mazraʿa*) that is the belly (*al-baṭn*), which produces, for good or for ill, the fruits of that with which it has been sown. Is it not said: 'Eat what you want, you will behave like what you eat'? (40). Above all, what seems important is the moral valence of what is ingested, assessed in light of the parameters of the licit and the illicit, the *ḥalāl* and the *ḥarām*. Eat *ḥarām* and you will be morally unsavoury; eat *ḥalāl* and your beautiful virtues will flourish. This is the foundation on which Muḥummadhun Fāl develops the prescribed rules of conduct for the belly.

It is forbidden to eat what has been acquired by extortion (*ghaṣb*) or theft (*al-sariqa*). It is unlawful to eat what someone has acquired through a false oath (*yamīn kādhiba*) at the expense of another. It is *ḥarām* to eat what has been obtained by trickery (*khadīʿa*) or fraud (*ghishsh*) or to 'betray the trust' (*khiyyāna*) of one who has entrusted you with property by consuming it. Payment for illegitimate sexual services (*al-zinā*) is also proscribed from the sphere of what is legitimately consumable, as is the fruit of the diviner's services (*al-kāhin*). Nor is it permissible to derive any (food-related) benefit from one's notoriety (*al-jāh*) alone, beyond the provision of services in exchange for the good obtained. 'Bribery' (*al-rashwa*), defined as giving a 'gift in exchange for falsifying a truth or accrediting a lie' and exemplified by practices that occur in the sphere of justice in particular, is likewise forbidden (145).

It is forbidden to consume the proceeds of gambling (*qimār*) or the retribution of praise (*al-madḥ*) when excessive or tendentious. It is also *ḥarām* to consume what comes from the remuneration allocated to singers and those who lend their services to mourn the dead (*al-nawḥ*).[35] All proceeds from legally invalid transactions, especially those associated with the various forms of usurious lending (*ribā*), are not *ḥalāl*. Also related, at least in part, to prescriptions concerning the belly are broader considerations that enter into the religious diet expounded by *Fatḥ al-ḥaqq*. Eating and drinking are a 'legal obligation' (*wājib*) if the purpose is 'to sustain life' (*imsāk al-ḥayāt*; 204), although one should, the *faqīh* points out, eat with obedience to Allāh in mind. While Muḥummadhun Fāl does not provide a catalogue of foods in their relation to good physical health, he notes that 'vinegar [unknown in his region] is the sauce of the prophets' (209). On the other hand, he goes on at length about what might be called 'table manners'. It is advisable, he writes, to eat with the right hand, without using intermediate instruments, using specifically the thumb, index and middle fingers (211). One should eat from one's own side of a common dish, and indeed from its 'periphery' (*jawānib al-ṭaʿām*). It is recommended that one chew one's food well and that one take 'small bites'.

It is advisable to stop eating 'before you are full' and to avoid eating 'lying down' (*muttakiʾan*; 214, 223). It is forbidden to eat two dates at once (at the possible expense of other diners). It is advisable to refrain from eating what your dinning partners avoid (because they would not find it good) to eat. It is inadvisable to squeeze food in one's hand in order to 'remove the liquid part' (*fasʿ al-ruṭuba*; 224) or to 'blow' (*al-nafkh*) on food, solid or liquid, with the intention of cooling it (224). If a fly should fall into one's meal, it should be immersed in it entirely because of a *ḥadīth* that says that it is a vector of disease on the one hand and an agent of healing on the other (229). One may, Muḥummadhun Fāl writes, thus putting a legal stamp on a local customary practice, abstain from eating in the company of certain people when tradition requires it (219). Without clearly stating it, he is thinking of the Moorish taboo (*saḥwa*) against eating in the presence of one's in-laws. It is expressly commanded (*yuʾmaru*) that one avoid sharing the meal of a great sinner (*ṭaʿām al-fāsiq*), as this would be to eat in the company of one who does not pray (223, 226). While it is permissible for fellow travellers to pool their food supplies for joint consumption as they travel (*al-nihd* or *al-nahd*; 216), the local practice known as *wangāla* is decreed to be prohibited by our author.[36] When a meal is finished, it is appropriate to lick one's fingers and the container in which it was held (214).

In the chapter on drinking, Muḥummadhun Fāl states that it is advisable not to drink during a meal, just as it is inadvisable (*makrūh*) to drink lying down (208). The vessel containing the drink should be held with the right hand (226). While it is lawful (*yajūz*) to stoop (*al-karʿ*) to drink from a large container, it is inadvisable to drink from the crack (*thalama*) of a chipped container (229, 231). The receptacle should be kept away from the mouth when breathing. Muḥummadhun Fāl issues precise instructions on the rhythm to which the one quenching his thirst is invited to act: three breathing pauses are recommended, and the drinking vessel should first be presented to the most honourable one (*al-afḍal*), who will pass it to his neighbour on the right, even if he is outranked (*mafḍūl*) by other guests, etc. Referring to al-Ghazālī and the *ḥadīth*, Muḥummadhun Fāl recommends that fellow diners wash their hands in the same vessel if they have one available that is large enough (221). It is appropriate for the host to be the one who serves the water for this hand-washing operation (231), and it is said that the guests should wipe their faces with their freshly washed hands (207) before cleaning their teeth (215).

In adhering to these instructions, formulated in the language of the Islamic system of obligations/prohibitions (*ḥalāl/ḥarām*, *mandūb/makrūh* ...), one should not forget to limit the costs of hosting guests to what is necessary and avoid unnecessarily ruinous sumptuary expenses.

Sex

'When Allāh created the penis, He made it lawful for it to find enjoyment with whom it is lawful to enjoy, wife or concubine' (150). Fornication (*al-zinā*), one of the greatest sins that can be committed, is *ḥarām*, but homosexuality (*al-liwāṭ*) is even worse. Anal intercourse with one's wife or concubine is, according to the most widespread opinion (*al-mashhūr*), prohibited (151). Muḥummadhun Fāl is somewhat more specific: it is not forbidden to take pleasure in caressing the periphery of the anal area (*al-tamattuʿ bi-ẓāhiri*), including through contact with the penis (*waḍʿ al-dhakar ʿalayh*), without going as far as the actual sexual act (*istimnāʾihi*). On the topic of legal provisions concerning sexual intercourse, the author asks whether a wife who refuses frequent sexual intercourse can be forced by a legal injunction (*yuqḍā ʿalayhā*) to accept this relationship. She must, the *faqīh* answers, be treated as one who has sold her services (*li-ʾannahā ka-l-ajīrati*) and have sexual relations at least once every four nights.[37] If, by contrast, a wife were to complain about infrequent intercourse with her husband, he may also be compelled to visit her every four nights, or, according to other opinions, every three nights (or even only once per menstrual cycle). In any case, Muḥummadhun Fāl continues, one must strike the right balance in such matters between relations that are too frequent, generating weariness, and those that are too spaced out and thus detrimental to the partners' mutual understanding. Moreover, he advises that the husband should not only be concerned with his own pleasure. He should try to take into account the benefits his partner derives from sexual relations and exercise the patience required for her to enjoy it as much as he does. As he points out, this promotes mutual affection (*al-maḥabba*). Departing somewhat from pure Islamic norms on the subject, Muḥummadhun Fāl prescribes that one should not neglect foreplay prior to the sexual act – specifying, at all times, that this must be 'lawful' (*mubāḥ*) – such as in the form of caresses and kissing, which, he says, is likely to win the partner over 'to what is expected of her' (*li-mā yurīdu minhā*).

Any penetration other than into the vagina (*al-farj*) with a woman with whom copulation is forbidden is prohibited, and contact between two vulvas is likewise forbidden (*mulāqāt al-mar'a al-mar'a bi-farjayhimā ḥarām*), although the author is not otherwise specific about female homosexuality. He also formulates a firm prohibition (*ḥarām*) against masturbation (*al-istimnā' bi-l-yad*, literally, 'ejaculation by hand'; 152). In a society where divorce must have been relatively common, and where it must have been equally common for ex-spouses to reunite, Muḥummadhun Fāl warns against having sex with a former wife – which is *ḥarām* – unless the act expresses an intention to re-establish the previous marital relationship. Similarly, it is forbidden to have sexual relations with a wife who has just given birth or is menstruating, or more precisely to approach the part of her body 'between her navel and her knees' at this time (154).

Under the heading 'intimate practices', Muḥummadhun Fāl specifies that it is forbidden to perform the cleansing of one's anal and genital area by means of stones (*istijmār*) near another's wall or one's own wall on the side of a public passageway.[38] The same prohibition applies to cleaning with anything that can be used as food for human beings or with paper with writing on it because of the respect due to letters (*ḥurmat al-ḥurūf*), whether they are in Arabic or in another language, and whether they are passages from the Thorah or the Gospels. It is forbidden to forgo this cleansing, and it is advisable to ensure that the anus and the penis are thoroughly cleaned, as cleaning the anus (*istibrā'*) after any emission of faecal matter is an obligation (*wājib*).[39] And while, our author details, it is relatively easy to ensure that the physical traces of defecation have been cleansed, 'because of the narrowness of the site of emission' (*li-quṣri maḥallihi*), more diligence is required with regard to possible urine residue, for the urine, due to the length of its flow (*li-ṭūli majrāh*), may not have been completely drained from the penis. The penis should then be held between the index finger (*al-sabbāba*) and thumb (*al-ibhām*) of the left hand, which should then be slid to the tip (*al-kamara*), shaking it slightly (*ma'a natrin khafīf*) to release the remaining urine. If nothing comes out on the first shake and there is no trace of moisture at the tip of the penis, one can be satisfied with this first gesture. If not, you have to do it again. There is no definite limit to the number of repetitions of this operation (154).

It is appropriate, Muḥummadhun Fāl adds, for one who is fulfilling his natural needs to 'think about the excretions that his organ is emitting' and what has become of them (154). Such excretion was (initially) something 'excellent' (*ṭayyib*), but now, just because of its use by man, it has become a hated defilement that one shuns. The same is true of clothing, which loses its lustre and freshness through prolonged contact with the body. This observation should make one realize the vanity of anything that does not help to promote sound religious practice, for the fate of the whole human body itself is no different: it will end up decomposed, without breath and given over to maggots (*al-dūd*), except in the case of the (*unalterable*) bodies of prophets (*anbiyā'*), scholars (*'ulamā'*), martyrs (*shuhadā'*) and established muezzins (*al-mu'dhdhinūn al-muḥtasibūn*) (154).

Hands and feet

Among the useful tasks assigned to the hands the author includes writing pious invocations (*dhikr allah*) and reminders addressed to others to prevent them from forgetting Allāh. On the other hand, 'it is forbidden to write what it is impermissible to write' (163). The hands must also give the legal tithe (*al-zakāt*), which falls under the heading of 'offering' (*al munāwala*). The feet, on the other hand, enable one to go to the mosque, to visit the sick, to pay visits to saints (either dead or alive) and to attend the educational institutions of the scholars (*al-ʿulamāʾ*). The obligations associated with the hands also include washing (*istinjāʾ*) the relevant organs after every excretion of urine or faeces. Various obligations/prohibitions relating to the duties of the hands and feet come under the heading 'intimate cleanliness'. It is recommended that one put one's left foot forward first when entering a latrine (*al-kanīf*; 241), and Muḥummadhun Fāl also indicates the prayer to be spoken upon exiting the toilet. It is also appropriate, he states, to be seated when relieving oneself. The *qibla* should always be located to the right of the one who is relieving himself (243), but one should not relieve oneself or copulate facing in its direction or with one's back to it.

Among the obligations assigned to the feet are walking to the Friday prayer, toward a drowning person to rescue him and more generally fulfilling all the obligations incumbent on any Muslim. It is forbidden to strut (*yaḥrum mashyu al-mutamaṭṭī*; 156) or to adopt a proud gait, just as it is forbidden to walk towards any sin (*al-maʿāṣī kullihā*). It is forbidden for the hands and the feet, or indeed the whole body, to put oneself in a situation that generates suspicion or a presumption of guilt (*mawāḍiʿ al-tuham*). It is forbidden to light a torch (*īqād sirāj*) in a dwelling where a wedding is being celebrated and where 'men and women' are gathered (*ajānib*).[40] It is likewise forbidden to bring wine (*khamr*) close to one who wishes to drink it or to bring any other intoxicant close to him,[41] unless this facilitates the swallowing of something on which he is choking (*ghaṣṣa*). It is forbidden to be a courier or peddler of the news of a great sinner (*fāsiq*), just as it is forbidden not to give to the needy that which one has in excess and which is necessary for the sustenance of life.

Under the category of actions or injunctions (negative or positive) of which the hand is the agent, Muḥummdhun Fāl reviews, with varying degrees of thoroughness, a whole range of gestures that relate to the care of the body, most of which he associates with an 'innate' requirement (*al-fiṭra*). Under this heading are included gargling (*maḍmaḍa*) and nasal cleansing (*al-istinshāq, al-istinthār*). There is also mention of the freedom to grow one's beard, the trimming of one's moustache, the removal of hair from the armpits (165) and trimming one's nails – for which there are no strict rules, we learn, except that, according to al-Nawawī (commenting on Muslim al-Nisābūrī),[42] it would be good to start with the right pinky finger, then the ring finger, then the middle finger, then the index finger and the thumb, with the reverse order advised for the left hand. It is not advisable to trim one's nails with one's teeth (174).

It is advisable to shave one's pubic hair (*ḥalq al-ʿāna*) once a week (every Friday). Shaving is preferable to plucking because the latter 'generates leprosy, relaxes the nerves and affects the ability to obtain an erection' (166). According to al-Nawawī, women may wax, but men must shave their pubic hair. It is forbidden to selectively pluck white hairs (*al-shayb*) from one's beard and head. White hair, the Prophet is reported to have said, 'is the light of the believer', and to pluck white hairs is to engage in deception about one's age (171). An abundant head of hair (for men) is also considered *sunna*. The use of henna dye is permitted. It is forbidden to remove hair from the face (*al-tanammuṣ*; 176), although this prescription is, the author points out, in tension with the one enjoining women to eliminate from their faces anything that might make them look like a man. Wigs and all forms of artificial hair lengthening are forbidden. Tattooing (*al-washm*) is likewise prohibited.

It is forbidden (for women; men are not mentioned) to attempt to create an artificial gap (*tafalluj*) between one's teeth.[43] Circumcision (*al-khitān*), which is a prophetic *sunna*, is also mentioned in the section concerning the hands. This procedure is discouraged at birth and must be performed at the age of 7. In connection with this, Muḥummadhun Fāl observes that if a full-grown man were to convert, he would have to perform his own circumcision, as it is forbidden for another adult to see his genitals (166–167). Excision (*al-khifāḍ*) is also strongly advised, but it should be conducted in a discreet manner, without any special ceremony or meal similar to those usually reserved for male circumcision.

Under bodily care carried out by the hand, the *Fatḥ al-ḥaqq* mentions the use of perfume (*al-taṭayyub*) and incense (*al-istijmār*). Unmarried women are advised against perfume, however, and widows should refrain from its use for four months and ten days after the passing of their husband (168). It is lawful for a young unmarried woman to dye (*takhḍab*) her hands, either uniformly or only certain sections, although the later licence is a matter of controversy among the *fuqahā'* (177). Women may also use kohl and wear jewellery, as long as they are not provocative. This is even recommended for the married woman because of 'her husband's right to anything that may beautify her' (177).

The swathed body

Clothes are an obligation, a 'human right' (*ḥaqq al-ādamī*) against cold and heat. But clothes are to be used in moderation. Wearing a shawl (*al-ridā'*) on one's shoulders is highly recommended (*sunna*) for the one praying (192). Similarly, it is recommended that the *imām* wear a head covering. A modest garment, in accordance with the tradition of the country, should be worn by women to ensure that they are free from any presumption of temptation (*al-āmina al-fitna*; 194). Despite Muḥummadhun Fāl's insistence on the (legal) need for women to conceal their bodies, he still admits that in (very) secluded spaces they are allowed to wash without their veils (*bilā izār*; 302).

The one who reads the Qur'ān should be dressed in beautiful white clothes. The male garment should reach mid-leg (*niṣf al-sāqayn*). The wearing of pure silk (*al-ḥarīr al-khāliṣ*) is prohibited. It is forbidden to wear clothes that are too loose or for a man to wear women's clothes, and vice versa. It is forbidden (*ḥarām*) for women to wear clothes that reveal the shape of their body. For men, this prescription only falls under what is considered 'inadvisable' (*yukrah*). It is not advisable for a man to tie his turban on his head without passing it under his chin (199). The man who ties his turban is advised to do so standing up (*qāʾiman*) and not to sit down until the operation has been completed. He is recommended to do the same when wearing trousers (*al-sarāwīl*). It is also forbidden for a woman to tie the neckline of her veil too loosely, which could reveal parts of her body that should not be seen (200). Putting on one's shoes while standing is another of the discussed topics, with the author signalling that one should always start with the right one (201). It is not advisable to walk wearing only one shoe.

The use of precious metals is also strictly regulated. It is forbidden to wear pure gold (*al-dhahab*) or silver (*al-fiḍḍa*), with the exception of a ring made of silver, or partially of gold, up to one-third of its composition (197). Moreover, this ring should be worn only with the intention of complying with prophetic practice. Devoting all of one's energy to the sole care of one's appearance (*li-mujarrad al-zīna*) is in any case strongly discouraged. The taboo against gold extends to other spheres. It is impermissible to decorate a mirror or a vessel with gold or to glue the pieces (*al-taḍbīb*) of a broken vessel back together with this metal. Nor is it permissible to use jewellery (*taḥliyya*) to decorate works of science and *ḥadīth* (198).

The body-subject

In reality, as Muḥummadhun Fāl points out, everything that has been said about the obligations imposed on the organs has been done in a metonymic mode (*ʿalā sabīl al-majāz*): the true subject of the legal injunction is, in fact, the soul (*al-nafs*), and the organs are only the instruments at its disposal (*al-mukallaf fī al-ḥaqīqa innamā hiyya al-nafs wa al-jawāriḥ ālāt lahā*; 156). There is thus a whole range of prescriptions that involve the 'external relations' of the organism as a totality, always beholden to the soul, in its relations with both human and non-human others. The external relations of the body-subject cover its relations with healers, relatives, neighbours and guests, the essential figures of religious authority, etc.

Therapists and therapies

Citing the *Tanqīḥ al-fuṣūl fī ikhtiṣār al-uṣūl* by the Egyptian *faqīh* Aḥmad b. Idrīs al-Qarāfī (d. 684 H/1285 CE), Muḥummadhun Fāl observes that there is no contradiction between submission to the divine will (*tawakkul*) and the legitimate quest for the restoration of disrupted health, as Allāh has ordered his creation to combine the two (177). The cosmos (*al-ʿālam*) and the spirits (*al-rawḥāniyya*, sg. *al-rawḥānī*) have no effect anyway through the saint (*al-walīy*), the bearer of the evil eye (*al-ʿāʾin*), or the magician (*al-sāḥir*), except by the will of Allāh (190). Salvation in all cases is obtained through prayer. It is lawful to heal with the help of the verses of the Qurʾān and the invocation of the names of Allāh. It is also lawful to heal oneself with the help of 'good words' (*al-kalām al-ṭayyib*) such as invocations (*al-adʿiya*) calling on the intervention of the prophets and the angels or the saints, provided the healer (*al-murqī*) understands the terms he is using (otherwise he cannot be called upon). This type of intervention is particularly useful for releasing people from evil spells (178).

It is permissible to use verses to heal by ingestion or lustration (*al-nashra*) by washing the surface on which they are written and ingesting the water. On the other hand, it is impermissible to use amulets (*al-tawala, al-taʾkhīdh*) to curry favour with a person, whether male or female (179). It is likewise impermissible to seek protection (*taʿawwudh*) from powerful demons (*murdat al-jann*). Lustration by spitting (*al-tafl*) is a religiously recommended therapeutic practice. Bringing relief (within one's means) to those stricken by demons is a legal obligation (*wājib*), but all therapeutic means that come close to divination (*al-kahāna*) are prohibited (*ḥarām*) (180–181). 'It is [nevertheless] permissible for the saint to make himself useful by his pious intention' (*yajūz li-l-walīy ʾan yanfaʿa bi-himmatihi*; 181), even though doing so may come close to these prohibited practices, especially when it comes to 'disenchantment' or exorcism (*istinzāl al-jinn*), which constitutes, by the author's own admission, 'a form of divination' (*ḍarb min al-kahāna*) (187). The bearer of the evil eye (*al-ʿāʾin*) is obliged to keep away from all potential victims and to stay at home. The same applies to carriers of contagious diseases, of which the author cites smallpox (*al-judrī*), leprosy (*al-judhām*) and plague (*al-ṭāʿūn*). However, he does not shy away from reporting doubts attributed to the *ḥadīth* concerning the reality of the contagion itself (182–183). Muḥummadhun Fāl provides instructions for curing victims of the evil eye, taken from various authoritative sources.[44] It states that it is permissible to use recitations of the Qurʾān to shorten distances (*ṭayy al-arḍ*). Magic squares, on the other hand, are criticized, especially if they are associated with astrology (*raṣd al-aflāk*). The use of procedures proven by experience to cure patients is lawful, but treatments using products considered to be defiling (*najas*) should be excluded. Cauterization with fire (*al-iktiwāʾ*) is also reported to be *ḥalāl*. In terms of contact between the healer and the patient, most 'doctors', it is related, allow for the examination of the patient's private parts (*al-ʿawra*) for therapeutic reasons. Enemas (*al-ḥuqna*) are of questionable legality. The lustration of a wound by applying pus from a smallpox infection is traditional practice, and therefore lawful. However, it is impermissible to buy pus from one suffering from smallpox. Proper sleep – in accordance with the *sunna* – is a part of good physical and moral health. One should avoid falling asleep in the midst of those who are awake. 'Naps increase intelligence', while sleeping after the *ʿaṣr* (afternoon) prayer is reputed by the author to cause a 'disturbance of the mind' (*fasād fī al-qalb*; 238). The sleeper should have already prepared to clean his teeth, something to perform his ritual ablutions and have written his 'testamentary will' (*waṣiyyatuh*; 235), if he has not previously performed this formality. The prophetic tradition recommends beginning the sleep cycle on 'the right flank' (*al-shuqq al-ayman*; 232). Muḥummadhun Fāl identifies the prayers that should be said before giving in to this temporary eclipse of consciousness. Before falling asleep, one must be in a state of ritual cleanliness (*ṭahāra*; 235). One must have resolved to engage in pious exercises (*ʿazmuhu ʿalā al-tahajjud*; 235) upon awakening. The author of the *Fatḥ al-ḥaqq* also provides the prayer to be spoken upon waking up. All of these arrangements and processes naturally take place in the shadow of the will of Allāh, from whom salvation should be sought by means of 'pious deeds', just as the intercession of the Prophet should be sought for this purpose (191).

The socia(b)l(e) body

As it is governed by the soul, i.e. subject to the injunctions and prohibitions established by the Creator, the body must move in a universe in which other human bodies evolve, to which it is bound by imperatives that it must take into account. These bodies draw in a very concrete, even physical, way the contours of one of the fields in which the body's activity unfolds.

Muḥummadhun Fāl writes that sociability (*al-mu ʿāshara*; 280) requires excellent conduct with others. This begins with 'obedience to parents' (*burūr al-wālidayn*), with insubordination being a mortal sin (*min al-kabā ʾir*; 282). Citing the commentary of the Tlemcenian scholar Aḥmad b. Zakrī (d. 899 H/1493 CE) on the essay pertaining to *taṣawwuf* by Zarrūq al-Fāsī (d. 899 H/1493 CE), *al-Naṣīḥa al-kāfiya li-man khaṣṣahu allāh bi-l- ʿāfiya*, Muḥummadhun Fāl specifies, organ by organ, the anathema of disobedience toward or hatred of one's parents. These offences fall, he says, under the category of 'contraventions of the *sharī ʿa* (*muḥarramāt*) spread in the body'. *Sharī ʿa*, he continues, obliges children to take care of their parents' material needs, including providing for the marriage expenses of a needy father in order to 'preserve his virtue' (*bi-mā yu ʿiffuhu*; 283). It is also appropriate, out of deference, to refrain from walking before them (*al-taqaddum amāma humā*; 284) and to honour their friends.

The 'rights' of children over their parents also pass through the body. The first 'right' a child has over his father is 'to choose his mother' (*ʾan yakhtāra ummahu*; 289). To this 'prenatal' right, the author adds another that occurs immediately upon the newborn's entry into the world. Reporting the story of a date that was chewed by the Prophet and administered at birth to ʿAbdallāh, son of Asmāʾ bint Abī Bakr (d. 73 H/692 CE) and al-Zubayr b. al-ʿAwwām (d. 36 H/656 CE), even before the baby had suckled his mother's breast, Muḥummadhun Fāl concludes that it is the father's duty to deliver to his child 'the first element of sweetness that will reach his stomach' (284). As the perspective here is that of a male subject, the author notes that the child is entitled to receive a 'beautiful name' from his father, to have his head shaved and to be circumcised, not at seven days but at seven years. Parents are obliged, he writes, to behave fairly towards their children. They must play with them and dress them in new clothes during festivals. They must also know how to forgive their children's misbehaviour, although it is specified that a father has the right to discipline his child and to impose particular tasks on him for this purpose.

Under the heading of a 'husband's "rights" in relation to his wife', Muḥummadhun Fāl enumerates obedience, consent to sexual relations (*al-istimtā ʿ bihā*; 310), activities necessary for the maintenance of her home according to local customs, and respect and friendliness towards her in-laws. A wife is not allowed to engage in supplementary prayers or fasts without the permission of her husband. She is also obliged to refrain from eating anything that may irritate him, such as garlic (*al-thawm*; 311).[45] Some of these rights are also given to the wife in relation to her husband. It is said that he should educate her and behave properly towards her (312). He must not impose on her tasks that she is not obliged to perform according to local custom. In particular, he may not force her to perform tasks for the purpose of earning an income (*al-takassub*; 314). Nor is the husband allowed to wear clothes or eat food that would annoy his wife (*mā yuʾdhīhā*; 312). He is also forbidden from divulging their secrets to third persons. Referencing al-Ghazālī, Muḥummadhun Fāl writes that the husband should copulate with his wife every fourth night, an act that should be preceded by the appropriate prayer (315). He must endeavour to bring her to orgasm (*yarfaqa bihā fī al-jimāʿi ḥattā tanzala*; 316) and to this end lavish her with caresses (*yulāʿibahā*; 318) before copulation; in particular, writes Muḥummadhun Fāl, he should caress her breasts (*yaghmaza thadyayhā*), as this increases her desire (319). He must enjoin (*yaʾmurahā*) her, after copulation, to lie on her right side to sleep (320).

The slave (*al-mamlūk*) also has 'rights' in relation to his 'owner' (*mālikihi*; 329). Once more referencing the authoritative work of al-Ghazālī, Muḥummadhun Fāl writes that the master must dress his slave in the clothes typically worn by slaves in the country and feed him as his fellow slaves are fed. He must lavish religious instruction on him, the extent of which is not specified, and provide him with the free time necessary for this purpose (325). The master is forbidden to take from a nurse-slave a quantity of milk that would compromise the health of her own baby. Beyond the domestic sphere, mention is also made of friends, neighbours, visitors and 'Muslims' in general. It is advisable to be pleasant with them, to listen to them and to pay attention to them. Even the great sinner (*al-fāsiq*) should be treated with flexibility and preached to gently, in the hopes of bringing him back onto the right path. The travelling guest (*al-ḍayf*) should be welcomed with kindness and fed without prejudice. Muḥummadhun Fāl recommends that it should be the head of the household who serves him in person.

Greetings, contact with visitors and casual encounters do not escape Muḥummadhun Fāl's attention. Under the heading 'laws governing greetings' (*aḥkām al-salām*), he notes that it is a religious obligation to return the greetings one is given. On the other hand, he points out, it is not advisable to address one's greetings to a muezzin calling to prayer (371). The handshake (*al-muṣāfaḥa*) is recommended by the majority of Maliki *fuqahāʾ* (375). On the other hand, the embrace (*al-muʿānaqa*) is discouraged. Muḥummadhun Fāl discusses the differences of opinion among the *fuqahāʾ* (Mālik himself, Ibn Abī Zayd, Zarrūq commenting on the latter's *al-Risāla*) concerning the practice of kissing the hand of an emir (*amīr*) or of a scholar (*ʿālim*), which is deemed 'recommended' (*yundab*; 377).[46] On the other hand, he advises against responding with any greeting other than those that fall within the repertoire agreed upon by the *sharīʿa*, such as when one says 'excellent morning' (379). There are differing opinions among jurists regarding the legal status of standing up to greet a visitor. Islamic sociability enjoins (*yajib*) that one should respond (*tashmīt*) with the consecrated formula to one who sneezes if he himself is heard to utter the ritual formula that accompanies this act: *al-ḥamdu li-llāh* ('thanks be to Allāh'). The same Islamic sociability also recommends placing one's right hand in front of one's mouth when yawning (389). Muḥummadhun Fāl states that Islam recommends visiting the sick (390), while attaching some restrictions to this recommendation in terms of the time of day, etc. Visiting saints (*al-ṣāliḥīn*), living or dead, is also recommended (393). When visiting a grave, however, it is advisable to approach from the direction of the deceased's legs, with the grave on one's right (407). Muḥummadhun Fāl extends the sociability of the Islamic body to contact with animals and plants, which also have 'rights' (*ḥuqūq*); animals, for example, should be addressed gently (340) and should be given water and properly fed (329). Forcing them to do tasks that they cannot perform is prohibited. While branding is permitted, it must be done without damaging the animal's face. It is permissible to castrate male animals for slaughter (332), and if a domestic animal should find itself in a desperate situation, it should be killed by cutting its throat, even if it is an inedible animal such as a horse. The ownership of dogs is permitted for herding and hunting, provided they are not vicious (335). In the case of plants and crops, the owner is obliged to maintain them (335), and while it is permissible to cut a few green branches to feed one's animals, it is forbidden to cut down fruit trees, among which Muḥummadhun Fāl mentions the 'palm tree' (*nakhīl*), the vine (*karm*) and the olive tree (*al-zaytūn*), although the latter two were absent from the Saharan ecosystem in which he lived.

Conclusion

The body may at first seem an unpropitious site when searching for possible traces of a thinking subject in a learned cultural tradition such as that of the *Bīḍān* populations of the western regions of the Sahara. Beyond or at the periphery of speculative space proper, where debates directly pertaining to the topic of the thinking subject unfold as they would in established Islamic disciplines, the body may contain traces of a normative relentlessness, inscribing the conduct and thought of the Saharan Islamic subject on a narrow path. From the legislative mark inscribed in the anatomy of the embryo to the extreme minutiae of the normative physiology recounted by Muḥummadhun Fāl w. Muttālī, we have seen how the dislocation of the subject operates as the very means by which he is transformed into an 'alphabet of the law'.

I have deliberately abbreviated, at the expense of the extraordinary diversity of disciplinary precisions ascribed to the prophetic tradition, Muḥummadhun Fāl's work in order to better highlight the purely legislative, enumerative, side of his approach, out of concern for the foundations of the law. 'Tradition' (*sunna*) alone, in his eyes, is enough. The unbridled ritualism expressed in his book is obviously not specific to the Muslim religion alone. One can easily find in its Christian, and especially Hebrew (Cohen 1991), roots a wealth of similar prescriptions. The dismemberment of the subject to which he devotes himself with such focus, the catalogue of obligations and prohibitions in reference to the Islamic norms that he delivers in great detail, organ by organ, only outlines the figure of a transregional and trans-historical generic subject whose recomposed archetype traces back to seventh-century Arabia. And even if, as Muḥummadhun Fāl writes, the legal injunctions addressed to the organs actually call out to the 'soul' (*nafs*), of which they are only metonymic vectors, the soul remains an impersonal entity, an abstract legal figure.

The body to which it strives to dictate its law has as its sole vocation submission to divine will. Nothing seems to dispose it to face the consequences of a way of thinking animated by a desire for autonomy, by a desire to reach an alternative 'truth' to that taught by the pious heritage of the forefathers. Such a body, imprisoned in such a soul, undoubtedly calls for a different '*hermeneutique du subjet*' (Foucault 2001) than that which is permeated by 'self-concern', by the injunction 'know thyself', and, finally, by a desire to think for oneself.

Notes

1 Among the most significant references in Arabic, see Aḥmad b. al-Amīn al-Shinqīṭī's *al-Wasīṭ* (1989); the twelve volumes of al-Mukhtār b. Ḥāmidun's encyclopedia, *Ḥayāt Mūrītānyā* (with special mention to *al-Ḥayāt al-thaqāfiyya*, 1990); and Yaḥyā w. al-Barrā''s *al-Majmūʿa al-kubrā: al-shāmila li-fatāwā wa nawāzil wa aḥkām ahl gharb wa janūb gharb al Ṣaḥrāʾ* (2009). The most comprehensive overviews conducted of Mauritanian manuscripts in European languages to date are Ulrich Rebstock's *Maurische Literaturgeschichte* (2001) and Charles C. Stewart and alii's *The Writings of Mauritania and the Western Sahara* (2016).

2 I am thinking in particular of Marcel Mauss's text 'A category of the human mind: the notion of person; the notion of self' (1968: 331–62), which was harshly criticized for its Eurocentrism and evolutionism (Carrithers 1985; Dumont 1983; Dupont 2018; Macpherson 1962). On the philosophical level, and as if in a distant echo of the question once posed by Kant, 'What is Enlightenment?' (Kant 1985: 497–505), I refer to the work of Alain de Libera, *L'invention du sujet moderne* (2015), and Etienne Balibar's *Citoyen sujet et autres essais d'anthropologie philosophique* (2011). Vincent Descombes (2004) develops an approach inspired by Wittgenstein in *Le complément de sujet*.

3 Recall that when Kant raised the question 'What is Enlightenment?' he replied: '*Sapere aude*! Have the courage to use your own understanding! That is the motto of the Enlightenment' (Kant 1985: 497).

4 The body also attracted the attention of Mauss, but from a different perspective than that discussed here. Mauss, as we know, was interested in the 'techniques of the body' (1968: 363–86), in gestuality, considered from the point of view of what he called the 'total man', or even of entire societies, since, in his opinion, societies can be read, compared and distinguished on the basis of the systems of gestures and bodily attitudes that they inculcate in their members.

5 Axel Honneth (2020 [2018]) associates the notion of the individual-subject in the European history of ideas with that of interaction, of recognition, the history of which he traces from Rousseau to Sartre via Hume, Mill, Kant and Hegel.

6 My translation from the French. All translations are my own.

7 Porqueres i Géné and Bilbao Zepeda (2020), however, emphasize the resistance of the ethics of human reproduction in contemporary modern societies to techniques (genetic manipulation, cloning, euthanasia, etc.) that threaten to substantially alter their course – a resistance that also invokes a kind of 'external intervener', the ethico-metaphysical entity that constitutes the singular human subject, whose transcendence, associated with the free play of the genetic lottery, is invoked as the supreme regulating authority of human reproduction.

8 This is debatable and widely discussed. Lévi-Strauss inscribes his approach in the problematic of exchange (of women, words, goods), inspired in particular by Mauss's 'L'essai sur le don'. Héritier and, in her wake, other researchers (such as P. Bonte, Ed. Conte), instead inflected the theory of incest towards the theme of sharing essential fluids (see Bonte 1994; Jamard et al. 2000).

9 'Prohibited to you [for marriage] are your mothers, your daughters, your sisters, your father's sisters, your mother's sisters, your brother's daughters, your sister's daughters, your [milk] mothers who nursed you, your sisters through nursing, your wives' mothers, and your step-daughters under your guardianship [born] of your wives

unto whom you have gone in. But if you have not gone in unto them, there is no sin upon you. And [also prohibited are] the wives of your sons who are from your [own] loins, and that you take [in marriage] two sisters simultaneously, except for what has already occurred' (*The Qur'ān* 1997: 4:23).

10 On the relation of the notions of hot and cold to male/female interactions, see Christina Figueiredo-Biton's (2001) observations on another Saharan society 'akin' to the *Bīẓān*, the Tuareg. Serge Tcherkézoff (1983) has summarized some of the essential texts in anthropology – from Robert Hertz (*La prééminence de la main droite*, 1909) to Rodney Needham (*The Right and the Left*, 1973) – on the theme of the left and the right and its hierarchical significance, based in particular on the work of Louis Dumont on the Indian caste system.

11 The content of *al-'Umda* was taken up and developed by a member of another illustrious family of traditional Saharan physicians (the Ahl al-Maqarrī): Muḥammad Bayba b. Sīd Aḥmad al-Maqarrī, in his *Jam' al-manāfi' fī al-ṭibb al-qadīm* (1997).

12 The *Mawsū'a* of w. al-Barrā' (vol. IX: 3766–805) reports seventy-three *fatāwā* related to breastfeeding by well-known *fuqahā'* and *awliyā'* ('saints') from the western regions of the Sahara. Among them are Shaykh Sīd al-Mukhtār (d. 1226 H/1811 CE) and his son, Shaykh Sīdi Muḥammad (d. 1242 H/1826 CE), Sīdi 'Abdullāh w. al-Ḥāj Brāhīm (d. 1233 H/1817 CE), Ṣāliḥ w. 'Abd al-Wahhāb (d. 1272 H/1855 CE), Shaykh Muḥamd al-Māmi (d. 1282 H/1865 CE), Maḥanḍ Bāba w. A'bayd (d. 1277 H/1860 CE) and Shaykh Sīdiyya (d. 1284 H/1868 CE). These *fatāwā* deal with various topics related to *riḍā'* (milk kinship): the consequences for a matrimonial union of the 'discovery' of a prohibitive milk relationship between the spouses; the conditions for the admissibility of a testimony of *riḍā'*, the effects of the husband's ingestion of his wife's milk, etc.

13 In the *Ṣaḥīḥ Muslim* (IV: 162), it appears in the following formulation: *yaḥrum min al-riḍā'a mā yaḥrum min al-wilāda*. Wensick (1936, vol. I: 452) provides references to other variants present in the works of al-Dārimī, Ibn Mājja, *al-Muwwaṭṭa'* and Ibn Ḥanbal's *Musnad*.

14 The *Lisān al-'arab* relates this term to *al-raḥim* ('womb') and associates it with a marriage interdiction.

15 Muḥummadun Fāl's nephew, Ḥaymidda wuld Ndyubnān (d. 1329 H/1910 CE), dedicated to his uncle a rhymed bio-hagiographical piece in rajaz metre in 240 verses, which he entitled *al-Jinān al-'āliyya fī al-sīra al-muttāliyya* (*Fatḥ al-ḥaqq*: 562–72). Pierre Bonte provides an analysis of the narratives relating to Bū-Bazzūl in his Récits d'Origine (2016: 453–82). In her PhD thesis, Erin Pettigrew (2014: 277–341) examines the history and (miraculous) healing powers of a small Wolof community in southwestern Trarza, the Ahl Gannār, who also claim Bū-Bazzūl as their ancestor.

16 With a view to an early 'connection', one may surmise, to an invisible universe of which he would be one of the greatest specialists in this region.

17 He briefly frequented the *maḥẓara* of al-Mu'ayyad b. Maṣyūb al-Kumalaylī and borrowed works by Aḥmad b. Muḥamd al-'Āqil al-Tawangalī (d. 1244 H/1828 CE), but this is all that is known about his education (Cf. *Fatḥ* 17–18).

18 We might mention, among others, his four sons (Aḥmadu, Muḥammadu, 'Abd al-Raḥmān and Ḥabīb) and his nephew and biographer Ḥaymidda w. Ndyubnān; al-Mukhtār w. Alummā al-Yadālī (d. 1308 H/1890 CE); see also Awfā b. Abī Bakr al-Idātfaghī (d. 1300 H /1882 CE), the best-known healer of his time. See *Fatḥ* 19.

19 It is worth mentioning, in addition to the *Fatḥ al-ḥaqq*, an abridgement of al-Mawwāq's exegesis on Khalīl's *Mukhtaṣar*; see also *Qurrat ʿayn al-niswān fī al-ʿaqīda wa al-sīra wa al-fiqh, Naẓm fī al-uṣūl* and its commentary, *Tasdīd al-naẓar* (a commentary on the *Mukhtaṣar* of al-Sanūsī devoted to logic). Cf. *Fatḥ* 21. Rebstock (2001, vol. I: 338–43) mentions fifty-six works/opuscules attributed to him; Stewart and Ould Ahmed Salim (2016, vol. II: 1406–15), refer to sixty.

20 In its western Maghrebian branch, originating from Aḥmad b. Nāṣir al-Dirʿī (d 1085 H /1676 CE) and his *zāwiya* of Tāmgrūt (Dra valley, Morocco), the *shādhiliyya* spread to the Mauritanian space through the teachings of notable figures such as Atfagha al-Khaṭṭāṭ (d. 1196 H/1781 CE), Nikhtāru b. al-Muṣṭafā al-Yadālī, Sīdi Muḥammad b. Sīdi ʿUmar al-Maḥjūbī al-Walātī (d. 1132 H/1719 CE), Sīd Aḥmad al-Tamagḷāwī al-Dayṃānī, Sīdi ʿAbdallāh b. Sīdi Bubakkar al-Tinwājiwī (d. 1145 H/1732 CE) and al-Ṭālib Aḥmad b. Ṭwayr al-Janna al-Ḥājī al-Wadānī (d. 1265 H/1848 CE) (Ibn Ḥāmidun 1990: 93–4). On the shādhiliyya, see also Geoffroy (2005: 355–75), which contains a brief note by Constant Hamès entitled 'La Shâdhiliyya dans l'Ouest saharien et africain: nouvelles perspectives'. The only known active branch of the *shādhiliyya* in this region is the *ghuẓfiyya*, named after its founder, al-Shaykh Muḥammad al-Aghẓaf al-Dāwūdī al-Jaʿfarī (b. 1128 H/1716 CE; d. 1223 H/1808 CE). Its 'heterodoxy' was underlined by some colonial observers, such as Laforgue (1928) and Beyriès (1935).

21 Related in particular with the actions of the brothers of the Trarza emir Muḥamd Laḥbīb w. Aʿmar w.al-Mukhtār, who, just after assassinating the latter (in 1860), tried to take refuge with Muḥummadhun Fāl. This, in the end, would not save them from the vengeance of their nephew, Muḥamd Laḥbīb's son Sidi, who would succeed his father (1860–1871).

22 With, as a variant, a verb with the same meaning in the third person singular of the imperfective: yaḥrum. It is known that the system of licences and prohibitions established by Islamic theologians distinguishes between *ḥalāl* ('licit'), *wājib* ('obligatory'), *mandūb* ('recommended'), *ḥarām* ('prohibited') and *makrūh* ('inadvisable').

23 With the variant: 'such action is sunna … ', i.e. highly recommended.

24 al-Ghazālī (d. 505 H/1111 CE), Khalīl b. Isḥāq (d. 767 H/1374 CE) and his many commentators, Ibn ʿAṭāʾ Allāh (d. 709 H/1309 CE), al-Suyūṭī (d. 911 H/1505 CE), etc.

25 Abū Ḥāmid al-Ghazālī (1997), abundantly quoted by Muḥummadhun Fāl, had already traced a similar path in his *Iḥyāʾ ʿulūm al-dīn*, and the great Alexandrian master of the shādhiliyya, Ibn ʿAṭāʾ Allāh, unfolded its mystical and ethical arcana in his *Ḥikam* (Ibn ʿAjība al-Ḥasanī n.d.).

26 Muḥummaḏun Fāl is referring here to the Mutazilites and their major figure, al-Jubbāʾī (d. 303 H/916 CE), whose views on the eternity of the world, the resurrection of bodies, etc., were opposed by the theological school to which he claimed to belong (Ashari), a school whose founder, Abū-l-Ḥasan al-Ashʿarī (d. 324 H/936 CE), had been al-Jubbāʾī's disciple for more than twenty years.

27 All of these faults and virtues, as well as those relating to the tongue, are amply developed in al-Ghazālī's Iḥyāʾ (1997, vol. III).

28 A dhimmī is a protected member of one of the three faiths (Judaism, Christianity, Zoroastrianism) tolerated by Islam on payment of a special tax called al-jizya.

29 The *Muqadimma al-waghlīsiyya ʿalā madhab al-sāda al-mālikiyya* is a summary of the Maliki/Ashari rite written by the Bougie (Algerian) scholar Abū Zayd Abdur-Rahmān al-Waghlīsī al-Jazaʾirī (751 H/1351 CE). Muḥummadhun Fāl refers to the

commentary on this work by the *faqīh* and mystic of Fez, Aḥmad b. ʿĪsā al-Barnasī, known as Zarrūq (d. 899 H/1493 CE).

30 al-Qāḍī ʿIyyāḍ b. Mūsā al-Yaḥṣubī al-Sabtī (d. 544 H/1149 CE) is a major figure in the intellectual history of the Almoravids. ʿAbd al-Bāqī b. Yūsuf al-Zurqānī (d. 1099 H/1687 CE) is an Egyptian commentator on Khalīl b. Isḥāq's *Mukhtaṣar*, the pervasive reference in Saharan *fiqh*.

31 This term includes all women with whom one is not related by birth or by milk, thus making them 'untouchable'

32 The opposite of *ajnabiyya*, which groups together all women whom a male can see/touch because of a particular blood or milk tie.

33 A practice that is not common in Moorish society. The mention of eunuchs here likely comes from Maghrebi and Oriental authors whom Muḥummadhun Fāl consulted.

34 No such rule applies to the relations between a master and his female slaves: he may dispose of them sexually as he pleases, according to Muslim law.

35 A practice that does not seem to be common in this context, and which is probably taken here from other works consulted by the author.

36 Wangāla involves a group of people taking turns to slaughter a sheep/goat, randomly dividing the (presumably equal) shares between the partners.

37 As if she shared her husband with the three co-wives tolerated by Islamic law. Again, this is likely material gleaned from other sources, as in the Moorish environment in which the author lived polygyny was generally not practised.

38 *al-istijmār bi-jidār al-ghayr ḥarām, wa kadhā jidāru nafsihi min jihati mamarri al-nās* (152). The term *bi* in *bi-jidār* can be interpreted as 'with the help of'. This instruction for anal hygiene likely has its source in other commentaries, since in the author's nomadic environment there were no walls.

39 All of the prescriptions considered in this book stem from the point of view of a male subject.

40 Literally: 'strangers', those who are not related by a blood or milk tie and are thus not allowed physical contact.

41 An indication taken from the literature consulted by the author, as there was no production of wine in Moorish society, nor is there any record of its import.

42 Muslim b. al-Ḥajjāj al-Qushayrī al-Nisābūrī (d. 261 H/875 CE) is the author of a famous collection of *ḥadīth* known as *Ṣaḥīḥ Muslim*. Yaḥyā b. Sharaf al-Khuzāmī al-Nawawī (d. 676 H/1277 CE) is a prominent shafi expert on the *ḥadīth*.

43 Diastema is a highly valued sign of beauty in traditional Moorish society.

44 In particular, al-Qāḍī ʿIyyāḍ and the great Tunisian scholar of the *ḥadīth*, Muḥammad b. ʿAlī al-Tamīmī al-Māzarī (d. 536 H/1141 CE) (185–6).

45 A vegetable largely unknown to western Saharan nomadic groups.

46 While one can nowadays find traces of this practice towards Sufi 'holy' figures, it seems that it has never been used with the *umarāʾ* (sg. *amīr*) of ancient Moorish society.

References

Canonical sources and manuscripts

Awfā b. Abī Bakr, *al-ʿUmda*, manuscrit, s.d.

The Qurʾān: English Meanings, 1997, Jeddah: Dar Abdul Qasim.

Ṣaḥīḥ al-Bukhārī, Beirut: Dār al-maʿrifa, s.d.
Ṣaḥīḥ Muslim, Beirut: Dār al-maʿrifa, s.d.

Other references

Balibar, E. (2011), *Citoyen sujet et autres essais d'anthropologie philosophique*. Paris: PUF.

Benkheira, M. H., A. Giladi, C. Mayeur Jaouen and J. Sublet, eds (2012), *La famille en islam d'après les sources arabes*. Paris: Les Indes Savantes.

Beyriès, J. (1935), 'Note sur les Ghoudf', *Revue des Études Islamiques*, 1: 52–73.

Bonte, P. (2016), *Récits d'origine*. Paris: Karthala.

Bonte, P., ed. (1994), *Épouser au plus proche. Inceste, prohibitions et stratégies matrimoniales autour de la Méditerranée*. Paris: EHESS.

Carrithers, M., S. Collins and S. Lukes, eds (1985), *The Category of the Person: Anthropology, Philosophy, History*. Cambridge: Cambridge University Press.

Cohen, A. (1991), *Le Talmud*. Paris: Payot.

Descombes, V. (2004), *Le Complément de Sujet. Enquête sur le Fait d'Agir de Soi-Même*. Paris: Gallimard.

Dumont, L. (1983), *Essais sur l'Individualisme*. Paris: Seuil.

Dupont, F. (2018), 'Comment Marcel Mauss croyait à l'origine romaine de la civilisation', *Cahiers 'Mondes Anciens'*, 11: 1–12.

Figueiredo-Biton, C. (2001), 'Conceptualisation des notions de chaud et de froid. Systèmes d'éducation et relations hommes/femmes chez les Touaregs (Imedégaghen et Kel Adagh, Mali)', thesis, Paris.

Fortier, C. (2000), 'Corps, différence de sexes et infortune: la transmission de l'identité et des savoirs dans la société maure de Mauritanie', thesis, EHESS, Paris.

Foucault, M. (2001), *L'herméneutique du sujet*. Paris: Seuil.

Geoffroy, E., ed. (2005), *Une voie soufie dans le monde, la Shâdhiliyya*. Paris: Maisonneuve.

al-ghazālī, A. Ḥ. (1997), *Iḥyāʾ ʿulūm al-dīn*. Beirut: Dār al-Fikr.

Godelier, M. (2007), *Au Fondement des Sociétés Humaines. Ce que nous Apprend l'Anthropologie*. Paris: Albin Michel.

Hamès, C. (2005), 'La Shâdhiliyya dans l'Ouest saharien et africain: nouvelles perspectives', in É. Geoffroy (ed.), *Une voie soufie dans le monde, la Shâdhiliyya*, 355–75. Paris, Maisonneuve.

Héritier, F. (1994a), 'Identité de substance et parenté de lait dans le monde arabe', in P. Bonte (ed.), *Épouser au Plus Proche. Inceste, Prohibitions et Stratégies Matrimoniales Autour de la* Méditerranée, 149–64. Paris: EHESS.

Héritier, F. (1994b), *Les deux sœurs et leur mère. Anthropologie de l'inceste*. Paris: Odile Jacob.

Honneth, A. (2020 [2018]), *La reconnaissance*. Paris: Gallimard.

Ibn Aʿbayd, M. B. (2016), *Muyassar al-jalīl fī sharḥ mukhtaṣar al-Shaykh Khalīl*. Nouakchott: Dār al-Riḍwān.

IbnAjība Al-ḥasanī, A. (n.d.), *Īqāẓ al-himam fī sharḥ al-ḥikam*. Beirut: Dār al-Fikr.

Ibn Ḥāmidun, M. (1990), *Ḥayāt Mūrītānyā, al-Ḥayāt al-thaqāfiyya*. Tunis: al-Dār al-ʿarabiyya li-l-kitāb.

Ibn Isḥāq, M. (1981), *Mukhtaṣar al-ʿallāma Khalīl*. Beirut: Dār al-Fikr.

Ibn, M. F. (2017), *Fatḥ al-ḥaqq fī ḥuqūq al-khāliq wa-l-khalq*. Casablanca: Najībawayh.

Jamard, J.-L., E. Terray and M. Xanthakou, eds (2000), *En substances. Textes pour Françoise Héritier*. Paris: Fayard.
Kant, E. (1985), *Critique de la faculté de juger*. Paris: Gallimard.
Laforgue, P. (1928), 'Une secte hérésiarque en Mauritanie: les Ghoudf', *Bull. du Comité d'Études Historiques et Scientifiques de l'Afrique Occidentale Française*, 11: 685–92.
Lévi-Strauss, C. (1949), *Les structures élémentaires de la parenté*. Paris: Plon.
Libera, A. de (2015), *L'invention du sujet moderne*. Paris: Vrin.
Macpherson, C. B. (1962), *The Political Theory of Possessive Individualism: Hobbes to Locke*. Oxford: Clarendon Press.
al-Maqarrī, Muḥammad Bayba b. Sīd Aḥmad (1997), *Jamʿ al-manāfiʿ fī al-ṭibb al-qadīm*. [n.l.]: Dār al-Ḥāwī li-l-ṭibāʿa wa-l-nashr.
Mauss, M. (1968), *Sociologie et Anthropologie*. Paris: PUF.
Pettigrew, E. (2014), 'Muslim healing, magic, and amulets in the twentieth-century history of the Southern Sahara', PhD diss., Stanford University.
Porqueres I Géné, E. and A. Bilbao Zepeda (2020), 'Récits des origines et individualisation de l'embryon: Afrique de l'Ouest', in A. M. Brisebarre et al. (eds), *L'anthropologie en partage*, 117–25. Paris: Karthala.
Rebstock, U. (2001), *Maurische Literaturgeschichte*. Würzburg: Ergon Verlag.
al-Shinqīṭī, Aḥmad b. al-Amīn (1989 [1911]), *al-Wasīṭ fī tarājim udabāʾ Shinqīṭ*. Cairo: al-Khānjī.
Stewart, C. C. and S. A. Ould Ahmed Salim (2016), *The Writings of Mauritania and the Western Sahara*. Leiden: Brill.
Tcherkézoff, S. (1983), *Le roi Nyamwezi, la Droite et la gauche: révision comparative des classifications dualistes*. Paris: MSH.
Wensick, A. J. (1936), *Concordance et indices de la tradition musulmane*. Leiden: Brill.
Wuld al-Barrā, Y. (2009), *al-Majmūʿa al-kubrā: al-shāmila li-fatāwā wa nawāzil wa aḥkām ahl gharb wa janūb gharb al-Ṣaḥrāʾ*. Nouakchott: al-Sharīf Mawlay al-Ḥasan b. al-Mukhtār b. al-Ḥasan.

10

The past and present of the *ghuzfiyya* Sufi order from the western regions of the Sahara

Yahya Ould al-Bara
University of Nouakchott

Introduction

A variety of considerations sparked our interest in the *ghuzfiyya* Sufi order (*ṭarīqa*), which has played a leading role in shaping religious, political and economic life in the Sahara-Sahelian regions in the past two centuries. These include the scarcity of available sources on the *ghuzfiyya* in comparison to other religious orders; the different opinions given by Islamic theologian-jurists (*fuqahā'*) concerning the *ghuzfiyya*; its impact on religious, economic and social life in the region (especially during the colonial period); widespread secrecy concerning the principles that govern it; the blatant opposition from certain Islamic scholars (*'ulamā'*) it has encountered; and finally, speculations about the political role it may play in contemporary Mauritania.

Since its creation in the eighteenth century until the first half of the twentieth century, this arcane Sufi order has been the subject of few scholarly studies. Most of what has been written about it has emerged from disputes among local scholars: sympathizers who seek to defend the *ghuzfiyya* and critics who wish to confirm (or even intensify) the accusations commonly levelled against it. Statements from members of the order have been rare, irrespective of the harsh criticism and controversies to which they have been subject. Despite my efforts, I was unable to find any written works in defence of the order, with the notable exception of Shaykh al-Maḥfūẓ ould Bayya's 'Epistle in defense of the *shādhiliyya*' (*Risāla fī al-Radd 'an al-shādhiliyya*; undated manuscript, c. 1955).[1]

The French colonial administration, for its part, gave some attention to the *ghuzfiyya*. From as far back as their early presence in the region (at the turn of the twentieth century), the French expressed their mistrust of the *ghuzfiyya* in numerous documents. The reason for this is certainly to be found in the opposition of some *ghuzfs* to the colonial project. In fact, Sīdī ould al-Zayn, responsible for the death of the French colonial administrator Xavier Coppolani in 1905, was a disciple of the *ghuzf*

Shaykh Muḥammad Maḥmūd 'al-Khalaf', who was openly hostile to French colonial penetration.[2]

This chapter aims to contribute to the understanding of the *ghuẓfiyya*'s distinctive characteristics and to make up for the deficits of previous works. The text is based on fieldwork conducted in February 2019 in a number of towns and villages in the Hodh region of eastern Mauritania, the most important of which are Timbedra, Legweirga, Adele-Bagru, Bassikhou and Nema. The chapter provides an account of the history of the *ghuẓfiyya* Sufi order from its emergence in the Hodh to its later 'resurrection' in the second half of the twentieth century, which resulted in its expansion into numerous other countries. In doing so, this chapter will elucidate the basic moral principles and teachings of the order, identify its essential characteristics and, more broadly, locate it on the religious and spiritual map of Mauritania and the Muslim world.[3] The evolution of the order, over a period of two and a half centuries and spanning different parts of the Muslim world, can be divided into distinctive phases:

1. An initial phase (second half of the eighteenth century) tied to the life of the founding shaykh, Muḥammad al-Aghẓaf, exclusively centred in the Hodh. The information on this early period indicates that the *ghuẓfiyya* was by then (considering their basic spiritual teachings and practices) very close to the *malāmātiyya*.[4] A high level of discretion, close to 'clandestineness' (*al-takhaffī*), was also valued during this period.
2. The second phase is associated with the *ghuẓfiyya*'s second shaykh, al-Mukhtār b. al-Ṭālib Aʿmar, who was chosen as the sole transmitter of the *ṭarīqa* by Shaykh Muḥammad al-Aghẓaf. It seems that its diffusion was by then limited to the Taganit and parts of the Rgayba (in the Assaba region of present-day Mauritania). It is marked by spiritual exercises, the elaboration of the order's characteristic teachings and ritual recitations (*awrād*, sg. *wird*), and the pursuit of mystical rapture (*al-jadhb*) and ecstatic utterances (*al-shaṭḥ*).
3. The third phase is marked by the transition to dynastic leadership, transmitted through the family of Shaykh al-Mukhtār's successor, Shaykh Sīd Aḥmad b. ʿAmmār b. al-Nāh. He was succeeded by his son Shaykh Muḥammad Maḥmūd al-Khalaf, who then passed the order's leadership onto his sons Shaykh Sīd Aḥmad al-Ghazwānī and Shaykh Muḥammad Aḥmad. Under their direction, the *ghuẓfiyya* expanded to the Adrar, Rgayba and Taganit. During this period, the *ghuẓfiyya* acquired its distinctive social form as a 'true' *ṭarīqa*, valuing the spiritual education of its members, stimulating their mystical experience and valuing work for the common good.
4. The fourth phase begins with Shaykh ʿAlī b. Āffa (m. 1909 CE), who brought the *ghuẓfiyya* back into the Hodh and diffused it widely throughout the region. He and his disciples also spread the *ṭarīqa* beyond Mauritania, leading to the establishment of communities in Sudan, Chad, the Hijaz in the Arabian Peninsula, Libya, Jordan and Turkey. This period is also characterized by militant proselytism and by rigorous efforts to defend the order – based in scholarly arguments – against accusations of heresy.

The early formative period (1758–1798)

The Hodh (Ar. *ḥawḍ*) is a natural geographic space with a geomorphology that resembles a type of bowl commonly used to scoop water – whence the literal translation of the name. Shaykh Saʿd Būh b. al-Shaykh Muḥammad Fāḍil b. Māmīn (d. 1335 H/1917 CE) provides a detailed description of the region and its inhabitants:

> Its extent, between Tishit and Segou, is forty days or more, and its extent between the Taganit and Nema is about a month. Among the territories created by god, it is the most peopled. Its southern part is inhabited by Blacks (*ḥabasha*, lit. 'Ethiopians'), that is, Bambara, Fulani, Massina, Soninké (*aswānik*), and Futanké (*ahl fūta*). These people live together in a region with big cities and villages. The northern part of the Hodh belongs to *zwāya* and *ḥassān qabāʾil* ('tribes'),[5] to nomadic herdsmen from the countryside and the cities, and to those living in the mountains.
>
> (*Kashf ḥijāb al-astār* (manuscript))

As this description shows, the region was populated by groups with different ethnic backgrounds, which testifies to its economic importance and the diversity of the productive activities undertaken in the region. The Hodh was profoundly influenced by the Black African empires of Ghana, Mali and Songhay; following their demise in the late sixteenth century, however, no centralized political system (comparable, perhaps, to the more recent emirates of the Adrar, Tagant, Brakna and Trarza) was established in the region. Instead, it was successively influenced by two 'tribal chieftaincies' (*mashyakhāt*, sing. *mashyakha*): that of the Awlād Mubārak, and that of the Mashẓūf. In the eighteenth and nineteenth centuries, the region saw a remarkable development of Islamic religious sciences and Sufi movements, giving rise to numerous distinguished scholars with notable social, religious and economic influence.[6] The *ghuẓfiyya* is included in this landscape, the origins of which lie in the argilliferous plains of the Kūsh. As the name suggests (it means 'stomach' in Azer),[7] the topography of this agricultural and pastoral reservoir allowed it to meet the alimentary needs of a large population.

The most important community in the Kūsh is the Awlād Muḥammad (Būḥummud) community, which currently constitutes around 80 per cent of the total population.[8] They immigrated from the Taganit in the late seventeenth century and by the nineteenth century were already permanently established there. They are organically structured in twenty-four factions, divided into two functional groups: Those who carry arms and follow 'warrior' traditions (*ḥassān*/ *ʿarab*) are called Awlād Būḥummud al-ʿArab (sixteen factions); the second group, composed of the remaining eight factions, specialized in religious matters (*zwāya*/*ṭulba*) and are known as the Ṭulbat Awlād Būḥummud (according to Ibn Māmīn's undated manuscript, *al-Ḍiyyāʾ al-mustabīn*).

The life of Shaykh Muḥammad al-Aghẓaf

This is the social milieu in which al-Shaykh Muḥammad al-Aghẓaf, the only son of Ḥamāh Allah b. Sālim al-Dāwūdī,[9] was born in 1128 H [1716 CE; d. 1223 H /1808 CE]

(Ibn Maynummu 1961). Citing his patrilineal ancestors, the historian-genealogist Mawlāy ʿAbdallāh b. al-Shaykh Mawlāy ʿAbd al-Mālik b. Mawlāy Ḥasan (d. 1348 H/1928 CE) writes: 'Sālim b. Laḥbīb b. Muḥammad b. Mūsa b. Abū Bakr b. Aʿbayd b. Haddāj b. Jaʿfar b. Dāwūd b. Aʿrūg b. Uday b. al-Ḥāmid b. Ḥassān b. Mūsā b. Maʿqil.'[10] This demonstrates that Shaykh Muḥammad al-Aghẓaf belonged to the al-Jaʿāfra faction, who, together with the Awlād ʿAllūsh and Awlād Zayd, formed the Awlād Dāwūd Aʿrūg *qabīla* (Ibn Maynummu 1961).

Following the early death of his father (who was purportedly killed by bandits), Shaykh Muḥammad al-Aghẓaf was raised by his mother, al-Quẓwiyya mint al-Nagnūg, from the Yāddās *qabīla*. His grandfather allegedly lived in Tishit or its surroundings, where he is said to have been one of the most eminent leaders of the al-Jaʿāfra, the owner of large palm groves, and a follower of *ḥassān* traditions. Rather than staying with his Awlād Dāwūd relatives, he lived with his Yāddās maternal uncles (*akhwālih*). Later, having already acquired the status of a saint, he joined the Tāfullālit,[11] who lived between Kunayb and Adele-Bagru.[12] He was then married and remained there for the rest of his life.

Different sources report that Shaykh Muḥammad al-Aghẓaf had multiple wives, most of them from the Awlād Buḥummud, and that he also had a 'secret marriage' (*tasarrā*) with the mother of his son al-Ṭālib Muḥammad. The exact number of the shaykh's children is disputed, but we can confirm with some certainty the existence of at least twenty-five: sixteen sons and nine daughters. Only seven of his sons passed on their lineage to the present day: al-Shaykh Sīdī Ṣāliḥ, al-Shaykh Sīdī Aḥmad Zarrūq,[13] Lujayba, Abū al-Ḥasan, Al-Ṭālib Yūsuf, Būna ʿĀlī and al-Ṭālib Muḥammad. The remaining nine sons were named Sīdī Bubakkar al-Kandarī, Shaykhna, al-Ṭālib Aʿmar, Abū al-Ḥasan, al-Ṭālib al-Amīn, al-Shaykh Sīdī al-Mukhtār, al-Shaykh al-Aghẓaf al-Ṣaghīr, al-Shaykh ʿAbd al-Qādir and al-Ṭālib Ṣiddīq. Six of them died at an early age, and the lineages of the other three ended before the present day. Paul Marty, writing in 1921 (1921: 91), mentions that 'all of the shaykh's descendants' (the Ahl al-Shaykh Muḥammad al-Aghẓaf; leaving out the Lujayba and Abū al-Ḥasan) lived between Bassiknou (Mauritania) and Sokolo (in present-day Mali), mainly around the villages of Madalla and Dwānkarā. Following their nomadic trails during the dry season, they approached the inlets of the Niger River towards Diawara and Macina. Today, the shaykh's direct descendants continue to live in different locations in the eastern Hodh.

Oral tradition maintains that as a child, Muḥammad al-Aghẓaf did not show any interest in the normal activities of children his age and that, showing signs of future 'sainthood' and confirmed sagacity (*al-ḥudhdhāq*), he was admitted to a *maḥẓara* (a traditional religious school; see the chapter by Baba Ahmed and Horma in this volume) for children with similar promise. When he had proceeded to the forty-fifth subdivision (*ḥizb*) of the Qurʾān and read the two verses '*al-raḥmān ʿallama al-qurʾān*' ('the Merciful taught the Qurʾān'), he was suddenly overtaken by a powerful emotion and retreated into anxious silence. He looked to the sky and remained transfixed in this position for a long time, to the point that his eyes became red and people began to fear for his life.[14] His teacher (whose name is not remembered) repeatedly tried to call him back to his writing board (*lawḥ*), but to no avail (Ibn Maynummu 1961). After he regained consciousness, he left the Quranic school and adopted a solitary disposition, remaining silent and avoiding encounters with others. He spent most of his time in the desert worshipping God and began to undertake long mystical journeys (*siyyāḥa*) that led him to all corners of his native region, and notably to Tishit, the home of his ancestors. He visited spiritual guides (*mashā'ikh*) of various traditions and led a truly ascetic life, wearing simple tunics made of rough cotton (*jīf*) and renouncing all personal possessions, fully entrusting himself to the will of God. When people asked him about his habit of travelling without any provisions, he answered that birds always travelled that way. When they objected, saying that birds had been given wings, he said that 'there are beings that can fly even without wings'.[15] After many years on this mystical quest, Shaykh Muḥammad al-Aghẓaf eventually reached the stage of accomplishment (*wuṣūl*) through an ecstatic mystical experience of God (*jadhb*), without the spiritual guidance of any master.

As a saint and Sufi master, Shaykh Muḥammad al-Aghẓaf is naturally credited with many miracles (*karāmāt*). A distinctive feature of these, also reported by later holy men of the *ghuẓfiyya*, is their relation to water. Some of the most important miracles that serve to confirm the shaykh's saintly powers revolve around Nwall, a salty well situated in the al-Rag region of eastern Hodh. Oral tradition recounts the story of Nwall as follows:

> A man of the Ahl al-Ṭālib Mukhtār came to a camp of *shurfā*, where he saw a girl in a state of mental illness. He asked for permission to marry her, assuring her family that she would be cured. The girl's parents accepted but warned him that she was in the clutches of a dangerous demon. He did not believe them, and the marriage was concluded. The day of the wedding, a storm suddenly descended and lifted the couple's tent into the sky. The man shouted the magic phrase, 'Oh auxiliary men' (*yā rijāl al-ghayth*), whereupon a group of saints, including Shaykh Muḥammad al-Aghẓaf, immediately appeared to help. They chased the demon away until they reached Nwall. Some of the saint's companions were thirsty and asked for water, but they were told that the water from this well was poisonous, and those—both men and beasts—who drank from it would instantly die. After invoking God's name, Shaykh Muḥammad al-Aghẓaf spat into the well, and its water was then safe to drink. Since then, the water of Nwall has been sought by the sick, who come from afar in search of its therapeutic properties.
>
> (Ibn Māmīn, al-Shaykh Muḥammad Fāḍil n.d.; see also al-Burtulī 1981: 5)

Another version of the Nwall miracle tells that a group of saints, including Shaykh Muḥammad al-Aghẓaf, camped at the well. When the time for prayer approached, they each declined to lead it, out of decency. The shaykh's rug then miraculously shifted to the imam's position, and he led the collective prayer (Ibn Maynummu 1961). This event is said to have earned him the titles 'master of masters' (*shaykh al-ashyākh*) and 'sultan of saints' (*sulṭān al-awliyā'*), as he would henceforth be known.[16]

Būna ʿĀlī b. Maynammu reports that when Shaykh Muḥammad al-Aghẓaf was 35 years old, Sharīf Zayn al-ʿĀbidīn b. Sīdī ʿAbdallāh al-Maghribī al-Fāsī, the famous scholar from Fes, learned of his existence by divine revelation. Zayn al-ʿĀbidīn had a vision that he would mediate Muḥammad al-Aghẓaf's ascension to gnosis and decided to leave Morocco to meet him in the Kūsh (south of the Hodh region of present-day Mauritania). He initiated him in all the esoteric secrets leading to the divine presence, returning to Fes only once he had accomplished this task (Ibn Maynummu 1961). The expression 'all the secrets' (*jamīʿ al-asrār*) indicates that the master from Fes authorized Shaykh Muḥammad al-Aghẓaf to pass on the secret prayers (*awrād*) of all the Sufi orders, not only those of a determined *ṭarīqa*.[17] This resonates with the fact that the early *ghuẓfiyya* seemed to incorporate the prayers and teachings of different Sufi orders and was thus considered either an independent order, as a branch of the *shādhiliyya*, or a 'mix' of the *shādhiliyya* and the *qādiriyya* (Boubrik 2000: 269).[18]

When Shaykh Muḥammad al-Aghẓaf was 40 years old, Būna ʿĀlī writes, *sharīf* Zayn al-ʿĀbidīn (also bearer of the title 'master of masters') returned once again to the Sahara to visit him (Ibn Maynummu 1961). He died shortly upon his arrival and was buried in Gnayb (in the Kūsh), the likely residence of Shaykh Muḥammad al-Aghẓaf at the time. Based on this information, Zayn al-ʿĀbidīn's death would have occurred in the year 1168 H/1755 CE.

The filial chain of the *ghuẓfiyya* is connected to the *ṭarīqa shādhiliyya nāṣiriyya*, a Sufi path that is considered to have been the most widespread among the inhabitants of the region over the past three centuries. This path is attached to ʿAbdallāh Muḥammad b. Muḥammad b. Muḥammad b. Aḥmad b. Muḥammad b. al-Ḥusayn b. Nāṣir al-Darʿī al-Tamagrūtī al-Aghlānī (d. 1085 H/1676 CE), one of the most eminent Islamic scholars of his time. The *zāwiya* of the *nāṣiriyya* in Tamagrūt (in the Draa region of southern Morocco) attracted followers from far and wide and enjoyed a high reputation, not only for its intellectual influence – extending throughout the whole Maghreb and the Sahara – but also for its outstanding social and political role in the region (Gutelius 2002; Hammoudi 1980; Katz 1992).

When Shaykh Muḥammad al-Aghẓaf was in his forties, he took up the task of offering education and spiritual guidance to those who came to him in search of knowledge. He received many visitors and disciples from all corners of the Hodh and from neighbouring regions. Some claim that he was the first to carry the title of 'spiritual guide' (shaykh) in this area.[19] He is said to have entertained close ties with other Sufi masters of his time, especially Shaykh Māmīn (1795–1869), founder of the *fāḍiliyya* branch of the *qādiriyya*, and Shaykh Sīdī al-Mukhtār al-Kuntī (1729 –1811), the famous 'renewer of faith' (*mujaddid*) who propagated and popularized the Sufi teachings of the *qādiriyya* in the western Sudan.

Apparently, Shaykh Muḥammad al-Aghẓaf initiated his disciples into the litany prayers (*awrād*) of the *shādhiliyya nāṣiriyya*, also adding, among others, elements from the *qādiriyya* tradition. It seems that the adepts of the *ghuẓfiyya* were first introduced to the teachings of the *shādhiliyya*, considered the basis of the order's spiritual path, and only after having demonstrated a certain degree of progress were they initiated into the *awrād* of the *qādiriyya*. It was believed that those who attained this level should always begin their ritual recitations with the *qādirī wird* and only then pronounce the *wird* of the *shādhiliyya* because, as Shaykh Muḥammad al-Aghẓaf claimed, Shaykh ʿAbd al-Qādir al-Jīlānī was 'jealous'.[20] The adepts of the *ghuẓfiyya* recited their own specific *wird* not collectively but individually after the five regular prayers of the day and were obliged to keep it a secret. The so-called *wird al-taʿmīr* (literally '*wird* of filling in [time]') was to be recited between the morning prayer (*fajr*) and sunrise and between the afternoon prayer (ʿ*aṣr*) and sunset. During these periods, disciples were to concentrate fully on their ritual invocations, refraining from talking. This rule explains the widespread delaying of the ʿ*aṣr* prayer by the *ghuzfs*, an element that has often been a point of contention. In his comment on Khalīl b. Isḥāq's *al-Mukhtaṣar*, the Islamic scholar from Kifa Muḥammad al-Amīn b. Aḥmad Zaydān al-Jakanī (d. 1935) wrote:

> I consulted the works of the mystics and of the authors of good advice, the books on the *ḥadīth* such as al-Bukhārī's, the treatises of *fiqh*, and the works dealing with their fundaments and branches, in search of what could justify the conduct of these people, and I learned as an unmistakable truth that this is a Satanic doctrine.
> (al-Jakanī al-Shinqīṭī (1993), vol. 1: 132–3)

The *ghuzfs* justified this delaying of the ʿ*aṣr* prayer by appealing to a principle known in Maliki *fiqh* as 'moving beyond dissent' (*al-khurūj min al-khilāf*). Muḥammad b. Sīdī al-Buṣādī (d. 1972) described this point of view in a *fatwā* in which he affirms that Shaykh Abū al-Ḥasan al-Shāḍilī followed the opinion of Abū Ḥanīfa (founder of the Hanafi school of Islamic law) concerning the appropriate time for the ʿ*aṣr* prayer.[21]

Shaykh Muḥammad al-Aghẓaf reportedly prioritized the acquisition of certain behavioural and mental traits which he considered more beneficial than those espoused by most legal scholars, who argued that renouncement (of certain vices) precedes the acquisition of certain spiritual qualities. He is credited with having said to his children and disciples: 'Purify yourselves, that's of more worth then studying', 'He amongst you who wants to emulate me shall put his head under an *um-l-bayna* [a plant with leaves that touch the ground]' (alluding to the value attributed to modesty and renouncement).[22] These combined factors account for the particular character of the *ghuzfiyya*, whose adepts are encouraged to live in seclusion and discretion, accord high value to a working ethos and contribute to public welfare.

Another distinctive feature of the *ghuzfiyya* is their individualistic approach to the initiation of disciples, i.e. the consideration their teachers are supposed to pay to their individual character traits when guiding their spiritual development. Some are encouraged to indulge in the order's ritual practices, while those with a different constitution are advised to devote themselves to the material service of the community.[23] Many of the order's adepts affirm that the prophet (PBUH) himself used this pedagogical strategy with his companions.

Shaykh Muḥammad al-Aghẓaf died in 1213 H (1798 CE), at the age of 84.[24] He was buried in al-Mabrūk (46 km south of Adele-Bagru, in present-day Mali), where his tomb still attracts visitors. According to local accounts, his last will and testament stipulated that his corpse was to be placed on the back of a camel, which was to roam free until it decided to rest, in this way determining his burial site.[25]

Soon after his burial, an anonymous 'Bambara of Ségou' is said to have erected a protective structure over the tomb. This man, who was a pagan, saw the shaykh in a dream in which the latter invited him to convert to Islam. He did in fact convert and decided to visit the shaykh's tomb. When he arrived at al-Mabrūk, the tomb was elevated in the air, and he resolved to erect a structure to protect it. As there was no one living in the vicinity of the tomb, he went to Akamb, a village in the Malian *département* of Nara, to seek assistance. After accomplishing his mission, he remained in the area for some time before returning to his homeland, where he proselytized among his people.[26]

The shaykh's first disciples

Among the shaykh's disciples, two deserve particular consideration for the outstanding reputation they enjoyed and the exceptional intellectual and spiritual influence they exerted on others: Shaykh Muḥammad al-Amīn b. al-Ṭālib ʿAbd al-Wahhāb (1254 H/1838 CE) and Shaykh Sīdī Muḥammad b. Aḥmad al-Aswad (d. 1259 H/1843–44 CE; Ibn Maynummu 1961).

Shaykh Muḥammad al-Amīn b. al-Ṭālib ʿAbd al-Wahhāb was part of the Tāfullālit faction of the Awlād Buḥummud *qabīla*. His love of knowledge is exemplified in the oral account that tells that when God revealed to him that he had just one year left to live, he took his wooden writing board (*lawḥ*) and spent his remaining time studying. He founded an important school of Islamic sciences (*maḥẓara*) and wrote a number of manuscripts in different genres, including a commentary on Khalīl b. Isḥāq's *al-Mukhtaṣar* (in fourteen volumes) and a long commentary on Ibn Abī Zayd al-Qayrawānī's (d. 385 H/922–996 CE) *Risāla*, *al-Talkhīṣ al-mufīd ʿalā risāla Ibn Abī Zayd*. Until recently, the latter work was the most important manual of *fiqh* used in the Hodh. Muḥammad al-Amīn b. al-Ṭālib was buried in Idrīs.[27] His only son, Shaykh Muḥammad Aḥmad, followed in his footsteps and was later replaced by his own son, Muḥammad al-Amīn.[28] It is clear, however, that this succession did not take place within the framework of the *ghuẓfiyya*, as Shaykh Muḥammad al-Amīn b. al-Ṭālib did not receive Muḥammad al-Aghẓaf's authorization to do so.

Shaykh Sīdī Muḥammad b. Aḥmad al-Aswad derives his name from his clan's founding father, Sharīf Mawlāy Aḥmad b. Muḥammad ʿAbdallāh b. Mawlāy ʿUmar (surname 'al-Aswad').[29] Aḥmad al-Aswad left Tindouf (where he lived) by the mid-eighteenth century to establish himself in the Taganit, among the Aghlāl, and later in the Hodh. He died in Tashamāmit, where his tomb became a place of pilgrimage and worship. Shaykh Būna ʿĀlī b. Maynammu presents Sīdī Muḥammad b. Aḥmad al-Aswad as an ascetic who took care of orphans, fasted throughout the day and prayed through the night (Ibn Maynummu 1961). He died in 1259 H (1843 CE) and is buried in Jagraga (20 km north of Djigueni, in the Hodh al-Gharbi region of present-day Mauritania).

There is no doubt that the Ahl Aḥmad al-Aswad were highly reputed in religious matters, but it is also known that with the rise of Shaykh Muḥammad Fāḍil b. Māmīn and his *ṭarīqa*, they joined his Sufi order (for the most part). Paul Marty (1921: 314) mentions that the famous saint Sīdī Muḥammad b. Ahl al-Khayr, who affirmed his filiation with Shaykh Muḥammad al-Aghẓaf, was also a *muqaddam* ('deputy', one authorized to initiate others into a *ṭarīqa*) of the *qādiriyya* and instructed numerous disciples from the Glāgma, al-Tanāgīd, Ijummān, Idawblāl, and al-Aghlāl tribal spheres. After his death in 1916, they all returned to their respective *qabīla*.

Shaykh Muḥammad al-Aghẓaf is also credited with having influenced Shaykh Muḥammad Fāḍil b. Māmīn: '[a]fter his death [Muḥammad al-Aghẓaf] poured water over Shaykh Muḥammad Fāḍil b. Māmīn from the glass of the accomplished path of sanctification' (Ibn Maynummu 1961). Shaykh Būna ʿĀlī b. Maynummu provides further details on what led Shaykh Muḥammad Fāḍil to visit Shaykh Muḥammad al-Aghẓaf. He tells us that a severe drought hit the region where Shaykh Sīdī al-Mukhtār al-Kuntī lived, and in order to put an end to this serious problem he tried to convince Shaykh Ibn Aḥmad b. ʿUthmān al-Tinwājiwī to pray for them. He sent him a letter in which he urged him to carry out the pilgrimage to Mecca. Ibn Aḥmad complied and prepared for the journey. On his way, he visited Shaykh Māmīn, who received him with great hospitality and presented his newborn son, Muḥammad Fāḍil, to him. Shaykh Māmīn asked his visitor to pray for his son and to bestow his divine *baraka* ('grace') on him, so that God would make him one of those rendering service to Muslims. Shaykh Ibn Aḥmad did as asked and informed the child's father of the scope of the divine gifts and the sainthood that he would later manifest in his life. He also revealed that this would be achieved through the intermediation of a 'friend of the house' (*ṣāḥib al-dār*) named Shaykh Muḥammad al-Aghẓaf. He then recommended the following to his host: When Muḥammad Fāḍil reaches adulthood, he should prepare a pious gift composed of a tent, some cows and various other objects and travel to Shaykh Muḥammad al-Aghẓaf's tomb, where he should stay for a week; this will lead to the awakening of the powers within him.

When Shaykh Muḥammad Fāḍil reached adulthood, after the death of his father, Shaykh Būna ʿĀlī b. Maynummu tells us, he fulfilled the advice given by Shaykh Ibn Aḥmad. He gathered the goods he'd mentioned and went to the tomb of Shaykh Muḥammad al-Aghẓaf, where he stayed for some time (some accounts mention several weeks). By God's grace, he was filled with wisdom and light. When it became clear to him that he had gotten what he had come for and was allowed to return home, he composed his famous poem:

> Oh God! By the grace of the man buried here
> The pillar of our times al-Aghẓaf of sound advice
> (*Yā rabbunā bi-ṣāḥib al-ḍarīḥ*
> *Quṭb al-zamān al-Aghẓaf al-naṣīḥ*)

Once he recited this, he received all he desired and returned home haloed by the light of right conduct, having accomplished his mystical journey (Ibn Maynummu 1961).

The retreat to secrecy

During the more than forty years that Shaykh Muḥammad al-Aghẓaf devoted to the instruction and spiritual orientation of his disciples, he attracted a great number of devotees, many of whom became distinguished scholars and saints. Shaykh Muḥammad al-Aghẓaf himself 'confirmed' (*ṣaddara*) the mystical accomplishments of many of his disciples, to the point that, it is said, he 'licensed' (*ajāza*) thirty-nine in a single afternoon.[30] Despite this, it seems that the shaykh authorized only one person to transmit the *ṭarīqa*'s *wird*: Shaykh al-Mukhtār b. al-Ṭālib Aʿmar b. Nūḥ (surname 'Bū-damʿa'), who hailed from the Īdaybūsāt. The account of Shaykh al-Mukhtār's authorization to transmit the order's distinctive teachings is supported by the fact that Shaykh Muḥammad al-Aghẓaf's eldest son, Sīdī Ṣāliḥ, was later initiated by Shaykh Sīdī Muḥammad b. al-Shaykh Sīdī al-Mukhtār al-Kuntī (d. 1242 H/1826 CE) into the *qādiriyya*.[31] The Īdaybūsāt *zwāya* status *qabīla* produced numerous judges, saints and poets. At some point, they were established in the Gibla (the southwestern region of present-day Mauritania) but then migrated to the Taganit, the Aoukar, the Adrar and finally to the Hodh.[32]

It seems that the formulation attributed to Shaykh Muḥammad al-Aghẓaf when certifying al-Mukhtār b. al-Ṭālib Aʿmar ('I hereby confer onto you the stallion's necklace'; Ibn Maynummu 1961), signals the ascription of exclusive authority over the order's propagation. The *wird* of the *ghuẓfiyya* was actually not transmitted by the numerous already initiated disciples, not even by his own sons, who were widely respected as 'honourable men' (*ṣāliḥīn*) and Sufi masters (*mashāʾikh*) in their own right. This suggests that the *ghuẓfiyya* was seemingly very selective in choosing its members, deciding to keep its ritual invocations (*awrād*) a secret. This surely contributes to explaining why it retained an aura of mystery and has remained an object of speculation for outside observers.

Shaykh al-Mukhtār b. al-Ṭālib Aʿmar's ascension to spiritual leadership

The genealogy of Shaykh al-Mukhtār connects him to his ancestor al-Ṭālib Aʿmar b. Nūḥ b. al-Ṭālib ʿAbd al-Fattāḥ b. Lamrābiṭ b. Ābba. His father, al-Ṭālib Aʿmar b. Nūḥ, left al-Bayrāt Īdaybūsāt (situated to the north of Butilimit) in 1155 H (1742 CE) and headed to the Taganit (Ibn Ḥāmidun 1970). There, he settled in a place called Tashāga, in the Tishit region, which remains the only available gateway to the Hodh, further south. This area had hitherto been known for the looters that used to take advantage of the strategic passage. It is said that he was the first person to light a fire there (travellers avoided doing so for fear of bandits). It is also said that a band of brigands were once surprised to discover that the fire they had spotted belonged to al-Ṭālib Aʿmar's tent, for in this location only a considerable force, one unafraid of being attacked, would have dared to light a fire. Al-Ṭālib Aʿmar's presence thus secured this area, making it a safe refuge for travellers. Soon, his Ahl Ābba 'cousins' and other Īdaybūsāt factions regrouped around him. They consolidated their control over the area and extended it to the Tāskāsit.[33] Al-Ṭālib Aʿmar likely hoped to ensure the security of his relatives on their nomadic routes, which sometimes led them to distant northwestern (*al-Sāḥil*) pastures in the cooler season, well into Rgaybāt-controlled areas. The Ahl Nūḥ attracted disciples from among them and consequently gained a high reputation and respect from this *qabīla*.[34] In addition, al-Ṭālib Aʿmar had to look after his relatives' security in the western Hodh, where they went with their herds in the dry season.

Oral tradition among the Ahl Nūḥ reports that al-Ṭālib Aʿmar had five daughters and seven sons: Muḥammad Būka, ʿAbdallāh, Aḥmad Fāl, al-Shaykh al-Mukhtār, al-Ṭālib Muṣṭafā, Khalīl and ʿAbd al-Jalīl.[35] Different interlocutors specified that Shaykh al-Mukhtār was the fourth of al-Ṭālib Aʿmar's sons and present him and his brother

Aḥmad Fāl as accredited scholars. In his search for knowledge, Shaykh al-Mukhtār travelled to Rgayba, where his mystical states intensified. His father then ordered him to look for a shaykh to guide him because, according to Muḥammad al-Amīn b. ʿAbdallāh b. Sayyid al-Qawm, those who experienced these mystical states were legally obliged to seek the tuition of a shaykh in order to learn the adequate ways to purify and free themselves of daemons. Shaykh al-Mukhtār sought a master to teach him and met a shaykh of the *shādhiliyya*.[36] He joined this shaykh's camp and stayed with him until he received his 'habilitation' (*ijāza*) in mysticism (*taṣawwuf*) and the authorization to transmit the teachings of the Sufi order. He then returned to where his relatives were settled (between Likhshab and Tishit) to teach and guide those aspiring to spiritual development. It is said that God granted him authority over wild animals, who became tame in his presence and came to him when he called them. This explains his riding a lion on his travels.

Būna ʿĀlī b. Maynummu tells that one day, when some of his disciples were digging a well and had already reached a great depth, the pit suddenly began to collapse. In unison, they exclaimed the holy invocation 'Oh auxiliary men!' (*yā rijāl al-ghayth*), thereby provoking God's intervention. The collapse halted, but they were now trapped underground. Their relatives, along with the shaykh, were desperate but saw no alternative to abandoning them. When night fell, a tall, light-skinned man in white clothes suddenly appeared in the cavern and offered the group food and water. They accepted his offer without asking who he was, and he went on to offer them milk, sitting and speaking with them as if he knew them. When they finally asked his name, he answered: Muḥammad al-Aghẓaf b. Ḥimā Allah b. Sālim. They committed his name to memory, and he continued to visit and to provide for them for a period of three months. None imagined they would still be alive, until Shaykh Muḥammad al-Aghẓaf appeared before Shaykh al-Mukhtār in his sleep and asked him: 'Why don't you look for your disciples, who are trapped alive under layers of earth?' Shaykh al-Mukhtār initially dismissed the episode as a confused dream, but every time he closed his eyes and tried to fall asleep, the shaykh re-appeared, instructing him to search for his disciples. Puzzled by this experience, he asked his visitor his name, and the latter told him he was Muḥammad al-Aghẓaf b. Ḥimā Allah b. Sālim. Būna ʿĀlī b. Maynummu's account continues: 'In the morning, he summoned the most respected scholars and notables (*ahl al-ḥall wa-l-ʿaqd*) and told them of his experience. They could hardly believe what they were hearing. As they could not apprehend the divine omnipotence at work, they did not know how to answer.' He told them: 'Assemble the population; we are going to dig. If we discover that I was lied to, that will only strengthen our faith in the futility of dreams. And if we discover that things are as we were told, we will know that this confirms divine omnipotence.' They agreed, and the population mobilized themselves in support. They went on to enlarge the entrance of the well and dug until the earth began to trickle onto the heads of those trapped below, who shouted: 'Oh you up there, don't kill us!' People joyfully called out to the buried disciples by their names, and they answered that all of them were alive. Carefully, they continued until all had been rescued. When people asked what had happened, the disciples reported: 'When we saw that the well was collapsing, we invoked the assistance of the good souls in

God's favour. A man called Shaykh Muḥammad al-Aghẓaf appeared above our heads, as if he were supporting the rubble that threatened to crush us.'

Būna ʿĀlī b. Maynummu's account continues:

> From that moment on, Shaykh al-Mukhtār was convinced that he could not pretend to be either a mentor (*murshid*), or a master of education (*murabbī*), or a guide to mystical accomplishment (*muwwaṣṣil*). He decided to seek out Shaykh Muḥammad al-Aghẓaf. A lion served as his mount. He prepared for the voyage, decided to ask his closest disciples to accompany him, and departed with only a few provisions, with no idea of the distance he would have to cover. The group traveled without rest until they were close to Shaykh Muḥammad al-Aghẓaf's camp. Outside the camp, they met a man wearing patched-up clothes following his herd of goats and sheep. He confirmed that this was the camp of the shaykh they were seeking. They entered and asked for the tent of the shaykh. They were told that he was away, likely in the desert, as was his custom. When the shaykh returned to welcome them, they saw that it was the same man they had met outside the camp. He then began to arrange for his guests' accommodation. When night fell, Shaykh al-Mukhtār informed Shaykh Muḥammad al-Aghẓaf that his lion needed to eat and that his usual diet consisted of a well-fed cow. The shaykh did not possess any cattle at the time; the only option was a young calf owned by a woman who lived nearby. Although the calf was hardly big enough to satisfy the lion's appetite, he asked her to sell it to him, but she initially refused. Shaykh Muḥammad al-Aghẓaf convinced her by promising that her cow would be returned to her unharmed. He then entrusted the animal to his disciple, al-Ḥājj al-Kawrī, and instructed him: 'When you bring the calf to the lion, whisper into its ear that I command it to eat the lion, with God's permission.' Al-Ḥājj al-Kawrī did as he was told by the shaykh. In the early morning hours, Shaykh al-Mukhtār sent one of his companions to check on the lion. He returned without saying anything, and nobody interrogated him further. Then al-Ḥājj al-Kawrī went to see what had happened to the lion, but he could find no trace of it. The calf was licking its chops. The shaykh's disciple was filled with pleasure and shouted: 'The cow has eaten the lion!' By the time the sun rose, the news had reached Shaykh al-Mukhtār, leaving him perplexed. He went to Shaykh Muḥammad al-Aghẓaf and told him that he could only return home on the back of a lion. The shaykh resolved to reward his straightforwardness and said to his disciple, Sīdī Ibrāhīm b. al-Ḥājj b. Buradda: 'Go to this place (giving him the name), and when you have arrived there, call the lions from everywhere as loud as you can; when they come to you, there will be one with such-and-such characteristics, coming from such-and-such direction, approaching you with a wagging tail; that is the one you are to bring back.

When Sīdī Ibrāhīm arrived at the location, following the shaykh's instructions, everything happened as he had predicted, and he told the lion: 'Shaykh Muḥammad al-Aghẓaf orders you to obey me.' He brought the animal to the camp, where Shaykh Muḥammad al-Aghẓaf equipped it with a harness and personally handed it over to Shaykh al-Mukhtār. He requested for forgiveness for what had happened and said goodbye, asking his guest to send his regards to his kin and to free the lion once he arrived home. Shaykh al-Mukhtār mounted the lion and left with his companions, but he soon began to feel remorse and shame, worrying about his reputation among his kin following this failure. He decided he could not return home this way and travelled back to the camp of Shaykh Muḥammad al-Aghẓaf, becoming his disciple and integrating himself into his community. He is reported to have lived there for twenty-four years, and then for another period of sixteen years, before Muḥammad al-Aghẓaf confirmed his accession to the 'divine presence' (*al-ḥuḍra al-muqaddasa*), to the rank of the Gnostics (*al-ʿārifīn*), ultimately entrusting him with the secret *wird* of the *ghuẓfiyya*. When he transmitted the *wird* to al-Mukhtār, Shaykh Muḥammad al-Aghẓaf is reported to have said: 'I hereby confer onto you the stallion's necklace' (Ibn Maynummu 1961). This expression signifies the transference of absolute responsibility for the order's leadership and propagation to Shaykh al-Mukhtār. Būna ʿĀlī b. Maynammu's comment closes the account of Shaykh al-Mukhtār's ascension to spiritual leadership, confirming his saintly qualities and his importance to the development of the *ghuẓfiyya*:

> Without these two men [Shaykh Muḥammad al-Aghẓaf and Shaykh al-Mukhtār], this Sufi order would not have come to light. But Allah does what He wants. He brought it into being. He inscribed its lights and secrets as a testimony to the creative wisdom He wished to reveal; and only the blind, those with a troubled nature, and heretics deny the miracles of the saints and the efficiency of the divine action. This account was received from the mouth of Shaykh al-Mukhtār, the leader of the *ghuẓfiyya*.
>
> (Ibn Maynummu 1961)

It was Shaykh al-Mukhtār who named the order the 'path of the *ghuẓf*, and thus he became known as the 'shaykh of the *ghuẓf*. He stayed with Shaykh Muḥammad al-Aghẓaf at the end of his life, for sixteen years, to prepare for his cleansing and burial upon his death, as well as the performance of the ritual prayer over his remains, over which he would preside. With the initiation of Shaykh al-Mukhtār and his return to the Taganit, the transmission of the *ghuẓfiyya*'s teachings in the Hodh was interrupted.

The return to his kin in the Taganit and the designation of his successor

When Shaykh al-Mukhtār returned from his sojourn with the shaykh, around 1214 H/1799–1800 CE, he re-joined the Ahl Ābba, who were now established south of Tamshikit. He stayed with them as teacher and spiritual guide, leading the ascetic life of a saint (according to Ibn Maynummu's manuscript). He is considered to have laid the foundations of the nascent Sufi order and to have mapped out its mode of teaching and internal organization, to the point that some refer to him as the true founder of the *ghuẓfiyya*. They justify this by appealing to the fact that he was called 'our shaykh' (*shaykhunā*) by the disciples and by the fact that it was he who was directly criticized in Shaykh Sīdī Muḥammad al-Kuntī's *al-ṭarāʾif wa al-talāʾid* (Patris 1948).

It is reported that thirty-nine relatives of Shaykh al-Mukhtār joined the *ghuẓfiyya*. Most of his kin, however, had reservations about the Sufi movement and denounced its mystical excesses. The shaykh's own brothers were apparently among the first to express their opposition to his cause.[37] Some of the Ahl Ābba even accused him of 'unbelief' (*kufr*). They complained about him to the emir of the Taganit, Muḥammad b. Muḥammad Shayn (d. 1236 H/1821 CE), who assured them that if they simply issued a *fatwā* proving his unbelief, he would have him executed.[38] They chose to ask the Idaw 'Ali Islamic scholar from Tijikja Sīdī ʿAbdallāh b. al-Ḥājj Ibrāhīm (d. 1233 H/1818 CE) to confront Shaykh al-Mukhtār. The two men debated for three nights at Tijigja, and at the end of the third night they headed to the mosque for prayer. Sīdī ʿAbdallah asked Shaykh al-Mukhtār to lead the prayer, at which point he experienced an acute mystical episode. While directing the prayer, he jolted around, flailing himself against the walls of the mosque, his tears flowing down his beard and spilling over onto those praying behind him. When the prayer was finished, Sīdī ʿAbdallāh said goodbye to Shaykh al-Mukhtār, who left Tijigja to rejoin the Ahl Nūḥ, who were travelling between al-Ghubba and Tishit. As soon as he turned his back to them, Sīdī ʿAbdallāh's disciples hurriedly asked their master about the validity of the prayer led by the strange shaykh, discussing whether they would have to repeat it. He answered: 'This is the prayer of the humble devoted (*al-khāshiʿīn*). Your forefathers (in the diminutive form) have never practiced it.'[39]

After returning to his kin, he dedicated his life to education and the spiritual guidance of his disciples. One of the peculiarities of his teachings was his strong criticism of tobacco use, which he opposed to such a degree that he ordered that a bowl that had been used by his older brother, who used to smoke, be washed three times before he used it himself. This anecdote substantiates the claim that the *ghuẓfiyya* order was strongly inspired by the (*shādhiliyya*) *nāṣiriyya*, known for its strict interdiction of tobacco.

After this period, which lasted for about two decades, Shaykh al-Mukhtār felt the need to set out on pilgrimage and to visit the prophet (PBUH). He prepared for the journey and informed his kin of his intentions. When the day of departure arrived, he assembled his disciples and called out the names of three of them, all hailing from the Īdaybūsāt: al-Shaykh Sīdī Aḥmad b. ʿUmāru, al-Shaykh Muḥammad and Muttār (or, according to another version, Aḥmad Billa). He asked each of them to express their wishes and promised they would be fulfilled.

Shaykh Sīdī Aḥmad told him he wished to master the world of knowledge (*al-fatḥ*) and to acquire the authority and capacity to act (*al-taṣarruf wa al-tamkīn*) in the invisible world. Shaykh al-Mukhtār assured him that his wish would be granted and appointed him as spiritual master (*murabbī*), heir to his mystical secrets and his successor. Shaykh Muḥammad told his master that he wished to achieve the highest perfection in Sufism, and this wish was also granted. He became famous for his clairvoyance (*walāya*) and his knowledge of the Qurʾān. Muttār finally asked for material well-being, which was also granted to him. He lived the life of a pious man and redistributed his wealth charitably among those in need. According to another account, the third man was named Aḥmad Billa (rather than Muttār), and he asked Shaykh al-Mukhtār to open the doors of knowledge to him. Later, he and his descendants became famous scholars in the region of Agān and west of Almijriyya (in the Tagant region of present-day Mauritania).[40]

When he left, Shaykh al-Mukhtār only had one son, Laghẓaf, still an infant at the time. He entrusted his care to Aḥmad Billa, asking him to teach him the Qur'ān and the weaving of ropes from alfa leaves.[41] Another account relates that he entrusted the care of Laghẓaf to his other disciple, the scholar and saint Muḥammad al-Amīn (Yubba) b. Fāl b. Aʿmar Nūḥ (an-Na) b. Muḥammad b. al-Imām b. Ābba, who was endowed with premonitory powers.[42]

During his journey to Mecca, in the course of which he would die, Shaykh al-Mukhtār had a second son, named Muḥammad Mūsā Ibrāhīm, with a woman named Fāṭma b. Muḥammad Būḍrāʿ, from the Liʿwaysyāt.[43] Shaykh al-Mukhtār had married her before leaving. It had been revealed to him that she would attain sainthood through his guidance. She had previously led a disordered life, dominated by the distractions of youth, including smoking and listening to music. One day, the shaykh gave his coat (*ridā'*) to one of his disciples, instructing him to hit her with it when her attention was elsewhere. From that moment on, she changed her ways completely, correcting her religious behaviour and developing a strong aversion to tobacco and music.

Following the birth of his son, he ordered his disciple, Sīdī Aḥmad, to bring the baby to his relatives in the Taganit and to take care of him until he reached adulthood. Muḥammad Mūsā became a *faqīh* and a specialist in the religious sciences, credited with having compiled a work called *Ḥamlat Muḥammad Mūsā ʿalā rasm al-qur'ān*.[44] Shaykh al-Mukhtār and his wife both died on the journey to Mecca. It seems that the two sons of Shaykh al-Mukhtār were not affiliated with the *ghuẓfiyya*. Al-Sālik b. ʿAbdallāh b. Sayyid al-Qawm explained us that their father withheld his *wird* from them and did not want to transmit it to anyone other than Shaykh Sīdī Aḥmad. Muḥammad Mūsā purportedly wanted to join the Sufi order, but his young brother Laghẓaf discouraged him from doing so.

Consolidation and dissemination of the order's teachings

To this point, the *ghuẓfiyya* had remained a largely individual endeavour, unlike other Sufi orders. It promptly developed in a radically different direction under the leadership of Shaykh Sīdī Aḥmad al-Kabīr b. ʿAmmār b. al-Nāh and his sons, however. Al-Shaykh al-Mukhtār had chosen his disciple al-Shaykh Sīdī Aḥmad b. ʿAmmār b. al-Nāh for the task of purification. After Shaykh al-Mukhtār's departure, the *ghuẓfiyya* left the Ahl Nūḥ to join another clan of the Īdaybūsāt, the Awlād Būyāḥamm. This period is marked by several qualitative changes to the *ghuẓfiyya*, which began to forge a strong public presence.

The first transformation consisted in the construction of a permanent base in Awjaft, whereas its leaders and adherents had hitherto led a nomadic life. The second alteration, related to the first, was the order's strong orientation toward manual labour: digging wells, constructing barrages, commercial activity and agricultural labour. At this stage of its evolution, the *ghuẓfiyya* instituted manual labour and its benefits as the first and easiest step toward approximating God. The third transformation concerns the path of transmission. Whereas transmission had hitherto been restricted to a single person, Shaykh Sīdī Aḥmad al-Kabīr authorized multiple disciples to carry the title 'shaykh of the *ghuzf* and to transmit its distinctive award, thus expanding the *ṭarīqa*'s influence throughout the western regions of the Sahara and beyond.

Reorientation under Shaykh Sīdī Aḥmad al-Kabīr

Shaykh Sīdī Aḥmad (surname 'Bū-ghuffāra', 'the man with the hat') was born in a place called Arādim, in the vicinity of Tāmshikiṭ (Patris 1948: 7–8). He belonged to the Ahl al-Nāh *fakhdh* (faction) of the Awlād Būyāḥamm *baṭn* (clan). When he returned to his kin, he propagated the *ghuzfiyya* among them. He had four brothers; two of them, Shaykh Sīdī (surname al-Jaffa) and Shaykh ʿAbd al-Raḥmān, joined the *ghuzfiyya* and followed him to Awjaft, where he lived. The other two, al-Ṭālib and Sīdī al-Mukhtār, both educated scholars, rejected the teachings of their brother Sīdī Aḥmad and eventually developed an open hostility toward him.[45] Shaykh Sīdī Aḥmad al-Kabīr was married to his *bint ʿamm* (patrilateral cousin) Ummu b. Aʿjī of the Idaghmayāma. They had two sons, Muḥammad Maḥmūd (known as al-Khalaf) and al-Tār, as well as four daughters, Fāla, Lālla, ʿAysha and Tūttu.

The foundational myths of the *ghuzfiyya*, as noted above, seem to be associated with the symbolism of water, starting with the story of the well of Nwall and continuing with the story of the four disciples trapped alive under the crumbling well in the Taganit. This theme also runs through a tradition that is based in a miracle ascribed to Shaykh Sīdī Aḥmad. When Shaykh al-Mukhtār decided to undertake his pilgrimage without informing Sīdī Aḥmad b. ʿAmmār, he resolved to continue following his master. He trailed behind him from a distance so that the shaykh would not order him to return home. Only when they were sufficiently far away from home and this was no longer an option did he finally join him. They continued along together until reaching the Fezzān (in present-day Libya), where Shaykh al-Mukhtār fell ill. He informed his disciple that his death was near and that it was his wish to be buried in this land. He ordered Sīdī Aḥmad to return home to his Ahl Ābba relatives and to wait for divine grace to fall upon him. This moment, he told him, would be announced by a sign: 'You will be visited by a man while sitting in the desert, under an acacia tree, in the afternoon, after the prayer of ʿaṣr. You will be surrounded by camels, under a sky filled with clouds announcing rain, and a man will press the palm of your right hand and disappear.'[46]

Shaykh Sīdī Aḥmad did as he was told and returned to the Ahl Ābba camp at Āwkār, where he is said to have spent many years – between thirty and forty – without receiving the promised sign. At the end of this period, purportedly around the year 1261 H/1845 CE, the deceased shaykh's prophecy finally materialized, and Shaykh Sīdī Aḥmad had a vision of a settlement in the Adrar named Awjaft, which was unknown to him.[47] After the mysterious divine messenger pressed his palm and disappeared, perfume filled the air. Full of joy, he returned to the camp, which was crowded with the students of Shaykh Muḥammad al-Amīn al-Jakanī (the son of Shaykh al-Mukhtār's sister). He asked everyone he met: 'Do you smell the perfume?' and everyone who also smelled it was immediately seized by mystical rapture (*al-jadhb*). Many people entered into this state, especially from among the *maḥẓara*'s students, until the number of the 'ravished' (*majāḍīb*) reached sixty during the night.

This collective mystical experience was met with reprobation by some of the Ahl Ābba, with their *fuqahā'* accusing Shaykh Sīdī Aḥmad of magic (*al-siḥr*) and charlatanism (*sha'wadha*). They burned his hut and ordered him to leave the camp. Some reportedly even planned to kill him, but this was revealed to him and pushed him to flee.[48] The shaykh departed with his disciples, heading for the unknown Awjaft. They travelled for some time until they reached the region of Butilimit, where they met a Smassid caravan on their way back to Awjaft. Shaykh Sīdī Aḥmad called all of them by their names and those of their ancestors and asked them where to find their destination. Impressed by his revelations, they were convinced he was a saint and offered to take him there. They arrived in Awjaft in the year 1278 H/1861 CE (Ibn 'Abd al-Jalīl 2014: 37, 87). The men of the caravan informed the inhabitants of the town of the arrival of a saint and his disciples, and they were received with great honour.[49]

Shaykh Sīdī Aḥmad al-Kabīr founded a large establishment for religious education, and his influence encompassed most of the Adrar and the Taganit. He attracted disciples, men and women alike, from various regions and social backgrounds. At the end of his life, his spiritual community purportedly comprised several thousand people. Shaykh Sīdī Aḥmad acquired the standing of a reputed scholar, saint, Sufi and ascetic subject to mystic states. He was given the title 'spiritual master of the *ghuẓf* (*shaykh al-ghuẓf*) because he was the first to effectively provide a framework for the order's teachings. He was a convincing *faqīh* who was widely heeded, and there was not a single problem or controversy in the whole Adrar that did not benefit from his elucidations. In his final years, he led a life of utter seclusion, and his son Shaykh Muḥammad Maḥmūd assumed the leadership of the *ghuẓfiyya* (Patris 1948: 7–8). Shaykh Sīdī Aḥmad died on 11 Dhū l-Qa'da 1292 H (6 December 1875 CE), and was buried in al-Tayshṭāya, 50 km south of Awjaft.

Shaykh Muḥammad Maḥmūd, 'al-Khalaf'

Shaykh Sīdī Aḥmad's son, Muḥammad Maḥmūd, was born around 1235 H/1820 CE in Libbayrāt, near Tamchikit. Like his father, he was respected as a saint and as a scholar who had dedicated his life to studying the Qur'ān and the *sunna* (Wuld Ḥāmidun 1970). He is attributed with the saying: 'The world is composed of three days: yesterday, which is in the past and over which you have no influence; tomorrow, which you may or may not experience; and the present day, which you should make use of' (Ibn 'Abd al-Jalīl 2014: 72).

It is reported that Shaykh Mā' al-'Aynayn once said that there is nobody in the world more qualified in the 'science of the secret of the letters' (*'ilm asrār al-ḥurūf*) and in the orientation of people's hearts than the shaykh of the *ghuẓf* of his time (who must have been Shaykh al-Khalaf). Astonished, one of his disciples asked him: 'How is this possible, when we know that the *ghuẓf* emit sounds (during their devotions) comparable to those of camels in the rutting season (*al-hadīr*)?' Shaykh Mā' al-'Aynayn said: 'This means that the disciples saw what would lead them to make these *hadīr*.'[50]

When Shaykh Muḥammad Maḥmūd assumed the leadership of the Sufi order, it had already begun to abandon the concept of the singular, individual transmission of its teachings. He had numerous disciples in various regions (the Adrar, the Taganit, the

Assaba and the Hodh) and had conferred the authority to transmit the *wird* to several of them. Among them were his two sons, Shaykh Sīdī Aḥmad al-Ghazwānī and Shaykh Muḥammad Aḥmad al-Kabīr, as well as Shaykh ʿĀlī b. Āffa and Sharīf Sīdī b. Mawlāy al-Zayn.

Shaykh al-Khalaf lived a long life of nearly one hundred years. Like his father, he lived in complete seclusion in his final years. He did not present himself to the French when they established their presence in the Adrar, whereas all the other notables of the region hurried to meet them. It seems that, like Shaykh Māʾ al-ʿAynayn, he was opposed to French colonial rule in the region. He died on 6 Shawwāl 1328 H (10 October 1910 CE) and was buried in Labba, near Atar, in the Adrar region of present-day Mauritania. He had ten children – five sets of twins, each composed of a male and a female.

Shaykh al-Ghazwānī and his brother, Shaykh Muḥammad Aḥmad

Shaykh Sīdī Aḥmad al-Ghazwānī took over the direction of the *ghuẓfiyya* in 1305 H (1888 CE), twelve years before his father's death (Patris 1948: 6). At the time, some of his father's disciples had started to exhibit behaviours that went against *sharīʿa*. He was a *faqīh*, perfectly versed in the history of the Arabs and their poetry, just as he was an accomplished Sufi (Ibn ʿAbd al-Jalīl 2014: 86). It was he who received the French colonel Gouraud in the Adrar on December 25, 1908, three years after the murder of Xavier Coppolani by a *ghuẓf*. He pledged allegiance in the name of the *zāwiya ghuẓfiyya*, thus formalizing a new stance in the relationship between the Sufi order and French colonial forces.

Following the death of Shaykh Muḥammad Maḥmūd, Shaykh al-Ghazwānī decided to put an end to the behaviour of certain *ghuẓf*s. He assembled them and announced that the shaykh of the *ghuẓf* and those who recognized him followed the example of the prophet (PBUH). Those who did not agree to change their deviant behaviour would have to leave. Confronted with this choice, the disciples split up into two groups. One of them, the 'community of the mosque and the Sunna' (*jamāʿa al-masjid wa al-sunna*), decided to stay, whereas another group, the 'community of the ravished' (*jamāʿa al-majādhib*), left with Shaykh al-Ghazwānī's younger brother Muḥammad Aḥmad al-Kabīr, who established his own Sufi community in the Taganit. Shaykh Muḥammad Aḥmad al-Kabīr thus became *khalīfa* of the *ghuẓfiyya*. When Shaykh al-Ghazwānī sensed that his death was approaching, he vowed that Shaykh Muḥammad Aḥmad al-Kabīr would continue to lead the movement until his own eldest son, still a child at the time, reached maturity. His son, also named Muḥammad Maḥmūd (known as ''Azrī Būmadayd'), succeeded him. When he died in 1998, his brother Muḥammad took over. Shaykh Muḥammad was replaced, following his death in 2010, by his son Muḥammad al-Mukhtār.

Shaykh al-Ghazwānī has built solid ties in the Maghreb countries and in West Africa. Under his leadership, the *ṭarīqa* developed a stronger educational vocation and advanced its expansion. Their disciples apparently tempered their devotion and avoided states of 'deliriousness', although Shaykh al-Ghazwānī was the only master of the *ghuẓfiyya* to proclaim his own sanctity (*walāyatih*), frequently evoking and promulgating his miracles, whereas the masters who preceded him preferred to keep them secret.[51] Under his leadership, the *ghuẓfiyya* also pursued political and economic ambitions. The *ghuẓf*s established significant commercial posts in Atar, Tijigja, and Gasr al-Barka (in the Tagant region of present-day Mauritania) and set up a successful long-distance caravan trade business between Guelmim (Morocco), Mali, the Hodh, and Senegal. The order's economic activities rested on the strict application of Islamic norms, such as a ban on engaging in commerce at night, the rejection of dubious transactions, and a methodical and precise organizational structure. Each economic sector (palm groves, caravans, agriculture, and the breeding of livestock) was entrusted to one of the disciples.

Shaykh al-Ghazwānī died in 1915 and was buried 3 km east of Tijigja (Ibn ʿAbd al-Jalīl 2014: 86). He left two young sons, Muḥammad Maḥmūd and Muḥammad Aḥmad. The French colonial authorities had planned to appoint Muḥammad Maḥmūd as the new leader of the *ghuẓfiyya* once he reached adulthood, but he died at the age of 20, in 1927.[52] His brother Muḥammad Aḥmad was then given the allegiance of the disciples of the *ghuẓfiyya* in his place and stayed on as *khalīfa* until his death in 1986. He was known as 'ʿAzrī Nwākshūṭ' ('the patron saint of Nouakchott'), where he lived and is now buried. After Shaykh Muḥammad Aḥmad's death, his son Muḥammad Maḥmūd took over the affairs of the *ghuẓfiyya* and remains its current leader.

Return to the Hodh and propagation in the Middle East (1895–1909)

After the death of Shaykh Muḥammad al-Aghẓaf, the teachings and distinctive prayers of the *ghuẓfiyya* nearly disappeared from the Hodh. His own sons did not follow in his path and apparently did not propagate their father's legacy among their contemporaries.[53] The families whose ancestors figured among the shaykh's disciples and received their education from him often joined other Sufi orders, especially the *mukhtāriyya* and *fāḍiliyya* branches of the *qādiriyya*. For nearly two centuries, the *ghuẓfiyya* did not have a significant presence in its own birthplace. Its resurrection in the Hodh was accomplished by Shaykh ʿĀlī b. Āffa, who left his native region on the current border with Mali to visit Shaykh Muḥammad Maḥmūd al-Khalaf in the Adrar, where he received his initiation. He finally brought the *ghuẓfiyya* 'back home', after Shaykh al-Mukhtār had been solely authorized to transmit its *wird*, and returned to his relatives in the Taganit with this authorization.

The community of Shaykh ʿĀlī b. Āffa al-Dulaymī

Shaykh ʿĀlī was the son of ʿAbdallāh b. ʿĀlī b. Sīdī Bubakkar b. Yūsuf ('Āffa'), who was himself a scholar and a teacher. He was born in 1281 H/1864 CE in the village of Sibta, the ancestral seat of his family.[54] His kinship group is attached to Yūsuf ('Āffa') b. Farba b. Sīdī b. Aʿmar b. Bukayr b. Aʿlī b. al-Ẓwaymir b. Aʿlī b. al-Shaykh, from the Awlād Dlaym.[55] Paul Marty (1921) reports that Yūsuf arrived in the Hodh at the end of the eighteenth century. He apparently renounced his ancestors' 'warrior' traditions for the sake of seeking knowledge and religious practice. His descendants founded the village of Sibta and were respected for their scholarly knowledge, their piety (*ṣalāḥ*), and their memorization of the Qur'ān.[56]

Shaykh ʿĀlī received his early education from his relatives and from *sharīf* Jaʿfar b. al-Mahdī and *sharīf* Ibn Ḥāmmannī al-Ghallāwī. He founded a *maḥẓara* of considerable reputation in the Hodh, and his contemporaries considered him an authority on Arabic. He was also a praised poet, writing much of his scholarly texts in rhyming and lyrical form. He published multiple works in the fields of *fiqh*, the recitation of the Qur'ān (*tajwīd*), and the oneness of God (*al-tawḥīd*), and he certified students in the recitation of the Qur'ān according to the canons of Warsh and Qālūn. We also know that he authored an anthology in which he discusses (among other topics) judicial principles and moral rectitude (*ḥisba*). In this collection, he denounces established habits and traditions of his social milieu that contradict the *sharīʿa*, such as the rejection of polygamy and the treatment of female slaves (*imā'*) as animals. Much of his intellectual legacy has disappeared, however, due to a fire that destroyed his personal library. Shaykh ʿĀlī died relatively young, in 1327 H/1909 CE, and was buried in Sanfāgha.

Shaykh Būna ʿĀlī reports that Shaykh ʿĀlī was residing in Tishit when he encountered a caravan of *ghuẓfs* returning to the Adrar. Seeking spiritual development, he joined them, expecting to meet Shaykh Muḥammad Maḥmūd al-Khalaf and to become his disciple. He was so impressed by him that he stayed there for a long time, frequently visiting the tomb of Shaykh Muḥammad al-Aghẓaf. After mastering the *ghuẓfiyya*'s path of mystic immersion, Shaykh al-Khalaf eventually authorized him to spread the order's secret *wird*.[57] At this point, he returned to his native Hodh propagating the *ghuẓfiyya* in the region.

The *ghuẓfiyya*'s return to the Hodh, however, was met with fierce resistance by certain *ʿulamā'*. Among the critics of the *ghuẓfiyya* was the eminent *faqīh* Muḥammad Yaḥyā al-Walātī, who was especially harsh in his denunciation. It is reported that he issued a *fatwā* for the wife of a Tajakānit, al-ʿĀlim al-Jakanī,[58] affirming her right to refuse to allow him to give their cows to his shaykh as a pious gift (*hadiyya*). Because of his affiliation with the *ghuẓfiyya* he had forfeited all of his property rights.

When Shaykh ʿĀlī decided to disseminate the *ghuẓfiyya* in the Hodh, he opted to leave his relatives, creating a new community together with his disciples. He is credited with having transmitted the *ghuẓfiyya*'s *wird* to more than one hundred people in his lifetime. He was also the first to propagate the *ghuẓfiyya* beyond the frontiers of the contemporary Islamic Republic of Mauritania. The Idawʿīsh, living in ʿAyn Idawʿīsh, 30 km south of Sanfāgha (Mali), are considered to have furnished some of his first disciples.

When the French began to penetrate Mauritania, his disciple Shaykh Muḥammad al-Amīn b. Zaynī al-Qalqamī initiated a collective exodus to the Middle East in 1322 H/1904 CE, leading about fifty *ghuẓf* families on pilgrimage to Mecca. According to different interlocutors, on the way they received support from the Ottoman administration and were escorted to the sultan, ʿAbd al-Ḥamīd, in Constantinople. After completing their pilgrimage, the community settled in Anatolia, where Shaykh Muḥammad al-Amīn created a *zāwiya* of the *ghuẓfiyya* that exists to this day. He created another *zāwiya* in ʿAmmān, the current capital of Jordan, where a few tribes from the east of the country settled nearby. His disciple Shaykh ʿĀyish al-Ḥawyān succeeded him as leader of the *zāwiya*. Shaykh Muḥammad al-Amīn is thus credited with having brought the *ghuẓfiyya* to the Middle East.

Other important agents of the *ghuẓfiyya's* revival and expansion

Among the distinguished Sufi masters affiliated with the *ghuzfiyya* in the Hodh, we must also count Shaykh Muḥammad Maḥmūd b. Aḥmad Khaṭṭārī b. Aḥmad Zaydān b. Muḥammad b. Bayya (Laḥbīb) al-Massūmī. He possessed a licence (*ijāza*) in the seven koranic lectures, which he had received from Shaykh b. Ḥāmmannī in Shinqīṭ, and created a large *maḥẓara* in the village of Legweirga that attracted many students and visitors from different regions. He also organized numerous caravans and developed a great interest in agriculture in order to provide for his community and those in need. It is reported that he initiated the cultivation of a large area of land between Legweirga Umm Lāṣu and Ghwayrgit Ahl Bayya, from which he extracted bountiful harvests.

Shaykh Muḥammad Maḥmūd encouraged the invocation of various *awrād* from different Sufi orders. Whereas the *wird* of the *ghuẓfiyya* was only to be recited individually by those who were initiated into the *ṭarīqa*, others, those of the *shādhiliyya*, for example, could also be invoked collectively in obligatory ritual prayers in the mosque. He did not view visiting the tombs of saints as problematic and is credited with advanced powers of clairvoyance (*kushūfāt*) and the accomplishment of miracles. One oral tradition recounts that some of his disciples were digging a well at a location east of Djiganī. At one point, they hit a rock formation that they could not break through. The shaykh told them to take a branch from the al-hajlīj (*tayshiṭ/Balanites aegyptiaca*) tree and to hit the rock with it. The rock broke, and water began to spring from it. The well was named 'well of the *ghuẓf*/well of the fortunate' (*biʾr al-ghuẓf*).[59]

One of his disciples was the *faqīh* and historian Shaykh Maḥfūẓ b. Muḥammad Maḥmūd b. Zaydān b. Muḥammad b. Bayya ('Laḥbīb'), referred to by the name Ibn Bayya (d. 1391 H/1971 CE). He is among the most outstanding figures in the recent history of the *ghuẓfiyya*, having written, alongside many other works, one of the rare texts countering the attacks against the *shādhiliyya* (and thus defending the *ghuẓfiyya*).

Another important student of Ibn Bayya was Shaykh al-Mukhtār b. Sīdī Aḥmad b. ʿAbd al-Raḥmān b. Yūsuf al-Tinwājiwī (d. 1360 H/1941 CE), a respected scholar, judge and Sufi master. He entertained close ties with the Ahl al-Ghazwānī and conferred licences on several disciples, among them his son Shaykh Abū Bakr (d. 1384 H/1964 CE), who became imam of the al-Ḥarām mosque in Mecca, and Shaykh Muḥammad al-Mukhtār, who emigrated to the holy land of Islam, passing through Mali, Niger, Nigeria, Chad and Soudan and instructing disciples in these regions.[60] After a sojourn in Mecca, Shaykh Muḥammad al-Mukhtār founded a mosque in Medina, where he instructed those who came in search of knowledge and spirituality. He then continued to travel around in the Sham (Syria, Lebanon, Palestine) and Turkey, adopting many disciples as he went.

Shaykh Muḥammad Maḥmūd died in 1337 H/1918 CE at the age of 63. He was succeeded by his son Muḥammad al-Shaykh, who was only 15 years old but had already been guided into mystical retreat (*khulwa*) and received the *wird* of the *ghuẓfiyya* from his father. Muḥammad al-Shaykh lived for forty-two years (d. 1364 H/1945 CE) and was buried next to his father in Legweirga. His brother Sīdna (Sīdī Muḥammad) b. al-Shaykh Muḥammad Maḥmūd then became the next shaykh in the lineage until his death in 1992, at the age of 79.

Another eminent member of the *ghuẓfiyya* in the Hodh was the Sufi scholar Mawlay ʿAbdallāh ('Būya') b. Mawlay ʿAbd al-Mālik b. Mawlay al-Ḥasan, who hailed from the Ahl Mawlay Ṣāliḥ of Nema and whose surname was Bāba Ḥasan al-Niʿmāwī. Shaykh Bāba Ḥasan was a disciple of both ʿĀlī b. Āffa and Shaykh Muḥammad Maḥmūd b. Bayya, who had initiated him into the *ghuẓfiyya*. It is reported that upon his initiation he declared that he had previously understood nothing of the true nature of the holy book and of faith (*īmān*), and he therefore repeated each of the obligatory ritual prayers he had performed from the time of his adulthood up to his affiliation with the *ghuẓfiyya*.[61] He became famous for his vast knowledge of the religious sciences (*ʿulūm al-sharʿ*), the corpus of the *ḥadīth* and for dispute resolution (Ibn Maynummu 1961). Shaykh Bāba Ḥasan was promoted to *qāḍī* of Nema, but it seems that his relatives and the other *fuqahāʾ* reproached him for his affiliation with the *ghuẓfiyya* and forced him out of office, citing his occasional practice of ritual dancing and the frequent gathering of *ghuẓfs* at his home.[62] He died in 1348 H/1929 CE and is buried in Nema.

Shaykh Bāba Ḥasan was succeeded by his son and disciple Shaykh Mawlay ʿAlī ('al-Dāh'). Shaykh Būna ʿĀlī b. Maynummu, whose comments on ʿAlī b. Āffa's poem have given us much insight into the *ghuẓfiyya*, was one of his disciples.

Notes

1 Among those who voiced their suspicions against the *ṭarīqa* were Shaykh Sīdī Muḥammad b. al-Shaykh Sīdī al-Mukhtār al-Kuntī (d. 1242 H/1826 CE), Muḥammad Yaḥyā al-Walātī (d. 1330 H/1912 CE), and Muḥammad al-Amīn b. Aḥmad Zaydān al-Jakanī (d. 1335 H/1916 CE).

2 Sīdī wuld al-Zayn has recently become a leading figure in the eyes of many Mauritanians, who consider him an icon of the *muqāwama* ('resistance') against French colonialism in the region (Ould Mohamed Baba and Freire 2020: 279).

3 This project couldn't have been carried out without the support of a number of people, whose efforts I would like to acknowledge: al-Shaykh ad-Dadda b. Muftāḥ al-Khayr, al-Shaykh Muḥammad al-Shaykh b. Muḥammad b. Daydda, Sīdī Muḥammad b. Sayyidī (head of 'Direction du Monde Arabe' in the ministry of the interior), ʿAbdallāh b. Muḥammad Qullī (responsible for the *maḥẓra*s in Timbedra), Muḥammad al-Amīn b. ʿAbdallāh b. Sayyid al-Qawm, Muḥammad al-Amīn b. al-Niʿma b. Sulṭānna, Sidāt b. Shaykhna, Muḥammad al-Amīn b. Āffa and al-Sālik b. ʿAbdallāh b. Sayyid al-Qawm.

4 The *malāmātiyya* Sufi order originated in ninth-century Khorasan and centres its distinct philosophy on blaming and humiliating the ego (*nafs*) to attain spiritual purification. Because of their extreme form of asceticism and the ecstatic rituals they practice, critics have accused them of deviating from orthodox Islam (Seale 1968).

5 The Hassaniyya-speaking populations of Mauritania can be described through a hierarchical distinction between those of free status and different tributary groups.

This design was consolidated in the second half of the seventeenth century, with a leadership role being given to 'warrior' (*ḥassān*) and 'religious' (*zwāya*) hereditary status groups following the Shurbubba War.

6 Al-Sālik b. Faḍilī recounts the biographies of several important personalities of the region in his introduction to the *Kitāb farḍ al-ʿayn*. See also al–Burtulī's *Fatḥ al-shakūr* (1981) and Shaykh Muḥammad ʿAbdallāh b. Bubakkar b. al-Bashīr manuscript (c. 1950, a copy of this work is kept in Sīdāt b. Shaykhna's private library in Nouakchott).

7 The Azer dialect is considered a Amazigh-influenced variant of the Soninke. It was once widely spoken but is now nearly extinct.

8 Interview with al-Imām b. Muḥammad Fāḍil (director of Islamic affairs and education in the wilāya of Hodh ech Charqui) in Amurj, 14 February 2019.

9 Remembered as a saint and praised for his moral rectitude. His tomb lies in Fudr Anāq Ḥmālla, not far from Adele-Bagru.

10 Taken from the *Waraqa fī nasab al-shaykh Muḥammad al-Aghẓaf* (undated manuscript, c. 1920), written by the Nema historian Mawlāy ʿAbdallāh b. al-Shaykh Mawlāy ʿAbd al-Mālik b. Mawlāy Ḥasan (d. 1928 CE).

11 This community is currently settled in the eastern vicinity of Adele-Bagru.

12 Kunayb is the name of a large cemetery located some 20 km southeast of Adele-Bagru, in present-day Malian territory.

13 His male descendants now number around 1,400, according to Muḥammad Niʿma b. Sulṭānna (interview in Bassiknou, 20 February 2019).

14 Muḥammad al-Amīn b. Sulṭānna (a descendant of Shaykh Muḥammad al-Aghẓaf) details that this period lasted for forty days (Bassiknou, 20 February 2019).

15 Interview with Muḥammad al-Amīn b. Sulṭānna (Bassiknou, 20 February 2019).

16 Interview with Muḥammad al-Amīn b. al-Niʿma b. Sulṭānna (Bassiknou, 20 February 2019).

17 This characteristic trait was later also adopted by the *fādiliyya*, whose teachings and principles resemble those of the *ghuẓfiyya* in many respects.

18 Sharīf Zayn al-ʿĀbidīn's voyage also reveals the effective bond between the Moroccan *makhzan* and the Saharan confines. This historical episode has been used by various actors at many different levels. In the context of this chapter, we would like to highlight the interconnected nature of different networks of Islamic scholarship which have linked the broader western Saharan region, the Maghreb and West Africa for centuries.

19 Interview with Muḥammad al-Amīn b. Nuʿma b. Sulṭānna (Bassiknou, 20 February 2019).

20 This was reportedly practised by the *ghuẓfiyya* shaykhs in the Adrar and in the Rgayba regions of present-day Mauritania.

21 The *fatwā* in question is reproduced in Supplement no. 1 of my collection *al-Majmūʿa al-kubrā* (2009: 209–10). For the Hanafi School, the time of the *ʿaṣr* prayer begins once the length of one's shadow reaches more than double the height of one's body. The period before this point, in their view, still corresponds to the preceding period of *ẓuhr*, or to an interstitial period between the two prayers.

22 Interview with Muḥammad al-Amīn b. Niʿma b. Sulṭānna (Bassiknou, 20 February 2019).

23 Interview with Muḥammad b. al-Tār (Nouakchott, 22 April 2019).

24 This is the date remembered by his descendants, which is also mentioned in Būna ʿĀlī b. Maynummu's manuscript. Some authors have expressed different opinions, for example al-Ṭālib Būbakar b. Aḥmad al-Muṣṭafā al-Maḥjūbī al-Walātī, who writes: 'I am ignorant of the exact date of Shaykh Muḥammad al-Aghẓaf al-Jaʿfarī's death; it might have been in the year 1218 H or later.'

25 Interview with Muḥammad b. Shayknna b. Būna, imam of the mosque of al-Mabrūk (13 February 2019). The narrative states that the camel roamed for forty days.
26 Interview with Muḥammad b. Shayknna b. Būna (al-Mabrūk, 13 February 2019).
27 Site of a well and of a cemetery located 10 km to the north of kilometre 47 on the road connecting Nema and Timbedra.
28 Muḥammad Aḥmad is buried in Gabda, 5 km northwest of the Malian village of Nioro.
29 Marty (1921: 313) reports that the father and the grandfather of Ahmad al-Aswad are both buried in Tindouf and that he owes his surname ('the black') to his mother, Ḥūriyya.
30 Interview with Muḥammad b. Shaykhna b. Būna (al-Mabrūk, 13 February 2019).
31 Hārūn b. al-Shaykh Sīdiyya is confirmed to have licensed (*ijāza*) Shaykh Sīdī Ṣāliḥ b. al-Shaykh Muḥammad al-Aghẓaf, born Jaʿfarī (of the al-Jaʿāfra fraction), to transmit the teachings of the *qādiriyya*, as well as the invocations and orientations of Shaykh Sīdī al-Mukhtār (in *Kitāb al-akhbār*; Nouakchott, n.d).
32 Muḥammad al-Amīn b. Sayyid al-Qawm affirms that before reaching the Gibla, they were established in the Adrar region of Mauritania.
33 A plain (*tayārit*) situated between two elevated plateaus. It is about 10 km wide and 100 km long, beginning in the Taganit, at the well of Maza, and extending to Tamshikit. Its favourable geography features numerous wells.
34 Interview with Sidāt b. Shaykhna (Nouakchott, 20 April 2018).
35 Shaykh al-Mukhtār's brother Khalīl had a son named al-Ṭālib, who provided the murderers of Coppolani with support at Tanouchart. He refused to proclaim his allegiance to the French and authorized his followers to kill the administrator, which they eventually did, in 1905. On the persistent repercussions of this episode, see Ould Mohamed Baba and Freire 2020: 266–8.
36 In some versions of this oral tradition, this shaykh is reported to have been a disciple of Shaykh Muḥammad al-Aghẓaf, although the later encounter between Shaykh al-Mukhtār and Shaykh Muḥammad al-Aghẓaf seems to contradict this account.
37 According to Ahl Nūḥ interlocutors I interviewed in Kiffa (22 February 2019).
38 Interview with al-Sālik b. ʿAbdallāh b. Sayyid al-Qawm b.al-Shaykh al-Mukhtār b. Laghẓaf b. al- Shaykh al-Mukhtār (Nouakchott, 19 April 2019).
39 Ibid.
40 Ibid.
41 Ibid.
42 It was this disciple whom Shaykh al-Mukhtār is said to have appointed as his successor when he undertook his mystical journey (*lammā sāḥa*; in al-Mukhtār b. Ḥāmidun's *Ḥayāt Mūrītānyā*, vol. *Īdaybūsāt*).
43 Interview with al-Sālik b. ʿAbdallāh b. Sayyid al-Qawm b. al-Shaykh al-Mukhtār b. Laghẓaf b. al-Shaykh al-Mukhtār (Nouakchott, 19 April 2019).
44 Ibid.
45 Interview with Sīdiyya b. Muḥammad b. Sayyidī, head of 'Direction du Monde Arabe' in the ministry of the interior (Nouakchott, 5 May 2019).
46 Ibid.
47 Interview with al-Sālik b. ʿAbdallāh b. Sayyid al-Qawm b. al-Shaykh al-Mukhtār b. Laghẓaf b. *al-* Shaykh al-Mukhtār (Nouakchott, 19 April 2019). See also Patris (1948: 7–8).
48 These events are at the origin of the persistent enmity between the Ahl Ābba and the *ghuẓf*.

49 Interview with al-Sālik b. ʿAbdallāh b. Sayyid al-Qawm b. al-Shaykh al-Mukhtār b. Laghẓaf b. al-Shaykh al-Mukhtār (Nouakchott, 19 April 2019).
50 Interview with Muḥammad b. al-Tār (Nouakchott, 22 April 2019).
51 Ibid.
52 The author of *Inārat al-afkār bi-tārīkh Awjaft wa Aṭār*, in his biography of Shaykh Muḥammad Maḥmūd, affirms that he died in 1924. His tomb is situated at Wādī Āgirj, in the vicinity of Bumdeid.
53 Interview with al-Dadda b. Muftāḥ al-Dīn in (10 February 2018).
54 Sibta is situated 70 km southeast of the town Timbedra and has been inhabited by the Mashẓūf.
55 This genealogy is affirmed in two documents written by al-Ḥasan b. Mawlāy Aʿlī al-Niʿmāwī and Sīdī b. al-Ṭālib ʿAmmār al-Filālī, the latter dated to 1253 H/1837 CE. Paul Marty (1921: 77) cites a slightly different genealogy: Āffa b. Sīdī (surname 'Farba') b. ʿUmar b. Būkar b. Muḥammad b. ʿAlī b. al-Labb b. Muḥammad b. al-Shaykh b. Dlaym.
56 Interview with Muḥammad al-Amīn b. ʿĀlī b. Āffa (Bassiknou, 19 February 2019).
57 Interview with Sidāt b. Shaykhna (Nouakchott, 20 April 2018).
58 The descendant of this man currently lives in Nema. He is a *faqīh* and the *imām* of the town's 'old mosque'.
59 Interview with Muḥammad al-Shaykh b. Muḥammad b. Daydda (Legweirga, 11 February 2019).
60 *Aʿlām al-Shanāqiṭa fī al-Ḥijāz wa al-Machrik* ('Les grandes figures mauritaniennes au Hijāz'), p. 152. Beirut: Dar al-Kitab 2015. Abu 'Ali Beheyda b. Cheikh Yerbana al-Kalkami al-Idrissi.
61 Interview with Muḥammad al-Shaykh b. Muḥammad b. Daydda (Legweirga, 11 February 2019).
62 Interview with Izīd Bīh b. al-Rābī, imam of Nema's 'old mosque' (Nema, 10 February 2019).

References

al-Burtulī, b. Bannān Muḥammad (1981), *Fatḥ al-shakūr* fī maʿrifat aʿyān ʿulamāʾ al-Takrūr. Annotated by Muḥammad Ibrāhīm al-Katānī and Muḥammad Hajjī. Beirut: Dar al-Gharb al-Islāmī.

al-Jakanī al-Shinqīṭī, Muḥammad al-Amīn b. Aḥmad Zaydān (1993), *Sharḥ Khalīl b. Isḥāq al-Mālikī (raḥamahu Allāh taʿālā) al-musammā Naṣīḥa*, vol. 1. Beirut: Muʾassasat al-Risāla.

Beyriès, J. (1935), 'Questions Mauritaniennes: 1. Note sur l'Enseignement et les Moeurs Scolaires Indegènes en Mauritanie; 2. Note sur les Ghoudf de Mauritanie', *Revue des études islamiques*, 9: 39–73.

Boubrik, R. (2000), 'Itinéraires initiatique du fondateur de la tarîqa Fâdiliyya (Mauritanie)', *Journal of the History of Sufism* (Special Issue: the Qādiriyya Order), 1: 259–74.

Du Puigaudeau, O. (1961), 'Mauritanie, république des sables', *Esprit*, 292 (2): 230–48.

Gutelius, D. P. V. (2002), 'The Path is Easy and the Benefits Large: The Nāṣiriyya, Social Networks and Economic Change in Morocco, 1640–1830', *The Journal of African History*, 43 (1): 27–49.

Hamès, C. (2013), 'La Shâdhiliyya ou l'origine des confréries islamiques en Mauritanie', *Islam et Sociétés au Sud du Sahara*, 3: 73–87.
Hammoudi, A. (1980), 'Sainteté, pouvoir et société: Tamgrout aux XVIIe et XVIIIe siècles', *Annales. Économies, Sociétés, Civilisations*, 35 (3–4): 615–41. http://anom.archivesnationales.culture.gouv.fr/ark:/61561/hj998ez6x3w.num=200.form=simple.start=2891.
Ibn ʿabd al-Jalīl, Muḥammad al-Amīn (2014), '*Inārat al-afkār bi-tārīkh Awjaft wa Aṭār*', 2nd edn, Nouakchott: 2md.
Ibn Aḥmad al-Muṣṭafā al-Maḥjūbī al-Walātī, al-Ṭālib Būbakar (2002), *Minaḥ al-rabb al-ghafūr fī dhikr mā ahmalahu fatḥ al-shakūr*. Edited by Elhadi Mebruk, Tripoli. Undated manuscript (c. 1860). Private library of the Ahl al-Ṭālib Būbakar, Walata, Hawd al-Chargui, 80 pages.
Ibn Mawlāy Ḥasan, Mawlāy ʿAbdallāh b. al-Shaykh Mawlāy ʿAbd al-Mālik (n.d.), *Waraqa fī nasab al-Shaykh Muḥammad al-Aghẓaf*. Undated manuscript (c. 1920). Private library of Hamaddi Ould Hajati (al-Mabrūk, Mali), 7 pages.
Ibn Faḍilī, Al-Sālik (c. 1910), *Muqaddimat kitāb farḍ al-ʿayn*. Undated manuscript. Private Library of Sīdāt b. Shaykhna, Nouakchott, approx. 250 pages.
Ibn Māmīn, al-Shaykh Muḥammad Fāḍil (n.d.), *al-Ḍiyyāʾ al-mustabīn*. Undated manuscript (c. 1860). Manuscript Center for Heritage and Culture 'Ennour Sati', Nouakchott, 450 pages.
Ibn Māmīn, Saʿd Būh b. al-Shaykh Muḥammad Fāḍil (n.d.), *Kashf ḥijāb al-astār ʿan wajh rumūz sullam al-iẓhār*. Undated manuscript (c. 1904 –1917). Manuscript Center for Heritage and Culture 'Ennour Sati', Nouakchott, approx. 300 pages.
Ibn Maynummu, Būna ʿĀlī (n.d.), *Sharḥ manẓūmāt ʿĀlī b. Āffa ḥayāt al-Shaykh Muḥammad al-Aghẓaf*. Undated manuscript(c.(1961). Private library of Shaykh ad-Dadda b. Mufāḥ al-Dīn (Adele-Bagru, Hodh al-Chargui), 31 pages.
Katz, J. (1992), 'Visionary Experience, Autobiography, and Sainthood in North African Islam', Princeton Papers in Near Eastern Studies, 1: 85–118.
Knysh, A. (2018), *Sufism: A New History of Islamic Mysticism*. Princeton, NJ: Princeton University Press.
Laforgue, P. (1928), 'Une secte hérésiarque en Mauritanie: Les Ghoudf', *Bulletin du Comité d'Études Historiques et Scientifiques de l'Afrique Occidentale Française*, 11: 654–65.
Marty, P. (1921), *Études sur l'islam et les tribus du Soudan. Tome III: Les tribus Maures du Sahel et du Hodh*. Paris: Ernest Leroux.
Ould El-Bara, Y. (1998), 'Fiqh, société et pouvoir: étude des soucis et préoccupations socio-politiques des théologiens-légistes maures (fuqahā) à partir de leurs consultations juridiques (fatwas), du xviie au xxe siècle', Thèse de Doctorat en Anthropologie sociale – PhD thesis in Social Anthropology, Paris.
Ould Mohamed Baba, E. and F. Freire (2020), 'Looters vs. Traitors: The *Muqawama* ("Resistance") Narrative, and its Detractors, in Contemporary Mauritania', *African Studies Review*, 63 (2): 258–80.
Patris, A. (1948), *Contribution à l'étude des ghoudfs*. Mémoire de stage d'administration coloniale, 82 pages.
Rebstock, U. (2001), *Maurische* Literaturgeschichte, 3 vols. Würzburg: Ergon.
Stewart, Charles C. and S. A. Ould Ahmed Salim (2016), *The Arabic Literature of Africa, Volume 5: The Writings of Mauritania and the Western Sahara*. Leiden: Brill. 2 vols.
Voll, J. O. (1992), 'Conservative and Traditional Brotherhoods', *The Annals of the American Academy of Political and Social Science*, 524 (1): 66–78.

Wright, Z. V. (2020), *Realizing Islam: The Tijaniyya in North Africa and the Eighteenth-Century Muslim World*. Chapel Hill, NC: The University of North Carolina Press.

Wuld Al-barrā ʾ, Y. (2009), *al-Majmū ʿa al-kubrā: al-shāmila li-fatāwā wa nawāzil wa aḥkām ahl gharb wa janūb gharb al-Ṣaḥrā ʾ*, 12 vols. Nouakchott: al-Sharīf Mawlay al-Ḥasan b. al-Mukhtār b. al-Ḥasan.

Wuld Bayya, al-Maḥfūẓ (n.d.), *Risāla fī al-Radd ʿan al-Shādhiliyya* (*Epistle in defense of the shādhiliyya*). Undated manuscript (c. 1955).

Wuld Ḥāmidun, al-Mukhtār (1970), *Ḥayāt Mūrītānyā*, volume *Īdaybūsāt*. Manuscript available at Institut Mauritanien de Recherches Scientifiques, Nouakchott, 130 pages.

11

Islamic traditional schooling in a globalized context: A case study from the *maḥẓara* of Teysir (southwestern Mauritania)

Mariem Baba Ahmed
CRIA – NOVA FCSH, Post-Doctoral Researcher at CAPSAHARA
and Zahra Horma
CRIA – NOVA FCSH, Junior Researcher at CAPSAHARA

Islam is about realizing the liberating power of a living and proactive confession of faith in an infinitely singular, omnipotent, and omnipresent God. This is the sense of Islam that the vast majority of Muslims experience in everyday life, and from which they seek spiritual and moral guidance.

–An-Naʿim 2008: 10

Muslims believe that the first ever prayer was uttered over 1,400 years ago in a cave in Mount Hira, on the outskirts of Mecca, when the Archangel Gabriel revealed the Word of God to Muḥammad b. ʿAbdallāh. Muḥammad, in turn, passed the Word of God to the willing, re-enacting the movements and reciting the verses, thus bringing into existence the ritual of prayer.

Today, prayers continue to be taught to children and youth who, day in and day out, learn to read, write and recite the Qur'ān in the *maḥẓara* – the main institution in charge of the initial transfer of Islamic knowledge in Mauritania. A distinctly Mauritanian institution, the *maḥẓara* represents 'traditional Islamic education', where the young are taught not only to memorize and recite the Qur'ān but also to read and write, while being introduced to the canon of Islamic religious sciences: the Islamic creed (*al-ʿaqāʾid*), mysticism (*al-taṣawwuf*), Quranic science (*ʿilm al-Qurʾān*), the so-called prophetic traditions (*al-ḥadīth*), the holy history of the Prophet Muḥammad (*al-sīra*) and Arabic language (*al-lugha*), grammar (*al-naḥw*) and rhetoric (*al-bayān*) (Ould Cheikh 2020: 5).

Throughout the region's history, and more recently, through state structures, the *maḥẓara* has played an active role in creating, maintaining and promoting religious identity and the use of Arabic. The French colonial period (1920–1960) was characterized by various attempts to subdue the influence of the *maḥẓara*, and yet it resolutely held its ground, questioning colonial policies and French laws that sought to impose a Western model of elementary education on Mauritania (Launay and Soares 1999: 502;

Ould Maouloud 2017: 2; Pettigrew 2007: 63; Seesemann and Soares 2009: 93–4). As a result, decades after Mauritania's independence (1960), the *maḥẓara* educational model remains a strong presence in both urban and rural parts of the country.

Understanding the link between the traditional education system in Mauritania and the nomadic way of life is thus of the utmost importance, since the social mores of the *maḥẓara* were shaped by life in the desert. In the popular perception, and especially in comparison with learners in the so-called 'modern' system, we encounter persistent clichés designating *maḥẓara* students as imprisoned by tradition and nomadic life. 'Bedouins', outdated, unadjusted to the times and – a new cliché – potentially radicalized.

Contrary to these sorts of prejudices, our study offers a more dynamic account of the *maḥẓara*. The young people we met seemed to be experiencing, at their own level, the same jolts as the rest of the country in terms of complexities, mixtures of genres and more or less defined expectations, all crowned by a tug-of-war between moral and religious values that are no longer solely the product of ancestral bookish interpretations, intermingled with other forms of shared, transnational religiosity.

This chapter contextualizes the *maḥẓara*, tracing its evolution from a nomadic context to the present. At the beginning of this study, the research included a quantitative element, with a questionnaire filled in by eighty-eight students in the *maḥẓara* of Teysir and Nouakchott. As the study progressed, the methodology shifted to a focus on life stories: nine paths that would be documented, in some cases by means of audiovisual recording sessions. Drawing mainly on this data (collected between November 2017 and March 2021), this chapter examines the role of traditional Islamic education in an increasingly urbanized society. We seek to understand, as evidenced by the students' own accounts, the prospects of reconciling this kind of learning with the aspiration of becoming a professional, a career path that would most certainly be pursued in an urban environment.

The field research was conducted in a particular *maḥẓara* (Teysir, among the most reputable in the country), where students recounted their entry into and exit from the learning cycle, what they thought of the kind of knowledge they'd acquired and the skills they'd obtained, the conversion of this immaterial knowledge into 'real-world' skills, and the existing (and at times newly created) pathways that in some cases led them to pursue their education at a university or in a professional setting unrelated to the *maḥẓara*. It became essential to understand these personal pathways against the backdrop of new techniques of learning and knowledge transmission, as new technologies, such as smartphones, took on an important role in this context. The individual trajectories identified in this chapter reveal an – often contradictory – context of multiple social, cultural and political interactions.

Society and culture among the Hassaniyya-speaking populations of Mauritania

Mauritania can be seen as a place of – not always peaceful – encounters between Arab-Berber populations (who are predominantly nomadic) and black African populations (who are predominantly sedentary). Their cultural differences are now rooted in the organization of social and political life in a multi-ethnic country which is nevertheless marked by the social and political preponderance of its Hassaniyya-speaking populations and, more specifically, by its 'noble'/'free' status groups, the Bīḍān (see Bonte 2016: 12; Ould Cheikh 2017: 56).

The Bīḍān society of the western regions of the Sahara was born out of the confluence between Arab groups entering the western regions of the Sahara (from the Arabian Peninsula, Egypt and Tunisia) and Amazigh groups already settled in these territories (Norris 1969). The overall social landscape was largely marked by nomadism until the late 1970s. It was only after a series of droughts that hit the region during this period that populations stopped basing their livelihoods on nomadic pastoralism and began to gradually settle in urban areas, leading to the emergence of large cities such as Nouakchott, or Nouadhibou (on the nascent development of Mauritanian cities, see Ould Cheikh 2017: 35).

Precolonial 'Moorish' society (a recent term, of colonial origin but now comfortably incorporated into the region's ethnic lexicon, identifying the Hassaniyya-speaking populations of the western regions of the Sahara) was characterized by a bicephalous type of power exercised by two dominant hereditary status groups: the 'warriors' (*ḥassān*), and the 'religious' authorities (*zwāya*) (Bonte 2016: 46; Brenner 2000: 147; Ould Cheikh 2020: 3).[1]

The *ḥassān* – descendants of the Banū Ḥassān Arab 'tribes' (*qabā'il*, sing. *qabīla*) who roamed the Maghreb and the Saharan confines, where they began to settle in the fifteenth century – were subject to a code of warrior virility (Bonte 2016: 29; El Hamel 1999: 64; Ould Cheikh 2017: 64). They possessed weapons and had mastered the art of war. Later, they also had centralized command of large parts of the western Saharan region through the establishment of four emirates (Trarza, Brakna, Adrar and Tagant, between the eighteenth and the nineteenth centuries; see Bonte 2016: 328, Ould Cheikh 2017: 65). The *zwāya*, by contrast, represented Islamic religious values. They taught and officiated various religious practices and were also organized according to a *qabīla*-centred system that determined social, economic and political activity and delineated the geographic reach of each group. Relevant positions within this scheme depended on ancestry, function and economic wealth. With this general distinction noted, this structure should not be reduced to a linear partition, however; indeed, the two elements within this structure complement each other in complex ways.[2] While accepted as fundamental organizational elements of Bīḍān society, hierarchy and status must be considered in relation to other processes, such as the emergence of the 'state', the market economy, changes to residential practices and migration to cities. Today, innovative social dynamics have given these structures a new appearance without completely overshadowing long-established patterns.

With Mauritania's independence, the state, inspired by the Western/French model, put in place mechanisms of democratic political control such as a Constitution, elections, political parties and a public administration. The implementation of this political model was inaugurated by the first president of the Islamic Republic of Mauritania, Moktar Ould Daddah (in power between 1960 and 1978). Despite these innovative political configurations, however, changes to social and political life were slow to take place. Even after decolonization, ethnic and tribal bonds continued to evolve in significant ways, but genealogy-based relationships continue to carry significant weight. As we will see, the type of education a child receives in Mauritania is still largely dependent on their ancestors' origin, tribal affiliation, gender and social status.

The *maḥẓara* and the transmission of religious knowledge

The maḥẓara *is where you should go before you go anywhere else.*
–Mohamed A., student at the *maḥẓara* of Teysli, Trarza, November 2017

The rural *maḥẓara*

The history of the Islamic expansion into the western regions of the Sahara goes back to the ninth century and the trans-Saharan caravan networks, which were followed in the mid-eleventh century by the armed proselytism of the Almoravids, which resulted in the spread of Islam and its development into a hallmark of the region (El Hamel 1999: 64; Launay and Soares 1999: 499–500; Ould Ahmed Salem 2012: 638; Ould Cheikh 2017: 159). Although an idealization of the Almoravid movement continues to permeate many social milieus and the Islamic landscape of the region (appropriated notably by the Islamic Republic of Mauritania's official narrative), it is the ulterior establishment of the Sufi orders (*ṭuruq; sing. ṭarīqa*) that most likely consolidated the western Saharan region's prominent role as an acknowledged Islamic actor (for a significant case study of Sufism in the western Saharan regions, see Ould al-Bara's chapter in this volume). From the beginning of the eighteenth century, the region thus witnessed the entrenchment of Islam and the development of structured religious teaching (Ould Ahmed Salem 2012: 638; Ould Cheikh 2017: 161).

As mentioned above, the Saharan *zwāya* thus became the legitimate bearers of religious knowledge and the guardians of spiritual practices (on the importance of this cultural milieu, see the chapter by Ould Cheikh in this volume). This group is largely responsible for teaching the Arabic alphabet, the Qur'ān and other topics related to Islam. The Arabic alphabet is memorized even before the child can read, using mnemonic processes (also known in the Maghreb) to facilitate memorization. It is common for mothers (or female family elders) to initiate the child into the memorization of parts of the Qur'ān and the life of the Prophet (Fortier 1997: 86).

At the initial level of instruction, the transmission of knowledge is performed by a master (*mrābit* or *ṭālib*), this time a man, who may be a close relative or someone outside the family. When boys from *zwāya* families have memorized and learned to recite the Qur'ān, they continue their Islamic education at a higher level, in a *maḥẓara* (El Hamel 1999: 66). At this level, mainly male[3] students learn and perfect their recitation skills – reading and writing Qur'ānic verses – as well as other subjects such as rhetoric, Islamic jurisprudence (*fiqh*), the life of the Prophet (*sīra*), Islamic moral rules of behaviour, Arabic language and literature, and logic:

> I first learned the entire text of the Qur'ān and passed the first [level]. Then I learned from a small book how to write the Qu'rān, [which took] four to five

> months of learning. Then [I spent] another four months with another book to learn how to recite the Qurʾān orally. Then I learned how to pray, how to be pure, how to worship the religion, from a big book (Shaykh Khalīl's), which takes about four years to learn. When we finish learning this book, we start learning the Arabic language itself and its rules; this is another moment in the life of the *maḥẓara*. The most reputable teaching is the one provided in the *maḥẓara*s in the southwest of Mauritania (with regard to learning the Arabic language). We also learn logic, Arabic figures of speech, poetry, and the basics of *sharīʿa*.
>
> (Interview with Mohamed, a student at the *maḥẓara* of Teysir, 13 August 2020)

Often, in order to continue their Islamic studies at a higher level, young *zwāya* boys must leave their homes, whether in the desert or in the city, and move to another location where they can learn from a renowned teacher. The inhabitants of these locations consider these boys foreign students (*tlāmīd al-ghurba*). As a rule, the teaching at the *maḥẓara* is delivered by a single teacher with encyclopedic knowledge of certain religious fields; if necessary, however, he may ask for help from his best students on a voluntary basis. This volunteer system helps students to fund their studies and accommodation at the *maḥẓara*, in remote locations in the Mauritanian hinterland. Whereas in the nomadic past payment was made with camels, as further explained by Pettigrew (2007), nowadays there are other ways for students to contribute to the *maḥẓara*:

> Not only were students expected to feed themselves while under this system of intense tutelage, but custom demanded that they bring livestock as a payment for their studies with the *mrabit*. According to Ibn Alamin, students normally brought their teacher one or two camels depending on what the teacher already owned. Students could pool the livestock and share the milk produced by the cows, camels, or goats.
>
> (Pettigrew 2007: 68)

Currently, in an increasingly urban and sedentary society, the regime of student contributions to the *maḥẓara* has undergone some changes, as witnessed by the account provided by Ahmed, a student at the Teysir *maḥẓara*. In any case, if a student moves to a *maḥẓara* in the interior of the country, his family must provide his means of support:

> If you are a student at a *maḥẓara* in Nouakchott there are no changes; it's like [going to] a normal school. On the other hand, if you are a student at a *maḥẓara* in the interior of the country, it is obligatory to make a food deposit, around 50,000 ouguyia[4] on average (sometimes it is much less). The students do not have a house; if the *maḥẓara* has money, it is good and the students are comfortable, but if it is a poor *maḥẓara*, the students are left to fend for themselves. The most representative *maḥẓara* is Tendeghmat, near Teysir, where students must build a dwelling place by themselves. You have to go into the dunes for seven days to

> build a hut ... that is how it was done in the past. These *maḥẓaras* I am talking about specialize in Arabic.
>
> (Interview with Ahmed, a *maḥẓara* student, 20 July 2020)

In the Trarza region (present-day southwestern Mauritania) in particular, the teaching curriculum at the *maḥẓara* is more diversified. In addition to studying the Qur'ān, students learn law, theology and the mystical sciences, as well as grammar (*naḥw*), prosody (*ʿarūḍ*), morphology (*al-ṣarf*) and the history of the Arabs (*tārīkh al-ʿarab*). After acquiring these skills, students complete their studies by learning the fundamentals of Islamic law (*uṣūl al-fiqh*), logic (*manṭiq*), rhetoric (*balāgha*) and mathematics (*ḥisāb*) (Fortier 2003: 238). A student can actually spend a large part of his life at a *maḥẓara*, sometimes as long as thirty years. After memorizing and thoroughly understanding all of the canonical Islamic texts, the student receives a certificate (*ijāza*), which authorizes him to start teaching the knowledge he has acquired (El Hamel 1999: 66). Unlike the education system of the 'modern school' (the name used in Mauritania for the official school), in the *maḥẓara* the student is not evaluated through examinations. One of the students, Mohamed, views this as a failure of the traditional Islamic *maḥẓara* educational model:

> Another thing that should change in the *maḥẓara* education system is that there are no exams, and the fact that there are no exams puts less pressure on the students. The big disadvantage of the *maḥẓara* system is the absence of periodic and cyclical assessment. For example, when I wanted to take the *bac* [*baccalauréat*, the exam qualifying successful candidates for higher education] I discovered three months earlier that I had a lot of potential and that I could learn a lot of things, and I didn't know that I had the capacity to memorize so many things at the same time, and this was revealed by the exam.
>
> (Interview with Mohamed, a *maḥẓara* student, 13 August 2020)

We have seen that Islamic knowledge in Mauritania is both a communications channel and a marker of social stratification. The transfer of knowledge within Hassaniya-speaking communities is one of the areas where inter-statutory, inter-order and gender differentiations are most clearly demonstrated. Strongly linked to *zwāya* culture, the *maḥẓara* constitutes what can be viewed as a 'rite of passage' for this group, an identity marker and a space for effective socialization when entering adulthood. The *maḥẓara* is the place where an eminently *zwāya* experience is materialized and which presently guarantees the students' 'social distinction', in Pierre Bourdieu's sense of the expression.

As related to us by teachers and students, the curriculum of the *maḥẓara* goes beyond the matrix of knowledge that is mandatory in Islam, towards an entire schematization of the Moorish ethos that is captured, developed and retransmitted in these institutions. At the same time, the schools represent the Borromean knot of faith in this region of the world: Sunni/Maliki/Ashari Islam. The *maḥẓara* is a traditional model of learning that corresponds in many ways to the university level in public schooling (al-Naḥwī 1987). The materials transmitted and the didactic methods used are essentially based on the Islamic sciences, the Quʾrān, the *ḥadīth*, the textual foundations of *sharīʿa* (in their theoretical and practical aspects) and the Maliki rite as a doctrinal basis according to Ashari doctrine. In the Trarza region, knowledge of Arabic language sciences, grammar, syntax, poetic metrics and logic is also transmitted and is renowned in the entire Arab-Islamic geographical area. Apart from these two 'modules', *sharīʿa* and Classical Arabic, the curriculum also includes a whole collection of texts which appear to be ancillary but central to everyday life, dealing with decorum, good manners and social behaviour in general.

Initially, this model was mobile, adapted to the nomadic and transhumant lifestyle common to the region until the late 1970s. In fact, while the *maḥẓara* has made a resounding name for itself in the Muslim world and beyond, in 'scholarly' cities such as Chinguitti, Ouadane, Tichitt and Walata it is its role as an itinerant education provider that has set it apart from the *madrasa* (Fr. *médersa*) and other educational centres found in North and West Africa (on the differences between the *madrasa* and the western Saharan *maḥẓara*, see El Hamel 1999: 65–6; Frede 2021: 301–3).

The *maḥẓara* combines the two human habitats debated long ago in Ibn Khaldūn's dyad, *al-badawī* and *al-ḥaḍarī* (the nomad and the sedentary). It is linked, both in practice and symbolically, to the *bādiyya* (the Saharan hinterlands) and to nomadic movements throughout the Sahara (which also reach the Maghreb and the Mashrek), whether in search of water or while journeying to the holy sites of Islam. As argued by Ould Cheikh and Ould Bah, the *zwāya* clerical groups – through the institution of the *maḥẓara* and the dissemination of Sufi orders – have established the norms that allowed *sharīʿa* to prevail in largely ungoverned territories, the famous *al-bilād al-sība*/'land of insolence' (Ould Bah and Ould Cheikh 2009: 103–4).

The presence of the *maḥẓara* in the region is usually associated – most likely for ideological reasons that served to inscribe Islam in the western regions of the Sahara at a very early date – with the Almoravid period, its (controversial) *ribāṭ* ('lodge') serving as a prototypal form of this teaching. It thus became well established much later, towards the seventeenth/eighteenth centuries, with the emergence of the Sufi *ṭuruq* (*Shādhiliyya*, *Qādiriyya*, *Tijāniyya*) and the blossoming of their *zawiyas* ('centres' of Sufi practice that can be interchangeably associated with schooling and religious practices) which continue to be important sites for the transmission of knowledge.

In addition to the influence of the abovementioned ancient cities, there are several other key names and patronyms belonging to different tribes that are closely linked to prestigious *maḥẓara*s. One of these is al-Mukhtār w. Būnā – an Ashari thinker considered one of the great stars in the constellation of Moorish scholars, with significant influence on Arabic grammar, rhetoric and other language sciences. Other figures, some of them mentioned in the *Fatḥ al-shakūr*, have also contributed to this reputation, including al-Shaykh Muḥammad al-Māmī, Lemjeidri (also spelled al-Mujaydirī), Ibn Mbūjā, ʿAbd al-Qādir w. Muḥammad w. Muḥammad Sālim, Muḥammad al-Ḥasan wuld Aḥmadū al-Khadīm and Aḥmad al-ʿĀqil.

*Maḥẓara*s like the one addressed in this chapter, settled in a rural environment, still carry the soul of the *frīg* (nomadic camp) and are most often led by a shaykh – an erudite descendant of a long line of masters, sometimes with distinguished, specific knowledge areas. The 'profile' of these *maḥẓara*s is (self-)inscribed in a tribe-related geography, and any attempt to define it immediately brings to mind a plethora of cultural referents specific to each tribal area, along with real and mythical attributes ascribed to each member of a particular lineage of scholars.

To better understand the specifics of the *maḥẓara* in rural areas in Mauritania, however, it is important to consider the structure and role of the *maḥẓara* in urban areas. Despite the daily dynamics and techniques that separate them, both are interested in deepening Islamic knowledge and its dissemination to the world.

The urban *maḥẓara*

The reflections in this chapter do not aim to provide an exhaustive study of an entire traditional teaching system that escaped being taken over by the state (contrary to what happened to hundreds of similar structures in the capital and other cities that also offered instruction in Qurʾān memorization and the study of fundamental texts of *sharīʿa*). Nor will we cover the phenomenon of the neo-*maḥẓara*, which is organized more along the lines of the Maghreb's *madrasa* or the Egyptian *kuttāb*, both providing a 'modernized' version of education featuring the Qurʾān, air-conditioning, meal trays and supervisors in arithmetic, and civic education.

In these types of schools, students are often urban and relatively wealthy, with parents who are anxious to instil a performance-driven spirit in them. The most popular of these is the so-called 'Dedew mosque', a *maḥẓara* located in Nouakchott's bourgeois Tevragh Zeina district. Reminiscent of the Middle Eastern style in its architecture and general atmosphere, it is very popular with the women/mothers of the Nouakchott bourgeoisie. Every year, dozens of children and teenagers who have memorized the Qurʾān are awarded prizes. This occasion, which is given extensive media coverage, is marked by festive ceremonies to which parents, neighbours and cultural and religious personalities are invited. Social networks brim with shared photos, increasing publicity; addresses are exchanged and digital pages created, promoting the best *maḥẓara*s in town – all this against the backdrop of calls for personal development, since the study of the Qurʾān is seen as a first step towards increased inner well-being and social achievement.

This phenomenon, directly associated with the complete recitation of the Qurʾān, has become widespread and is now part of the social calendar in urban middle-class neighbourhoods, where it is common for children to take religious education classes in parallel with conventional schooling, dividing the daily rhythms between mornings dedicated to regular schooling and afternoons working with the *lawḥ* (a traditional wooden tablet that provides textual support for learning the Qurʾān). This practice has become a distinctive mark of the 'model family'. As mentioned by one of the students who had trained at a conventional elementary school in parallel with learning the Qurʾān at home:

> I started by doing elementary school, and then I did the *maḥẓara*. This is a common practice in my environment. Often, we prefer to let the child go to elementary school first, so he has the basic skills – he has a national number at the Ministry of Education – and then we let him do the *maḥẓara*. In my social environment, this is how we do it (…) When I was in elementary school, I had a Qurʾān master with me at home who taught me the basics of learning the Qurʾān, and then I had

> no problem entering the *maḥẓara* because when we come from school, it is always easier to enter. The *maḥẓara* is a mixture of everything; there are those who know a lot and those who know less.
>
> (Interview with Ahmed, a *maḥẓara* student, 20 July 2020)

While adapted to urban tastes and habits, this new form of relating to religion (in which Islamic knowledge is passed on to children) is undoubtedly a social asset and a reference point, especially to those with the means to provide this hybrid schooling and the employment of private 'religious' tutors. Thus, in the villas, the guards' lodgings are increasingly occupied by private religion professors (men who often come from rural *maḥẓara*s) who circulate among houses. This demand for proximity to a religiously legitimized actor is reflected in the common expression 'to have the Qurʾān' (*ʿəndū al-Qurʾān*). This phrase expresses the idea of being able to recite the Qurʾān in full, but it also denotes the idea that, in addition to the Qurʾān's intrinsic value as the core of faith and spiritual enrichment, it has value as a source of (sometimes quite sizeable) income. For these urban *mrabit*s and for those who came from the neo-*maḥẓara*, the question of money and pecuniary contributions is not always straightforward. In the learning centres, this basic service is rarely provided without the performance of charitable works in return, an exchange that is made without the explicit notification of any authority.

As witnessed by the comments made by mothers of children who attended such schools (neo-*maḥẓara*s), teaching their children the Qurʾān in addition to modern schooling has a calming effect on both parents and children. It is said to contribute to better results at the regular school and seems to reassure parents, even if they themselves cannot recite the Qurʾān and have a rudimentary knowledge of Islam, as reported by a mother in the Ksar district of Nouakchott:

> Every day, when they come from school, the children have to eat quickly because right after the *ẓuhr* prayer the *mrabit* is waiting for them at the center for the Qurʾān class. My 14-year-old daughter will soon 'have' the whole Qurʾān! They finish two hours later; they can play or go out, but they must not stay up too late because at 5:00 am we have a teacher here at home who makes them recite until the *ṣubḥ* prayer at about 6:00 am, when they stop to pray, have breakfast and get ready for school. In this world without roots which we live in today, it is necessary for the children to have this knowledge, especially the girls.
>
> (Interview in Tajihla, mother of a *maḥẓara* student, 12 April 2018)

At the end of a religious education class in the district of Tevragh Zeina, where we were set to meet the parents, a queue of luxury cars waiting for pupils served as a reminder of the extent of the interest – and the economic standing – of the students' families. It would not be an exaggeration to say that the sacred texts are indeed in the process of becoming commodified in this context – of becoming 'assets', the 'knowledge' they contain becoming increasingly disembodied. It should also be noted that this same type of urban *maḥẓara* can be found in less luxurious peripheral neighbourhoods such as Dar-Naim, Arafat and Toujounine, where those who arrived in the capital more recently tend to be concentrated.[5]

Maḥẓara attendance first peaked in the 1990s, with the religious fervour drenched in the activism of the Islamist movements of the time. Those who were interested in this kind of education at the time were themselves engaged in Islamist discourse and activism. They responded positively to the engaging, at times militant, rhetoric of the Muslim Brotherhood (*al-Ikhwān al-Muslimīn*), up to the ousting of the Ould Taya regime (1984–2005). Things are very different today. Even though the political movements are still active, they seem to have adapted to the current situation, in which religious education is not correlated with ideological commitment or specific sympathies. This unbiased approach makes this model appealing to different social and economic strata of the population. Parental participation is not mandatory, and attention seems to have shifted to the youth, creating a contagion effect in which the sons and daughters of *Ikhwān* leaders are taken as a model.

These urban Islamic trends, though not central to the arguments developed in this chapter, deserve to be mentioned and further explored.[6] As noted above, our study is centred on a rural *maḥẓara*, based on the following idea, as articulated by Bensaid and Lajdal:

> Emerging in the desert, the *maḥẓara* effectively adapted its functions, lifestyle, educational systems, social operations, and overall intellectual makeup in order to better suit the local life conditions of the desert, whilst effectively sustaining its role and presence dating back to the Almoravid period.
>
> (Bensaid and Ladjal 2019: 152)

Teysir, the village around the *maḥẓara*

Local classifications tend to represent *maḥẓara* institutions of the east and central Mauritania as specializing in *fiqh* and in the Qur'ān. Unlike in the Middle East, *tajwīd* (the rules of recitation of the Qur'ān) is not a part of the curriculum, with recitation being carried out in the local style. Also absent from the curricula in these *maḥẓara*s is the *sīra* ('biography') of the prophet as a historical subject. In this respect, what is taught is the *ḥadīth* – 'the knowledge of men', i.e. the biographies of the Prophet's companions and the first actors of Islam. The *maḥẓara*s located in the Trarza region are presented as temples of Arabic, with a purist approach based on syntax, poetry and rhetoric but also reflecting a shift towards poetry written in Hassaniyya Arabic. Alongside the core curriculum, students also learn about *ʿibādāt* (the worship of God), *muʿāmalāt* (relations between individuals) and *ghnē* (local poetry).

As mentioned in the introduction, this chapter is based on a survey taken by students at the *maḥẓara* of Teysir, in Tiguent, southwestern Mauritania (a town bordering the Nouakchott-Rosso road, about 105 km south of Nouakchott). We worked with students who were also affiliated with the University of Nouakchott,[7] asking them about the scholarly materials they used, their methods of study, their level of text retention and their use of these texts in the context of a more profession-oriented general education.

The *maḥẓara* of Teysir was established at the beginning of the nineteenth century and was associated with the teachings of Mawlūd w. Aḥmad al-Jawād, Abū Muḥammad

w. Mawlūd, Muḥammad Mawlūd w. Abū Muḥammad, Aḥmadū al-Khadīm and its current head, Muḥammad al-Ḥasan w. Aḥmadū al-Khadīm, who was trained by the renowned Aḥmad Sālim Alummā, also in Teysir. It has been at its current location since the early 1970s. Teysir is an administrative part of the Moughataa of Mederdra and the *commune* of Tiguent. During the peak season (between June and September), it boasts approximately 1,500 students between the ages of 13 and 26. Between November and May, it hosts approximately 800 children and youth. We also observed the presence of approximately 200 foreign students, the majority of whom were from other African countries (including Senegal, The Gambia, Mali, Nigeria, Algeria, Tunisia and Morocco). At the *maḥẓara* in Teysir, there were families from South Africa, Tunisia and some couples in the area temporarily, from northern Europe. As we will see in what follows, attention to the daily lives of the students at this institution reveals important spaces of change.

Housing

In Teysir, housing is constructed from three types of material: fabric, bricks and wood. These small, semi-urban settlements, many with running water and electricity, combine nomadic and sedentary modes of construction in almost equal measure. In those houses that do not have a tin or concrete roof, families in Teysir have at least one room, a *m'bar* (a medium-sized shed constructed with wooden beams and props), and a tent (except in the rainy season). The students of the *maḥẓara* are housed in the same type of dwelling, usually grouped by tribal affiliation.[8] Despite the existence of these houses, new affinities have also led those from certain groups to associate according to urban/rural criteria (with rural young people choosing to live with other rural young people, and with those from more 'urban' backgrounds staying with other urban young people), and even according to age. Having a computer or a few books made certain students more attractive and added new layers to this housing cartography. This transformation of the norms of student settlement is only one of the observed changes that shape daily life in the *maḥẓara*.

Initially, the construction of the houses was funded by contributions from those first to arrive or by donations (*waqf*) from the Shaykh of the *maḥẓara*, prominent local figures, and foreign benefactors who had a connection to the Shaykh or wanted to give alms. The furniture is always very basic, most often amounting to some mats or carpets, a few cushions and kitchen utensils. Each student keeps a few personal belongings in a trunk or bag: a few books, a blanket and, increasingly, extra school supplies, notebooks, a tablet, a smartphone and in some cases even a laptop computer.

The village of Teysir is divided into different sections. At the centre is the mosque and the homes of the permanent inhabitants of the village and of families related to the Shaykh of the *maḥẓara* (who is also the head of the village, assisted by one of his sons, who teaches by his side). This central area is encircled by an area inhabited by the students, who live in both the traditional houses described above and common rooms and *m'bars*. The next district is inhabited by students from neighbouring African countries: Senegal, Mali, The Gambia and Niger. Some foreign families have also settled there, with converts being well integrated with the rest of the inhabitants (we were told of French and American students who had recently left, but we only met South Africans and Northern Europeans, notably from Norway and Denmark).

Admission and eligibility

Admission at Teysir is permitted based on a simple decision by the future student or his tutors, the fundamental prerequisite being that the student has memorized the Qur'ān. The new urban *maḥẓaras* are more hybrid in nature and receive young children who are still working through the first learning cycle. In Teysir, we met children between 8 and 12 years of age who were being taught the Qur'ān directly by their families.[9] They formed a separate group alongside the adolescents and young adults who had already advanced in their studies. The presence of a few migrant children accompanying elders on their journeys was also observed. These children were housed in the West African 'neighbourhood' provided for foreigners:

> When you arrive here, you go to see the son of the Shaykh, who is responsible for the organization of village life. We are welcomed; we are not asked any questions – personal information will be known later anyway. Sometimes we are told which house to go to, a recommendation or something like that; sometimes we already have a place to stay. Here you just have to arrive with your *lawḥ* (wooden tablet) or your notebook and be patient, because at the beginning there are habits to develop … but you get used to it quickly, and in particular, you make friends.
>
> The Shaykh is one of the few people still alive who teaches all disciplines. You don't need to say that you want to learn this or that chapter; you just open your mouth and start reading him the verses or part the meaning of which you want to learn … The Shaykh knows all his texts by heart.
>
> (Interview Abdellahi, *maḥẓara* student, February 2018)

While admission to the *maḥẓara* is free, daily life, at first sight also without additional costs, is governed by implicit, deeply respected codes. The rules of conduct for both the students and the inhabitants of the village are well delineated. The students are supervised by their families and by the Shaykh. In case of illness, they are taken care of, and in return they perform various services ranging from cleaning, slaughtering animals, small household chores and even herding animals. Nevertheless, there is an ostensible gap with regard to regulating the collective behaviour of the youth of the *maḥẓara*, which will be explained below.

A typical day at the *maḥẓara* begins with the Shaykh's teaching after the *ṣubḥ* (daybreak) prayer, although the students may arrive at the previous call, around 4.00 am, generally two hours before sunrise. This pre-lesson is a repetition of the text learned the day before, sometimes involving recitations of the Qur'ān for better retention or to test different readings and their modes.

Around 7.00 am, most of the students begin to arrive. The first to come are the first to learn. The Shaykh is located at the centre, in the shadow of a wall, under the *m'bar* or tent, and a circle of students gather around him. A student begins to read a text from a notebook or his tablet, sometimes stopping at each hemistich (a half-line of verse) to listen to the master's explanation. Two students can work together and 'advance' in the same text by having it explained to them and listening at the same time. The Shaykh moves from Shaykh Khalīl to Ibn Mālik's *al-Alfiyya*, from the *al-Ṭurra* to the *al-Iḥmirār*, from *al-Kifāf* to the *al-Risāla* and to the *al-Shāṭibiyya*, continuing the review until the *ẓuhr* prayer. During these four to five hours, there are few interruptions: at the time of the *ḍuḥā* prayer, supplementary prayers are performed by the teacher. During the lesson, the Shaykh often sits to the side, cross-legged, leaning or lying on the floor. He delivers his lesson dressed in regular clothes, without any specific ritualization, and is sometimes interrupted by his family, at times commenting on issues not directly related to the lesson. The space in which the class is held is fully integrated in village life, and the content of the exchanges between the students and their teacher can be heard by passersby. The women in the houses can listen to the readings and the various interpretations given by the Shaykh if they are so inclined.

The Shaykh's explanations are at the heart of the lesson. The *sharḥ* ('explanation') would not seem to aim at either simplification or intellectualization, however. The explanation seemed to us to be a re-formulation, a re-composition in another mode, of the text in question. The model of learning practised in the *maḥẓara* can be compared to a continuous round-trip journey; when moving in one direction, we pass through the central work, and on our return we visit various supplementary works, which do not literally explain the central text but rather 'reposition' its contents. The cognitive operation set in motion by this method involves comprehending various historical attempts to answer a certain question, as opposed to a more modern, literal interpretation of the text.

From the students' perspective, the content of the courses taught in Teysir can be very complex: the lessons are both sacred and secular in both form and technique. The irreplaceable Shaykh Khalīl,[10] for example, remains a central focus of the curriculum, but the reminder of the textual sources are not fixed.

Student life

In Teysir, where the local community is strongly attached to the *Tijāniyya* Sufi order, students do not necessarily attend the mosque and do not perform the collective rituals of this *ṭarīqa*. Cultural differences are very strong, and student life is not always peaceful. Although open confrontation is rare, student co-existence can be marked by palpable withdrawal, avoidance and sometimes even poetic jousts and challenges (for example on the football field).[11] Despite this, different interlocutors have also mentioned that *maḥẓara* life affords the students certain freedoms that they do not enjoy in their local communities:

> When we are in the *maḥẓara*, the list of prohibitions is narrowed; we can commit all sorts of petty crimes, minor offences, without this falling on us or making an indelible mark on our reputations or those of our parents, contrary to other places in our nomadic lives where exemplary conduct is very strict. For example, when we are in the *frīg*, we represent society almost in a theatrical sense, which means that we have to stick to a role, master it and be satisfied with it.
>
> (Interview with Ahmed, a *maḥẓara* student, 20 July 2020)

Having student status allows for some leniency in daily life and in relationships with the local population, who informed us, with good humour and without any hard feelings, of the occasional disappearance of chickens or vegetables from their garden at night and of small pranks to which the family of the master was subjected. As Ahmed, a student of several *maḥẓara*s, explained:

> The *tlāmīd* [*maḥẓara* students] will be the future references in matters of religion, the most serious and sacred; the silly acts we commit should not follow us. Also, society allows us to restart our 'counter' at zero after we leave, as we arrive here [at] around 13 years [of age] and must then learn the common basis of the Shaykh Khalīl for three-and-a-half years, plus two more years for the *qirāʾāt* and the *al-Kifāf* in parallel, along with other minor works (…) At this stage, one is well prepared to be a *ʿalīm* (…) as we are already familiar with the texts, codifying the syntax and the rhetoric in classical Arabic.
>
> (Interview with Ahmed, a *maḥẓara* student, 20 July 2020)

Tradition and modernity

> My main concern is language; I want to master English and French first. My ambition is to be able to teach Islamic religious sciences one day, from a modern perspective. I would like you to understand its value and know what the *maḥẓara* means. I want to explain *maḥẓara* in a modern way so that it does not die out and becomes well known.
>
> (Interview with Ahmed, a *maḥẓara* student, 20 July 2020)

For centuries, the *maḥẓara* has remained a timeless space in terms of its content and methods. In the last two decades, it has tended, if not towards 'modernization', then at least towards the incorporation of two aspects of both practical and symbolic significance: the incorporation of new technologies and the greater involvement of students in shaping the curriculum.[12] Since the beginning of the 2000s, various changes have been taking place in Mauritania. The gap between tradition and modernity has been the most marked in 'original education', the official term used in Mauritania for religious schools. In the following, we will use the expression 'modern school' to denote the teaching framework established by the state, which includes many subjects that are not part of the curriculum traditionally taught in the *maḥẓara*s.[13] We wanted to question students on the legendary immutability of the *maḥẓara*, perceived from the outside and readily understood by society as a guarantee of continuity. And yet, at first sight, there is a clear negotiation at work in this context between the new and the old – the creation of new ways of 'receiving' the sacred and, above all, of being its bearer. From this standpoint, one could ask what effect global interconnections of all kinds, coupled with a generalized questioning of Islam, have had on the *maḥẓara* as an institution. What has remained permanent, and what is being transformed? Or better, what have the subjects in this context chosen to treat as permanent, and what is seen as transformable, permeable to change?

Figure 11.1 Teysir's mosque, March 2021 (© Zahra Horma).

It is not difficult to imagine what the specificity of the *maḥẓara* model in the western regions of the Sahara and its mutations, even if relative, can bring to our understanding of contemporary Islam. In this part of the Muslim world, Islamic scholarship has always been linear in terms of its reproduction. What is noteworthy here is that space is being made for a new link in this chain, located for the moment in the field of the learner himself. As Mohamed explains, when asked about his professional ambitions for the future:

> Right now I'm learning English because I want to access all the literature about the Muslim world or Muslim knowledge that is written in English. Arabic speakers are somewhat deprived of all that is written about Islam in English … And it also opens up the possibility of working, for example in the media, like [in] journalism.
> (Interview with Mohamed, a *maḥẓara* student, 13 August 2020)

Mohamed's words confirm that, despite the centrality of traditional religious practice to the educational system of the *maḥẓara*, there is a growing demand for new cultural elements and knowledge structures from the Western world, which are described as 'modern' and whose legacies trace back to the colonial presence, in particular to the bilingual educational system of the modern school. While on the one hand Mohamed believes in the importance of valorizing and expanding the Muslim religion in the world, on the other hand he defends opening up the *maḥẓara* to a globalized world.

The testimonies of the *maḥẓara* students we interviewed for this study reveal that it is possible to link traditional Islamic education with modern formal education. For the majority, it is essential to complement the education received at the *maḥẓara* with a modern, bilingual (Arabic and French) school education, such as that provided in Mauritania. Obtaining the *baccalauréat* and learning languages other than Arabic, such as French and English, is something that most students view as imperative to completing a traditional religious education adapted to the modern world. Many end up finishing their *maḥẓara* studies, some having gone through several *maḥẓara*s over the years, seeking to complete their training with modern education to prepare for the job market in a globalized world. Like Mohamed, who aspires to learn English in order to access all the available literature on Islam and as a vehicle for eventually working in the field of journalism, Ahmed advocates learning law and economics as important tools for understanding not only world history but also the history of Muslims in the world:

> I chose to take law, and also economics, because I had an American professor when I left *maḥẓara* in 2016, in an English study center. I enrolled in this English center and met this American Muslim teacher, who told me that the best subjects I could take today were economics and law. So, I graduated from high school and enrolled in law school at the university. I participated in a competition at the Institute of Religious Sciences and was among the first, and I decided to also enroll in economics there because I am convinced that law and economics are disciplines that are important for understanding Human history, especially that of Muslims.
>
> (Interview with Ahmed, a *maḥẓara* student, 20 July 2020)

In Teysir, the use of new technologies is now a feature of the *maḥẓara*. According to the students we met, this has developed gradually, 'as a natural shift and without any prohibition being pronounced by the shaykhs. There is a *ḥadīth* that recommends ways and means that facilitate any enterprise as long as they are not categorized as illicit. Cell phones and photocopy machines have helped us a lot lately' (Interview with Sidi, a student in Teysir, February 2018).

While wooden tablets and notebooks are the main means of study in the classroom, at rehearsals and post-session revisions with the Shaykh, smartphones, recording devices and even laptops are becoming common. During the interviews, the students often spoke of when books – of which there were few – had circulated among the students, which was arduous because 'you had to wait your turn or copy all the time' (Interview with Sidi, a student in Teysir, February 2018).

When we asked students to list those objects they considered new to the life of the *maḥẓara* but directly related to their courses, smartphones were always mentioned first:

> My phone is first of all my torch; it gives me light for evening revisions, when I go out around 5:00 am to go to class, when we travel.
>
> (Interview with M. L. A., a student at the *maḥẓara* of Teysir, March 2019)

> My phone is my text storage place. I have links to Middle Eastern libraries, but I also have texts from here that I note down, that I take photographs of. I take screenshots of everything that interests me.
>
> (Interview with M. B., a student at the *maḥẓara* of Teysir, March 2019)

> My phone allows me to record recitations of texts, by myself or my friends, or by the Shaykh. We share them, and so we are always present in one way or another in the course; for example, in our evening revisions, since we have smartphones, we have more things to share with the recordings.
>
> (Interview with N. M., a student at the *maḥẓara* of Teysir, March 2019)

> Those of us who want to have information about university courses, the dates of the competitions, the sites to visit, can access [this information] from Teysir and plan our trip, make an appointment or register by email on the portals of the Ministry of Education. Before, we were cut off from this other life until we were finished at the *maḥẓara*; now we know what is going on and what to do even before we arrive in Nouakchott. (…) We communicate a lot with our parents. Before cell phones, our older brothers were cut off from their families until they returned. Now we are always informed about the affairs of our villages. We schedule our returns better; sometimes we only return once a year because we maintain sufficient contact.
>
> (Interview with Y. V. C., a student at the *maḥẓara* of Teysir, November 2018)

While the students praise the merits of connectivity and digital tools, it seems that web content is kept at a distance and never incorporated into the traditional curriculum of the *maḥẓara*, which has remained almost unchanged, as Frede (2021: 307) confirms:

> Despite the changes to teaching methodologies and knowledge transmission and authority within the institutions, texts taught within traditional Mauritanian institutions have not yet been replaced by reformed text books. Most *maḥẓara* institutions still teach the curriculum as former generations did: a locally produced didactic literature that has been derived from ninth- and tenth-century texts, written mainly by Andalousian and North African authors.

What is noteworthy is the attempt to recognize and make use of 'unconventional' texts through virtual explorations and use them to flesh out the acquired knowledge. The works of great Islamic figures from the Middle East are 'downloaded' (the word is always used in English by students), read and appreciated. It seems that the texts studied in the *maḥẓara* have their own source of validation which is precisely the process described above: a 'disarticulation-reconstitution' which makes it a local appropriation. At the same time, it also operates as a safeguard, ensuring that any novel elements are always surrounded by traditional ones and cannot effect fundamental change. The observable changes seem in fact to guarantee a certain continuity.

In our interviews, the young people for the most part said that their priority once they left the *maḥẓara* was to learn English, so as to gain access to English-language

Islamic literature. When asked whether different texts would one day be taught in the *maḥẓara* if the acquisition of other Islamic texts became widespread, a relative of the Shaykh of the Teysir *maḥẓara* explained:

> The *maḥẓara* has already 'changed'! For example, at the beginning of the last century, we did not teach the texts of the *ḥajj* (pilgrimage) to all the entrants in the *maḥẓara* because the *ḥajj* was a luxury available to only a few people, wealthy men and scholars. On the other hand, the primary concern was the teaching of commercial transactions (*al-bayʿ*); in fact, we were all traders at the time. This tells you that the *maḥẓara* is evolving, and I know that it has evolved a lot amongst young people and what they do with their training after the *maḥẓara*. There has also been change in this area, as we have smartphones and we see new things. If we continue with Shaykh Khalīl during our time in the *maḥẓara*, then when we arrive at the university we are more inclined towards philosophy, history, and law, and we like it! We are not 'glued' to Shaykh Khalīl, but we also can't abandon our traditional books. We know that there is debate on the passages on slavery and women's inheritance, but what sticks with us when we leave the *maḥẓara* is not these chapters; what we retain is what will help us to pass the *baccalauréat*! Not everything that we read is applicable, we know that, but this is a big subject, and a difficult one.
>
> (Interview with M. A. O. A., a relative of the Shaykh of the village of Teysir and a former student of the *maḥẓara*, November 2017)

Google search engines and platforms like Wikipedia are frequently visited by the *tlāmīd*, who nonetheless relate with some irony the reverence that must be shown to *Shaykh* Google and *Mufti*-wiki. Exchanges of this sort are not without effect on the general transmission of religious knowledge in Mauritania, shaping young people's management of the modes of knowledge acquisition.

Figure 11.2 Students' housing in Teysir, March 2021 (© Zahra Horma).

Conclusion

The *maḥẓara* student is at the heart of multiple connections, both internal and external, on an unbridled search for a future, driven by the feeling that he has taken the 'high road', which is not always available to those 'from below', left on the fringes of employment and economic integration. Despite the *maḥẓara* student's commitment to the academic path, however, traditional Islamic studies do not render the student as competitive in the labour market as their proponents might hope. It is therefore imperative for the *maḥẓara* student to take a more active role in integrating modern, marketable skills into the *maḥẓara* curriculum.

On the question of whether the time has come to organize the *maḥẓara* sector, those we interviewed answered in the affirmative, but they demand 'good intentions' and significant consultations in which they are equal partners. As for the possibility of replacing the modern school with the *maḥẓara*, or vice versa, according to our interlocutors a fusion of the modern school within the *maḥẓara* would be preferable.

In terms of the possibility of protecting the *maḥẓara* from deterioration or even disappearance, the students with whom we spoke insist on the importance of two elements: first, the predisposition of scholars to teach for the love of God, and second, state assistance for this sector, on the condition that this backing does not corrupt the autonomy, the qualities and the thinking of the *maḥẓara* Shaykhs.

Is there still room for the *maḥẓara* to grow and develop? The students' answers to this question were brief; this would require financial and scientific support that nonetheless respects the autonomy of the institution, which does not appear to be on the horizon, given the situation both within the country and internationally. Do the students and teachers of the *maḥẓara* want to change their materials, equipment and pedagogical processes? Our interlocutors said that anything that can facilitate learning and does not lead to harm is desirable. Ould Mohamed Baba Moustapha (2014: 62) confirms these new forms of engagement between the religion and its followers, as well as active state support for religious education through media platforms:

> The media in Mauritania have followed the Islamization movement soundscape. Radio Qurʾān broadcasts, as its label implies, the Qurʾān but also exegesis and prophetic *ḥadīth* and hagiography, as well as Islamic teachings. Radio Qurʾān is therefore completely religious. On the other hand, public television and radio in Nouakchott devote more and more of their programming to religious topics. During Ramadan, all forms of secular broadcasts are preempted. Even Arabic soap operas are replaced by religious programs devoted to the Prophet Muḥammad, or the lives of his Companions, as well as great Muslim heroes and battles. The most popular show on public Mauritanian TV remains *al-Sahra al-Ramaḍāniyya* ('Ramadan Evening'), which features a physician and a religious scholar answering questions about public health and religious concerns.

According to the latest estimates, the number of *maḥẓara*s is expected to reach six thousand in the near future, a third of which are concentrated in Nouakchott.[14] The students argue that the state must take global, not partial, measures. They have called for the integration of *maḥẓara* teachers and their students into the civil service and for the rehabilitation, reorganization and reform of the education sector so as to integrate the two systems – a perspective that has recently been signalled by Britta Frede, noting the natural development of 'hybrid knowledge conceptions' (2021: 308).

Notes

1 Other groups, of subordinate status, included smiths (*m ʿallemīn*), the descendants of slaves (*ḥarāṭīn*), griots (*iggiw*) or musicians, and slaves (*ʿabīd*) (Bonte 2016: 45; Ould Cheikh 2020: 3). This stratified model is featured throughout the Sahara/Sahelian regions in many other populations.
2 On the contemporary articulation of postcolonial debates associated with the rivalry between the two predominant elements of this social structure, see Ould Mohamed Baba and Freire (2020).
3 On women's expectations regarding traditional Islamic education, see Frede (2021: 309).
4 Approximately US$1,300. See, for example, p. 2 of the World Bank International Development Association Report No: PAD3362, http://documents1.worldbank.org/curated/en/505861585879349315/pdf/Mauritania-Decentralization-and-Productive-Cities-Support-Project.pdf.
5 This clearly touches on the phenomenon of a consumerist and bourgeois 'market Islam', as discussed by Patrick Haenni (2006: 132).
6 On religiosity in Nouakchott, see Ould Mohamed Baba Moustapha (2014).
7 On the importance of the Islamist sphere in Mauritania's universities, see Ould Mohamed Baba Moustapha (2020: 93–5).
8 An example of this is the 'Tajakant House' (*Dār Tajakānit*), where students are grouped according to tribal affiliation and to which students from other social backgrounds can be invited, provided they are from tribes of the same region (and often related to the Tajakant).
9 In compliance with the research ethics provisions of the Capsahara project, these subjects were not interviewed.
10 Khalīl b. Isḥāq (d. 1374 CE) remains the most important reference in western Saharan Maliki thought (cf. Ould Cheikh 2016: 61).
11 At Teysir, young students (12–16) often played football in the afternoons. The teams were sometimes mixed, and students of different nationalities and regional origins could be found wearing the same regional jersey or playing on rival teams.
12 It is important to note that the *maḥẓara* is in principle open to all, but access to learning has traditionally been reserved for the *zwāya*. This inequality of access to learning institutions has been signalled as a form of maintaining statuary inequality (El Hamel 1999: 66). The *maḥẓara* currently receives many students of *ḥassān* background. Dah ould Sidi ould Amar Taleb, for example, the current Minister of Islamic Affairs and Original Teaching, comes from a 'warrior' status family.
13 On the incorporation of 'modern' technologies and innovative schooling methods by Mauritanian *ʿulamāʾ* in the early twenty-first century, see Freire (2005: 281–3).
14 Reports, no doubt underestimated, mentioned the existence of 800 *maḥẓara*s in 1905 (i.e. one *maḥẓara* for every 500 inhabitants), and 691 at the end of the colonial period (Bonte 2003, in Maouloud 2017: 19).

References

An-Na'im, A. A. (2008), *Islam and the Secular State: Negotiating the Future of Sharia*. Cambridge, MA: Harvard University Press.

Al-naḥwī, K. (1987), *Bilād Shinqīṭ: al-manāra wa-l-ribāṭ*. Tunis: Alecso.

Bensaid, B. and T. Ladjal (2019), 'The Struggle of Traditional Religious Education in West Africa: The Case of Mahdara in Mauritania', *Journal of Ethnic and Cultural Studies*, 6 (1): 152–61.

Bonte, P. (2016), *Récits d'Origine, Contribution à la Connaissance du Passé Ouest-Saharien (Mauritanie, Maroc, Sahara Occidental, Algérie et Mali)*. Paris: Karthala.

Bonte, P. (2017), *Identités et Changement Socioculturel dans l'Ouest Saharien (Sahara occidental, Mauritanie, Maroc)*. Paris: Karthala.

Brenner, L. (2000), *Controlling Knowledge: Religion, Power, and Schooling in a West African Muslim Society*. London: Hurst.

Eickelman, D. F. and A. Salvatore (2006), 'Public Islam and the Common Good', *Etnográfica*, X (1): 97–105.

El Hamel, C. (1999), 'The Transmission of Islamic Knowledge in Moorish Society from the Rise of the Almoravids to the 19th Century', *Journal of Religion in Africa*, 29: 62–87.

Fortier, C. (1997), 'Mémorisation et audition: l'enseignement coranique chez les Maures', *Islam et Sociétés au Sud du Sahara*, 11: 85–105.

Fortier, C. (1998), 'Le corps comme mémoire, du giron maternel à la férule du maître coranique', *Journal des Africanistes*, 68: 199–223.

Fortier, C. (2000), *Corps, Différences des Sexes et Infortune. Transmission de l'Identité et des Savoirs en Islam Malékite et dans la Société Maure de Mauritanie*. Paris, EHESS, PhD thesis in anthropology.

Fortier, C. (2003), 'Une pédagogie coranique. Modes de transmission des savoirs islamiques (Mauritanie)', *Cahiers d'Études Africaines*, 169–170: 235–60.

Frede, B. (2021), 'What Does Traditional Islamic Education Mean? Examples from Nouakchott's Contemporary Female Learning Circles', in O. Kane (ed.), *Islamic Scholarship in Africa: New directions and Global Contexts*, 300–20. New York, NY: Boydell & Brewer.

Freire, F. (2005), 'La Ligue des ulémas de Mauritanie: débats religieux et politiques dans une république islamique', *Annuaire de l'Afrique du Nord 2003*: 279–88. Paris: CNRS.

Freire, F. (2010), 'Portugal (ainda) nos confins saharianos: leituras identitárias sobre três tribos do litoral da Mauritânia', in M. Cardeira da Silva (ed.), *Castelos a Bombordo: Etnografias de Patrimónios Africanos e Memórias Portuguesas*, 172–91. Lisbon: Livros Horizonte.

Freire, F. (2013), *Tribos, Princesas e Demónios: Etnografias do Encontro Pré-Colonial no Sudoeste da Mauritânia*. Lisbon: Colibri.

Haenni, P. (2006), 'La France face à ses musulmans: émeutes, jihadisme et dépolitisation', *Esprit*, 10: 112–45.

Ladjal, T. and B. Bensaid (2017), 'Desert-based Muslim Religious Education: Mahdara as a Model', *Religious Education*, 112 (5): 529–41.

Launay, R. and B. F. Soares (1999), 'The Formation of an "Islamic Sphere" in French Colonial West Africa', *Economy and Society*, 28 (4): 497–519.

Maouloud, Mohamed Salem Ould (2017). 'L' éducation Islamique Non-Formelle Mahadra de Mauritanie', *Revue Internationale d'éducation de Sèvres*, 74: 18–24. https://doi.org/10.4000/ries.5767.

Norris, H. T. (1969), 'Znāga Islam during the Seventeenth and Eighteenth Centuries', *Bulletin of the School of Oriental and African Studies*, 32 (3): 496–526.
Ould Ahmed Salem, Z. (2007), 'Islam in Mauritania between Political Expansion and Globalization: Elites, Institutions, Knowledge, and Networks', in B. F. Soares and R. Otayek (eds), *Islam and Muslim Politics in Africa*, 22–46. New York, NY: Palgrave Macmillan.
Ould Ahmed Salem, Z. (2012), 'Les mutations paradoxales de l'Islamisme en Mauritanie', *Cahiers d'Études africaines*, 206–207: 635–64.
Ould Ahmed Salem, Z. (2013), *Prêcher dans le Désert: Islam Politique et Changement Social en Mauritanie*. Paris: Karthala.
Ould Ahmedou, E. G. (1997), *L'Enseignement Traditionnel en Mauritanie: La Mahadra ou l'École 'à Dos de Chameau'*. Paris: L'Harmattan.
Ould Bah, M. and A. Ould Cheikh (2009), 'Moral Entrepreneurs and Islamic Financial Networks in Mauritania', *Afrique Contemporaine*, 231: 99–117. https://doi.org/10.3917/afco.231.0099.
Ould Cheikh, A. W. (1985), 'Nomadisme, Islam et pouvoir politique dans la société Maure précoloniale (XIes.- XIXes.): Essai sur quelques aspects du tribalisme', PhD thesis in sociology, Université de Paris V - René Descartes.
Ould Cheikh, A. W. (1998), 'Cherche élite, désespérément: évolution du système éducatif et (de)formation des "élites" dans la société mauritanienne', *Nomadic Peoples*, 2 (1): 235–51.
Ould Cheikh, A. W. (2016). 'De quoi le Sahara est-il le nom? Images du Sahara et des Sahariens dans Kitâb al-Bâdiyya d'al-Šaykh Muhamd al-Mami', In Rahal Boubrik and Ahmed Joumani (eds), *Le Sahara: Lieux d'histoire et espaces d'échange*, 51–69. Rabat: Centre des Études Sahariennes.
Ould Cheikh, A. W. (2017), *La Société Maure: Éléments d'Anthropologie Historique*. Rabat: Centre des Études Sahariennes.
Ould Cheikh, A. W. (2020), *Les (Res)sources de l'enseignement 'traditionnel' maure*. https://www.academia.edu/44018218/Les_res_sources_de_lenseignement_traditionnel_maure.
Ould Mohamed Baba Moustapha, E. (2014), 'Negotiating Islamic Revival: Public Religiosity in Nouakchott City', *Islamic Africa*, 5: 45–82.
Ould Mohamed Baba Moustapha, E. (2020), 'Islamisme, tribalisme et ethnocentrisme sur le campus de l'Université de Nouakchott', in L. A. Villalón and M. Bodian (eds), *Entre le Savoir et le Culte: Activisme et Mouvements Religieux dans les Universités du Sahel*, 85–113. Dakar: Amalion.
Ould Mouloud, M. S. (2017), 'L'Education non formelle islamique *mahadra* de Mauritanie', *Revue Internationale d'Éducation de Sèvres*, 74: 18–24.
Pettigrew, E. (2007), 'Colonizing the *mahadra*: Language, Identity, and Power in Mauritania under French Control', *Ufahamu: A Journal of African Studies*, 33: 2–33.
Pettigrew, E. (2019), 'The History of Islam in Mauritania', *Oxford Research Encyclopedia of African History*. Oxford: Oxford University Press. https://doi.org/10.1093/acrefore/9780190277734.013.628.
Seesemann, R. and B. F. Soares (2009), '"Being as Good Muslims as Frenchmen:" On Islam and Colonial Modernity in West Africa', *Journal of Religion in Africa*, 39 (1): 91–120.
Soares, B. F. (2014), 'The Historiography of Islam in the West Africa: An Anthropologist's View', *The Journal of African History*, 55 (1): 1–10.
Stewart, C. C. (1973), *Islam and Social Order in Mauritania: A Case Study from the Nineteenth Century*. Oxford: Clarendon Press.

12

Islam, blasphemy and realpolitik in Mauritania: The Mkhaitir affair

Francisco Freire
NOVA FCSH

Introduction: The Mkhaitir affair

In December 2013, Mohamed Ould Cheikh Ould Mkhaitir, a 30-year-old Mauritanian national, posted comments (in Arabic) on the social media platform Facebook that led to a public outcry in his home country. In the post, he exposed what he considered to be unfair uses of Islam, indicating examples ranging from the times of the Prophet Muḥammad to contemporary Mauritania. Days after the posting, large crowds took to the streets calling for his immediate punishment. In the city of Nouadhibou, where Mohamed Mkhaitir resided with his family (including his father, a high-ranking, state-appointed public administrator/*ḥākim*), the crowds were particularly large. In what seems like a direct response to this public pressure, he was promptly imprisoned on 2 January 2014.

Almost a year later, on 23 December 2014, Nouadhibou's Regional Court found Mkhaitir guilty of apostasy and sentenced him to death under Article 306, paragraph 293 of Mauritania's Penal Code. The majority of the country's Islamic scholars considered capital punishment the appropriate measure and approved the court's decision (Abdel Wedoud 2014; Cervello 2015). Although Mkhaitir appealed the sentence, Nouadhibou's Court of Appeal upheld the initial ruling. This second ruling was also appealed, and in November 2017, after reopening the trial, the Supreme Court commuted the death sentence to two years in prison. This decision scrupulously followed what was then inscribed in Mauritania's Penal Code: accepting the repentance of someone who insults the Prophet Muḥammad – an act punishable by a maximum of two years in prison. On 29 July 2019, Mohamed Mkhaitir was freed and taken to neighbouring Senegal, from where he flew to France after spending more than five years in jail.

This chapter, with the title 'Islam, Blasphemy, and Realpolitik in Mauritania: The Mkhaitir Affair', was originally published in 2021 as an article in the academic journal *Africa Today* (68 (2): 57–79; Print ISSN: 0001-9887; https://muse.jhu.edu/issue/47101#info_wrap). I would like to thank the Indiana University Press for authorizing its republication.

The most controversial part of Mohamed Mkhaitir's online post stated that the Prophet Muḥammad had been unfair when he assented to the execution of the Banū Qurayẓa (a Jewish tribe from the Arabian Peninsula) upon their surrender in the so-called Battle of the Trench (Ar. *Ghazwat al-Khandaq*) in March 627. Mkhaitir used the fact that the Prophet had not applied the same sort of punitive action against his own Qurayshī relatives, who had already defied his authority on several occasions, as one of his main arguments. He thus claimed that the actions of the Prophet of Islam during this episode amounted to a form of nepotism.[1]

From this seventh-century reference, Mkhaitir moved on to contemporary Mauritania, affirming that a chosen corpus of Islamic scholarship had been used for segregationist purposes in the western regions of the Sahara. For him, Islam had often been put to unsound use, corrupting the noble principles on which it had been established. He argued that biased interpretations of Islamic texts had been established mostly by the *zwāya* ('religious') hereditary status groups, who for centuries have been considered the legitimate interpreters of Islam in the region (Norris 1969; Ould Cheikh 2017: 67–73; Stewart 1973). Mkhaitir unequivocally claimed that many of the *zwāya*'s scholarly works legitimized a stratified order that was particularly harsh on his 'oppressed brothers' the *m'allemīn* ('blacksmiths'), another of the hassanophone hereditary social categories and one of the most clearly stigmatized of these groups.

Various commentators have pointed out that Mkhaitir presented a simplistic and somewhat naïve analysis of Islamic history and the forms it takes in Saharan social landscapes, and some even appealed for the pardon and release of the young accountant, whose online argument, they claimed, was merely puerile, albeit highly provocative. The intervention by the pre-eminent Islamic scholar Muhammad al-Mukhtar al-Shinqiti was precisely along these lines. Drawing on the *Qur'ān* – where one finds evidence supporting freedom of religion (Rehman 2010: 5) – and the prophetic *sunna*, he provided examples of several cases of people renouncing Islam without facing subsequent punishment. In his insightful appraisal, al-Shinqiti defends religious affiliation as a choice given to each individual and advised the Mauritanian authorities to be merciful with Mkhaitir (al-Shinqiti 2014).[2]

Long before Mkhaitir's public intervention, other voices, notably associated with abolitionist movements, had already raised similar arguments criticizing the persistence of a stratified social model and its association with Islamic scholarship (McDougall 2010; Ould Ahmed Salem 2009).[3] It is possible that these movements played a role in Mkhaitir's case, and, ultimately, in the Mauritanian government's implementation of stricter anti-blasphemy legislation. This chapter argues that the social malaise of large parts of the population and the political pressures exerted through the actions of these various actors explains this most recent attempt by the Mauritanian government to stifle all forms of critical thought that drew a connection between traditional Islamic scholarship and status-based social inequality in the country.

Despite my extensive field research in the Islamic Republic of Mauritania, the government's decision to introduce substantial changes to the existing anti-blasphemy legislation (following a close reading of Maliki jurisprudence) was neither part of the discussions I followed nor (apparently) of significant interest to the more recent scholarly debates taking place in Mauritania's Islamic spheres. The incorporation of an amendment to the Mauritanian penal code regarding blasphemous practices thus came as a surprise, marking a stark contrast with the implementation of its previous version in 1983 (which made apostasy a criminal offence), preceded by a passionate public debate led by renowned Islamic scholars such as Mohamed Salem Ould Adoud and Hamdan Ould Tah.

This chapter explores why this legislation was so abruptly implemented in a country widely acknowledged as 'an inspiring example to neighbouring countries like Mali and Niger' (Bisa Williams, the US Deputy Assistant Secretary in the Bureau of African Affairs; cf. Freire 2019: 493). Was the implementation of this anti-blasphemy law intended to curb the movements that had more recently started to question traditional interpretations of Islam? Or was it encouraged purely by religious ideals and a sudden impulse to bring the country's penal code into full accordance with the Maliki jurisprudence preponderant in the country?

The reflections presented here draw on field research in Mauritania and on the analysis of a diverse corpus of documents emanating from existing scholarly literature and from various media outlets (newspapers, televised broadcasts and social media) that closely followed Mkhaitir's case. Although it focuses on the events that led to the enactment of stricter anti-blasphemy laws in Mauritania, this chapter does not aim to provide a comprehensive overview of Islamic legal readings on apostasy/blasphemy. It is centred on Mauritania's state policies, its complex relation to relevant Islamic spheres and the reconfigurations of the social design specific to the Hassaniyya-speaking populations of the western regions of the Sahara. While focused on a clearly identifiable case study, this chapter also contributes to the extended literature on Islamic law and Maliki jurisprudence in north and West Africa and Islamic governance more broadly.

Mauritanian Hassaniyya-speaking spheres and its smiths

Mauritania's multi-ethnic social landscape is composed of Hassaniyya speakers and three Black African communities: the Pulaar, the Soninké and the Wolof. All three are based on a hierarchical distinction between 'free' status groups and different tributary populations. In hassanophone spheres, this social design was consolidated in the second half of the seventeenth century, with a leadership role being given to 'warrior' (*ḥassān*) and 'religious' (*zwāya*) hereditary status groups following the conclusion of the Shurbubba War (by the mid-1670s; see Wuld As-Sa'd 1989; Bonte 1989; Curtin 1971; Norris 1969; Ould Cheikh 1991). In his online text, Mkhaitir centres solely on this context and its tributary social categories, signalling the unjust treatment given not only to the *m'allemīn* but also to the *ḥarāṭīn* (of slave descent) and the griots (Hassaniyya: *iggāwen*).

Research on Mauritania has investigated the reconfigurations of this stratified model, but it has seemingly ignored the actors at the lower levels of this structure, with the notable exception of the *ḥarāṭīn* (McDougall 2015; Ould Ahmed Salem 2009; Rossi 2009; Villasante-de Beauvais and Acloque 2000). Recent references to the *m'allemīn* are relatively rare (Cervello 2004; Fortier 2006; Seesemann 2004), contrary to what occurred in the second half of the twentieth century, when the case of the blacksmiths in Africa was extensively discussed (Bisson et al. 2000; McNaughton 1988; Rasmussen 1995). The reason for this shift of scholarly focus is beyond the scope of this chapter, but a suggestion regarding western Saharan social landscapes can be made: a preoccupation with religious traditions (largely associated with the *zwāya*) and (reportedly) Arab genealogical discourse and its immanent political machinations (largely associated with the *ḥassān*) have shifted interest away from other Saharan groups, notably those that have remained largely estranged from the 'noble' fields of politics and religion. The abovementioned focus on the *ḥarāṭīn* case could be regarded precisely within this framework as *ḥarāṭīn* activism played a key role in the reconfiguration of Mauritanian politics by openly questioning the role of Islamic scholarship in the preservation of a stratified social model, as promoted by its regional 'tutors', the *zwāya*. It is thus notable that the contemporary analysis of these very diverse social spheres has for the most part disregarded actors such as the griots, the *znāga* ('herders') and the *m'allemīn*. The analysis of Mohamed Mkhaitir's court case reiterates the presence of these figures in the Mauritanian political landscape and their incorporation – if far from exemplary – in a national project.

Blacksmith identity in Africa has often been associated with artisanal work (metal, jewellery, leather and woodworking) but is not limited to it. In the case of the Saharan Hassaniyya-speaking populations, these groups were intimately related to nomadism, having recently adapted to urban settings (similarly to the overwhelming majority of Mauritania's nomadic groups), where they continue to perform multiple tasks, mostly concomitant with their technical expertise (Cervello 2004: 133; for an example of the contemporary role of blacksmiths in urban Africa, see also Badi 2012; MacGaffey 2009). This apparently successful adaptation to urban functionalities has not curtailed a fundamental marker of social opprobrium directed toward the lower-status representatives of the hassanophone social pyramid: the strict endogamy practised by the *m'allemīn*. *M'allemīn* groups are also associated with an imprecise origin – which some have related to a remote Jewish presence in the Sahara (Prussin 2005), others claiming their singular familiarity with profane metaphysical powers (Richards 1981) – which disqualifies them from any attachment to the 'honourable' genealogical projects that continue to constitute a central element in the definition of identity. This genealogical obscurity may have facilitated the categorization of the *m'allemīn* as 'outsiders' in relation to a 'respectable' social milieu that continues to stigmatize these groups. With this noted, however, this chapter is concerned not with the social intricacies associated with the role of the smiths in Africa per se, but rather with Mohamed Mkhaitir's *m'allemīn* identity, with the transformations felt in hassanophone social spheres and the with growing prominence of these voices in public debate.

In 2008, the so-called M'allemīn Movement (*ḥirāk lam'allemīn*) took centre stage in Mauritania, calling for equality and for the public rehabilitation of the group's role in society. Like *ḥarāṭīn* activists, members of this movement referred to the manipulation of knowledge (both religious and historical) by the *zwāya*, who in their opinion were directly responsible for the perpetuation of the moral prejudice levelled against the *m'allemīn*. They expressed their revolt in televised broadcasts and through messages displayed in public. In direct response to this, President Ould Abdel Aziz (2009–2019) took action, installing three leading figures of the movement in significant roles in the administration (he appointed one ambassador, a new Minister of Rural Development and promoted a mid-ranked military serviceman to the position of General). These isolated actions are clearly insufficient to curb the stigma still attached to having smith ancestry, but they signal an initial success, as well as the state's acknowledgement of the pertinence of these claims. This first step taken by President Aziz must be kept in mind when interpreting his regime's response – a decade later – to Mohamed Mkhaitir (who clearly anchored his online post in statements by other actors, notably of *m'allemīn* status, who had voiced similar concerns).

An Islamic republic in the Sahara

Mauritania's political leadership did not question any of the courts' decisions, and then-President Mohamed Abdel Aziz publicly supported all of the judicial rulings related to Mkhaitir. In fact, despite the complex socio-juridical jigsaw at play, in which the streets (and the courts) faced significant pressure from some Mauritanian citizens/activists and from international players arduously campaigning for Mkhaitir's release (Amnesty International 2015; Pinto 2016), President Aziz capitalized politically on the demonstrations, demanding that Mkhaitir be punished. By then, the very nature of Mauritania – and particularly its official status as an Islamic Republic – seemed to be called into question. President Aziz took special care to emphasize that Mohamed Mkhaitir's punishment was not only a legal matter but was in fact demanded by the massive gatherings that took to the streets, calling for the execution of the 30-year-old: 'I've listened to the Mauritanians who protested against this blogger's writings, and they were the ones demanding that he be condemned to death' (Châtelot 2016).

The so-called al-Nuṣra Party (the 'Party of the Supporters [of the Prophet]'), presided over by the controversial Shaykh Rihda (currently under investigation for running a Ponzi scheme that led to the bankruptcy of hundreds of Mauritanian families), planned most of the large-scale public protests against Mkhaitir. According to al-Nuṣra, the international community's vehement demands for Mkhaitir's liberation amounted to 'foreign interference' aimed at imposing a Western-centric legal model on an Islamic republic. Such intrusions were also associated with an allegedly biased and Islamophobic understanding of Islamic jurisprudence as merely punitive and incompatible with such values as freedom of speech and human rights.[4]

The mobilization of protests in the streets could also be a sign of the potential high-level orchestration of the anti-Mkhaitir movement – which was most likely tacitly approved by the Mauritanian regime. Shaykh Rihda may have expected to restore his reputation through a public performance of religious zeal (hoping that some would forget his involvement in murky financial operations), while the state may have been interested in the adherence of the general public to this 'pro-Islam' stance, while capitalizing on a generalized 'antipathy' towards blacksmith status groups. At that point, President Abdel Aziz declared that the court sentences supporting Mkhaitir's death penalty embodied the Islamic essence of Mauritania.

Mauritania's 'Islamic Republic' label could in fact be seen as the ultimate target of many of the critiques voiced by Mohamed Mkhaitir (and others before him). The actors whom he accused of using Islam to maintain an unjust social stratification – the *zwāya*, hailing predominantly from the Trarza region of southwestern Mauritania – are widely accepted as the protagonists of the country's transition from colony to state. Moktar Ould Daddah, the country's first president (1960–1978), was himself a product of southwestern Mauritanian scholarly traditions (Ould Daddah 2012). Contrary to what happened further north, where colonial control was disputed well into the 1930s, political alliances with the French had pacified much of the southwestern Mauritanian region by the early twentieth century (Harrison 1988; Ould Mohamed Baba and Freire 2019: 8–9; Robinson 2001). This familiarity with colonial educational programmes and administrative procedures eased the way to political prominence for many of the region's elites during the country's founding period. Separating Islam from the particular sort of religious understandings developed by the zwāya (also known by the French as marabouts), some critical voices addressed this circumstance in a humorous tone, stating that the French acronym for the country's official name – RIM (République Islamique de Mauritanie) – should in fact read RMM, as in 'République Maraboutique de Mauritanie'. Mauritania's adoption of the Islamic Republic label can be attributed to different reasons, but the *zwāya*'s prominence in the country's transition to independence is incontestable. More cynical commentators might also point to the country's need to formally distance itself from neighbouring Morocco, Algeria, Mali and Senegal and from the secular paradigm (*laïcité*) associated with French colonization.[5]

The different uses – or instrumentalizations – of the Islamic Republic moniker led political scientist Zekeria Ould Ahmed Salem to define Mauritania as a 'pseudo-confessional' state, where Islam mainly served institutional protocol but was not considered a structural force in the definition of state policies (Ould Ahmed Salem 2013: 53–60; see also Tamburini 2019). This analysis, if understood as suggesting the independence of state practices from more complex societal processes (where Islam is clearly a significant factor), represents a limited approach to statehood. In fact, in Mauritania, the state has often adapted legislation and its overall policies in order to accommodate pressures coming from religious spheres.[6] The historical importance of Islam and Islamic culture in the greater western Sahara region, as well as their role during the colonial chapter and the transition to independence, raises questions about whether it was the state that made instrumental use of Islam or whether it was certain social actors, authorized by their knowledge of Islam, who in fact used the state.

These difficulties, associated with the state's Islamic character, extended to the country's legal system, where – until now – we could not find full adherence to the Maliki school of jurisprudence (*madhhab*), which guides Islamic legal interpretation in the region.[7] Mauritania inherited civil law from colonial times, but its Islamic Republic status gives prominence to Islamic law. Its application, however, must be translated into national law before being applied in the courts (cf. Articles 2 and 5 of the Mauritanian Constitution of 1991). Mauritania initially continued to apply French colonial law following independence, but in the early 1980s it introduced sharia-inspired civil and penal codes and, without repealing the pre-existing French model, established an Islamic court system (Kamali 2019: 321). Among other retributions, such as flogging and hand amputation, these courts had the power to impose capital punishment for specific offences. It is through this intricate relationship between Islamic jurisprudence and state law (particularly the penal code) that Mkhaitir's case became even more complex.

The legal debate

The influence of the eighth-century Islamic scholar Malik Ibn Anas over the western regions of the Sahara is signalled through the establishment of a canon composed of four main figures: Ibn Qāsim (d. 806), Ibn Abī Zayd al-Qayrawānī (d. 965), Khalīl ibn Isḥāq (d. 1374; by far the most important reference in western Saharan Malikism; cf. Ould Cheikh 2016: 61) and Ibn ʿĀṣim 'al-Gharnāṭī" (d. 1426; Ould al-Bara 2001: 118–22). This corpus, which largely inspired modern Mauritanian legal codes, does not allow blasphemers the chance to repent and imposes a mandatory death sentence for such offenders (on Maliki traditions in the western regions of the Sahara, see Ould al-Bara 2009; see also Hall and Stewart 2011: 109–74; Lydon 2009; Ould Bah 1981).[8]

It is precisely on this point that the main legal claims concerning Mkhaitir's case were made. On the one hand, a majority of the country's Islamic legal scholars reiterated the mandatory death penalty for offenders of the Prophet according to the Maliki school.[9] On the other, Mkhaitir's defence stated that this demand contradicted Article 306 of Mauritania's Penal Code, which acknowledges repentance – a formula that constitutes an 'integral part of Islamic penal philosophy' (Kamali 2019: 149) and that Mohamed Mkhaitir used in his pre-trial hearing – and limits the maximum sentence of imprisonment to two years:

> Tout musulman coupable du crime d'apostasie, soit par parole, soit par action de façon apparente ou évidente, sera invité à se repentir dans un délai de trois jours. / S'il ne se repent pas dans ce délai, il est condamné à mort en tant qu'apostat, et ses biens seront confisqués au profit du Trésor. S'il se repent avant l'exécution de cette sentence, le parquet saisira la Cour suprême, à l'effet de sa réhabilitation dans tous ses droits, sans préjudice d'une peine correctionnelle prévue au 1er paragraphe du présent article. / Toute personne coupable du crime d'apostasie (Zendagha) sera, à moins qu'elle ne se repente au préalable, punie de la peine de mort.
>
> (Mauritania's Penal Code, 1983, Article 306; original text in French)

The interpretation of the concepts of *ridda* and *zandaqa* (in Arabic; *zendagha* in Hassaniyya) varies significantly among different Islamic locations (Baker 2018; Rehman 2010; Vikør 2005: 296), resulting in frequently ambivalent and even contradictory uses (Wagner 2015: 530). Under certain interpretations, blasphemy implies a repudiation of faith, and in this way it is often understood as an implicit declaration of apostasy (O'Sullivan 2003: 205). This argument, well grounded in history, has been pushed to its limits by Frank Griffel, who views the assassination of Islam's third caliph as a paradoxical example of the intricacy of such debates, as some (notably among the Kharajites) thought that ʿUthmān's (d. 656) actions amounted to unbelief, thus making his execution lawful (Griffel 2001: 339; see also Wiederhold 1997: 57–8). Presently, an extended consensus affirms the ambiguities of the legal distinction between 'blasphemy' and 'apostasy' in Islam, confirming that 'blasphemy against God, the Prophet Muḥammad, and his Companions, when committed by a Muslim, was discussed by the legal scholars in the context of apostasy (ridda) and unbelief (kufr)' (Wiederhold 1997: 43–4; see also Kamali 2019: 142–7; Lewis 1953: 58–60; Powers 2002: 175).

In Mauritania – confirming the complex use of this lexicon – the concept of *ridda* is globally understood as an 'insult' to the Prophet ('heresy'), while the term used for apostasy is *zendagha*. Mohamed Mkhaitir's defence pointed out this distinction, stating that the Mauritanian courts filed the claim under an inaccurate category, erroneously condemning Mkhaitir as a *zendīghī* (in Hassaniyya; *zindīq* in Arabic). This was precisely the argument taken in consideration by the Supreme Court, which led to the reopening of Mkhaitir's case and to a final sentence of two years in jail.[10]

Despite acquiescing to the court's final decision, the state ensured that similar cases would not lead to the same outcome in the future. Through an amendment altering the provisions of Article 306, Mauritania's Penal Code now codifies the impossibility of repentance in cases of blasphemy:

> Chaque musulman, homme ou femme, qui se moque ou outrage Allah ou Son Messager (Mohammed) . . . ses anges, ses livres ou l'un de ses Prophètes est passible de la peine de mort, sans être appelé à se repentir. Il encourt la peine capitale même en cas de repentir.
>
> (Amendment to Mauritania's Penal Code, Article 306, with the title '*Attentats aux mœurs de l'islam: Hérésie, apostasie, athéisme, refus de prier, adultère*'; original text in French)

The main difference between the version under which Mkhaitir was sentenced and the new text is the inclusion of an amendment stating that offences against the Prophet are to be punished by death without the opportunity of repentance. The incorporation of this element might be understood as a political response to the public outcry that affirmed the need for a 'Maliki punishment' for Mkhaitir, despite the fact that it could possibly jeopardize the Mauritanian government's alignment with some of its more significant international partners. The harshening of the anti-blasphemy law is also likely to worry many of those who fought for Mkhaitir's freedom and likely did not anticipate the hardening of the country's penal code. This 'conservative' turn can still be interpreted as a response on the part of the state to the arguments developed by different activists and political actors pushing for a redefinition of the country's stratified social design (more recently associated with a partisan use of Islamic knowledge).[11]

While conducting field research in Nouakchott in 2018, I witnessed that a novel Islamic voice, based in the southern outskirts of the capital, was starting to be noticed. Even if not formally accepted by many as an Islamic scholar (Ar. *faqīh*), his work as a *ḥarāṭīn* community leader and educator was widely acknowledged. In the recent past, he had been known as 'IRA's *muftī*' (*jurisconsult*), before leaving the movement in 2013.[12] His words coincide with the arguments presented by Mohamed Mkhaitir regarding social stratification and the instrumentalization of Islamic knowledge. His statement, cited below, describes a large political spectrum currently associated with one fundamental element: the reshaping of the country's social landscape.

> The Quran and the Sunna propose a liberating path for each individual, whilst fiqh can differentiate between free and non-free men. The sacred text comes directly from God and cannot be questioned, but the interpretations that men make, those can be debated!
>
> I thought it was necessary to change the way fiqh was being implemented in Mauritania, especially in its treatment of slavery. One knows that fiqh is very often dependent on governments, on political authority, and on local traditions … I have intervened next to people who have had slaves, trying to change their minds and to develop a fair view of society.
>
> There was an anti-slavery movement in Mauritania called Al-Hor. I thought, at one point, that they would be able to change things. I was part of that movement, but then I changed my position. I thought that through a more moderate approach we would achieve better results. After that I was with Biram's IRA. But after the burning of the books event I left the movement. But these sort of actions are not new in the Muslim world! Books, like Ibn Hazm's, have been burned many times … In fact, this has been done since the time of the Almoravids!
>
> Actually, the state promoted a very discriminatory narrative against one man—Biram—not showing any interest for the profound roots behind this movement. They insisted that we were part of an extremist organization simply in order to limit the reach of our ideas.
>
> I believe that Islam in Mauritania, both now and in the past, has been instrumentalized. We really wanted to alter this sort of behavior … associated with a particular group. And Islam in Mauritania cannot be understood as the privilege of a particular social group.
>
> (Vall 2018)

Although this clarifies the local context, it is also important to consider the international repercussions of Mkhaitir's case. Mauritania's new legal amendment introducing the death penalty for blasphemy without the possibility of repentance does not make the country exceptional with regard to this sort of legislation.[13] Besides Mauritania, twelve other countries have written the death penalty for blasphemy or apostasy into the law: Afghanistan, Brunei, Iran, Malaysia, Maldives, Nigeria, Pakistan, Qatar, Saudi Arabia, Somalia, the United Arab Emirates and Yemen (Sudan revoked the death penalty for apostasy in July 2020). A balanced position between the Mauritanian state's right to self-determination, the country's status as an Islamic Republic and its future engagements with key international partners seems hard to reach at this stage, especially in what concerns such sensitive issues as human rights protection. The implementation of a new anti-blasphemy law may in fact jeopardize the state's relations with many of its international partners, as the amendment to Article 306 blatantly undermines the European Union's aspirations to prohibit capital punishment globally (to take just one example).

The EU, in agreement with the European Convention on Human Rights, has consistently opposed the death penalty worldwide, considering it inhumane, degrading and unnecessary – an effort that would seem to be at odds with the 'simplified approach' to capital punishment stemming from the new amendment to the Mauritanian Penal Code. In addition, the wider issue of human rights may also be at stake. One of the stated objectives of the Cotonou Agreement, which has served as the legal base for the EU's relations with Mauritania since 2000, is to foster the protection and development of human rights among its signatories. Given the latest political and legislative developments in Mauritania, it could be argued that the money spent by the EU on democratization and the support of human rights in Mauritania is not achieving its objective. Moreover, the very definition of human rights can also be put under scrutiny; the Mauritanian National Commission on Human Rights, for example, was quick to express outrage over Mohamed Mkhaitir's writings (Abdel Wedoud 2014). Voicing its indignation, the institute declared that Mkhaitir's Facebook post constituted an 'offence to the beliefs of Mauritanian people and their collective rights' and fully supported his condemnation to death. Of course, the EU is not oblivious to the existence of human rights abuses in Mauritania (Bøås 2017), and there were already calls for the EU to follow the example of the US and limit trade benefits with Mauritania in relation to another blatant abuse of human rights – slavery (Lazareva 2019).

Will political and economic relations between Mauritania and the EU be strained as a result? In withdrawing its aid on human rights grounds, the EU may exacerbate inequality in the country, leading to more damage in the long run. As the working document of the EU 2020 budget made clear, Mauritania will continue to receive significant financial contributions aimed, in part, at 'addressing human rights abuses and enforcing rule of law'.[14] The EU's stance in this case – with no formal opposition expressed to the removal of the repentance clause from Mauritania's Penal Code – could be interpreted in light of the necessity of safeguarding an important strategic partnership: Mauritania is one of the EU's privileged interlocutors on security and development in the Sahel. It should also be noted that, after being freed, Mohamed Mkhaitir found refuge in a European Union country (France).

A televised repentance

Before leaving his post, President Abdel Aziz finally resolved the case of Mohamed Mkhaitir: he was released from prison and taken abroad, to neighbouring Senegal, just one day before the new president of Mauritania – Mohamed Ghazouani – took office. The events leading to this outcome demonstrate the difficult balance that President Abdel Aziz has tried to achieve throughout this process. More than a merely legal battle, Mkhaitir's case was acknowledged in Mauritania as a crucial moment in the country's sovereignty and the significance of its Islamic credentials. Throughout this process, President Aziz had to reconcile the Islamic character of Mauritania with a penal code that contradicted traditional Maliki legal reasoning. At the same time, he had to respond to demands for Mkhaitir's release that were loudly voiced by some of the country's more relevant international partners. The term realpolitik would seem to capture president Aziz's actions perfectly during this period, as he astutely tried to win political gains from a pious local population, from the Persian Gulf Arab monarchies and indeed from Western countries (with which Mauritania has significant economic relationships).

Feeling the need to engage with an Islamically framed performance, President Aziz promoted a meeting with a selected group of Muslim scholars in order to give the case closure. This group is an integral part of the state apparatus, with members serving in state-run Islamic cultural agencies and educational institutions. They are not best described as the leading figures of Islam in Mauritania, but rather as a group of state-dependent religious officials. This professional group, generally identified with the term *qāḍī* (judge), plays a role that is inscribed in the foundations of Islamic law, which establishes a distinction between non-state muftis and state-based *qāḍīs* and *faqīh*s (Nelson 2017: 235).[15]

Before being set free, Mkhaitir was 'asked' to declare his repentance. This act was staged in Nouakchott's Ibn Abbas mosque (the venue for official celebrations), in the presence of the forty Islamic scholars convened by President Aziz. Mkhaitir's repentance, which barely received any coverage by international media outlets, was broadcast on Mauritanian state TV and extensively debated locally (on media uses and religion in Africa, see Hackett and Soares 2015). Ahmedou Ould Mrabit, the imam of Nouakchott's largest mosque (commonly known as the 'Saudi Mosque') and the appointed speaker for this group, issued a statement following Mkhaitir's televised declaration in which he noted that the Maliki tradition did, in fact, point to Mkhaitir's death sentence. But, he continued, *qaḍāʾ* ('justice', a reference here to Mauritania's Penal Code) provided another sentence compliant with the current laws of the state, and it is these that must be followed.[16]

After stating their personal allegiance to Maliki legal terms, these scholars also acknowledged the state's commitment to a binding penal code, which ultimately led the group to adopt what they called a strictly 'juridical decision' (Ar. *qarār qaḍāʾī*). Their declaration does not conform to normative Islamic law, which would normally lead to a *fatwā* ('legal opinion') being issued or a *naṣīḥa* ('advice') concerning the case. Their decision confirms the plurality of legal formulas available to scholars of Islam under state authority (Grote and Röder 2012; Jackson 1996), ultimately contradicting opinions that have asserted the (moral) incompatibility of Islamic governance and modern statehood (Hallaq 2014). It also testifies to the authority of a state that is now capable of implementing significant legal changes without the need to consult the country's more respected Islamic actors. This particular declaration, as well as the amendment to the penal code, was made at a bureaucratic level, without public debate or the significant intervention of relevant Islamic scholars. This 'administrative' intervention points to highly significant transformations to the country's institutions, confirming the state's capacity and autonomy in addressing Islamic matters.

The group of forty Islamic scholars recognized the existence of significant differences in the punishments for apostates – even though Mkhaitir always denied been one – set out by the main schools of Islamic jurisprudence, and with the decisions of the Mauritanian courts in mind, they declared that the final decision should be made by the person in charge of the government of the local Muslim community (the *walīy al-amr*). It has been noted that the passionate debate on blasphemy that constituted a pivotal point of discussion among Islamic scholars in the fourteenth century established the incorporation of theological concepts into legal discourse, as applied, up to the present, in particular Islamic settings (Wiederhold 1997: 70). In this sense, the decision taken by the group of forty scholars over the Mkhaitir case is pursuant to the regional/North African tradition of *fiqh*, confirming the judge's central role in the treatment of contemporaneous social problems not covered by the Qur'ān (Ould al-Bara 2001: 111–12), through what has also been described as a 'constructivist' approach (Warscheid 2018: 361).

Invited to make a final decision, President Aziz opted to abide by the Supreme Court's ruling, and Mohamed Mkhaitir was finally freed from prison.

Conclusion

Mohamed Mkhaitir's trial connects social critique, Islam and the emergence of 'non-authorized' voices in Mauritanian public spheres. The actors involved in this case are not associated with the centres of Islamic thought acknowledged in the region: traditional Islamic schools (*maḥẓara*) and Sufi orders. They are distinct from the religious elite which has defined the region's cultural history and remain outsiders to the political class that has led the country since independence. The agenda they recommend represents an innovative approach to the state and Islam as both a political and a culturalized expression, where social inequalities are explicitly addressed. These voices are now being heard in public spheres (both physical and virtual), where they have managed to garner the attention of more diverse, and indeed global, audiences.

Processes of this type do not constitute a novelty in the Muslim world, where they have been signalled and thoroughly addressed (Eickelman and Piscatori 1996: 122). In Mauritania, the incorporation of new protagonists in the political and the religious sphere has faced resistance from a pervasive opponent: the hierarchized social order associated with the country's Hassaniyya-speaking populations. The popular backlash in response to Mkhaitir's Facebook post seems to confirm the stigma that still attaches to *m'allemīn* populations and their alleged unpreparedness to address intricate Islamic questions.

The removal of the chance to repent from Mauritania's Penal Code was made at a bureaucratic level, without public debate and without the noticeable involvement of significant Islamic scholars. This merely technical intervention seems to have been introduced almost surreptitiously, although it represents a highly relevant transformation. Similar legislative codifications have been signalled as a technique used by states to limit the interpretative freedom of Islamic authorities (usually legitimized by tradition, and, in the Mauritanian case, mostly through genealogical ascendance) or as an instrument for silencing dissent (Griffel 2001: 340; Hallaq 2004: 255). In this sense, the amendment introduced into Mauritania's Penal Code may ultimately confirm the downfall of traditional religious authority in the country and the consolidation of power in the hands of the state. Paradoxically, the flexibility of

Maliki law (Lydon 2009: 293) – at times accepting almost arbitrary interpretations (al-Alwani 2011: 102; Rehman 2010: 5) – which hindered the definition of a standard legal view on blasphemy/apostasy, allowed political agendas to operate almost freely in relation to this sensitive topic.

After his arrival in France, where he was given refugee status, Mohamed Mkhaitir gave interviews in which he declared he had been treated unjustly because of the stratified social order in Mauritania. The fact that his family was part of the high-level political apparatus of the state notwithstanding, he claimed that others had made similar or even more damning critiques of Islamic culture in Mauritania without suffering any consequences. He stated that his father 'was one of the few elected m'allemīn and *ḥarāṭīn* to whom the state gave a good job, in order to give an appearance of openness to (Mauritanian) society' (Verdier 2019). He also stated that his trial had nothing to do with the application of Islamic justice: 'My prison conviction was racist. Some have acknowledged that, but too late … One day Mauritania will change, and then I will come back' (Verdier 2019).

Notes

1 Mkhaitir's Facebook post was translated into French by the Mauritanian news blog Chez Vlane, available at https://chezvlane.blogspot.com/2014/01/voici-enfin-la-traduction-du-texte-du.html.

2 In court, Mkhaitir attested that he remained a Muslim and that the only intention behind his online post was to highlight a socially unfair use of religious knowledge in Mauritania, never considering himself an apostate.

3 The outspoken protagonist for this cause is Biram Ould Dah Ould Abeid (Freire 2019: 499–500), whose interventions have made him the most active figure promoting the rights of the Mauritanian *ḥarāṭīn* populations. A public intervention staged in April 2012 gave IRA and its leader widespread notoriety. After Friday prayers, the movement's leaders burned works of Islamic jurisprudential literature outside a mosque in a popular neighbourhood in Nouakchott's outskirts. They declared that these texts had been deliberately used for centuries to justify and maintain the Hassaniyya-speaking groups' attachment to a hierarchized social model. On the main formations acting over the slavery problem in Mauritania, see Malluche's chapter in this volume.

4 This idea can relate to changes noticeable in Nouakchott's public life. A spontaneous and acephalous movement, identifiable through the French label '*Café Tunisien*', describes the laic cultural atmosphere that can be found in Nouakchott more recently. This movement is associated with the debates maintained in coffee houses that have recently opened in the Mauritanian capital. These spaces, all of them with terraces open to the public, attract crowds and provide a contrast with Nouakchott's famous, and secluded, salons, where debates took place by invitation, always behind closed doors. On the alterations of Mauritanian public spheres, see Choplin 2009; McDougall 2015; Taine-Cheikh 2007; Wiley 2018. For modern Islamic topographies in Mauritania, see Frede 2014; Hill 2012; Ould Mohamed Baba Moustapha 2014.

5 The Islamic Republic label used by Mauritania (1960) is shared with Pakistan (1956), Iran (1979), and Afghanistan (1992). One might feel tempted to incorporate

Malaysia, Saudi Arabia and Sudan in the group of nations that, despite their non-adherence to this label, have experimented with the role of Islam in modern state definition.

6 President Aziz sponsored major changes in the country's Islamic institutions: he opened a 'Fatwa Office' (with the aim of coordinating a state-sponsored version of Islam), he got Radio Qur'ān to start broadcasting, he facilitated and financed the opening of the Mahadra TV channel, and he announced the future construction of the country's largest mosque in Nouakchott—an undertaking that has not yet begun. For a deeper analysis of his time in office, see Ould Mohamed Baba's chapter in this volume.

7 Conformity to Maliki jurisprudence is not prescribed in any official state document (such as the Constitution and the penal code), but it is acknowledged through the practices and historical background of the scholars defining the country's legal traditions.

8 An argument disputed by David Powers (2002: 175–6), who states that regarding apostasy, Maliki jurisprudence was not unanimous in proscribing the possibility of repentance.

9 Mandatory capital punishment is universal to all Sunni legal schools in the case of an insult to the Prophet: 'According to all Sunnite schools repentance prevents the punishment for apostasy (except for apostasy on the ground of insulting the Prophet Mohammed)' (Peters 2005: 27; see also Stern 1979; and Powers 2002: 176, limiting the reach of this statement).

10 Regarding Egyptian and Malaysian legal systems and their attempts to articulate blasphemy and heresy, see Bälz 1997; and Kamali 2019: 147–9.

11 Supporting this argument, more recently (June 2020), a 'crackdown on online dissent' led to the imprisonment, on blasphemy charges, of Eby Ould Zeidane, author of a social media post that 'condemned religious fanaticism in Mauritania and said his compatriots have deviated a lot from the path of Prophet Muhammad' (Media Foundation for West Africa 2020a). In an attempt to ban reporting on prickly social issues, Mauritanian authorities have summoned the representatives of several international news outlets, asking them to abstain from covering news that could 'disturb social peace' (Media Foundation for West Africa 2020b).

12 The political agenda developed by Biram's IRA is often perceived as non-religious, with a strict focus on social change. Incorporating a so-called 'mufti' in this movement clearly contradicts this, highlighting the comprehensive character of Islamic cultural expressions in Mauritania. For an inspiring example from Mali, on the limits of lineage-based scholarly status and the ulterior recognition of slave-status figures as Islamic scholars, see Berndt 2008: 297–336.

13 On a regional level, it is worth noting that the legislation incorporated into Mauritania's Penal Code (April 2018) opposes Morocco's January 2017 ruling on the same subject, which holds that apostasy in Islam is not punishable by death (Jabrane 2017). Mauritania's legal realignment might thus suggest a closer engagement with the Arab world, setting it further apart from its continental neighbours.

14 In 2018, the Sahel / Lake Chad region received €1,721 million in approved projects and other EU actions. These contributions came from the European Development Fund, the EU budget and some member states, with Germany and Italy contributing €175 million and €112 million, respectively (European Commission 2019).

15 These figures have often played the role of mere state operatives: 'Islamic legal literature is replete with references to the precarious and dubious role of qadis as agents of corrupted politics' (Hallaq 2004: 249).

16 Only one of the religious scholars who attended Mkhaitir's repentance contested its outcome. In a press release, this *'alim* reiterated the country's alignment with the Maliki consensus (*mashur*, epitomized in Khalil's *Mukhtasar*), through which, he argued, execution was the appropriate punishment for Mkhaitir. This scholar refused to elaborate when I visited him in Nouakchott (September 2019), and he requested that I contact the Ministry of Islamic Affairs, as he did not wish to comment further on what he considered to be a closed case.

References

Abdel Wedoud, I. (2014), 'Communiqué de la CNDH sur les Propos Blasphématoires Tenus à l'Encontre du Prophète', *CRIDEM*, 7 January. http://www.cridem.org/C_Info.php?article=651667%23.

Agrama, H. A. (2010), 'Secularism, Sovereignty, Indeterminacy: Is Egypt a Secular or a Religious State?', *Comparative Studies in Society and History*, 52 (3): 495–523.

al-Alwani, T. J. (2011), *Apostasy in Islam: A Historical and Scriptural Analysis*, Washington: The International Institute of Islamic Thought.

al-Shinqiti, M. O. al-M. (2014), 'Attacking the Sanctity of Prophethood: Between Winning Their Hearts and Minds and Capital Punishment', *Anhar*, 7 January. http://anahar.info/node/3392.

Amnesty International (2015), *Joint Public Statement: Mauritania Must Immediately Release Mohamed Mkhaïtir, Blogger Sentenced to Death for Apostasy*. https://www.amnesty.org/en/documents/afr38/0002/2015/en/.

Badi, D. (2012), 'Cultural Interaction and the Artisanal Economy in Tamanrasset', in J. McDougall and J. Scheele (eds), *Saharan Frontiers: Space and Mobility in Northwest Africa*, 200–12. Bloomington, IN: Indiana University Press.

Baker, M. (2018), 'Capital Punishment for Apostasy in Islam', *Arab Law Quarterly* 32 (4): 439–61.

Bamyeh, M. A. (2019), *Lifeworlds of Islam: The Pragmatics of a Religion*. New York, NY: Oxford University Press.

Berndt, J. R. (2008), 'Closer than Your Jugular Vein: Muslim Intellectuals in a Malian Village, 1900 to the 1960s', PhD diss., Northwestern University.

Bisson, M. S., T. Childs, P. de Barros and A. Holl (2000), *Ancient African Metallurgy: The Sociocultural Context*. Boston, MA: Altamira Press.

Bøås, M. (2017), *State of Play of EU-Mauritania Relations*. Luxembourg: European Parliament Publications Office. https://op.europa.eu/en/publication-detail/-/publication/3b6e414e-ffdf-11e6-8a35-01aa75ed71a1/language-en/format-PDF/source-111380578.

Bonte, P. (1989), 'L''Ordre' de la Tradition. Evolution des Hiérarchies Statutaires dans la Société Maure Contemporaine', *Revue des Mondes Musulmans et de la Méditerranée*, 54: 118–29.

Cervello, M. V. (2004), '"They Work to Eat and They Eat to Work": The M'allemiîn Craftsmen, Classification, and Discourse among the Bidân Nobility of Mauritania', in by J C. Berland and A. Rao (eds), *Customary Strangers: New Perspectives on Peripatetic Peoples in the Middle East, Africa and Asia*, 123–54. Westport, CT: Praeger.

Cervello, M. V. (2015), 'La Condamnation à Mort de Mohamed Cheikh Ould Mkhaitir: Un Cas de Dysfonctionnement de la Justice Mauritanienne', *Academia*. https://www.academia.edu/10577145/La_condamnation_%C3%A0_mort_de_Mohamed_Cheikh_ould_Mkhaitir_un_cas_de_dysfonctionnement_de_la_justice_mauritanienne.

Châtelot, C. (2016), 'Il n'y a Pas d'Effervescence Islamiste en Mauritanie', *Le Monde*, 9 December 9. http://www.lemonde.fr/afrique/article/2016/12/09/il-n-y-a-pas-d-effervescence-islamiste-en-mauritanie_5046599_3212.html?xtmc=abdel_aziz%26xtcr=1.

Choplin, A. (2009), *Nouakchott au Carrefour de la Mauritanie et du Monde*. Paris: Karthala.

Corten, A. (2014), 'EU-Mauritania Fisheries Partnership in Need of More Transparency', *Marine Policy*, 49: 1–11.

Curtin, P. (1971) 'Jihad in West Africa: Early Phases and Interrelations in Mauritania and Senegal', *The Journal of African History*, 12 (1): 11–24.

Eickelman, D. F. and J. Piscatori (1996), *Muslim Politics*. Princeton, NJ: Princeton University Press.

European Commission (2019), *Draft General Budget of the European Union for The Financial Year 2020*. Bruxelles: European Union. https://ec.europa.eu/info/sites/info/files/about_the_european_commission/eu_budget/draft-budget-2020-wd-11-web-1.4_coverfull.pdf.

Evrard, C. and E. Pettigrew (2019), 'Du Baptême du Nouvel Aéroport de Nouakchott à la Réforme Constitutionnelle (fin 2015–2018). Politiques de l'Histoire en Mauritanie', *L'Année du Maghreb*, 21: 295–319.

Fortier, C. (2006), 'Intelligence pratique du berger et art magique du forgeron dans la société maure de Mauritanie', *Cahiers d'Anthropologie Sociale*, 1 (1): 55–65.

Frede, B. (2014), 'Following in the Steps of ʿĀʾisha: Ḥassāniyya-Speaking Tijānī Women as Spiritual Guides (*Muqaddamāt*) and Teaching Islamic Scholars (*Limrābuṭāt*) in Mauritania', *Islamic Africa*, 5 (2): 225–73.

Frede, B. (2021) 'In an Era of Terror Threats. Negotiating the Governance of a (Trans) Local Islamic Heritage in the Islamic Republic of Mauritania', in J. E. Dağyeli, C. Ghrawi and U. Freitag (eds), *Claiming and Making Muslim Worlds*, 131–57. Berlin: De Gruyter.

Freire, F. (2019), 'Weapons of the Weak, and of the Strong: Mauritanian Foreign Policy and the International Dimensions of Social Activism', *The Journal of North African Studies*, 24 (3): 490–505.

Griffel, F. (2001), 'Toleration and Exclusion: Al-Shāfiʿī and al-Ghazālī on the Treatment of Apostates', *Bulletin of the School of Oriental and African Studies*, 64 (3): 339–54.

Grote, R. and T. J. Röder, eds (2012), *Constitutionalism in Islamic Countries: Between Upheaval and Continuity*. Oxford: Oxford University Press.

Hackett, R. I. J. and B. F. Soares, eds (2015), *New Media and Religious Transformations in Africa*. Bloomington, IN: Indiana University Press.

Hall, B. S. and C. C. Stewart (2011), 'The Historic "Core Curriculum" and the Book Market in Islamic West Africa', G. Krätli and G. Lydon (eds), *The Trans-Saharan Book Trade: Manuscript Culture, Arabic Literacy and Intellectual History in Muslim Africa*, 109–74. Leiden: Brill.

Hallaq, W. B. (2004), 'Juristic Authority vs. State Power: The Legal Crises of Modern Islam', *Journal of Law and Religion*, 19 (2): 243–58.

Hallaq, W. B. (2014), *The Impossible State: Islam, Politics, and Modernity's Moral Predicament*. New York, NY: Columbia University Press.

Harrison, C. (1988), *France and Islam in West Africa, 1860–1960*. Cambridge: Cambridge University Press.

Hill, J. (2012), 'The Cosmopolitan Sahara: Building a Global Islamic Village in Mauritania', *City & Society*, 24 (1): 62–83.

Ibn Kathir (1998–2006), *The Life of the Prophet Muhammad*. 4 vols. Leicester: Garnet Publishing Ltd.

Jabrane, E. (2017), 'Morocco's High Religious Committee Says Apostates Should Not Be Killed', *Morocco World News*, 6 February. https://www.moroccoworldnews.com/2017/02/207505/moroccos-high-religious-committee-says-apostates-should-not-be-killed/.

Jackson, S. A. (1996), *Islamic Law and the State: The Constitutional Jurisprudence of Shihāb al-Dīn al-Qarāfī*. Leiden: Brill.

Kamali, M. H. (2019), *Crime and Punishment in Islamic Law: A Fresh Interpretation*. New York, NY: Oxford University Press.

Katsarova, I. (2013), *EU-Mauritania Fisheries Agreements: Library Briefing*. Bruxelles: EP Library. https://www.europarl.europa.eu/RegData/bibliotheque/briefing/2013/130562/LDM_BRI(2013)130562_REV2_EN.pdf.

Lau, M. (2000), 'Islam and the Constitutional Development in Pakistan', in I. Edge (ed.), *Comparative Law in a Global Perspective*, 293–323. Leiden: Brill - Martinus Nijhoff.

Lazareva, I. (2019), 'Europe Must Cut Ties with Mauritania, Anti-Slavery Politician Says', *Reuters*, 9 January. https://www.reuters.com/article/us-mauritania-slavery-europe-idUSKCN1P316M.

Lewis, B. (1953), 'Some Observations on the Significance of Heresy in the History of Islam', *Studia Islamica*, 1: 43–63.

Lydon, G. (2009), *On Trans-Saharan Trails: Islamic Law, Trade Networks, and Cross-cultural Exchange in Nineteenth-century Western Africa*. Cambridge: Cambridge University Press.

MacGaffey, W. (2009), 'The Blacksmiths of Tamale: The Dynamics of Space and Time in a Ghanaian Industry', *Africa*, 79 (2): 169–85.

Mandani, M. (1996), *Citizen and Subject: Contemporary Africa and the Legacy of Late Colonialism*. Princeton, NJ: Princeton University Press.

Media Foundation for West Africa (2020a), 'Mauritania Passes Law on False Publication Amidst Crackdown on Online Dissent'. https://www.mfwa.org/country-highlights/mauritania-passeslawon-false-publication-amidst-crackdown-on-online-descent/.

Media Foundation for West Africa (2020b), 'Mauritanian Government Gags Foreign Media from Reporting on Slavery, Racial Discrimination'. https://www.mfwa.org/country-highlights/mauritanian-government-gags-foreign-media-from-reporting-on-slavery-racial-discrimination/.

McDougall, E. A. (2010), 'The Politics of Slavery in Mauritania: Rhetoric, Reality and Democratic Discourse', *The Maghreb Review*, 35 (3): 259–86.

McDougall, E. A. (2015), 'Hidden in Plain Sight: Haratine in Nouakchott's "Niche-Settlements"', *International Journal of African Historical Studies*, 48 (2): 251–79.

McNaughton, P. (1988), *The Mande Blacksmiths: Knowledge, Power, and Art in West Africa*. Bloomington, IN: Indiana University Press.

Nelson, M. J. (2017), 'Islamic Law in an Islamic Republic. What Role for Parliament?', in A. Bâli and H. Lerner (eds), *Constitution Writing, Religion and Democracy*, 235–64. Cambridge: Cambridge University Press.

Norris, H. T. (1969), 'Znāga Islam during the Seventeenth and Eighteenth Centuries', *Bulletin of the School of Oriental and African Studies*, 32 (3): 496–526.

O'Sullivan, D. P. (2003), 'Punishing apostasy: The case of Islam and Shari'a Law Re-considered', PhD diss., Durham University.

Ould Ahmed Salem, Z. (2009) 'Bare-Foot Activists: Transformations in the Haratine Movement in Mauritania', in S. Ellis and I. van Kessel (eds), *Movers and Shakers: Social Movements in Africa*, 156–77. Leiden: Brill.

Ould Ahmed Salem, Z. (2013), *Prêcher dans le Désert: Islam Politique et Changement Social en Mauritanie*. Paris: Karthala.

Ould Al-bara, Y. (2001), 'Fiqh, société et pouvoir: Étude des soucis et préoccupations socio-politiques des théologiens-légistes maures (fuqahâ) à partir de leurs consultations juridiques (fatāwā) du XVIIème au XXème siècle', PhD diss., École des Hautes Études en Sciences Sociales.

Ould Al-bara Y. (2009), *Al-majmū 'a al-kubrā: al-shāmila li-*fatāwā *wa nawāzil wa aḥkām ahl gharb wa janūb gharb al Ṣaḥrā* ', 12 vols. Nouakchott: al-Sharīf Mawlay al-Ḥasan b. al-Mukhtār b. al-Ḥasan

Ould Bah, M. E. M. (1981), *La Littérature Juridique et l'Évolution du Malikisme en Mauritanie*. Tunis: Publications de l'Université de Tunis.

Ould Cheikh, A. W. (1991), 'Herders, Traders and Clerics: The Impact of Trade, Religion and Warfare on the Evolution of Moorish Society', in J. Galaty and P. Bonte (eds), *Herders, Warriors and Traders: Pastoralism in Africa*, 199–218. Boulder, CO: Westview.

Ould Cheikh, A. W. (2016), 'De Quoi le Sahara est-il le Nom? Images du Sahara et des Sahariens dans Kitâb al-Badiyya d'al-Šaykh Muhamd al-Mami', in R. Boubrik and A. Joumani (eds), *Le Sahara. Lieux d'Histoire et Espaces d'Échange*, 51–69. Rabat: Centre des Études Sahariennes.

Ould Cheikh, A. W. (2017), *La Société Maure: Éléments d'Anthropologie Historique*. Rabat: Centre des Études Sahariennes.

Ould Daddah, M. (2012), *La Mauritanie Contre Vents et Marées*. Paris: Karthala.

Ould Mohamed Baba Moustapha, E. (2014) 'Negotiating Islamic Revival: Public Religiosity in Nouakchott City', *Islamic Africa*, 5 (1): 45–82.

Ould Mohamed Baba, E. and F. Freire (2019), 'Looters vs. Traitors: The *Muqawama* ("Resistance") Narrative, and its Detractors, in Contemporary Mauritania', *African Studies Review*, 63 (2): 258–80.

Peters, R. (2005), *Crime and Punishment in Islamic Law: Theory and Practice from the Sixteenth to the Twenty-First Century*. Cambridge and New York, NY: Cambridge University Press.

Pinto, M. (2016), 'Urgent Appeal Regarding Mohammed Shaikh Ould Mohammed Ould Mkhaitir', *Freedom Now*, 28 November. https://www.freedom-now.org/cases/mohammed-shaikh-ould-mohammed-ould-mkhaitir/.

Powers, D. (2002), *Law, Society, and Culture in the Maghrib, 1300–1500*. Cambridge: Cambridge University Press.

Prussin, L. (2005), 'David in West Africa: "No More Forever"?', *Yale University Art Gallery Bulletin*, 88–109.

Pulcini, T. (2017), 'Cyber-Apostasy: Its Repercussions on Islam and the Interfaith Relations', *Journal of Contemporary Religion*, 32 (2): 189–203.

Rasmussen, S. E. (2017), 'Pakistan: Man Sentenced to Death for Blasphemy on Facebook', *The Guardian*, 11 June. https://www.theguardian.com/world/2017/jun/11/pakistan-man-sentenced-to-death-for-blasphemy-on-facebook.

Rasmussen, S. J. (1995), 'Art as Process and Product: Patronage and the Problem of Change in Tuareg Blacksmith/Artisan Roles', *Africa: Journal of the International African Institute*, 65 (4): 592–610.

Rehman, J. (2010), 'Freedom of Expression, Apostasy, and Blasphemy within Islam: *Sharia*, Criminal Justice Systems, and Modern Islamic State Practices', *Criminal Justice Matters*, 79 (1): 4–5.

Richards, D. (1981), 'The Nyama of the Blacksmith: The Metaphysical Significance of Metallurgy in Africa', *Journal of Black Studies*, 12 (2): 218–38.

Robinson, D. (2001), *Paths of Accommodation: Muslim Societies and French Colonial Authorities in Senegal and Mauritania, 1880–1920*. Athens, OH: Ohio University Press.
Rollier, P. (2019), 'We're All Blasphemers': The Life of Religious Offence in Pakistan', in P. Rollier, K. Frøystad and A. E. Ruud (eds), *Outrage: The Rise of Religious Offence in Contemporary South Asia*, 48–76. London: UCL Press.
Rossi, Benedetta, ed. (2009), *Reconfiguring Slavery: West African Trajectories*. Liverpool: Liverpool University Press.
Roy, O. (2008), *La Sainte Ignorance: Le Temps de la Religion Sans Culture*. Paris: Seuil.
Seesemann, R. (2004), 'The Shurafa and the "Blacksmith": The Role of the Idaw 'Ali of Mauritania in the Career of the Senegalese Shaykh Ibrahim Niasse (1900–1975)', in S. Reese (ed.), *The Transmission of Learning in Islamic Africa*, 72–98. Leiden: Brill.
Stensvold, A., ed. (2021), *Blasphemies Compared: Transgressive Speech in a Globalized World*. London: Routledge.
Stern, M. S. (1979), 'Al-Ghazzālī, Maimonides, and Ibn Paquda on Repentance: A Comparative Model', *Journal of the American Academy of Religion*, 47 (7): 589–607.
Stewart, C. C. (1973), *Islam and Social Order in Mauritania: A Case Study from the Nineteenth Century*. Oxford: Clarendon Press.
Taine-Cheikh, C. (2007), 'The (R)urbanization of Mauritania', in C. Miller, E. Al-Wer, D. Caubet and J. C. E. Watson (eds), *Arabic in the City: Issues in Dialect Contact and Language Variation*, 37–54. Abingdon/New York, NY: Routledge.
Tamburini, F. (2019), 'The "Islam of the Government": The Islamic High Councils in Algeria, Morocco, Mauritania and Tunisia', *Journal of Asian and African Studies*, 54 (7): 1–17.
Vall, M. (2018), Interview with author, 2 February. Nouakchott, Mauritania.
Vercelletto, F. (2019), 'Condamné à Mort pour Blasphème', *Ouest-France*, 12 December. https://podcasts.ouest-france.fr/broadcast/3713-Condamn%C3%A9-%C3%A0-mort-pour-blasph%C3%A8me.
Verdier, M. (2019), 'Dans les Prisons de Mauritanie, le Calvaire d'un Apostat', *La Croix*, 30 September. https://www.la-croix.com/JournalV2/prisons-Mauritanie-presque-six-ans-sans-bouger-2019-10-01-1101051087.
Vikør, K. S. (2005), *Between God and the Sultan: A History of Islamic Law*. London: C. Hurst & Co.
Villasante-De Beauvais, M. and B. Acloque, eds (2000), *Groupes Serviles au Sahara: Approche Comparative à Partir du Cas des Arabophones de Mauritanie*. Paris: CNRS.
Wagner, M. S. (2015), 'The Problem of Non-Muslims Who Insult the Prophet Muḥammad', *Journal of the American Oriental Society*, 135 (3): 529–40.
Warscheid, I. (2018), 'Le *Livre du Désert*: La Vision du Monde d'un Lettré Musulman de l'Ouest Saharien au XIXè siècle', *Annales. Histoire, Sciences Sociales*, 73 (2): 359–84.
Wiederhold, L. (1997), 'Blasphemy against the Prophet Muhammad and his Companions (*Sabb al-Rasūl, Sabb al-Sahābah*): The Introduction of the Topic into Shāfi'ī Legal Literature and Relevance for Legal Practice under Mamluk Rule', *Journal of Semitic Studies*, XLII (1): 39–70.
Wiley, K. A. (2018), *Work, Social Status, and Gender in Post-Slavery Mauritania*. Bloomington, IN: Indiana University Press.
Wuld As-Sa'd, M. al-M. (1989), 'Émirats et Espace Émiral Maure: Le Cas du Trârza aux XVIIIe–XIX Siècles', *Revue des Mondes Musulmans et de la Méditerranée*, 54: 53–82.

Postscript

Reflections on research ethics in complex contexts: Navigating politics, pragmatics and positionality

Leonardo Villalón
University of Florida
and Irina Branco da Silva
NOVA FCSH

The social, political and ecological spaces on which the studies in this book focus are complex and constantly shifting, sometimes slowly and barely perceptibly, like sand dunes in the desert. In his introduction to this volume Francisco Freire suggests that carrying out research in the region is like attempting to see clearly through the haze produced by the fine sands carried by *assāvi* breezes of the Sahara. Maintaining a clear vision of the core ethical requirements of social research – to safeguard the rights and well-being of the research participants in the field, and to represent them accurately and fairly – is no less challenging a proposition. The difficulties are compounded in a project such as this, in which the levels of analysis, the objects of study and especially the relationship of the researchers to the subjects of study, are so widely varied.

The Capsahara project had the ambitious goal of critically (re-)assessing the sociopolitical and cultural dynamics of the populations scattered across the vast western expanses of the Sahara. The project is built on the logic of the historical and social interconnectedness of this region, yet in the past century it has also been geopolitically subdivided and socially transformed in many ways by factors both internal and external. Making sense of this complexity requires by definition a plurality of perspectives, skills and disciplinary frameworks, and the brilliance of European Research Council funding for large projects of this sort is in making that possible. In the case of the Capsahara project, this Herculean task was undertaken by assembling an international team of researchers and academics hailing from Europe, West Africa and the United States. By design, the cultural, sociopolitical and academic backgrounds and worldviews of the team members varied widely.

The ethical considerations involving such a diverse team of researchers were twofold: 1) the external, related to adhering to established practices and procedures intended to safeguard the moral obligation of protecting participants in the field; and

2) the internal – concerning the management of potentially competing subjective interpretations of the research objectives by individual researchers themselves, while respecting their own moral integrity and academic freedom. Both are complex and complicated issues, filled with ambiguities and uncertainties that require attempting to specify both a clear set of ethical principles, and heuristics for their implementation.

The external expectations set out by the funding institution, in this particular case the European Research Council, were clear and straightforward: the researchers should follow the extensive and nuanced guidance provided in a document entitled 'Research Ethics in Ethnography/Anthropology' issued by the European Commission Directorate General on Research and Innovation (Iphofen 2021),[1] as well as those of the 'Global Code of Conduct for Research in Resource-Poor Settings' developed by the TRUST consortium on 'equitable research partnerships' (TRUST 2018). Both of these documents are rich and thoughtful considerations of a wide variety of issues, and each was developed with the aim of creating a more equitable global research environment. The specific procedures attempting to ensure their implementation were detailed in the project's Grant Agreement. The provisions for continuous monitoring, facilitated by the competence and accessibility of the ERCEA officers in Brussels, fully met the formal requirements: risk assessments detailing potential harms and contingency plans for each field trip were carried out, and periodic ethics reports delivered as scheduled in the course of the project.

Such formal processes for safeguarding ethical research, now well-entrenched and institutionalized as part of the research approval process in Western academic settings, provide important guidelines that are both useful and constraining. These guidelines, however, offer only frameworks for addressing the ethical and related conundrums of fieldwork, which inevitably intertwine on the ground with pragmatic, situational and political considerations that are not always foreseeable. As the ERC Research Ethics document noted above stresses, 'ethical decision making is not a static, one-off exercise. Only the field researcher truly confronts the unanticipated aspects of research as it occurs spontaneously while the project is ongoing' (Iphofen 2021: 3). And as Glasius et al. have noted about the inevitable 'dilemmas and trade-offs' of fieldwork: 'There are no easy fixes … for the tension between transparency and responsibility towards respondents' (2021: 3).

The institutionalization of ethics in ethnographic research

The rise in the formalization of ethical prescriptions has itself become an important topic of debate in anthropological research, and there is a widely shared sentiment that since the discipline was always based on deep interpersonal connection between researcher and interlocutor – a connection without which the very production of knowledge in anthropology is barely possible – any attempt to 'institutionalize' ethics can have unintended consequences. Indeed, some go so far as to interpret this formalization as a manifestation of 'a bureaucratic controlling gaze' emerging out of 'pressures from an audit culture and archaic methods with less trust in individual judgment' (Okely 2020: 25, 47). While not all would share such interpretations, it nonetheless remains indubitable that the concept of 'trust' is deeply entrenched in the ethnographic method. As eloquently expressed by Pels et al., in social sciences in general and in anthropology in particular '... methods and ethics are mutually supportive, congruent and sometimes even identical. They rest on the same epistemological foundation of a process of mutual learning that builds social relationships on varying degrees of trust' (2018: 394).

If we consider the evolution of research ethics governance in recent years, it appears prima facie that ethical considerations have become intrinsically enmeshed with legal ones. When the new personal data protection provisions of the European Union (Regulation (EU) 2016/679 or GDPR) became effective in May 2018, the large amount of personal and often sensitive data that researchers employing ethnographic methods collect and manage was confronted with new legal considerations. Indeed, the additional data management restrictions imposed by the regulations led some to provocatively ask such questions as 'Is anthropology still legal?' (Yuill 2018). Even though data collection and management for research purposes fall under several exemption clauses [e.g. recital 33, Art. 5(1)(b), Art. 89(1)], under GDPR provisions data subjects are given significant rights (Art. 12–23), and therefore the way personal data is handled may have serious consequences for data processors and controllers – the researchers themselves and their host institutions. As Dilger, Pels and Sleeboom-Faulkner have argued, in this context there is an incentive to design elaborate ethics protocols more with the purpose of shielding the researcher and the institutions from legal claims than for the protection of research participants per se (Dilger et al. 2019: 5). This incentive (including in ethnographic research), of course, raises some significant ethical issues in itself. This concern notwithstanding, and despite the increasing importance of legal considerations, these are not usually at the centre of the anthropologist's preoccupations when entering the field. Rather he or she is inevitably met with the need to make a plethora of moral choices from the very inception of research, and these choices are confronted with pragmatic, political and indeed personal and emotional considerations.

As a solution to the tendency for increased bureaucratization and formalization of ethics governance in research, some have proposed the idea of training designed to produce an 'ethical researcher' capable of 'ethical praxis' that is independent of formal guidance (Pels et al. 2018: 406). Though attractive in theory, the level to which ethical rules can be taught and internalized so that they 'come naturally' to an individual cannot be sufficiently anticipated, and, therefore, some inevitably will act 'ethically' through natural disposition (or 'virtue'), while others will need instead to be guided by a set of deontological prescriptions. In either case, and following an Aristotelian (and, in some senses, Wittgensteinian) logic, the continuous practice of making ethical decisions in the course of fieldwork might incrementally contribute to the development of the virtue of 'becoming' an ethical researcher, shifting the motivating logic of fieldwork choices over time.

In this complex terrain between bureaucratic constraints and individual judgements on moral praxis, the internal considerations of field research ethics require that each researcher improvise, negotiate and navigate in each interaction, and in each social setting. These considerations are inevitably more complicated, and we would suggest that they are also more important – and more interesting. Taken together, a central element of the richness of this volume lies in the multiplicity of perspectives and positions reflected in the diversity of the backgrounds and identities of the research team members. While an exhaustive examination of the impact of this diversity on the conduct of research is beyond our scope here, following a presentation of the specificities of the specific research context, we provide in this Postscript some reflections on the internal dimensions of the ethical imperative faced by the Capsahara project.

Context: State, society and Islam in the Saharan west

The specific ethical conundrums, trade-offs and dilemmas of the research for this project can only be understood in light of the specificities of the western Saharan context. The contributions to this work collectively describe the historical, social and political features that constitute the complexity and singularity of this geographic region. It may be useful, however, to provide a short (and certainly oversimplified) summary description of that context here, as laid out more fully in the substantive chapters.

The history of the people currently living in the western regions of the Sahara can be very briefly summarized as a 'series of encounters' between nomadic pastoralist Arab and Berber groups from the north and the west and the mostly sedentary agriculturist Black African populations in the south (see the chapter by Baba Ahmed and Horma). Before the infamous Berlin Conference of 1884 and the subsequent European 'scramble for Africa', borders or frontiers in this space were virtually non-existent, with different ethnic and socio-cultural communities or tribes living in a sort of 'punctuated equilibrium', finding their modes of cohabitation in these vast, mostly arid, and at times utterly inhospitable areas of the Sahara (see López Bargados' chapter in this volume).

With the arrival of colonial powers under the pretext of their putative 'civilizing missions', specifically France and Spain in this particular region of Africa, the area was politically divided into 'zones of influence' which took no account of the traditional uses of territory by the populations who had inhabited it for centuries. Through that process the territory of what is now Mauritania became a French colony within l'Afrique occidentale française (AOF) and what now forms the disputed territory of the Western Sahara (or Morocco's 'southern provinces' as the authorities of that kingdom insist that it be called)[2] became *el Sahara español*.

The subsequent fate of this latter territory is of particular centrality in shaping the current regional context. In the aftermath of a hasty and poorly organized decolonization process following the sudden withdrawal of Spain in 1976, it quickly fell prey to the expansionist agendas of the neighbouring countries: Morocco, Algeria and Mauritania. Following a series of political manoeuvres, Morocco managed to get the upper hand rather quickly after the Spanish withdrawal, and has since been de facto 'administering' a large portion of the former colonial territory, the length of its Atlantic coastline (see Bengochea Tirado's and López Bargados' chapters in this volume). Part of the Saharan population fled across the Algerian border, establishing refugee camps near the town of Tindouf, under Algerian government auspices. These camps continue to exist, governed by the Polisario as an administrative part of the Sahrawi Arab Democratic Republic, though its inhabitants still harbour hopes (see chapters by Boulay and by Gimeno Martín and Carboni in this volume) for a return to the land of their forefathers as citizens of an independent state. Decades of alternating engagement or neglect by the African Union, the UN, the European Union and the United States have not resolved – and in many ways have complicated – the situation, with no clear end in sight.[3]

The central point to bear in mind in this brief summary is that the territory that is the focus of the Capsahara project went from being an interdependent space of complex and linked socio-cultural processes to one currently divided by the borders of nation-states – Morocco, Mauritania and Algeria (notably those parts harbouring the Tindouf refugee camps) – but borders which remain sharply contested, both locally and internationally. The historically related populations who have long lived across the area still share a common language (the Hassaniyya dialect of Arabic), pervasive forms of social stratification and deeply rooted Islamic traditions, yet these characteristics are also in flux and being transformed by the decades of division and socialization into very different political discourses.

Within this complex and vast terrain, the Capsahara team members carried out intensive research on a very diverse set of thematic issues. Several of these focused on the diverging trajectories of ongoing nation-building project (see chapters by López Bargados; Bengochea Tirado; Boulay and Meidah; and Gimeno Martín and Carboni). Others explored transformations in the traditional socio-cultural hierarchical stratification of Saharan populations (Malluche; Freire), or on the important continuities and transformations of Islamic traditions and knowledge transfer processes (Ould Cheikh; Ould El-Bara; Baba Ahmed and Horma). Engaging with current trends, other chapters explored specific economic and political dynamics of central interest (Taleb Heidi; Ould Mohamed Baba Moustapha). In this diversity, the project and this book have grouped these studies together under three broad themes: ***State, Society and Islam***. Within each of these areas one can discern different forms of ethical considerations and dilemmas that need to be navigated, and different needs and requirements, where pragmatic considerations may conflict with abstract principles. We can offer some brief observations on each here.

State: As we have noted above, the organizing logic of the book is historical and socio-cultural, and the delimitation of the area of study is prescribed by the extent of the dominant Hassaniyya ethno-linguistic group. But in fact the divisions of this space by political boundaries complicate the conduct of fieldwork, and hence the ethical considerations the researcher must face, in at least two ways. On one hand, these diverging political contexts have come to shape new norms and expectations of individuals as citizens of these entities. These involve new identities, with dominant ideologies, codes of conduct and sensitivities to be navigated. These are starkly evident in the different codes of speech and behaviour that might be expected in public discourse by citizens of the 'popular, democratic and revolutionary' Saharawi republic, versus those of Mauritania whose code of public morality is subject to the expectations of an 'Islamic Republic'. In addition, Mauritania, whose state-building efforts can be enacted within physical boundaries that are no longer subject to debate, nevertheless remains centrally divided by contrasting visions of the 'Arab' or 'African' identity of the Mauritanian nation, and of who belongs. In sharp contrast, Saharawi identity exists on the premise of an established 'nation' (and an explicitly 'Arab' one, as Freire notes in his Introduction), while even the bare outlines of a state remain elusive.

A second way in which the state context impacts the ethical position of the researcher arises from the challenges of how to balance political considerations in representing the purpose of fieldwork for securing official authorization. In this respect, the most central difficulty that ultimately confronted the project was the impossibility of carrying our research in areas under Moroccan jurisdiction. The barriers of access to communities living in the territories under the control of Moroccan authorities were not explicit – research activities in the Moroccan 'southern provinces' or the disputed territory of the Western Sahara are not per se prohibited. Instead, the difficulties were more 'technical' in nature – most notably a simple inability to establish collaboration with local research centres, a necessary step in securing the local data protection clearance. While some established Rabat-based institutions were initially receptive and signed research protocols with the Capsahara project, these subsequently withdrew. The pleas for support or for intervention with Moroccan authorities that were sent to international organizations remained unanswered.

This situation presented ethical (and political) questions of the necessary extent for transparency in the presentation of the project, and the (non-)acceptability of tolerating (perhaps self-imposed) pre-emptive censorship on topics of study. It is not our intention to speculate on the reasons why the local research centres were unable to offer collaboration, but the fact remains: independent academic research on these particular environments was in the end out of reach even for this international research project funded by the European Commission's Research Council. Beyond interpreting this fact as a 'limitation' of the project, we propose, it must been seen as an important empirical observation about the reality of the western Saharan regions, and hence a research finding in itself.

Society: In fundamental ways the underlying premise of the protocols for ethical research conduct elaborated in Western research settings assume the universality of the ethical frameworks of democratic liberal modernity. While, no doubt, researchers based in such institutions (almost) universally share these values, the societies in which they work may not. This reality adds significant complexity to the ethical choices that must be made in field encounters with well-established and locally accepted – but illiberal – social structures and understandings. As is the case across the Sahel (Jourde 2021), the Hassaniyya-speaking societies of the western Saharan regions are historically highly stratified, and socially acceptable interactions with any given individual are often shaped by his or her place in such hierarchies. To varying degrees depending on their own identity and context, researchers may face strong expectations of adherence to such social norms.

To be sure, such social structures are often, and increasingly, themselves subject to intense local contestations, debate and even conflict. In the context of such contestations and debates, a researcher's choices based on a premise of the universality of the liberal perspective is anything but neutral; in fact this puts him or her in the position of taking sides on a subject of potentially intense local debate. Fieldwork choices based on ethical judgements about established social facts in which 'universal' (i.e. Western dominant) conceptions do not necessarily align with local social understandings thus present both moral and practical conundrums. In the Saharan region, social inequalities based on hereditary status or 'caste', notably among very marginalized groups such as blacksmiths, and especially the status of slave or slave origins, present particular challenges, as the chapters by Malluche and Freire reflect. Questions of gender of course may present similar considerations, again with ethical consequences. In a recent highly insightful consideration of liberal approaches to peacebuilding premised on Western notions of gender equality, for example, Maliha Chishti (2020) notes the unintended negative consequences for women. What stance must the researcher take when an approach to fieldwork prescribed by notions of liberal equality in fact bears the potential for causing unintended harm? In a related vein, Suleman (2016) points to the particular challenge of grappling with problems of consent for some Muslim women in contexts of marriage.

These particularities of western Saharan social structures give rise to situations marked by specific dilemmas and trade-offs in which the researcher must make choices in the face of local social realities and norms to which the researcher needs to conform. What attitude or approach should a researcher adopt in fieldwork circumstances where inequalities due to social status, or specific behaviours (such as deference or submission) that may be expected of individuals, clash with the ethical considerations of equal treatment and the agency of all individuals? How is consent to be understood in social contexts where the deference of some to others is the shared norm? And in what ways must the identity of the researcher – and especially his or her own relationship to the society in question – shape such behaviours?

Islam: These considerations take on very specific forms in the context of Muslim societies, where individual behaviour and social interactions are often guided by highly developed sets of legal and ethical codes of conduct and expectations. As the chapters by Ould Cheikh and Ould Bara highlight, there is a rich, intricate and complex tradition of Islamic scholarship and debate in the Sahara, and these traditions are highly salient to contemporary social questions. Yet at the same time, Islamic traditions are themselves at times contested, and subject to reinterpretation and transformation within evolving political contexts, as highlighted in Bengochea Tirado's discussion of the evolution of legal practices in the Sahrawi national project.

In an international project such as Capsahara, focused on Muslim societies and involving researchers from diverse social, national and religious backgrounds, the question of the relevance of the identity of the researcher to ethical considerations is inevitably complicated. In a review of the literature on scientific research in Muslim contexts, Suleman (2016) points to 'the importance of normative Islamic sources within the research ethics discourse in contexts where Muslims may be subjects of research and/or conducting research. Although the application of Islamic principles is varied and inconsistent', he notes, there is a need to be conscious of 'the role of religion and religious authority in underlining research priorities, guidelines, and conduct'.

Suleman's discussion suggests the particular challenges for Muslim researchers working on an 'international' research project – that is, a project sponsored by institutions from the global north. Such scholars face areas of 'religio-cultural contention between what is expected according to global secular standards and what can be implemented in a context where researchers' and participants' values may require consideration'. These issues are far from resolved and of increasing salience when endeavouring

> to ensure that participants' interests and safety are upheld whilst balancing the professional and personal considerations of the researcher … Muslim scientists, researchers, ethicists, theologians and legal scholars need to address [such] questions using tools from within their own tradition to provide coherent guidelines to enable researchers to engage in moral reasoning that is congruent with their own religio-cultural values, whilst presiding within the necessary international governance standards.
>
> (Suleman 2016: 55)

Ambiguities: Navigating complex issues

As the above discussion suggests, and as Goduka pointed out as early as 1990, the ethical norms for research that have emerged in the Western liberal world can end up in 'disjunctures' (1990: 329) when applied in different political and social contexts. The principles of fairness, respect, care and honesty enshrined in the 'Code of Conduct for Researchers in Resource-Poor Settings' that are claimed to be 'universally applied to research in any discipline' (Schroeder et al 2018: 1) undoubtedly aim at a laudable objective of fighting double standards, universalizing research ethics and building trust. Yet these standards were originally adopted as a reaction to exploitative practices taking place in biomedical and other health-related research, such as in clinical trials. Applied to ethnography, the implementation of such recommendations proves to be less than straightforward, particularly when studying a non-Western society. The significant areas of ambiguity inherent to the ethics of ethnographic research in complex environments are well known by now, but some further reflections on how they were manifested in this specific project may be useful.

Representing the European Union?

Because the Capsahara project was funded by the European Commission (of which the European Research Council is an organic part), and the interlocutors were informed of that fact *ex-ante* (in conformity with ERC ethics requirements), the researchers themselves and their actions might be taken as 'representative' of the EU's interests and intentions, and expected to act accordingly. Under these circumstances, how does a researcher conscious of this positionality situate him or herself vis-à-vis the EU's values and strategic goals?

The founding Treaty of the European Union states that it ' ... seeks to advance in the wider world: democracy, the rule of law, the universality and indivisibility of human rights and fundamental freedoms, respect for human dignity, the principles of equality and solidarity, and respect for the principles of the United Nations Charter and international law' (Art. 21.1, TEU). After harsh criticism of the lack of coherence in European dealings with the rest of the world, the EU shifted to a global strategy guided by 'principled pragmatism', a concept laid out in a document entitled 'Shared Vision, Common Action: A Stronger Europe' issued by the European External Action Service (EEAS) in June 2016: 'We will be guided by clear principles. These stem as much from a realistic assessment of the current strategic environment as from an idealistic aspiration to advance a better world. Principled pragmatism will guide our external action in the years ahead' (p. 8).

Nathalie Tocci, a strong advocate of principled pragmatism, insists that it should not be interpreted as giving up on principles and values altogether in order to accommodate utility-informed interests (2017). Rather, it means taking off the 'rose-tinted' spectacles and engaging with the complexity of the world and recognizing the ambiguity and uncertainty that other actors introduce in the picture, while still being guided by the core values of 'accountability, representativeness, responsibility, effectiveness and transparency' (2017: 152). In practical terms this shift in approach signified that as much as the EU would continue to advocate for a better world based on the 'idealistic aspiration' (EUGS 2016: 8) of rule of law and human rights, each particular situation will be dealt with pragmatically on the case-by-case basis (EUGS 2016: 39) based on a 'realistic assessment' of situations.

Considering ethnographic methods of research through this same EU framework, the guiding priorities become less than clear. How to balance 'principles' and 'pragmatism' in the day-to-day practices of research in the field? Should anthropologists concern themselves primarily with the prescribed ethical procedures (and the potential legal consequences) of their method of work, or should they focus on pragmatic adaptation essential to establishing human rapport and building trust, indispensable for research validity? While studying a society historically and culturally segregated by social status and ethnos where, for example, 'blacksmiths' are not allowed to marry outside their social strata and slavery is still implicitly flourishing despite being officially outlawed – how does one establish relations of trust and mutual respect and understanding with an elusive 'other' who, by some Western standards, may not deserve respect and, therefore, cannot be trusted or, alternatively, should be made aware of their options for emancipation and empowerment?

Positioning the researcher

Questions such as these cannot be answered independently of the position of the researcher towards the subjects of study. 'The ethnographer's identity serves to locate him or her vis-à-vis others within the field', McLean and Leibing remind us, and thus 'can work to facilitate or impede access to institutional knowledge and the subjective worlds of others' (2007: 264). As we have noted, the Capsahara project involved a highly diverse group of researchers: both local and outside, senior and junior. Researchers also varied in terms of age and life experience, another variable whose subtle influence is not always fully recognized. For the 'outside' scholar who has spent decades involved and working in a community, relationships change over the life cycle: 'informants' of the earlier periods fade to become old friends, and at times collaborators, partners or indeed long-time dependents. Each such position entails a different relation to the subjects of study, and hence each researcher finds him or herself working under different moral and ethical expectations and code of behaviour on the part of the interlocutors.

Particularly in its positivist paradigm, ethnographic research has often assumed a 'transcendental right to cultural objectification' (Albert 1997: 54) of the populations it aims to study, often assuming a position of realist ontology readily lending itself to epistemological discovery through observation and analysis of empirical facts. Within post-positivist and interpretivist paradigms, the ethnographic researcher delves into 'local' experiences of the research subject in order to sense, interiorize and translate their meaning (inevitably through his or her own subjective and value-tinted lens), aiming to distil a certain 'universal' truth from the process. Even when aiming to strike a balance between positivist and interpretivist approaches, and intellectually attempting to be an impartial witness and a 'reporter' rather than an actor in the social reality under investigation, a researcher can barely be humanly expected to completely withdraw personal value judgements and emotions.

The gap between *emic* (from within, i.e. the research participants' point of view) and *etic* (from outside, as presented to the researcher) perspectives can be particularly wide in situations involving moral judgement on the status of individuals. Whether an individual is inherently a 'victim' of a violation of rights by his or her social status, or is in a position of 'vulnerability' demanding special consideration or protection, may be points of strong contention both between researcher and subjects and within a community itself. Such is often the case in the Sahara with tributary status social groups, whose position older participants might consider an absolutely 'normal' and correct state of affairs, while a younger generation often socialized by experiences with alternative frameworks might decry as unjust, and crying out for social change and reform.

Research participants from populations undergoing processes of self-determination and even 'ethnogenesis' (see Malluche's chapter in this volume) often predicate their participation in the research project on the assumption of empathetic support and even advocacy for their cause by an anthropologist. As one interviewee noted to a researcher in a Sahrawi refugee camp: 'If you are here, it is because you are with us, we don't need "tourists" here.' Given the fact that access to the Sahrawi refugee camps is controlled by the visa regime established by the Polisario itself, it is fair to assume that many participants believe that by talking to a Western researcher they will advance the movement's cause, and that the information they provide will be communicated to the public as advocacy. Whether and how to correct such an assumption when in fact advocacy is not the researcher's intent presents a difficult ethical issue, and a practical problem. As one of us noted long ago in reflecting on a specific field experience, there is 'a constant difficulty for the Western social scientist to explain his or her peculiar questions and interests without misrepresentation, but also without alienating his interlocutors … Attempting to correct misperceptions without insult is a delicate and precarious undertaking' (Villalón 1995: 12).

In addition, the issue that a participant may attempt to see advanced when engaging with a researcher need not necessarily be the large causes of a collective group, but might well be a more subjective, restricted, or even a personal, cause. A Western researcher involved in collaborative research with local scholars may thus sense, for example, that his or her presence is being instrumentalized with the goal of eliciting support for a specific interpretation of a religious text, such as one dealing with slavery, as a means to strengthen one side within a local scholarly dispute. Or, as in a telling example from the Capsahara project, when the delicate issue of 'blacksmiths'' (*mʿallemīn*) status was evoked in a joint interview carried out with a Sahrawi poet, the local researcher also present during this interview posed questions seemingly designed to use the presence of the Western researcher to put the interviewee 'on the spot' and to force a specific response. Such situations are of course ethically fraught, yet they may also lend significant insights into local tensions and power relations, as well as into the conditions of ambiguity and constant negotiation of meaning in which the Capsahara researchers had to operate.

The phenomenon of 'anthropological advocacy' is by no means a new one in ethnographic research, and the ways that researchers negotiate and justify their involvement with the research participants reveal deeper paradigmatic premises of their epistemic and ontological stances. It is not a secret that 'ethnographic discourse has become a strategic tool' (Albert 1997: 57, 59) for the legitimization of social movements and societal transformations, posing a dilemma for the scholarly enterprise. But as Albert has argued in the context of a discussion of ethnogenesis: 'many anthropologists are inclined to get involved in the politico-symbolic maieutics that underpin it. But, whatever the sympathy they may have for their hosts' struggles, it does not imply an agreement to limit the exercise of anthropology to a mere apologetic reproduction of their ethnic discourse, which would lead to a complete renunciation of any scholarly enterprise' (Albert 1997: 59). Navigating between convictions, moral and deontological imperatives and research validity, as well as maintaining academic freedom and access to the research field, is a multifaceted and dynamic process. Described as 'working uneasiness' (Albert 1997: 60) and as 'discomfort in ethnography' (Boulay 2017), this 'articulation between values and knowledge' is exactly what gives to anthropology its 'true quality as a critical humanism' (Albert 1997: 60).

Consent, anonymity and objectivity

The informed consent of the research subject and the right to anonymity are core values enshrined in prescriptive research protocols. Yet the questions of how consent is granted and signalled, what has in fact been agreed to, who controls an interview and who has the authority to report what to whom, are the subject of subtle negotiation and relations of power and authority. In situations of hierarchy and authority, a researcher may well arrive at a predetermined appointment only to find that a figure of authority has taken charge of the protocol, convened dependents and followers to appear, prescribing who will speak on what matters, and what topics will be discussed. The insistence or assumption that the researcher has the authority to control the exchange of information in itself raises thorny ethical issues of power and agency.

In the context of Saharan societies, guided primarily by Islamic values of duty and obligations, signing a document is not something likely to be done casually but rather 'is reserved for special transactions' (Osman 2017: 64). No matter how well-intentioned, the presentation of printed paperwork (information sheets, consent forms, contact information) for signature by a Western researcher to a potential interviewee, may well be read as demanding a 'quasi-contractual' (Pels et al. 2018: 394) relationship between researcher and participant, with the potential for creating an atmosphere of suspicion and mistrust rather than of transparency and respect. Informed consent, as a 'social construct' that emerged in the global north (Visagie, Beyers and Wessels 2019: 167), reflects the modus operandi of Western institutions, but it sits uncomfortably in societies with a strong sense of community and where kinship-based social structures and personal relations of trust are central in shaping the interactions of individuals.

Gaps in the differences in worldview and in the avowed versus ascribed evaluation of the situation between researcher and participant are reflected in differing understandings of the purposes of anonymity or authorship, and of objectivity. A number of participants in the studies collected here valued an opportunity to 'tell their story'. This was especially the case for actors engaged in a concerted collective political agenda of nation-building, such as those from the Sahrawi populations of Tindouf. Such individuals did not appreciate the anonymity that our consent forms promised them, and rather wanted researchers to use their real names, to film them, to record their testimonies and to distribute these online and elsewhere for public access. Under such circumstances, it is easy to understand how ethical and moral consideration by the researcher would suggest the need to respect the wishes of the participants, yet this also suggests pitfalls of falling into a stance of advocacy, thus compromising ethnographic objectivity (Adler 2007). The tensions inherent in the concept of 'objective' and 'value-neutral' research when it comes to the moral integrity of researchers faced with pressures to become advocates for their interlocutors raise questions of academic responsibility and freedom and indeed become an ethical consideration in their own right.

Guiding a research project that aims to produce balanced results by giving airtime to different parties involved, especially when these parties are in a relation of smouldering conflict, brings with it additional challenges. This project began with the goal of carrying out research across the Hassaniyya-speaking populations of northwest Africa, including those residing in Mauritania, the territories of Western Sahara under Moroccan control and in the Tindouf refugee camps. Given the complex political context we have discussed above, however, academic support and collaboration was only successfully established in Mauritania. The Tindouf camps were accessed thanks to the established collaborations of senior research consultants on the Capsahara project, while the territories under Moroccan governance remained out of reach. In a divided society, such as that of the Western Sahara, distributed between the territories under Moroccan administration and the Polisario-controlled refugee camps, the risks are high of a 'contamination of the field' (Iphofen 2021: 17–20, 73), that is, of alienating the participants and making the society under study unlikely to collaborate in further research. In situations when trust as a core element of research integrity is lacking by default, if any of the feuding parts suspects that the researchers are biased or supporting the cause of the opposite side, a degree of field 'contamination' seems rather unavoidable.

Multiple perspectives on a complex object of study

One of the great achievements of the Capsahara project was bringing together local academics and early career researchers from the area of study with other scholars based in Europe and North America. Chapters in this volume by local researchers bear witness to the richness of work produced by those scholars whose birth and upbringing have imbued them with deep cultural awareness, language skills and intimate access. For their part, researchers working outside their own country, and hence more detached from the social pressures and the personal political aspects of the research environment, may at times be better placed to situate the social structures that are the object of study in 'objective' context. Yet as we have discussed throughout this essay, each positionality brings with it its own limitations, and raises ethical considerations for which the answers are never straightforward.

The subject of anthropological research is, by definition, the human being, and the central ethical concern is thus the respect for human personhood and dignity as embodied by the participants themselves. We can imagine the ethical relation to the 'other' in line with what Amartya Sen envisioned in his 'capabilities approach', that is instead of measuring the other with what one might think they 'should' want and desire, the researcher comes from a position of respect for what the person him or herself already 'has reason to value' (Sen 2009: 231). And yet, the relationship of the researcher to those very things of value inevitably shapes the perception of the place of that individual in the social fabric. Taken as a whole, the Capsahara project faced these issues in complex and multiple ways, depending in large part of the identity of the researcher and his or her position in regards to the social field of study: member, newcomer, experienced visitor, friend, sympathetic militant …

Collectively, this diversity makes for great richness of this book, and we would posit in addition that reading through the chapters not only for the material they provide us on the contemporary dynamics of Saharan societies, but also with an eye to the complexity of questions of ethics and positionality of the researcher, allows us a much more accurate picture of the whole. In a dialogic exploration of the twin perspectives of the researcher and of the subject of research in a specific field experience, McLaughlin and Sall (2001) open their discussion with the words of a character from the novel *Arrow of God* by the great Nigerian writer Chinua Achebe: 'The world is like a mask, dancing. If you want to see it well you do not stand in one place.' This book offers us multiple perspectives on the slowly shifting world of the Hassaniyya-speaking populations who inhabit the Saharan spaces, by a set of scholars who are certainly not 'standing in one place'. Collectively the chapters thus give us a deep and rich sense of the whole in all of its complexity, and help us to 'see it well'.

Notes

1 The previous version of the document, Iphofen 2013, contained similar provisions. The updated document can be found at: https://ec.europa.eu/info/funding-tenders/opportunities/docs/2021-2027/horizon/guidance/research-ethics-in-ethnography-anthropology_he_en.pdf

2 It is beyond our scope here to attempt to discuss the politics of the disputed territories of Western Sahara. For some detailed accounts, see e.g. Correale (2017); Ojeda-García (2017).

3 In December 2020, and as part of a deal to have the kingdom recognize Israel, outgoing President Donald Trump announced that the US would henceforth recognize Moroccan sovereignty over Western Sahara. Despite calls for him to do so, as of mid-2022 President Joe Biden had not reversed this decision. On 19 March 2022, the Spanish government endorsed the Moroccan plan for a solution to the stalemate, eliciting angry responses by both the Polsario and by Algeria, which recalled its ambassador to Spain.

References

Adler, R. (2007), 'But I Do Academic Anthropology!: Advocacy, Ethics, and the Politics of Research', *Practicing Anthropology*, 29(2): 20–3. doi: 10.17730/praa.29.2.60xv20220228724v.

Albert, B. (1997), '"Ethnographic Situation" and Ethnic Movements: Notes on post-Malinowskian Fieldwork', *Critique of Anthropology*, 17 (1): 53–65.

Boulay, S. (2017), 'Discomfort in Ethnography: Methodological Questions, Choices, and Tools in Sensitive Contexts', *Prace Etnograficzne*, 2: 213–28.

Chishti, M. (2020), 'The Pull to the Liberal Public: Gender, Orientalism, and Peace Building in Afghanistan', *Signs: Journal of Women in Culture and Society*, 45: 3.

Correale, F. (2017), 'Les origines de la "question du Sahara Occidental": enjeux historiques, défis politiques', in M. Balboni and G. Laschi (eds), *The European Union Approach towards Western Sahara*, 33–60. Bruxelles: Peter Lang.

Dilger, H., P. Pels and M. Sleeboom-Faulkner (2019), 'Guidelines for Data Management and Scientific Integrity in Ethnography', *Ethnography*, 20 (1): 3–7.

EUGS (2016), *Shared Vision, Common Action: A Stronger Europe. A Global Strategy for the European Union's Foreign and Security Policy*. European External Action Service, Brussels. https://eeas.europa.eu/archives/docs/top_stories/pdf/eugs_review_web.pdf.

Glasius, M., M. de Lange, J. Bartman, E. Dalmasso, A. Lv, A. Del Sordi, M. Michaelsen and K. Ruijgrok (2018), *Research, Ethics and Risk in the Authoritarian Field*. Cham: Palgrave Macmillan.

Goduka, I. N. (1990), 'Ethics and Politics of Field Research in South Africa', *Social Problems*, 37 (3): 329–40.

Iphofen, R. (2021), *Research Ethics in Ethnography/Anthropology*. DG Research and Innovation, European Commission, Brussels. https://ec.europa.eu/info/funding-tenders/opportunities/docs/2021-2027/horizon/guidance/research-ethics-in-ethnography-anthropology_he_en.pdf.

Jourde, C. (2021), 'Social Stratification in the Sahel', in L. A. Villalón (ed.), *The Oxford Handbook of the African Sahel*, 631–48. Oxford: Oxford University Press.

McLaughlin, F. and T. S. Sall (2001), 'The Give and Take of Fieldwork: Noun Classes and Other Concerns in Fatick, Senegal', in P. Newman and M. Ratliffe (eds), *Linguistic Fieldwork*, 189–210. Cambridge: Cambridge University Press.

McLean, A. and A. Leibing, eds (2007), *The Shadow Side of Fieldwork: Exploring the Blurred Borders Between Ethnography and Life*. Oxford: Wiley-Blackwell.

Ojeda-García, R., I. Fernández and V. Veguilla, eds. (2017), *Global, Regional and Local Dimensions of Western Sahara's Protracted Decolonization*. New York, NY: Palgrave Macmillan.

Okely, J. (2020), *Anthropological Practice: Fieldwork and the Ethnographic Method*. Abingdon and New York, NY: Routledge.

Osman, S. (2017), 'Ethical Issues Involving Informed Consent in the Arab Region', in H. Silverman (ed.), *Research Ethics in the Arab Region*, 59–72. Cham: Springer.

Pels, P., I. Boog, J. Henrike Florusbosch, Z. Kripe, T. Minter, M. Postma, M. Sleeboom-Faulkner, B. Simpson, H. Dilger, M. Schönhuth, A. von Poser, R. C. A. Castillo, R. Lederman and H. Richards-Rissetto (2018), 'Data Management in Anthropology: The Next Phase in Ethics Governance?', *Social Anthropology*, 26 (3): 391–413.

Regulation (EU) 2016/679 of the European Parliament and of the Council of 27 April 2016 on the protection of natural persons with regard to the processing of personal data and on the free movement of such data, and repealing Directive 95/46/EC (General Data Protection Regulation), OJ L 119, 4.5.2016: 1–88.

Schroeder D., J. Cook, F. Hirsch, S. Fenet, and V. Muthuswamy, eds (2018), *Ethics Dumping: Case Studies from North-South Research Collaborations*. Springer Briefs in Research and Innovation Governance. Cham: Springer. https://doi.org/10.1007/978-3-319-64731-9_1.

Sen, A. (2009), *The Idea of Justice*. Cambridge, MA: The Belknap Press.

Suleman, M. (2016), 'Contributions and Ambiguities in Islamic Research Ethics and Research Conducted in Muslim Contexts: A Thematic Review of the Literature', *Journal of Health & Culture*, 1(1): 46.

Tocci, N. (2017), *Framing the EU Global Strategy: A Stronger Europe in a Fragile World*. Cham: Springer-Palgrave Macmillan.

TRUST (2018), Global Code of Conduct for Research in Resource-Poor Settings, ed. D. Schroeder (ed.). doi: 10.13140/RG.2.2.19106.27848. https://www.globalcodeofconduct.org/

Villalón, L. A. (1995), *Islamic Society and State Power in Senegal: Disciples and Citizens in Fatick*. Cambridge: Cambridge University Press.

Visagie, R., S. Beyers and J. S. Wessels (2019), 'Informed Consent in Africa – Integrating Individual and Collective Autonomy', in N. Nortjé, R. Visagie and J. S. Wessels (eds), *Social Science Research Ethics in Africa*, 165–80. Cham: Springer.

Yuill, C. (2018), 'Is Anthropology Legal?', *Anthropology in Action*, 25 (2): 36–41.

Index

Abdel Aziz, M. O. (president of Mauritania) 87–103, 315, 320–1
abolitionist movements 124–5, 126, 195–228
  see also anti-colonialism
Action pour le Changement (AC) 207
activism
  artisanal gold mining 108, 124–5
  gender and feminism 143–66
  Ḥarāṭīn 195–228
  MLA 30–1
  politics and funeral orations 177, 178, 179, 181
ADIL political party (Mauritania) 91, 95
Adrar, emirate 198
Advanced Organization for the Liberation of the Sahara (OALS) (*Ḥarakat al-Taḥrīr*) 43–4, 50, 52
adwābe (sing. *adabay*) agricultural hamlets 200, 203
Āffa al-Dulaymī, ʿĀlī b. 279–81
African counter-nationalism 204–6
Afrique-Occidentale Française (AOF) 146
al-Aghẓaf, M. (Shaykh) 263–70
agriculture 126, 129, 200
Aḥmad al-Aswad, S. M. b. (Shaykh) 268
Aḥmad, M. (Shaykh) 278–9
Ahl Bayrūk (Āyt Mūsā ū ʿalī) 21
Aïn ben Tili *jamāʿa* of May 11th, 1959 36
Al Aaiún refugee camp 49, 80–1
Al Vadhila political party (Mauritania) 95
Algeria 35–6
Alliance Populaire Progressiste (APP) political party (Mauritania) 208–9
Amghar Sa'id 25
al-Amin b. al-Ṭālib ʿAbd al-Wahhāb, M. (Shaykh) 268
Amlu village 26
AMS *see* artisanal mining sector
anawāl 72–3, 75, 78–9, 81
anti-colonialism 28–9, 43–4, 47–8, 50
  Ḥarakat al-Taḥrīr 43–4, 50, 52 *see also* liberation movement
Antil, A. 88, 91, 99
anti-slavery laws 211–12
APP *see Alliance Populaire Progressiste* (APP)
Arab Spring 87, 152
artisanal gold mining in Mauritania 107–42
  AMS in Africa 109–12
  field research data 108
  field study 114–19
  living conditions 118, 123
  mining locations in northwestern Mauritania 110
  Mauritanian mining context 112–13
  nomadism and sedentarization 121–2
  organization of work 122–3
  politics and society 123–6
artisanal mining sector (AMS) 109–12, 124–5
  'illegality' 117–19
  permit costs 113
  reasons for joining 117–19
ascension routes of the *ḥarāṭīn* elites 88
Asebti North & South refugee camps 80–1
Ashʿari theology 43
authoritarianism 89–90
Awlād Muḥammad (Būḥummud) community 263, 264, 268
al-ʿAynayn, M. (Shaykh) 28
Āyt Arbaʿīn ('Council of Forty') 46, 53, 54, 178
  Sahrawi nomadism 70, 72, 74–5, 78
Āyt Bāʿamrān (fractions) 19–20, 21–2, 24, 25
Āyt Billa 21
Āyt Jmal 21

Āyt Laḥsan 24, 26
Āyt Ūsā 26, 33
Azevedo, R. 187

Baathist political currents 200–1, 213
Bābānā, H. wuld 32
Balandier, G. 31
al-Ballāl, L. wuld 35
Bambara populations 198
Banchirigah, S. M. 126
baraka 176, 199–200
Bargados, A. L. 47–8, 75–6
Baroja, J. C. 47, 73–4
barrios 80–2
Bassiri, S. B. 178
Batallón de Tiradores 26–7
batrônat (businesswomen) 149
Beiba, M. Ali 168, 179–81, 186, 188–9, 190
Benichab mining sites 114–19
benj music 202–3
Bensaid, B. 298
bīḍān 21, 28, 167
  gender and feminism 146–9, 156
  rise and fall of the MLA 28
  slavery, race and social order 197–200
  traditional schooling 291 *see also* abolitionist movement; *ḥassān*; *zwāya*
bīḍāniat 151
Bilād Shinqīṭ 48–9
Bilal, M. Ali 215
Bir Moghrein 28
Bir Moghrein mining sites 114–19
blacksmith *see m'allemīn*
blasphemy and realpolitik 311–29
body-subject 249
Boex, C. 188, 189
Bolay, M. 126
Bornand, S. 168
Borromean knot of faith 294–5
Bourdieu, P. 294
Brakna emirate 198
breastfeeding 234–6
BTI Country Report of 2020 151
Bū'ayda, A. 27, 30, 34–5
Bujchaibiyya *makhzan* 34
al-Bukhāri al-Bārakī, M. al-M. b. 47
Buss, D. 122
Butel, E. 188–9
Būyhāt fraction of the Rgaybāt 28

Campbell, B. 111
canonicity of funeral tributes 185–7
Capaz (colonel) 23–4
CAPEC (savings bank) 93
Caratini, S. 46, 80, 81
Chami mining sites 114–19, 122–125, 126
Charter of Human Rights 154, 155
Chevrillon-Guibert, R. 119
child labour 123–4
circumcision (*al-khitān*) 238, 248
classical Arabic orations 172–4, 181–5
CLTM *see* Confédération libre des travailleurs de Mauritanie
Coalition Vivre Ensemble (CVE) 214
colonial schools 201
colonialism 5–7
  artisanal gold mining 112
  ghuẓfiyya Sufi orders 261–2
  Ifni territory 20
  law in Sahrawi society 43, 47–52
  potlatch frontiers 22–3
  rise and fall of the MLA 27–30
  Sahrawi nomadism 75–6
  sugar pylon policy 31
  traditional schooling 289–90
Comité national pour l'éradiation des séquelles de l'esclavage en Mauritanie (CNESEM) 208
Commission for Human Rights 2010, Mauritania 210
Committee for the Liberation of the Sahara 34
competitive authoritarianism 89–90
Confédération libre des travailleurs de Mauritanie (CLTM) 207
Constitution Mauritania (1961) 150
Constitution Mauritania (1991) 57, 58, 207
Constitution and 'national community' 215–16
constructivism 197
Convention on the Elimination of All Forms of Discrimination against Women 150

Convention on Human Rights 320
Coppolani, X. 5, 261–2
Correale, F. 31
Council for the Command of the Revolution 56
Country Partnership Framework (World Bank) 126
'culturalized Islam' 155
CVE *see Coalition Vivre Ensemble*

Daddah, M.-T. 150
daily motions, Sahrawi nomadism 71–2
Dakhla urban centre 55–6, 80–1, 82
dawā'ir (sing. *da'ira*) 54, 80–1, 82
death and funeral orations 167–194
death penalty 311, 315, 317, 318, 319–20, 321
declaration of Guelta 1975 53
democracy 207, 208
  see also Islamic Republic and democracy; Sahrawi Arab Democratic Republic
Derive, J. 168
dictatorship 47–8, 89–90
Dimi Mint Abba 180
dismembered body 239
diya 46–7
al-Dulaymi, Ālī b. Āffa (Shaykh) 279–82
Dupont, F. 187

École Normale Supérieur (ENS) 93
economic instability 117, 125
Ed Jal refugee camp 80–1
El Aaiūn urban centre 55–6
El Hamel, C. 198
El-Hor movement 201–6, 207, 209–10, 214
El-Ouali, M. Sayed 178, 179, 189–90
emancipation 195–228
  gender and feminism 150
  Ḥarāṭīn activism 201
embryology 232–6
Enubke refugee camp 80–1
Esmra, S. 179
Espoir publication 25
Esquillat (Lieutenant-Colonel) 36
ethno-racial tensions
  FLAM and African counter-nationalism 204–206 *see also* abolitionist movement; slavery
European Union (EU) 210, 320

Fāl b. Muttālī, M. 231–59
Fatḥ al-ḥaqq (Muttālī) 231–53
Fatḥ al-shakūr 295
Fatwa Office 152–3
F'Derick mining region 120
feminism 143–66
  academy and nation-building 146–9
  power, Islam on women's terms 153–7
  pseudo-confessional state and pseudo-feminism 149–53
fiqh (jurisprudence) 45, 48, 50, 58, 267, 292–3, 322
  fuqahā (*fiqh* specialists) 45, 47, 49
firgān (sing. *frīg*) nomadic camps 46, 54, 70, 71–3, 76, 78–83
FLAM *see* Forces de Libération Africaines en Mauritanie
FLSM *see* Fron de Libération du Sahara de la Mauritanie
FNDD *see* Front National pour la Défense de la Démocratie
FNDU *see* Forum national pour la démocratie et l'unité
fora (NGOs) 148
Forces de Libération Africaines en Mauritanie (FLAM) 204–6, 207, 210–11, 214
Fortier, C. 147–8, 154–5, 199
Forum national pour la démocratie et l'unité (FNDU) 212
Foucault, M. 231
Franco regime 47–8
Frede, B. 153, 154–5
French colonial schools 201
French colonialism
  ghuzfiyya Sufi order 261–2
  law in Sahrawi society 43, 49–50
  rise and fall of the MLA 27–30
  traditional schooling 289–90
Front de Libération du Sahara de la Mauritanie (FLSM) 32

Front National pour la Défense de la Démocratie (FNDD) 209
Front uni pour l'action des Haratines (FUAH) 209
funeral orations 167–94

Gaddafi 54
Geertz, C. 144–5
gender
  and feminism 143–66 *see also* women
Ghana, gold mining 126
al-Ghazwānī (Shaykh) 278–9
ghuẓfiyya Sufi order 261–87
  consolidation/dissemination of teachings 275–9
  early formative period 1758–1798 263–75
  return to Hodh and propagation in the Middle East, 1895–1909 279–82
Gleib N'Dour 121
Godelier, M. 232
gold mining in Mauritania 107–42
gold panning 113
gold treatment facilities 124
Grarrat Lentilaga refugee camp 73, 80–1
Griffel, F. 317–18
griots *see iggāwen*
Grupo de Tiradores 26
Guelmin 25
Guelta, declaration of, 1975 53
Guinea, gold mining 126
Gulf War 207

Haalpulaaren populations 198, 202–3
ḥadīth 294–5
Hall, B. 198, 211
ḥalla 74
Hamada of Tinduf 73
Ḥarakat al-Taḥrīr 43–4, 50, 52
ḥarakat anṣār al-taghyīr ('Movement of the Supporters of Change') 215–16
Ḥarāṭīn 115
  blasphemy and realpolitik 313, 318–19
  gender and feminism 148
  women 154–5
Ḥarāṭīn activism 195–228
  FLAM and African counter-nationalism 204–6
  institutional politics and advocacy 207–8
  political change and revitalization post-2005 208–16
  post-slavery and citizenship struggles 193–7
  revolution 200–4
  slavery, race and social order 197–200
ḥarkas (military campaigns) 18–19, 23, 29, 30, 33, 34
Ḥasan, M. (Ḥasan II) 34–5
Hassan, M. 178
ḥassān ('warrior' status groups) 20, 21
  artisanal gold mining 115
  blasphemy and realpolitik 313
  gender and feminism 146–7
  slavery, race and social order 198
  traditional schooling 191, 291
Hassaniyya-speaking groups 2–5, 21–2, 26–7, 43
  funeral orations and politics 167–8
  kwār populations 198
  society and culture 290–2
  tribute poetry 174–7
Hatem political party (Mauritania) 95
al-Hay Assakin neighbourhood 94
al-Hayba, A. 28
heresy *see* blasphemy
High Council of Youth (HCY) 97
ḥijāb 155
'hijacking' of tributes 181, 186, 187–9
Hill, J. 153, 154–5
Hodh region (*ghuẓfiyya* Sufi order) 261–87
housing
  Teysir village 299–300, 306
Huggins, C. 121, 122
human rights 155, 211–12, 320
  see also activism
ḥurr (free/noble) 198–9
  see also bīḍān
hybrid morphologies of northern frontier 19–23

ibn Isḥāq, K. 211
Ibn Khaldūn 295

identity, blacksmiths 313–15
Ifni territory 20, 23–7
Ifni-Sahara War 26, 49–50
tabores (military companies) 26–7
Tiralleurs Battalion of the Ifni 26–7
iggāwen (griots) 167–8, 180–6, 188, 190, 198, 215, 313
immobile nomadism 78
incest 232–3
Inchiri region and artisanal gold mining 118
institutionalization of Sahrawi legislation 56–9
International Development Association 125–6
intersectional approaches to gender 144
IRA-Mauritanie (abolitionist movement) 124–5, 126, 209–13, 215–16
Iran–Iraq war 188–9
Iraq
Gulf War 207
Iran–Iraq war 188–9
IRA's *mufti* (jurisconsult) 318–19
Isidoros, K. 54, 79, 80
Islam 229–329
blasphemy and realpolitik 311–29
Fatḥ al-ḥaqq (Muttālī) 231–59
gender and feminism 143–66
ghuẓfiyya Sufi order 261–87
'hijacking' of *rithā* tributes 189–90
traditional schooling 289–310
'Islamic legal triangle' 45
Islamic Republic and democracy 87–103
crusade against political classes 93–7
intermediate political categories 88–90
populism and mismanagement 90–3
youth 97–9 *see also* Sahrawi Arab Democratic Republic
Islamic Republic in the Sahara 315–17
Islamic Republic of Mauritania 200–1
Istiqlāl party (Morocco) 24, 25, 26, 27–31
Izargiyyīn 30, 34–5

jamā ʿa (pl. *jamā ʿāt*) tribal assembly 34, 36, 46, 50, 53

al-Kabīr, S. A. (Shaykh) 276–7
Kādiḥīn communist-Maoist movement 150, 157, 201
Kantorowicz, E. 189
Kawtal (NGO) 212
Khaddad, M. 186
Khaïtoure, S. Mint 152
al-Kharr, M. 29
khayma 76, 148
khayma kbīra 54
Kinross mining company 117, 126
Kitāb al-bādiya (al-Bārakī) 47
klām al-bīḍān language 198
Kopytoff, I. 17, 19
Kurdish liberation movement (PKK) 177
kwār populations 198

Ladjal, T. 298
Lahlaoui, B. 178, 189–90
Laman, M. A. 44
law, artisanal mining sector 117–19
lawḥ (wooden slate) 49
Lefwāsim, Rgaybāt 35–6
legal practices among the Sahrawi 1958–2019 43–67
1958–1975 late Spanish colonialism 47–52
1975–1991 revolutionary period 52–6
1991–present, institutionalization 56–9
Lesourd, C. 88, 91, 99, 157
Lévi-Strauss, C. 232–3
Liberation Army of the North African colonies 47–8
liberation movement 52–56, 177
liff systems 21
living conditions for artisanal gold miners 118, 123
Lonsdale, J. 197
'luck' economy and artisanal gold mining 119–21
lullabies 150
Lydon, G. 21, 43

madhhab (Maliki school of jurisprudence) 316–17
Magrin, G. 119
maḥāẓir 154–5
Maḥmūd 'al-Khalaf', M. (Shaykh) 261–2, 276, 277–8, 279, 280
maḥṣar (pl. *mḥaṣir*) 72–5, 81–3, 289–310
and modernity 302–6

religious knowledge 292–8
rural 292–6
Teysir village 298–302
urban 296–8
Mahadra TV 152–3
Maham, A. 91
Mahbes 1974 72
Mahmood, S. 143–4
maḥẓaras 48–9
makhzan 18–19, 28, 29–30, 34
Mali
gold mining 126
Malian migrants 123
Maliki *fiqh* 267, 294–5, 316–17
Mālikī interpretations of *sharī ʿa* 45–6, 48–9
Malikite Islam 154–5
m ʿallemīn 123, 313–15
al-Māmūn, M. (Shaykh) 28
'Manifeste des 19' 204–5
Manifeste des Haratines 213–14
Manifeste du Négro-mauritanien opprimé 205
Maouloud, A. M. 98
marāthī (sing. *marthiyya*) 168–71, 178–9, 184–5
marriage 24, 33, 34, 264
Martin, G. 80
Marty, P. 38, 136, 264, 268, 279
martyrdom 168–9, 177–9, 188–9
Mauritania
Abdel Aziz (president) 87–103
blasphemy and realpolitik 311–29
gender and feminism 143–66
gold mining 107–42
maḥẓara/traditional schooling 289–310
online politics and funeral orations 167–94
post-slavery and *Ḥarāṭīn* activism 195–228
Maynummu, Būna ʿĀli b. (Shaykh) 269
McDougall, E. A. 143, 206
medḥ (artistic genre) 202–3, 215
Meidah, A. 184
Meidah, M. Mint 180–8
Meidah, M. Salem 184–6, 188
memory, death and funeral orations 167–94
Mesti village 26
Mhamed, K. Sidi 184–5
mineral resources (gold mining) 107–42
Mines de Cuivre de Mauritanie (MICUMA) 112
Mines de Fer de Mauritanie (MIFERMA) 112–13, 120, 124–5
Mining Code of 1999 113
mining pits in northwestern Mauritania 114
mining trenches Tasiast gold mine 116
Ministry of Finance 113
Ministry of Mines 113, 118, 122
MINURSO 76
M'Jeihidatt mining region 120
Mkhaitir affair 311–29
Islamic Republic in the Sahara 315–17
legal debate 317–20
televised repentance 320–1
Montéil, V. 21–2
Moroccan Communist Party 25–6
Moroccan Liberation Army (MLA) 23, 26, 27–30, 32, 33, 34–5, 36
mosques 25, 143–4, 296, 303
motions refugee camps
frīg/refugee camp analogies 78–83
immobile nomadism 78
and spatial histories 1975–1991 79–83
Movement of the Supporters of Change 215–16
Muḥammad V (Sultan) 25, 27–8
al-Mukhtār b. al-Ṭālib A ʿmar (Shaikh) 270–5
al-Mukhtār w. Būnā, 295
al-Mukhtaṣar (book on classic Maliki jurisprudence) 211
music/musical instruments 202–3, 215
see also song
Muslim Brotherhood 298

An-Na'im, A. A. 289
Naïmi, M. 21, 28, 29–30, 33
nasab (Rgaybāt) 33
Nasserist political currents 200–1
National Assembly 151, 208–9
national heroes and martyrdom 168–9, 177–81
National Society of Import and Export (SONIMEX) 93

'National Unity Pact' 53
National Women's Front (MNF) 150
nationalism 25–6, 197
Alliance populaire progressiste 208–9
Ḥarāṭīn activism 204–6, 208
'Négritude' movement 201
'neo-orality' 186–7
neopatrimonialism and dictatorship 89
Niger 299–300
non-governmental organizations (NGOs)
gender and feminism 151, 152, 157
Ḥarāṭīn activism 207–8, 210, 212, 215
Sahrawi nomadism 80–1 *see also* SOS-Esclaves
Nouakchott 92, 93
gender and feminism 152–3
Ḥarāṭīn activism 211–15
maḥẓara 293–4
al-Nuṣra Party (Mauritania) 315

OALS *see* Advanced Organization for the Liberation of the Sahara
online politics and funeral orations 167–94
Organisation pour la libération et l'émancipation des Haratines 201–4
see also El-Hor movement
Ouad Lhme refugee camp 80–1
Ouenet Bellagra refugee camp 80–1, 82
Ould A. Fettah 98
Ould Abdellahi, C. 91
Ould Abeid, Biram Dah 124–5, 126, 209–13, 215–16
Ould Ahmed Salem, Z. 88, 98–9, 100, 150, 152–3
Ould al-Bara, Y. 47, 49–50
Ould al-Zayn, S. 261–2
Ould Bah 295
Ould Beye, S. 207
Ould Boulkheir, M. 203–4, 206–9
Ould Bousseyri, B. 49
Ould Cheikh 200, 295
Ould Cheikh Abdallahi, S. 208–9
Ould Daddah, A. 95
Ould Daddah, M. (president) 112–13, 151, 203, 204–5, 291–2, 316
Ould Eleywa, K. 95
Ould Eleyya, E. Salem 171–2, 187–8
Ould Ely, B. 178–9
Ould Ghazouani, M. 213
Ould Haidallah (president) 94, 203–4
Ould Lemseydev, M. Y. 174–7, 187–8
Ould M. al-Waqf, Y. (prime minister) 91
Ould Mahfoud, H. 180
Ould Meidah, M. S. 183–4
Ould Messaoud, B. 207, 208, 214
Ould Mohamed Vall, E. 168, 170, 171–7, 186, 188–9
Ould Noueigedh, M. 91
Ould Saleck 205
Ould Sid'Ahmed Taya, M. 180
Ould Sneib 97
Ould Taleb, M. 172–174, 185
Ould Taya, M. 91, 94, 95, 97, 98, 151, 203–4, 205–6, 207, 298
Ould Waghef 91
Ould Weddad, L. 95
Oum Dreyga encampments 76–7

Palestinian PFLP 52
Pan-Arabism 200–1, 207
Paris-Dakar rally 153–4
Parti radical pour une action globale (RAG) 212, 213
Parti Républicain Démocratique et Social (PRDS) 95, 208
patriarchy 150
see also feminism
Penal Code of Mauritania 317, 320
Pettigrew, E. 293
Picón, R. 80
PKK *see* Kurdish liberation movement
pluralism 45, 48, 207
PNDD-Adil political party (Mauritania) 95
Polisario Front 43–4, 49–50, 53–4, 55
funeral tributes to Sahrawi personalities 178, 184–5
Ḥarāṭīn activism 200–1
'hijacking' of *rithā* tributes 188–90
politics and funeral orations 167–8
political morphologies at northwestern Saharan frontier 17–42
contingent alliances 30–2
demise of social order 32–6

hybrid morphologies 19–23
Ifni territory 20, 23–7
impossible demarcation 17–19
rise and fall of the MLA 27–30
politics
categories of the Islamic Republic 88–90
and funeral orations 167–94
Ḥaraṭın activism 207–8
and political class 93–7
artisanal gold mining 123–6
Popular Front for the Liberation of Saguia el-Hamra and Rio de Oro *see* Polisario Front
populism 90–3
poverty 117
see also economic instability
Pratt, M. L. 17
PRDR *see* Republican Party for Democracy and Renewal
PRDS *see* Parti Républicain Démocratique et Social
primordialist conception of ethnicity 197
prisons 179–80
pseudo-confessional state and pseudo-feminism 149–53

qabā ʾil 21, 28, 45–9, 53, 199–200
rise and fall of the MLA 28
Sahrawi nomadism 70–1, 72, 74, 75, 78, 82–3 *see also ʿurf* ('customs')
qāḍī (judge) 45–8, 50–1, 55, 58
qawlāba (rock collectors) 121–2
Qur ʾān 49, 51–2, 58
see also Islam; *sharī ʿa*

race
slavery and social order 197–200
see also bīḍān
Radio Qur ʾān 152–3
RAG *see* Parti radical pour une action globale
Rally of Democratic Forces (RFD) 95
realpolitik 28, 311–29
refugee camps 43–5, 46, 48–9, 52–60, 69–86, 167–8, 181–2
Republican Democratic and Social Party (PRDS) 95, 208
Republican Party for Democracy and Renewal (PRDR) 95
revolution
Ḥarāṭīn activism 200–4
martyrdom tributes 178 *see also* abolitionist movement; activism
RFD *see* Rally of Democratic Forces
Rgaybāt 19–20, 28, 30, 31, 33, 34–6, 46
ridda concepts 317–18
rithā tributes 177–9, 181, 187–9
Royal Armed Forces (FAR, Morocco) 30, 33, 34–5
Ruf, U. P. 148
rural *maḥẓara* 292–6
Rutherford, B. 122

SADR *see* Sahrawi Arab Democratic Republic
SADR TV 179, 181
Saguia al-Hamra 18, 19–20, 33
Saharan embryology 232–6
Sahelo-Saharan mining 111–12
Sahrawi Arab Democratic Republic (SADR) 43, 44, 53–4, 56
Council for the Command of the Revolution 56
funeral tributes to Sahrawi personalities 177–8, 179
'hijacking' of *rithā* tributes 189–90
institutionalization 56–7
Sahrawi nomadism 69–86
daily motions 71–2
exceptional motions 74–7
frīg/refugee camp analogies 78–83
seasonal motions 72–3
spatio-temporal organization, 20th century 70–1
Sahrawi personalities 177–9
Sahrawi legal practices 1958–2019 43–67
Sa'id, A. 25
Said wuld al-Jumānī, K. wuld 28
Sakina mining sites 115, 121
Sand War 32
satirical poems (*shemt*) 180, 189
'Sawab'/Baathist political currents 213
schooling
French colonial schools 201
maḥẓara 289–310
Scott, J. C. 5, 35
Seck, M. L. 215–16
Second Arab Spring 87

'secondary orality' 186–7
'secret marriage' 156, 264
sedentarization 200, 208
  artisanal gold mining 121–2
  gender and feminism 154
  political morphologies of northwestern Saharan frontier 35–6
  politics and funeral orations 170
  Sahrawi nomadism 69, 70, 75–6, 78
Sellahi, A. 181–2, 184
Senegal River valley 204, 206, 207, 212
Senghor, L. S. 201
sex 245–6
'sexularism' 143–4
sharī 'a
  gender and feminism 149–50
  legal practices among the Sahrawi 1958–2019 43–67
al-Shaykh, M. 281–2
shemt (satyrical poems) 180, 189
Shinqīṭ 48–9
al-Shinqiti, M. al-Mukhtar 312
shurfā lineages 20, 45
sība 47
Sidi Innu mosque 25
Sierra Leone, gold mining 126
'silent' resistance 49–50
as-sirriyya ('secret marriage') 156
slavery
  anti-slavery law 211–12
  race and social order 198–200 *see also* abolitionist movement
Smara urban centre 55–6
smiths 313–15
socia(b)l(e) body 251–3
Société Nationale Industrielle et Minière (SNIM) 112–13, 120, 124–5
society 105–228
  artisanal gold mining in Mauritania 107–42
  death and funeral orations 167–94
  gender and feminism 143–66
song 167–94
SONIMEX 93
Soninké populations 198, 202–3
SOS-Esclaves NGO 207–8, 209–10, 211–12
South *shurfā* 48–9
Spanish colonialism
  Ifni territory 20
  law in Sahrawi society 43, 47–52
  rise and fall of the MLA 27–30
  sugar pylon policy 31
spatialities of refugee camps 81–3
'spoiled rice' affair 91
ṣhūyū (fractions) 21–2, 24, 25, 26
ṣulḥ (amicable settlement) 45, 46–7, 50–1, 54, 58, 59
state 15–103
  democracy in an Islamic Republic 87–103
  legal practices among the Sahrawi 1958–2019 43–67
  political morphologies at northwestern frontier 17–42
State Security Court (Sahrawi law) 57
student life, *see also maḥẓara*
sūdān 198–9
  see also bīḍān
Sudanese migrants 123
Sufism 43
  ghuẓfiyya order 261–87
sugar pylon policy 31
'Sultanian' governance 87–8
Supreme Council of Justice (Sahrawi law) 53–4, 58
Supreme Court (Mauritania) 311, 317, 318, 322

'tactical Islam' 156
Tagant emirate 198
Tarfaya province 34–5
targhība 46–7
tasarrā ('secret marriage') 156, 264
Tasiast mining region 116, 120, 126
Tauzin, A. 147–8, 154–5
Tawāṣul party (Mauritania) 95, 155, 157
tebrā ' poems 170
Teide-Écouvillon operation 36
Tenoumer mining region 120
'Teranim' (NGO) 215
Tevragh Zeina district (Nouakchott) 297
Teysir village (Mauritania) 289–310
  admission and eligibility 300–1
  housing 299–300, 306
  mosque 303
  student life 301–2
therapists and therapies 249–50

tidal frontiers (Kopytoff) 19
Tijirit mining region 120
Tikna 19–20, 21, 24, 26, 27, 33
Tindouf refugee camps 167–8, 181–2
Tiris mining sites 109, 112, 121
Tiznit prison 179–80
t'mari (lullabies) 150
Trāb al-Bīḍān 28, 43
traditional schooling/*maḥẓara* 289–310
  and modernity 302–6
  Teysir village 298–302
  transmission of religious knowledge 292–8
transitology 89–90
'transnational Islam' 155
transnational traders, women 149
Trarza emirate 198
Trarza region 294–5
tributes to the deceased 167–94

ʿudūl (sing. *ʿadl*) 50, 58
UNHCR *see* United Nations High Commissioner for Refugees
Union des Forces Démocratiques (UFD) 207
Union des Forces Progressistes (UFP) 95
United Nations (UN) 157, 210
United Nations High Commissioner for Refugees (UNHCR) 206
UPR party (Mauritania) 213, 214
urban *maḥẓara* 296–8
urbanization 200, 208
ʿurf (customs) 29–30, 45, 46, 50

Vall, M. 319
Villa Cisneros 25, 49
violent resistance 49–50
'virtuous Islam' 156

Wad Draa 19, 21–2, 23–4, 27–8, 29, 33
Wad Nun basin 18, 19–20, 29–30, 33, 34
walā concepts 199–200
Western Saharan War 189–90
wilayāt (sing. *wilaya*) 55–6, 58, 80–2
Wiley, K. A. 148
Wilson, A. 5, 44–5, 78–9, 81
Wolof populations 198, 202–3
women
  academy and nation-building 146–9
  breastfeeding 234–6
  funeral orations and politics 188
  gender and feminism 143–66
  ḥarāṭīn 154–5
  Rgaybāt and marriage 33
  rithā tributes 288
  Sahrawi nomadism 81–2
workers safety 123–4
World Bank 111, 125–6

Yūsuf, S. M. b. 24

zandaqa concepts 317–18
zawiyas (centres of Sufi practice) 295
znāgā (tributary status groups) 47
Zouerate mining site 120, 121
zwāya ('religious' status groups) 20, 21
  artisanal gold mining 115
  blasphemy and realpolitik 313
  gender and feminism 146–7, 155
  legal practice of Sahrawi societies 45–6
  slavery, race and social order 198–200
  traditional schooling 295

www.ingramcontent.com/pod-product-compliance
Lightning Source LLC
Chambersburg PA
CBHW052140300426
44115CB00011B/1461
* 9 7 8 0 7 5 5 6 4 3 4 8 6 *